Keith Oatley shows how emotions are central to understanding human action and mental life, serving a crucial function when the unexpected occurs and when priorities must be set. *Best Laid Schemes: The Psychology of Emotions* draws from fields making up cognitive science – psychology, philosophy, linguistics, artificial intelligence, and anthropology – together with other approaches such as narrative literature and psychiatry, to inform readers about a wide range of writings and research on emotions and to offer an integrative understanding of the role of emotions.

Studies in Emotion and Social Interaction

Paul Ekman
University of California, San Francisco

Klaus R. Scherer
Université de Genève

General Editors

Best laid schemes

Studies in Emotion and Social Interaction

This series is jointly published by the Cambridge University Press and the Editions de la Maison des Sciences de l'Homme, as part of the joint publishing agreement established in 1977 between the Fondation de la Maison des Sciences de l'Homme and the Syndics of the Cambridge University Press.

Cette collection est publiée co-édition par Cambridge University Press et les Editions de la Maison des Sciences de l'Homme. Elle s'intègre dans le programme de co-édition établi en 1977 par la Fondation de la Maison des Sciences de l'Homme et les Syndics de Cambridge University Press.

Best laid schemes

The psychology of emotions

Keith Oatley

Centre for Applied Cognitive Science
Ontario Institute for Studies in Education
and Department of Psychology, University of Toronto

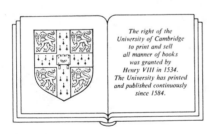

The right of the
University of Cambridge
to print and sell
all manner of books
was granted by
Henry VIII in 1534.
The University has printed
and published continuously
since 1584.

Cambridge University Press

Cambridge
New York   Port Chester   Melbourne   Sydney

Editions de la Maison des Sciences de l'Homme

Paris

Published by the Press Syndicate of the University of Cambridge
The Pitt Building, Trumpington Street, Cambridge CB2 1RP
40 West 20th Street, New York, NY 10011-4211, USA
10 Stamford Road, Oakleigh, Victoria 3166, Australia
and
Editions de la Maison des Sciences de l'Homme
54 Boulevard Raspail, 75270 Paris, Cedex 06

© Maison des Sciences de l'Homme and Cambridge University Press 1992

First published 1992

Printed in the United States of America

Library of Congress Cataloging-in-Publication Data
Oatley, Keith.

p. cm.

Best laid schemes : the psychology of emotions / Keith Oatley.

Includes bibliographical references and index.

ISBN 0-521-41037-1. – ISBN 0-521-42387-2 (pbk.)

1. Emotions. 2. Emotions and cognition. 3. Emotions in
literature. 4. Emotions – Sociological aspects. I. Title.
BF511.O37 1992
152.4 – dc20   91–17589
                                                          CIP

A catalog record for this book is available from the British Library.

ISBN 0-521-41037-1 hardback
ISBN 0-521-42387-2 paperback
ISBN 2-7351-0429-X hardback (France only)
ISBN 2-7351-0431-1 paperback (France only)

To Hannah

The best laid schemes o' mice and men
    Gang aft a'gley,
An' lea'e us nought but grief an' pain
    For promis'd joy.

Robert Burns
To a mouse, on turning up her nest
with the plough, November 1785

Contents

Figures and tables

Figures

Tables

Acknowledgments

This book has greatly benefited from discussions with colleagues. Like many books, it is in many ways a joint effort.

A major collaboration has been with Phil Johnson-Laird. We have written together several papers on the cognitive theory of emotions and some of this work is incorporated in Chapters 1 and 3 of this book. The theory, which is called here the communicative theory of emotions, is a joint product. The process of working together on the psychology of emotions and on semantic analyses of emotion terms has been invaluable and invigorating. Many of the ideas described here have been conceived or refined in this collaboration. The main ideas behind the semantic analyses were Phil's.

Steve Draper has also been a close collaborator and discussed many of these ideas with me in the context of our work on theories of planning in artificial intelligence. In response to my early thoughts about writing this book, Steve wrote a survey of emotion theories and a commentary on them. He also read and commented on a draft of the book. The idea that planning theories in cognitive science are too narrowly defined and that their constraints need to be relaxed is Steve's, and these ideas are discussed in Chapter 1. He also suggested the idea that emotions are based on monitoring each of our plans and goals, not just the active ones. I thank him warmly.

My thanks, too, go to Jenny Jenkins, who discussed both the words and the concepts with me in detail, in many different ways and with great insight. Jenny has been most sensitive to the relation of the parts to the whole of this book. She has detected many of my diversions and tangents and been insistent on my developing and maintaining the book's thematic quality. Without her and her encouragement, the book would be much the poorer.

I am grateful to the stimulation and contribution of the graduate students who worked with me on emotions. Joint work that I have done with them has helped this book: Winifred Bolton (life events and depression), Chris Perring (plans and psychopathology), Elaine Duncan (emotion diaries), Charles Button (Richard Power's model of conversation), and Judy Ramsay (people's emotions in interacting with computer systems).

I have been much helped by two recent books. One is Nico Frijda's *The Emotions* (1986). The fact that independently Johnson-Laird and I came to a similar theoretical formulation to Frijda's seems to indicate that a theory of this kind has the right general shape. There are differences, but they are small in comparison with the similarities, and I have discussed them at appropriate points. Most especially I would like to acknowledge Frijda's comprehensive review of the psychological literature – his book is a model of its kind. Its existence allows me to offer my book, as I say in the Prologue, as complementary to his, with a different kind of purpose. In writing my final drafts I have been much helped by Frijda's work, as well as by interesting discussions with him.

The second book that had a very large effect on my final drafts was Martha Nussbaum's *The Fragility of Goodness: Luck and Ethics in Greek Tragedy and Philosophy* (1986). This has been another happy convergence. Frijda's book was on the same subject as mine, but with a different stylistic approach. Nussbaum's project has a similar style and intention, drawing as I do on literary texts, but in a different field, the philosophy of ethics. It is from Nussbaum that I have realized that my project is Aristotelian in conception. I have also based something of the structure of my book on hers.

I have been much helped in thinking about the issues of stress and psychiatric epidemiology by the writing of George Brown and by stimulating discussions with him. My thanks also to Tirril Harris, who trained me in the Bedford College Life Events and Difficulties Schedule, and to Tom Craig, who trained me on the Present State Examination.

My introduction to cognitive science was by the influence of the late Max Clowes, close friend and collaborator on a number of projects. Among these projects was a seminar and we wrote a paper together (Clowes & Oatley, 1979) in which, I realize in retrospect, some of the early ideas for this book were being developed.

I am grateful to a number of people for opening up to me the world of psychoanalytic therapy. This occurred by the influence of the Philadelphia Association. In particular, Ronnie Laing influenced me, both through his writing and personally. John Heaton introduced me to the phenomenological philosophers and their connections with psychotherapy. My thanks also go to Tony Ryle, who was responsible for helping me with the synthesis between psychoanalytic and cognitive ideas. Ben Churchill and Nancy MacKenzie have been of profound help in my experience of some of the issues discussed here. Peter Smith has been responsible for my induction into the ideas of group dynamics and has influenced me with his theories of psychological change in therapy and groups. George Craig has been a delight in his discussions of the potent and disturbing qualities of literature and its close relationships with psychotherapy.

I have much enjoyed conversations with Stephen Medcalf, who shares an interest in the question of inner and outer experience that pervades much of Chapter 5. He introduced me to the works of Collingwood, one of which is an influential source for Chapter 9. I have also enjoyed conversations with Mary Sissons, who introduced me to folk theories of medicine.

I thank George Mandler for discussions and criticisms that he kindly offered on a paper written in the early stages of developing the theory on which *Best Laid Schemes* is based. His papers and books on conflict theories of emotions have influenced me considerably and have been models of scholarly understanding in this field.

I thank Paul Ekman both for illuminating discussions of his work on emotions and nonverbal behavior and for his extensive and careful writings. His pioneering empirical research, more than anyone's in recent years, has carried forward Darwin's and done much to place the topic of emotions into the serious scientific arena.

I am grateful to the members of four seminar groups: The Clinical and Psychotherapy Research Seminar, started by Tony Ryle, Peter Smith, and myself, that was organized for several years at the University of Sussex; the undergraduate members of a seminar I gave on Freud's "Dora" – Wendy Bell, Jo Smith, Elodie Magnus, and Tanya Stevens, who read and commented on a draft of Chapter 7; the members of the informal group on stress with whom stimulating discussions have taken place – Chris Brewin, Paul Gilbert, Richard Moore, Glenys Parry, John Teasdale, and Fraser Watts; the members of a seminar group who met for a year at Sussex to discuss the implications of joint planning and dialogue in cognition.

Past and present members of the Laboratory of Experimental Psychology at the University of Sussex have been my close colleagues for a number of years and I greatly benefited from the intellectual atmo-

sphere of the laboratory, from the many discussions, and from the toler-
ance of people there toward my nonexperimental approaches to psychology. In particular, Bob Boakes, Mic Burton, Alan Garnham, Tony
Marcel, Richard Power, Richard Totman, and Nicola Yuill have contributed directly to ideas in this book. I have also benefited widely from the
growth of cognitive science at Sussex, where Maggie Boden has been an
influential colleague and Aaron Sloman has shared an interest in cognitive approaches to understanding emotions.

Most of *Best Laid Schemes* was written while I was a member of the
Psychology Department at the University of Glasgow. I am grateful for
the interest of colleagues in the cognitive group – Anne Anderson,
Simon Garrod, Tony Sanford, and Paddy O'Donnell – and the Construc-
tive Interaction Group, which also included members of the Psychology
Department of Strathclyde University – Tony Anderson, Christine
Howe, and Terry Mayes.

For two years I was a visiting associate professor in the Department of
Psychology at the University of Toronto, where I received warm intellectual and personal hospitality. My interest in Jaynes's work was sparked
by Bob Lockhart. My interest in emotions was stimulated there by Ber-
nard Schiff. Judy Katz of York University, Toronto, wrote and discussed
with me a paper on emotions that has influenced my thinking considerably.

I thank the members of the International Society for Research on Emotions, and Joe Campos who was the first executive officer of the society.
Not repeating mention of those who I have already thanked, I am grateful for understandings that I have gained listening to and conversing
with Jim Averill, Gordon Bower, Jerry Clore, Paul Harris, Marty
Hoffman, Alice Isen, Richard Lazarus, Michael Lewis, Cathy Lutz, Carol
Malatesta, Tony Manstead, Andrew Ortony, Ira Roseman, Jim Russell,
Klaus Scherer, Phil Shaver, Nancy Stein, and Tom Trabasso. The results
of these discussions have found their way into this book in various
places. To other members of the society I am grateful for the stimulation
and understanding that, though more diffused, has also influenced *Best
Laid Schemes*. Versions of this work have been presented at con-
ferences/workshops: "Emotion-Cognition Interrelations," held in Winter Park, Colorado (1985), organized by Joe Campos and supported by
the National Institutes of Mental Health; "Consciousness," organized by
Edoardo Bisiach and Tony Marcel; "Aspects of Consciousness" (1988),
organized by Peter Bieri and Philip Smith, and a research group "Mind
and Brain" (1989–1990), organized by Peter Bieri and Ekhart Scherer –

both sponsored by Zentrum fur interdisziplinare Forschung at the University of Bielefeld; a symposium "Emotion and Cognition" at the British Psychological Society annual meeting at Sheffield (1986), organized by Vernon Hamilton; a NATO Advanced Research Workshop "Emotion, Cognition and Motivation" held at Il Ciocco, Lucca, 1987, organized by Vernon Hamilton, Gordon Bower, and Nico Frijda, and another NATO Advanced Research Workshop "Computational Theories of Communication," Trentino, 1990, organized by Olivero Stock, Jon Slack, and Andrew Ortony. I am grateful to these organizers, funding agencies, and other participants for the invaluable opportunities of meeting and understanding the work of leading emotion researchers at these conferences and workshops.

I thank the universities of Sussex and Glasgow for supporting my work on this book. I thank the British Research Councils for graduate scholarships: to Win Bolton and Chris Perring from the Medical Research Council, to Elaine Duncan from the Economic and Social Research Council, to Charles Button from the Science and Engineering Research Council, and to Judy Ramsay from the Joint Research Councils Cognitive Science/HCI Initiative.

Anna Black was of great assistance with corrections to a draft, saving me from some baleful effects of a malfunctioning word processor, and Maria Guzman was most helpful in the final stages.

I am grateful to Eric Wanner who stimulated me to write this book and offered suggestions at an early stage; to Julia Hough and Iris Topel at Cambridge University Press, and to Paul Ekman and Klaus Scherer the editors of this series. I also thank Mary Louise Byrd for copy editing the manuscript.

Finally I would like to thank most warmly for their reading and comments on the whole or parts of this book: George Brown, Steve Draper, Simon Garrod, Jenny Jenkins, Phil Johnson-Laird, Paddy O'Donnell, Tony Sanford, Klaus Scherer, and Phil Shaver. For the most part I have gratefully taken their advice. The remaining defects are my own.

Acknowledgments of permission for use of material

Parts of this book have been published in different form elsewhere. I am grateful to the following publishers for permission to reprint their material. A shorter version of parts of Chapter 3 was published in K. Oatley, "Do emotional states produce irrational thinking?" In K. J. Gilhooly, M. T. G. Keane, R. H. Logie, and G. Erdos (eds.) *Lines of Thinking: Vol. 2,* pp. 121–131, Chichester: Wiley, copyright © 1989 Wiley, reprinted by permission of John Wiley & Sons, Ltd. A shorter version of Chapter 7 was published in K. Oatley, "Freud's psychology of intention: the case of Dora." *Mind and Language, 5,* 69–86, 1990, Oxford: Basil Blackwell, used by permission. Part of an earlier version of Chapter 9 was published in K. Oatley, "Expression of emotions in psychotherapy and art." *Teorie & Modelli, 4,* 19–35, 1987, Bologna: Pittagora Editrice, used by permission. Tables 3 and 5 are from K. Oatley and P. N. Johnson-Laird, "Towards a cognitive theory of emotions." *Cognition and Emotion, 1,* 29–50, 1987, Hove: Erlbaum, used by permission. Figures 1, 3, 4, and 5 are from K. Oatley, "Plans and the communicative function of emotions: a cognitive theory." In V. Hamilton, G. H. Bower, and N. H. Frijda (eds.) *Cognitive Perspectives on Emotion and Motivation,* pp. 345–364, Dordrecht: Kluwer, 1988, reprinted by permission of Kluwer Academic Publishers.

I am grateful for permission to use the following: my paraphrase of Chapter 6 of *Moon Tiger* by Penelope Lively to Murray Pollinger, Literary Agent, and Andre Deutsch Ltd. and Penguin Books Ltd. For quotations from Marcel Proust's *Remembrance of Things Past* (Trans. C. K. Scott Moncrieff, T. Kilmartin, and A. Mayor) © 1981, Random House, Inc., by permission. C. A. Trypanis's Translations from Sappho, a fragment "Love the loosener of limbs . . ." and the poem "Some say that the most beautiful thing" in Constantine A. Trypanis, ed. and trans., *The Penguin Book of Greek Verse,* Harmondsworth: Penguin, 1971, reproduced by permission of Penguin Books Ltd. and copyright © Constantine A. Trypanis, 1971. Sappho's poem "Richly enthroned immortal Aphrodite" from D. Page's translation (1955), *Sappho and Alcaeus: An Introduction to the Study of Ancient Lesbian Poetry.* Oxford: Oxford University Press, by permission of Oxford University Press. Sappho's poem "He is a god in my eyes" from Mary Barnard, *Sappho: A New Translation,* copyright © 1958 The Regents of the University of California, © renewed 1984 Mary Barnard, by permission.

Prologue

Like good inductive scientists, they have kept their eye
on the facts, but (a disaster against which inductive
methods afford no protection) the wrong facts.
R. G. Collingwood
The principles of art, p. 31

A wider range of evidence

To understand emotions we must consider a wider range of phenomena
and evidence than is usual in psychology.

The topic of emotions has been slow to take its place alongside other
aspects of scientific psychology. Nonetheless, understanding has grown
since Darwin's work of 1872. I will discuss some of that understanding,
but I wish to do more. Emotions have been considered from many
perspectives, from within psychology and from outside it, across a
range from biology to philosophy, in areas as seemingly diverse as the
theater and computer simulation. I propose that in understanding emotions we need attend to insights from these differing perspectives and to
set them in relation to each other.

It is usually thought that scientific methods afford reliable understanding, and that the knowledge they deliver is superior – other
knowledge is labeled prescientific or unscientific and becomes at best of
historical or recreational interest. Psychologists armed with experiments
and statistics have been as insistent on methodological hegemony over
mental life as other scientists over their areas.

In this book I put a different case, the case of pluralism. We will not
comprehend emotions unless we draw from several areas of understanding, including some from outside natural science. We should not

1

adopt this view simply to be heterodox, but because unless we do so we will fail to grasp fundamental aspects of our subject matter.

What reasons are there for admitting methods other than natural scientific ones? Natural scientific psychology has been largely experimental. With the recent rise of cognitive science, researchers in artificial intelligence have, however, argued that experimentation does not guarantee an understanding of mentality. As Newell (1972) has put it: "You can't play twenty questions with nature and win." He was commenting on the lack of cumulative understanding that has occurred as a result of experimental psychologists asking binary questions about their subjects' performances – questions like: "Is this due to nature or nurture?"

One may add to Newell's contention: Experimenting, when it is the sole method in psychology, has not only failed to cumulate in many areas, it has offered views of its subject matter that have only local interest to those doing similar research. I wish to propose that of all aspects of mentality emotions need a broader approach to understanding.

The approach I have taken means that in increasing coverage of fields not usually included in a psychology book, I have had to select a smaller amount of source material from the psychological literature than is usual and be less intricate in my discussion of this literature. Instead, I have tried to describe the psychological evidence I present in enough detail for the reader to draw her or his conclusions and to be in a position to argue with mine as necessary. In pursuing this course I hope to have avoided some of the problems of bias and of seeming to select arbitrarily because there is a book available, Frijda's *The Emotions*, which is a complete, scholarly, and critical survey of the psychological literature on emotions. Its existence, I hope, allows me to pursue a complementary aim to Frijda's of widening the discussion into areas not usually considered by academic psychologists. On matters in which a reader finds I have missed something or been selective, I apologize and suggest reference to Frijda's book or to Strongman (1978).

The Romantic movement

In European literature a movement began a little before the time that Burns wrote his poem "To a mouse" and lasted until the middle of the nineteenth century. Known as Romanticism,[1] its adherents stressed people's relationship to nature, to the spontaneous and even to the impulsive in human life. They explored the adult's relation to childhood. They celebrated the ordinary, as well as realms of fantasy and dreams.

They traveled, making contacts with the exotic and the unknown. Above all, Romanticism was about emotions – emotions felt intensely, expressed with directness, and explored in order to reach an understanding. The movement occurred in reaction to the classical ideals of the Enlightenment, in which form was the important principle and rational thought the guiding human virtue.

Since Nietzsche's (1956/1872) description of the Classical and the Romantic as Apollonian and Dionysian, respectively, in tension with each other, it has become more difficult to argue that human life is to be understood in terms of only one of them. Yet in cognitive psychology this is what has happened. Computation has offered analyses of human mentality in terms that are entirely Apollonian.[2]

This book is not Romantic; but in it I seek to explore in psychology some of the issues that were introduced into literature by the Romantics and thereby to reestablish the tension between Apollonian and Dionysian threads in psychological understandings of emotions. Any serious understanding in this area needs to draw both on formal structure and on our experience of emotions.

An integrative theory

If we extend the range of emotional phenomena that are to be considered, a theory is needed that will be appropriate to the Gestalt that emerges. The theory I propose derives from cognitive science – the study of how knowledge is acquired, represented, used, and communicated in intelligent beings. The book's proposal is that emotions are part of a solution to problems of organizing knowledge and action in a world that is imperfectly known and in which we have limited resources. If this is correct, emotions are not on the periphery but at the center of human cognition.[3]

The theory presented here is based on planning and action. Its core ideas have been familiar in European culture since the time of Plato and Aristotle, with the concept of *techne*, technique or skill, depending on *episteme*, reliable knowledge. *Techne* enables forward planning toward defined goals. The philosophical term epistemology is derived from the notion of *episteme*, and cognitive science is the modern descendant of the philosophical pursuit of understanding the nature of knowledge that began with Socrates and Plato.[4]

Natural science is the means for producing knowledge that is reliable enough to be used in prediction and technology. Much of it is about causes and mechanisms. What might be called human science or social science is less well defined. It can be thought of as descended from Aristotelian considerations. It is concerned with understanding ourselves though not in an exclusively technical way. It is marked by the centrality of human intention, which is absent from the material studied in natural science, and which cannot be fully understood as mechanism, at least in terms of any mechanism that we now understand.

Cognitive science uses computation as its theoretical language and takes as its central concern the uses of knowledge in goals and plans. In so doing it is potentially capable of integrating the twin strands of natural and human science.

Emotions arise continually in the course of human action, although no equivalent phenomena occur in technical plans. This difference is an important pointer to the function of emotions. It hints that emotions are biological solutions to just those problems in the management of human action that cannot be tackled in technical plans.

The theory proposed is a product of collaboration with Phil Johnson-Laird (Oatley & Johnson-Laird, 1987; Johnson-Laird & Oatley, 1989). This core of theory has been fundamental to developing the approaches made in this book. Like any other theory it is provisional and corrigible. What we claim for it is that, in giving up some of the precision of exclusively experimental observation, the overall Gestalt is more adequate to the subject of human emotions. We hope that it will have something of the right overall shape. This is not to say that it is specified so vaguely as to be incapable of falsification. Indeed, I compare it with alternative accounts and indicate how discriminations among rival theories can be made.

A theory of the general kind presented by Johnson-Laird and myself is needed to integrate the fields in which phenomena of emotion have been explored. With such a theory the apparently heterogeneous set of phenomena that are usually referred to as emotional takes on a comprehensible structure.

Style and the question of insight

Thus far, cognitive science, with its formal computations, its syntactic analyses, and careful experimentation, has lacked nothing of the elegance of Apollonian formalism. With the inclusion of a Dionysian element a change in style is needed.

One reason for this is a discrepancy that has confronted me in reading the psychological literature on emotions. Many of us are very interested in emotions, particularly our own and those of people we know. This interest extends to spending large amounts of time vicariously experiencing emotions in novels, theater, cinema, and television; to discussing emotions with each other; and to seeking the experience of emotions by listening to music or taking part in sports and other activities. Yet, somehow, books on the psychology of emotions do not always explain this kind of interest, let alone create it.

William James complained: "The descriptive literature of the emotions is one of the most tedious parts of psychology. . . . I would as lief read verbal descriptions of the shapes of rocks on a New Hampshire farm as toil through [the classic descriptive works on emotion] again" (1890, p. 446). Though some of the works published since James's time engage our attention, in reading others his sentiments spring to mind. Something is going wrong when a topic so intrinsically interesting should somehow tempt writers to be boring.

The main reason, I believe, why there is a mismatch between a ready interest in emotions and the potential tedium of psychological writing on the subject is the assumption that psychology is exclusively a natural science. A natural scientific stance implies possibilities of technical application. This in turn implies a style in which knowledge is independent of the knower so that it can be exported from one situation to another, and from person to person without ambiguity. Procedures, observables, and inferences are described separately from one another. Technical terms are elaborated, quantitative data presented, formalisms created. In the end we are seeking reliable, repeatable procedures of prediction and production in our environment.

A psychology of the emotions will not, however, be of interest just for its technical applications. It should also enable us to derive insights. This is where some works on the psychology of emotions have faltered. They are written in the style favored by academic psychology that implies technical application, when it is insight that is being sought.

If natural science and technology allow us to operate reliably in the outer world, we can think of insight as allowing us to understand our own inner world and the inner worlds of others. For this to be possible we must be able to make aspects of such worlds of our selves and others accessible and even salient. This requires a style of the kind more traditionally associated with poetry, theater, novels – with narrative.

This question of style had high priority in the earliest European discussions of cognition and emotion, the dialogues of Plato and the teachings of Aristotle. I suggest that style must again be taken seriously. In a psychology of emotions in which there is the possibility of insight, styles are needed that engage our emotions and thereby allow us to reflect on them.

Cognitive science carries the possibility of both usefulness and insight (Oatley, 1987a). The topic of emotions demands an alliance between the two, if any topic in psychology does. A style appropriate to this dual aim is necessary: a style that is neither just formalism, data-packed text, and technical description on the one hand, nor just dramatic and engaging narrative on the other. This book involves an attempt to create such a style.

So, rather than writing in a purely technical voice, I include narrative. And in the hope of avoiding too much ambiguity, I also invite the reader to understand emotional phenomena by means of a testable theoretical framework. My intent is to offer sufficient structure for the reader to be able to see emotions in new ways, and to be able to reflect on their significance.

I have not succeeded fully in creating such a style. One indication of this is that the book contains some passages that are mainly technical. I suggest that the reader wishing to follow the main flow of the book skips these. At the beginning of each part I give some directions about the sections that can be skipped without losing the overall sense.

Organization and content of the book

This book is organized into three parts. Part I presents a theory of emotions appropriate to the integrative task described above (Oatley & Johnson-Laird, 1987; Johnson-Laird & Oatley, 1989). We call it the communicative theory of emotions. It applies both to organization within the individual cognitive system and, because many emotions are social, to what takes place between people. Part II tackles specific issues of conflict within and between cognitive systems, as this is where emotions most often become problematic. Here I deal principally with three basic types of emotion: anger, sadness, and anxiety. Part III ends more cheerfully, dealing with the nature of happiness and with the expression of emotions in creative art. Here I try to draw conclusions about a problem that underlies the whole book, the problem of the function of emotions. To anticipate, I argue that emotions function to help us humans construct new parts of our own cognitive systems.

I have structured the book around ten pieces of literature in which emotions are explored. The two that carry most of this weight are the great nineteenth-century novels, Tolstoy's *Anna Karenina* and George Eliot's *Middlemarch*, with the first carrying some of the argument in the first stages of the book and the second in later stages. Then I have chosen some ancient poetry: Homer's *Iliad* and two love poems of Sappho. From the later Renaissance is John Donne's *Valediction: Forbidding Mourning*. Then there is Freud's *Dora*, arguably the piece of literature that brings to a conclusion the Victorian period and marks the beginning of the modern era in literature. From the modern period I briefly refer to Proust's *Remembrance of Things Past*, then at more length to Joanna Field's autobiographical *A Life of One's Own*, and to Penelope Lively's novel *Moon Tiger*. All these pieces of literature have an emotion, or emotions more generally, as a central concern. In my treatment of these works I give some literary criticism appropriate to psychological purposes, and say enough to introduce them to those who do not know them, though without giving too much away to those who will wish to read them whole. More specifically I seek to show how each of them allows us to press forward with an understanding of emotions that carries recognition and insight to its readers.

Though I have argued that we will not understand emotions without a basis that is sufficiently broad I regret that there is some unevenness in the level of discussion. Although, for instance, I treat some topics in the developmental psychology of emotions, this field has been growing rapidly and it is underrepresented here in terms of its importance. I have also been sparing in references to work in physiological psychology and ethology, mainly because they would take the issues too far away from concerns with human emotions toward those of animals. I am also aware that my selections from literary and philosophical texts have been patchy. In an attempt to make stark contrasts I have concentrated on early times and then on the nineteenth and twentieth centuries. My coverage of the great writers on emotions from the Middle Ages, the Renaissance, and the eighteenth century is sparse: Aquinas I do not mention at all; Shakespeare only in passing; Descartes, Spinoza, and Hume just a little. I can only squirm and apologize for not having done as well as I would have liked in these and in other matters where the book is unrepresentative.

Each chapter is somewhat self-contained – though, of course, the chapters in sequence also form the steps of an argument.

PART I

Theory and function

Perfection belongs to machines, and the imperfections
that are characteristic of human adaptation to need are an
essential quality in the environment that facilitates.
Donald Winnicott
Playing and reality, p. 163

What kinds of things are emotions? Perhaps the most basic observation
about emotions in Euro-American culture is that adults report experiences of subjective feelings that they describe as emotional. These experiences are consciously preoccupying. They are often accompanied by
bodily disturbances and are seen in facial expressions and gestures.
They also tend to prompt people toward actions or interactions that are
characteristic of the emotions. Emotions are not only consciously preoccupying – we are fascinated by them. Subjectively, they claim our attention and direct our interest. The fascination of emotional experiences
itself can be sought.

Emotions are, to some extent, involuntary. We experience and express
them without being able to choose them exactly. They are passions
rather than actions. We can, however, affect the timing of emotions,
modify them in various ways, inhibit their expression to some extent,
and vary their interpersonal implications. We can choose activities that
will maximize some emotional effects or distract us from others.

We give off emotional expressions in a way that is different from the
behavior that we consciously control. And these expressions are of a
distinctive type in that they often seem not to be steps toward achieving
any specific goal.

On the one hand, then, we have private, conscious experience of our
emotions that is not available to anyone else. On the other hand, experience of our own emotional expressions is visible to others but not fully
available to us. This difference between private experience and public

9

expression leads to an odd conclusion. Whereas a person and an observer can agree on whether some voluntary action has occurred, for instance, the raising of a hand at a meeting, this contrasts with emotional expressions, where private experience and public manifestation may be discrepant. There may even be doubt as to whether first-person descriptions and third-person descriptions of emotions refer to the same things.

When an emotion is experienced we sometimes do not understand it. To start with, there may be some inchoate sense, a kind of protoemotion. Only after thinking about it, perhaps discussing it or expressing it in various ways to various people, may we come to understand that emotion. Moreover, emotions may occur in waves, and their meanings may shift. A disturbance, experienced at first as frustration in some task, may become more clearly recognized as anger at some person. Behavior that at first seems to indicate contemptuous lack of interest in someone may be followed by sexual desire.

Not only are there transformations over hours or days, but life changes in its emotional patterns from infancy to adulthood. Emotions in childhood seem more salient, more intense, more frequent than in adulthood. There are clear continuities, but there is also the question of whether adult emotions concern different matters than those of childhood. Many of our strongest emotions are not so much individual but social. They arise out of our relationships with others, and they can affect those relationships. Emotions experienced as private may have profound consequences for others.

This brief survey of the characteristics of emotions is certainly incomplete, but it does touch on those issues that any theory of emotions must address.

This book is Aristotelian in conception. It starts with human appearances and intuitions about emotions. It also takes up evidence widely found in the human world, from opinions accepted "by everyone, or by the majority or by the wise" (Aristotle, *Topics,* 100b). After showing the relationships of some of these kinds of evidence to each other, I try to move toward understandings that resolve inconsistencies and avoid some of the errors inherent in the opinions from which we start. Of the great classical philosophers, Aristotle had the most to say about emotions. It is no accident that his interest in emotions is related to his interest in action. And so this book is based on an analysis of action, treated in a functionalist way.

In Aristotle's *On the Soul*,* the word *psuche*, though usually translated as "soul," more properly means something like "livingness" or "that which animates." Aristotle's proposal is a functionalist one. We can understand *psuche* as follows: "It is substance, in the sense of formula (*logos*)" (412b). Substance is made up of matter and form. So a vase might be made of bronze matter, but its form makes it an actual vase. Form in this sense is not just shape, but is that which enables a function to be fulfilled. It is, as Aristotle says, actual, whereas matter is potential.

To put this argument in relation to living things, Aristotle uses the metaphor of an ax. "Suppose that an implement, e.g. an axe, were a natural body, then the substance of the axe would be what makes it an axe, and this would be its soul (*psuche*); suppose this were removed, and it would no longer be an axe" (421b). He goes on to say that if the eye were a whole animal, its substance (or formula, or principle) would be sight. Aristotle's inquiry into what makes it possible for things to live starts from the functionalist position of what formulas or principles there might be that animate living things.

Aristotle's work has been superseded in many fields of inquiry by experimental science. In much of physics, for instance, his conclusions have been shown to be plain wrong. Cognitive science, however, can be seen both as continuous with classical preoccupations of epistemology that stretch back to Plato and Aristotle and, because of the computer, as a wholly fresh start. This new start is made not from a Platonic position, but from a position of Aristotelian functionalism.

Modern functionalism includes the doctrine that to understand something is to be able to make a model of it, certainly a mental model and nowadays a computational model. In the strong form of the argument, computational processes need not merely simulate mental processes; they could *be* mental processes. In other words, a formula (*logos*) of such processes, if fully understood, could be implemented on mechanisms other than biological ones. *On the Soul* begins with criticisms of earlier work and then offers its startlingly original treatment by proposing that *psuche* is to be understood in functionalist terms such as those just stated, the discussion opening with the analogy of the ax to help explain the functionalist idea. Aristotle asserts, in effect, that there is an analogy between an ax and a living organism.

Analogies between things that are different each point to a functional

---

* I use Hett's translation of *On the Soul* from the Loeb edition because for this issue it is clearer than the edition edited by Barnes.

principle that is common to them, and that is their essence. Aristotle uses analogies frequently in his biological work. In *On the Soul*, he wonders whether the soul might not be like the sailor in a ship. Later, he points out the far from superficial analogy between the roots of plants and the mouths of animals, both serving the function of nutrition. Elsewhere he explains movements of animals as like "automatic puppets, which are set going on the occasion of a tiny movement (the strings are released and the pegs strike against one another)" (*Movement of Animals*, 701b).

Making models depends on the possibility of particular functions, including psychological ones such as perceiving and making inferences, being accomplished in a variety of matter. In cognitive science we are now able to assert that such functions can be based on carbon in living things or on silicon in computers. That one thing could ever be a model of something else depends on such equivalences. Cognitive science has undergone a revolution because with computers we can make much better models of living and mental processes than formerly, and this allows understandings that complement empirical inquiry. Now we need not just make observations and do experiments to find out how a biological system works. We can see what principles are involved when we try to make comparable systems.

In Part I, I analyze emotions using a functionalist approach to action, discussing the underlying principles that make intelligent action possible for any kind of being, human or otherwise. In this domain, Aristotle's work has not been superseded. Rather, computation has enabled us to pursue an Aristotelian research program in a way that was not previously possible. We can start from and compare intuitions. We can also try to discover by writing computer programs to simulate mental processes how our arguments might become internally consistent.

The main idea of Chapter 1 is to contrast a technical view of planning with human action. I show how a realistic theory of intended action requires processes that function to organize transitions among sequences of action and to establish priorities. Finally, I introduce three issues that I claim are essential to understanding the relation of emotions to human action: first, that human action has many goals not just one; second, that such action takes place in a world in which we have limited resources and imperfect knowledge; and, third, that much of human action is undertaken jointly with others.

In Chapter 2 I argue that emotions are not just a heterogeneous collection of events to be dismissed as the misleading constructs of folk theory, and I do so by examining approaches from different directions. From one direction I discuss understandings that depend on folk theory and are embodied in English emotion terms. From another I present the main postulates of the natural scientific theory on which this book is based. I discuss empirical evidence relevant to each postulate, as well as the implications of cross-cultural studies. This chapter is partly addressed to the cognitive science community as a methodological proposal, explaining why I start the book with scenes from literature and from intentional terms rather than from laboratory experiments. Chapter 2 is the most technical in the book. Some readers may wish to skip it altogether, or maybe they will judiciously skip parts, such as the semantic analyses of English emotion terms, that are technical.

Chapter 3 takes up the issue of whether emotions are functional and have a rational basis, or whether they are untrustworthy, atavistic elements of our lives – a question that is central to any understanding of emotions. The discussion is based on the conceptualizations and evidence of the ethological and experimental psychological literature on emotions from Darwin to the present. I counter proposals that emotions are without function and that they distort proper adult mental processes like thinking. Indeed, I claim that the idea that emotions are especially irrational is based on an inadequate understanding of the nature of both thinking and emotions, which the theory of planning is capable of improving. Chapter 3 is concerned with our limitations, including the impossibility of knowing the world perfectly.

Chapter 4 is based on how emotions function in our relations with each other. After a discussion of work in artificial intelligence on how two agents may organize joint plans, I use this work as a basis to inquire about what is distinctively human in our interactions and what the function of emotions might be in those interactions. Most of the emotions that people find either interesting or troublesome are those that emerge in such interactions. I propose that human beings are cognitively specialized for interacting with other cognitive beings in joint plans. This leads to an analysis of social interaction quite different from any based on individual plans in which other people are treated as objects or resources. Again, the reader may wish to skip some technical passages, perhaps especially those that deal with linguistic analyses.

1. The structure of emotions

Man is a synthesis of the infinite and the finite, of the
temporal and the eternal, of freedom and necessity.
Søren Kierkegaard
The sickness unto death, p. 146

Body and mind

We live in two worlds: a finite world of embodiment in time, place, and
biological nature and an infinite world of imagination, language, and
culture. It is perhaps the transition from the nineteenth to the twentieth
century that prompts the substitution of "nature" and "culture" for
Kierkegaard's "finite" and "infinite." Despite the rather old-fashioned
tone of Kierkegaard's aphorism,[1] the problems of synthesis of these two
worlds could scarcely be more apt to a discussion of the structure[2] of
human emotions.

As to nature: Emotions are concerned with the bodily, with facts, with
our limitations. Often emotions occur as a kind of necessity, outside
voluntary control. As to culture: Emotions are concerned with our imagination, with plans and aspirations, which continually change and are
limitless. Emotions arise with the meeting of these two worlds of nature
and culture. This book is concerned with exploring and understanding
this meeting.

Scenes of emotion

Here, from Leo Tolstoy's *Anna Karenina* (1980/1877) is a scene of emotion:
Anna and her husband, Alexis Alexandrovitch, are watching a cavalry
officers' race when one of the riders falls (Tolstoy, 1980/1877):

14

The officer brought the news that the rider was unhurt but that the horse had broken its back.

On hearing this Anna quickly sat down and hid her face behind her fan. Karenin saw that she was crying, and that she was unable to keep back either her tears or her sobs that were making her bosom heave. He stepped forward so as to screen her, giving her time to recover.

"For the third time I offer you my arm," he said. (p. 210)

Then, later in the carriage on the way home:

"Perhaps I was mistaken," said he. "In that case I beg your pardon."

"No, you were not mistaken," she said slowly, looking despairingly into his cold face. "You were not mistaken. I was, and can not help being, in despair. I listen to you, but I am thinking of him. I love him, I am his mistress, I cannot endure you; I am afraid of you, and I hate you." (p. 212)

Tolstoy depicts here the class of nature and culture: When the accident happened, "a change came over Anna's face which was positively improper. She quite lost self-control" (p. 209). She was unable to restrain her show of concern for her lover, Vronsky, who was riding in the race. When she heard that he was alive after his fall, she was still less able to act voluntarily. She was caught up in emotions, in events of nature, precipitated by the fact of her lover's near death. At the same time, the meaning of this event in the lives of Anna and her husband is a product of culture, of their aspirations, of the rules and expectations of marriage, and the implications of having an adulterous affair in that part of Russian aristocratic society.

Karenin says he is sorry if he was wrong. He had tried to prevent others seeing his wife's emotion following her lover's fall, and suggested that they leave. He apologizes because he has had suspicions of her fidelity previously, and she had mockingly rebuffed them, making him feel ridiculous. He apologizes because he wants, against the evidence, to believe his wife faithful. He wants to be, and be seen to be, an irreproachable member of society. It is for Anna's public show of concern for her lover that he has reproached her.

In the terms of the nineteenth-century novel, emotions are depicted. Anna weeps – from relief that her lover is not killed. Karenin declares sorrow that inadequately masks jealousy clinging to a shred of hope:

"Perhaps I was mistaken. . . . If so, I beg your pardon" (p. 212). Karenin's apology is more formal than one might expect in the conversation of husbands and wives – but he is formal and becomes more so when angry. He finds it easier to reproach Anna for public indiscretion than to talk of any regrets he might have at the loss of her love. In any case, he makes an apology. On it, and on what is said next, hang the future of Karenin's and Anna's lives, individually and with each other. Around this moment between Karenin's apology and Anna's reply the novel turns. Anna expresses hatred, rebuffing him after her forbearance and then her deceit: "No, you were not mistaken," said Anna. . . . "I love him. I am afraid of you, and I hate you" (p. 212).

Two common conventions of the nineteenth-century European novel are that plots turn on such moments of emotion and that the emotions are not straightforward but are expressed in subtle ways. Though emotions may affect us strongly, often their meanings are not obvious. The insights of the great novelists include the light they throw on the meanings of emotions. Tolstoy's Anna struggles with herself in her life with Karenin. Then her ardent nature finds an object in Vronsky. Karenin is not an emotional man. Even in this moment of severe disappointment, he can only express his emotions with a coldness of face and an overformality of manner.

What is an emotion?

What is an emotion? This is the title of a famous paper by William James (1884) – and, indeed, it is a good question.

We all might agree that Anna, as she is sobbing, is undergoing an emotion, but to define emotion is difficult. Some argue that it is impossible. Mandler (1984) observes that there is no commonly or even superficially acceptable definition of the term, and, he adds, too many psychologists fail to understand this. Emotion may merely be an ordinary language usage that points to a quite heterogeneous set of phenomena. Though we may all agree on some states as examples of emotion, we may disagree about others.

Fehr and Russell (1984) asked 200 subjects to write down examples of emotion terms for 1 minute. In their analysis, Fehr and Russell treated syntactic variants of a term as the same, for example, "anxious," "anxiety," and "anxiously" all counted as the same term. They found that 196 such terms were mentioned by at least two people. Some seem obviously good examples of emotions, like "happiness," the most common and mentioned by 152 subjects. But what about "hurt," with 16 mentions, "lust" with 8, "stress" with 4, "thinking" with 3, and "insecurity" with 2?

These examples are quite varied; the full list of 196 terms is even more so. Is it possible to make sense out of such emotional vocabularies? James (1890) thought not:

> If one should seek to name each particular one of them [emotions] of which the human heart is the seat, it is plain that the limit to their number would lie in the introspective vocabulary of the seeker, each race of men having found names for some shade of feeling which other races have left undiscriminated. If we should seek to break the emotions, thus enumerated, into groups, according to their affinities, it is again plain that all sorts of groupings would be possible, according as we chose this character or that as a basis, and that all groupings would be equally real and true. (p. 485)

James thought the answer to his question would lie elsewhere. His answer was that emotions are perceptions of bodily states.[3] Because indefinitely many such perceptions are possible, just as there are indefinitely many perceptions of the outside world, there is an infinite number of emotions and they will be variously described.

This book is based on the theory that emotion is a coherent concept, and that emotions are mental states that can be defined, that can be talked about in ordinary language, and that have functions. Two competing proposals will be compared with this theory. One proposal I will call the heterogeneity argument. James's theory is an example, and it is considered in this and the next chapter. The heterogeneity theory holds that emotion terms arise from folk theories in ordinary language, but they have no coherent psychological status. Instead, bodily changes and physiology should be investigated and related to eliciting events using natural scientific methods. The other alternative is discussed in Chapter 2. This theory states that emotions are vestiges of our animal and infantile history that tend to distort adult mental functions.

James proposed that folk theories have no relation to any future scientific account, but that there are such things as emotions: They are perceptions of bodily events. A more extreme version of the heterogeneity argument is that when we have a scientific account of physiological and perceptual processes, scientific discourse will not include emotion terms at all, except perhaps as a shorthand or in passing (cf. Churchland,

1986). Today we no longer discuss personality or disease in terms of humors. Saying that someone is melancholy or phlegmatic has an archaic sound. A yet more radical variant of the heterogeneity argument might be put as follows. The failure of universally accepted theories of emotion to emerge despite more than a century's research may indicate that the very enterprise of trying to create even such theories as James's is mistaken.

James's "What is an emotion?" may have misled us. Just because it sounds like a question does not mean that it has an answer, any more than does "Why is the moon made of cream cheese?" Draper[4] has put it as follows: Hypotheses of the form "All emotions are X" invite counterexamples, and that for the theories so far advanced in the psychological literature these are not difficult to think of. So, for James's theory that emotions are perceptions of bodily states, one could ask: What about emotions that occur when listening to music? It was to combat such an argument that James developed the idea of the coarse emotions that involve strong bodily perturbations. Thus only some emotions are covered by his theory.

According to the radical heterogeneity argument, examples can always be found that will not be covered by any possible unifying proposal. This is because, as Draper continues, it may make no more sense to ask what an emotion is than to ask what intelligence is. Emotion, like intelligence, is a term used variously to indicate aspects of the functioning of the whole cognitive system. It is not a property of any specific subsystem or a description of a specific kind of process.

An answer to William James's question

In contrast to these arguments of heterogeneity, I propose that emotions are mental states with coherent psychological functions and that they are recognizable by empirical and theoretical criteria. When these criteria are applied, apparent heterogeneities and ambiguities disappear. Emotions can be described scientifically in a way that corresponds recognizably to emotions as referred to in ordinary language. We should continue to refer to emotions as mental states, just as we talk about seeing and hearing even though more than a hundred years of research has taught us much more about them than is known to a layperson.

What, then, are emotions from this viewpoint? And how do they differ from bodily states like feeling cold or from personality traits like shyness? An emotion is a distinctive mental state that normally occurs in identifiable eliciting conditions. It has distinctive parts and recognizable consequences.[5] I describe these rather generally at first, indicating typical emotions, and then extend the analysis to all emotions.

Eliciting conditions of emotions

Emotions occur in distinctive circumstances, but the events that elicit them are not purely physical. Rather, they are psychological. By physical, I mean that when a stimulus is applied it has a reliable effect, irrespective of to whom it is applied or the recipient's evaluations. For instance, if someone is put in a cold environment, bodily changes, such as shivering, occur. Pursuing this kind of argument, Ekman, Friesen, and Simons (1985) have shown that startle is not an emotion. It is a reflex reaction with stereotyped characteristics that can be triggered reliably by a physical stimulus, a loud, sharp sound.

Emotions are not elicited in this way. There is no physical situation that will reliably initiate particular emotions, because emotions depend on evaluations of what has happened in relation to the person's goals and beliefs. For instance, I may suddenly feel frightened if the vehicle in which I am traveling seems to be heading for an accident. I evaluate a perception in relation to my concerns for safety, though not necessarily consciously. This may be the common experience in such situations. But a person confident that an accident would not occur, perhaps the one who is driving, or the one who is unconcerned about personal safety at that moment, may not feel fear.

We do, however, think of emotions as more or less appropriate to circumstances. So it would be strange not to feel fear in response to a believable threat of torture. Clinicians often categorize the anxiety of patients as abnormal when they can see no reason for it. So we expect people to feel sadness at a loss, anger at being thwarted, happiness at meeting a friend, and so on. The relation is not always simple, though, and novelists who chronicle events that elicit emotions often comment on how appropriate the emotions are to those events (cf. also De Sousa, 1987).

The two components of an emotion

Action readiness. If we ask what the core of an emotion is, the best answer based on our present state of knowledge is that it is a mental state of readiness for action (Frijda, 1986), or a change of readiness. Such a change of readiness is normally based on an evaluation of something happening that affects important concerns (e.g., Lazarus, 1966; Frijda, 1986; Roberts, 1988). This evaluation need not be made consciously.

An emotion tends to specify a range of options for action. When frightened, we evaluate a situation in relation to a concern for safety and become ready to freeze, fight, or flee. We stop what we are doing and check for signs of danger (Gray, 1982). In an emotional state we are pressed toward a small range of actions in a compulsive way. In fear, it may seem impossible to act except in ways to make ourselves feel safer. When angry, we are prompted to attack. When sad, we may not feel able to do anything very much.

Phenomenological tone. This description of emotions as states of action readiness points to an underlying function of emotion. Emotions also have a distinctive phenomenological tone, of which we may be conscious. Each emotion can typically be felt as different from contrasting emotions and from nonemotions: Sadness feels different from happiness and from states like deductive reasoning or sleepiness. Sometimes we may not be consciously aware of an emotion, though others can see signs of it in our behavior. Sometimes emotions seem inchoate, and we do not quite know how we feel.

The conscious feeling of an emotion, of sadness, fear, or the like, is not identical with the evaluation or the state of readiness. An underlying mental state is the core of an emotion. In common with most mental states, only limited aspects of it are conscious.[6] Mechanisms of generating the action readiness are not conscious. In Western culture, however, it is common (wrongly) to identify the underlying mental state of an emotion with its conscious feeling, for example, "I *feel* sad," as if the conscious feeling were the whole emotion.

The usual accompaniments of emotions

As well as the underlying mental state and its associated feeling tone, emotions are typically accompanied by one or more of the following.

Conscious preoccupation. Emotions have attentional properties. They often include a preoccupying and even compulsive inner dialogue. When in an emotional state, we may find it difficult to stop thinking about the issue. When angry, for example, we may dwell on thoughts of revenge.

Bodily disturbance. An emotion is typically accompanied by a bodily disturbance involving the autonomic nervous system and other physiological processes. In anger, skin temperature tends to rise; in fear, it may fall, and the face becomes pale.

Expressions. Emotions are often outwardly expressed by recognizable facial gestures, bodily postures, and tones of voice that are not entirely voluntary. For instance, happiness typically involves smiling, particular patterns of muscle movements around the eyes, and a lightness and spontaneity of speaking.

Action consequences of emotions

The consequences of an emotion are that we may act, perhaps somewhat involuntarily. So Anna acts by speaking to her husband: "No, you were not mistaken," she said. . . . "I love him. I am afraid of you, and I hate you" (p. 212). Such speech acts, like all actions, may change the world. Anna is at the beginning of a sequence of actions of withdrawing from her husband.

Typical emotions

A fully developed, typical emotion is a kind of readiness elicited by some event that impinges on a person's concerns. It will have a tone that is experienced consciously and it will include accompaniments of conscious preoccupation, bodily disturbance, and expression. It will also issue in some course of action prompted by the emotion.

In certain episodes of emotion, however, an eliciting condition, a feeling tone, some of the accompaniments, or an action consequence may not occur or may not be noticed. In other words, ordinary instances of emotions may differ from the typical emotion just described by lacking one or more of these features. In a study in which subjects kept structured diaries of episodes of emotion, Oatley and Duncan (1992) found that 77% of emotions of happiness, sadness, anger, and fear included a subjective inner feeling of emotion, 77% included a bodily sensation, 81% were accompanied by involuntary thoughts, and 90% involved a consciously recognized action or an urge to act emotionally. Most episodes of emotion included all these features, but in some one or several features were absent.

The emotion process

Frijda's (1986) conceptualization of emotions is similar to that described here, and he discusses thoroughly the evidence for his formulation. He has proposed that emotions are processes of the following kind:

> event coding→appraisal→significance evaluation→action readiness→action

Each step is itself complex. For instance, appraisal involves comparing the coded event with the person's concerns, evaluation involves diagnosing what can be done about it, and so on. Some steps may have conscious accompaniments, and the action that occurs may include emotional expressions, physiological changes, and physical actions on the world.

A difference between Frijda's account and that offered here is that Frijda argues that an emotion is not a state but a whole process from event coding to action. I argue that it is more straightforward to see emotion as a mental state of readiness based on an evaluation and with a specific phenomenological tone, but to distinguish this for purposes of analysis from eliciting conditions, from accompaniments, and from action sequences. These are minor divergences, and their reasons are discussed in Chapter 2.

We often recognize an emotion in others, says Frijda, like this:

> At some moments when observing behavior that behavior seems to come to a stop. Effective interaction with the environment halts and is replaced by behavior that is centered, as it were, around the person himself, as in a fit of weeping or laughter, anger or fear. (1986, p. 2)

Tolstoy depicts just such an event. Anna ceased to concentrate on the race, and stopped behaving in the way that one does when watching a sporting event. It was on seeing this that her husband tried to shield her display from others who might guess at its significance.

The duration and intensity of emotions

As well as qualitative features emotions have quantitative dimensions, specifically of time and intensity. An emotion may start suddenly or slowly and decay either fast or slowly. The interval between an eliciting event and the start of an emotion may vary. At any moment an emotion will have a specific intensity, which can be measured by facial, physiological, or phenomenological indices.

Emotional expressions of the face and the physiological perturbations of emotions last typically for seconds or minutes (Ekman, 1984). People's subjective experiences of episodes of emotion can last for much longer. Frijda et al. (1991) had people draw graphs of the time course of emotion episodes. The shapes of such graphs were rather variable, and there was often periodic fluctuation of intensity, as the emotion returned in waves. Frijda et al. found that it was not unusual for emotions to last for several hours and that a few bridged across a period of sleep into the following day. They use these observations to argue that emotion is a process. In the diary study of Oatley and Duncan (1992), 33% of episodes of happiness, sadness, or anger lasted 5 minutes or less, 34% lasted 5 to 30 minutes, and 33% lasted longer than 30 minutes. The diary method and the method used by Frijda et al., however, are insensitive to more fleeting emotions.

Informally the picture is this: Depending on factors such as the importance of the concern involved, an emotion may rise to a peak and perhaps fade after some minutes or hours or until the issue is resolved interpersonally or in some other way. Intensity may wane and then increase in further waves, or an emotion may be replaced by another emotion focused on a different aspect of the issue that elicited the original emotion. The duration of an emotion, a few minutes to several hours of preoccupation with an emotional event, corresponds to an emotion occurring at a point of transition. Emotions are changes in action readiness, and other cognitive changes accompany them. If an emotion lasts a long time it is because the transition that is occurring is not just a switch from one state to another. The starting up of new plans and other cognitive reprogramming that may be involved can have extensive implications that occupy a person mentally for some time.

People do experience emotional states that last for days, weeks, months, and even years, as the sadness that follows bereavement. Emotional states that last for more than a few hours are referred to as *moods*, particularly when the subject is unaware of how the state started. Moods tend to be of lower intensity, perhaps punctuated by waves of more distinct emotion. So, for the purposes of description, we see emotions as discrete states of some intensity, typically noticeable to the self or to others or from recording of autonomic nervous system indices, and lasting for finite periods.

Moods are emotional in that, like episodes of emotion, they are based on exactly the same kinds of readiness. Moods are, however, longer lasting background states that, rather than being associated with changes and interruptions, resist further changes and interruptions. They do not have the compulsiveness of an emotion episode – other actions may be superimposed upon them. Thus, we may see Anna's sobbing as indicating a discrete involuntary emotion, and her outburst at Karenin as another. But the state of longing in which she later waits to see her lover Vronsky again after returning home is best thought of as a mood, during which she would no doubt do things quite unrelated to it.

The functions of emotions

The account given so far has been descriptive. Even though emotions have been identified as types of readiness for action, why should this be important for understanding mental life? The most fundamental question for a psychological understanding of emotions is "What are their functions?" The answer that I propose is based on the idea that most human action has many simultaneous aims but limited resources. It takes place in a world that is imperfectly known and in conjunction with other people. Emotions function in the management of action when all the consequences of such action cannot be fully foreseen.

In cognitive psychology it is axiomatic that actions do not occur singly or haphazardly. They occur in ordered sequences and achieve purposes. An ordered sequence of actions that achieves a purpose is known as a plan. So it is to the principles of planned action that we should look to understand the functions of emotions.

Simple plans

Plots and plans

The plot of a story or play is a sequence of actions, a *plan*, of one or several protagonists. The cognitive representation of a plan can be thought of as follows:

    Goal (preconditions)→actions→effects

This is to be read as: A goal (when the right preconditions exist) prompts a series of actions that in turn produce effects in the world.

A goal is an aim, or as Frijda puts it, a concern. It is a description of a possible state of the world represented symbolically in a cognitive system. I will use the term *goal* in a way that is neutral as to whether or not it is conscious. A goal-directed system works to achieve a correspondence between the world and the goal by changing the world through an ordered series of actions, a plan. Preconditions are states of the world that affect whether and how a plan can be accomplished. Again, I will use the term *plan* in a way that is neutral as to how conscious it is.

Marriage is a plan, a long-term one requiring two actors to carry it out jointly. In our society, marriage is the very paradigm of a joint plan eagerly adopted. Into its course unforeseen circumstances intrude. For Karenin, in Tolstoy's novel, the plan of marriage was meant to accomplish, among other goals, a faultless display of respectworthy adult life that would support his role as an important person with a public position. By becoming married, Anna had entered into the joint plan with Karenin and pursued a goal that was somewhat similar to his. Only when her lover was in danger did emotions cause her to bungle an aspect of it. Her show of emotion revealed that she was simultaneously conducting another plan, with another goal that was incompatible with the first. A juncture occurred at which her two plans collided. At this point the possible outcomes of each were evaluated very differently than before.

Emotions emerge at just such significant junctures in plans. The reevaluations that occur are communicated to oneself and somewhat involuntarily to others. European novels of the nineteenth century are representations of the ways in which emotions occur in the course of our most serious life plans. At the same time, emotions are communicated to readers who identify with one or more of the characters, and in so doing may activate experiences of their own. The implication is that in such novels each reader may reflect on issues of action in relation to others.

Novels and plays have been able to depict and transmit emotions because they have plots. Within psychology, however, emotions may have been difficult to understand partly because the psychological structures corresponding to plots, namely, plans and narrative accounts, in some ways have been neglected.

The hierarchical arrangement of plans

In a conscious plan some effects of actions are imagined in advance and can form the basis of an intention. Here is another passage from *Anna Karenina*, describing a plan of a single actor. Early in the book, Vronsky drives to the train station to meet his mother, who is arriving in Moscow

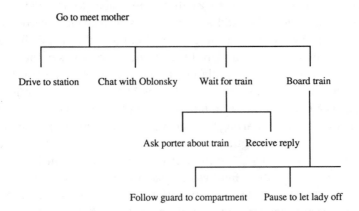

Figure 1. Fragment of a hierarchical plan tree representing a sequence of actions from Tolstoy's *Anna Karenina*. (Modified from Oatley, 1988a.)

from St. Petersburg. The train arrives, and a guard tells him what compartment Countess Vronsky is in.

> Vronsky followed the guard to the carriage, and had to stop at the entrance of the compartment to let a lady pass out.
> The trained insight of a Society man enabled Vronsky with a glance to decide that she belonged to the best Society. He apologised for being in her way and was about to enter the carriage, but felt compelled to have another look at her. (p. 60)

A basic formulation of cognitive science is that the structure of plans can be represented as a hierarchy or tree. Hierarchy was postulated by Miller, Galanter, and Pribram (1960) as the major principle of plans. A plan is an organization of action similar to a computer program. It has an overall goal, to be achieved by fulfilling a set of subgoals. Miller, Galanter, and Pribram speak of a goal as a kind of image of how the world might be, so that action can then be devoted to making the world like the image. In turn, each goal can evoke lower-level goals and so on down a hierarchical tree that terminates in actions.

Using this formulation, we can express some of Vronsky's plan as in Figure 1. The top-level goal is to meet his mother. Tolstoy describes the action as involving various subgoals: drive to station, chat with Oblonsky (whom Vronsky meets by chance), wait for train, and board train. Terminal nodes of this tree are actions such as ask porter about train.

A novelist assumes that only a few elements need be mentioned, often in terms of subgoals and actions: Vronsky drives to the station, chats with Oblonsky, asks the porter when the train will come, follows the guard to his mother's compartment, and so on. We, the readers, use these cues to build from our own knowledge a mental model[7] of the scene and a plan tree of an actor corresponding to that in Figure 1. A mental model is a means of simulating states of the world; a plan tree represents a sequence of actions made meaningful by the goals they accomplish. From such a model and such a plan tree we fill in the gaps in the narrative.

The cognitive psychology of plans

To meet one's mother at a station is to enact a plan. Vronsky imagines a state of affairs: meeting his mother. He also has a model of himself. This includes the knowledge that he can act to achieve such a state of affairs. One formulation would be that by operating with his mental models (involving, perhaps, times, routes, places) he assembles a series of sub-goals, and hence the actions he will perform, to achieve the overall goal. After assembling the plan in the simulation space of his mind, he can act, directing himself, as it were, by reading off the actions in sequence. This idea of the planning hierarchy captures a principle of what we mean by acting intentionally. It also allows us to connect this fundamental piece of human cognition with computational accounts of action.

The analysis given in Figure 1 has actions like asking and receiving a reply as primitives at that level of detail. Part of the interest for psychologists is the idea that a plan tree can be applied at any level of detail.[8] A similar hierarchy could be constructed in which muscle movements of the mouth and throat are the primitives in a hierarchy that specifies the articulation of certain sounds when speaking. At a yet finer level a hierarchy based on primitives of individual muscle fiber contractions could be constructed. The idea of hierarchical organization has often been invoked in brain research as an organizing principle, as evidenced by the common use of such terms as higher and lower brain functions.[9] Computer programs are constructed in the same way. Programs in high-level programming languages are implemented as programs in lower-level languages.

Goals in narrative. At the level of detail shown in Figure 1, human actors can talk about their goals and subgoals. To give a reason for an action or subgoal is like reading off the goal at the next highest node. For instance,

Vronsky might say: "I waited because I wanted a train which had not yet arrived." The subgoal was not achieved immediately because the precondition of the train's arrival was not yet fulfilled. For the next higher level of analysis (not shown in Figure 1), higher goals are referred to. Tolstoy informs us about them: In novels, such goals constitute "character": Vronsky meets his mother not because he loves her, but because, "in accordance with the views of the set he lived in, and as a result of his education, he could not imagine himself treating her in any but one altogether submissive and respectful" (p. 60).

So we begin to understand that Vronsky acts partly to fulfill goals set by convention and propriety. In the wake of his ambivalence about these, in the scene at the station, a potentially conflicting plan is hinted at, with a goal of a quite different kind. The first nuance of a sexual plan is implied. Anna is the woman at whom he takes another look as he goes to enter the railway carriage. This is their first meeting.

Mental models. A plan implies forethought. Craik (1943) proposed that thinking consists of translating perceptual information into the terms of a model of the world, then operating on this model, and finally doing a retranslation into terms of the world again, for example, into actions. Models allow the representation of effects of actions without inappropriate, expensive, or dangerous consequences that wrong actions might have in the real world.

Search in constructing plans. The idea of a plan itself has been modeled in artificial intelligence programs. To plan means to search for courses of action in a simulated model world. To construct a plan means starting up a model of the world and searching sequences of actions until a path from the current state to the goal is discovered.[10] Typical planning programs search backward from the goal because this makes it easier to keep account of the reasons, that is, the goals, for each action. When a solution is discovered – the sequence of actions that connects the goal to the starting point – it is remembered. Then this stored sequence can be unreeled in the opposite direction in the actual world.

Procedures. Plans are often decomposed into parts each of which achieves a subgoal. In computation such parts are procedures. A computer program is a simple hierarchical plan. If it is to be understood or developed it needs to be composed of procedures. Figure 2 illustrates such a hierarchical structure of a plan, with subgoals at each level, dominating

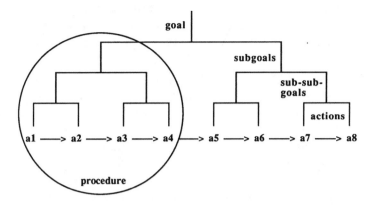

Figure 2. A simple plan: a sequence of actions a1 to a8 organized to achieve sub-sub-goals, which are organized to achieve subgoals, and the whole organized to achieve an overall goal. The circle encloses a separable procedure that achieves a subgoal.

lower-level goals downward to primitive actions. Procedures, such as the one circled, result from decomposing a complex plan into parts that can be more readily understood. Each procedure is relatively self-contained, and each is relatively free of side effects. Procedures can be nested together so that one procedure, higher in the hierarchy, can call other subprocedures with as many levels of embedding as necessary.

When it is run, then, the action sequence in Figure 2, a1 to a8, is orchestrated by procedures invoking one another in the hierarchy – the overt action of a plan, then, depends on unseen inner structure. The virtue of composing plans from procedures is that procedures can be tested and developed on their own and then the problems of assembling them can be tackled.[11]

Plans and technical skills

All this is, in a sense, familiar to the European or American mind. The idea of rational planning to achieve a goal is indeed a conception expounded nearly two and a half thousand years ago that has profoundly influenced the Western tradition. One of the accomplishments of this tradition of Socrates, Plato, and Aristotle was to formalize the idea of *techne,* meaning a craft or skill, and to apply it to all sorts of situations.[12] *Techne* is the skilled application of plans, for giving speeches, for navigating ships, for curing diseases, and so on. *Techne* requires reliable knowledge, *episteme*, or, as cognitive scientists might now say, an accurate model of the world. *Episteme* is technical knowledge that allows plans to be constructed, and *techne* is a simple plan (like that in Figure 2) for achieving a defined goal or "good," as classical writers called it. Technical knowledge is exportable to other people, but it is usually applicable only to a single domain.[13] So a person can learn the skill of rhetoric but may know only how to organize information to give a speech, a navigator can learn about stars and coastlines, a doctor about diseases.

The classical philosophers distinguished means and ends. As in an artificial intelligence plan, the planning phase involves first considering the goal and then the steps to achieve it. Enacting a plan takes place in the reverse order: Actions are followed by the goal. The Greeks described the hierarchical organization of skills whereby the finished product of one craft becomes the raw material of another: Chunks of marble produced from the quarry become blocks shaped by the mason that become the components arranged by an architect.

Techne is perhaps the most successful of all ideas in the history of ideas. On its applications the world in which we now live depends. It is embodied in technology based on procedures of science that produce reliable *episteme*. The computer is a device by which means can be related to ends. It is itself a means that can undertake a *techne* like skilled people. And, for the first time, because its processes are open to investigation, we can compare artificial knowledge-based systems achieving plans with our own less accessible mental operations. The cognitive conception of a simple plan as a hierarchy of subgoals that might be accomplished by a single robot actor forms an all-important kernel of understanding action. It is indeed the fundamental principle of cognitive science that accomplishing an intended action involves a plan based on a model and organized in this way. It is, moreover, the kernel that is needed for understanding emotions.

How, exactly, does the idea of emotions as changing readiness for action connect with this principle of planned action? The connection is that the principle of planning takes us some way toward understanding human action, but not far enough. Despite the idea of *techne* being such a good one, even the early philosophers had to restrain their enthusiasm in trying to apply it to everything. Are there aspects of human life where the principle of planning does not fit? Plato, in *The Republic*, argues, for instance, that though justice is a good (a goal), attaining it is not a technical matter. Aristotle, in the *Nicomachean Ethics*, is even more skeptical of the universal applicability of *techne*. A *techne* of ethics would require a universal metric against which the results of all personal and political actions could be measured in order to make rational choices in relation to some single top-level goal. If some subgoals are incompatible with others, however, no such *techne* of ethics can exist (Nussbaum, 1986). In *Anna Karenina*, we, too, may wonder whether Anna's uncontrollable sobbing at the races, or even Vronsky's actions as he goes to meet his mother at the station, are really the results of simple plans that involved exact goals or a complete model of the world, in the way that artificial intelligence plans do.

The idea of goals and operations in a mental model world provides a fundamental principle, as Aristotle might say, the *logos*, of human action. Yet human actions, including conducting a love affair or meeting one's mother at the station, are clearly different from anything yet programmed in a computer. To understand issues of human intention, the simple idea of a plan as described so far is necessary, but not sufficient. In an attempt to explain ordinary human action, we must augment the basic theory. As we do so, we discover that it is no accident that a simple technical plan such as a computer program has nothing emotional about it. As we introduce the augmentations to basic planning theory, we find we must also consider the function of emotions in human action.

Augmented planning

Table 1 shows differences between simple technical plans and everyday human action. The principle of a basic plan corresponds to that of a simple technical plan, as indicated in the left-hand column of Table 1. This is close to the classical Greek conception of *techne*, or skill. Cognitive analyses of plans are mainly of this kind, for the good reason that this is how things are done technically in the world. For cognitive science to characterize everyday human action, however, we also have to understand the issues in the right-hand column. Some of these have distinctly nontechnical attributes. Many involve issues of emotion.

I shall now describe three types of augmentation needed to extend these principles toward those of everyday human plans. The types of augmentation correspond to the three groupings in Table 1.

Augmentation 1: multiple goals

Unlike the sequences directed to a single main goal in a simple or technical plan, human intended action is influenced by multiple goals.[14] To characterize even an apparently simple intended action, several goals

Table 1. *Comparison of computational and other technical plans with everyday human plans, in three major groupings*

Computational and other technical plans	Everyday human plans
1. Goals: number, specification, engagement	
Single top-level goal	Multiple goals
Exact specification of goals	Vague specifications of goals
Nothing corresponds to engagement with one particular goal	Human actors can become engaged in a plan or with a goal
2. Completeness of knowledge and resources	
Accurate and complete model of domain	Imperfect and incomplete model of domain
Adequate resources of time and materials to reach goal	Limited resources of time and materials
Plans enacted ballistically, often with only intermittent feedback	Actions proceed piecemeal with much feedback
Construction and execution are different phases	Construction and execution are intermingled
Debugging takes place off-line in construction phase	Errors often occur during execution
3. Number of agents	
Usually directed by a single cognitive system	Often involves coordination of more than one person

Source: Draper and Oatley (in preparation).

may be relevant. Thus, when Vronsky goes to meet his mother, as well as wanting to accomplish that goal he also might want to go for a drive. As a man of the world he might like being out and about.[15] Perhaps he may have wanted something to do when he might otherwise have been bored. Or maybe on the occasion of his mother's arrival he had to defer some other goal. At the station new goals emerge. Vronsky takes an opportunity to speak with Anna.

Often multiple goals give rise to conflicts. Because we have only imperfect models of the world, and of the implications of our goal structure, the pursuit of some goals may only become overtly problematic in

Table 2. *Wilensky's classification of multiple goal states*

	Single actor	Two actors
Goals are compatible	Goal synergy	Goal concord
Goals are not compatible	Goal conflict	Goal competition

Source: Wilensky (1983).

unforeseen circumstances. The hypothesis that most human action is influenced by multiple goals has until recently been neglected in cognitive psychology, though not in literature or in clinical psychology.[16]

Wilensky (1983) has argued that the main characteristic of human planning, as compared with technical planning, is the ability to reason about the problems arising from multiple goals. He proposes a four-way classification (see Table 2; I have substituted "goal synergy" for his "goal overlap"). Wilensky calls the process of goal resolution "metaplanning." It includes such principles as "Don't waste resources," "Achieve as many goals as possible," "Maximize the value of the goals achieved," or "Avoid impossible goals." Resources include time and money, and account must be taken of physical limitations. All these can give rise to goals being compatible or incompatible.

According to Wilensky, we have a large number of stored plans – how to get food from a shop, how to travel by car or foot, how to talk to someone by phone, and so on. His theory of planning has both a forward and a backward application. The forward application is in the ability to arrange pieces of stored plan using metaplanning principles to generate action. Thus, we often find that we need to replan as new opportunities to achieve goals or new interactions among goals are discovered. The backward application is in understanding human action. For instance, most stories are about goal conflicts and goal competition. To understand a story is to make inferences about goals and to see how conflicts between goals may be resolved.

Wilensky's approach differs from others in artificial intelligence planning research principally in that it starts with the issue of multiple goals. It is the closest of such approaches to the one adopted here.

As well as being multiple, human goals can be vague. In contrast to simple technical plans with specified steps and an exact goal, much human action takes place somewhat independently of an explicitly conscious goal. So, although someone can give a reason for an action when asked, we may wonder whether that reason is indeed the one that motivated the action. In other words, some of our goals may be unconscious. This occurs in two main ways, which may be distinguished as Helmholtzian and Freudian.[17]

The Helmholtzian sense is at the center of cognitive psychology. It is that although mental processes operate on knowledge structures, only a very few conclusions of such processes ever become conscious. Consciousness is a small part of mental processing, and may be primarily concerned with new adaptations, as, for instance, when we construct new plans to deal with problematic events (e.g., Mandler, 1985). When there is nothing problematic, behavior runs off automatically. Goals, it seems, may be conscious, but they can also be unconscious, and in this case action may not be completely voluntary.

The Freudian sense of an unconscious goal arises from our having multiple goals with only partial consciousness. So action can occur without conscious intention, or with one intention attributed by the actor, while other intentions, in conflict with the attributed one, are disowned. According to this hypothesis, conscious intentions may not cause an action, although rationalization may be offered later. In other words, plans may be scheduled by processes that are not fully integrated with any consciously accessible representation. They may be run off in plans of action that are detached from the goal they had been constructed to serve, or they may occur in circumstances inappropriate to any relevant goal.[18] Correspondence between the cognitive-theoretical idea of goals that direct plans and the reasons people give for actions therefore becomes problematic. Many of our actions hover on a borderline between the voluntary and the involuntary.

We can say that a human action is fully intended only when the person acts with a goal and knows consciously that she or he can accomplish the goal in a specific way. An intention is a conscious mental construction that depends on having a model of self that includes knowledge of the ability to accomplish the goal by actions of the kind intended. In human action a model of self is important. A person can be more or less engaged in a plan. Engagement is an identification of the self with the goal of the plan.[19] The question of engagement does not arise in technical plans. It is only in the context of multiple goals and plans that a person's motivation can be divided, and that a curious kind of behavior, going through the motions of one plan while wanting something else, may occur. Perring, Oatley, and Smith (1988) make the distinction between explicit conflict, as when a person has two roles such as a career and bringing up children that may compete for resources, and implicit conflict, in which a person is doing something without engagement. In the implicit case the person may say that an activity, a job for instance, feels alien to the self.[20]

Augmentation 2: imperfect knowledge and limited resources

A major augmentation of simple plans is required for purposeful action when the actor has only an imperfect model of the world and limited resources. The ordinary world, in contrast to worlds where technical operations occur, cannot be modeled either completely or accurately. We can have beliefs or opinions about it, but real *episteme*, reliable knowledge, is usually not possible.

Most human intended action, therefore, takes place with imperfect knowledge of the precise effects that actions will have. Most robot plans, by contrast, could not cope with much deviation in the world from their models of it. To work well they typically need perfect knowledge embedded in a model that represents all contingencies. To match this requirement, simplified synthetic worlds have been built so that robot systems can model those worlds accurately. This is a common type of engineering solution. In a similar way, large parts of the world have been made hard and flat to accommodate the restricted engineering properties of wheeled traffic. It is a major problem for cognitive science to understand how to augment the idea of the simple plan into plans that use imperfect knowledge in finite systems that will work in limited time.

A fundamental principle of human intended behavior is captured in the idea of a plan with goals and of construction of plans deriving from models of the world. But an equally important idea, expounded by Suchman (1987), is that of flexibly responding to circumstances as they arise in progressing toward a goal, using the limited resources available – what she calls "situated action." We have very limited resources of strength, movement, skill, and particularly time. Though technology has been successful in expanding these in various ways, we human beings still have most of our original limitations intact when we are not executing technical plans. Under such circumstances, as Suchman would argue, human action becomes a series of attempts, not always successful, at continuous ad hoc problem solving.

Augmentation 3: multiple agents

Not only is human intended action influenced by multiple goals, it often includes coordination among two or more agents who may arrange a plan mutually by distributing subgoals and actions among themselves. Much of our intended action requires the interdependence of several actors.

The problems of coordinating joint action among individual human agents are comparable to those coordinating action among different goals in a single individual. If we have multiple goals, then one way of treating them is to see each as associated with an almost separable procedure and knowledge about how to achieve the goal given certain preconditions. The distribution of agency into specialized subtasks indeed seems to have been the main means by which the human species has overcome its limitation of resources – and indeed technology depends on such division of labor and skills among different people.[21] The modern skill of management involves organizing individual agents to achieve defined subgoals within an overall plan with a specified top-level goal.

Emotions and augmented planning

The proposal here is that each of these three kinds of augmentation of simple plans produces a recognizable kind of problem for cognitive organization. Each requires an elaboration beyond those successfully tackled so far in cognitive science. The problems are those of managing multiple and ill-defined goals, of acting with imperfect knowledge and limited resources, and of coordinating several agents.

So what designs could cope with these augmentations? One solution already exists – the biologically based system of emotions. In each of the three augmentations of simple planning, changes of evaluation of plans or goals occur during the course of action, and it is at such junctures that emotions arise. Emotions do not necessarily allow such occasions to be dealt with perfectly; often such junctures allow no perfect solution. Rather, emotions set the cognitive and bodily systems into certain modes of readiness for small sets of action patterns that have evolved to cope with specific kinds of juncture as they occur.

Tolstoy's portraits of emotions

Tolstoy was concerned with representing a world in which human interaction could be understood. Although there are no technically perfect solutions to many of the problems of human action, our fascination with them shows we do not stop trying to understand. The opening passages of *Anna Karenina* offer many examples. I will use some of them to illustrate three kinds of modification based on emotions by which the principle of a simple plan needs to be augmented in order to bring it closer to the kinds of actions characteristic of human beings.

Of multiple goals. Tolstoy lets us know that Vronsky's behavior toward his mother is "in accordance with the views of the set he lived in" (p. 60). Vronsky's relations with his mother are, in other words, quite disengaged. He does not love her. He nonetheless acts toward her in a respectful way, but "the more submissive and respectful he was externally, the less he honoured and loved her in his heart" (p. 60). Tolstoy thus gives us an account in terms of goals. Vronsky's model of self allows a discrepancy: One goal is of being respectful, but he also feels contempt, indicating that a quite different goal is also present.

In an incident that occurs as Vronsky, his mother, and Anna are about to leave the station, a railwayman is killed as the train is being shunted. The man's wife had flung herself on the body. Vronsky takes an ad hoc opportunity. After Anna said: "Can nothing be done for her" (p. 64), Vronsky slips away to leave 200 rubles for the man's widow. He is perhaps gratified that Anna notices his generosity. Thus, Vronsky had gone to the station with the goal of meeting his mother, but he is not fully engaged in this. He has other goals, too, waiting for an occasion. A suppressed conflict between the goal of acting respectfully toward his mother while having other goals related to his lack of love for her leaves, as it were, an inviting gap for intrusions of the kind that occur with the diversion of his attention toward Anna.

Tolstoy lets us see how the merging of Vronsky's goals at the station is not quite seamless. The gap appears not in Vronsky's consciousness, however, but in Anna's. Anna had come to Moscow to visit her brother, Stiva Oblonsky, and his family. Stiva had met her at the station, and following the death of the railwayman, Anna and Stiva depart in a carriage. Anna's brother "noticed with surprise that her lips were trembling, and that it was with difficulty that she kept back her tears. . . .

'What is the matter?' . . . 'It's a bad omen,' she replied" (p. 65). Later, when Anna tells Kitty, her unmarried sister-in-law, about her meeting with Vronsky, Anna omits to tell her about the 200 rubles. "For some reason she did not like to think of them. She felt that there had been something in it relating personally to her that should not have been" (p. 73).

Tolstoy depicts emotions: Anna's excessive agitation apparently triggered by the railwayman's death and the disagreeable feeling attaching to the incident of the 200 rubles. What do we, as readers, make of them? That Anna, a heroine somewhat in the romantic tradition, has strong and responsive emotions? Yes, no doubt. More importantly, though, the emotions imply that all is not as it seems.

Often, conflict between goals gives rise to difficulties only in certain circumstances. As well as having imperfect knowledge of the outside world, we also have imperfect knowledge of our own goal structures and their implications. So, after Anna's arrival in Moscow we learn that Vronsky had been courting Kitty, Anna's sister-in-law. He had wanted the excitement of courtship but not the implication that courtship leads to marriage. Only after Anna's arrival and the occasion of a ball that was soon to be held did problematic implications of this goal conflict emerge for him.

Tolstoy also lets us know that Vronsky's divided goal structures are mirrored by Anna's. Just as his contradictory motives allow his attention to be caught by a woman met by chance when he is getting into a train, and allow him to be pleased that she sees a piece of his generosity, so does Anna's lack of attachment to her husband contribute to making Vronsky attractive to her. We begin to discern the possible existence of some of Anna's goals, though not all consciously elaborated by her. She may not just be coming to Moscow to visit her brother's family. She has been enacting a major plan of her life, her marriage to Karenin, without being completely engaged in it. Ostensibly, she came to Moscow to help heal the rift between Stiva and his wife, Dolly, following Dolly's discovery of her husband's affair with a governess. Was she also visiting Moscow perhaps with a vague idea of a respite, an excursion into something less deadening than her married life, an adventure? We are not sure. And if she could have been asked, she herself may not have been sure.

When one of several goals is unconscious or only partly conscious, an emotion that occurs in the course of action can nevertheless become quite intrusively conscious, as with Anna's agitation in the carriage. But under such circumstances the emotion will not be easily understood. As with Anna's sense of an omen, it might be understood in terms other than those that actually caused the emotion. This suggests one of the functions of emotions for us as conscious beings. By inserting issues into consciousness, and because they imply goals that may be inexplicit, emotions can point to aspects of our goal structures that we may have been unaware of.

With imperfect knowledge and partial intent, human beings work toward goals that are more vaguely formulated than in a simple plan. Anna's goal in coming to Moscow might have been unclear. Perhaps she just hoped for some enlivenment. Corollaries are that steps in many human plans are not typically unreeled in exact sequences of action. They are taken one at a time in the general direction of goals that may themselves be vague. With such a procedure we experience both fortunate outcomes and those that are later regretted.

A few days after Vronsky and Anna met at the station, they meet again at the ball. The manner of their conversation indicates to themselves, to each other, and to onlookers that they are sexually attracted. Their individual conscious intents for any sexual encounter were barely conscious at first. Now they have become explicit, and a mutual intention is constructed. Vronsky had been expected to propose to Kitty at this ball. Though he has been greatly enjoying his courtship of her, he had not wanted the next step, marriage. He had thought that the flirtation was, as people say to themselves in such circumstances, harmless, with no further consequences than itself. Kitty had a quite different interpretation. She discovers, at this ball that was to be her triumph, that a mutual goal was not mutual at all.

Happiness is the emotion of single-minded engagement in what one is doing, of action without conflict. Though there is much to experience in such a state, there seems relatively little to describe, as a happy person is, in a sense, simply doing what he or she is doing. By contrast, in the myriad forms of unhappiness, discrepancies and contortions occur with a great deal to discuss. Tolstoy, like many novelists, has more to say about dysphoric and conflictual emotions than happy ones. But some examples of happiness do occur. One of them is when a new mutual plan is being created – falling in love.

Tolstoy shows Vronsky and Anna finding themselves, apparently unexpectedly, falling in love. They experience the emotions of complete absorption in their activities together that contrasts with the disengagement of their other relationships. Kitty thinks to herself as she sees

Anna: "No it's not the admiration of the crowd that intoxicates her, but the rapture of one . . . can it be *he?*" (p. 80). Tolstoy describes Anna's expression: "a smile of pleasure curved her rosy lips. She seemed to make efforts to restrain these signs of joy, but they appeared on her face of their own accord" (p. 80). The normally self-possessed Vronsky, too, looks at Anna adoringly: "His face had an expression which she had never seen before" (p. 81). They are engrossed in each other, excluding all else. Anna's involvement makes her disattend her usual observance of convention and her usual lively concern for others. At this moment Kitty is thrown in on herself, in an unspeakable despair, while Anna's actions flow outward into conversation with Vronsky.

To engage in what one is doing unself-consciously is to be happy. In such activities, it is not that impediments are absent; indeed, love stories are invariably tales of impediments. But they are ones that can be relegated in importance. They are overcome in the context of an unconflicted top-level goal and with resources that one is optimistic enough to think will come to hand as the love relationship proceeds.

Of imperfect knowledge and limited resources. In the ordinary human world, resources of knowledge, time, and materials are limited, and perfectly smooth action is not always possible. The unexpected happens often. Almost every action is patched up in an ad hoc way, usually from existing resources. Quite unexpectedly Vronsky bumps into Stiva Oblonsky. They both have to wait for the train to arrive, neither having timed his arrival perfectly. Later, Vronsky adds to his plan by following the guard to his mother's carriage. When getting into the train he stops short of the carriage door because, unexpectedly, someone is coming out. He pauses in his planned path. No exact model of the world equips him for any of these events.

Yet human augmentations of simple plans include the ability to cope with the unexpected, to incorporate ad hoc steps into our actions in the general direction of one or more goals. Later, we think, new information will become available to suggest further steps. Human action involves constant adjustments made in response to circumstances of the local situation and to events caused by what we have already done.

When human actors substitute a new action sequence into an ongoing plan from readily available resources, then either no emotions occur or the actor will feel happy that subgoals are being achieved. Vronsky steps aside to let someone pass before getting into the train. Such an action, where the substitute plan is available and concerns are unaffected, requires no reevaluation. There is thus no emotion. In this case, though, Vronsky perhaps derives a little extra pleasure from seeing a woman he finds attractive. Here the basic plan is augmented successfully and smoothly by incorporating an ad hoc modification, and an extra step is added to Vronsky's plan of being out and about in the world.

By contrast, dysphoric emotions occur when available resources are inadequate, when replanning seems impossible. So, when at the officers' race Anna sees Vronsky fall, there is for both Anna and Karenin an unexpected event. For Anna there is the sudden possibility of Vronsky's death that strikes at the root of the plan around which she has been constructing her life. For Karenin there is the sudden realization that his wife is unfaithful and, apparently more important to him, that she is broadcasting that their marriage is not what it seems. Their emotions signal that new cognitive work will be necessary. For each there are clearer indications of goals that might have been obscure.

Just as Tolstoy is able to indicate important nuances that accompany the conflicting goals of Vronsky in his relations with his mother, and Anna in relation to her husband, so at the races the emotions he describes are complex though recognizable. The race was known to be dangerous, and the crowd was excited. Karenin is contemptuous of such sports and looks not at the riders but in a bored way at the spectators. The race starts and he notices his wife, white-faced, peering at one man, with her hand convulsively clutching her fan. Then he notices another lady very much moved too. "'It is quite natural,' he said to himself." He examines Anna's face again, "trying not to read what was so plainly written on it, but against his will he read in it with horror that which he did not want to know" (p. 209). As one of the riders fell, he "saw clearly by Anna's pale, triumphant face that he whom she was watching had not fallen" (p. 209). Then another officer fell and was fatally injured, but Karenin sees that Anna did not even notice. Despite her engrossment she gradually realizes that Karenin has been staring at her. She glances round, looks inquiringly at him, and slightly frowning turns away. "'Oh, I don't care,' she seemed to say to him, and then did not once look at him again" (p. 209).

The race was an unlucky one. More than half the officers were thrown and hurt. Toward the end, "Everyone was loudly expressing disapproval . . . so that when Vronsky fell and Anna gave a loud exclamation, there was nothing remarkable about it" (p. 209). It was then, however, that the change came over Anna's face that really was beyond decorum. She utterly lost her head. "She began to flutter like a captive bird. She said to her friend Betsy: 'Let us go.' " It was at this moment that Karenin went up to her and "politely offered her his arm saying 'Come if you like' " (pp. 209–210). It was only after Karenin asked her a second time, and she drew back saying, "No, no, leave me alone, I shall stay here" (p. 210), that the news came that Vronsky had not been killed, and Anna sat down quickly, hid her face behind her fan and sobbed.

We would agree that Anna's emotions of fear and relief are comprehensible at such a juncture as this; such emotions are appropriate to events in which one's lover is in danger and almost killed. What Tolstoy proposes, though, is that a varying set of emotions can occur, and also that emotional expressions can be ambiguous. A simplistic account, that sadness occurs at a loss, need neither be complete nor correct. Anna weeps not when she thinks her lover is dead, but when she hears he is not dead.

Tolstoy's narrative makes the emotions of Anna and Karenin believable. We are a world away from the enactment of a technical operation in which the domain is fully understood, a plan has been perfected, and runs predictably.

Of multiple agents. Many human emotions arise with the construction and dissolution of joint plans. The disruption of such plans is distressing because many strands of interdependency may become part of long-term mutual plans. Disruptions are also revealing in that some of the most intense of human emotions emerge from such dissolutions, and these indicate the importance of the structures that had been assumed.

When Anna's attachment to Vronsky finally becomes plain, Karenin becomes, shall we say, angry. Here, as in other such dissolutions of mutual plans, he first experiences disbelief – everything until then had been consonant with the idea that he and his wife had been carrying out the plan. The degree to which inference was involved in assuming the extent of his wife's participation was underestimated. As well as rage and disappointment, there is an element that springs directly from the discoordination of two actors who had been engaged in a plan they had constructed jointly. There is a sense of betrayal, not so much of disappointment but of broken trust. Karenin had a mutual understanding with Anna that their marriage involved sexual exclusiveness and public propriety. He is not so much grieved at losing her as angry that Anna has not kept her agreement about their public status, has not fulfilled this part of the mutual plan.

After the incident at the races, though, when Anna informs him on the way home of her affair with Vronsky, Karenin suppresses an anger that for him is triggered whenever he sees anyone weeping. He knows himself to be irrational when angry, and not wanting to say anything he might regret, he sits with an expression of deathlike rigidity. He also feels a pang of jealousy. When he is on his own he is caught up in an inner dialogue. He feels relief that now he knows what had been poisoning his existence and enchaining his attention for some time. Now he can live and think of something else. He is able now to think of Anna as a corrupt woman. He is able now to think she has committed a crime. He considers a duel, and rejects this as irrational; then of divorce, rejecting this as unseemly and furthermore allowing Anna to throw in her lot with Vronsky. Finally, he conceives the solution that Anna should continue to live with him, preserving the external forms and giving up her lover. He thinks of how he has not done anything wrong and therefore will not be unhappy, but this will make her unhappy, as she properly deserves.

We have here a man for whom it is important to be in control. He is not a bad man, but he goes through self-serving contortions of a kind that may be familiar to us, putting his decisions to himself in terms of justice and the minimum discomfort for himself as the innocent party, unable to recognize in himself his desire to punish his wife. The emotions that occur at such junctures are emotions of being betrayed in what had seemed like a mutual arrangement. Such emotions occur when two people, having reached an understanding, had been enacting a mutual plan. The understanding turns out to have been a misunderstanding. A coordinated plan has not flowed from one goal shared by two people, but, rather, different plans have been produced by discrepant goals.

From Tolstoy's portraits to psychological theory

We may start from paradigmatic cases such as those that Tolstoy has outlined, recognizable to us though depicted as occurring in a kind of society that none of us has experienced. I think it can be accepted, too, that Tolstoy's reputation as a great novelist implies that events that elicit emotions, and the consequences of such states, are recognizable – Tolstoy's representations are tolerably correct.

The hypothesis of this book is that emotions derive from cognitive processes for integrating multiple and sometimes vague goals and for managing the associated plans that are enacted with limited resources in an uncertain environment, often in conjunction with other people. Happy emotions occur when coordination between plans is being achieved and unanticipated events are assimilated. Distressing emotions occur when coordination fails, or when some plan goes badly, when a problem emerges that cannot be solved from current resources or when an important background goal is violated. Emotions function to allow otherwise disparate aspects of a complex system to be coordinated. Tolstoy's portraits did not directly suggest the theory that I am proposing here, but they do offer characterizations that the theory is designed to meet. The basic account of emotions as evaluations of goals and plans, active and dormant, and as changes of readiness gives the beginnings of an understanding, I think, of the emotions portrayed by Tolstoy.

Emotions as communications

This analysis of augmented planning points to a significant feature of the human cognitive system. Almost all plans involve subplans, and each of these subplans may be achieved by a part of the system that is somewhat separate. Orchestrating a whole plan, then, involves coordinating separate parts or procedures. This in turn involves communication among the parts.

Oatley and Johnson-Laird (1987) have proposed that the function of emotions is communicative: Emotions communicate both to ourselves and others; within the cognitive system they communicate among the different parts of the system; and in a social group they communicate among individual people. (During the discussion I will refer to the Oatley and Johnson-Laird theory as the "communicative theory"; the pronoun "we" in the context of this theory means Johnson-Laird and myself.)

The reason for communications within the individual is, we argue, because parts of the cognitive system are somewhat autonomous. With incomplete access and incomplete control of each part by others, the topmost level receives signals from lower-level parts and may invoke them to try and achieve their goals as components of larger plans. We propose that conscious awareness is a function of the topmost level of the cognitive system that contains some model of the system's goal structure and knowledge base. Only the conclusions of this top level become conscious (see also Johnson-Laird, 1983a, 1983b). We assume that people elaborate the model of self in the course of life, and that the Delphic injunction to "know yourself" implies that for integrative tasks it is better to have more accurate rather than less accurate representations of our abilities, habits, and goal structures.

Part of the purpose of this model of self is to allow the system to integrate disparate pieces of new information or to add a new goal or plan to the system in a way that minimizes incompatibility with the existing structure.

Modularity

Let us suppose that the parts of the cognitive system are modules, each like a procedure in computation. In each module knowledge is represented to achieve a specific goal. This knowledge relates to preconditions and to pieces of the plan to accomplish such goals. Minsky (1986) describes such modules as agencies, each specializing in a particular kind of activity and able to accomplish it when invoked, given the right data and preconditions. He calls this the "society of mind."[22]

As a way of thinking about a mental module, imagine a crayfish or squid. These animals have escape mechanisms that, when activated, remove the animal rapidly from a noxious stimulus. The neural mechanism associated with this response is a functional module. Its goal is to escape, and its plan is to contract the large specialized muscles that propel it backward. The knowledge embedded implicitly in the escape procedure allows the genetically programmed plan of escape to be activated when the mechanism is invoked. Of course, no plan is in the animal's mind. The idea of a plan is a way we have of understanding the mechanism functionally.

The modular theory of mind is an elaboration of this idea. There are many different processors, or agencies, in a complex cognitive system, each capable of performing a specific function. The evidence for modularity of the cognitive system is of two kinds. First, there is a general argument from the design of cognitive systems. It makes sense for any complex system to have functional parts, each of which has some autonomy. In programming, this means writing programs as sets of procedures that call each other rather than as tangled transfers of control that are impossible to understand. One feature of modular systems is that, once begun, a procedure runs either until its goal is achieved or until it is interrupted. In a homogeneous or unstructured system, by contrast, one can scarcely talk of starting or completing any process, and consequently sequencing becomes difficult.

Second, Johnson-Laird (1983b) suggests an argument specific to human cognition. From the dissociations that occur in mental life, it is clear that one (conscious) part often does not always know what another part is doing. Phenomena of this kind range from psychiatric and neurological symptoms such as hysterical dissociations and Parkinsonian automatisms to more common experiences such as involuntary emotions or thoughts and inabilities in controlling ourselves in dieting. Though each of these phenomena may seem minor on its own, collectively they point to the important conclusion that some mental processes are separable from others and do not have complete control over others or access to the conclusions of others.

Modular systems can have problems of coordination. Modules may produce conflicting outputs to the motor system, or two modules may need a particular input, but each may be waiting for this input from the other.

In genetically specified systems, maladaptive organizations are selected against during evolution. But the human mind, as well as having some innate organization, is capable of learning, or assembling new procedures. There is, therefore, a constant possibility of constructing new conflicts, deadlocks, and other pathological organizations. It is primarily in a system that constructs new pieces of itself that the need arises for processes with the functions of emotions. Emotions insert problems into consciousness, so that the individual can use a model of self to help integrate new pieces with existing parts of the system.

Conflict and evaluation theories of emotion

Oatley and Johnson-Laird's theory is one of a family of theories known as conflict and evaluation theories of emotions.[23] Its basic postulate is that emotions occur when a psychological tendency is arrested or when smoothly flowing action is interrupted. The mental disturbance of this interruption is experienced as an emotion. Mandler (1984) says that Paulhan (1887) first proposed this idea. Freud's work on conflict had resonances with it, and more recent work in the behaviorist tradition, as by Seligman (1975), has involved similar principles.

The specific theory that emotions are based on interruptions has been held, among others, by Dewey (1894, 1895), Hebb (1946), and Mandler (1975). Within cognitive science, Miller, Galanter, and Pribram (1960) discuss interruptions of plans giving rise to emotions, and Simon (1967) argues that the problems of understanding how to deal with multiple goals with finite resources are coextensive with the problems of understanding emotions. Insofar as emotions have been considered by cognitive scientists, theories based on conflict and evaluation are the only ones that have seemed at all appropriate to the phenomena. Evaluation theories deriving from that of Lazarus (1966) are founded on the related idea that emotions arise with appraisals or evaluations of events. The events at issue are typically those in which there is a potential conflict of whether an actual outcome presents a match or mismatch to a desired goal.

In systems that work with multiple goals in finite time there will be a need for interruptions, when one goal, unexpectedly, becomes more urgent than the one controlling the current process. Such interruptions disturb what was going on, but the disturbance allows a change of priorities that was not foreseen. Computational ideas deriving from this are reviewed by Pfeifer (1988). Among recent computational theorists is Sloman (1987), who has argued that emotional disturbances occur whenever new thoughts or motives interfere with or modify other mental processes. Perhaps the computationally most advanced are Frijda and Swagerman (1987), who have a working program, Acres, that manages goals, or as they call them, "concerns," in an uncertain environment. Computational analyses of emotions assume that disruptions of any activity are inevitable in information processing systems with multiple goals and limited resources.

Mandler (1984), in reviewing the history of the conflict theory of emotions, describes how it has been periodically forgotten and reinvented. Why should this be? The proposal that emotions are based on conflicts and interruptions seems like a good idea, but perhaps it has a defect, so that it does not command continuing assent. Perhaps this defect is that although negative emotions like frustration are easily explained in this way, not all emotions are like this. How does the theory deal with happy emotions?

Positive emotions. Frijda's characterization of an emotion occurring as we cease focusing on action in the world and become focused on ourselves is a classic statement of the conflict theory, but it seems not to apply, for instance, to Tolstoy's description of the interaction between Vronsky and Anna at the ball. The usual way in which conflict theories deal with positive or happy emotions is somewhat like this: Being in love requires for its typical experience in the Western romantic tradition a certain amount of delay and impediment, as described by Berscheid (1982). These interruptions of a strong tendency give it an emotional excitement, which can have a happy tone. One can even wonder whether Anna ceases being happy when she is finally free of her husband. Along similar lines, Meyer (1956) has proposed that the enjoyable experience of music depends on the interruptions of tendencies set up in some passages and not completed until much later. Gaver and Mandler (1987) have extended Meyer's idea: Enjoyment of music is related to the discrepancies that arise when a listener tries to assimilate a piece of music into existing schemas.

Such proposals do not cover all instances of positive emotions, however. Among the proposals of Oatley and Johnson-Laird's communicative theory is one that meets this hitherto unsatisfactory state. According to our hypothesis, an emotion occurs in relation to a person's several plans and goals when there is a significant change in assessment of the outcome of a goal or plan. Thus we can define a positive emotion as one that occurs when a goal is achieved, and even more frequently positive emotions occur when a plan is progressing well, when subgoals are being achieved, and when the probability of a main goal being achieved is increased.

Enjoyment occurs where some overall goal is important, as with being in love. It also occurs where there is no pressing overall goal, in states where the mind is full as in listening to music, in creative activities, in play, or when social participation is more important than any end result. Being happy requires that there be no distressing reevaluations, but rather the easy incorporation of new elements into the activity. Enjoyment is therefore less usually the final achievement of a main goal than engagement in what one is doing and the reaching of small subgoals using available resources.

Happiness is distinctive and preoccupying. Like dysphoric emotions it is behaviorally recognizable and is communicated to others. So Anna's happiness at the ball is obvious to onlookers, and the knowledge that she is acting against the interests of others she cares about could be assimilated into her major plan. It does not interfere with her engrossment with Vronsky. (Questions of the nature of happiness are discussed further in Chapter 8.)

Negative emotions. When in the course of action a problem arises that we think we cannot cope with, when a new goal has to be inserted into an ongoing sequence but the person concerned does not know how to do it, when a previously unrecognized conflict is discovered, or when a threat arises, a negative emotion tends to occur.

We can call emotions positive if the probability of attaining a goal is increased and negative if such a probability decreases. A comparable distinction has been proposed by Gordon (1987) and by Carver and Scheier (1990). This usage, however, is easily confused with the common psychological idea (as proposed by Ortony, Clore, and Collins, 1988) that each emotion has a fixed primary valency of pleasantness or unpleasantness. This idea I believe to be incorrect, because it makes it difficult to understand why, for instance, anyone should ever watch a thriller, the object of which is to induce anxiety. (This problem is discussed further in Chapter 2.)

A negative emotion is not always unpleasant, not necessarily avoided. It occurs as we evaluate a problem as not readily solved, when decreased progress toward a goal is detected. The structures of unselfconscious activity or habit break down. Most radically, negative emotions can signal that an important goal cannot be achieved or that a major plan has failed. The emotions that then occur may indicate that a large structure of habit, skill, and knowledge is obsolete. It may need to be entirely rebuilt to fit new circumstances.

Default plans are then brought to readiness, and we may begin to assemble new pieces of cognitive structure. Two properties of the consciousness of negative emotions occur, and they contrast with the effects of positive emotions. First, restrictions are made in the set of plans and options to be considered and old, established, fallback plans are made ready or brought into operation. For instance, when in fear, our action and thought are concentrated on safety, and the basic plan of freezing may occur. Restriction of action may account for some of the compulsive qualities of strong emotions. Second, the emotion may include inner debate, with attempts either to understand the problem or to create new plans to meet the situation. Part II of this book is devoted to discussing negative emotions.

The central postulate of the communicative theory

Though the communicative theory of emotions is a recognizable member of the family of conflict and evaluation theories, a modification of the usual formulations is needed. Most conflict theories hold that emotions occur when a tendency is arrested, when a person becomes focused not on the ongoing activity but on himself or herself. Though this behavioral image is not unrepresentative, it emphasizes the weakness of conflict theories in dealing with happy emotions. According to the communicative theory, the best analysis involves a focus not on behavior and its interruption but on goals. This allows the usual difficulty of conflict theories in coping with positive emotions to be resolved.

The formulation of evaluation theories is that events are evaluated along certain dimensions, such as pleasantness or controllability. The outcome of any evaluation then determines what emotion will occur. The weakness of this approach is that an indefinitely large range of evaluations of events can occur. Often it is unclear which kinds of evaluation might be specifically important for which emotions. According to Oatley and Johnson-Laird (1987), events are not just evaluated but are also evaluated in relation to an individual's goals. We follow Draper's (1985) suggestion that the progress of each plan toward its goal is monitored, and when there is a significant change in this progress an emotion occurs. More recently, Carver and Scheier (1990) have made a similar proposal, postulating a metamonitoring system that detects such changes and underlies emotions.

Emotions derive from our many goals and plans, active and dormant, that may encounter unexpected events and conflict. The central postulate of Oatley and Johnson-Laird's communicative theory can be stated as follows:

> *Each goal and plan has a monitoring mechanism that evaluates events relevant to it. When a substantial change of probability occurs of achieving an important goal or subgoal, the monitoring mechanism broadcasts to the whole cognitive system a signal that can set it into readiness to respond to this change. Humans experience these signals and the states of readiness they induce as emotions.*

Goals and plans are not necessarily subparts of a larger hierarchical plan – they may be unintegrated. The emotional monitoring mechanisms are like burglar alarms that go off when there is an intruder. They are signals that imply that something needs attention.[24] They need to be taken account of in the current sequence of action, although they do not indicate exactly what has happened or what should be done.

Positive signals of increasing probability of goal attainment focus attention on the ongoing activity itself. They tend to assimilate events to the ongoing plan, maintaining it, promoting modifications, and disattending other events. Negative signals of decreasing probability of goal attainment, such as those of anger, sadness, fear, or disgust, promote change from the current activity. They tend to interrupt current action, to make ready new plans appropriate to the emotion.

Two kinds of mental communication

Monitoring mechanisms evaluate both ongoing and dormant plans and goals. They communicate these evaluations to other modules, including the one at the top level that contains a model of the whole system. Conclusions of this module may become conscious. This module can reorganize goals and plans, using the model of the whole system, including its goal structure. Such restructuring of goals can be contrasted with the kind of learning in which beliefs are changed, that is, where modifications are made to a knowledge base.

Oatley and Johnson-Laird argue that emotions occur at junctures when there are changes of evaluation of the likely outcome of plans. When such junctures are recognized, a special kind of message is broadcast, like a burglar alarm signal. We call this type nonpropositional because it does not need to be parsed or interpreted, in contrast to the kinds of message more usually considered in cognitive science, which we call propositional because they assert predicates. Following a suggestion by Sloman (1990), I have been convinced that the terms *control messages* and *semantic messages*, respectively, more nearly catch our meaning. Control signals are nonsemantic; they tend to alter the control structure of the cognitive system, with the intensity of the signal increasing this tendency. By contrast, semantic messages refer to something.[25]

Semantic messages. Semantic messages include those associated with recognizing and understanding events. In a hierarchy, such as that in Figure 3 (which has a similar structure to those in Figures 1 and 2), the messages that pass between modules are semantic. They have syntactic structure, which must be parsed and which reflects the structure of what they refer to.

Semantic messages have destinations and they must be interpreted. Computer programs use messages of this kind. By use of such messages, procedures can be invoked from the next higher level, for instance, by specifying the name of a lower-level procedure. Ordered sequences can be built by triggering procedures in turn. Each can signal that it has achieved its goal, and then the next can be triggered. Procedures may also be invoked in a nonordered fashion by specifying a pattern to be matched to all available procedures, any of which triggers if the pattern matches. Pattern matching can extend the strictly up and down flow of messages in the system. Semantic messages thus refer to

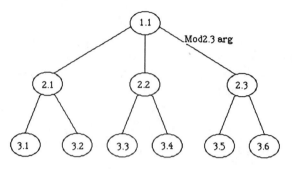

Figure 3. Modules in a hierarchy passing a semantic message to a destination. The message mod2.3 arg passes from module 1.1 to module 2.3. (From Oatley, 1988a.)

addresses, to procedures by name, to states of affairs by calling patterns, to data, to representations, to results, or to elements for building new procedures. They are a sophisticated way of controlling functions in organized plans.

Figure 3 shows a message "mod2.3 arg" being passed from the operating system module (1.1) along the top right branch. This can be understood as a message that invokes module 2.3 and supplies it with some data (called an argument, arg) that it needs to accomplish its goal. In a system with a single main goal, such messages and a hierarchy of control are sufficient. Each processor is invoked by the next higher level, making it begin its computation, which may include response to inputs from other sources such as the environment. The whole operation can have the structure of a technical plan.

Control messages. Imagine, though, a set of modules each of which has its own goal, where these modules are not hierarchically organized. Many kinds of pathology could occur. Goals of different procedures might conflict for the use of a resource such as the action system, processor 4.1 might need a signal from processor 4.2 before it could start computing, but 4.2 is waiting for a signal from 4.1. Such configurations would prevent the system from working.

Among nonhierarchical solutions is the possibility of organizing modules into compatible sets to operate cooperatively without pathological conflicts and deadlocks. Oatley and Johnson-Laird propose that nonsemantic control signals within the cognitive system set up and maintain just such compatible arrangements. These messages spread nonspecifically from any module in the system so that they may affect all the

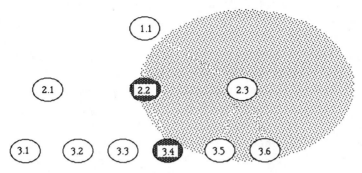

Figure 4. Control message spreading out diffusely from a single module. It can affect the other modules in the system in a simple way, by turning them on, turning them off, or otherwise setting them into a specific preprogrammed state induced by the particular message. In this example, the signal emitted from module 2.3 has reached modules 2.2 and 3.4 and switched them into a specific preprogrammed state, but it has not affected modules 3.5 and 3.6. (After Oatley, 1988a.)

others, as shown in Figure 4. They are simpler, cruder, and evolutionarily older than semantic messages. The structure of the message is not of informational significance to the system, so it need not be parsed or interpreted. It is like the siren of an emergency vehicle that does not tell us where that vehicle is going or what has happened. Its function is merely to be heard and to induce drivers to pull to the side of the road until the vehicle has passed.

In the cognitive system, control messages simply tend to turn some modules on or off or invoke some prespecified action in them. There is just a small set of such signals that propagate pervasively through the system. They can be sent from any module, and any one such signal tends to set all the modules into a single compatible organization or mode.

Quasi-autonomous modules can be organized in this way without needing to receive specific inputs from higher levels of the hierarchy. But groupings of such processors will work only if their activities are mutually compatible. For instance, if the squid's escape response is invoked, muscles that control swimming forward are inhibited, though other muscular activities might be unaffected. The compatible set, therefore, includes switching on one procedure, switching off others, and leaving others to do what they were doing.

The hypothesis is that in mammals and birds, control messages, arising from lower or higher modules, activate sets of modules that have evolved to act compatibly. Among the characteristic modes of the cognitive system, therefore, are organizations in which modules are cooperating in specific and well-defined ways. Emotion signals are a kind of control message, one invoking, for instance, the modules concerned in fearful vigilance and another the preparedness to attack. Comparable control signals that are not emotions invoke sleepiness or the reluctance to move that is characteristic of pain.

Control signals are propagated to the body and different parts of the nervous system by processes that are parallel to semantic signaling. Control signaling presumably includes nonspecific neural pathways, classical endocrine pathways, and perhaps also the more recently discovered peptide transmission systems (e.g., Panksepp, 1982, 1989). Why is this more primitive system necessary in a properly organized neural hierarchy? Why, for instance, cannot any module that detects an important event send to the operating system a semantic message: "A dangerous situation is at such a place," or "Wound in the left leg," or "Goal x is not achieved"? The operating system could schedule appropriate actions in the light of other goals. This is a possible solution, and in a sense no other seems necessary. It is related to the idea that emotions have no place in rational beings.

No doubt we inherit control signals from primitive origins and less developed nervous systems, but inasmuch as the systems of control signals have not been selected against in evolution, the hypothesis remains that this kind of signaling is important even in more lately evolved cognitive systems.

Basic emotion signals have two properties with continuing advantages. First, they make the system capable of rapid and unified response, interrupting ongoing activity and causing transition to readiness for a new one, without parsing, interpretation, or other computations that could be lengthy and may not reach completion. Second, longer-term maintenance becomes possible so that the system can stay in one of the organized states, or moods, that resist further transitions or the intrusions of other concerns.

Five basic emotions

Oatley and Johnson-Laird's hypothesis is that there are control signals that correspond to basic emotions. Each occurs when a particular kind of juncture is recognized. Table 3 shows five basic emotions, the junctures in action that typically trigger them, and the transitions of action read-

Table 3. *Five basic emotions with the junctures at which they occur and the transitions they accomplish*

Emotion (mode)	Juncture of current plan	State and goals to which transition occurs
Happiness	Subgoals being achieved	Continue with plan, modifying if necessary
Sadness	Failure of major plan or loss of active goal	Do nothing/search for new plan
Fear	Self-preservation goal threatened or goal conflict	Stop current plan, attend vigilantly to environment, freeze and/or escape
Anger	Active plan frustrated	Try harder, and/or aggress
Disgust	Gustatory goal violated	Reject substance and/or withdraw

Source: Oatley and Johnson-Laird (1987).

iness that they accomplish. An emotion is experienced when one of these pervasive signals is broadcast through the system.

Among the criteria for a basic emotion are that it is physiologically and expressively distinctive and that it has a biological basis. What is there to suggest just a small number of basic human emotions? Many writers have postulated certain fundamental emotions: George Eliot read Sophocles because of his "delineation of the great primitive emotions" (Haight, 1985, p. 195); and even William James, despite his claim that it was pointless to try and organize emotions into groups, referred to a set that he called the coarse emotions.

Potential evidence about whether there are basic emotions is available from phenomenology, from preoccupying cognitive states, from physiological and expressive accompaniments, from eliciting conditions, from the action consequences of emotions, and from the ways in which emotions develop in infancy. Not all such evidence is easily interpretable, however, so I will review just three kinds of evidence: on distinctive eliciting conditions for emotions, on physiological specificity of emotions, and on certain cross-cultural emotional expressions.[26]

Eliciting conditions in an ontology of mammals and birds. The communicative theory states that emotions signal that some change has occurred in the evaluation of the likely outcome of a plan toward a goal. The hypothesis follows that of Plutchik (1984) in the postulation that a small number of basic emotions is linked to a small number of junctures of plans that are recognizable and that recur.[27] Danger might be a commonly occurring circumstance; fear is the emotional response to it. Loss is another common circumstance; sadness is its emotional result. These eliciting conditions are not conditions of the environment as such. They are, rather, evaluations of conditions of the environment in relation to an individual's several goals.

One way to ascertain whether there is a small set of distinctive and recurring circumstances that could be evaluated in relation to goals is to consider the ontology of the life of birds and mammals and its commonalities among different species. There are just a few kinds of individuals of one's own species with whom plans are enacted. The psychological accompaniment of being a mammal or bird is being reared by an adult, and typically to have an attachment relationship with a parent or parent substitute. This is a specific, partly innate, set of joint plans, and individuals who do not enact them will, with rare exceptions, die quickly. In many species attachment is later repeated in adult sexual relationships.[28]

Three kinds of juncture are basic to attachment plans: (1) There are the junctures of establishment or reestablishment of the relationship, occasions for happiness. In ethology comparable effects are seen in the rituals of maternal-infant signaling and in sexual courtship displays. (2) Attachment relationships can be interrupted; occasions for fear or anxiety and for protests of various kinds. (3) Relationships can be lost, occasions for sadness.

As well as attachment figures (parents, offspring, and mates) there are two other kinds of significant conspecific figures, cooperators and competitors. Cooperation occurs when animals hunt together or signal the presence of food to each other. As with attachment relationships, formation and re-formation of groupings are associated with happiness. Competition is of various kinds – sexual rivalry, dominance, and territorial. All these have been understood as having evolutionary advantages in social species, and are accompanied by expressive displays of anger and fear, which can be complementary to each other (Lorenz, 1967/1963). Aggression tends to occur with anger at a competitor. Ritualizing fighting may take place with angry displays characteristic of the species. A beaten competitor becomes fearful, perhaps flees or shows submission. So, for instance, a dog beaten in a fight may turn on its back and urinate a little.

Two significant kinds of individuals from other species are prey and predators. It is generally assumed that in animals the action of hunting prey is not itself emotional (though in humans it can be very much so). Our argument would be that hunting would be a happy experience if an individual successfully incorporates ad hoc modifications into a sequence of action. Perhaps a dog hunting a rabbit has this quality. If an automatic action pattern is simply fired off, however, no emotions are involved because no changes of evaluation occur. Being preyed upon is usually fear-producing, though sometimes anger may occur, as in birds mobbing predators. Other kinds of individuals, such as symbionts and parasites, are generally not involved in emotional issues in different ways from those described elsewhere in this ontology.

Finally, there are inanimate substances: resources such as territory, dangerous articles, events, food, toxins, and infections. Happiness is associated with discovery of food or resources; fear with physical dangers like bush fires or being trapped. A specialized emotion is associated with toxins and potentially infectious agents: Disgust is the emotion that includes nausea at contaminated food and that has the consequence of rejecting it. This is a mental rather than a purely physical process, as shown in one of Darwin's (1872) anecdotes. A native of Tierra del Fuego touched with his finger some cold preserved meat that Darwin was eating and showed his disgust at its softness. Darwin himself became disgusted at his food having been touched, although, as he says, the man's hands did not seem to be dirty. Though based on specialized gustatory evaluations, disgust may also provide a prototype for other kinds of withdrawal, which might be called hatred, including its social forms such as contempt and disdain (see below for further discussion of this).

According to this ontology, there are just five distinctive junctures associated with changes of goal evaluation that occur in the life of birds and mammals. Each has a distinctive basic emotion, as indicated in the second column of Table 3.

What makes emotions seem heterogeneous, and makes the question of whether there is a basic set so difficult, is the many-to-many mapping of eliciting conditions to specific emotions (Ekman, 1984). A specific condition might elicit different emotions in different people having different plans in different cultures. A specific emotion may be associated with different eliciting conditions. A rival might elicit anger, fear, or contempt; likewise, a person might feel happy in an interaction with a parent or a sexual partner or in discovering a territory. But this does not indicate a lack of orderliness. Because emotions are psychologically elicited, not physically, to understand the relation of eliciting conditions to emotions the person's goals and plans must be known, together with idiosyncratic and cultural conventions. This ontology indicates that starting with distinctive types of evaluation of goals, just a small set of basic kinds of emotion can be postulated.

Distinctive physiological accompaniments. Evidence that each basic emotion is associated with a physiological state that is distinct from those of other basic emotions has been reported by Ekman, Levenson, and Friesen (1983). They studied surprise, disgust, sadness, anger, fear, and happiness, and sought autonomic changes corresponding with each. In one task, actors and scientists were coached to contract specific facial muscles in patterns appropriate to each of the six emotions. In another task the same subjects were asked to remember experiences of each emotion and to relive them in imagination.

Ekman, Levenson, and Friesen found that making facial expressions was accompanied by autonomic effects that could be discriminated from one another. In the facial expression task, higher heart rate was characteristic of anger, fear, and sadness. A lower heart rate was characteristic of happiness, disgust, and surprise. Skin temperature allowed a further discrimination among the high heart rate emotions, with high skin temperature being characteristic of anger and a lower skin temperature characteristic of fear and sadness. With the relived emotion task, the distinctions between the high heart rate and high skin temperature of anger and the lower heart rate and lower skin temperature of happiness were confirmed. In addition, sadness was accompanied by larger decreases in skin resistance than other negative emotions of disgust, anger, and fear. In all but one of their subjects the pattern of autonomic activation was similar to that found in the mean data. Moreover, although Ekman and co-workers wrote that they avoided suggesting emotion labels to subjects or asking about them, they also said that other subjects performing facially directed action tasks of the same kind reported that they experienced the relevant emotions strongly.[29]

This study indicates that specific emotions are each associated with a distinctive physiological state. It does not tell us exactly how many such emotions there are. There is also evidence from animal studies that distinctive physiological patterns are associated with particular emotions (Panksepp, 1982, 1989).

Pancultural facial expressions. A third kind of criterion depends on the thesis that although emotions undergo cultural variation and idiosyncratic modification, their biological bases can be determined through cross-cultural studies. Related to this is the idea that basic emotions might emerge early in individual development, though not necessarily in the earliest months of infancy. Most of the empirical work on this problem has concentrated on recognition of facial expressions, of people in different cultures, and of infants. There has now been a series of such studies.[30]

Ekman and Friesen (1971), in an influential study, tested 189 adults and 130 children of a cultural group called the Fore in New Guinea. Subjects were chosen who had had minimal contact with Westerners, who spoke no Western language, had seen no films, and had not been employed by a Westerner. A native speaker of the Fore language told the subjects short stories that had been gathered as prototypical of emotions from this same cultural group. Each centered on an emotion that was mentioned explicitly – one was about the arrival of friends, so the person felt happy; one about a close relative dying, which made the person feel sad; and another about fear at an encounter with a wild pig in the house when the subject was alone. As a story incident was told, the Western researcher displayed a set of three photographs of facial expressions, taking care (by looking at the tape recorder) to give no non-verbal cues as to the correct photograph. Subjects were asked to indicate the appropriate emotion for each story. For four emotions, happiness, anger, sadness, and disgust, between 69% and 92% of people chose the faces that the researchers had hypothesized as being appropriate to the story that was told. People only performed at chance level when discriminating fear from surprise, though they were 64% correct or better in discriminating fear from happiness, sadness, anger, or disgust. In the experiments with children, subjects were asked to choose between just two photographs, and very similar results were obtained.

Ekman and Friesen then had Fore people make facial expressions appropriate to particular emotions. Video recordings of the poses were later correctly identified by Americans (Ekman, 1973).

From such cross-cultural studies, Ekman has concluded that there are eight different emotions that might be considered basic: happiness, sadness, fear, anger, disgust, contempt, surprise, and interest. Each can be identified by a specific panculturally occurring facial expression.

Which emotions are basic? Problems of surprise,
disgust, contempt, desire

Ekman and his collaborators suggest that surprise is basic because it has a facial expression that is recognizable panculturally. A difficulty with the proposal is that facial expressions of surprise are not easy to discriminate from fear. Johnson-Laird and I have also argued that because surprise may accompany any emotion, it is not distinctive. If, however, a distinctive pattern of surprise were found without any other emotion, this would suggest that it might be counted as a basic emotion.

The basis for Oatley and Johnson-Laird's treatment of disgust and contempt is less satisfactory than that for happiness, sadness, anger, and fear. Rozin and Fallon (1987) have shown that disgust is a fully developed emotion. It has a distinctive pancultural facial expression, a distinctive readiness for the action of withdrawal from the offensive object, a physiological manifestation (nausea), and a phenomenological tone (revulsion). They also argue that disgust properly applies to food, to possibilities of contamination, and to ideas that take on properties of what we eat, and that it develops in the first eight years of life. But there are also occasions for emotions of withdrawal and revulsion that are interpersonal. Ekman and Friesen (1986) have discovered a facial expression unique to contempt.[31] It involves raising and tightening the corner of the upper lip on one side. The expression is recognized by people in a variety of cultures.

The difficulty about the question of basic emotions is this: If contempt were a basic emotion, we might expect it to occur at distinctive junctures, have a distinct facial expression, a distinct physiology, and to be based on a distinctive control signal. Although Ekman and Friesen have shown that contempt has a unique panculturally recognizable facial expression, evidence on the other defining features is equivocal or not available. Oatley and Johnson-Laird regard the emotions of interpersonal withdrawal and revulsion as being founded on a basic emotion of disgust/hatred. The term *disgust*, as Rozin and Fallon point out, is properly applied to revulsion from food and contamination. When people experience such feelings toward a person, the emotion is described as contempt, disdain, or hatred.

Attitudes of esteem and contempt are applied very generally in society. They are the measures by which we assess ourselves and others, criteria by which we associate or dissociate ourselves from social actions and people who perform them. Some theorists (e.g., Spinoza 1955/ 1675) have regarded hatred as the paradigmatic negative emotion, whereby we mentally reject something that we cannot tolerate: According to Spinoza's scheme, so-called negative emotions are elaborations of this general reaction of mental rejection.[32]

Oatley and Johnson-Laird (1990) were prompted to rethink the issue of whether there might not be more basic emotions than the five we had postulated. If disgust/hatred is an emotion of rejection of some object or person, we have wondered whether to consider an opposite emotion of attraction to an object or person that might be called "desire," with "interest" being the name for its maintained mood. If this were so, the basic structure of our argument would not be affected, though modifications would be needed. We would need to add desire/interest to Table 3. This addition would help our semantic analysis of emotion terms (discussed in chapter 2) because it would account for a group of terms (desire, lust, and the like) that refer to emotional goals and are otherwise difficult to explain.

The state of research at present, I think, is that most theorists accept that happiness, sadness, anger, and fear are distinctive and separable for research purposes. Some theorists, including Johnson-Laird and myself, also believe these emotions to be basic. In addition, and awaiting further debate and evidence, are surprise, disgust, hatred, and contempt, as well as desire/interest. All these have some properties that, we have argued, indicate they could be basic, although evidence on other properties is equivocal.

The most prudent course is to be agnostic as to exactly how many basic emotions there are. Oatley and Johnson-Laird (1987) proposed that there are five, as I also propose here.

What states are not emotions?

Temperaments and personality traits are not emotions. Rather, they are best thought of as dispositions to particular kinds of emotion (e.g., Malatesta & Culver, 1984).

Bodily states such as shivering and erection of genitals are not emotions. They can be reliably evoked by eliciting conditions that are physical rather than mental. Some bodily states may give rise to emotions, and some accompany emotions. Some can even be triggered mentally. The point of differentiation is that emotions are not bodily states as such, and not initiated by physical stimuli as such. They are mental states, typically initiated mentally as evaluations of events that affect goals and plans.

Hunger, thirst, greed, maternal caregiving, ambition, and the like are motivations, not emotions. Emotions can accomplish transitions among motivational states, and they select a repertoire of plans and goals. They may have the effect of amplifying certain motivations.[33] But emotions, according to our theory, are not motivations as such. They are mental states that enable the priorities of multiple motivations to be managed.

Two states, sleep and pain, are based on control modes that share many of the properties of emotions, without themselves being emotions. Sleep is a distinctive mode of the brain, with its own neuronal rhythms and some distinctive neurochemical bases. Its primary function seems to be to provide animals with phases of activity and inactivity that keep in time with the alternation of light and darkness in the environment.[34] It has nothing to do with voluntary goals or plans. And whereas an emotion can have semantic content, for instance, about what caused it, sleep never has. Pain is concerned with bodily events. It is often used as a metaphor for distress, though it itself is not an emotion. It has, however, some of the same organization. In severe pain a particular mode can be initiated suddenly and also be maintained for a period. It organizes certain bodily processes, such as inducing inactivity that may facilitate healing. The mode can be suspended if some more urgent priority intervenes. Thus people who are injured in battle or in sport may not feel pain until the action has finished. This mode is associated with the actions of specific neurochemicals, the endogenous opiates, peptides that act as transmitter substances at synapses in the pain system, and also pervasively. (See Wall and Melzack, 1984, for an account of pain.) Pain is, however, not an emotion. It is ordinarily elicited not mentally, but by physical injury or physical pathology.

This has been only a brief catalog of control states that are not emotions. It is also possible to define states based on semantic activity that are not emotions. Conscious planning is one such. It seems to occur without invoking compatible sets of goals in a pervasive way. Only semantic signals are relevant.

Combined semantic and control signals

For the most part, emotions are based on both semantic and control messages experienced as a single event. The part that is semantic can indicate the cause of the emotion and, in some cases, an aspect of a plan. For instance, anger is an emotion, but we typically know what made us angry, and we direct the emotion toward the person responsible in the form of aggressive plans. The part that concerns control propagates through the system to set it into an appropriate mode and provides a distinctive phenomenological tone.

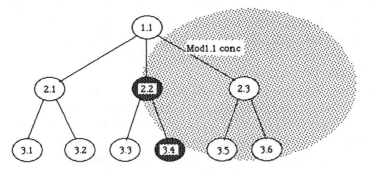

Figure 5. Combined semantic and control messages such as occur in a typical emotion. (After Oatley, 1988a.)

Figure 5 indicates the combination of these two kinds of signal: A semantic message, namely, a conclusion (conc) about an event is sent from module 2.3 to the operating system module 1.1, and a control message spreads out from module 2.3, which has just evaluated this event as important for a goal or plan. Violation of an important goal, for instance, can be signaled both by the control signal reaching the operating system and semantically by realization of what event elicited the emotion. Although usually both parts of an emotion are bound closely together, the connection between the control and semantic parts is not necessary. The potential for dissociation enables long-lasting moods to occur, as well as emotions happening for no apparent reason.

We argue that emotions can be reflected by emotion terms in English like "fear," indicating just a basic emotion without any implication of what caused it or what its object is. Other terms indicate combined control and semantic parts. So "to frighten" means that someone or something causes fear. "Embarrassment" means fear with the semantic content of being an object of unwelcome attention, and so on. A semantic analysis of emotion terms is discussed in Chapter 2.

Moods and emotions that occur without apparent cause

The phenomenon of an emotion occurring for no apparent reason, as a free-floating emotion mode, is not common, but it is significant. It occurs when a control emotion mode is set up but without conscious semantic information about its cause. Oatley and Duncan (1992) asked 57 students to keep structured diaries in which they recorded details of five successive episodes of emotion that happened in their ordinary lives. We found that happiness, sadness, anger, and fear all occasionally occurred without any cause discernible to the subjects. Some 6.3% of all emotion episodes were of this free-floating kind. We did not ask systematically about disgust/hatred.

The most striking of such acausal states, widely described in the clinical literature, is free-floating anxiety. It involves an overwhelming feeling of dread that something nameless is about to happen. The sufferer does not know what will happen or what caused it. Only the feeling of dread and perhaps the bodily accompaniments of fear occur. Corresponding to this, in the diary study of everyday emotions, we found that fear/anxiety was the most common of the emotions to occur without apparent cause.

Moods are states based on control modes that last longer than the few seconds of a facial expression or the minutes or hours characteristic of an episode of sadness, fear, or anger. They are emotional, but rather than being transitions between one sequence of action and another, they are maintained states. They occur when an emotion mode is set up that resists further transitions. When a person is sad, he or she will not be distracted by anything funny; when angry, it is difficult to eschew vengeful thoughts.

Oatley and Johnson-Laird's communicative theory is, we believe, the only cognitive theory of emotions that gives a principled account of moods. We assert that moods are based on control signals maintaining the system in a particular state (e.g., sadness or irritability) beyond any immediate event in the outer world and even beyond memory of what caused it. Moods depend on the dissociability of control emotion signals from semantic information about causation. For instance, irritability is a mood that can be maintained in which a person feels angry but may not know why. Perhaps he or she waits for an occasion when an outburst of anger at somebody or about something can occur.

The physiological state associated with each emotion mode has a specific neurochemical basis. Associated with this, psychologically active drugs can trigger and maintain the system in a specific mood state, making a person feel happy, frightened, or sad for no semantic reason, or alternatively, decrease the intensity and tenacity of moods, again without anything in the outer world having happened. The fact that the system responds to such alterations of physiology that are not themselves dependent on a cognitive evaluation and are not "about" anything at all in the outer world provides evidence for the dissociability of semantic and control signaling that we postulate.[35]

Moods that occur intensely and are maintained over a period of a week or more, without apparent connection to external events, are regarded as psychopathological. Each is primarily associated with one of the emotions that we have postulated as basic, although such states typically also include symptoms that are not emotional.

Corresponding with happiness is the pathological state of mania or the more common and less intense state of hypomania, without any special outside reason to be happy. People in such states feel expansively euphoric, often infectiously so. They perform actions unconstrained by fear of social consequences. Manic episodes in people I have known have included giving away money, possessions, and large presents even though they had little money, and in another case, driving fast and elatedly down one-way streets in the wrong direction, saying that one should not be concerned about petty social constraints.

Moods of sadness with bursting into tears many times a day occur in depression. But depression is not just an emotion. It includes other features, such as a loss of self-esteem. Anger can occur in several pathological states, for instance, in some that are diagnosed as paranoid. Such states may often involve people in ruminations along the lines of "What I would like to do if only I could get my hands on. . . ." Fear has as its psychopathological extensions – phobias, panic attacks, generalized anxiety states, and obsessive-compulsive disorders. Phobias are intense fears of specific objects or circumstances. A panic attack is a strong autonomic disturbance with an irresistible urge to escape to safety. Anxiety states may have no apparent object. Obsessive-compulsive disorders involve ruminations, or checking and rechecking actions. In all cases clinicians think the fear is inappropriate to possible causes. Disgust occurs psychopathologically in anorexia nervosa; it includes a revulsion from food, sometimes to the extent of starving to death.

Bower (e.g., 1981) and Teasdale (e.g., 1988) have shown that moods can constrain memories and thoughts. So, for instance, a person in a sad mood has thoughts of sad events coming to mind. In a related way it has been found (e.g., MacLeod, Mathews & Tata, 1986; Broadbent & Broadbent, 1988) that anxious subjects deploy their attention toward signs of danger in the environment, and these tend to have the effect of maintaining a mood of fear. There is widespread interest in the hypothesis that such self-reinforcing moods might be an important basis of pathological moods, an idea consonant with the theory presented here.[36]

Phenomena in which control signals can occur separately from semantic content support a main proposal of the communicative theory of emotions. They allow Johnson-Laird and me to give principled explanations of free-floating emotions, drug effects, moods, and the emotional aspects of psychopathological syndromes. They provide additional information on what emotions might be basic and what their properties are. Unfortunately, they also make for theoretical difficulty with regard to emotions of withdrawal, hatred, and disgust, because these seem to need an object; by definition, they seem to need semantic content. One must hate something, be disgusted at something.[37] We solve this problem by supposing that such emotions are capable of being aroused independently of events and sustained as moods, but then attributed to some object or other. In anorexia, for instance, a mood of revulsion from anything that might make the sufferer fat is maintained and is then projected into specific foods which then appear revolting. More generally, disdainful moods without a fixed object occur in psychopathological states with schizoid features.

Inner and outer communication

There are interpersonal equivalents of the messages sent within the cognitive system. Verbal utterances have semantic content and syntactic structure. By means of such messages we can affect the cognitive systems of other people, by suggesting and agreeing with new goals or new plans or by passing pieces of belief about the world. The equivalent of control messages between people include emotional expressions such as facial and bodily gestures and tones of voice. These need to be recognized by means of processes that involve interpretation. But in their unconventionalized forms their structure does not have significance for what is being communicated. The shape of the brow does not indicate the cause of anger.

Fear provides a clear example of the inner and outer communicative functions. Gray (1982) has described the internal events when fear or anxiety occur: Action is halted, the environment is carefully monitored, and default plans such as freezing, fighting, or fleeing are made ready. As to external communications, if a predator is noticed, members of many social species become frightened and communicate fear to others by alarm calls. Environmental monitoring is enhanced by many eyes and ears scanning the environment. Only one member need spot a predator to alert the rest by a signal that propagates throughout the community.

Seyfarth, Cheney, and Marler (1980) found that vervet monkeys have three kinds of alarm call. One signals a leopard. Monkeys hearing it climb trees and look downward. A second signals a snake, and the monkeys look around on the ground. The third signals an eagle, and the animals hide in the undergrowth and look upward. Alarm signals are typically less complex than those discovered by Seyfarth and colleagues, which are control signals in that they do not have to be parsed by the system that receives them. But they also have a minimal semantic content in referring to different kinds of predators. The typical pattern is that a danger can be detected by any of several modules in an individual's cognitive system, visual, olfactory, or acoustic. The internal signal sets the modules into a cooperative mode appropriate to danger, and then an external alarm call sets all the nearby individuals into a similar mode.

Among humans we can distinguish interpersonal communications that are control signals, biologically based, and occurring panculturally from those that are based on conventions. Crudely, emotional expressions are of the former kind; written language is of the latter kind. Face-to-face communication combines semantic and control signals. We say things, but in a particular tone of voice and with particular facial expressions.

Communications at moments of transition. As they begin their courtship, Anna and Vronsky experience delight and start relegating existing plans. Later, when Vronsky falls at the officers' race, Anna experiences an unexpected event of great threat. When she reacts to the news that Vronsky has not died, a conflict emerges starkly. She can no longer maintain her respectable marriage to a highly placed government official and her affair with a cavalry officer in the fast set as separate plans. Emotions mark the turning points of the plot in novels. If novelists are correct, they mark moments when plans undergo transition.

Emotions are communications to ourselves arising as evaluations change. As such, they produce feelings related to these evaluations. They allow us to continue, relinquish, or modify plans and goals. They also communicate to others, allowing new states of action readiness to be recognized.

Communicative effects. Because emotions can become conscious, we can, by reflection, infer aspects of our own goals and plans that might be unknown to us. It is partly this property that makes emotions so interesting to us. They point to goals and plans of which we may be unaware. Their realization can lead to more conscious assimilation. We can compile an account of these goals into the model we have of ourselves, which we experience as our self. Thus we may modify the cognitive structure that we inhabit and from which our actions flow.

Emotions also communicate to others in a way that is not quite deliberate, which is sometimes desired, sometimes more or less effectively suppressed. It allows others to know also of important junctures in the stream of our action, and not just to know but also sometimes themselves to be moved by the same or by complementary emotions.

In an emotion the cognitive system switches into a characteristic mode under the control of an emotion signal to accomplish a transition. In a mood a state is maintained against further transitions by this signal being sent continuously. Were we operating with just a single plan in a perfectly known world, there would be no need for such arrangements. They become necessary because the world and ourselves are partly unknown. Our plans must allow for modifications, and we incorporate unanticipated goals. We create new parts of our cognitive system as we go along.

We can think of functions of emotions, then, in three different ways. Basic emotion signals communicate directly to ourselves and tend to constrain our actions, thus managing happy continuations of existing plans or dysphoric transitions to new ones. They also communicate to others, tending to induce in them states similar to or complementary to our own, and thus prompting continuations or transitions in those with whom we interact. Finally, we communicate semantically by talking about emotions to ourselves and to others. What we say in such dialogues also has effects, ranging from the building of models of our self to influencing others in the way they think and act.

2. Intuitive and empirical approaches to understanding

The ability to puzzle on both sides of a subject will make
us detect more easily the truth and error about the
several points that arise.

Aristotle
Topics, 101a

Literature, language, and emotions

The cognitive revolution in psychology has extended methods for studying mental life beyond those of behaviorism. How wide should the
range of methods be? It is often assumed that art is of only mild interest
for scientific purposes, perhaps for stimulating ideas or for occasional
examples or quotations. In itself, however, art is subject to error and
deserves no serious attention. Thus, it may seem whimsical to base the
opening chapter of a book about the cognitive psychology of emotions
on scenes from a novel and to treat seriously such terms as "happiness"
and "anger" drawn from ordinary language, while referring to experiments and physiological data only to test specific hypotheses. Nevertheless, I propose that this is the way to proceed. I suggest that rather than
experiments being the main source of psychological knowledge, as is so
often assumed by academic psychologists, that methods based on making our intuitions explicit are more important for understanding emotions, at the current stage of development. A purely experimental approach would not take us as far toward understanding.

I argue for starting an understanding of emotions using Aristotelian
methods based on making explicit our intuitions, comparing everyday
understandings with those deriving from art and with those deriving
from science. After discussing the role of folk theory in understanding
emotions generally, I examine the folk theory of emotions implicit in

English emotion terms. I then move to stating explicitly seven main opinions embodied in Oatley and Johnson-Laird's theory of emotions, bringing forward empirical evidence on each. Next, I discuss evidence from other cultures that would potentially question the Eurocentric view expressed up to this point. Finally, I discuss the role in understanding of emotions in narrative literature.

Distrust of fiction and other intentional accounts

I will first cite some arguments in favor of a purely natural scientific, experimental approach for psychology and then explain the methods I claim are more appropriate here.

Fiction. Reasons for distrusting fiction go back at least to Plato, who was suspicious of art because he thought that, like drugs, it aroused emotions and thereby subverted rationality. In *The Republic,* he argued that art, rather than being based straightforwardly on truth, is based on imitation, *mimesis.* For people to imitate others, as actors do in a play, is to be deceptive. Such representations can be amusing and provide an escapist pastime, but they are, by definition, untrue. We can imagine Plato's argument clearly, I think, if we see it as suggesting that in a better kind of society than ours, soap operas would have no place because they untruthfully represent a glamorized world for the sake of diversion, escape, and cultural propaganda rather than presenting truths about society as it is, truths that might inform right action.

Ordinary language accounts. It is not only fiction that is problematic. According to a natural scientific approach, accounts by people other than novelists may be just as misleading, even when they describe what actually happened.

Suppose the scene at the races in *Anna Karenina* had occurred and conversations had been transcribed from recordings. How would we understand, for instance, Karenin's later actions? He believes Anna unfaithful, and he thinks about a duel, then about divorce. He later writes a formal letter to her saying she must eradicate the cause of their estrangement and maintain their marriage. He thinks this will make her unhappy, as she deserves. Imagine the letter was written and we have the text together with his thoughts spoken aloud, recorded and transcribed. Would these data be superior to what Tolstoy provides?[1]

Intentionality. In some ways recorded accounts are superior to fiction. But ordinary language accounts of all kinds include emotion terms and are described by philosophers as intentional. This quality itself makes them suspect in natural science. *Intentional* is used to describe mental states that are about something – belief about something, desire for something, anger that something, and so on.[2]

Stich (1983) and Churchland (1984) have argued that such intentional accounts are theories, and I agree: They are implicit theories to explain and predict our own and others' actions. Following Clark (1987), we can describe Karenin's intentional explanations to himself in the following kind of way:

> Karenin desires that his dignity be maintained.
> He believes that his dignity is threatened by Anna's infidelity.
> Therefore he acts to prevent further unfaithful behavior by Anna.[3]

Tolstoy, although he wrote fiction, uses the theoretical apparatus of desires and beliefs that we all use in ordinary life. He assumes that such intentional states explain action.

The idea that folk theory is bad theory. The statements of the theory of beliefs and desires are comparable to statements about why planets move as they do. Just as Newton proposed that planetary motions are caused by gravity and inertia, so folk theory contains the postulate that beliefs and desires cause behavior, and from them, one can make predictions. According to Stich (1983) and Churchland (1984), the difference between this kind of theory and theories in physics such as Newton's is that folk theory is bad theory. It is no better when derived from transcripts than from novels.

Stich compares this kind of folk psychology to earlier theories in physics. "Folk astronomy was false astronomy, and not just in detail," says Stich (1983, p. 229). By extension, folk theories of psychology are also likely to be wrong. Unlike scientific theories, they are not affected by evidence. Folk psychology is speculation like early cosmology, distinguished from it only by its persistence, which is stagnation. Proper scientific theories make progress. The failure of such folk theory to explain the behavior of animals indicates also that it is parochial.

Stich (1983) and Churchland (1984) propose that cognitive science should abandon explanations based on intentional constructs and get on with being real science. Nerve impulses, not beliefs and desires, cause behavior. If we were to adopt this proposal, we would segregate observations from their interpretation and draw only on observations that are repeatable, as in experimental psychology or neurophysiology. There is evidence that patterns of nerve impulses cause muscle contractions, and proper scientific explanations of behavior can be built up from such concepts. There is no scientific evidence that beliefs or desires cause anything at all.[4]

Support for this kind of position comes from experimental social psychology. Nisbett and Wilson (1977) and Nisbett and Ross (1980) have shown how bias occurs in judgments based on folk theory. We are affected by vivid and immediately available information even when it is unrepresentative or has no causal effect, at the expense of less vivid but more accurate information. Thus, people are usually affected more by anecdotal remarks than accurate and representative statistics.

So what basis could there be for starting with fictional representation and ordinary language explanations?

Saving the appearances: an Aristotelian approach

Recent research on the brain and behavior has been conducted in the largely Platonic way that Churchland (1984) and Churchland (1986) say is proper. Plato recommended a vantage point outside the merely human world, free of the distortions and biases of worldly appearances. From such a point we can reach understandings of timeless and incorruptible truths. Natural science is the direct descendant of Plato's ideals – an approach to reliable truth. It is based on repeatable observation, measurement, and mathematics. It creates reliable knowledge, *episteme,* the paradigm of truth.

Natural science and technology as cultural inventions have, of course, been astonishingly successful in physical domains. In comparison, the Aristotelian method of starting from human "appearances" seems to have failed, and this seems to reinforce the antiintentional view.[5] The revival of mentalism in psychology, however, has occurred because for all the cogency of the argument in physics, science that is exclusively natural science has not been so successful in psychology.[6] My proposal is, therefore, that another approach is needed, instead or in addition: the Aristotelian one in which "the human being is the measure of all things."[7] Unsuccessful though this seems to have been in physics, it identifies both a starting point and a point to which explanations need to return if we are to understand ourselves.

Aristotle's recommendation is that

> We must set down the appearances (*phainomena*), and first working through the puzzles, in this way go on to show, if possible, the

truth of all the beliefs we hold about those experiences; and, if this is not possible, the truth of the greatest number and the most authoritative. (1145b, Nussbaum, 1986, p. 240)

In other words, instead of escaping from mere appearances of the human world to attain a god's-eye view, we start with human appearances and attempt to reconcile them with each other. *Phainomena* are our ordinary interpretations of experience and our human intuitions about them.[8] Because knowledge is distributed in the community (cf. Putnam, 1975), we consult also the opinions of the many and the wise, comparing understandings with each other. The wise include the natural scientists. Then we make comparisons to reveal inconsistencies among different kinds of evidence. Thus, as it were, we bootstrap ourselves toward more reliable understandings of general principles. Moreover, "It is through reputable opinions about them that these [principles] have to be discussed, and this task belongs properly, or most appropriately, to dialectic; for dialectic is a process of criticism wherein lies the path to the principles of all inquiries" (*Topics*, 101b).

Nussbaum (1986) shows that Aristotle's method is neither naive nor obsolete. Even in physics, it is the recommendation that we try to bring together ordinary understanding with the understanding of experts (the wise), and that the path to knowledge is a social one involving proposals, criticisms, alternative explanations, and discussion.[9]

It seems as if, *a fortiori*, this argument should apply to human and social sciences. Here, not only is the process of critical discussion similar to that proposed by Aristotle, but initial appearances are less likely to mislead than they did in some early physics. We know that they are the appearances to start from because they are the ones that are important to us ordinarily in explaining behavior, and arguably it is in gaining insight that our ordinary understanding may be improved. In physics, early scientists seem to have been misled not by a form of reasoning but because the salience of certain physical phenomena prompted them to think that these were the significant observations from which to start. As it has turned out, in the natural world many phenomena invisible to ordinary senses are more important for explanatory understanding than things that are directly visible.[10]

To us humans, the appearances of emotions are salient. They press upon us and demand that we try to understand them. Emotions figure largely in our explanations of ourselves, and that suggests why narrative literature is important. It provides paradigm cases of such explanations.

Nisbett and Ross (1980) have shown that we often make judgments on the basis of what is salient, but that this is often a poor guide to what might have causal significance. They propose that people in everyday judgments are acting as intuitive scientists, not pure scientists for whom a great expenditure can be lavished on testing a theory but more like applied scientists or scientist-practitioners who use rather than test theories and have to make practical decisions with limited time and resources. For us as intuitive scientists, these theories are the folk theories of our culture. Within these theories we attribute causal significance to that which is vivid and salient and neglect factors that are less vivid and less salient. Just as theories help to assimilate data, so that we may make sense of the information, they can filter and distort data, so that what happens does not always make us change what we believe even when it ought to.

This could mean that in trying to understand emotions we should only attend to evidence collected scientifically and disattend all intuitive judgments, all data filtered by folk theory. This, again, is the Platonic position. What I am arguing for is an alternative. We are indeed often deceived by the salience of some information on which we base everyday inferences. But, as Nisbett and Ross (1980) go on to argue, this does not mean that only behavioral or natural scientific evidence is ever worth attending to. What it means is that implicit folk theories need to be made explicit and opened to critical discussion in order to understand their effects, improve them where possible, and bring them into register with scientific theories. Even if we were to find that emotions have less causal significance than we think, we must come to that conclusion by taking seriously the intuitive idea that emotions are important. I shall return to the biases in human intuitive judgments in Chapters 3 and 6.

Pursuing an Aristotelian program in this chapter, in the next section I consider the significance of natural language terms for the theory I have been expounding. Following that I take up empirical evidence from Western culture and then cross-cultural evidence about emotions. Finally, I discuss the role of narrative literature and the question of insight in understanding emotions.

Ordinary language and emotion terms in English

Although according to Paul Churchland and Patricia Churchland all explanations in ordinary language are likely to be wrong, Clark (1987) argues that their persistence over time means quite the opposite. Folk theories are good at predicting our own and others' behavior. Certainly we are vastly better using these methods than we would be if we were confined to analyses of stimulus and response.[11] Mentalistic concepts, therefore, reflect a basic competence in psychological explanation. They are not comparable to being mistaken in theories of cosmology or quantitative mechanics, but to being essentially correct in our implicit grasp of physical principles like gravity or the properties of liquids without which we would be unable to grasp a handrail to steady ourselves on a staircase or to place a cup of coffee on a table without spilling it. Thus, we should try to discover what psychological concepts are implicit in the ordinary language of emotions.

Johnson-Laird and Oatley (1988b, 1989) have analyzed emotion terms in English with a view to approaching this kind of understanding. The proposal of our communicative theory is that there is a small number of basic states of action readiness, each with distinctive phenomenological tone. Emotions typically occur in response to an event that affects a goal, though they may also occur for no apparent reason. They may be accompanied by conscious preoccupation, by physiological events, and by emotional expressions. The consequence of an emotional state may be distinctive forms of action that are the opening phases of a new plan.

According to this theory, people can recognize basic emotion modes just as they can recognize hunger, sleepiness, or physical pain. If this is so, then in a typical natural language there will be terms that denote such basic feelings.

The theory also indicates that terms denoting events associated with emotions but which are not themselves emotions, such as eliciting conditions ("successful"), preoccupations ("thinking"), physiological descriptions ("tense"), emotional expressions ("crying"), or attributes of action prompted by emotion ("aggression") will be found in a language. All these terms in parentheses were offered by at least two of Fehr and Russell's (1984) subjects who were asked to write down examples of emotions for two minutes.[12] The heterogeneity of such terms need not imply that the concept of emotion is incoherent, merely that ordinary language is not itself a theory that indicates the mechanism of eliciting conditions, accompaniments, and consequences of emotions.

Meanings of emotion terms

Johnson-Laird and Oatley (1989) have analyzed a corpus of 590 English emotion terms and used it to see if the communicative theory can explain the semantics of such terms.[13] The concept of emotion (singular) is a superordinate, and is sometimes used as a placeholder for a disjunctive set of specific emotions – happiness, anger, and so on. Specific emotions are mental states that usually occur in particular contexts. Basic emotion terms refer only to the state of readiness or to a distinctive phenomenological tone, not to the environmental context as such.

Happiness is an example of a basic emotion term. Although I can describe conditions in which it might arise, the term itself does not imply any particular circumstance. Happiness can be experienced for no apparent reason. The linguistic test is to ask whether it makes sense to say: "I feel happy today, but I don't know why." This is not anomalous in any way. We propose this "don't know why" test as a linguistic test of a basic emotion. Because we can refer to emotions as occurring when we do not know what caused them, such usages can refer to emotion modes without conscious semantic content.[14]

Most emotion terms, however, denote a mental state that is a basic emotion and also imply a context in which the state arose. We can call these contextual terms. People are usually aware of the events that have caused an emotion. If such matters are important in a culture, then terms emerge to refer to them. For instance, if in a culture it is regularly found that a state of revulsion is aroused by substances, persons, or events, and this matter is of interest, then the verb "to hate" becomes useful. So when Anna says to Karenin, "I hate you," she is asserting that she feels a basic emotion in relation to him, a readiness to withdraw from him.[15] There is no reason to suppose that ordinary language is wrong in referring to an emotion arising in such a context. Indeed, as Gordon (1987) has argued, the reverse is the case: It would be almost impossible to understand certain kinds of human behavior if we were not allowed to use emotion terms.

Using a contextual emotion term like "hate" implies an emotional control state combined with the semantic signals that indicate context, namely, the cause and/or object of the emotion. In this case Karenin is both cause and object: He has caused the state, and Anna warns that she will withdraw from him. It would be anomalous to say, "I feel hatred, but I do not know who or what I am hating." The term "hate" refers both to a control state and to some aspect of its cause or object.

There is also a set of emotion terms that we call "complex," in which the context includes the self. Jealousy is one such term. It occurs to Karenin at the races and to Kitty at the ball. It is an elaboration of the contextual emotion "hatred," with a context that involves the possible loss of a loved one to a third person in a way that will diminish the self. Again, it is anomalous to say, "I feel jealous, but I do not know why," though one can be jealous and not know who because one might be mistaken in one's suspicions. To talk of being jealous refers to a control state in relation to a sense of outrage for the self because of a second person on whom one has some claim and in relation to a third person who could supplant one in the affections of that second person.

As Roberts (1988) has put it, an emotion typically unites a feeling and such matters as its cause. We do not usually just feel something and know separately about its eliciting cause, accompaniments, and object. Putting this in terms of our communicative theory, when we experience emotions the control state and semantic information are usually bound together in a unified mental conclusion, a semantic content about the context with distinctively emotional tone and readiness.

Emotions, concepts, words

Emotions, concepts of emotions, and words referring to emotions should be distinguished: Johnson-Laird and Oatley (1989) make the distinctions. An emotion is a mental state of readiness that has a phenomenological tone. A concept is a mental construct categorizing that experience. A word enables what is experienced to be spoken of. The meanings of words are concepts that have been found useful in communication. When we use a word to refer to something, it points to a conceptual meaning. If the communication is successful, a corresponding meaning is evoked in the mind of the listener. Emotions may be experienced privately, or we may infer from other people's behavior that they are having emotions. Therefore, the relations among experience, concept, and word are somewhat different from those in which there is an external referent like a chair.[16]

The meanings of emotion terms are not open to introspection, and emotional vocabulary has grown up unsystematically. Perhaps the impression that emotion terms are heterogeneous arises because many are ambiguous. Terms may refer to an emotion, to a predisposition, or they may be metaphors. Many, perhaps most, of the 196 terms volunteered by Fehr and Russell's (1984) subjects are ambiguous. For instance, "hurt" was cited as an emotion term by 16 people in that study. Without context there is no clear way of deciding whether or not "hurt" is an emotion. Used in a sentence the ambiguity disappears. For instance:

"I felt so hurt when she went off with that other man."

does refer to a specific emotion, probably jealousy. But

"When I sprained my ankle it hurt quite a bit."

does not refer to an emotion at all, but to physical pain.

Emotion words have meanings in the ordinary sense: They contribute to the truth conditions of the utterances (as described by Miller and Johnson-Laird, 1976). So, if Anna says she is afraid of Karenin, she means she feels fear of him, referring either to an emotion present at the time of speaking or to a general attitude. This idea of emotions indicating truth conditions requires that meanings of other terms are understood and some basic concepts are taken for granted. But the rules of language are capable of defining the notion "afraid of." Moreover, if the term is understood, inferences can be made. We may validly infer that she supposes something about him causes her to feel fear, though the term does not allow a valid inference that he caused her fear intentionally. The further inference of intended frightening would be carried by such a term as "intimidate."

According to the communicative theory, emotions are not just a heterogeneous set of psychological concepts. It is possible to give an orderly account of the semantics of emotion terms. When properly used we know what these terms mean.

Semantic primitives: basic emotion terms

What, then, are the meanings of emotion terms, starting with the basic ones? Basic emotion terms arise from the set of basic emotion modes that correspond to control signals that can have a conscious tone. Such feelings may be vague when they are of low intensity. Hunger and headache, too, are insubstantial under such circumstances, but we still suppose that the terms refer to concepts of discriminable experience.

Emotion terms are often ambiguous, so that emotions themselves may be confused with aspects of their context, with predispositions, motivational states, and so on. It is these matters that make understanding emotion terms problematic. Basic emotion signals have no internal structure that is parsed and interpreted within the system, and words referring to subjective experiences of these modes cannot be analyzed semantically. Like pain, experiences of basic emotions are phenomeno-logical primitives.

The acquisition of emotional vocabulary depends on more than the experience of basic emotions. Not only is an experience necessary, but so also are an awareness of what caused it and a knowledge of its accompaniments and consequences. As a child, we may learn that the absence of someone to whom we are attached elicits a particular feeling, and find that we are crying. We may learn that the experience occurring with these eliciting conditions and accompaniments is called sadness. When we see others in similar conditions or making similar expressions, we can attribute a similar experience to them.

Although the eliciting conditions and accompaniments are necessary for us to learn how to use emotion terms, they are not necessary to the meaning of the basic emotion words. If they were, it would be anomalous to make such assertions as:

"I feel sad for no reason."
"I feel sad even though I don't show it."

One can certainly make default inferences from utterances that include emotion terms. If someone says:

"I feel sad"

we can infer that a loss has probably caused the emotion and that the sadness may be expressed in behavior. But eliciting condition and expressions are not emotions. We can refer to them separately. Frijda (1986) describes the emotion process as including an eliciting event, a feeling, and consequences. But basic emotion terms in English refer just to unanalyzable modes of readiness that can be experienced consciously.

The structure of the semantic field of emotions

Miller and Johnson-Laird (1976) have described a procedure of questioning to reveal how a basic term is semantically elaborated. Drawing on this work, the first question one can ask about a potential emotion term is whether it can be used to refer to a feeling. If it can, then one asks whether it is a bodily sensation such as pain or a mental feeling such as fear (see Figure 6). If it is mental, one can ask whether it can be experienced for no apparent reason or only as a result of a known cause. The existence of terms referring to feelings that can be experienced for no known reason is explained by the basic emotion modes.

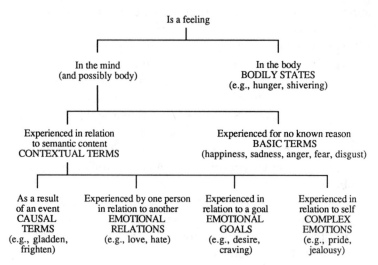

Figure 6. Classification of words referring to emotions. Types of
emotion terms are in capital letters and examples are in parentheses.
(Modified from Johnson-Laird & Oatley [1988b].)

Here, the folk theory of emotions embedded in English meets the
psychological theory that the cognitive system includes these signals
and these modes. Although lay ideas do not bear strongly on the scientific veracity of the theory of emotional control signals in the cognitive
system, as laypeople we know of recurring mental states that we call
emotions.

Syntactic categories. Johnson-Laird and Oatley (1989) have argued that the
vocabulary of emotions contains nouns, verbs, adjectives, and adverbs.
Many roots take suffixes that enable them to serve in all these categories.
Thus, "fear" is a noun and a transitive verb, but also the root of adjectives – "fearful," "fearless," "fearsome" – and their corresponding adverbs – "fearfully," "fearlessly." The adjectives can also become nouns,
as "fearfulness." Though these words have the same root, they may
differ in connotation and usage. So the verb to affect means to move the
emotions generally, but the noun affection denotes just a positive feeling
toward someone. "Dread" is intense fear. "Dreadful" is more common
and almost always used metaphorically.

Many English words refer to basic emotions, and modifications can
indicate intensity. To be "contented" is to be mildly happy, to be "joyful"
is to feel very happy, and to be "ecstatic" is to feel such extreme happiness that everything else becomes insignificant.

Contextual emotion terms. Though some words can refer just to basic emotions, others signify a feeling in conjunction with a semantic content. Hume (1739) proposed the idea that some emotions are direct and essentially unanalyzable, whereas others include qualities that can be described and that he called indirect. His distinction corresponds to that of Johnson-Laird and Oatley between basic terms, and terms that can be called contextual, which can be subcategorized as follows (see also Figure 6).

CAUSAL TERMS. There are contextual terms to indicate caused emotions. So, if someone truthfully says, "I am glad," that person feels happy and implies that something caused the feeling.

Terms for caused emotions are related to those called causatives, which are the inverse of this pattern. Causatives include verbs describing causation of an emotion in someone, for instance, "gladden." Examples of causative emotion verbs in the other four basic modes are "sadden," "frighten," "aggravate," and "disgust." There are also verbs that imply causing emotions more generally: "upset," "thrill," "provoke," and "disturb." Some causative verbs also refer to the restoration of emotional equilibrium during sadness ("comfort," "console"), to the alleviation of fear ("encourage," "hearten"), or to lessening anger ("mollify," "placate").

EMOTIONAL RELATIONS. Some words have meanings that depend on basic emotions but also express their objects. In Figure 6 these words are called "Emotional Relations." They imply emotions directed toward or experienced in relation to people or other entities. "Love," "grief," "fear of," "resentment," and "hatred" are terms in each of the five categories of basic emotions that imply relation to objects.

EMOTIONAL GOALS. Though we have argued that emotions should be distinguished from motives, emotions are sometimes spoken of as motives. In Figure 6 these are referred to as "Emotional Goals." Thus, "to desire" is to have a feeling whose object is a particular goal. The usual connotation is sexual. Ambiguity of vocabulary is evident: "Craving" may signify an emotion or a motivation or it may be used as a metaphor.

COMPLEX EMOTIONS. Complex emotions are contextual, but with the context including an evaluation of the self. They are discussed in Chapter 4.

SUMMARY. Contextual terms are the most frequent emotion terms in English. In them, we begin to see the work of explanation in terms of the folk theories that support ordinary language. Contextual emotion terms are intentional; the emotions to which they refer are about something. Emotions are understood as being caused by events, as capable of affecting our behavior, and as capable of being directed at people.

Johnson-Laird and Oatley have shown, then, that far from being heterogeneous, emotion terms in English have an orderly semantics, implying that emotions are mental states usually caused by events, and that can explain actions. The folk concepts on which these semantics are based do not constitute a scientific theory. What we claim is, first, that these concepts are used within statements deriving from the folk theory of beliefs and desires, and, second, that they are consistent with the cognitive scientific theory that emotions are important in managing goals and plans.

Semantics and pragmatics. The fact that we offer a semantics of emotion terms does not imply that language is the business of describing things.

In all cultures, it seems, people strive to understand themselves and make their behavior and that of others relatively predictable. Emotion terms are used pragmatically to talk about oneself and others in order to evaluate actions, to discuss people's moral status, and to negotiate joint plans. The uses to which emotion terms are put in discourse serve these aims. The main discussion of these issues is in Chapter 4.

The structure of the affective lexicon

A project close in spirit to Johnson-Laird and Oatley's has been conducted by Ortony, Clore, and their colleagues.[17] In one part of this work, Ortony, Clore, and Foss (1987) started with a corpus of affect terms in English and undertook a componential analysis to understand which terms referred properly to emotions and which did not. They did this by making as few assumptions as possible in a way that was not specific to any particular theory of emotions, including their own.

Within affective conditions they distinguish external and internal. External conditions include descriptions of behavior, like "sexy," or of the objective state of affairs, like "abandoned," as in "Moses was abandoned in the bullrushes." Such terms, though they often have affective connotations, do not themselves refer to emotions. Next they distinguish among internal conditions. Mental conditions like "angry" are distinguished from nonmental ones like "sleepy" and "hungry." Thus far, their analysis is similar to ours.

Clore, Ortony, and Foss (1987) have found that not just they, but undergraduates who acted as subjects as well, could distinguish emotional states from nonemotions on the basis of a linguistic test. The test relies on whether each of the 585 terms from their corpus of affect terms, like "angry" or "abandoned," implied a mental state when used with verbs of feeling and verbs of being. Subjects agreed that both to feel angry and to be angry imply an emotion, and therefore "angry" properly refers to an emotion. Subjects thought, however, that feeling abandoned refers to an emotion, whereas being abandoned does not. Thus "abandoned" is not a genuine emotion term.

Ortony, Clore, and their colleagues thus have cleared away some of the confusion from terms in the affective lexicon. Mandler (1984) has pointed out that there is no definition of emotion. But neither Johnson-Laird and I, nor Ortony, Clore and their colleagues accept this as meaning that no useful taxonomy can be constructed. There is no definition of a sentence, but this does not stop linguists from using the term. Their object, like ours, is to create an explanatory theory.

It is at this point that our analysis diverges from that of Ortony, Clore and their colleagues. Their next distinction is in "affect focal," "behavior focal," and "cognition focal" categories. We have no quarrel with these distinctions. Perhaps they will be useful for exploring the inferences that can be made from emotion terms in computational text understanding. Our purpose is somewhat different (cf. also Oatley & Johnson-Laird, 1990). We argue that commitment to a theory is important. Our next distinction, then, is dependent on our theory, and is between basic and contextual terms (see Figure 6).

Emotions as prototypes

An objection to the semantic analysis of Johnson-Laird and Oatley is that emotion terms are not definable classically in terms of their contributions to truth conditions, but that they are based on prototypes, like the terms "dog" and "water." According to this argument, the apparent disorder among emotion terms is resolved by considering that the concept of emotion is prototypical.[18] We have two kinds of reply.

First, is the concept of emotion a prototype? Some words have a meaning that can be communicated to other people in ordinary language. If someone asks us what "borrow" means, we can explain that when we borrow something from someone we intentionally obtain it from its owner, who permits us to use it on the understanding that we must return it. The definition requires that we know about intention, obligation, owning, getting, and returning, which can be explained in terms of still other concepts. Given such concepts, the meaning of "borrow" can be analyzed in terms of its contribution to the truth conditions of sentences in which it is used. Then we can make valid inferences: If I borrowed something, did I own it? – No.

By contrast, some words refer to entities that are not well understood. When we refer to a natural kind such as "dog," we may have little idea of the true nature of dogs. The term is used because of a convention that a word refers to a stereotype (cf. Putnam, 1975) or prototype. The meanings of such words support few, if any, valid inferences. If I were asked the meaning of "dog," I might describe a prototypical dog, perhaps saying it barks and has four legs. Our knowledge of the word depends on having seen and heard dogs or having learned about them to build up the prototype, but there are no concepts that describe the contribution that "dog" necessarily makes to the truth conditions of sentences. Notions such as "barks" or "with four legs" function only as attributes to be assumed by default. Someone might refer to a dog that did not bark or had lost one of its legs.

The proposal that emotion concepts are prototypes may be seen in relation to Frijda's theory that emotion is a process consisting of encoding an event, evaluating it, generating readiness, and acting.[19] According to this idea, different emotion terms are more or less good exemplars of this process. No one fully understands the process. Ordinary emotion terms, therefore, will tend to refer to this natural phenomenon in a prototypical way.

Fehr and Russell (1984) and Shaver et al. (1987) have presented data to support the idea that the apparent disorder among emotion terms is resolved if "emotion" is prototypical, lacking necessary and sufficient conditions for its definition. Different emotion terms are more or less good exemplars of the concept of emotion. For instance in Fehr and Russell's table of 196 emotion terms, "happiness" was a core example with 152 people listing it when asked to supply examples of emotion terms. "Hurt" was more peripheral with 16 people listing it, and "insecurity" marginal with only 2 people listing it.

It is not at all easy to demonstrate prototypicality. It is not demonstrated merely by showing that subjects rate instances of a concept as varying in typicality and are faster to verify good exemplars than poor exemplars. Armstrong, Gleitman, and Gleitman (1983) point out that such phenomena are not decisive, because they occur with concepts that do have necessary and sufficient conditions.

Theorists sometimes argue that prototypicality is established where there is no clear boundary between what are and what are not instances of the concept. But this argument is uncertain because it tends to identify meaning with verification.[20] Miller and Johnson-Laird (1976) distinguish between a concept and the perceptual process of identifying its members: Concepts imply functions and attributes of entities and their relations to other entities. So, a difficulty in identifying instances of a concept need not reveal the underlying nature of the concept. The concept "bachelor" can be analyzed as an eligible adult male who is unmarried. But this gives us only uncertain clues as to how to identify bachelors in a crowd of people. The problem is made worse by different people having different concepts and varying in the completeness and accuracy of their knowledge: Is a Catholic priest a bachelor? Is a widower a bachelor?

People do indeed have difficulties in deciding whether or not a particular word refers to an emotion. The problem is caused in part by the considerable ambiguity of emotional terms, so subjects rating isolated words may well consider different meanings of the same words. "Love," for instance, was the fourth most frequently chosen example of an emotion by Fehr and Russell's (1984) subjects. The idea of "love" as an erotic passion is indeed properly thought of as an emotion. Presumably, however, loving one's neighbor is a kind of commitment, and is neither a sudden emotion nor a mood.[21]

The only secure way to establish that a concept is prototypical is to show that it supports default inferences, such as the inference that a dog barks, rather than valid inferences, such as the inference that if one borrows something one does not own it. Does the concept "emotion" support default inferences? Well, yes, to some extent. If people are asked what follows from the assertion

Jane was experiencing an emotion

they might make the default inference that she was agitated or showing expressions of the emotion. But they might also say, validly in our view, that she must have been angry or frightened or having some other specific feeling.

So, although the general concept of "emotion," in English, does support some default inferences, it is also like "furniture" in that it is a superordinate that refers to a disjunctive set of instances – namely, basic emotions or their contextual variants. In some languages, there is no superordinate term for "emotion" (see, e.g., Lutz, 1982). The ordinary concept of "emotion" is, therefore, more like a placeholder for a set of separate mental states – specific emotions – that people do know about in all cultures and that contrast with other kinds of states like hunger or sleepiness.

From contextual emotion terms one can make entirely valid inferences. If I truthfully say I am furious, you can infer that something has caused my anger, and you can ask me what has happened. If I say I am ashamed, then you can validly infer that something I have done or am associated with has damaged my sense of self. If, by contrast, we take an emotion to be the whole process, then only default inferences would be possible, because this process would be only partly understood.

Recently, Russell (1991) argued that the way people actually behave suggests that emotion concepts are based on prototypes, although classical definitions of emotion concepts, such as those offered by Johnson-Laird and Oatley, are more appropriate to scientific analyses of emotions. In many ways this is a helpful suggestion. Johnson-Laird and I, however, have a different position. We take the phenomenological tone associated with a change in readiness as an unanalyzable primitive, and terms indicating combinations of such states with their eliciting conditions, accompaniments, or consequences as capable of being analyzed. We make sense of our emotions via cultural folk theories of them, and hence classical definitions are possible as they are of borrowing or bachelors. A scientific hypothesis from psychology makes sense of folk concepts of emotion and their semantics in natural language.

The importance of intuitions

Folk theory has no claim to truth by virtue of being folk theory. There are many folk theories. Some contradict others, and many are just plain wrong. In Chapter 3, I argue that the folk theory that emotions are irrational, as compared with thought, which is rational, is false.

In summary, I make three proposals. First, following Clark (1987), I assume that the folk theory implicit in mentalistic talk that desires and beliefs affect action should be taken seriously because it allows us to predict and explain our own and others' actions quite well – better than any other class of theory and certainly better than any foreseeable theory based on neurophysiological or behaviorist terms. If I say I will meet you at a certain place, there is a high probability that you and I can predict my behavior, and the degree of this predictability is comparable to or better than that of many physical systems. Second, I propose that when we talk of emotions, we refer to something important for us, particularly in our interpersonal lives. Psychologists should explore the significance of what is referred to and see if it can be made sense of. Third, decisions about which aspects of ordinary understanding are reliable can be made by comparing different intuitions with each other, and with scientific data, saving those appearances and intuitions that survive critical scrutiny and replacing those that do not.

Johnson-Laird and Oatley claim not that the semantics of emotion terms reveal a folk theory of emotion terms that is necessarily true. Rather, we claim that a test of the (scientific) communicative theory is to see if it is consistent with the ordinary language of emotions. If it were inconsistent, this might mean that folk concepts, here as in astronomy, are muddled, or that our theory is wrong, or that both our theory and folk concepts are wrong.

We have not found our theory and folk concepts in ordinary language to be inconsistent with one another. For a corpus of 590 English emotion terms we used our theory and the methods described here to decide whether each term is or is not an emotion and offered a semantic analysis of those that are emotions. We found no genuine emotion terms that we were unable to analyze in this way, and we take this to suggest that our approach is useful.

Concepts of emotions are unlike those in physics, first, because they refer partly to subjective phenomena rather than public ones. Second, contextual emotions refer to regularly occurring associations, for instance, between emotions and causes, that have taken place many times in each person's experience and have been subject to much cultural learning. No substantive evidence has been advanced to make one doubt that people can report such associations: When a loss happens and we feel sad, the loss caused the sadness. Someone frustrating a previously agreed plan causes anger. The method of starting with such ordinary interpretations, *phainomena,* and comparing them with each other, and also with scientific theories, seems appropriate to the problem of understanding emotions in human terms.

It is the opposite view, of considering only empirical work on behavior or physiology, as relevant to understanding emotions that seems absurd. If psychologists were to adhere to such a program, they would no doubt arrive at the conclusions of animal learning theorists in the 1950s about what happens to an animal when reinforcements are or are not predictable. Can it be accidental that even when the behaviorist program was dedicated to avoiding mentalistic terms, a kind of shorthand was introduced? Behavior was labeled "elation" when, as discovered by Zeaman (1949), rats ran faster in a runway when the size or their reward was increased; "frustration" when an anticipated reward did not appear (Amsel, 1958); and "anxiety" when there was anticipatory avoidance (Mowrer, 1960).

Hebb (1946) has argued that rather than using emotion terms apparently as a shorthand for behavioral phenomena, the concept of emotion itself is essential for understanding certain kinds of behavior. He observed chimpanzees in the Yerkes Laboratories, and found that some animals had become unpredictable during the reign of behaviorism when research assistants were forbidden to "anthropomorphize" in the daily notes they kept on the animals. He gives examples: An animal, Bimba, was friendly and responsive to the attendants, but would occasionally become angry and attack if she were slighted. He contrasted this with another animal, Pati, who seemed to hate humans, and would attack an attendant deliberately after appearing friendly. But there was no observable difference in the nature of the attacks of the two animals, and no short-term observations of behavior would predict them. But, by allowing animals to be described using "concepts of emotion and attitude . . . a newcomer to the staff could handle the animals as he could not safely otherwise" (p. 88).

Theory and evidence

In contrast to analyses of the folk theory embedded in emotion terms, I shall now approach the issue from an empirical direction. I shall state seven main postulates of Oatley and Johnson-Laird's communicative theory of emotions. Not presented here is the evidence for the general family of conflict and evaluation theories of emotion, among which there has been substantial convergence. Mandler (1984) and Frijda (1986) have presented such evidence admirably, with the latter reviewing the literature comprehensively up to about 1984. This is also not the place for a comprehensive review of literature since then, which is given by Oatley and Jenkins (1992). This evidence in general supports an understanding of common principles among researchers on the cognitive approach to emotions.[22]

In this section I set out the seven postulates with the main arguments and empirical evidence relevant to each, and while acknowledging the convergence between the communicative theory and other cognitive theories, to indicate the differences.

1. Function

The normal function of an emotion is to change goal priorities and to load into readiness a small suite of plans for action. At the same time information is inserted into consciousness, prompting interpretations of the event that caused the emotion, and sustaining attempts at problem solving in planning. Emotions have a consciousness-raising function in allowing us to infer goals that might have been obscure, and hence to build models of our own goal structures.

In my view the most compelling argument that human emotions have such functions is as follows. Any intelligent being that has multiple goals, that operates with finite resources in an environment that is not fully knowable, and that cooperate with other similar beings would have to solve pressing cognitive problems – particularly if the being changes its own cognitive organization as it goes along. These problems center on the management of goal priorities and the generation of ad hoc situated action. We humans are such beings. The system that seems to undertake these functions is the mechanism underlying emotions.

The analytical problem is to carve nature at the joints. Do the emotions we experience correspond to cognitively functional processes? To take an analogy: Arguing from salience could be like proposing 100 years ago that flapping wings were crucially necessary for heavier-than-air flight. Such a theory is neither descriptively nor explanatorily adequate. In explaining a process it is important to name parts that are functional and that will be functionally significant. Two potential fallacies are mistaking a name for an explanation and being misled into thinking that a name implies something functional.[23] So, according to this argument, emotions as we experience them may figure large in folk theories, but they may not be functional. They may be epiphenomena.

So far as I know, there is no empirical evidence that decisively refutes this view. In the same way it is impossible to demonstrate that consciousness is not an epiphenomenon. My method of meeting this kind of argument is to show that emotion concepts account for a range of mental phenomena that would otherwise be incomprehensible.

The argument is that the folk theoretical term "emotion" properly refers to states such as happiness, anger, and so on, which are coextensive with processes that are functionally important in cognitive systems operating with multiple goals in uncertain environments.

2. Folk theory and natural science

Distinct emotions correspond to phenomenologically distinct mental states that have cognitive functions. At least some folk categories of emotions correspond to scientific categories, and they are a means of understanding our own and others' actions.

The term "emotion" does not explain emotions, but it has psychological meaning just as the folk theoretical term "seeing" refers to a functionally coherent set of processes, which in cognitive science we think of as being accomplished by the visual system.[24] Many psychologists, including myself, think that mental terms should not be eliminated. We should not confine ourselves, as the behaviorists did, to physiological and behavioral measurements. We should include verbal data that depend on mental constructs, or at least admit such verbal categories as happy, sad, and so forth as appropriate for analysis. Three kinds of evidence are relevant, though they are suggestive rather than conclusive.

First, Harris (1989) has shown that children in the first few years of their lives acquire the folk theory that emotions are mental rather than behavioral states and that they are caused by events relevant to goals. Children use this theory to understand the minds of other people, and they are severely handicapped in social life if they are unable to do so.

Second, Gordon (1987) presents a range of arguments to show more generally that some kinds of human action are impossible to understand if one is not allowed to use concepts of emotion. He shows, for instance, that certain actions can be understood if seen as prompted by anger in retribution for an injury or by jealousy, but they are unpredictable by behavioral or instrumental theories. In one example he discusses how people may destroy belongings of sexual partners by whom they had been deserted, even though there could be no instrumental purpose in doing so.[25]

Third, Johnson-Laird and Oatley (1989) have offered a semantic analysis of English emotion terms described earlier in this chapter. We argue that the systematic quality of this semantic field indicates that emotions are not hopelessly heterogeneous. The folk theory embedded in English converges with scientific theory, in that terms for basic emotions are primitives and other terms denote a basic emotion bound to some semantic indication of a cause or object.

3. Basic emotion signals without awareness of cause

Emotions are based on control signals that communicate pervasively within the cognitive system and tend to set up distinctive emotion modes. These modes can occur without any conscious semantic knowledge of their cause. They are referred to as moods when they become self-maintaining and remote from their initial cause.

Though emotions are usually elicited by goal-relevant events (see postulate 5), emotions and moods occasionally occur for no consciously known reason. Oatley and Johnson-Laird's theory explains this, but acausal emotions are troublesome for theories that state that emotions are always based on appraisals of events (e.g., Ortony, Clore & Collins, 1988). Our communicative theory is founded partly on the occurrence of control states that need not have conscious elicitors.

A piece of research that discriminates between the theory of Oatley and Johnson-Laird and other theories on this issue is that of Oatley and Duncan (1992). We asked 57 student subjects to keep structured diaries giving details of five emotion incidents of any assortment from happiness, sadness, anger, and fear that were strong enough to cause bodily perturbations, intrusive thoughts, or urges to act in an emotional way. Most incidents were recorded within 2 hours of occurrence and hence were less subject to regression to stereotypical responses than those in which people judged vignettes or events remembered from days or weeks previously.[26] We found five, three, one, and nine instances, respectively, of happiness, sadness, anger, and fear described as seeming "not to be caused by anything in particular." Overall, 6.3% of emotion episodes were described as acausal in this way. This result is predicted by the communicative theory and not by other cognitive theories. Certain emotions can occur without any semantic awareness of their cause.

Our theory that basic emotions may seem to be uncaused by anything external allows a principled account of what a mood is – a control mode being maintained irrespective of current events. Except for Schachter and Singer's (1962) theory, which has been rendered implausible on other grounds, rival cognitive theories to ours give no principled account of moods or acausal emotions. According to us, a mood occurs when the cognitive system is maintained in an emotion mode for a period. Events that might change that mood are not able to do so because the mode is to some extent self-sustaining.

Basic emotion states can be caused by such events as drugs, electrical stimulation, infections, and hormonal changes. They can be induced without semantic content by music, and this method has been used in the laboratory. Kenealy (1988) has shown that effects of music can be independent of any verbal instructions to subjects either to get into a mood suggested by a particular piece of music or to get into a mood that is different from one suggested by the music.

Schiff and Lamon (1989) have shown another kind of induction independent of semantic meaning. They have found that contracting muscles in the left side of the face induces sadness, whereas contracting muscle on the right side produces emotion effects that are more positive and more difficult to characterize exactly.[27] Zajonc, Murphy, and Inglehart (1989) have also induced small emotion effects without semantic content by having subjects contract certain facial muscles. Dissociation of the control part of an emotion from its semantic part can be revealed by surgury. Gazzaniga (1988) has reported on patients whose corpus callosum had been surgically severed and to whom pictures could be shown to the right hemisphere, which is not associated with language. One such woman, having been shown in this way a film of a person throwing another into a fire, said: "I don't really know what I saw; I think just a white flash. Maybe some trees, red trees like in the fall. I don't know why, but I feel kind of scared. I feel jumpy. I don't like this room, or maybe it's you getting me nervous" (p. 235). The explanation here, it seems, is that a basic emotion signal is not interrupted by callosal section, but it can be experienced consciously though not connected to semantic information about the events that elicited it.

Moods without semantic content occur in psychopathology. So, although depression and anxiety usually relate to events in the life of the person concerned (see, e.g., Brown and Harris, 1978), psychiatrists also recognize endogenous states in which people become elated, depressed, or fearful for no apparent external reason.

There is much recent evidence that a mood tends to allow easier recall of memories that are congruent with that mood (see e.g., Bower, 1981; Bower & Cohen, 1982; Teasdale & Fogarty, 1979; Teasdale, 1988, for influential studies; or Leventhal & Tomarken, 1986; Blaney, 1986, for reviews). We argue that the function of such phenomena is related to goals and plans being associated with knowledge made relevant by an emotion mode. Because moods tend to make certain kinds of semantic material available, some remembered events or imaginings occurring in this way can act as further elicitors of the same basic emotion and hence help to prolong a mood. Neither the existence of moods, nor mood-dependent cognitive effects, nor the elicitation of emotions by means other than evaluations of external events can be assimilated to current cognitive theories other than ours except in an ad hoc way.

4. Interpersonal communication

As well as communicating within the cognitive system, emotions can be communicated interpersonally, by innately based nonverbal means such as facial expression and tone of voice. When such a communication is received, it can set up a corresponding signal, as in empathy, or a complementary one, as in a fearful response to anger.

Oatley and Johnson-Laird (1987) propose that emotions are not just internal. They are communications that often go beyond the skin. There is a parallelism between the communications of emotions within the cognitive system and among individuals – both types, we claim, involve basic signals. Whereas the internal signals have not yet been identified, the interpersonal signals of basic emotions are carried by facial expressions, gestures, and tones of voice – by media other than semantic meanings of words.

Principally because a large amount of evidence has been gathered carefully by Ekman and his colleagues, the most compelling data of emotional communication are those of facial expression. Ekman and his co-workers (see, e.g., Ekman, 1984, and the discussion in Chapter 1) have found facial expressions specific to discrete emotions, which are both produced and recognized panculturally and therefore are likely to be biologically based.

Not just recognition of faces, but the communication of emotional effects has been documented. Eibl-Eibesfeldt (1972) has filmed and described a range of emotional expressions in different cultures that have effects. Thus, a smile and briefly raised eyebrows encourage social contact. A frown discourages it. Such expressions are made even by people born deaf and blind, implying innately based facial expressions. In addition, there is comparable evidence that tones of voice carry emotion signals interpersonally (Frick, 1985; Scherer, 1985).

It is clear to any parent of a young infant that in the early years of life the most salient expression of emotion is crying. Though this can take on different characteristics in different circumstances, it is largely an undifferentiated response, graded in intensity and duration. Its function is to command the attention of the mother or other caregiver. As such, of course, there is no special reason why there should be crying of different kinds. It is simplest to think of crying as deriving from rather generalized distress. So, although this distress may be one of the bases from which negative emotions develop, to start with, it is elicted in situations that we think of as causing emotions like separation, loss, frustration, and the perception of danger, but also with states that are not emotions like pain, hunger, or being unable to sleep. As the child grows older, the characteristics of specific emotions are discernible within the generalized distress in the child's facial expressions, as recorded by Camras (Izard, Malatesta & Camras, 1991), who kept a log and made video recordings of her infant daughter. At the same time, Bell and Ainsworth (1972) propose, as development proceeds, the amount of crying decreases with the mothers' attunement to needs and the elaboration of infants' repertoires of communication.

Against this background, there is evidence that distinct facial expressions are both made and recognized by infants soon after birth. Thus, Field et al. (1982) found that children aged 36 hours were able to discriminate three kinds of facial expression: happiness, sadness, and surprise. With repeated presentations of any one of these expressions by a live model, the infants habituated and spent less time looking at it, whereas their interest was rearoused when the model posed a different expression. Moreover, the babies were able to reciprocate the expressions, so that judges blind to the expressions posed by the model were able to recognize on the babies' faces expressions that corresponded to those of the model.

Campos et al. (1983) and Harris (1989) have reviewed literature on early infant recognition and display of emotions, and have concluded that a small number of emotions emerge in infancy and develop in relation to caregivers and others.

A worthwhile account of emotional development in infancy (Johnson et al., 1982; Emde, 1983) emphasizes a close interplay between developmental factors and the communication of emotions between infant and caregiver. This account is as follows. To start with, a baby's expressions, including generalized crying, may best be seen as simply biological, perhaps reflex. But caregivers interpret many of them as emotional and intentional: The baby is irritable and has the goal of wanting to be fed, or is happy and wants to exchange glances. Moreover, adults judge photographs of infant facial expressions in categories that seem to be universal – joy, sadness, anger, and surprise (Izard et al., 1980). Caregivers act as if infants' expressions are signals to make transitions appropriately into specific modes of caregiving: to feed, to gaze lovingly, and so on. Emotions thus become important in social interaction. This starts early in infancy and continues throughout life. Initially, involuntary expressions acquire significance for the child through interactions with the caregiver. The child also becomes sensitive to emotions of others and uses these as signals to regulate her or his own actions. Later in childhood emotions will be experienced consciously and also used in understanding other people.

There is evidence of the innateness of interpersonal communicative signals of emotions and their effects. Haviland and Lelwica (1987) had mothers interact with their 10-week-old babies and, when asked, to display for 15 seconds each happiness, sadness, or anger while saying, "You make me so happy (sad or mad)." Though they did not just mirror the mother's expressions, babies' responses were distinctive to each emotion. The results were clearest in the first of the four presentations of each emotion by the mother. Babies tended to look happy in response to the mother's happy expressions and voice, inhibiting mouth movements and showing interest. In response to the mother's angry expressions and voice, the babies looked angry and interest decreased. In response to their mother's sad expression and voice, they did not mirror with sad expressions, but mouth movements increased and they tended to look away.[28]

Communication of emotion is important in the initial stages of exploring and acting in the world. Thus, Campos et al. (1978) describe the phenomenon of social referencing in which an infant monitors the emotional expression of its caregiver to see how to act in novel situations. Klinnert (1984) found that 36 infants 12 months old and 36 infants 18 months old, when presented with an unusual toy, monitored their mother's faces. The baby sat in a corner of a small room playing with some ordinary toys, and the mother sat 3 meters away. Then a large, new toy – a moving dinosaur, a large, black spider, or a head popping out from a box – was introduced by remote control at the other end of the room. The 12-month-old babies looked at the mother with a mean latency of 35 seconds and the 18-month-olds with a mean latency of 16 seconds. Having been instructed by the experimenter, the mother posed an emotional or neutral expression while looking at the new toy. As the toy appeared, her infant approached more closely toward her when she made a fearful expression than when she looked happy.[29]

Infants regulate their interaction and their own emotions by the emotions they perceive in the person with whom they are interacting. They become distressed, for instance, if they see their mother's face becoming blank or showing a dysphoric emotion. Trevarthen (1979, 1984) has suggested that this kind of intersubjectivity is a very basic human attribute that can be observed from the earliest months and that very generally forms the basis of timing and tone of interactions.

Communication of anger can be demonstrated from an early age. Cummings, Ianotti, and Zahn-Waxler (1985) found that children were affected by angry arguments between adults that took place in their sight and hearing. A laboratory was set up to simulate a living room and kitchenette. Two-year-old children came with their mothers and were paired with another child and mother. As the two mothers sat and chatted, the children played with toys that were provided. The observation session was divided into five periods of 5 minutes and a sixth of 2 minutes. In the second, fourth, and sixth periods two actors came into the kitchenette to create an emotional background. The first period was neutral with no background of actors. In the second the actors entered talking in a warm and friendly way. The next period was neutral again. In the fourth period the actors again entered and had an angry verbal argument about the other not doing a fair share of work around the laboratory. It did not involve the children or their mothers in any way. Then there was another neutral period, and finally, in the shorter sixth period, the actors reentered, reconciled their differences, and were again friendly with each other. Some of the children were exposed to this sequence in a further session a month after the first. A control group of children with no exposure to anger at all was also observed.

During the period of the angry argument, children were much more distressed than at other times, with more than 50% showing distress in their posture (e.g., by freezing or seeking their mother), in their facial expressions, or vocally. Moreover, children's aggression toward each other, in the form of hitting, kicking, pushing, and the like or of attempting to take something from the other child, was measured. During the neutral period following the adult argument, aggressive acts were markedly and significantly higher than during the other periods. The effect was largest of all in the repeat session a month after the first, and here children spent a mean of 17 seconds in intensely aggressive acts toward the other child during the 5-minute neutral period following the adult argument. The children's aggression was not based on modeling of the

Intuitive and empirical approaches   97

adult actors, as at no time did the actors make contact with each other or attempt to take anything from each other.

Among older children, aged 11, this sensitivity to others' angry emotions continues. Jenkins, Smith, and Graham (1989) have shown how children are sensitive to their parents' quarrels. The degree of children's psychopathology is predicted by the amount of parental quarreling. But children also regulate their own behavior judiciously in respect to episodes of quarreling, so 71% of children reported trying to intervene in the quarrels in some way to stop or alleviate them.

Emotional expressions can prompt children into actions toward the person making them. Dunn and Kendrick (1982) observed the behavior of children aged 2 to 4 and found that these children comforted their younger siblings when they were in distress. This was effective in that by the age of 14 months a third of the younger children went to their older siblings for comfort.

Zahn-Waxler and Radke-Yarrow (1982) traced the development of children giving comfort to others. Children of 10 to 12 months tended either to look on disinterestedly when someone was in distress or to become distressed themselves. During their second year, however, signs of distress in an observing child decreased during such episodes, and they tended instead to touch or pat the distressed person, and by 18 months efforts to comfort or protect the other became more complex. Children also desist from taking a toy from another child if that child shows signs of distress as this action occurs. By 3 years old children base moral ideas on such emotional effects on others, judging actions as bad if they distress others, but less bad if they merely transgress a parentally made rule (Smetana, 1981). These reactions to other people's emotional displays seem to indicate that empathy has, at first, a direct basis in emotional communication, though, of course, this is assisted by parental encouragements and prohibitions.

Some children do not behave comfortingly; they may tease and hurt others who are in distress. Very striking in this regard is the work of Main and George (1985), who have compared children aged 1 to 3 who had suffered physical abuse with other, nonabused children from similar socioeconomic backgrounds. Abused children did not respond with concern to a distressed child of the same age in a day-care setting, though some made mechanical patting gestures or looked on. Most often they responded negatively, for instance, by making threatening facial expression, or by physically attacking, or by becoming themselves upset and fearful. Among the nonabused children, only one made a threatening gesture and none became distressed. One explanation is that the abused children were responding to a crying child as if that child were angry. More likely, though, they were adopting the role of the abusing adult.

Summing up this kind of evidence, Dunn (1988) discusses how children are affected by other people's emotions and become sensitive to their goals. They may be directly affected by a kind of emotional contagion, and this is observed from early on. Then, starting in their second and third years they sometimes act to comfort and help others or to react to their emotions in other ways. Evidence on the communication of emotion in young children before they are fully aware of semantic meanings is now very compelling. It is clear that it offers an important kind of datum for any theory of emotion. Social development does not occur successfully without it.

5. Elicitation by events relevant to goals

The most typical causation of an emotion in adults is by an evaluation of an event relevant to a goal. Often the evaluation is conscious and forms the semantic part of an emotion. Each goal has a monitor that recognizes events that change the probability of its fulfillment. Emotions caused in this way are not perceptions of external or internal events as such, however, but of events as they change the probability of goal attainment.

Perhaps the most fundamental postulate of Oatley and Johnson-Laird's theory is that emotions are elicited not by events as such but by evaluations of events relevant to goals. Researchers in the area agree that emotions are psychologically rather than physically caused. For the most part, they also agree that emotions are related to goals, or as Frijda (1986) says, "concerns," and to adapting an organism's response repertoire to environmental stimuli. In our theory, however, our commitment to evaluations being relevant to goals makes us eschew categorization of emotion-eliciting events as such. To make this point clear, let me contrast it with an alternative approach of Ellsworth and Smith (1988a, 1988b) in which eliciting situations are differentiated by values on nine attributes: pleasantness, anticipated effort, attentional activity, certainty, human agency, situational control, perceived obstacle, importance, and predictability. Each emotion is then defined by its profile of values of these attributes. This approach also offers an alternative to the semantics of emotion concepts offered by Johnson-Laird and Oatley (1989).

Smith and Ellsworth (1985) asked subjects to remember in turn incidents associated with each of 15 different emotions and then to rate the emotion on the nine attributes.[30] The researchers found that happiness was pleasant, associated with low effort, high certainty, and high attention. Shame and guilt were difficult to distinguish on these features. Both were unpleasant, requiring a large amount of effort with moderate certainty about the situation. In later studies Ellsworth and Smith (1988a, 1988b) asked people to remember incidents where something either unpleasant or pleasant occurred and the subject had made some particular appraisal – that is, that he or she remembered being in control in the situation, remembered a strong attentional effect, and so forth. Then the incident was rated on all nine attributes.

Such analyses of the appraisals of eliciting events are complemented by similar analyses of the consequences of emotions, principally in terms of readiness for action. Thus Frijda (1987b) has found in a questionnaire study that subjects associated emotion terms with particular forms of action readiness: Happiness is associated with exuberance and wishing to be with others, sadness with apathy and submissiveness, fear with avoidance and inhibition, anger with antagonism and excitement.[31] Frijda, Kuipers, and ter Schure (1989) found that patterns of action readiness showed associations with 32 emotion words that were as strong and distinctive as with patterns of appraisal of eliciting events. Also, Tiller (1988) has found that people are accurate at knowing what English terms are consequences of emotions. He asked people to give examples of events that had happened when they had experienced certain feelings; for instance, for "unhappy/miserable/sad," people gave one-sentence scenarios like, "Went for a long walk just to get away from it all." Different subjects were then good at sorting such sentences into 12 sets corresponding to 12 types of emotion that had occurred.[32]

Such analyses as these[33] have been informative as to the antecedent and consequent features that differentiate emotions in Western people's folk theories, and they also attest to the generality and consistency of these folk theories. They tend, however, to blur a distinction between causes of emotions and inferences that can be made from emotion terms, as in narrative. To put this crudely: Tears or a certain kind of attribution may be part of the profile of an emotion, but they need tell us nothing about what caused it.

Contrast this with a theoretical focus on goal-relevant events. For instance, Stein and Levine (1989) asked 3-year-old and 6-year-old children and adults to make judgments about short stories in which goals and outcomes of goals were varied. Children and adults were similar in being able to infer what emotions the protagonist would feel when different attributes of goals and the outcomes of goals were described in the story, and they were able to say what plans the protagonist would be likely to have next. Happiness was inferred when a valued goal was achieved or prolonged, and it was followed by plans to maintain or enjoy it. Both anger and sadness occurred with goal failure and were followed by plans to reinstate, replace, or forfeit goals. Anger occurred most typically with those goal failures that could be described as aversive states such as being in pain, whereas sadness tended to occur with losses. Adults and 6-year-old children tended to infer anger following intentional harm rather than when a natural event caused the harm, but all age groups tended to infer anger rather than sadness when aversive states occurred, thus indicating that another person's intention is not a necessary component in anger (see also Stein & Levine, 1990).

Soon after birth, emotional evaluations relevant to goals occur, indicating that they are biologically based. Rosenstein and Oster (1988) presented sweet-, salty-, sour-, and bitter-tasting fluids to infants at 2 hours of age. Childrens' recorded facial expressions were judged as appropriate to pleasure with the sweet taste and to displeasure with the salty and bitter tastes. Some of the displeasure responses may be forerunners of disgust expressions. Blass, Ganchrow, and Steiner (1984) observed evidence of distressing emotions such as angry facial expressions and crying and whimpering in 2-day old babies when sweet-tasting stimuli were not given as expected in learning experiments. In babies 7 months old, Stenberg, Campos, and Emde (1983) observed angry facial expressions when a teething biscuit was presented and then withdrawn.

In other words, even very young children have emotions related to goals, and by 3 years of age, children know that emotions are followed by plans to maintain, reinstate, relinquish, or change goals. This kind of study, then, approaches more closely the question of how people understand the causes of emotions in relation to goals and their consequences for subsequent plans.

Concentrating on the causes of emotions in goal-relevant evaluations, I think we can take the implications of analyses of patterns of appraisal farther, that is, toward the kind of theory these analyses imply. To do this, I again will contrast our theory with the work of Scherer (e.g., 1984). He argues that emotions involve "a rapidly occurring sequence of hierarchically organised stimulus processing steps" (p. 306) where each step is a stimulus evaluation check. The first check is for novelty, the second for pleasantness, the third for goal conduciveness, the fourth for coping potential, and the fifth for compatibility with norms. Scherer also argues that the evaluation process is continuous and that stimuli are constantly reevaluated, perhaps with some of the steps being skipped. The result is that different kinds of evaluations can combine as facets, as in a kaleidoscope. This is different from the model founded on basic emotions as proposed here. Scherer (1990) has also demonstrated a computer program, the first expert system predicting emotions on the basis of evaluations. Interacting with it, a person is asked to remember an incident of emotion and is then prompted sequentially to make evaluation checks about it as indicated by Scherer's theory. The program then suggests what emotion was involved.

Because it is universally agreed among cognitive emotion theorists that elicitation of an emotion involves perception, it is worth making a comparison with classical perceptual theory. Scherer's proposal, like those of Ellsworth and Smith and of Frijda, is a feature analysis theory of the kind advanced in perception by Selfridge (1959).[34] According to such theories an object is recognized by a series of feature checks. So, in simple terms, the letter *A* might be recognized by the presence of a horizontal feature and two oblique ones.

There are alternatives to this type of theory. For instance, according to feature detection theories only presence or absence of features is relevant, whereas in theories involving structural descriptions, relations between features are also critical. Further, whereas in a feature detection theory the presence of distinctive features identifies an object, in inferential theories cues are used to invoke stored schemata that then form the bases of interpretations and inferences about the object (see, e.g., Oatley, Sullivan & Hogg, 1988).

Comparably, we can propose a schema-driven mechanism of emotion elicitation by the evaluation of an event in relation to a goal. It can be described in three stages. First, an event is evaluated by one or more cognitive modules indicating a change in the probability of achieving either an active or a latent goal. On detecting this change, the module sends out a distinctive emotion control signal. In the second stage an emotion mode is set up by this signal. The mode becomes one element in a cognitive conclusion that is constructed like other cognitive conclusions (cf. Helmholtz, 1962/1866). The emotional state then has the tone of this emotion mode. Typically, this tone is bound to the semantic content of what caused the emotion or of what the emotion is directed toward – feeling happy at something going well or angry at someone who behaves inconsiderately. Sometimes, however, the emotion mode occurs without any semantic content being consciously bound to it. The third stage is that with the shift of cognitive resources that an emotion accomplishes, attention is focused on what has happened and on possibilities of doing something about it. Changes in interpretation can occur because the emotion mode is not permanently bound to particular semantic content – so there may be changes of interpretation, as well as of intensity, if the event and the emotion it has elicited continue to be problematic. Moreover, as problem-solving searches occur to determine the cause of the emotion or what new plan might be appropriate, new matches or mismatches with goals can occur and trigger new emotional states in different modes. This happens, for instance, if when trying to understand a loss, we start to anticipate a hopeless future. Then we may feel panicky.

How, then, can research on rating vignettes, stories, and remembered episodes of emotion help differentiate among theories? For the most part, research on componential cognitive approaches, although giving us information about what characterizes specific emotions, does not discriminate strongly among evaluation theories. By contrast, Oatley and Duncan's (1992) diary study does allow some differentiation among theories. We found that 61% of emotions were elicited by events involving action or lack of action by the subjects or by other people. Moreover, 77% of the emotion episodes were classifiable as occurring in relation to achievements, losses, frustrations, and threats. This is consistent with the first stage of evaluation described earlier, in that emotions typically occur with changes in the probability of attaining a goal, as well as with the second stage idea that emotions usually have explicit semantic content. The 6.3% of emotion episodes that occurred acausally supports the idea that in the second and third stages control modes are not tied rigidly to such content.

We did not search for changes of interpretation within emotional modes, as described for the second phase of interpreting an emotional event, but we did find evidence of the third phase of emotion processing, in that 30% of emotions changed from one basic emotion to another in the course of an episode. Moreover, 8% of emotion episodes occurred not as a result of an immediate event but as a result of something remembered, indicating that people replay emotional episodes, perhaps to understand them better.

To sum up evidence bearing on this fifth postulate: Emotions are typically elicited by events that change evaluations of goal attainment.

The evidence is cloudier than one would like, however, partly because of a paucity of information on the elicitation of different kinds of emotion in ordinary life.

Two contending kinds of theory can be thought of, as like that of Ellsworth and Smith (1988a, 1988b) and of Scherer (1984), on the one hand, or like that of Oatley and Johnson-Laird (1987) and of Stein and Levine (1989), on the other. The former emphasizes stimulus evaluations over a range of features, of which goal relevance is one, whereas the latter emphasizes just evaluations of events relevant to goals. No doubt further evidence will allow a choice between these two kinds of evaluation.

Currently, there is no evidence to contradict the idea that emotions are most frequently elicited by events that change the probability of goal attainment. But, as predicted by postulates 3, 4, and 7 of the current theory, not all emotions are elicited in this way.

6. Basic emotions

There is a small number of basic emotions including happiness, sadness, anger, fear, and disgust. Each has its own distinctive physiology and its distinctive state of readiness. Basic emotions show equivalence within classes. For instance, for elicitors, happiness results from achievements of several kinds, sadness from a variety of losses, and so forth.

There has been much discussion of basic emotions in the psychological literature, with some authors arguing for them (Plutchik, 1984; Oatley & Johnson-Laird, 1987) and others against (Mandler, 1984; Ortony & Turner, 1990). Mandler specifies no distinct physiologically based emotions, but merely an arousal dimension. Frijda (1986, 1987a, 1988) proposes positive and negative evaluations as primitives. Ortony and Turner (1990) say there is an indefinite number of emotions just as there is an indefinite number of natural human languages.

Among the arguments for basic emotions is that there is a small number of panculturally recognizable facial expressions (see discussion under postulate 3); that some but not all emotions can occur acausally with others being based on them (see discussion under postulate 4); that emotions change readiness in a small number of identifiable ways in response to certain recognizable and recurring events that affect goals (see discussion under postulate 5); and that specific emotions have specific physiological accompaniments. As to this last type of evidence, happiness tends to make people active, whereas fear is accompanied by frequent and sometimes intense autonomic perturbations, such as changes in heart rate, perspiration, trembling, and so on. Disgust has been found to be associated with small numbers of such bodily perturbations (Wallbott & Scherer, 1986). More direct physiological monitoring of autonomic nervous activation (Ekman, Levenson & Friesen, 1983) during the activation of specific emotions indicates that headway can be made with testing the hypothesis that each basic emotion is associated with a distinctive physiologically based mode.

In animal studies, Panksepp (1982) has shown how emotion modes inhibit one another, so that although he postulates only three basic emotions, mechanisms of mutually exclusive modes can be investigated. Oatley and Johnson-Laird (1987) started with this idea that basic emotions would tend to inhibit one another and that mixtures of emotions would occur only rarely, when the system was unable to settle into a single mode. Oatley and Duncan's (1992) study has disconfirmed this thesis. In more than a third of emotion episodes recorded in diaries of emotion incidents, people reported that they experienced two basic emotions simultaneously, the most common pairing being sadness and anger. This effect is not like mixing two primary colors to generate a different color. It is as if, in mixed emotions, two basic emotions occur simultaneously like two interpretations of an ambiguous figure. The proposal, then, is that mixed emotions are not to be understood in terms of merged primary emotions, but of a small number of basic emotions with simultaneous and different semantic contents corresponding to different interpretations of an emotion-eliciting event.

The proposal that there is a small number of basic emotions has been vigorously denied by Ortony and Turner (1990). They argue, as does Mandler (1984), that theorists who propose basic emotions do not agree on their number or identity and that this disagreement makes the idea unconvincing. This is not a strong argument. Most theorists do agree that happiness, sadness, anger, and fear are basic; difficulties principally come with what other emotions might also be basic. Further, this issue is not about voting; it is about theory.

Data on facial expression cross-culturally and in early infancy are generally agreed to be the most extensive and the most difficult to explain away by theories that allow emotions to be indefinitely variable. Nevertheless, Ortony and Turner (1990) give such an explanation. They argue that not emotions as such but the components of emotion are biologically hardwired, as can be seen from facial expressions. In anger, for instance, frustration elicits a furrowed brow, the desire to aggress is accompanied by an open mouth with teeth showing, determination by clenching of the lips (perhaps in an attempt to inhibit the aggression display), and eyelids are raised indicating attention to the visual field.

Such components, argue Ortony and Turner, often occur together not because they are biologically tied in basic composite expressions, but because the environmental circumstances for their elicitation often occur together. A virtue of this suggestion is that it offers an additional theoretical basis for componential cognitive appraisal theories, among which there is no necessary postulate of basic emotions, but rather of several features allowing differentiation among many emotions. There is only a small theoretical distance between their position and that of Ellsworth and Smith (1988a, 1988b).

There are some difficulties with Ortony and Turner's suggestion, however, not least of which is its incomplete state of development – anger is the only emotion for which a sketch of components is offered, and then not in much more detail than my account above. Also, what they are really offering is a proposal of human fixed action patterns, computationally equivalent to a set of production rules.[35] One puzzle aroused by the proposal is why, if it were correct, would we have emotions at all? Why not just these action patterns as stimulus-response elements?

Ortony and Turner say that theories of basic emotions are inexplicit – but they can be quite explicit: Oatley and Johnson-Laird say that basic emotions depend on discrete differentiable cognitive modes set up by control signals, perhaps transmitted hormonally, by peptides, or by certain kinds of neural signal. This proposal suggests tests by modifying emotions with drugs but without cognitive appraisal processes. Such manipulations, we claim, will affect only emotions that are basic.

Theories of basic emotions can be empirically tested in other ways: All such theories, I think, must predict equivalence within the class of emotions grouped around each basic emotion. This should be empirically observable in several ways, for instance, in studies of elicitation of facial expression, of mood-specific cognitive effects, and of physiological accompaniments. To put the matter crudely: One can become happy (with the same facial expression, the same mood-dependent cognitive effects, the same physiological accompaniment) in response to different events, as predicted by Oatley and Johnson-Laird's theory. We predict a basic emotion of happiness to occur with subgoal attainment, with single-minded engagement in an activity, with interpersonal communication of happiness, or with physiological triggering of happiness: respectively, perhaps a gainful event, absorption in a favorite activity, responding to a smile from a close friend, taking heroin. Comparably, one would expect the basic emotion of fear in response to a near traffic accident, to the perception that one will not finish an important assignment on time, to an interpersonal threat when watching a thriller at the movies, or even for no apparent reason at all. In all such cases one would expect the variance of measurements of any index of emotion to be small within each basic emotion category across a variety of predicted eliciting conditions. One would expect the variance of measurements of this index between basic emotion categories to be large.

Here are two examples of empirical studies to illustrate this kind of principle. The first is a clever experiment by Etcoff (1990). She argues that if there were basic emotions, we might expect facial perception to be categorical. Happy faces should be sorted into one category, sad ones into another, and so on. In other words, recognition of faces should be comparable to the categorical perception that occurs in speech perception. For instance, what distinguishes a spoken "bit" from "pit" in English is a few milliseconds of onset of voicing. For equal physical increments of voicing onset time, people are bad at making discriminations either side of the b–p boundary but good at discrimination across the boundary. Comparably, Etcoff argues, if she could create equal physical increments in a scale from happy to sad faces, for example, then there would be a boundary. On one side of it people would see faces as happy, and on the other as sad. Then, on either side of the boundary, discrimination between equal increments should be poorer than across the boundary.

Etcoff created the equal increments using the cartoon-generating computer program of Brennan (1985), which allows a photograph of a face to be traced by hand onto 169 landmark points. The program then fits curves through these points. The result is quite detailed drawings of faces with a concentration of information in the eyebrows, eyelids, and mouth. Etcoff traced 21 photographs from Ekman and Friesen's (1976) pictures of facial affect from three models each posing expressions of happy, sad, angry, afraid, disgusted, surprised, and neutral. Brennan's program allows averaging, so Etcoff created scales of 11 faces between pairs of emotions. Thus, in one scale the first and eleventh faces were the digitized photographs of happy and sad faces of one of the models. Intermediate faces were made up from the average position of ten sets of points from the happy face plus one from the sad, nine sets from the happy plus two sets from the sad, and so on. Using standard psychophysical methods, she found the abrupt shift of discriminability between faces on these scales that is expected with categorical perception for all pairs of emotion faces except "surprised–afraid" and between emotion faces and neutral faces, though gradations of neutral faces were more discriminable than of emotion faces.

A second line of evidence concerns the representation of emotions in memory. Conway and Bekerian (1987) found in a series of preliminary studies using similarity judgments and suchlike that emotion terms fell into groups corresponding to basic emotions: happiness/love/joy, misery/grief/sadness, fear/panic/terror, and anger/jealousy/hate. They then used lexical decision tasks to investigate the representation of these concepts in memory. In one such experiment two sentences that had previously been judged appropriate to (say) "hate" were shown on a screen. When the subject had read the sentences, a string of letters in the form of a word was shown. It was either an emotion word from the same basic group, as "anger" (though not "hate" itself), or an emotion word from another group, as "sadness," or a nonword matched to "anger" or a nonword matched to "sadness." The subject's task was to say whether what he or she saw was a word or a nonword. Interspersed with emotion trials were similarly structured trials with emotionally neutral filler sentences and words and nonwords. The usual counterbalancing of orders of presentation was included. It was found that reaction times for words within each basic emotion group appropriate to the priming sentences were significantly shorter than to words from the nonappropriate basic emotion groups.[36]

The categories corresponding to basic emotions found by Etcoff, Conway, and Bekerian are those of English-speaking cultures. They nonetheless indicate by methods that are familiar in the experimental psychological laboratory that the categories of basic emotions have implications for perception and memory well beyond consciously made judgments of similarity and difference. Ortony and Turner (1990) have asked what one might mean by basic emotions, and what would count as empirical evidence for or against them. They say that "current uses of the notion do not permit coherent answers to be given to such questions" (p. 329). The case for basic emotions has not convinced everybody, as evidenced by the lack of conviction it carries with Ortony and Turner. But it is false to say that such theories are not meaningful or testable.

7. Simulated plans

As well as being able to receive innately based communications of facial expression and tone of voice, people can mentally simulate the plans of others and understand their emotions, just as they can run simulations of their own plans and test their own emotional reactions in advance. In understanding narrative a subject may identify with the protagonist of a plan, and the simulation can have many of the properties of real plans, including the property of eliciting emotions appropriately to the junctures that the plan reaches.

It seems to need no empirical demonstration that people experience emotions when listening to or reading purely verbal stories. What does need empirical study are matters such as the age at which this occurs, and whether it occurs to people frequently. As to when, the ability to infer emotions from narrative seems to occur by the age of three (Stein & Levine, 1989). By this age children become happy, sad, anxious, and so on, in the course of listening to stories that are read to them.

As to how often this kind of thing occurs in adults, Oatley and Duncan (1992) found that 23% of emotion episodes recorded by 57 subjects were caused by things remembered, imagined, read, seen, or heard about, that is, by matters removed from any actual event. Here emotions are not elicited by external events but mentally. Moreover, though it is assumed by many componential emotion theorists that a pleasant/unpleasant dimension, or valency, is among the most important evaluations, we found in our sample that 13 of 244 episodes arose from things the subject "read, heard, or saw on TV, film, theatre," and that of these 13 episodes 9 were negative emotions. Because we can assume that the subjects were reading, watching TV, and so on, voluntarily, it is not clear that these were unpleasant or to be avoided in any straightforward sense.[37]

Most current emotion theories are weak in predicting this kind of occurrence. In the communicative theory we assume that emotional events signal something that is cognitively problematic and give rise to sadness, fear, and so forth. We actively seek such states in stories, perhaps because they allow us to experience trying to attain goals and exploring implications that are unavailable in everyday life. This may in part be why people find goal-based stories fascinating. Stories allow people to experience and explore emotions embedded within the parentheses of a wider plan such as "reading," the goal of which may be to explore implications of problematic interactions or to escape into someone else's goal problems.

A theory is required, I think, based on an ability to plan in simulated worlds, to understand the emotional effects of stories at all. In addition, we need to postulate that a person can identify with a protagonist taking on goals and plans as if they were his or her own as a narrative unfolds. Then a reader or listener can experience emotions appropriate to the occurrences in the story. Stories involve an inner mental simulation of plans – games are a kind of external simulation. In a game we take on goals offered by its structure. Similar effects apply to those of stories, such as the bracketing off of experience. Hence we are able to enjoy the anxiety that we may lose, as we try nevertheless to win.

Understanding stories involves being able to simulate other minds, or perhaps to have a theory of other minds. Wimmer and Perner (1983) told children stories using dolls as props, in which Sally comes into a room, puts a marble in her basket, and goes out again. Then Anne comes in, takes the marble out, and hides it in a box. The question put to children is where will Sally look for her marble when she comes back. Three-year-old children think she will look in the box, while four- and five-year-olds think she will look in her basket. The older children are able to imagine Sally's beliefs about the location of the marble as being different from their own.

Autistic children offer a test of the idea that emotional development includes this ability to imagine what is in the minds of others – these children lack sympathy for others, are emotionally impoverished, and are severely handicapped in interacting with others. Baron-Cohen, Leslie, and Frith (1985) have compared a group of such children with normal children and Down's syndrome children in Wimmer and Perner's task. Although the normal and Down's children were selected to be below the autistic children in verbal and nonverbal intelligence, 85% knew that Sally would look for the marble where she left it. By contrast, 80% of the autistic children thought that Sally's knowledge was the same as their own as viewer of all the events, and that she would look for her marble where it actually was. Gordon (1987), Harris (1989), and Leslie and Frith (1990) argue that this ability to simulate mental states, including those of others, is the basis for intuitive understanding of others' emotions and hence being able to take part in social interactions.

Any theory of emotions without a postulate about being able to simulate other minds and that is not based on goals and planning seems unable to deal in a principled way with understanding stories or the emotional effects that stories can have.

Conclusion from European and American empirical evidence bearing on the theory

This selection of evidence is incomplete, and further predictions from our theory can be generated. On the whole, evidence supports the theo-

ry I am proposing. The communicative theory was, however, not generated by induction from Baconian facts, but from trying to make explicit
human intuitions about emotions and then proposing a testable hypothesis about a mechanism to support the effects that emotions seem to
have. The role of evidence of the kind just described is to indicate
whether the theory is plausible in particular respects or whether it needs
to be modified or abandoned altogether.

There are two kinds of test of the theory I have proposed. The more
serious kind can be called Lakatos's test (Lakatos, 1978). It is that like any
other theory the theory proposed here will be acceptable if in comparison with its competitors it can assimilate more of the evidence that
the research community considers important. It will fail if other theories
assimilate more of this evidence.[38] At present, other cognitive theories
of emotion tend to be narrower in scope than the communicative theory,
and although it is not my role to make such a judgment but, rather,
yours as reader, I suggest that they do not so easily assimilate so much
of the evidence in a principled way.

The second kind of test we can call Popper's test (Popper, 1962): There
should be specific predictions from a theory that are vulnerable to single
pieces of evidence that have yet to be gathered. If the evidence turns out
not to be as predicted, the theory should be abandoned. Every such test
that the theory survives strengthens it. Thus the communicative theory
is vulnerable to demonstrations that emotions occur as reactions to
events with no necessary relevance to a person's goals, to tests of basic
emotions as described under postulate 6, to tests of whether a natural
scientific account of emotion categories is at variance with folk theories
embodied in a range of languages, and to demonstrations that all emotions have semantic content.[39]

Cross-cultural evidence

The evidence discussed so far has been largely derived from Western
culture and largely from English speakers. I have discussed this evidence under seven postulates to indicate the evidential base of the theory that I present in this book. Cross-cultural studies, however, clearly
provide an important test not just for the communicative theory but for
cognitive theories generally, and so I discuss them in a separate section
here.

Cognitive theorists have unashamedly used terms and concepts from
Western folk theory. If analyses of terms and concepts in cultures other

than Europe and America yielded results that were very discrepant from those presented so far, this would argue that folk theories are indeed parochial and largely irrelevant to cognitive science, as Stich (1983) has proposed. Also, by implication, most cognitive theories of emotions, including that of Oatley and Johnson-Laird, but with the exception of Simon's (1967), Mandler's (1984), and Sloman's (1987), would be ethno-centrically misguided.[40]

General considerations. Questions of ethnopsychology are difficult because there is no fixed position on which to stand, no Archimedean point outside culture. Anthropologists take on the valuable role of travelers to other cultures, immersing themselves in them and bringing back reports.

Lutz (1988b) has brought back reports from the Micronesian atoll of Ifaluk, about a square kilometer of land no more than 5 meters above sea level with few other islands nearby. It is a society of 430 people who live by fishing, gathering fruits, and subsistence horticulture. It is cooperative and nonaggressive.

Perhaps the most striking characteristic of Ifaluk society, from a Euro-American point of view, is the idea of the Ifaluk people that one must be, as much as possible, with others. To be alone exposes oneself to fear-inducing consequences, as their mythology emphasizes. Most people live in family groups averaging 13 in size. Only one person, a senile man of 70, sleeps alone, and he eats with relatives (Lutz, 1985a). Lutz nicely gives an appropriate perspective, I think, with her portrait of herself, a young, middle-class, American woman, asking for a hut in which to live. She was taken aback by the idea of sleeping on a mat overlapping with others in a hut with more than a dozen other people. At the same time, the Ifaluk people were appalled at anyone undergoing the loneliness of sleeping in a hut of one's own.

The culture shocks of visiting other societies allow us to gain, as it were, a meta-view, by comparing our own culture with others. This method is indeed one of the most valuable ways of making intuitions explicit, because as Lutz (1987, 1988b) has argued, by getting things wrong that we think are entirely straightforward, we simultaneously expose intuitions that we have and that members of another culture have.[41]

Lutz (1985b) gives an example of how ordinary language draws on fundamental cultural concepts. In the early weeks of her stay on the island, she had said to a group of young women who had come to visit her: "Do you want to come with me and get drinking water?" The women's faces fell, and Lutz realized that she had committed a solecism. On later reflection she realized that it probably had to do with her pronouns. On Ifaluk, when people are together they assume they will act, perceive, and decide as a group. Pronouns such as "we" are therefore commonly used. In America, the individual is the source of all actions and decisions. Joint action, then, has to be suggested or negotiated between one individual acting as "I" and others as "you," as Lutz was attempting. To do this on Ifaluk implies the peculiar idea that one is separating oneself from others. People may do this, for instance, when they are angry or upset; it is typically only under such circumstances that people are likely to act on their own. Even then this does not always happen, so people also say "we are angry (*song*)" (Lutz, personal communication). When the young women had come visiting, Lutz's pronouns had implied a separation of herself from them, which upset them. She realized on the basis of later understanding and reflections that what she should have said was something more like: "We'll go get water now, OK?"

This making explicit of intuitions is basic to cognitive science, but it is not "objective," in the sense of being outside culture. Anthropologists are not usually in a position to visit exotic cultures to bring back answers to such questions as: "Is it possible for people not to feel anger?"[42]

Aristotle's attitude toward cross-cultural evidence. Aristotle started from particular human understandings and compared them with others. He did not assume an acultural status for any particular appearances. Despite a ready interest in ethnography in his intellectual circles, he eschewed comparisons with remote peoples. Nussbaum (1986) suggests the following reason, drawn from *The Politics,* I and II: Human beings are the only ones who experience the good and the bad, the just and the unjust. We are neither beasts nor gods. Therefore, if we discuss concepts like justice they depend on our experience of justice being important to us, though scarce and hard to attain. Gods, for instance, would have no concern with such matters. There would be no term for justice in their language, and no point in trying to discuss it with them.

It is for this reason that it is so important to get the entry level into cross-cultural discussions of emotion about right. It had better not be at the level of issues like "justice," because we could imagine societies in which this was not much of an issue, perhaps because adjudications between people were dealt with in a way that nobody questioned (cf.

Howell, 1981), or perhaps because social interactions were so regulated that people hardly ever felt aggrieved, like the Malaysian Senoi (Stewart, 1969). By contrast with a view from America and Europe, we could easily believe concern with justice was universal because for us it is so salient and surrounded by social institutions. Injustice is a potent cause of angry feelings and vengeful action. Much of our mythology, in cowboy, detective, and thriller genres, as well as the more serious theater, is devoted to exploring these issues.

Cross-cultural discrimination of anxiety and depression. There are examples of getting the entry level wrong. Leff (1981) assumes, for instance, that Western emotional categories can be translated into other languages and applied to other cultures. He writes: "Where there is little or no choice of action in relationships, there is also a restriction on the possibilities of consciously experiencing a variety of emotions. In traditional societies, where relationships are more or less stereotyped, emotions remain unexplored and undifferentiated" (p. 72). Leff concludes that as society moves from the traditional to the modern, freedom of action in relationships increases and individualism emerges. Introspection flourishes and people experience emotions as psychological rather than somatic. As Lutz (1985a) puts it: In this way Leff accounts for his finding of a decreasing ability of people to distinguish feelings of depression from those of anxiety as one travels further from London.

What is wrong with this idea, as Lutz points out, is that we do not hear of studies in which people in London are asked to make judgments about emotions using concepts from a non-Western culture. From another point of view we could ask: Why are Euro-Americans so frequently aggressive?[43]

Are there human universals? In proposing the communicative theory of emotions, Johnson-Laird and I do not assume that somewhere there is an objective stance that will be provided by natural science from which we can understand emotions "correctly" and be no longer deceived by the flickering shadows of our own subjective experience. Indeed, in this book I am proposing the alternative, that only by examining a wide range of evidence will we be able to see what kinds of problems are common across human understandings of emotions and action and thereby attain some generality.

I have two assumptions of universality. One is that there is some biological basis for evaluating events in relation to goals. The other is that people try to understand themselves and each other: We speak of actions and interactions in everyday discourse in ways that allow us to make inferences about goals and plans (cf. White, 1980). In this way we humans try to make our own and others' behavior more understandable. Thus we can make effective joint plans, in which we depend on one another.

This necessitates some separation of self from others: In all cultures the moral status of one person's actions is potentially separable from that of other people's actions (Hallowell, 1955). This does not imply that the self is preexisting, unique, and separate from society. That is a particular folk theory of self that is distinctively Euro-American, and as Geertz (1975) points out, the idea is peculiar in the context of other societies. Worldwide the conception of self takes on many forms. For instance, Geertz describes how in Bali there is "a persistent and systematic attempt to stylize all aspects of personal expression to the point where anything idiosyncratic . . . is muted . . . the masks they wear, the stage they occupy, the parts they play, and most important the spectacle they mount remain and constitute not the facade but the substance of things, not least the self" (p. 50).

Nor does the communicative theory propose that emotions are essences of an individualized self, as compared, for instance, to the idea that emotions arise from our relationships (cf. Lutz, 1986).

Oatley and Johnson-Laird propose that the best entry level into a discussion of emotions is the one deriving from an ontology of mammals, presented in Chapter 1, and from the junctures in plans indicated in the second column of Table 3. Thus we start discussing emotions in terms of achievements of subgoals, of losses and frustration of goals, of threats, and so on. In this we agree with Lutz (1988a), who gives the following list of universal goal evaluations in social life, equivalent to our ontology and to Table 3 here.[44]

1. Conflicting goals or multiple actors, or others' violations of cultural standards
2. Ego's violation of cultural standards or anticipations of these
3. Danger to ego or significant others
4. Loss of significant relationships or threat of such loss
5. Receipt of resources, tangible and intangible

Such considerations provide not just the semantic content of emotions but also determine what goals are monitored by the emotion system and give rise to control signals when changes in evaluation occur. The hypothesis is that evaluations related to goals and plans are more likely to be universal than concepts such as justice, the value of introspection, freedom of action in relationships, or the importance of the individual.

Emotion terms in other cultures

The communicative theory of emotions was conceived within Euro-American culture. Johnson-Laird and Oatley's semantic analysis of English emotion terms is explicitly of this ethnopsychology. The cognitive theory on which it is based, however, is intended to apply to all cultures. It is a set of hypotheses, not a cultural assumption.

From the analysis of Johnson-Laird and Oatley two main kinds of predictions can be made about emotion terms in other languages. First, there should be terms that refer to five or so biologically based emotions. We expect that states of either phenomenology or action readiness or both, elicited by a small number of general types of evaluation of plans and goals similar to those of Table 1, will be found in all cultures. We would expect that people in widely different cultures would agree that basic emotions sometimes occur for no apparent reason, but we do not assume that people everywhere would recognize acausal emotions because they may be disattended, just as we typically disattend phenomena like afterimages within the eye. Students of perception have to train themselves to notice such entoptic phenomena. Terms for such phenomena are not in ordinary usage. We do not say that a focus on the phenomenological quality of emotions always occurs. People in many cultures attend more closely to external events, to relations with others, to actions, and to the body than to introspection. Second, we claim, all cultures will have terms that are contextual, that refer to semantic information bound to basic emotional modes. There will be terms that imply that an emotion is caused by something or prompts some action in relation to other people. A weaker prediction is that in many cultures emotion terms will refer to relatively complex situations having consequences for the status of the self in relation to others, though some societies may enable such moral evaluations to be made without much reference to emotions (cf. Howell, 1981).

Emotion terms on Ifaluk. Lutz (1982) has given us an outline of emotion words on Ifaluk. There is no term for "emotion" as such, but 31 words identified as being "about our insides" were selected by asking literate informants to sort, into as many piles as they wished, cards on which these words were written. A hierarchical clustering analysis revealed five clusters. These corresponded to emotions of pleasantness including happiness, emotions of danger including fear, emotions of connection and loss including sadness, and emotions of human error including anger. Then there were emotions of inability in a looser cluster with two subclusters, one having to do with discomfort and disgust and the other with suddenly feeling bad, conflicted, or bored.

Even though this culture is very different from our own, there seem to be similarities. The Ifaluk think these states have to do with their insides and that they occur in specific kinds of situations, particularly interpersonal ones. Lutz's results thus tend to confirm our hypothesis that Ifaluk emotion terms fall into groupings.[45] More particularly, on Ifaluk, although there are few exact equivalents, most terms, as I understand them, are contextual. Although very different from English terms, they convey the idea of something inside relating to a semantically explicit cause or object.

Fago, for instance, is a common term that Lutz translates as "compassion/love/sadness." It is an emotion of important relationships, and it means feeling sadness or empathy for someone who is in an unfortunate state, or if the person is out of reach so that something bad may happen to him or her while the person is absent. In our terms it is a sadness caused by a perception or thought that someone one cares about may lack material or interpersonal resources at that moment. It prompts one to do something for that person. Another common term that has no exact translation is *song*, "justified anger." This is feeling bad inside at the realization that another has contravened some social rule, perhaps has not shared food properly.

Though broadly consistent with Oatley and Johnson-Laird's theory, the results of Lutz's studies do not imply that Ifaluk people have the same conceptions of emotions as do Westerners. Far from it. They do not value feeling as such, and there seems to have been no Ifalukian Jefferson asserting a right to the "pursuit of happiness." Ifaluk subjects sorted words not on the basis of feelings as such but according to situations in which emotions arose. Emotions include moral evaluations of oneself in relation to others. A person is also evaluated as good or bad in terms of which emotions occur. So one is a good person to have uncomfortable feelings in certain circumstances, for instance, in solidarity for others in some difficult situation. Thus one will properly *fago* someone who one loves. And although *song* also feels bad, it is culturally connoted as good, because it indicates that one has taken proper notice of a social violation and will thereby remind the perpetrator of it. Here, again, the idea that emotions are primarily positive or negative is called into question.

Other ethnologies. I will consider briefly two cultures that I take to be very different from Europe and America and relatively unaffected by Western culture.[46] They might reveal principles that refute the assumptions made on the basis of English analyses or those from Ifaluk, which perhaps are only fortuitously similar.

I have not been able to be exhaustive, but a culture of which I have been able to find descriptions that seems very unlike the Euro-American one in lifestyle and attitudes is the Chewong, of Malasia, a small group of aboriginal hunter-gatherers and shifting cultivators. Emotions seem not at all salient in this culture. It was with difficulty that Howell (1981) drew up a list of emotion words at all. They are very few, in comparison with terms in English. From her list, only *chan* (angry), *greno* (sexually aroused), *hanrodn* (proud), *hentugn* (fearful), *lidva* (ashamed), *meseg* (jealous), and *mund* (miss) seem to correspond at all directly to emotions as Euro-Americans would think of them. Moreover, Howell says the faces of these people register little change as they speak or listen. Indeed, they rarely use gestures of any kind. They seem calm, restrained, and never "lose control."

The Chewong seem to offer a serious challenge to the ideas of universality of emotions. Nonetheless, Howell does not come to this conclusion. Instead, she documents a large set of social rules, about what to do in a wide set of social situations, that are carefully articulated and followed by members of the group. For instance, *maro* is an unpleasant consequence, inducing symptoms such as dizziness that will occur if a visitor comes to one's house and is not offered food. *Pantang* means forbidden; and among the things that are *pantang*, as it turns out, are expressions of emotions or demonstrative behavior during life crises, such as birth or death. Rules of different kinds indicate different types of penalties for particular transgressions, such as illnesses, attacks by tigers, and so forth.

These rules, Howell argues, indicate that despite their apparent undemonstrativeness, the Chewong do experience emotions – but some of their rules are about suppressing them. Other rules give guidance about what to do on various occasions when in other cultures emotions would be described as prompting certain kinds of behavior. So, Howell argues, in this culture it is not that emotions do not exist, but that they are either suppressed or not separated from thoughts. According to our theory, this means that the focus is on semantic content related to how to act or refrain from acting. Control feelings are disattended. Expressions and actions are suppressed, as is known to be possible in our own and other cultures (Ekman, 1982).

Another group that contrasts with that of English speakers in having very few emotion terms is the Gidjingali. They are aboriginal Australians, studied by Hiatt (1978), who seem to have a set of just six root morphemes meaning to be angry, to be afraid, to be sorry or sad, to be jealous, to sulk, and to feel good. This group, despite its small vocabulary of terms, seems to support the idea of a small number of basic emotions. Four of the terms seem to correspond rather closely to basic emotions, though they are also used contextually, so that, for instance, a syntactic variant of the term for anger also means to fight. The terms meaning to be jealous and to sulk are, as I understand it, invariably contextual. The latter means a state inviting appeasement, while at the same time threatening aggression – not entirely unlike states recognizable in Euro-American contexts.

No reports that I can find, or that are reviewed by Lutz (1988a), portray a society in which nothing corresponds to emotions or where emotions seem not to correspond to important junctures in people's plans.

Are emotions entirely social constructions? An argument deriving from cultural differences that is opposed to my argument is the neo-Wittgensteinian one of Harré (1986). He proposes that emotions are entirely culturally constructed with, so far as I can understand, no biological basis whatever. Analyses of the kind that Johnson-Laird and I are proposing are, says Harré, deeply in error and suffer from the illusion "that there is something *there*, the emotion of which the emotion word is a mere representation" (p. 4, emphasis in the original). According to Harré, there is nothing "there" except "linguistic resources and social practices" (p. 4). The book contains chapters by various contributors describing emotions that do not occur in most of modern Euro-America: There is *amae*, a happy Japanese emotion of rather sweet clinging dependency, *verguenza* a Spanish emotion of shame brought about by the inadequate or incompetent behavior of another, and *accidie* a medieval emotion of dejection, boredom, or disgust in one's religious duties.

Harré proposes that emotion terms may be used when there is a bodily agitation. They are intentional, entailing a moral order of rights, obligations, duties, and conventions of evaluation. I have no quarrel with these proposals, nor with Harré's insistence that we pursue ordinary language analyses, nor with the idea that emotions are socially constructed. Johnson-Laird and I differ from Harré in thinking that when someone speaks truthfully about feeling an emotion there is something "there" – a distinctive cognitive state. Harré's argument depends entirely on the assertion that bodily agitation is not the thing there, "since it has been clearly demonstrated that one and the same agitation can be involved in many different emotions" (p. 7). I have presented evidence that this assertion is false. To suppose that what is "there" could only be a bodily agitation quite wrongly accepts William James's (1884) theory as the only alternative to the social constructivist one.

Yes: Emotions are in part socially constructed, but they are constructed around a biological basis – a basis of mental states concerned with the cognitive management of priorities in our everyday plans and actions. The occasions for these states depend strongly on the culture in which we live.

Emotions in 27 countries on 5 continents. Because emotions depend on goals, the mapping between simple eliciting conditions in the environment and emotions is not one-to-one. The specificity of particular emotions is related to specific kinds of evaluation of their eliciting conditions in relation to aspects of a person's goals, plans, and beliefs about the self.

Scherer, Wallbott, and Summerfield (1986) found evidence in a large sample of European subjects of personal goals in understanding emotions. Whereas recent episodes of fear were frequently due to nonpersonal events such as near traffic accidents, joy, sadness, and anger were typically experienced in interactions with others, which implies important goals of social interaction.

Wallbott and Scherer (1986), in developing this method further, have reported preliminary results of a very large questionnaire survey with samples of 100 or so students, distributed roughly equally in sex, from each of 27 countries. There was a predominance of European samples, including two from Eastern Europe, five samples from Black African states, two from the Near East, three from the Far East (Hong Kong, India, Japan), two from Oceania (Australia and New Zealand), one from South America (Brazil), and one from North America (United States). All subjects were given standardized questionnaires, translated into the subjects' native language, in which they were asked to think of situations in which they had vividly felt joy, fear, anger, sadness, disgust, shame, and guilt. For each of these they were asked to complete about two pages of questionnaire responses.

The authors hypothesized that there would be differences in the time since the occasion on which the emotion had been felt, in its duration, in its intensity, in the bodily symptoms, in the extent to which subjects tried to hide or control it, and so on. They then performed factorial analyses of variance on each of these emotion variables, looking for differences in recency, duration, and the like, attributable to the different emotions, and to the range of countries. There were significant differences, which were often large, among the seven emotions on measures of recency, duration, and so on. There were also some significant effects of country, but the amount of variance explained by country was less than for different emotion types,[47] though differences in intensity were affected substantially by country.

Wallbott and Scherer conclude that neither the view that emotions are entirely determined by culture nor the view that they are entirely determined by biology is tenable. This finding of both similarities and differences is important. As they say, their findings are too nonspecific to discriminate among current cognitive theories, all of which converge on the postulate that emotions are based on evaluations of situations, though the question of which features of situations are evaluated is still a matter of discussion.

Emotions of childhood in England and other countries. Harris and colleagues have carried out a series of studies of the culture of childhood (see also Harter & Whitesell, 1989). How do children understand emotions? Harris, Olthof, and Terwogt (1981) concluded that children six years old tend to think of other people's emotions as being directly linked to their own. They find it hard to conceive that anyone has an emotion without showing it. By the age of ten, children realize that it is possible for people to have feelings that they do not show.

Harris (1983), in studying these issues more closely, reported three experiments in which children were told stories. In the first, subjects six, seven, and ten years old rated the emotions of characters in the stories by pointing to schematic faces ranging from very sad to very happy. They indicated that sad emotions are provoked by events like a bicycle being stolen or a pet dog dying, and that the sadness lasts longer than the situation that caused it, so that it would still be present later that day.

In the second experiment, Harris asked children about further stories in which conflicting emotions might be expected. One incident was about a dog that had been lost all day and returned late at night. Another was about the dog having its ear cut in a fight. Some children were told stories of the incident of the dog returning and the dog being hurt separately. Others were told of conflicting incidents in the same story, the dog returned and was hurt. The children were told to imagine that they were the person in the story and then asked how they would feel. Younger and older children agreed that they would feel negative and positive emotions appropriately to story incidents when these were told in separate stories. They more rarely said they would feel both a negative and a positive emotion at the same time when the conflicting incidents were combined simultaneously. The younger children volunteered conflicting emotional responses less frequently than the older ones.

The children were also asked explicitly whether it was possible to feel happy and sad at the same time and to say why. The younger ones, in line with a rather behaviorist theory of such matters, typically said things like: "No, because you can't make your face go down and up" (p. 500). When either younger or older children said they could experience two emotions at once, they invariably gave as a reason a conflicting situation: "Cos I can feel happy and sad at the same time like at the dinner table – when I can eat, but they're quarrelling" (p. 500).

In the third experiment in this series, Harris asked children about stories in which an intense emotion occurred and was still persisting when another event occurred that would tend to elicit an opposite emotion. Both younger and older children thought this would be likely to cause mixed feelings.

It seems clear that, like adults, European children have a theory that assumes that emotions are caused by certain distinctive kinds of events and that they may persist for some time. Harris and his collaborators have extended their studies to explicitly cross-cultural research. Harris et al. (1987) have found that children in a remote Himalayan village, isolated from most Western influences, knew about what situations elicited specific emotions and were similar in this way to European children. Their knowledge became increasingly accurate with age. By the age of 10 to 14 they gave accounts of emotion elicitation that were articulate and recognizable to Western adults – although also giving a poignant account of the concerns of their culture, with pleasure associated with certain foods in an otherwise bland and monotonous diet, depression and pity at the proximity of death and illness, fear of wild animals, and sadness and frustrations about the vicissitudes of agricultural labor.

In another study, it was found that Chinese and Western children age four and six knew that emotions extended beyond the event that caused it and waned over time (Harris et al., 1985).

Harris et al. (1986) told children at English schools stories about emotions that it would be appropriate to hide. Six-year-old children were able to understand the distinction between feeling an emotion and hiding it, whereas four-year olds showed a more limited grasp of this idea. Gardner et al. (1988) replicated this result with Japanese children, concluding that this is a distinction that depends on the growth of cognitive competence and is relatively unaffected by patterns of socialization.

Children's understanding of emotions seems to be similar to that of adults from a relatively early age, with differences being mainly those of universal developmental processes. In general, as Harris (1989) argues, emotional development involves not only an increasing sophistication in differentiating and recognizing one's own emotions, it involves an increasingly acute understanding of the emotions of others. If Harris's account is correct, it seems that in all cultures one may expect social competence to be based, at least in part, on an understanding of emotions and how they affect ourselves and others.

Part of the process of children acquiring the folk theory of emotions in their culture involves being able to simulate mental states, of being able to imagine the emotions of others. This allows them to understand and enjoy stories. The question of how any of us, child or adult, might be able to do this is the subject of the final section of this chapter.

Emotions, intuitions, and insight

A professor of psychology, when interviewing prospective students for his course, used to advise any who said they wanted to understand themselves and others that they would be better pursuing a degree in literature. His remarks were intended to question both the applicant's aspirations and the study of literature and to imply that psychology has more important things to be concerned with. By contrast, I suggest that if psychologists do not consider narrative literature and its concerns, at least in our understanding of action and emotions, we will be missing something fundamental.

In this section I propose that the reason for starting from literature and natural language is that psychology is not just a technical subject, allowing us to do things effectively in the outer world. We look to psychology for insight, for a better understanding of ourselves and of each other. Whatever natural scientific understandings we reach must connect with our everyday sense of ourselves, with natural language, and with the story form that we use in explaining things to ourselves and each other. If we were to achieve a natural science of emotions that eliminated semantic considerations, intentional terms, and functionalist explanations, and consisted only of causal explanations of behavior and physiology, then at best we would have created a neuroscientific *episteme* allowing us to do things to brains. There would be no place for understanding ourselves.

Despite its different strands, cognitive science has been much concerned with the Platonic program of discovering an *episteme* and a *techne* of intelligent systems, be these systems human or computational. This can be thought of as the rationalist program of research.[48] I suggest that narrative, a style quite different from that needed for technologically directed research, is an appropriate medium for a psychology that might allow us to understand ourselves.

Comparing the appearances

One of the most important contributions to cognitive science was Chomsky's (1957, 1965) work based on the idea that an understanding of tacit knowledge of syntax could be acquired by asking native speakers of a language to consult their intuitions. Readers are asked, in effect: Is it not intuitively clear that this example of a sentence is anomalous, or that it is ambiguous, or that it will support a particular paraphrase? Such data form the evidence on which much modern linguistic research and theory are based.

My proposal is that comparable data on action and emotions have been provided by poets, playwrights, and novelists for 3,000 years.[49] The practice of literary criticism, begun in the *Poetics*, is similar to the appeal by linguists for people to consult their intuitions as native speakers. As members of a culture, and drawing on implicit folk theories of beliefs and desires, you may consult your intuitions about the emotions you experience in the theater. When you witness a tragedy like Sophocles' *Oedipus the King*, Aristotle asks, do you not find yourself moved to fear and pity? Is it not the plot, made up from situations and the beliefs and actions of the characters, that has this effect? Novelists and playwrights succeed in communicating emotions. We are not just told about things. We are moved. Aristotle proposed that it was the universal aspects of human action that allowed people to experience emotions such as fear and pity at the theater.

Because the story form can be a vehicle for the propagation of mere opinion and for exerting social influence, to sell soap powder or to promote cultural values, Aristotle's ideas may seem implausible compared with the Platonic view. The Platonic view is that art may be more or less attractively packaged, more or less persuasive, more or less resonant with preoccupations of particular cultural groups, but because it rests on make-believe, it can be put to use in the service of any ideology. It depends, in short, on an emotional appeal. The very term emotional is one of derogation, an assertion of irrationality.

In the nineteenth century, literature and the arts were promoted as humanizing in European society. Whether these aims were achieved is a matter of assertion. It is Plato's view that has, on the whole, prevailed. The theater may be enjoyable, but for truth we look to mathematics and natural science as engines of rationality. My argument is not the nineteenth-century one that art is humanizing in some undefined way and certainly not that a bit of Tolstoy will lighten the weight of empirical argument. My proposal is that if cognitive psychology is to be not just technical but insightful we must take the Aristotelian approach to understanding emotions, not the Platonic one.[50] We should seek to increase understanding by comparing things that are related but have differences. To put this another way, rather than focusing only on methods that might allow occasional Platonic glimpses in natural science, we content ourselves with seemingly more pedestrian Aristotelian comparisons and dialectic. Rather than trying to collect unchangeable nuggets of pure truth, we accept the idea that truths can only be approached, not often attained, by comparing and modifying conclusions from different methods. We must, therefore, be in a position to make relevant comparisons.

The Aristotelian argument about the theater is consistent with this: It is the idea that emotions aroused in ourselves as an audience can be compared with those of the characters in the play. If emotions are stirred, a playwright or novelist is not necessarily doing this to persuade or manipulate us technically. We are being given an opportunity to run a simulation of a literary character, plausible in its coherence, through dilemmas of intention in our own minds. So it is to this important process of literary simulation that I now turn.

Literature as simulation

The innovation that ushered in the cognitive revolution was the computer. With computers we make simulations, including some with properties of mentality. A common term to indicate the novelist's portrayal of a scene is "representation." This is also a usual translation of the Greek *mimesis*, imitation of the kind that playwrights and poets create. In terms of cognitive science *mimesis* is simulation. In novels and plays a simulation runs not on a computer but on the minds of readers or of a theater audience.[51] Here, too, is created a world, recognizably like our own though not actually that world, in which the effects of actions can be examined and understood.

Bruner (1986) has argued that what I have called the "technical" contrasts with the "narrative." These correspond to two quite different kinds of cognitive functioning, each with its own form of verification. "The one verifies by eventual appeal to procedures for establishing formal and empirical proof. The other establishes not truth but verisimilitude" (p. 11). Bruner goes on to say that this latter deals with meanings, with possibilities, and with the vicissitudes of intention.

Aristotle put the issue clearly: The plot of "a tragedy is an imitation (*mimesis*) of an action that is complete in itself" (*Poetics*, 1450b). As we watch a play or read a novel, the words summon up our schematic knowledge, and we run the action as a plan in the simulation space of our minds. We regard playwrights and novelists as great in part if their simulations not only run on our minds, but if they are also internally coherent, recognizable, and typical.[52]

Intuitions about narrative and emotions

Certainly, narrative literature provides a basis that we can scarcely neglect. As I will argue in Chapters 5, 7, and 8, its properties of allowing us to generate our own understandings are particularly important. For these first two chapters, however, I have had the simpler purpose of treating literature as an explicit form of folk theory, an externalization of cultural intuitions and paradigm cases of emotions and their implications, selected by cultural approval, so that they can be discussed, compared, and tested.

As in a computer simulation, in the *mimesis* of narrative the interrelations among the parts can be understood more clearly than in real life. Literature can propose: "This is an emotion. This is how it comes about. These are its compulsive effects on this person and that one. Are they not?" So, in *Anna Karenina*, Tolstoy puts it to us as readers that this is what a passionate love affair is like. These paradigmatic cases are important in our culture for understanding ourselves and each other.

Narrative involves simulation. But narrative is unlike a computer simulation of, say, a meteorological system, in which if it rains nothing gets wet. In the mental simulation of a narrative, we experience emotions as the action unfolds. Our self is used to understand the actions and we experience some of the consequences of what we are simulating.

If we were to work entirely in the mode of natural science, the task of understanding emotions might be that of accurate description. If we asked whether *Anna Karenina* were an accurate account of human actions that actually occurred, we would say of course not. But if we want our psychological understanding also to be insightful, then we need somehow to make a connection with our own cognitive systems. Narrative literature such as *Anna Karenina* allows us to ask of ourselves not just: "Is this the kind of thing that happens in general?" but also, "Are Anna's feelings mine?" We are not just making explicit our intuitions, as in Chomsky's invitation. A play or novel allows us to compare an explicitly simulated set of actions and their results with emotions that are our own and that may move us considerably.

Katharsis *and the communication of emotions*

Whereas Plato thought that emotions were aroused by art to manipulate people, and hence to divert them from rationality and truth, Aristotle argued that the audience's emotions in the theater allow *katharsis* with respect to the acts that have emotional consequences.

Katharsis is the single most problematic term in the whole of Aristotle's *Poetics*. Nussbaum (1986) has shown that the term is widely misunderstood. Two common types of implication prompt its usual translation either as purification of a moral kind or as purgation of a quasi-medical kind.[53] Both interpretations imply that there is something wrong with emotions. They need to be purified, or somehow to be gotten rid of. Perhaps if we go off to the purgatorium of the theater to eliminate these unfortunate elements then they will not intrude into our serious adult lives. Plato's views have a strong hold on modern translators. Both these interpretations are really extensions of Plato's distrust of art. If we can either sublimate or get rid or emotions, we can be rational.

Such arguments are quite inconsistent with the bulk of Aristotle's writings about both emotions and art. They misunderstand the likely meaning of *katharsis*. Nussbaum shows that although this term can mean purification or purgation, such meanings are secondary. The central meaning, common before Aristotle, used frequently by Plato, by Aristotle himself, and continuing after Aristotle's time, was that *katharsis* and related words (e.g., *kathairo, katharos*) meant clearing up, clarification, clearing away obstacles, including the cognitive meaning of seeing or understanding clearly and without obstacles. The spiritual term purification is a derivation, indicating an absence of obscuring blemish. The medical one is also secondary, indicating freeing the body from internal obstructions.

Nussbaum puts it that *katharsis* in the theater was a cognitive process: "The function of tragedy is to accomplish through pity and fear, a clarification (or illumination) concerning experiences of the pitiable and fearful kind" (1986, p. 391). And this, as she then adds, is an appropriate translation of Aristotle's famous passage (1449b) in which *katharsis* is mentioned.

Comparing basic and semantic parts of emotions

I propose that one of the important functions of narrative literature is to allow us to bring together the phenomenological experience of an emotion and its understanding, its control part and its semantic part. It is in this that clarification can occur, and insights may happen.

Art is an approach to truth different from and complementary to science. It is not just propaganda, or even education in the usual sense. Much of it depends on simulations that run on our own cognitive systems, in order to clarify aspects of the relation of emotions to goals and action, and hence help improve our models of self. The fact that we can run other people's plans in our minds derives from our ability to run our own in this way. This ability is central to human planning (I take up the issue further in Chapters 7 and 9).

Aristotle proposed that in the theater the important vehicle for transmitting emotions is the plot. If we experience basic aspects of emotions in the theater or when reading a novel, this has occurred by a communication that is semantic. In cognitive terms a plot is typically a plan of one or more characters. The plan meets some vicissitude. Because a plot allows spectators or readers to run the plan in their own minds, they are liable themselves to experience emotions at such junctures.[54] As Aristotle says, this is usually aided in the theater by the actor's appearance, verbal expression, by music and so on, that is, by nonsemantic means. But the primary means of communication is the plot.

Small ripples of sound or a tiny quantity of ink on a page can thus summon up a world of meaning. Fictional works do not so much describe the world as it is or one that has been. They allow us to create worlds that could be and engage ourselves in them. Utterances, whether in art or conversation, are programs that run on other minds. In tragedy, according to Aristotle, part of the purpose is to allow the audience to experience the effects of significant choices and actions and experience in themselves the tragic emotions of pity and fear that may derive from actions performed, as always, without full knowledge of consequences. In the classical Greek theater, comparisons with the self were promoted by a chorus, switching our attention from emotions as experienced by the protagonist to these same emotions seen from outside.

In *Anna Karenina* such devices as a chorus have been replaced, but opportunities for comparison are still strongly present.[55] We can experience the meanings and emotions of seeing Anna's lover fall and of a passage of words with a disappointed husband. Two things may happen. First, we may feel emotions in ourselves. Second, we have the writer's indications of the fictional character's emotions: As Anna sits down, hides her face, and is unable to control her tears, we have the opportunity to compare our own feelings with hers. An insight can occur, as knowledge we have of our own and others' actions is extended, or something is put together in our own experience in a way that we might not have accomplished ourselves. This is the opportunity for *katharsis,* clarification, as the emotionally significant event happening to these simulated characters is assimilated into the schemata of our own sense of self.

Process and content

Cognitive psychology includes descriptions of processes and representations of knowledge that enable us to see, think, converse, understand, and so on. Some branches of the subject concentrate specifically on processes, for instance, the process of encoding visual information into memories stored for later retrieval. Others define the representations of mental knowledge, describing how problems might be mentally represented to affect their ease of solution.

In understanding emotions, however, more is at issue than process and representation. We need also to understand something of the content of the knowledge on which emotions are based and to do so in a way that is not merely technical. This content must not be just generalizations, as in natural science. We must understand specific goals and individual emotions, of ourselves and others, as we do in narrative. It is for this reason that this book differs in presentation from many books on cognitive psychology. This, I believe, is what we must attempt in a psychology of emotions. It would be no good just to give a natural scientific account of emotions, from a viewpoint outside the human world, even if such a view were attainable. We must start within the human world and articulate our insights.

I started Chapter 1 with a quotation from Kierkegaard, and said that emotions occur where biology and culture meet. Understanding emotions will depend on whether we can compare these two worlds, bring them into register, worlds that conventionally are separated into natural science and human narrative.

3. Rationality and emotions

Nothing is more usual in philosophy, and even in common life, than to talk of the combat of passion and
reason, to give the preference to reason, and to assert
that men are only so far virtuous as they conform
themselves to its dictates.

David Hume
Treatise of human nature, p. 154

Are emotions irrational?

As Karenin and Anna returned home in their carriage after the officers'
race, Anna admitted her affair with Vronsky and began to weep. Karenin
felt furious, but suppressed it by assuming a deathlike rigidity because
he was "aware at the same time of a rush of that emotional disturbance
always produced in him by tears." Tears made him angry, so that he
"utterly lost all power of reflection."

At the center of the debate about emotions is the question of the
difference between emotion and thought. I started Chapter 1 with folk
theories, and in Chapter 2 I advocated an Aristotelian approach as preferable to Platonic distrust of emotions. Here I discuss the common folk
theory that emotions are irrational. Karenin, like many of us, believes
this. As a man committed to rationality, he therefore says nothing at all
after his wife's revelation until they reach home.

Toward the end of Tolstoy's novel we see indeed a harrowing portrait
of the irrationality of emotions. Anna and Vronsky, now living together,
start to quarrel. Both know that they are destroying what is most important to them. Anna starts trying to restrain Vronsky from activities outside the house. Sitting at home she becomes jealous and starts to suspect some of these activities. She feels she depends on him for her very

130

existence. She knows that to act on this feeling of dependency by trying to curtail him is to drive him away and lose his love. But this consideration is unable to do more than form itself into intentions. She is unable to avoid questioning him and making demands. They quarrel, saying things that neither is able to control.

There is no question about what is meant when emotions are referred to as irrational. When experiencing compelling emotions, people often act with consequences that can be foreseen and are contrary to some of their purposes, even to their apparently most important purposes.

Published observations support the idea that strong emotions, notably fear, make one irrational. Tyhurst (1951) found that during fires or floods only some 15% of people behaved in an organized way. About 70% showed a mixture of organized and disorganized behavior, and some 15% became completely disorganized, running around screaming or becoming aimless. In battle only a small proportion of soldiers fight. For instance, in interviews of World War II veterans, Marshall (1978) found that an average of 15% of men actually fired their weapons during battles, with this proportion rising to 25% in the best units. In most actions about 80% of the troops were in a position to use their weapons. When seriously upset, people may be unable to act sensibly. When depressed, a parent may neglect children (Pound et al., 1985), or when angry or anxious, may hurt or scold them in ways that clearly do not benefit anyone.

That emotions may make us involuntarily irrational is seen in the cultural practices of law. To kill someone when angry or jealous carries less severe penalties than killing in cold blood, with malice aforethought or while executing a plan of robbery (see, e.g., Averill, 1982). Special consideration is given for an uprush of involuntary irrationality.

The conclusion that there is something irrational about emotions need not be labored.

Emotion implies compulsion in our thinking and action. If voluntary actions are the means by which we change the world, emotions seem to change us. They were defined by Descartes as passions for this reason.[1] These passions have been attributed to biological causes such as instincts or the autonomic nervous system. Nonconscious social processes may also act on us.[2] In grief, guilt, or envy, our preoccupation may be unwelcome; in love, and sometimes in vengeful anger, we may accept the compulsion eagerly.

The usual assumption is that thought is distinctively human and based on reason, but that instincts and emotions are bestial or infantile, misleading and irrational. The twentieth-century Western distrust of emotions seems related to Plato's articulations of the ways in which emotions can subvert rationality and distort truth. Nor is it accidental that the very emblem of rationality is the kind of technical plan that I have called simple, which has a single goal to which everything relevant is assimilated and which is executed in a perfectly known world. Hume (1888/1739) proposed that passions are the motivating forces of life, and reason the machinery to calculate how to act in response to these motivations. But his proposal has not replaced this dichotomy of reason versus emotion.[3] In ancient times and today, the idea has been elaborated that emotions are the principal cause of human suffering. Coming after Plato and Aristotle, the Stoics took up the idea, regarding emotions as diseases of the soul, to be cured by proper thinking.[4]

My objective in this chapter is to question the dichotomy reason versus emotion and to suggest that it be abandoned. I have argued for starting from folk theories. Aristotle, among others, has adopted this dichotomy, duly consigning emotions to the nonrational part of the soul. So we start from this concept. But I will claim that as we examine it we find that it is mistaken. It is one of those folk theories that Stich (1983) identified as wrong. I will criticize the idea that emotions are irrational and thinking is rational. Though Aristotle's concept here is mistaken, applying his method to this dubious dichotomy allows a fuller understanding.[5]

Do emotions have functions?

The question of rationality can be answered only if we decide whether emotions have functions.[6] The primary functional argument (discussed in Chapter 1) is that emotions have a fundamental role in mental life. They are important in setting goal priorities. A subsidiary hypothesis is that there are specific mechanisms or processes that subserve this function. The contrary argument, that emotions are nonfunctional and their effects irrational, takes several forms. I will discuss four influential versions: that emotions are frills on the serious business of organizing behavior, that they provoke disorganization, that they, or at least their expressions, are vestiges of behavior that once was functional but is so no longer, and that emotions can be the seeds of neuroses.

Emotions as by-products. As Draper (1985) has argued emotions may be superficial characteristics of behavior, the salience of which tempts us to believe that they are significant. Noise, for instance, is salient in many mechanical processes, but it has no functional status. It is a by-product, even though it is inherent and often cannot be removed. We would scarcely want to ask how many kinds of noise there were, or whether explanations of machines in terms that do not mention noise are convincing or complete. Perhaps more directly, Nisbett and Ross (1980) have shown that salience biases the inferences we make. Emotions are particularly salient to us, so perhaps we would be particularly misled in our judgments about them (see also Wilson, Laser & Stone, 1982).

The most distinguished proponent of this view was James (1884, 1890).[7] He proposed that emotions are perceptions of our voluntary and involuntary bodily reactions to events. The best he found to say about their function was that without them, the perception of external events "would be purely cognitive in form, pale, colorless, destitute of emotional warmth" (1890, vol. 2, p. 450).

Let me remark on three matters here. First, James explicitly proposed his theory as a scientific one in opposition to the folk theory, "our natural way of thinking" (as James 1890, vol. 2, p. 449, put it) that emotions have a causal effect on behavior. Second, as Gordon (1987) says, James and his followers like Schachter and Singer (1962), who are discussed later, trivialize emotions. For them, emotions at best are a kind of froth on the top of the real business of behavior. Third, of course, are the empirical arguments against James's theory. The theory was subjected to energetic criticism by Cannon (1927), who presented evidence that artificial induction of internal bodily changes does not induce emotions, and that diminution in the neural excitations from within the body does not diminish people's capacity to experience emotions.

In a recent test of James's idea, Bermond et al. (1991) conducted careful interviews with subjects with spinal injuries that had resulted in motor and sensory paralyses, cutting them off from the major sources of bodily excitation. Subjects were asked to recall an incident of fear before their injury and one after it that was as similar as possible in eliciting circumstances. Comparable data were also collected for incidents of anger. There was no evidence of lowered subjective intensity of fear or anger following the injury. Indeed, for these two emotions the remembered subjective intensity of the emotion was significantly greater following the injury, although, as expected on pure anatomical grounds, lowered intensity of physiological disturbance was reported.[8]

I am sure this will not be the last word: James's theory seems constantly to be on the point of collapse, but just as constantly people come forward to support it. So, for instance, Zajonc (1985) and Zajonc, Murphy, and Inglehart (1989) argue that emotions can derive from changes in brain temperature, which produce local changes in transmitter substance release. These temperature changes are themselves produced by alterations of flow in the cerebral blood vessels caused by different kinds of contraction of facial muscles. Though, however, some small changes of affect can be produced in this way, there is no reason to believe that most emotions depend on such mechanisms.

Emotion as physiological disorganization. A common type of theory that is still alive is that strong emotions disorganize behavior and thinking.[9] Attention can become too narrowly focused, action stereotyped and conventional. Recent research has added the concept that strong emotions in response to stress may lead to psychiatric breakdowns or psychosomatic illness or both.

THE YERKES-DODSON LAW. One expression of this idea is the so-called Yerkes-Dodson (1908) law, that there is an optimal level of arousal or activation for any task. Performance is efficient at this optimal level, but at low levels of arousal boredom and tendencies to sleepiness or distraction occur. At high levels overexcitement causes disorganization. Arousal is thought to be produced by the nonspecific reticular activating system, alerting the organism to sudden events and maintaining a background level of neural tone. Emotion, according to this idea, is equivalent to a high level of arousal.[10]

THE CANNON-BARD THEORY. This theory, which holds that emotional arousal arises from subcortical regions of the brain, is a relative of the idea that emotions disorganize. It was not perhaps a concept of disorganization as such, but that unthoughtful processes have irrational effects. Though Cannon (1927) attacked James's theory comprehensively, apparently he was unable to resist taking over James's idea of emotions giving warmth to experience. According to Cannon, impulses from the thalamus reaching the cortex contribute the "glow and color" to otherwise neutral cognitive states. Cannon also argued that normally the thalamus is under a degree of inhibition by the cortex. Emotional expressions of high intensity occur if this inhibition is removed either surgically, as in the sham rage of decorticated cats, or pharmacologically, as in the aggressiveness or sentimentality of drunkenness. The explanation of the strong emotions of infancy and childhood is that the cortex has not yet achieved its adult level of inhibitory control. The idea also explains the involuntariness of emotions:

> powerful impulses originating in a region of the brain not associated with cognitive consciousness and arousing therefore in an obscure and unrelated manner the strong feelings of emotional excitement that explain the sense of being seized, possessed, of being controlled by an outside force and made to act without weighing of the consequences. (pp. 123–124)

EMOTIONS AS STIRRED-UP FEELINGS. The idea that emotions are disorganizing was discussed by Leeper (1948), who argued that this was the predominant view of emotions in psychology at that time.[11] It appeared in influential textbooks such as Woodworth's (1945), in such words as "Emotion is a . . . stirred up state of feeling" (p. 410), and "The degree of emotionality depends on how free the lower centers are at any time from domination by the cerebral cortex. . . . We can say that activity is unemotional in proportion as it consists in observing and managing the situation" (p. 431). Leeper said the idea probably gained force from its resonance with the eighteenth-century cultural arguments that civilized adult humans should be rational and from psychoanalytic theories that irrational impulses well up from an underground unconscious. Perhaps such ideas, current in ordinary culture, have more influence on scientific ideas about emotions than some other kinds of evidence.

Seen in this way, proposals about emotions being due to unchecked intrusions from subcortical structures restate Hughlings-Jackson's metaphor of higher, more evolved structures of the brain keeping down the lower in the same way that a government controls the anarchic tendencies of the people.[12] The question remains as to how far this metaphor of higher influences controlling lower processes is insightful.

It is clear that there are many instances in which strong emotions are disorganizing. These are important data to be explained. What is required, however, are explanations in terms of psychological processes. Theories such as "disorganized (or compulsive) emotional behavior occurs because of intrusions of unchecked disorganizing (or compelling) influences" do no more to explain the phenomena than did the doctor in one of Moliere's plays who sagely explained that the action of opium in inducing sleep was due to its "dormitive potency."

SCHACHTER AND SINGER'S EXPERIMENT AND THEORY. Nevertheless, the idea that strong emotions are disorganizing has given rise to many studies in which arousal and pharmacological states are manipulated to see whether behavior is influenced by this nonrational means. The most influential piece of psychological research on emotion in recent years is Schachter and Singer's (1962) neo-Jamesean study of emotion as bodily arousal with a detachable attributional label.

Schachter and Singer injected adrenaline into subjects who believed they were taking part in a study of the effects of the injected substance in a visual task. They were unaware of the real experimental purposes: to test whether arousal induced by adrenaline would be experienced as emotion when subjects were in a social situation conducive to happiness or anger. The experimenters assigned each subject to one of several conditions. Some subjects were given adrenaline injections; others were given placebo injections that had no physiological effect. Of those given adrenaline, some were correctly informed of its physiological effects and therefore had a ready explanation of the effects, which lasted for 15 or 20 minutes and included hearts pounding, hands shaking, and faces getting hot. Others were misinformed. They were warned of possible effects that adrenaline does not have, that they might feel numbness, itchiness, and a slight headache. Others were given no information about the effects of the injections.

Each subject was asked to wait for the injection to take effect. In the room where each waited was an accomplice of the experimenters, posing as another subject. He was either behaving euphorically and encouraging the real subject to do likewise, or acting angrily because both had to complete a long and intrusively rude questionnaire.

Schachter and Singer predicted that subjects injected with adrenaline who were ignorant or misinformed of its effects would become more happy or angry than those who were informed or who had received the placebo. These effects would be reflected both in subjects' reports of their feelings and in observations of their behavior with the experimental accomplice. The subjects who had received adrenaline without a correct explanation indeed felt more emotion than those who had adrenaline with a correct explanation of its effects or than those who had the placebo.

Schachter and Singer explained their results in terms of subjects' interpreting unexplained physiological arousal as emotion: An emotion is arousal plus a cognitive label for it in terms of anger, joy, or the like. According to this idea, adrenaline-injected subjects who were ignorant of the effects were physiologically provoked into a distortion of perception. They became more happy or more angry than those who were physiologically normal.

Schachter and Singer's theory was immensely attractive to psychologists. However, two reviews of the extensive literature testing it conclude that the evidence leaves something to be desired. Manstead and Wagner (1981) argue that unexplained arousal attributed to different circumstances is the most distinctive attribute of the theory. But, of the large volume of research on the topic only three studies tested it directly and one gave partial support. The other tended to refute it. In another review, Reisenzein (1983) further clarified aspects of the theory and identified three main deductions about increases and decreases in the intensity of felt emotions. Only one, that misattributed arousal from an extraneous source intensifies emotions, has been substantiated. Two others are that reduction of arousal and attribution of an emotionally induced arousal to an alternative source lead to reduction in the intensity of emotion. The first of these is not supported and the second is equivocal.

Some experiments on misattributed arousal from an extraneous source have a certain charm, despite the duplicity always involved. An example is Dutton and Aron's (1974), in which male subjects approached by a woman research assistant on a high and apparently precarious suspension bridge wrote more sexually explicit accounts of the encounter and made more persistent efforts to meet the woman subsequently than men meeting the same woman on a lower, and apparently safer, bridge. This was explained by the idea that increased arousal tends to intensify emotional states.

One may conclude that to the extent that the arousal is incidental to the situation – when it is induced by apprehension of heights, by drugs, by physical exercise, by bogus feedback of autonomic arousal, and so on – the effects are irrational. They depend on processes other than reason that influence behavior to disorganize or reorganize it in nonrational ways. The importance of this in discussing the supposed irrationality of emotions is that Schachter and Singer argue that emotional arousal is frequently misattributed. Emotions can substantially influence judgment and action even when they may have only an inappropriate connection with actual events.

Oatley and Johnson-Laird's communicative theory of emotions follows Schachter and Singer in some respects. We also postulate that emotions have a generalized part, which we call the basic control signal, and an interpretive part, which we call semantic. Basic emotion signals can have effects that have nothing to do with thoughtful understanding of the outside world. To this extent, emotions allow a special type of irrationality. We depart from the usual emphasis of this theory, however, in that we do not suppose that this kind of irrationality is a central characteristic of emotions. It arises only rarely, because emotions can be set off by events outside their usual range of operation, just as perceptions of light can be induced by pressing the side of the eyeball in the dark. Though emotions can sometimes occur in ways unconnected with meaningful events, usually they are caused by events that affect goals and are functional responses to such events.

Darwin's theory. The most venerable version of the theory that aspects of emotion are nonfunctional is Darwin's (1872). He accepted that emotions are well-defined phenomena, but argued that their expressions occur even though "they may not be of the least use" (p. 28). Otherwise, of course, we would say that behavior is rational, adaptive, functional.

Darwin's work was the beginning of modern empirical investigations of emotions.[13] For his book he drew on a wide range of observations collected over many years, including his own observations of adults and children and of domestic and wild animals. He collected photographs, paintings, and literature and obtained descriptions of expressions from the director of a large psychiatric asylum. He did not neglect cross-cultural comparisons, and he received replies to questionnaires he sent to missionaries who were in a position to observe non-European peoples.

There were clear commonalities between humans and other mammals. Examples included behavioral patterns that involved the voluntary musculature, involuntary musculature, and glands (see Table 4).

Darwin (1872) was mainly concerned with the following problem: Whereas certain kinds of behavior, such as recoiling from a poisonous snake, can be functional, they can also occur inappropriately. Here is a typical Darwinian observation:

> I put my face close to the thick glass-plate in front of a puff-adder in the Zoological Gardens, with the firm determination of not starting back if the snake struck at me; but, as soon as the blow was struck, my resolution went for nothing, and I jumped a yard or two backwards with astonishing rapidity. My will and reason were powerless against the imagination of a danger which had never been experienced. (p. 38)

Table 4. *Emotional expressions discussed by Darwin, the motor apparatus used, and the type of emotion expressed*

Expression	Motor apparatus	Emotion example
Blushing	Blood vessels	Shame, modesty
Body contact	Somatic muscles	Affection
Clenching fists	Somatic muscles	Anger
Crying	Tear ducts	Sadness
Frowning	Facial muscles	Anger, frustration
Laughing	Breathing apparatus	Pleasure
Perspiration	Sweat glands	Pain
Piloerection	Dermal apparatus	Fear, anger
Screaming	Vocal apparatus	Pain
Shrugging	Somatic muscles	Resignation
Sneering	Facial muscles	Contempt
Trembling	Somatic muscles	Fear, anxiety

Note: Few if any modern theorists regard pain as an emotion.
Derived from Darwin 1872.

Darwin amassed examples of actions that were, on occasion, super-fluous. As I have put it previously, he described "Tears that do not lubricate the eyes, hair that stands on end adding nothing to the skill of an animal's attack, laughter that seems not to improve the execution of any task. He would have been fascinated by the facial expressions of people talking on the telephone" (Oatley, 1989, p. 33).

His hypothesis was that emotional expressions were accounted for by three principles. One was that expressions can be due to building up habits: "Movements which are serviceable in gratifying some desire, or in relieving some sensation, if often repeated, become so habitual that they are performed whether or not of any service, whenever the same desire or sensation is felt, even in a very weak degree" (p. 347).

The physiological basis of habit is that the "conducting power of the nervous fibers" (p. 29) is increased by repetition, so that particular expressive movements will result when certain states of mind are induced, even "though they may not then be of the least use" (p. 28). Darwin supposed that "some actions ordinarily associated through habit with certain states of the mind may be partially repressed through the will, and in such cases the muscles which are least under the separate control of the will are the most liable still to act, causing movements which we recognize as expressive" (p. 28). Thus, crying is the vestige of a habit of screaming established in infancy and only partly inhibited in adult life.

He also proposed the Lamarckian idea that habits practiced over a number of generations can be inherited.

The second principle is of antithesis: When a state of mind directly opposite to a habit is induced, then a movement characteristic of the antithesis may occur. Shrugging is a gesture opposite to a threatening one, expressed when aggression might be expected. The third is the principle of movements occurring because of the inherited structure of the nervous system: "Nerve force is generated in excess" (p. 66) when the sensorium is strongly excited. It flows, therefore, into channels not strictly necessary for behavior. Sneering, the partial retraction of lips covering the canine tooth, is a vestige of a snarl and preparation to bite inherited from our animal ancestry.

These issues pose a problem about communicative properties of emotion. Darwin alludes to it in his last chapter: Although emotional expressions are often communicated, Darwin doubted whether communication was ever the intention of an animal or person undergoing an emotion because, as he says, emotional expression is largely involuntary.

Darwin came on his idea of the pathways of habit, antithesis, and inherited nervous structure into which neural force would flow "only at the close of [his] observations" (p. 27). What he does not say is that this type of explanation forces something of a paradox upon us. The theory, as he said, "confirms to a certain limited extent the conclusion that man is derived from some lower animal" (p. 365), and even that expression "is certainly of importance for the welfare of mankind" (p. 366). Darwin was careful not to say that the function of emotions is to communicate. Had he said emotions were communicative it would have undermined his proposal that emotional expressions are recognizable as actions that on occasion are without function. It would also have questioned aspects of his theories of habit and excess neural force.

VESTIGES OR AUTOMATIC BEHAVIOR MECHANISMS? I would like to distinguish two aspects of Darwin's theory. One is the idea that emotions are nonfunctional vestiges of a bestial and infantile past. This is the paradigm of the view directly opposed to the one I am proposing in that it supports the idea of emotions as irrational. The second aspect, which is not easy to disentangle from the first, is conceptually different. It is concerned with how automatic behavior mechanisms might have been installed during evolution, how they might be triggered, and how making ad hoc modifications to them might not always be appropriate.

Darwin's research in its first aspect does not lead to a theory of emotional expression at all. Rather it takes emotional expression as evidence for evolution. It consigns many of our emotional expressions to a class of not-quite-dead fossils. If evolution is a process in which new forms are generated, emotional expressions are undiscarded behavioral debris from this process. Certain functions that may appear salient are no longer serviceable in a given organism. They had value at some earlier stage of individual development or of genetic evolution, but that value is lost, perhaps because the proper occasion for it no longer exists. These residues of older procedures survive because selection pressures may not have eliminated all nonfunctional features. Behavioral vestiges linger, just as do anatomical ones such as the bones at the base of the human spine which are vestiges of a tail.

The second aspect of Darwin's work is a theory of emotional expression as such. It can be seen in terms of functions of behavioral mechanisms, and expressed as follows. Darwin concentrates on a kind of behavioral mechanism, the habit. Habits are useful and are built up by repetition to become automatic. According to Darwin, they can be inherited. He drew on a line of thinking that was current in his time. G. H. Lewes, for instance, had coined the phrase "lapsed intelligence" for instincts that had been constructed as means to achieving consequences but had then become automatic.[14] We now commonly distinguish automatic processes that are instinctual from those that are learned and make the sharp separation of the Weismann doctrine, that adaptations made by the individual cannot be passed on genetically.[15]

In terms of a computational metaphor, we might talk of both genetically specified and individually acquired behavior patterns as procedures that had been compiled and then discuss them in terms of the knowledge embedded in them.[16] It is a useful property of such a mechanism that it is not accessible to alteration. It may be invoked by an eliciting condition for which it was designed, but the difficulty is that for the mechanism to work well in its designed setting it will also be invoked by a similar, but slightly different pattern – for example, a "desire or sensation" – in circumstances other than those for which it was designed. Such automatic patterns may appear irrational and partly unserviceable.

The idea is an important and general one. There are two issues. First, it is advantageous to compile plans as habits, storing sequences that have been practiced for later use.[17] Without habits, we humans become inept, as witnessed by our difficulties in adapting to any substantial

change in lifestyle. Next, habits must be triggered by distinctive circumstances, and a trigger mechanism often works best if it is based on a
simple discrimination. But with such an advantageous mechanism,
sometimes the triggering circumstance will not be discriminated accurately by the recognition device. Darwin's experience with the puff adder at the zoo had nearly all the characteristics of a situation in which it
would be a very good idea to spring backward. The apparent inap-
propriateness is really due to a limitation in the discriminative ability of
the recognition mechanism to take into account the plate glass. It was
not a defect in the idea of compiled action sequences. Second, there are
problems of dynamics: Time enters the analysis, and behavioral mechanisms have inertia. It takes time to generate or modify good plans. As
Darwin's experience with the puff adder attests, compiled plans cannot
be modified instantaneously just because in some instances this would
be rational.

A slightly different interpretation is in terms of optimizing multiple
constraints.[18] If in evolution many different constraints are being satisfied, then not all of them can be fulfilled adequately and simultaneously
in any one species. There will be conflicts and hence trade-offs of various kinds. For example, anatomical size may be an advantage for some
purposes, such as speed of locomotion, but it makes requirements of the
strength of bones and hence weight. Human bones are sometimes broken, and human backs often give trouble. Certain size-strength-weight
problems have not been optimized for humans, at least in some situations.

Emotional expressions may also indicate that multiple constraints
have not been optimized for all circumstances. An automatic mechanism
evolved to fit situation A will be less adapted to situations B and C,
which might share some aspects of A. Once again, emotions seem to be
related to the idea of human agents pursuing many goals. Clashes,
trade-offs, and conflicts occur and give rise to dislocations of functioning, which appear to be a nuisance. Darwin's idea about neural overflow
amounts to saying that neural mechanisms have not been optimized for
all circumstances. Despite habits having serviceable properties, they
also have properties that are a disservice in some situations.

Neisser (1963) drew attention to this aspect of our mental lives in his
paper comparing the biological mind to the computer. When computer
programs are developed, side effects are best minimized. Traces of previous versions of a program should be eliminated immediately because
their continued existence as vestiges will cause inefficiency and make
the rational structure of the program more difficult to understand. But

human beings ordinarily are not faced with the same task as the programmer. The programmer typically develops a rational solution to a single technical task in a limited domain. By contrast, as human beings we have to develop new pieces of program as we go along. These new developments have to meet current contingencies about which we have not been informed by our genetic start-up program, and they also have to serve as bases for further developments in a future that we cannot foresee.

The phenomena that Darwin studied are ambiguous as to their interpretation as vestiges or as problems of optimization in animals that compile knowledge and change in their own lifetime.

DARWIN AND FREUD. Although Freud did not propose a theory of emotions as such, his ideas are close to Darwin's on this issue. According to Freud, people undergo stages of psychosexual development. Habits of relating that are appropriate in childhood persist in adulthood where they seem no longer to have a proper place. A metaphor occurs in *Civilization and Its Discontents* (1961/1930), as Freud asks us to imagine that we stand in the city of Rome. Imagine the city not as a physical habitation where most of the earlier settlements have been destroyed and overlaid by later ones, where stones of classical buildings have been pillaged to build more recent structures, but as a psychic habitation in which by some slight head movement, one can see the classical, Renaissance, and modern buildings, all occupying their places simultaneously and all looking much as they were. According to this idea the mind may be added to, but it is hard to make deletions. Features that might have been replaced live on and can give us glimpses that we call emotional.

Both Darwin and Freud proposed the idea of repression. Although in detail their formulations differ, for both the core meaning is the inhibition of behavior that has become unwanted. The inhibition does not, in either formulation, remove the behavior mechanism. Nor is it usually fully successful in switching it off. With Freud's as with Darwin's idea, we are left with a question: Are we as adults like puppets, still being pulled by the strings of childhood that can compel us into atavistic activity? Or is it that for development on the time scale of a human life, there needs to be a means of integrating knowledge compiled genetically, with knowledge acquired individually in many different settings?

ACCRETION AND DEVELOPMENT. It is not easy to see what better mechanism there could be than one that bases new solutions to unforeseeable problems on foundations that already exist. The process is one of accretion and gradual modification. It allows some backtracking, but not complete rebuilding from the foundations, for new starts, new individuals, new cultures, or new species can occur, depending on the time scale. If we wish to question this arrangement the question is not: Doesn't this all seem rather clumsy? but What might be the alternatives?

Action tendencies with involuntary attributes remain with us. Are they vestiges or necessary features of difficulties of optimization? The alternative in which Darwin was most interested was that emotional expressions are vestiges of a bestial or infantile past. This alternative has, I believe, been misleading and corresponds to a prevalent theory already present in our culture. This alternative resonates with Plato's distrust of emotions, with Aristotle's separation of the rational from the irrational mind, and with the aspirations of the eighteenth-century Enlightenment to eliminate the effects of this irrational part. The idea has been thoroughly incorporated into many Euro-American prejudices.

Darwin's main aim was to seek continuity between ourselves and other animals and between adults and infants. Assimilated with other cultural ideas, however, his idea is not one of continuity but of contrast. Darwin himself was not above making this contrast and knew of its relation to cultural attitudes. In one of his notebooks compiled in preparation for *The Descent of Man* and the *Expression of the Emotions*, he wrote: "Our descent, then, is the origin of our evil passions!! – The Devil under form of baboon is our grandfather" (Gruber, 1974, p. 123). Bestiality and infantility are the opposite of adult human rationality. When supposed vestiges occur they are best denounced as inappropriate to our higher, adult life, at least to the life of slightly less than 50% of us, the males.[19]

Repressed emotions. One theory that has common currency is that we can have pent-up feelings. If distress is not experienced fully when it first occurs, then it can be somehow stored and have baleful effects. This was Freud's earliest psychodynamic idea, in which he postulated that hysteria was due to traumata that were not remembered but repressed and, like foreign bodies, continued to work within the psyche. Therapy then involved consciously remembering the circumstances surrounding a trauma and "discharging" the emotion associated with it (Freud & Breuer, 1955/1895).

Though Freud abandoned this theory, and indeed did not propose it as a theory of emotions as such, it has now been revised and restated on a full and thoughtful basis by Scheff (1979).[20] Scheff and I both think that a wide range of evidence is appropriate to understanding emotions. Scheff argues from evidence that ranges from intuitions and the processes of psychotherapy to the cross-cultural occurrences of ritual and drama. His argument includes the presentation of transcripts of therapy sessions in which people have experienced emotions in a very intense way. (Cf. also Davis, 1988, who reports a case of catharsis with physiological and subjective mood measures being taken.)

One patient described by Scheff was a 40-year-old man newly separated from his wife and children and feeling tense and lonely. He had been inexpressive emotionally. Between the ages of 16 and 40, he could remember crying only once. He was subject to severe and frequent attacks of migraine and hyperacidity.

In a daylong psychotherapy group he had recounted an experience of his childhood, and felt a lump in the throat but no other feelings. In the group some other members had episodes of crying, and he felt somewhat envious of them. In the evening at the home of a friend, retelling his experiences in the group, he began to cry. This crying lasted about 30 minutes, at first tensely and then in a more relaxed way. After a few minutes' rest, he began shaking and sweating but without feeling fearful, and this too lasted for about 30 minutes. After another brief rest he began to feel angry, and started shouting and cursing but without any sense of what he was angry about. Later still, he began laughing, a deep and relaxed laugh. After about six months, he experienced another period of intense emotional catharsis, after which he felt refreshed and relaxed. For about a year he cried almost daily. As his psychosomatic disturbances gradually lessened, he reported a change from having previously felt neither pleasure nor pain to a life that included highs and lows.

Scheff proposes that normally when a traumatic event occurs a person experiences a distressful emotion. If he or she expresses the emotion while at the same time observing it then the events can be assimilated and their implication remembered for later use. Scheff calls this a cathartic experience. By contrast, if the distressing event or events are too overwhelming, are not balanced by sufficient reassuring events, or if they are somehow kept at a distance, then repression can occur. The events are then not available in memory, or in a different kind of storage malfunction they can be reexperienced involuntarily in flashbacks in a syndrome now called the posttraumatic stress disorder (see Wolf and Mosnaim, 1990, for a review). Scheff argues that when this has occurred the person's subsequent life is affected by behavior becoming rigid, with ill-defined tensions, cognitive distortions, inability to experience positive emotions, and social isolation.

Therapy can be directed to the possibility of creating conditions for catharsis, for creating the correct "distance," as Scheff calls it, from the traumatic event(s). These can then be reexperienced, and the emotion appropriate to them can occur in a cathartic way, with a diminution of symptoms.

Scheff argues that repressed grief can result in diffuse and lasting sadness, headaches, and feelings of hopelessness. Important events appear emotionless. At a proper distance, grief is experienced with tears and sobbing, perhaps lasting over a considerable period. In the normal course of events, emotional experience and expression can be aided by proper societal rituals, for instance, funerals and other bereavement practices. Scheff's account of other emotions is that at the correct distance fear is experienced by shaking and cold sweat, embarrassment by laughter, and anger by hot sweat and laughter.

The phenomena of being unable in some way to assimilate the distress of traumata are important. They occur quite frequently, and they clearly involve emotions in irrational effects. The questions raised are not those of the phenomenology and natural history of such states, which have been described repeatedly during the last 100 years, though with differences in emphasis and detail, but of their explanation and the implications for therapy.

The irrational effects of emotions that Scheff describes are different from those in which emotions are by-products, disturbing influences, or vestiges. The reason is that the irrational effects are not of emotions as such, but of failure to experience emotions fully in relation to their eliciting events. Effects of stress and their relation to emotions are discussed further in Chapters 6 and 9.

Function and the perception of internal disturbance

With Darwin proposing that physiology is the carrier of no longer functional habits, and James (1884) that emotions are perceptions of internal physiological states, it was left to Dewey (1894, 1895) to propose a synthesis. He showed how Darwin's and James's work could be related: If an event elicits habitual actions, we will not feel emotions. It is only when a conflict occurs or an act cannot be completed properly that we experience an emotion. Thus, walking under some cliffs I notice that I am about to be cut off by the tide. I run and do not feel any particular emotion. Only when I find that I have left it too late, and waves are already smashing on the rocks, will I start to feel fear. The physiological activations involved in running, breathing deeply, the heart pumping the blood faster and so on are started up, but the actions they usually accompany cannot occur. The perception of these physiological patterns is the emotion, says Dewey: "There is temporary struggle and partial inhibition. This is reported as *affect*, or emotional seizure" (1895, p. 32). In Darwin's terms, the increased heart rate is without any current purpose because the action cannot be carried out in its customary way. In James's terms, it is the perception of just such bodily events that constitutes the emotion.

A difficulty with this and other lines of reasoning deriving from James is that they fend off the issue of function. James assumed that at least some emotions have arisen in a quasi-accidental way. At first sight, there seems no problem in supposing emotion to include perception of a bodily state. A principle of perception is that perceivers make use of wide ranges of evidence in forming perceptual judgments, and they might therefore use evidence from bodily events.[21] If we ask the question about function, however, a problem with the formulation appears: What serious function might perceptions of bodily disturbances have?

The function of internal perceptions. Tomkins (1979) is admirably direct. He proposed an attentional function. Emotions derived from internal perceptions amplify motivation. They make some aspects salient and important to us. It is this that separates "hot" cognition, in which there is emotional involvement, from "cold" cognition, such as deductive reasoning. The effect of arousal in increasing the intensity of an emotion is, furthermore, one of the few predictions of Schachter and Singer's (1962) theory supported by later experimentation. This seems to be a plausible function for emotions linked with a hypothetical mechanism and open to empirical testing.

A problem still emerges when we ask why amplification of salience, or indeed any other function, should be mediated by organs external to the nervous system.[22] Why not just send neural messages, such as: "This is a specific phenomenological tone; this is to be salient; this motivation is to be amplified"? Routing of emotion signals via organs outside the brain seems quite superfluous. Such a mechanism seems odd and confusing.

The confusion is revealing. The idea that emotions are largely dysfunctional and irrational gives rise to empirical difficulties and theoretical incoherence because function is central to psychological theory. If we make the assumption that emotions have no real function, then theory in any area involving them becomes problematic.

Counterargument to proposals of nonfunctionality. Arguments need to be answered, and the answers to the three kinds of ideas that emotions are without functions are, I think, as follows.

The first such idea, that emotions are noncausal by-products, has not fared well empirically. This is shown by the difficulties of providing evidence in support of James's or of Schachter and Singer's theory, even though these were probably the most influential theories of emotions that there have been. The second idea, that emotions are merely irrational intrusions, is scarcely serious. As such, emotions would be non-evaluative influences on cognition and action. The idea amounts to saying that emotions are disturbing because they arise from disturbing intrusions. Though it is clear from the effects of drugs that there are effects of this kind, to say that all emotions are like this begs almost all the questions about them. The third idea, that emotions are vestiges, is the most serious of the nonfunctional arguments. It is countered as follows: Emotions do indeed have an evolutionary history, but so also do thinking and walking. Darwin tried to persuade his readers of the truth of evolutionary theory and was perhaps overenthusiastic about some of the evidence for it. For those who now accept this theory there is no reason to doubt that emotions may indicate some of the history of our species. At the same time there is no reason why in mammalian evolution emotional expressions should have been shielded from selection pressures to provide a museum of evolutionary fossils. On the contrary, because emotional expressions, and presumably the underlying emotions, are more common among mammals than reflective thought or upright walking, it is overwhelmingly likely that they have important, widespread, and continuing functions.[23]

I will now examine the other side of the antithesis "the heart or the head" to see how far thought is indeed rational, in the sense that is commonly assumed.

What is rationality?

In its usual sense, rationality means possessing reason or being based on reason. If reason implies deriving conclusions by conscious thought, irrationality means decision without due thought or action uninfluenced by thought. If we were to accept such a definition, then to the extent that emotions occur involuntarily, they are irrational. But that is almost tautology. We need a less superficial understanding of rationality. One such is that rationality implies inferences made validly from premises to a conclusion. With this more informative definition the term can be used of beliefs and of actions, and we can ask how far emotions or thinking are rational. I aim to show in this section that although emotions do often lead to irrational actions, thinking also is often irrational. Therefore the idea that thinking is rational in contrast with emotions, which are irrational, is incorrect.

Why the idea of mental logic is implausible

Some influential psychologists, notably Piaget, have argued that thinking depends on the adult mind working by logical principles and that cognitive development is the attainment of these principles. Children do not think logically at first, but in the mature adult: "Reasoning is nothing more than the propositional calculus itself" (Inhelder and Piaget, 1958, p. 305). If this were true, rationality could be understood in terms of whether a belief or conclusion followed from laws of logic. Beliefs derived without following such laws would be irrational.

Johnson-Laird (1983a) has shown that there are considerable difficulties with such a doctrine. For instance, human thinkers, including professional scientists and logicians, often make systematic mistakes, some of which are grossly illogical. There are many demonstrations of this. I will discuss just two series, by Wason, Johnson-Laird, and their collaborators and by Tversky, Kahneman, and their collaborators.[24]

Confirmation bias. In one experiment, Wason (1960) asked university students to consider the three digits "2 4 6" and to find what general rule he had in mind that connected them. To do this subjects had to create new examples of strings of digits, noting down why they offered each example. The experimenter then said whether each example they offered obeyed his general rule. Subjects were to go on proposing examples until they thought they knew what the general rule was. Then they had to write it down, and the experimenter told them if that was what he had in mind.

Most subjects announced at least one incorrect general rule before finding the correct one and 28% failed to discover the rule at all. They proceeded mainly by offering examples that could confirm their current hypothesis. If they thought that the rule was "three successive even numbers in ascending order" they might offer "6 8 10," then "22 24 26," and so on. After generating several such examples they would announce their hypothesis as the general rule. Much less frequently did they offer examples that might disconfirm the hypothesis they were entertaining, as "1 3 7."

The rule that the experimenter had in mind was this: Any three numbers in ascending order. To discover it, subjects typically had both to vary their hypotheses and generate examples that would be contrary to them. In this way one subject offered "10 6 4," giving as her hypothesis "the highest number must go last." After entertaining several hypotheses and generating nine examples, one (just given) negative to the hypothesis she was entertaining, she announced the rule correctly in 17 minutes. The tendency to perseverate on positive instances has been called the confirmation bias: People seldom follow the procedure that Popper (1962) regards as basic to science, of generating instances that might disconfirm hypotheses.

Illogic in selection. In another experiment, Wason (1968) gave subjects four cards labeled as follows.

E   K   4   7

Subjects knew that all the cards had a letter on one side and a number on the other. They were asked to test, by turning over any cards they wished, whether the following rule was true of these four cards:

> If a card has a vowel on one side, then it has an even number on the other side.

The large majority of people, including some professional logicians, thought that "E and 4" or just "E" should be turned over. Both answers are wrong. They involve invalid inferences and are irrational. The correct answer is "E and 7." An odd number on the other side of the "E" card would falsify the rule, as would a vowel on the reverse of the "7" card.

Turning over the "4" card does not test the rule. Although it would apparently confirm the rule if it were found to have a vowel on the other side it would not disconfirm the rule if it had a consonant on the other side, because the rule is silent about the letters that even-numbered cards have on their other side: It allows them to have vowels or consonants. Turning over the "4" card is, therefore, irrelevant to testing the rule. The aspect that seems hard to grasp is that turning over the "7" card is necessary. (If you doubt that the problem is hard, try it on your friends.) The failure of people to select the "7" card seems to be related to the confirmation bias.

When a similar task was put in a more concrete form, people behaved rationally. Johnson-Laird, Legrenzi, and Sonino-Legrenzi (1972) asked subjects to imagine they were post office workers sorting letters. They were given four letters. Two were shown with the flap side visible; one had the flap unsealed, the other had it sealed. The other two had the stamp upward: one was a 5d and the other a 4d stamp, as follows.

sealed   unsealed   5d   4d

Subjects were asked which letters they should turn over to test this rule:

If a letter is sealed it has a 5d stamp on it.

The experiment included a condition similar to that of Wason's (1968), and in this situation the subjects acted as Wason had found. But in the task described in terms of sorting letters, 21 of the 24 subjects behaved rationally. They turned over the sealed letter and the letter with the "4d" stamp visible. It seemed that this was a demonstration of a more general finding that people are often incompetent in tasks posed in an abstract way. Faced with formally similar but concrete tasks, about which they have some knowledge they can think effectively about the problem, and they do much better.

Another experiment in this series showed this was not the whole reason. Manktelow and Evans (1979) asked subjects to choose cards to test the rule:

If I eat beef, then I drink gin.

They found that people were again usually irrational, with their performance being similar to that of the abstract task.

A nice variation on the theme of alcoholic beverages, by Cox and Griggs (1982), is people testing the rule:

If a person is drinking beer, then they are over 18.

Here, as in the Johnson-Laird, Legrenzi, and Sonino-Legrenzi's experiment, people mostly acted rationally. They knew to turn over the "under 18" card.

These experiments have many implications. Three are relevant here. First, if the mind were a logic engine we would expect people to be as good or better at abstract tasks as concrete ones, as one would assume that the abstract form is closer to symbols that a mental logic engine would work on. Second, it seems that people's actions are being triggered by elements in the situation in much the same way that Darwin's action of leaping backward was triggered by the snake behind the plate glass. The abstract situation is not enough to trigger the selection of the "7" card, but the letter-sorting scenario does trigger the selection of the envelope showing the "4d" stamp. Third, moral or legal propriety seems to be part of the eliciting condition for selecting the "4d" stamp with its implication of defrauding the post office and the "under 18" card with its implication of underage drinking, though moral issues are not usually thought to have much to do with rationality.

It seems better, therefore, to describe thinking as drawing inferences from a mental model[25] in the service of goals rather than as applying formal logic to problems.

Reasoning about probability. When people are reasoning about probability, Kahneman and Tversky have shown that people's intuitions are as bad as for logic. Although mathematical methods work well in this area, people use heuristics that are rather like rules of thumb. Several of these have been identified (see, e.g., Kahneman, Slovic & Tversky, 1982).

THE REPRESENTATIVENESS HEURISTIC. People are asked about sequence of coin tosses (where H is a head and T is a tail). They regard the sequence HTHHTT as random, but not HHHTTT or HHHHTH. People see patterns with alternating heads and tails as representative of randomness, and expect even short sequences to have equal numbers of each outcome. In thinking about coin tossing, or the sequence of boys and girls in a family, we underestimate the number of runs there will be. The gambler's fallacy, that if a roulette wheel has just come up with a run of reds, then it will be black next time is another failure of correct intuition. In fact, the probability stays the same on each spin, unaffected by previous outcomes. Our rule of thumb for randomness is based on a representative stereotype, which is not accurate.

The representativeness heuristic leads to other mistakes. Imagine Linda who is "31 years old, single, outspoken, and very bright. She majored in philosophy. As a student she was deeply concerned with issues of discrimination and social justice and also participated in anti-nuclear demonstrations" (Kahneman, Slovic & Tversky, 1982, p. 92). The experimenters ask subjects to consider statements, including

> Linda is a psychiatric social worker,
> Linda is a bank teller,
> Linda is a bank teller and is active in the feminist movement . . .

Subjects were asked to rank eight such statements, from the most likely to the least likely. More than 80% of people, including those who were sophisticated at statistics, said that it was more likely that Linda was a bank teller and a feminist than just a bank teller, even though the number of women who are bank tellers must exceed the number who are both bank tellers and feminists. Kahneman and Tversky say the problem is one of assessing probabilities of known frequencies. People are misled by the information about Linda at college that is entirely irrelevant. They use it to summon up a stereotype and then apply this inappropriately to a problem on which it has no bearing.

THE AVAILABILITY HEURISTIC. Further biases can be discovered by asking subjects questions like the following: Is the letter *R* more likely to occur in the first position or the third in English words? In response to this, 105 out of 152 subjects said the first position was more common. It is not.

In another experiment subjects were asked to estimate within 5 seconds the size of the number produced by

$$8 \times 7 \times 6 \times 5 \times 4 \times 3 \times 2 \times 1$$

The mean estimate of 87 subjects was 2,259. Another group of 114 subjects was asked to estimate the size of the same sequence in reverse order. The mean estimate was 512.

Kahneman and Tversky argue that in both cases the biases occur because some data are more easily available than others. More words beginning with a particular letter come to mind than words with a particular letter in the third place. And in 5 seconds, subjects estimating the product of the sequence starting with $8 \times 7 \times 6$ will have seen that 56×6 and so on is going to be a big number. Those starting with $1 \times 2 \times 3$ may get up to $2 \times 3 = 6$ and perhaps to $6 \times 4 = 24$ and guess that the number is not going to get big.

Interpretations of irrationality. There are two general views about such experiments. The first, which may be tempting, is to marvel a little at how silly people are. In reading the studies we are let into secrets and it is hard not to feel superior.

More thoughtfully though, rather than seeing such instances as indicating that the brains of some or all of us have been miswired, we can see them as a clue, that our intuitive theories are better at some things than others. Where we are not good we should use cultural prostheses like mathematics. Among the areas in which our naive psychology is not good are generating potentially refuting hypotheses (the issue in Wason's 1960 experiment), formal logic (the paradigm for Wason's 1968 experiment), and probability theory (the reference point for many of Kahneman and Tversky's experiments). We also, as Nisbett and Ross (1980) point out, tend to rely on information that is vivid rather than properly representative. In such areas it has required clever people working over generations and preoccupied with a narrow range of problems to invent the necessary pieces of theory. Then the rest of us can carefully learn the procedures that will allow us to reason validly in the areas of scientific experimental method, formal logic, probability theory, sampling theory, and so on. Just as pencils and paper are prostheses for our memory, and telescopes extend our senses, such pieces of theory are cultural prostheses that we can adopt and add to our implicit theories if they become important for us. They will allow us to think in ways that we have not been genetically adapted to. Without the cultural learning, we can be irrationally triggered into wrong responses.

Criteria for rationality of belief

Wason (1983) has considered Hudson's (1980) view of criteria for rational belief. Hudson says that an incomplete set of criteria for rationality of a belief, though not a definition of rationality, is the following:

1. Self-consistency – its parts must not contradict each other
2. Evidential corroboration – it must be supported by relevant evidence
3. Held open-mindedly – the person must be willing to surrender a belief if a good reason to do so is found
4. Conforming to a rational system of belief

Hudson says that these do not necessarily exhaust the criteria for rationality, and that the fourth is different from the others. It describes societal procedures that regulate what counts as making sense and the ways in which assent is or is not given to beliefs in a specific society.

Baron (1985) comes to a similar conclusion in more detailed terms. Deriving his approach from that of Dewey (1933), he proposes four phases in goal-directed thinking:

1. Search for possibilities
2. Search for goals

3. Search for evidence
4. Use of evidence

All these require search procedures, and Baron has shown how the data in which human thinkers have irrational biases can be characterized as terminating search inappropriately, typically too soon. This applies to the demonstrations of bias by Wason and to those by Kahneman and Tversky.

Rationality, therefore, does not imply adherence to any specific static criterion like logic. It refers to an ideal to aim at, and to the virtues of certain procedures for approaching valid beliefs. Characterizing rationality more specifically is difficult. The fact that we listen to each other's arguments, however, suggests that the goal of rationality may be approached. This also points to perhaps the most neglected fact in this area, that rationality is a social not an individual phenomenon. When one person gives up the search on a problem, others can continue. When one scientist is (irrationally) convinced of the truth of a hypothesis, another can suggest refutations. As one set of people imagine that this time the roulette wheel will do as they hope, others can search for principles of probability theory. If any procedure had the quality of rationality, it would be the social activity of critical discussion, not the private activity of individual thought.[26]

Thus, irrationality is not especially characteristic of emotions. Many examples of irrationality occur in thinking, which can be quite unemotional. When thinking emotionally, people sometimes terminate search too quickly, or fail to consider alternatives, just as they do when thinking unemotionally. Perhaps future research will show that premature termination of search is more marked under the press of some emotions in some situations.

This brings us to a more productive contrast of emotional and unemotional thinking. When experiencing an emotion it is typically the individual who has to generate an immediate practical solution to a problem that is new to him or her on that occasion. By contrast, when reasoning unemotionally we can often draw on cultural experience and a range of aids. Thinking that succeeds in being rational is largely based on defined and soluble problems in limited domains, involving skill or technical considerations, and it is assisted by methods available in our culture. When problems are new to us we often get them wrong, if indeed they have correct solutions. Emotional thinking may seem more irrational than nonemotional thinking because it is often applied to insoluble problems.

Rationality as effective action

A second way of describing rationality is in terms of effective action. In social science the idea of action that efficiently achieves an end corresponds closely to the idea of rationality. This is, of course, exactly equivalent to the idea of *techne*, which is rational to the extent that it is based on reliable *episteme* and that it efficiently achieves a defined goal.

Here Weber (1968/1922) has given the kind of definition generally accepted by economists and sociologists. Behavior is "instrumentally rational" when conducted according to expectations of behavior of objects and people, with these expectations being used as preconditions and means for the attainment of calculated ends. Behavior is "value-rational" when determined by a conscious belief in the value for its own sake of some ethical, aesthetic, religious, or other behavior independently of prospects of success. Weber goes on to say that other types of social action, namely, affectual action, determined by an actor's specific emotions or feeling states, and traditional action, determined by ingrained habit, are often on the borderline, or on the other side, of what can be considered rationally oriented action.

In cognitive terms, Weber's suggestions as to the nature of rationality imply acting according to a plan, either successfully to achieve a specific goal or so that the action itself has some desirable characteristics.

Human error. There are many studies of irrational action. Biases comparable to those of representativeness and availability discovered in research on reasoning are present and seem to be major causes of error. As with errors of reasoning, there is a large literature.[27] I will present here just a small set of studies, mainly from the work of James Reason.

Errors can be divided into slips in which an intention miscarries in action and mistakes where a person has a wrong understanding. There are many ways of studying errors. Questionnaires can be used (Broadbent et al., 1982). Perhaps more telling for understanding the structure of action, examples can be collected by incident diaries (Reason & Mycielska, 1982) and taxonomies can be created to cover them (Norman, 1981). Norman's theory of action derived in this way includes the idea that first an intention is formed, then procedures (such as those illustrated in Figure 2) are selected and made ready. Then they are triggered by specific perceptual patterns. Errors can occur in intention formation, in incorrect selection, or in triggering by an inappropriate event.

In experimental studies manipulation of conditions can show how errors can be induced, as in the study of Lucas (1984, cited by Reason, 1984), who interrupted his subjects and thereby induced place-losing slips as they recited multiplication tables. An experiment by Jenkins and Ward (1965) to demonstrate mistakes rather than slips comes close in spirit to Wason's (1960) finding of the confirmation bias in reasoning. In this study, people were asked if they could press some buttons to switch on two signal lights, and if they succeeded to say how they did it. In fact, the lights came on independently of anything the subjects did, but so long as they came on fairly often subjects always said they had found out how to control the lights by pressing buttons. In other words, subjects attended to the absolute frequency of the desired events, and did not think that to find out whether their actions were causally effective they should compare the frequency of the desired event following their button presses with its frequency when buttons were not pressed. As in Wason's (1960) experiment, they did not consider alternative hypotheses. Jenkins told me (personal communication) that when he was running one of the experiments in this series he thought that one subject had discovered that the lights were independent of his actions because, in contrast to most subjects, who pressed buttons more and more frequently, this one pressed the buttons less frequently as the experiment progressed, finally ceasing to press them altogether and sitting with his arms folded. Jenkins grew anxious that as the experiment ended he would be angrily abused by the man about how he had been hoodwinked into thinking that the buttons had anything to do with the lights – but no: The man said, "I see. You turn the lights on by doing nothing."

Perhaps most dramatically case studies of serious accidents can be analyzed. Though this method is post hoc, and therefore potentially more misleading than experimental studies, it illustrates how irrational action is a very practical concern. I shall briefly give three cases of accidents. Two were based on slips of action; in the other, there was something much more like a mistake in understanding.

In the first case Reason (1984) reports an accident in which six people were killed. A double-decker bus in South Wales had its top deck sheared off as the driver tried to pass under a low bridge. As he said at the inquest, he normally drove a single-decker bus. Psychologically the important feature is that a highly skilled or habitual action can be triggered inappropriately if the ordinary conditions for its elicitation change. Norman (1981) calls this a capture error because the more habitual pattern captures an action sequence that should be under the control of a less habitual pattern.

Perhaps, however, the bus driver's case was atypically simple. In many accidents multiple factors contribute, so we should examine this more complex type of occurrence too. In the second case (Reason, 1984), the worst disaster in the history of air travel, the fundamental error seems similar to that of the bus driver, but it was indeed surrounded by other possible contributory factors, such as delays, a bomb scare, a diversion with an unscheduled landing at Tenerife Airport, which had no ground radar, and fog. The pilot of one of the Boeing 747s involved in the crash started his takeoff when he was given permission to fly at a particular course and height. An accident report noted that this pilot's principal job was as chief training officer of KLM. As such, he habitually worked with a simulator. Although he also had to do routine flying, on this occasion he had not flown for 12 weeks. In the simulator, runway and takeoff permission were always given at the same time as course and height permission. At Tenerife, clearance to take off was not given at the same time as the course and height information. In the fog the aircraft gathered speed for takeoff – and crashed into a Pan-Am Boeing 747 on the runway.

The heart rates even of experienced airline pilots are raised above normal during takeoffs and landings (Smith, 1967), and in this case stress may have been increased by the fog, delays, and other factors. On the one hand, the KLM pilot seems to have committed a completely typical capture error of the kind that occurs frequently when conditions change even when there is no suggestion whatever of stress. But there is also a possibility that stress made it more likely that he would forget to wait for permission to take off. Reason (1988) concludes that although stress may increase the extent of irrational biases that contribute to such slips, overall it is an infrequent contributor to their occurrence.

Slips of action range in seriousness from pouring orange juice instead of milk into one's coffee, to surgical operations being done on the wrong leg, to accidents that kill hundreds or thousands of people. No doubt they occur proportionately more frequently in settings like the kitchen where their implications are trivial than in situations such as hospitals, transport, chemical plants, and the like where procedures have been constructed to reduce their frequency. Whenever and wherever humans make them, however, nonemotional slips of action are just as involuntary as those in which emotions prompt actions.

Finally, let us consider another kind of error, which is not so much a slip as it is a mistake. Though again the analysis is post hoc, and although as in the Tenerife disaster many factors contributed, including mistakes of managers and planners, the immediate causes of the Chernobyl nuclear power plant disaster in 1986 were mistakes of the plant's operators. Reason (1987) describes some of the errors contributing to the accident, which happened during an experiment to test a new safety feature.

The feature was designed to bridge a 3-minute period when power for the reactor's controls might have to be supplied from an alternative source if the power supply from the national grid failed, and at that moment the plant had to be shut down in an emergency. From the time they were switched on, the standby diesel generators took about 3 minutes to generate sufficient power, so the idea was that during this period electricity for the reactor's controls could be supplied directly from the plant's turbine generators as they freewheeled to a stop. There was just a limited time available to test the new safety equipment, and the plan was for the operators to run the plant at 25% of full power and to collaborate with a team of electrical engineers who would test the power generation of the turbines freewheeling and the new mechanism they had built.

The reactor had what is known as a positive void coefficient, with the implication that it would tend to run away with itself at low power settings. Because of this, operation below 20% of full power was forbidden. To reduce power to conduct the experiment the operator switched off the automatic controls and tried to drive the plant manually. He overshot the 25% output target, and the power went down to 1%. After about half an hour's struggle with the controls, the operators were able to run the plant at a power output of 7%. Reason remarks that this was in its most unstable range, and at this point the test experiment should have been abandoned.

The next move by the operators, ignoring yet another regulation forbidding the plant to be run with more than six cooling pumps operating, was to switch on all eight of these pumps, perhaps with some intuitive idea of providing the maximum core cooling during the experiment. Reason notes that this showed a profound misunderstanding of the reactor. Its consequence was that the increased water flow absorbed more neutrons and automatically caused a control system to withdraw more of the control rods. This in turn made the plant yet more unstable, running as if it were without brakes. In struggling to control the plant while at the same time continuing to establish conditions for the test experiment, the operators switched off yet more automatic safety mechanisms. (Reason gives more details of the sequence of events.) Twenty minutes after the eight pumps were started two explosions occurred – and people are still dying from their effects.

Part of the interest in errors is the light they shed on the theory of action. Taking up just three related points relevant to the analyses of rationality in this chapter: First, capture errors are slips of action that are similar to errors prompted by the availability heuristic described by Kahneman and Tversky. They occur because a highly practiced sequence of action is readily available. Second, many slips are triggered by patterns that are similar but not identical to those for which they were designed, and so their analysis is scarcely different from that of the fearful impulse reported earlier in this chapter, when a snake struck at the plate-glass window at the zoo, and Darwin leapt backward. In both cases, then, the automatic action is triggered by a pattern designed for simplicity and that underspecifies the necessary conditions for triggering (Reason, 1986), so that if circumstances change a slightly different pattern will trigger the action. Third, in the Chernobyl errors, the availability heuristic with partial pattern matching again seems to be at work: We see a picture of operators driving the reactor using intuitions readily available perhaps from the analogy of driving a car. The operators seemed to think that less power made control easier. Here quite inappropriate knowledge was being applied, like a theory being laid onto evidence that it does not fit with that vigor that makes disconfirming evidence invisible and that ignores any possibility of alternative theories. Notice, too, that in the analysis of errors of action, though stresses and deadlines sometimes contribute to accidents, the analysis of what goes wrong is primarily in the inappropriate use of skilled technical knowledge, not typically in emotions causing irrationality.

Could the confirmation bias be advantageous? We have seen from Wason (1960), from Jenkins and Ward (1965), and from a possible contribution to the Chernobyl disaster that the bias of seeking only confirmations of a current hypothesis occurs in most people and is potentially dangerous. Why, then, does it exist?

If we look at the problem from an evolutionary perspective, it seems that rather than being an unfortunate mental defect, there may be advantages for a mechanism that continues looking for evidence that will allow a plan to continue once started. There are considerable costs in interrupting a current plan and starting up a new one, and in an uncertain environment, with a range of interpretations for many perceptual phenomena, single, apparent disconfirmations may not mean much. On average over the period when these mechanisms have evolved, the costs of interruptions may have outweighed benefits. What appears as a defect in rational thinking may be a positive attribute of planning that allows us to concentrate on what we are doing, looking for positive information that will allow us to continue, rather than taking negative evidence as demanding an interruption and the inefficiency of starting up some quite different plan. In evolution backtracking may have been selected against – hence the irritation of an interruption when we are engaged in some plan, and hence a built-in bias that makes it difficult to consider large-scale alternatives at each step.

Situations where a single contrary indication to a scheme would be significant may have been rare until the controlled observations of science were developed. And, until the power of technology made some mistakes very dangerous, effects of the confirmation bias may have been less salient. Indeed most such effects are trivial still. It is hard to see that backtracking in response to every disconfirmation in the course of ongoing action would be advantageous. Instead, prioritizing specific kinds of disconfirmation was an important step in the history of science allowing the invention of a way of thinking that, as a cultural prosthesis, extends our innate capacities.

Why humans rarely attain rationality

Just as people can hold irrational beliefs it is clear that human plans often go wrong. If there is a kind of reasoning that can construct perfect plans, or a mechanism that can enact them without error, we humans do not possess it. There are two main reasons for this. First, as discussed in Chapter 1, our models of the ordinary world are imperfect. Within delimited domains they can be more or less useful for specific purposes. But even here there is a hint of paradox: To be rational implies not being necessarily right, but being prepared to be wrong. A rational belief, like a scientific theory, is corrigible. Often there is a contradiction between using a mental model rationally and believing it to be perfect. Second, many human plans serve multiple goals, so there are potential conflicts. Even the ideas of optimizing or of compromise can become problematic.

The general idea of reason can only be rather loosely indicated, perhaps in terms of what information is necessary to a mental model for particular problems or plans. Reasoning is not governed by any mechanism or process that is certain to discover truth independently of context or to construct perfect plans for all situations. Rather, reasoning and planning depend on making models that are more or less fallible and mirror more or less well some specific aspects of the world.

Because of our uncertain knowledge and multiple goals, many of the problems we face have no fully rational solutions. Emotions are a biological solution to this problem. This question has also been treated by De Sousa (1980, 1987), who has come to a similar conclusion to mine.[28] He says that people are somewhere between biological machines, like ants, and purely rational beings, like angels, both of which are characterized by complete determinacy. As he points out, the issues of salience, and of whether one line of action seems more pressing than another, are not susceptible to logic. The same is true for choosing strategies for existing goals: One could act to minimize losses, or to maximize gains, but there is no rational way in general to know which is better in all situations. As De Sousa says, we could even make up a principle to determine strategy for these problems: "But no [such] principle can claim to be dictated by rationality alone" (1980, p. 136).

Economically irrational action. Apart from issues such as choosing among incompatible preferences, there are actions prompted by emotion that seem against self-interest. They might broadly be called economic. There have been several treatments of this phenomenon. In a recent one, Frank (1988) explicitly labels certain kinds of action as emotional, points out that they cannot be assimilated easily to any straightforward view of individual instrumental rationality, and then goes on to argue that under a particular kind of interpersonal rubric these actions could be seen as sensible after all. Frank proceeds by a series of thought experiments. Suppose, for instance, you have been wronged financially by someone, for example, by buying a service that was defective. You may take this person to court, even though this action will cost you more than you could hope to get back. Evidently you are driven by an angry emotion in the pursuit of fairness or of getting even, even though in terms of self-interest you will be worse off if you pursue the case than if you let it drop. Or consider why if self-interest is what motivates us, should we not terminate a sexual relationship whenever a person comes along who seems better than the one we are with? Frank provides further examples of acting against our apparent self-interest, giving money secretly to charities, returning property that has been found, helping people in ways that expose us to danger or expense, and so forth.

Frank's answer to the apparent irrationality of all such types of action is that the terms of the immediate self-interest model of rationality of the kind usually assumed by economists and other social scientists are too narrow. They specify only what might be rational for an individual's goal if the incident is isolated from any other social context and occurs on a single occasion. The real issue, he argues, is one of commitment over time and over a number of potential occasions. If person A knows that person B is committed to fairness, or to making sure of retribution for wrongdoing, then person A will be unwilling to risk taking advantage by offering a shoddy product or engaging in sharp financial practice. Comparably, if person A is in the marriage market (here the economic metaphor intrudes yet further), then person B will be more attractive with a reputation for emotional commitment than for mere opportunism.

Putting the matter in slightly different terms, in this book I have considered the issue of acting without a complete model of the relevant aspect of the world. Frank's point is related: When buying some kinds of product or when choosing a sexual partner, we act with very incomplete knowledge. People with whom we interact can make our interaction easier by signaling their commitment to principles. If these principles are then violated, emotions do indeed occur, quite appropriately, and may drive behavior in ways that cannot be explained by momentary individual self-interest. Thus, once again, though from a different angle, we see that it is not so much that emotions are irrational, but that they are means of managing situations where no fully rational solution is possible. These issues of long-term commitment to recurring episodes of planning that involve other people is discussed in more detail in Chapter 4.

Reason versus emotion: a false dichotomy

The assumption that emotions are inherently irrational and nonemotional thinking is inherently rational is a wrong distinction. This particular folk theory is false. If my analyses are correct, the dichotomy of reason versus emotion dissolves. Rationality is always hard to attain. It needs knowledge, experimentation, learning of skills, time, the opportunity to make mistakes, cultural prostheses, and the possibility of social interaction and critical discussion; and it is only attained in limited domains.

Both emotional and nonemotional thinking typically relate to plans of action that are constructed and enacted with respect to goals. Although people caught up in emotions often behave irrationally, this is not well described by saying that their behavior has come under the control of some nonrational process, or is influenced by primitive regions of the brain, whereas at other times a cortical logic engine makes rational decisions. Occasionally, processes occur in which, for instance, the cognitive system is influenced by drugs or chemical imbalances. Usually, however, an emotional state relates to a meaningful event that elicited it. It is characterized by (1) a limited set of goals becoming salient, (2) some of these goals being linked with default plans that have been selected and consolidated during evolutionary or individual history, (3) unequal distribution of attention to the available evidence relevant to these plans, and (4) the possibility of invoking new plans, which like any new plans will be liable to error.

If we leave aside instances of emotional states being induced by drugs and the like, we can compare actions prompted by emotions and those directed by unemotional thinking. Even when an emotional action does not seem voluntarily intended, or does not achieve an advantageous end, it is explicable in terms of the goals and the knowledge embedded in the procedures that direct action. Exactly these considerations are at stake in explaining unemotional thinking.

In an emotional action irresolvable conflicts may be present, and some goals may even be unconscious. Some plans may have been compiled, and the knowledge embodied in them may be procedural, not declarative. They may have been socioculturally or biologically determined and they may be triggered inappropriately. Emotional action is more often irrational than thinking in the service of a technical problem. But there is nothing in any of this that makes the mental processes of emotions necessarily less rational than deliberative thinking or skilled action. In deliberative thinking and skilled action, too, processes by which inferences are drawn are unconscious and sometimes involuntary. Here, too, mental models may be inadequate, search may terminate too soon, decisions or action sequences may be triggered inappropriately, and so on.

Any full explanation of an action refers to goals and tacit or explicit knowledge on which it is based. Rationality depends on lack of goal conflict and on how appropriately knowledge bases are used. This holds both in emotional and nonemotional instances.

Replacing the dichotomy of reason versus emotion. There is, therefore, a relation of emotions to irrationality: It is that emotions are biological adaptations to problems that have no fully rational solution. So there will be differences between thinking under the influence of an emotion and thinking when enacting a technical plan or solving an intellectual problem. In one case an emotion mode has cognitive properties adapted to imperfect knowledge, to possibilities of goal conflicts, and to coordinating action with other people. In the other case we can sometimes hope for fully rational solutions.

We can, and certainly should, strive for rationality. But we humans attain it fully only in circumstances that correspond quite closely to the technical. Rationality can sometimes be attained in limited stationary domains, as in certain branches of mathematics, in games like chess, or in technical plans such as those of a car-assembly robot.[29] These circumstances are hardly ever those in which a lone thinker comes de novo to a rational conclusion. They are ones in which cultural elaborations have taken place over years or centuries until rational modes of thought have been perfected, their properties explored by many people, and passed on by education. Rationality implies the possibility of having explored the implications of all possible mistakes.

The idea of planning helps shift the emphasis from the eighteenth-century idea of men as rational beings to people as cognitive beings. Cognitive theory holds that an actor acts from knowledge. We are now more aware that knowledge may be fallible and that much of it is tacit and not available to consciousness.

To refer to irrationality is to imply that, from some perspective other than the actor's, a thought or action is questionable, and therefore that a knowledge base, or the actor's use of it, could be improved, goals changed, or an action sequence replanned. Rationality is not a procedure and not a property of thought. It is a process of converging on solutions or, alternatively, a standard by which thought or action can be judged if one knows a great deal about the domain in question, a standard to which thought or action can aspire.

Overcoming limitations of individuals

The potential irrationality of individual thought points to methods by which limitations may be overcome. In this section I briefly examine some of these methods as a counterpoint to the analysis of errors of individual thinking and to show how they can augment simple planning, thus solving some of the limitations of simple plans discussed in Chapter 1. There are two parts. The first is about building individual skills by learning from mistakes and cultural learning, and the second about the social arrangements that extend the capacities of the individual.

The construction of skills

Thinking about thinking must take into account the finite resources, the time course, and the multiple mistakes of thinking. Somehow the idea has spread that clever people think quickly without mistakes. Whistler is said to have replied when challenged about whether he asked 200 guineas for two days' labor on a painting: "No I ask it for the knowledge of a lifetime" (Seitz, 1913, p. 40). He knew that the acquisition of knowledge takes a long time.

Habits were the culprits in Darwin's analysis of why some actions seemed to be without function. But they are members of the same family as skills, which we prize among our most useful assets. Both may be called "automatisms," the term used by Bryan and Harter (1897) in their study of the acquisition of skill in telegraph operators. They reported that operators constructed automatic procedures first for letters, then for words, then for phrases. The importance these authors attached to acquisition of skilled habits can be gauged from the ringing maxims in their discussion: *"There is no freedom except through automatism"* (p. 369; emphasis in original); "Automatism is not genius, but it is the hands and feet of genius" (p. 375).

Automatisms have two faces: Just as they release attention and consciousness for other things, they also prompt actions that are inappropriate in some circumstances. They are the bases for the expressions that Darwin called emotional because they can seem superfluous, and they also account for many slips of action. In both cases an action can be released by patterns from a wider range than triggering recognition devices should ideally accept. Habits may be compiled genetically or individually. The advantages are comparable, and so also are the opportunities they afford for irrational actions. There is no reason for treating emotional expressions that Darwin studied in a fundamentally different way from errors of skilled performance. Instincts, habits, and skills confer advantages in efficiency and speed, but they have a price in breeding the possibility of errors.

The generation of new action sequences is slow, laborious, and uncertain.[30] It may need resources that are not readily available, and assembly of fragments in new ways. We may refer to this as thinking, creativity, development, or research. Research takes much longer than one thinks, even after one has taken into account that it will take longer than one thinks. Only afterward do we see it could have been done quicker, with fewer mistakes.

A computer program that learns from mistakes. Sussman's (1975) computational project explores the process of compiling skills by learning from mistakes. His program builds simulated structures of toy building blocks with a simulated robot arm. It starts with a set of primitive actions like picking up blocks and putting them down. It demonstrates some of the difficulties that occur when trying to execute an unskilled plan. For instance, if the program tries to pick up a block that has another block on top of it, it discovers an error because the constraints of its robot arm make this impossible. It must first remove the upper block and place it on the table. Then it can pick up the lower one.[31]

Sussman's program is an exploration of how to write a program that will learn about issues of this kind, of establishing preconditions for certain actions before others can be performed, of sequencing actions, and of conditions that might cause conflict with other goals or subgoals. To learn from its mistakes (bugs), the program writes new pieces of itself, which Sussman calls patches. Sussman argues that in order to improve its building skills, the program must have knowledge of the effects of actions in the blocks' world, a library of programming techniques, and a way of classifying bugs so that these can suggest the kind of patch that might work.

Most importantly, the program must have not one but two accounts of the relevant actions. One is the sequence of operations, stacking blocks in a particular order. This is the account that is usually recognized as a computer program. It corresponds to the terminal nodes, the actions, of a plan tree. The second component is a parallel set of statements about the goal each action is to achieve. A plan is the action sequence plus a statement of the goal of each action.

In a tree diagram of a plan, such as Figures 1 and 2, goals are depicted as higher level nodes. But in the usual computer program these statements occur as names of variables and procedures, as comments, in documentation, or only in the mind of the programmer. None of these is of any significance to the computer (cf. Searle, 1980, 1990). For a program to be a real plan, or for it to understand a mistake and write a better piece of itself, it must be able to compare the effects of each action with an intention. This means that the intentions must be explicitly represented in code that is parallel to that which specifies actions. This parallel code, of goals, is as important a part of a plan as is the sequence of action specifications. It is essential if a plan is ever to be modified.

In order to install a patch in a piece of program, Sussman found that he had to invent a mode of testing a rewritten piece of program, which he calls "careful mode." In this mode, each step of the program is tried out to see whether any action undoes any preconditions for the whole plan, or if it violates any of the subgoals specified in the parallel code, that the whole performance will require. This is a slow and laborious activity.

Human thought when it occurs in research is like planning in careful mode. How successful it is depends on how good the theory is on which it is based and what eventualities can be foreseen. What typically happens in research is that simulation procedures involving pens, paper, calculators, and so on are applied. Procedures are tried out one at a time in an equivalent of the environment in which the research will be run. They can then be debugged before being assembled into an action sequence for a full study. The whole process of doing research in protected environments like laboratories corresponds to running in careful mode before action in the ordinary world is undertaken, or until a result is offered for criticism by other researchers. During the process the person involved becomes more skilled. She or he acquires a better model of both the substantive and methodological issues.

Cultural transmission of skills. Culture allows us to pass on skills developed by an individual to others. Scientific procedures and concepts, for instance, are learned by carefully drawing lessons from historical examples. Newton's understanding of the motions of planets had taken more than 2,000 years of European culture and the conduct of many discussions, of thinking through many errors, the writing of many books, and the application of many minds to the problem. Newton modestly wrote to Hooke in 1676: "If I have seen further it is by standing on the shoulders of giants" (Anthony, 1960, p. 209). A result of the cultural transmission of ideas is that when an intellectual giant does appear, we can all stand on her or his shoulders. Social transmission often also occurs in protected environments like classrooms and libraries, and it enables thinking to move toward rationality, that is, well adaptedness to particular problems.

In the domain of action rather than declarative knowledge, training allows actions to be rehearsed. Military training, for instance, drills people in certain actions and in giving obedience in the service of goals formulated higher up in the hierarchy. In battle, junctures are reached where individual thought is inappropriate. The trouble with training, however, is that one tends only to practice specific procedures. When it is time for these procedures to be connected, disorganization again occurs, as military history testifies.[32]

Supplementing intuitive theory. In this subsection on constructing skills I must return to the question raised at the beginning of Chapter 2, about our irrationality as intuitive theorists. Perhaps the proper alternative is thoroughgoing adherence to nonintuitive scientific method, and using only the reliable knowledge that it provides as a guide to action. Nisbett and Ross (1980) raise the same question. They come, as I do, to the conclusion that we should build on human intuitive methods rather than despair of them. They propose that this should be done by recognizing sources of human error – that we are not good at judging covariation, that we can be misled by vivid data that are easily available to us, that we hold on to our beliefs despite refuting evidence – and by being reading to substitute scientific judgments where appropriate. They also point out that mere scientific veracity is often not the issue, both because it may cost more to use scientific methods than would be lost by making a wrong decision and because decisions that affect action must often be reconciled with many goals, social and personal.

In my judgment, Nisbett and Ross do not go quite far enough. Behind their analysis I detect an assumption that for any decision there is a best procedure, often in everyday life an intuitive one, but sometimes, particularly with important decisions, one based on scientifically collected evidence. The point emerges in their discussion of cost-effectiveness of decisions. They imagine a game contestant who must choose between two closed boxes, one containing a $10,000 check and one an old shoe. They say: "There are some decisions that, although of critical importance, have outcomes that are unknowable in principle" (p. 279). In this case the contestant should flip a coin. My argument of this chapter is that they understate the case. Their game-show example is exotic, and implies rarity, but decisions with outcomes that are unknowable in principle are very common. It is not just that the intuitive scientist may not make the best decision, but that for many problems in a world that is not knowable even statistically, and with incommensurable goals, we often do not even know if there could be a best decision-making procedure.

Social augmentation of limited abilities

Education is just one example of the cultural enhancement of rationality. In general, social arrangements allow us to overcome limitations of individuals by constructing joint plans in which agency and resources are shared among individuals, as well as between individuals and artifacts such as computers. Hutchins (1985) has proposed that by distributed cognition we can overcome some of the biases of individual thinking. So, individually we seek confirmatory evidence, and do not notice evidence that might disconfirm it. In distributed thinking, however, if one person presses forward with a hypothesis, another can act as critic.[33]

Hutchins discusses natural science as a social procedure for making inferences from evidence and attaining reliable knowledge of the kind on which technical plans can be based. It is often assumed that individual scientists are clever and think rationally. Maybe they are. But the procedure of science could not be accomplished individually. Hypotheses and conclusions of scientific research are offered to a community of others who offer counterevidence, criticisms, and alternative theories. Science is not a procedure of individual rationality. It is a social procedure, based on publication so that ideas become open to critical commentary from people who may be interested in disconfirming hypotheses, who may see the evidence in different ways, who may compare procedures with others that have been previously found to have particular properties, and so on. It is a process of comparison and dialectic, as Aristotle described.

Hutchins points out that distributing cognition among several agents may improve rationality by increasing the creative generation of models and by allowing people to take up different roles, proposer and critic, rather than the more difficult task of having to switch between roles. Thus the confirmation bias is not typically overcome by the individual learning to collect evidence that will disconfirm a hypothesis. People who have the goal of discrediting the hypothesis are very good at producing such evidence, so rationality is achieved by taking notice of their arguments and by social organizations that make this likely.

Contrary to the idea that rationality is an inherent feature of adult human thinking, we might say it is usually achieved by social interaction. Hutchins points out that another cultural invention, the trial with adversarial lawyers and a jury who do not take part in the public discussion but who make the decision, again instantiates thinking with several roles. It guards against those biases and mistakes that are dramatically portrayed in individually based systems of prosecution such as the witch hunt.[34]

The division of labor. I wish to make a proposal that is scarcely new but is fundamental for questions of both rationality and emotion. Yerkes said: "One chimpanzee is no chimpanzee" (Lorenz, 1967/1963, p. 89). The sentiment is true also of humans. Individual humans are not effective. It is only in cooperation, by means of culture, by shared plans, that the human species has been successful. We cooperate in plans ranging from sexual relationships, child rearing, and sharing of food to construction of cities and civilizations. In other words, much human cognition is inherently social.

In Chapter 1, I proposed the idea of a simple plan, by which a single agent performs a sequence of actions to achieve a defined goal. Such plans are essentially technical. Technical plans are, however, seldom as simple as I implied.

If they are performed by a single agent, the procedures typically will have been invented, debugged, and developed by others, then passed on by cultural transmission to the current agent. Also, the preconditions of one plan are typically the products of another. As Plato pointed out, the stones to which the *techne* of the mason are applied are those produced by the *techne* of quarrying. Plans of commercial production are separated into procedures that achieve subgoals, each performed by a separate agent. Adam Smith (1970/1776), in his treatise on the idea that wealth is created by the division of labor, gives the example of the manufacture of pins needing 18 distinct procedures, which "in some manufacturies are all performed by distinct hands, though in others the same man will sometimes perform two or three of them" (p. 110). It is hard to think of any commonly used article not produced by division of labor.

Smith proposed that becoming skilled at one operation and not having to stop and start up new procedures, including the preparation of preconditions, are among the reasons why division of labor is efficient and the key to producing wealth in modern nations. He explained that when all the workers exerted themselves in a pin factory he studied they could turn out 48,000 pins a day, equivalent to the ten workers making 4,800 pins each. If one man had to do all the operations himself, and without having been educated to the business, Smith declares, he would scarcely be able to make 20 pins, perhaps not even one.

Many, perhaps most, human plans involve distributed agency. We rely on others to perform parts of plans. Just as within the brain cognition is distributed among modules, so in social life cognition is distributed among people. Arguably, this distribution, more than any other factor, is characteristic of our species, and is responsible for our successes. But just as I argued in the first chapter, that distributed agency within the cognitive system brings with it the necessity for management of the multiple goals and uncertainties that arise, so comparable systems are needed where cognition is distributed among people.

Emotions are present in distributed cognition. Here as elsewhere they function to set tones of friendly cooperation or aggressive competition. Divisions of labor on which technology is based, although benefiting the majority, are accompanied by greed among some of those who invest capital and envy among some of those who sell their labor. The improved rationality of science is not unconnected with people becoming elated at the idea of the fame that accompanies discovery and with the contempt in which holders of one view denounce others. Decisions prompted by emotions are not perfectly rational, but the mental processes on which they are based have had the advantage of surviving evolutionary selection when fully rational solutions were not available.

Assembly of fragments into complex plans

The discussion of this chapter allows us not only to go beyond the dichotomy of reason and emotion but to understand more fully the problem of orchestrating action when it involves multiple goals, uncertain environments, and multiple agency, and to see that understanding emotions is just part of a more general issue about how cognitive processes are distributed both within and between individuals.

Automatisms, whether genetically specified or individually acquired, are means by which individuals can capitalize on the laborious activity of solving problems, and saving the means for reuse. The difficulty is that the fragments of plans that we create acquire a life of their own. The cognitive problem becomes one of management. We have to manage a set of quasi-autonomous procedures, each capable of achieving a subgoal. We have to deal with the problem of imperfect knowledge and also manage our interactions with other agents with whom we are cooperating. How is this done?

There have been a number of attempts at solving the problem. I will outline three general kinds and juxtapose them with the solution that Johnson-Laird and I think is offered by emotions.

One general kind of approach to this problem interested both Darwin and Freud. What happens, they asked, when an instinct or habit becomes inappropriate or comes into conflict with another one? Their answer was that because deletions from the behavioral repertoire are impossible, an attempt is made at inhibition, or repression, as they called it. Both Darwin and Freud noticed that this did not often provide a fully successful solution in that the repressed behavior mechanism survived with some degree of autonomy, leaving more or less intrusive traces of its existence.

A second type of solution was offered by Lorenz (1967/1963) in his chapter on "the great parliament of instincts." He, too, noted that the problem becomes manifest if animals create new behavior mechanisms in their own lifetime. Lorenz argued that when a new mechanism is acquired it takes part in what he calls a "parliament" with the many other instincts, ritual behaviors, and habits. He says that "since it is a more or less complete system of interactions between many independent variables; its true democratic nature has developed through a probationary period in evolution" (p. 72). The "parliament" produces, he says, not complete harmony but tolerable compromises. Each big drive, such as hunger, sexuality, aggression, or fear, can have in its service smaller servant behavior patterns, which can also be somewhat autonomous and also make their voices heard. The problem is to decide which shall control the motor system at any time.

Lorenz quotes a simile, proposed by Huxley, that a human is like a ship commanded by many captains, all on the bridge and all voicing their opinions. By doing this they can often reach a wise decision. In animals, although the multiplicity of potential commanders exists, a mechanism allows only one on the bridge at any one time. Lorenz says that though such processes do indeed exist, in reality in animals all sorts of possible combinations also occur – evolution, however, subjects the combinations to selection pressure. Lorenz is famous for arguing, for instance, that although most carnivores have both the weapons and skills to kill members of their own species, they rarely do so. In them aggressive skills are reserved for species preservation purposes, and they coexist with an effective mechanism that ritualizes them or prevents them from being directed in earnest at members of the same species.

The third solution is one hinted at by Huxley, that of rational resolution of conflicting drives and habits. It requires that each goal be represented and reasoned about. In artificial intelligence the principal attempt to address the problem is by Wilensky (1983). His sketch of how to accomplish this kind of management in everyday life suggests that it is achieved by "metaplanning," using a number of heuristics. These include to "achieve as many goals as possible" and to "maximize the value of the goals achieved." Wilensky proposes that multiplicity and the occasional incompatibility of goals are the major problems, and he has offered what might be thought of as a computer scientist's solution: to reason about goals using heuristics, and then to choose how to act.[35]

The proposal of Oatley and Johnson-Laird (1987) is that there is, not instead of these mechanisms but in addition to them, what might be called a biological social solution. It is related to those of Darwin, Freud, Lorenz, Huxley, and Wilensky but distinctively different: Cognitive systems at least of birds and mammals contain monitoring devices on *each* goal and plan of each individual agent. Each monitoring device checks on whether events occur to change the probability of achieving the goal it is attached to. If so, it draws the attention of the rest of the cognitive system, and sometimes of other individuals, to the kind of goal-relevant event that has occurred, a subgoal achievement, a goal loss, a goal conflict, or the like. The control signal tends to set the cognitive system into a distinctive mode appropriate to this kind of event. It makes ready a certain repertoire of actions, and it creates a preoccupation with what has occurred that assists further planning.

The mental states called emotions are based on modes that have been selected as bases for continuing or substituting plans when there is uncertainty either about the world or the relative value of goals. This individual mechanism is pressed into social service in the communication between interacting individuals and the management of joint plans.

The conflict theory of emotions

This kind of mechanism began to be explored by theorists who conceived conflict theories of emotions. When there is a change in evaluation of any substantial plan or goal, disturbances and changes of attention may occur.

The earliest version of such a theory seems, according to Mandler

(1984), to have been proposed by Paulhan (1887). It was that emotions arise where action tendencies are arrested: "Sudden appearance and lack of co-ordination of the phenomena" occur. Such discoordinations imply that "affective phenomena are due to the imperfect functioning of the mind" (p. 48). Paulhan stated how the phenomena tend to invade the whole field of consciousness, and "a considerable quantity of energy is released without being able to be used in a systematic manner" (p. 57). Conflict theories thus make the relation of emotions to individual consciousness clearer. Interruptions function to insert a problem into consciousness.

Mandler (1964) reintroduced the relation of interruptions to emotion into experimental psychology. In the quite different domain of music, Meyer (1956) recognized that a schema accommodating to new data will necessarily be disorganized at least temporarily, but the emotion need not be dysphoric. It may be euphoric, and it may signal the creation of a new mental construction.

Such formulations of conflict theory give a promising sketch of the relation of emotions to action and consciousness, but they seem not to take the issue far enough. Emotions often spring from interruption and often do provoke disorganization, but such disorganization is not an irrational nuisance. It is part of an arrangement by which new plans can be generated to meet conditions that change in an unpredictable way. Mechanisms that cope with limited and imperfect resources are not to be regarded as failures of rationality. They are among our most highly sophisticated cognitive features. We have yet to emulate them artificially.

Compiled action plans are given priority within basic emotion modes. They provide a set of general default solutions that have been selected to cope with commonly recurring situations of uncertainty or conflict. These solutions can be invoked quickly. We do not have to think about them. If this evolutionary argument is correct, these general solutions have been, on average, superior to solutions such as thinking that require the large resources of long search, backtracking, elimination of bugs, and the like.

When we consider examples of rational thinking, we may forget that solutions that are rational have been constructed in safe environments, free of interruption, with the use of cultural artifacts, rather than in more dangerous arenas of immediate action. Where danger may occur, and where goal conflicts may be uncovered, thinking has been selected against. It is too slow, too uncertain, too liable to mistakes that could be fatal.

Emotions make default plans ready and establish conscious priority

In individuals, emotion modes first make ready a small suite of plans, already assembled either in evolution or individually, that can be called upon when time or other resources are scarce. Running fast in the direction of least resistance may not be the best thing to do in a fire, if "best" is defined from the position of an omniscient observer. But usually there are no such observers to advise. The strategy of panicky flight may be a general default option that has survived better than other options during evolution. It is not fully rational, but it may be useful. Thinking out what to do would be worse, and take too long. Second, emotions act to insert a particular goal or set of goals that have become problematic into consciousness with high priority. The high priority of a goal seems potentially advantageous in that substantial cognitive resources, including concentrated thinking, are then devoted to the problem. This is often experienced as preoccupation with an emotional problem.

Thinking in an emotional way may be very important if a new problem is to be solved, and I will discuss this in Chapter 9. But it may involve limiting the search space and have other characteristics that are quite damaging. Examples occur when people are caught up in a depression, in vengeful plans, in an anxiety state. In such cases, reasoning may go round in loops or become stuck in some local valley. The person is unable to consider matters beyond those relevant to goals evoked within the emotion mode because, though other goals may be relevant, they are unable to win priority.

Though we may correctly speak of emotions being irrational, emotions need not distort thinking. Rather, it may be the specificity of goals invoked by an emotion that creates problems. The resignation of depression, the vengefulness of anger, the imperative of safety in anxiety, all involve compelling goals. Then it may be best for the person not simply to rely on her or his own resources but to enter a dialogue with others who may not be under the press of such goal constraint.

The difficulty of questioning a goal was the root of Anna Karenina's growing feeling of dependency on Vronsky. To say that jealousy prompted her to behave irrationally is scarcely an explanation. To explain what occurred we must understand that two of her major goals were in conflict. She wanted to keep Vronsky constantly by her side because now her whole life revolved around him. At the same time she wanted to avoid constraining him because she knew this would drive him away. There was no solution in those terms. Her behavior lurched between being driven by one goal, then the other. A successful solution would have required not so much thinking about the problem more rationally but modifying one of her goals or forming some meta-goal.

She was unable to do this partly because though her emotions flowed directly from her relationship with Vronsky, her attempts to express these emotions to him, and thereby to readjust their relationship, failed. The importance of emotions in changing and maintaining relationships, in longer term joint plans, is the subject of Chapter 4.

The idea that emotions are adapted to coping with junctures at which fully rational solutions are not possible should not be taken to indicate that any part of my argument is against rationality. I believe rationality to be fundamentally important, and that it should be approached wherever possible. Nor should the argument of this chapter, or of the book, be taken to imply that all action is instrumental or goal directed. Many actions occur that have no immediate goal other than the action itself. We may do things for their own sake and not for any instrumental reason whatsoever. And many actions occur without their goals being at all clear to ourselves or anyone else. Though goalless actions are no doubt frequent, they are less easy to analyze cognitively than those in which we can talk about goals. My proposal is merely that we first pursue analyses in terms of goals and plans, then see how far this takes us and what we can explain satisfactorily. We can then see what is omitted. Then we can progress to the yet more difficult problems.

4. Mutual plans and social emotions

Every community is established with a view to some good.

Aristotle
The Politics, 1252a

Cooperation

In Chapter 1, I proposed that human cognitive systems are composed of modules, each somewhat autonomous, each able to achieve a limited goal. Such an arrangement leads to problems of management, especially when the system creates new parts of itself as it proceeds. Emotions function in that management. In Chapter 3, I showed how some of the limitations of human rationality are helped by social means. Here I extend the argument about social organization to describe how emotions function in associations of people rather than in associations of modules. We ourselves are elements, each somewhat autonomous, cooperating in larger systems of interaction with others.

In the individual cognitive system emotions manage transitions between plans, and moods maintain a goal and its associated plans despite events that might tend to disrupt them. In the social world joint plans are units of analysis equivalent to the individual plan. A role is the social equivalent of the individual habit or stored plan in which people expect to continue joint plans that they have established. Social emotions help manage transitions to new joint plans and help to maintain them. The emotions of falling in love help effect the transition to doing things as a couple, and a prolonged state of love can help to maintain the roles involved in a long-lasting sexual relationship, for example, involving cohabitation.

Each basic emotion can enable transition into a particular kind of joint plan or can maintain it. So happiness is the emotion that encourages

178

cooperation and attachment. Sadness is the emotion of giving up one's part in a joint plan and of detachment from it. Anger is the emotion of competition and dominance, but also of the readjustment of joint plans. Fear is the emotion of separation from an attachment figure or of social degradation. Hatred is the emotion of withdrawal from an interaction. Each emotion and its interpersonal communication, then, can prompt people toward structuring their interactions in these ways, sometimes without quite knowing why they are doing so. When communicated between people, emotions have the quality of setting the highest level goal of the interaction – to be friendly or hostile, dominating or submissive, and so on. Some such structures, particularly when they involve love, anger, or fear, have a compulsive quality.

Here I discuss some features of joint planning and the conceptualization of role. Then I will discuss how emotions function in role transitions, and extend the semantic analysis begun in Chapter 2 to terms that refer specifically to socially constructed emotions.

Why are so many of our emotions social?

In an uncertain world and with multiple goals, even the best laid schemes gang aft a-gley.[1] When they do – when a plan is reevaluated because of an unexpected event, a conflict is uncovered, a smooth performance is disrupted, an expectation is contradicted – emotions tend to occur. Emotions communicate this juncture in a simple way among the modules of the individual's own cognitive system and bring the issue to consciousness.

If we ask why so many human emotions concern our interactions with others, an answer suggests itself. Planning that is distributed among people adds to the possibilities of unexpected events and to the number of goals, our own and those of others, that may affect action. When interacting, each person's reliance on the other may or may not turn out to be justified, and though helpful cooperation may be constructed, conflicts of goals can also occur among participants.

If, in general, emotions occur in monitoring plans where unforeseen events and goal conflicts may occur, then if many of our plans involve distributed agency, correspondingly many of our emotions will be social. Joint planning increases opportunities for happy and creative elaboration of plans – and for the dysphoria of interruptions, disruptions, and disappointments.

As in the individual cognitive system, joint plans and goals must be managed and priorities set without full knowledge of implications. Biologically the system of emotions is the basis for interpersonal management, just as it is for intraindividual management. The management of distributed planning requires communication. According to the communicative hypothesis of emotions, the intrapersonal control and semantic messages of the cognitive system have equivalents in the messages passed between individuals.[2] In humans, nonverbal emotional expressions are accompanied by linguistic messages with semantic content.

Joint planning: other agents as instruments or associates?

In Chapter 1, I outlined a cognitive theory of planning and showed how emotions become necessary when simple plans are augmented. How, then, are we to conceptualize planning that involves other people, and how does this provide a basis for social emotions?

There is a tradition in psychology in which the individual is seen as instrumentally controlling the world. Within it, if we think about planning, other people must be conceptualized as instruments in plans, as objects or resources. The social world then presents no new problems of principle: People are merely more complex than most of the physical world. We merely need more elaborate models of them to carry out our plans.[3] By contrast, my proposal is that the problem of interacting with other people involves a wholly different set of principles from those of individual plans in the physical world. These depend on the fact that we do not typically treat other people instrumentally. We enter into arrangements with them, into plans that are jointly agreed and jointly executed.

The extra processing capacity needed for social interaction has little to do with increased unpredictability of objects that we might wish to manipulate. Its problems include agreeing with other people about goals and plans that are to be enacted jointly, communicating about beliefs relevant to such enactions, and representing our own and others' goals, plans, and beliefs. All these matters, and others, are involved in treating other people as people.

If we were to act with each other merely instrumentally, the emotions of social life would be those identified in analyses of instrumental behavior, perhaps pleasure when subgoals are being achieved, elation when things go better than expected, or frustration when things go worse.[4] But we know our emotions have a wider range. The possibilities of interreliance bring about emotions of joy and love as we join with others in common plans. Grief occurs when a close person is lost, anger when one person in a joint plan does not act in a way he or she seemed to have agreed to. Shame occurs as others censure some action we have performed, guilt as we censure ourselves in a similar way, and so forth.

None of these can be analyzed in terms of treating others instrumentally. Other people are not merely objects that happen to be complex. When asking for pasta at a restaurant, actions toward the waiter or the chef have little in common with actions toward the pan or the pasta when we are cooking. Other people are not preconditions, instrumental means, or resources in plans. They are actors and planners too. So we enter into associations with them in pursuit of goals that we share. We plan jointly to attain goals that are jointly agreed. Even when one partner is very subordinate and the other very powerful, the subordinate will contribute remarks like, "What did you mean when you said . . . ?" or "How do you want me to . . . ?" which are quite different from anything that occur when using a tool.[5]

Can we conceptualize joint planning in terms that are adequate both to cognitive science and to human understanding? I will offer a cognitive science analysis of joint plans, drawn from computation, that has some of the necessary properties. Then, using this analysis we will be able to see more clearly where our human abilities go beyond these of computational metaphors, and ask how emotions contribute to joint action. We start with the propositional system of verbal utterances and the deliberate formulation of joint plans.

Conversation as mutual planning

Power (1979) has written an artificial intelligence program to investigate distributed agency. The program simulates two robot agents conversing purposefully to do things that neither can accomplish alone. It provides a conceptualization of basic issues and indicates how far we must go to explain some of the problems formally.

Purposeful conversation offers an informative example of mutual planning. As well as the purpose of the conversation itself, each participant acts with common goals that operate within the conversation to guide it. Rules, of the kind described by Grice (1975), are followed by participants. Grice proposed that conversation is based on a cooperative principle, and he sketched what was implied: When conversing, people need to say about the right amount for the purpose in hand, to be truthful, to be relevant, and to be clear.

Figure 7. Diagram of the simple world of Power's (1979) model of conversation.

Power's program is based on the idea that the unit of conversation is an exchange, most commonly a pair of utterances by two speakers, perhaps a question and a reply or a suggestion and an assent.[6] Conversation is the paradigm example of formulating and enacting a joint plan. Understanding conversation enables us to understand how plans are constructed and distributed among several actors. In the rest of this section it is assumed that just two actors are involved.

Cooperation in a simple world. Power simulated two robots on either side of a door with a bolt (see Figure 7). This world has just four entities, and each can be in just one of two positions: Each of the two robots can be either In or Out, the door may be Open or Shut, and the bolt may be Up or Down. The robots, John and Mary, can each have a goal. A goal is a state of the world. If their goals agree they can cooperate to achieve that state. A robot can attempt just three actions. "Push" is an attempt to change the position of the door. "Move" is an attempt of a robot to change position. "Slide" is an attempt to change the position of the bolt. There are also laws of nature. So, when a robot Moves, it changes position if the door is Open. When it Slides, the bolt changes position if the robot is In.

To explore the interactions of these robots, a run of the program may start from a particular state of the world, with each robot either knowing or being ignorant of certain laws of nature and each with beliefs that may be true or false. A robot will change a belief if a more complex belief is offered by the other, or if something unexpected happens following an action. Normally, each robot can perceive the state of the world, but, in the dialogue that follows, one of them is blind. The program is started by setting up initial conditions, beliefs, and so on and giving goals to one or both the robots. They then converse to negotiate joint goals, construct plans, exchange knowledge, and act. The program is an exploration of how common goals can be achieved when neither robot acting alone could accomplish them. A recognizable conversation arises naturally out of attempts of the robots to cooperate in creating and executing a mutual plan.

Transcript from Power's conversational program. Here is a transcript from a run of Power's program. John is Out, and has been given the goal to get In. He believes that if he Moves nothing happens. The bolt is Down, securing the door. Mary is In and can operate it, but she is blind. She does not have a goal to start with, so she accepts the goal suggested by John, having nothing else to do. The conversation proceeds by formulating and checking subgoals and plans and passing knowledge back and forth.

In the following fragments I have labeled the utterances in pairs corresponding to exchanges, with (a) being the opening utterance and (b) the completion.

1a. John: Mary.
1b. Mary: Yes.

2a. John: I want to suggest a goal.
2b. Mary: Go ahead.

3a. John: Will you help me get in.
3b. Mary: By all means.

4a. John: Shall we make a plan.
4b.

5a. Mary: John.
5b. John: Yes.

6a. Mary: May I ask you something.
6b. John: Go ahead.

7a. Mary: Are you in.
7b. John: No.

The first exchange is a summons and an acknowledgment, the second a suggestion and an assent, the third a request and an agreement to it. At the end of 3, Mary has learned John's goal, and John has learned that she is willing to help. John then makes a further proposal, 4a, that they should make a plan. The sequence is here interrupted by Mary, because she does not know whether the goal of the proposed plan is already achieved. Had she been given more extensive powers of inference, she might have guessed this from 3a, but like a good robot she always checks the state of the world to see if a goal has been attained, and this is what she is doing from 5 to 7.

The interruption causes both robots to forget 4a and start a new sequence, embedded in the previous one. Mary now takes the initiating role, starting up, as it were, a new procedure.

8a. Mary: Shall we make a plan.
8b. John: OK.

9a. Mary: John.
9b. John: Yes.

10a. Mary: May I ask you something.
10b. John: Go ahead.

11a. Mary: Can you move.
11b. John: Yes.

12a. Mary: John.
12b. John: Yes.

13a. Mary: May I ask you something.
13b. John: Go ahead.

14a. Mary: Is the door open.
14b. John: No.

15a. Mary: I suggest that we get the door open and then you move.
15b.

Now John interrupts:

16a. John: Mary.
16b. Mary: Yes.

17a. John: I want to explain something.
17b. Mary: Go ahead.

18a. John: If you move, nothing happens.
18b. Mary: I disagree.

19a. Mary: If you move when the door is open, you change position.
19b. John: I see.

20a. Mary: I suggest that we get the door open and then you move.

Mary's interruption starts a set of exchanges in which John explains his belief about a law of nature: If one Moves nothing happens. Then Mary makes two utterances. First (18b) she disagrees with John's belief, then (19a) she suggests a revision. Since the robots substitute more complex laws for simpler ones, John accepts it. Next (20a) Mary re-suggests the plan she first suggested at 15a and forgot at the interruption.

Private thinking and public discussion. It has been implicit in cognitive science that private thinking is primary, and speaking is a secondary activity that one does to convey something to another person. The alternative is that the social is primary, and that private cogitation is an internalization of public discourse. However this may be, it is clear that to analyze conversation we need both kinds of thinking, private and public.

An informal idea of how the program works is as follows. When they are given goals, the robots think privately, trying to formulate plans to achieve these goals, running what Power calls routines. When one of them, say, John, finds there is something he cannot complete alone, he contacts Mary, by calling her name. This causes both to break off their private thoughts and conduct a conversation. When this is over they return to their private thoughts, but now including changes that have been made to their minds in the conversation, so that if John had asked something, he now knows it or knows that Mary does not know it.

When a robot is thinking publicly, that is to say, conversing, it uses what Power calls conversational procedures. In the example I have called the first move in each conversational procedure (a) and the second (b). Power has programmed seven such procedures, including asking for help in achieving a goal (e.g., exchange 2), arranging for another conversational procedure (exchange 3), asking for information (exchange 7), and explaining a law of nature (exchanges 18 and 19).[7]

A conversation, then, is made up of conversational procedures for two agents in which each takes a different role. Conversation is like getting these procedures loaded and running in sequence in both minds. In their conversation the robots undertake two kinds of activity.

First, they build planning trees and enact as much of the plan as they can while they converse. It is the building of the joint plan by incrementally agreeing on goals, knowledge, and pieces of the plan that holds the utterances of the conversation together. Each robot constructs and keeps a copy of the plan tree, and in the program everything is done to ensure these copies are similar. Joint plan trees are similar to the single agent's tree described in Chapter 1 and illustrated in Figures 1, 2, and 3, but with two modifications: that some goals can be joint and that actions can be conducted by either agent. Thus, after Mary has agreed to it, the topmost goal is joint: To get John In. As for the terminal actions, whereas John will do Move, Mary will do Slide to change the position of the bolt.

Second, the robots develop their mental models of the physical world and of the mind of the other robot. In this example, John updates his model of the world by perception, though there are laws of nature that he needs instruction on. Mary, being blind, needs to update her model of the world by asking John questions. In addition, each develops a model of the other. For instance, at 11, Mary learns that John can Move. These models are updated either by information from the other or by experience, that is, from a change in the state of the world following an action.

Power's work clarifies several issues in understanding social interaction. Experience, we may take it, is private. This includes access to one's own models of the world and to those of other agents. Some kinds of thinking can also be private. There are, however, social facts that are shared among actors. The rules by which conversations are managed are social, existing in culture before being adopted by individuals. A conversation and other public actions are social facts, though each actor may remember a somewhat different version. Joint goals and joint plans are also shared. Again, participants may have somewhat different versions.

Power's program clarifies the psychological basis of the meaning of utterances. A meaning in purposeful conversation is not a reference directly to the world but to a mental object relevant to a plan – for example, to a part of the plan, to a model, to a goal, or to a precondition.[8]

Many adult human plans are mutual. They are distributed among two or more actors. They must be created simultaneously in the minds of all the relevant individuals by implicit or explicit agreement, as with Power's robots. The bases of social interaction include roles, which are joint plans in which further planning episodes are expected.[9] Many emotions depend for their understanding on such concepts.

Why emotions are not needed by Power's robots. Joint planning is an augmentation of simple planning. Simple planning with multiple goals and imperfect knowledge inevitably leads to junctures in which new planning sequences are needed, although resources for them are not readily available. As humans, we tend to experience these junctures as emotional. Joint planning suffers from similar problems, but multiplied because of the necessity for communication between people. A system has evolved to allow this communication. As within the individual cognitive system there are two kinds of message: the older system of emotional expressions and gestures and a newer system based on linguistic conventions of verbal messages with semantic content.

It is remarkable that interpersonal communication is possible, that one mind, with an idiosyncratic history and a unique structure of ideas and beliefs, can communicate with another. Draper (personal communication) has pointed out that direct telepathic transfer of mental contents would be impossible even if we had occult powers or the technology. We could not pass thoughts directly between two brains for the same reason that programs written on one computer will not run on another made by a different manufacturer. I have neural mechanisms that can initiate appropriate nerve impulses controlling my muscles and making my intended action occur. But my procedures for operating my muscles would probably not run on a different nervous system.

Instead, there has evolved a specialized people-interfacing system, of verbal and nonverbal communication in which mental objects can be transmitted. These communications are not raw thought. If I think of doing something, speaking allows me to try to insert specific kinds of objects, such as suggested goals, plans, and beliefs, into other people's minds. If they wish to, they may accept my communication, and if they have compatible goals they can cooperate by programming their nervous systems to accomplish actions.

So what are people trying to do when they speak? Are they trying to use other people to implement parts of their own plans? Sometimes no doubt. But Power's solution is more radical, and more interesting. It is that people propose, negotiate, agree, and revise joint goals. They then communicate about the knowledge and arrangements necessary for building a joint planning tree that both actors make a copy of. They propose and repair plans and carry out actions that can be performed as they are going along. Each must know when to act, and each must rely on the other to do as arranged.

There is, however, nothing in Power's program that corresponds to emotions. Chapter 1 has informed us why not. Power's program stays close to technical planning. If robot John were a person, he might feel glad if Mary agreed to help him get In, but there is nothing in Power's program that would be functionally assisted by such a state.

I think there are several reasons for this. First, among humans, cooperation presupposes either some mutual advantage – as in contracts of exchange of money for goods or in contracts of employment – or it depends on a power imbalance involving fear, or it depends on an affectionate emotion with the people involved liking or loving the other. In the communicative theory of emotions, liking and loving are seen as directed emotions of happiness that prompt continuation of the current plan. In other words, happy emotions have the quality of creating a top-level goal of mutual cooperation. In natural conversations we often see this top-level goal being reaffirmed by smiling and laughter, which has the effect of promoting adherence to the joint activity. Laughter also occurs when it seems that a plan of one person has become discrepant with that of the other.[10]

Power finesses the problem either of contracts or emotional commitment by simply implementing the rule that a robot agrees to a suggested goal if it has nothing else to do.

A second reason why emotions are not necessary in the robots' conversation is that inferences about the other are avoided and there is no question of the extent to which each may rely on the other agent. The robots' planning can encounter problems that neither robot foresees. For example, Mary could not foresee that John would be ignorant of the law of nature that if one Moves and the door is Open then one changes position. Nevertheless, the copies of the plan tree that each builds are kept in full correspondence. No ambiguities occur about the plans or goals of the other participant. There are no misunderstandings, no variations of the agreed actions. There is a single plan with a single top-level goal. Absent are the interpersonal emotions when goals other than those agreed upon intrude into the field of action, for instance, when one participant is not reliable or wants adjustment of the performance of the other after a plan has been launched. Nor are actions carried out other than those intended. Moreover, there is no opportunity following any variation of what had been agreed for participants to contemplate the advisability of further joint plans in which knowledge of the other's reliability or otherwise could be carried forward from one episode to the next. All such matters, then, might be thought of in terms of the extent to which one may trust one's partner in joint plans.

Interpersonal emotions come into being when cooperation is not certain in the first place and when the extent of trust is problematic. They can occur when understanding of the other is inherently imperfect, when goals other than the agreed ones claim attention, and when one agent perceives the performance of the other as being different from what was agreed explicitly or understood implicitly.

If emotions are to be understood in terms of plans, social emotions are to be understood in terms of joint plans. If emotions occur when an evaluation of progress toward one of several goals changes, social emotions occur when joint plans are monitored as they are constructed, enacted, or abandoned.

Why are social emotions experienced as individual emotions?

This sketch of an analysis raises a question. If emotions that concern the coordination of joint planning are social, why are they primarily felt as individual and not experienced as aspects of the relationship?[11] An informative analysis comes from Berscheid's theory of close relationships (1982, 1983). She defines a relationship between two people, Xavier (X) and Yolande (Y), as close if X has a frequent influence on Y and if this influence is strong, distributed across a diverse set of activities, and continues for some time. For the relationship to be properly close, Y must also affect X in similar ways, though there can be asymmetries in the effects that people have on each other. In other words, in close relationships, each partner interacts with the other in many episodes of joint planning and in several different types of roles.

According to this analysis, dysphoric emotions occur when there are interruptions of organized sequences of behavior, particularly within plans that are fulfilling higher order goals. Interruptions involving others may be of two kinds. They may occur either when another person in the same behavioral field inserts a new goal at some important point or when another person causes the absence of a precondition for the protagonist's current plan.

Some interruptions may occur without any explicit arrangement between the two people. But there are frequent occasions when a person apparently has agreed to a part in a mutual plan, but then does not do it. Suppose Xavier has a chain of action $a1 \rightarrow a2 \rightarrow a3$, and Yolande has agreed to do $b1 \rightarrow b2$. For Xavier to be able to do his $a3$, Yolande must do her $b2$ that is a precondition for it. If she does not, his chain is broken and he will experience an interruption and possibly a dysphoric emotion. The key that Berscheid suggests for understanding the kinds of emotions that occur in closer relationships is that although plans are joint, or will have been supposed to be joint, the emotions associated with interruptions are experienced by an individual, who then tends to attribute any problem to the other participant.

This paradigm emotion for Berscheid's analysis is anger, most notably the sense of indictment when another person does not take a step in a plan that had been expected or agreed. We can imagine comparable analyses for other emotions involving unresolved differences between individual experience and the expectation of mutuality. In all social emotions, it seems that the individual experiences an emotion while semantic content can be based on what is jointly known. This is true whether this arrangement is explicit as in a contract or implicit like a cultural understanding of the moral obligations of social roles.

Acts of both omission and commission can damage joint plans. Examples occur in the passages from *Anna Karenina* quoted in Chapter 1. At the ball, Vronsky omits to ask Kitty to dance the mazurka, thus destroying her plan of enjoying the evening and becoming engaged to be married. At the races Anna commits a show of concern for Vronsky, thus disrupting Karenin's plan of displaying the smooth face of marital decorum.

Projection. What kinds of models of other people do we have, then, in order to enter into the enmeshed relationships that Berscheid calls close. They tend to involve elaborate inferences and the projection of assumptions about the other that may be contradicted as events unfold. Misunderstandings produced by such projections can provide some of our most distressing emotional experiences.

Laing, Phillipson, and Lee (1966) recount a story of a couple who, on their honeymoon, had their first seriously angry argument, one from which it was hard to recover. They were having a drink in the bar of their hotel. The new wife struck up a conversation with another couple. To her dismay, her husband refused to join in. He became aloof, gloomy, and antagonistic toward her and the other couple. Perceiving this, she became angry for creating this awkward social situation. Tempers rose. Each became bitter, and later accused the other of being inconsiderate. This was the extent of their report, but Laing describes how eight years later they and he were able to see more deeply into it.

She had thought that as a wife she could practice an interesting new role, as a member of a married couple, conversing with other couples, and she had looked forward joyfully to such opportunities. What better time than the honeymoon to try this out. He had thought that the honeymoon was the one occasion when he could expect to be alone with his wife, ignore the rest of the world, be sufficient unto themselves, and explore each other. He felt that when his wife struck up the conversation she was offering a direct insult, telling him that he was not man enough for her, that he was insufficient to fulfill her demands. She made him feel inadequate and angry.

Though their emotions were pointing to something that had gone wrong in their joint plan for their honeymoon, they were unable to make the full repairs until eight years later, when they could laugh at it. The reasons were that many of the apparent agreements involved inferences that turned out to be incorrect and had not been explicitly negotiated at all. Though the top-level goal "have a harmonious honeymoon" was shared, subgoals and subplans about how this was to be accomplished were not shared. Unlike Power's robots, the copies of the planning tree that each held were different.

Berscheid points out that emotions associated with romantic love are enhanced by restrictions that delay the mutual plan for sexual congress. Many of the engagement customs of the past restrict the amount of real interaction between prospective partners. Hence disappointments of the kind described in Laing's story are unlikely to occur until after a full commitment has been made. Indeed, it may be that the bittersweet experience of romantic love could not exist without delays and interruptions. Such indeed is a persistent theme of stories of romantic love. Romantic love is, moreover, a good example of how the conflict theory of emotions can account for happy as well as dysphoric emotional states.[12] One might imagine that the real function of much of courtship customs is to maintain projections and fantasies in an untested state until full commitment has occurred.

Emotions in human development

Unlike Power's robots, who have to arrange cooperation as independent individuals, programmed to accept a goal offered by the other if they have none of their own, we grow up in a context of cooperative action. Much of this context is not semantic but based on direct emotional communication. A baby's cry that summons its mother is a communication, though in the first weeks of life crying is presumably not voluntary. It may be thought of as a message of some benefit to both sender and receiver. Communication is a property of pairs of individuals or of larger groups.

In the case of mother and baby, the communicative function is central to a set of inherited joint plans. Though mother and baby have slightly different overall biological goals, they also have a joint biological goal of enabling the infant to survive healthily into adulthood. The interactions

Table 5. *Examples of social emotions developed from biological emotions of a single actor*

Juncture of plans	Basic emotion	Infant social emotion	Adult social emotion
Subgoal attainment	Happiness	Emotions of attachment, joyfulness in inter-action, de-light	Adult love, joys of cultural pursuits
Goal deprivation	Sadness	Emotions of loss – grief and dis-tress	Depression, disappoint-ment
Goal conflict or self-protection goal violated	Fear	Separation anxiety	Conscious anxi-ety, embar-rassment
Plan frustration	Anger	Rage, envy	Vengefulness, bitterness
Gustatory goal violated	Disgust	Disgust at feces, etc.	Hatred, loath-ing

Source: Adapted from Oatley and Johnson-Laird (1987).

of mother and baby may properly be thought of as resulting from joint plans, some of which are genetically based.[13] Emotional expressions, instinctive interpersonal actions, and the later acquisition of proposi-tional language are parts of a communicative system on which coopera-tion and mutuality depend.

Human infants, in comparison with those of other species, are born very immature. We start life in a close relationship with another person, a caregiver, on whom we depend. We are equipped with a repertoire of expressions – to cry, to gurgle, and so on. They allow us, apparently because of an innate ability to do joint planning, to cooperate with our caregiver so that we are fed, changed, comforted, and so on, even when much of our muscular system is very inept. Some discussion of the development of emotions was given in Chapter 2. Here I will continue this theme.

Table 5 indicates how emotions develop. The leftmost column is a set of characteristic junctures in mammalian plans that give rise to emo-tions. The second column shows the corresponding basic emotions. These junctures and emotions correspond to those of single agents' plans, as described in Table 3. In early childhood further crucial junctures occur that are social. They concern the relations between caregiver and child and among caregiver, child, and siblings. Some early social emotions engendered in this way are shown in the third column.

There is no doubt that emotions are crucial to social development. The early social emotions seem to be programmed innately just like those communicating the equivalent junctures in nonsocial plans. These then form bases for elaborations of social interaction. Campos et al. (1983) have reviewed socioemotional development in infancy and describe a range of ways in which emotions develop from a genetic basis, how they are related to goals, and how they give structure to social interaction (see also Field & Fogel, 1982). The following are five principal aspects of this development.

1. *Attachment:* As Ainsworth (e.g., 1967) has shown, attachment relationships and their associated behavior are similar in widely different cultures. Infants show distinctive happy behavior with their mother or other primary caregiver, and the relationship with this person affects other action and interaction. Other emotions, particularly of anxiety and sadness, are related to the absence of the caregiver (Bowlby, 1969, 1973, 1980).

2. *Social referencing:* Infants recognize emotional expressions of others, especially caregivers, and rely on these as guides to their own action in the physical world and to their interactions with others. (These phenomena are reviewed in Chapter 2 in the section on evidence concerning the interpersonal communication of emotions.)

3. *Role taking:* Dunn and Kendrick (1982) and Dunn (1987, 1988) have shown how children as young as two interact with their mother or with a sibling in role structures as cooperating, helping, antagonizing, or demanding attention, based on emotions (e.g., responding to another's expressed goals, sadness or anger, or prompted by their own envy or longing). They are often able to comment verbally on their own and others' emotions in such situations.

4. *Empathy:* Hoffman (1978) has reviewed studies of empathy, the process whereby an emotion felt by one person is transmitted to another. This process is of course related to the direct transmission by various signals of alarm in social groups. It develops early, as indicated by Dunn's studies, and is of wide general significance.

5. *Temperament:* This can be thought of as genetically programmed emotional style that appears in infancy, apparently before much learning

has occurred. It has an effect on how caregivers react to their infants, which in turn affects the infants' experience of themselves and of social interaction (Graham, Rutter & George, 1973; Dunn, Kendrick & MacNamee, 1981).

These five principal emotional bases of social interaction form the foundations for a wide range of social interactions, and there is reason to believe that emotional habits that develop in childhood are the bases for our interactions with others in adulthood. To put these processes in terms of the theory of planning, as infants develop, their activities diversify. They enter into what can be thought of as joint plans that require understanding of others' intentions, inferences about their emotions and other mental states, commitment to joint activities, and so forth. The age of two is a good time to observe this because, although toddlers like social interaction and have both the emotional abilities to accomplish it and can sustain their parts with adults, at this age they are not yet skilled enough to negotiate joint goals with other toddlers. One can see the interesting spectacle of two two-year-olds running toward each other in happy anticipation and then not quite knowing how to continue. As language develops, though, this problem is soon mended, and children start to delight in elaborating games involving roles.

Moving right along any row of Table 5 follows a developmental sequence of increasingly more elaborate semantic interpretations that modulate the structure of basic emotions and become part of the actor's understandings of them. Only adult humans reach the last stage (column 4).[14] By then, the instinctual structures of attachment have provided foundations for culture and language, and a model of self has become active.

In this developmental progression, Darwin's and Freud's descriptions of adult emotions as vestiges of childhood are reinterpreted. Instead of seeing adult emotions as vestiges of an evolutionary and infant past, one can see an elaboration from early foundations into the purposes of communication among members of a species whose success depends wholly on social organization and cooperation. The elaboration is partly semantic. But it is built on basic emotion modes that can mediate relationships by invoking particular kinds of joint goals without explicit agreement having to be negotiated.

We distribute cognition in the pursuit of social objectives that we could not accomplish individually. Emotions form the bases of our social interactions by organizing groups of two or more of us into compatible agents acting in coordination with each other.

The self as a cognitive structure for accomplishing joint plans

One of the striking features of emotional development is the appearance of the self, which seems to become fully developed in adolescence (Damon & Hart, 1982). At that time emotions that relate to the self emerge in characteristic ways. Embarrassment can occur rather forcibly as we become aware of ourselves as possible objects of attention, particularly of sexual attention. Depression, a state that rarely occurs in childhood, becomes a possibility. As children, we may be problems for our parents; as adolescents and adults, we can become problems for ourselves.[15]

The self has been a problematic concept in philosophy. In Western culture it has perhaps taken the place of the soul as the center of individuality and the source of voluntariness. Without denying this sense of selfhood, I propose a quite different interpretation: The self is primarily social. It is the cognitive device that enables us, as we grow beyond childhood, to cooperate in repeated episodes of joint planning.[16]

Cognitively, the self is a representation of our goals and abilities; but importantly it also represents aspects of our relations with others. The self is a representational structure, a model of our bodies, abilities, and habits, mainly in relation to other people. How might the nervous system contain such a model, and what might the contents of the model be?

Johnson-Laird (1983b) has argued that the human cognitive system has evolved to contain a model of itself. The mind can be aware of itself, at least to some extent. Part of the mind's ability to construct models involves the ability to embed models of our own mind in our own mind, recursively. John Donne (1967/1628) put it that the difference between the knowledge of man and beast is "that the beast does but know, but the man knows that he knows" (p. 336).

In deliberate action, we not only act according to a goal, but we know that we are able to plan toward this goal. It is this knowledge of our own ability that is re-presented in a model of the self. Only with such a representation could we be said to have an intention to act. One may assume that this recursive sense of self is a human universal. As to content, however, our model of self is primarily social. It develops from culture and language, and in Western culture this has been investigated by Selman (1980). During adolescence, people start to talk of this self as able to monitor and control some thoughts and emotions.[17] Only with this development of a recursive sense of self does the full set of adult emotions occur. These vary in propositional content from culture to culture. Some adult emotions depend on a person feeling the self to be enhanced, for example, by falling in love. Some are of the self being damaged, as in betrayal by others, or by events that contradict one's definition of self.

The self as implied by complex emotion terms. The sense of self in relation to others has been reflected in emotion terms that have grown up in English. Johnson-Laird and Oatley (1989) call these emotions complex, and their experience requires comparison of an event with a model of the self, when this self is a means for relating us to other people and to society.

Many complex emotions correspond to what Adam Smith (1976/1759) called the moral sentiments, the bases of approval and disapproval, which he distinguished from our propensities for self-interest. He regarded these sentiments as being founded on sympathy and as depending on our being able to take an external view of ourselves as well as being able to put ourselves in the position of another, to be moved by his or her case, and thus to have desires that are not just self-interest.

A complex emotion, in the analysis of Johnson-Laird and Oatley, is a contextual emotion that has propositional content involving evaluation of performance in relation to a model of self but that might be related either to the self, as in shame at one's own action, or to another, as in sympathy for his or her unhappy plight. Complex emotions, according to us, are founded on basic emotions. But they are specific to evaluation of events and plans that may vary from culture to culture and from person to person. Here is an example of the complex emotion of jealousy from *Anna Karenina*, which takes a form specific to European and American culture.

Tolstoy describes how, on an occasion after Vronsky had danced with Anna at the ball, but before their affair had begun in earnest, Vronsky and Anna meet, not really by chance, in the drawing room of Vronsky's cousin, the fashionable Princess Betsy. Vronsky sits with Anna. During their conversation he declares his love. She struggles to tell him he must not say such things. Karenin had seen nothing unusual in their sitting together away from the general company. He leaves the gathering earlier than the others, and when he reaches home he feels agitated. Though he had not seen anything striking, he had noticed that others saw the eager conversation of Anna and Vronsky as improper. For that reason it now seems to him improper. He makes up his mind to speak to Anna about it.

Jealousy is a typical complex emotion term. It can be understood only in terms of the customs of the culture in which it is used. To indicate this, Tolstoy builds up elaborately to the scene of Anna and Vronsky at Princess Betsy's. He describes the social circles in which Anna moved and their sexual customs, the mischievous interest of Princess Betsy, her invitation to Vronsky, the views of the others in her social set who saw conquests of respectable married women by dashing young men as titillating subjects for conversation.

When he arrived home, Karenin went to read in his study but was unable to concentrate. Tolstoy tells us: "He was not of a jealous disposition. Jealousy in his opinion insulted a wife" (p. 141). In restless reflection he awaits Anna's return, and during his account of this reflection Tolstoy describes the onset of jealousy: "It was the first time that the possibility of his wife's falling in love with anybody had occurred to him, and he was horrified" (p. 142). Jealousy involves a basic emotion (Tolstoy suggests it is fear), with the semantic content of being caused by something (here indicated by the passive of the causative verb "horrify," meaning to cause horror). The cause is the idea that his wife might love someone else. More generally, we can say jealousy is based on hatred (and on the basic emotion disgust or contempt, though perhaps on anger or fear in particular episodes) at the prospect of being supplanted by a third person in a relationship previously thought to be exclusive.

Basic emotion terms can refer both to basic and to complex emotions. Where a particular complex emotion occurs frequently in a culture, or where it is convenient to refer to it, a special term enters the language. Such terms for complex emotions are restricted to them, and are not interpretable as referring solely to the underlying basic emotion. So, though Tolstoy makes "horrified" refer to the social emotion of jealousy, the term jealousy only refers to a complex emotion, and not to just any instance of horror or hatred.

Terms for complex emotions have a complex semantic structure. To use them properly, we need an understanding of the semantic content of the evaluation that creates them. Specific emotion terms could not have been created or maintained in the language unless this semantic information were available to members of a language community.

Tolstoy's scene of Karenin waiting for Anna's return indicates two further features of social emotions. First, as well as any understanding of the emotion's semantic content, there are rules about the appropriateness of experiencing or expressing the emotion. The reason Karenin "was not of a jealous disposition" (p. 141), although we, the readers know that he was experiencing jealousy, is because he regards this emotion as shameful, as an insulting lack of confidence in the love that his wife has for him. Second, social emotions typically prompt people to do something to readjust the relations between themselves and others. In this case Karenin decides to reprimand Anna for attracting attention, although he explains to her that it was not he who observed the behavior in question, but everyone else at Betsy's. In other words he makes a move to restrain Anna from further displays that might excite comment. She disdainfully affects not to know what he is talking about, but thinks that his way of putting the matter in terms of social disapproval confirms her sense that he does not care for her.

Katz (1980) proposed that emotions occur in relation to past, present, or future events, and this feature is included in Johnson-Laird and Oatley's analysis of complex emotions. Such emotions, according to us, are experienced as a result of a conscious self-evaluation, and this evaluation can be made either about one's own state or in relation to others, and may concern past actions, current situation, or future goals. Retrospective feelings about one's own state include nostalgia and regret. Emotions such as pride or boredom concern the current situation. Emotions such as hope and hopelessness concern future goals.

Emotions that depend on relating the self to others may be feelings that a person has about herself or himself: To feel a sense of belonging is to feel happy that one fits in with a group. To feel lonely is to feel sad because one lacks company. Similarly, embarrassment and shame are emotions that depend on an evaluation of self in relation to other people. As well as these feelings that refer to the self, there are also emotions in which the comparison with others yields a feeling about them, for example, various forms of sympathy and empathy and the more bitter feelings of envy and jealousy. Figure 8 sketches our analysis of complex emotion terms.

Although there are no cases in which the meaning of a complex term lies outside the basic modes,[18] some complex emotions can produce specific autonomic responses, such as blushing because of embarrassment.

Consciousness and the self. Representations of the self first become accessible in consciousness as a result of relationships with others. Mead (1912)

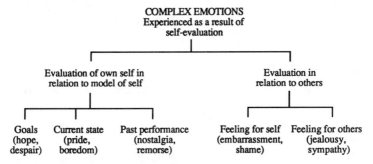

Figure 8. Classification of complex emotion terms, with examples in parentheses. (After Johnson-Laird & Oatley, 1988b.)

wrote: "Inner consciousness is socially organized by the importation of the social organization of the outer world" (p. 141). This aspect of self is not simply a source of experience, it can be an object of thought. This is expressed grammatically in the accusative "me." It corresponds to the model of self. Mead also argued that this aspect of self acts, in a manner that had been suggested previously by Adam Smith (1976/1759), to monitor ongoing activity, "criticizing, approving and suggesting, and consciously planning" (Mead, 1913, p. 145). Though without the computational metaphor, Mead thus described some of the functions and reasons for an operating system containing a model of the whole system, including some of its goals and characteristics of some of its operations.

Cooley (1902) argued that "me" is a "looking-glass self," the self as seen in the social mirror of others' esteem and contempt. It remained to Mead to explain how in childhood such a self might be constructed by language in the world of adults and peers. The sense of paradox, or of infinite regress, in the idea of the self having a model of itself is avoided by the idea that "me" is a construction from the experience of others' reactions to us.

At first it is parents who hold up the social mirror:

> The child can think about his conduct as good or bad only as he reacts to his own acts in the remembered words of his parents . . . and the self which is a fusion of the remembered actor and this accompanying chorus is somewhat loosely organized and very clearly social. Later the inner stage changes into the forum and workshop of thought. The features and intonations of the

dramatis personae fade out and the emphasis falls upon the meaning of the inner speech, the imagery becomes the barely necessary cues. (Mead, 1913, pp. 146–147)

If I may suggest another metaphor: Communications based on emotion modes and their semantic content program new cognitive structures in the child. The individual skull is, as it were, permeable to these communications, which can help to create new mental modules. One of the important structures so created is this higher level model of self, the "me." Being able to reflect on ourselves implies the modular state of mentality, of being able in adulthood to think about oneself in something like the way we think of others, of being able to talk of looking after ourselves, controlling ourselves, and so on.

The model of self also contains each person's distinctive abstraction of rules and conventions of a community. It provides the agency by which values are maintained and propagated from one generation to another.

Mead went on to remark how in normal activity, self-consciousness is rare. People's actions are in register with their monitoring self and correspond to habit, to character, to what they expect, and to what others expect of them. It is only when "an essential problem appears, there is some disintegration in this organization, and different tendencies appear in reflective thought as different voices in conflict with each other. In a sense the old self has disintegrated, and out of the moral process a new self appears" (Mead, 1913, p. 147).

This phenomenon of becoming self-conscious when a problem arises in a social plan is a typical part of the experience of adult emotion. The idea is indeed close to the conflict theories of emotion expressed by Paulhan and Dewey (discussed in Chapter 3). An emotion mode generates pervasive signals that coordinate modules and perhaps initiate bodily changes. By running the issue in the conscious simulation system of the mind, emotion signals concentrate attention and preoccupy the operating system. In the state of being-in-love, it becomes hard to stop thinking about the other person. With a severe loss the inner dialogue becomes a rumination about the loss. After insult or injury, we feel angry and the inner debate may concern the means and advisability of retaliation. In general, conscious reflection arises from the critical juncture. It concerns such matters as consequences for goals and plans. Often these matters are ambiguous, especially in the negative emotions, and so the inner debate may be about whether to adjust the model of the self or the model of the other, and about what new plans may be appropriate, or even what new goals. Plans are evaluated in mental simulations in which conflicts can be detected among the multiple goals of the goal hierarchy. The semantic messages associated with conclusions from such operations rise to consciousness, "as voices in debate."

The self as an archive of interpersonal history. With this account of the self, it seems that our model of ourselves is a kind of archive of our history of relating. It contains both elaborations of the strategies of relating that we have practiced and some abstracted experiences of ourselves in interaction with others.[19] What happens when a mode is activated, then, is that some amalgam of strategies is made ready and modes of experience of the self associated with them are activated.

There is now substantial empirical evidence to indicate that when happy, happy memories come to mind, and when sad, sad memories come to mind (Blaney, 1986). Bower (1987) has suggested that in depression, only cognitive states that were initially involved in causing an original state of depression are preferentially remembered.

The most studied effects have been those of depression. Beck (e.g., Beck at al., 1979) proposed that people are vulnerable to depression insofar as incidents in adulthood reactivate schemata based on negative personal experiences in childhood. These schemata tend to activate ideas of personal defeat and worthlessness of the self. More recently, Teasdale (1988) has proposed a variation of this idea, consistent with the theory proposed here, that once a person has entered a sad or dysphoric mood the cognitive system is biased to activate schemata based on the same mood. Such activations contribute to a mood's persistence because dysphoric autobiographical memories come to mind (cf. also Conway & Bekerian, 1987). As a person remembers demeaning implications of an event, these tend to maintain the dysphoric mood, and it is difficult to initiate optimistic plans.

The hypothesis here is that part of the effect of emotions is to give differential access not only to types of readiness appropriate to each emotion, but aspects of personal autobiographical experience germane to particular moods, because, due to the development of the cognitive system by accretion throughout life, these will be stored together and there will be advantages in relating knowledge and compiled strategies appropriate to each type of eliciting situation and hence to each basic emotion mode.

According to this theory, unusual persistence or severity of depression occurs, not because of any defect in this useful mechanism, but because for some of us, the sense of self built up from our early relationships may be characterized by failure, rejection, punitiveness, or injunctions toward perfectionism. Such experiences can be damaging – we live in a society where failure and rejections are often viewed harshly, and our model of self is affected by this.

Role as a basis for social interaction

The bases of relating are models of self and others, first formed in childhood and reissued in a number of versions, more or less adapted to different social settings. Such structures are roles, the social equivalent of habits, outline enactments in which self and other play complementary parts. The outlines of these roles are known to the participants, and give them scripts for particular types of performance with each other. Mead thought that roles are learned in childhood play by taking up the position of the other; and, indeed, he supposed that this ability is central to all social interaction. Hoffman (1986) has shown that emotional empathy is related to our ability to interact with others in role relationships.

Role is a term that has slipped so easily from social science into common speech that now it seems barely technical. Social philosophers of the last century seem to have been hampered by the lack of this concept. Or perhaps the former absence of the term indicates that a social change really has occurred. People have become interchangeable. Perhaps only recently has it become usual that roles in employment, negotiation, and even close relationships exist as patterns that are partly independent of the player. They can be slipped into by anyone with certain attributes who can give plausible performances of the parts afforded.

Two metaphors inform this idea: the theatrical performance, from which the idea of role is directly taken, and games that provide roles for players who use the rules of the game to structure their interactions.

The theater, since ancient times and in many societies, has been a place where consequences of human action could be modeled and explored. In classical Greek tragedy, the protagonist stands for everyone, implying universality of the predicaments enacted. The actors are masked, implying both concealment and the presentation of a particular face. The actions are commented on by society represented by the chorus. The protagonist experiences powerful emotions in a world that it is impossible to understand fully in advance, but in which she or he must nevertheless act and take responsibility for actions.

Games are also ancient. They are models of recurring types of interaction in society, perhaps those that fascinate us or demand the development of abilities of motor skill or problem solving that are too difficult or risky for real life. Chess is a safe version of medieval battles with nobles as the cavalry able to dash about in an exciting way, and peasant foot soldiers able only to plod slowly and liable to be killed easily. Each player performs feats of reasoning in a limited universe that would be quite impracticable in the ordinary world. Monopoly is an allegorical reenactment of commercial competition and the accumulation of wealth, preferably by putting other people out of business, which would be crass if it were enacted in ordinary commerce. Tennis requires skills of coordination and prediction of the other's actions that would be hard to acquire if being beaten meant being killed or maimed as in sword fighting. As Stephen Draper (personal communication) has said, it may be rash to disagree with Wittgenstein, who claimed that games have no ready definition, only family resemblances. Nonetheless, games seem as if they may be defined as activities that offer players top-level goals. Players adopt these goals and then see what it is like to interact with others on the basis of a given system of rules and operations.

The classical definition of role was given by Linton (1936). To enact a role is like playing a certain position in a football team. A position, quarterback or whatever, is not the role – enacting it is. A role gives the skeleton of one part of a joint plan, which allows a performance that will coordinate with other actors and be recognizable to others in pursuit of certain agreed goals and subgoals.

Goffman (1961) describes entering into a role interaction as entering through a semi-permeable membrane, within which certain rules apply and within which there are an official top-level goal and an officially recognized focus of activity corresponding to this top-level goal. In a game there is only one official top-level goal. In football it is to win, by as large a margin as possible. In real life, however, there may be several goals that any individual is pursuing. So any interaction may be ambiguous as to which goals are in play. Part of interaction is to agree at any time with other participants on one of them or on a small set. Only then will an interaction, a joint plan, be able to take place smoothly.

In real life, though not always in games, the official focus changes, sometimes abruptly and sometimes often. So new interpretations of an interaction can occur. Perhaps one participant at the office says: "It's late. Let's call it a day, and get a drink." At this point participants exit through the membrane that contains "office discussion," its roles of work colleagues, and the rules that apply there. They pass through a membrane and change roles to those of sociability, with different rules and a different recognized focus and goals. Other types of changes may occur. In one of Goffman's examples, at mealtime in a psychiatric ward one of the patients "asks for the salt in voice that covers the whole table with misery and gloom" (p. 24). The patient has stopped enacting the role of having a meal with others, and redefined the situation in terms of the role of his or her misery and implied complementary roles of others' sympathy.

In individual action problems may be raised by unanticipated events and by the different goals that the individual has. Emotions prompt continuation or change of plans. In interaction entirely comparable decisions are taken. There are two possibilities at such junctures. In one, a joint plan continues with participants modifying it as necessary to meet unexpected contingencies and disattending distractions. In the other, the participants change the focus, exit through one membrane, and perhaps reconvene inside another.

Though emotions are not always recognizable at such junctures of social interaction, they often are. They signal when a joint plan can be maintained and when it can be changed. In the first case emotions are happy; in the second they tend to be dysphoric. In the rest of this chapter, and in Part II of the book, I treat mainly dysphoric emotions. Discussion of more cheerful emotions and their relation to this formulation is in Chapter 8.

Interpersonal schemata of emotions

Lutz (1987) proposes on the basis of her work on Ifaluk that emotions function in four main schemata that are predominantly interpersonal. The schemata are organizations of cultural knowledge into which we are inducted by parents and others. Lutz's idea, I think, advances ideas of prototypes, emotion processes, scripts, and paradigm scenarios,[20] in that instead of assuming that this issue concerns largely the causation of emotions, her schemata also specify what leads to what in terms of interpersonal implications.

The relation between an eliciting condition and an emotion that may properly occur as a result constitutes Lutz's first schema, as follows:

Schema 1 is: If event X, then emotion Y.

Typically event X will have interpersonal significance. For instance, if someone has traveled away from the island of Ifaluk, one feels *fago* (compassion/love/sadness) for that person. If there has been a rule violation by the self, or if one is called to eat by someone unfamiliar, one will feel *metagu* (fear/anxiety).

Schema 2 is: If we experience emotion X, then we may perform act Y.

For instance, if we feel happy, we may laugh, talk a lot, misbehave, and "walk around," that is, neglect work or show off. And if we feel *fago* (compassion/love/sadness), we might refuse to speak or refuse to eat. Action Y on Ifaluk will typically be interpersonal or have interpersonal significance.

Schema 3 is: If we experience emotion X, then another person should or might experience emotion Y.

So if one person feels or expresses *song* (justifiable anger), then the person to whom this is expressed will tend to feel *metagu* (feat/anxiety). Or if one person feels *tang* (frustration/grief), others will feel *fago* (compassion/love/sadness).

Schema 4 is: If we experience emotion X, we may later experience emotion Y.

Some examples are that following *rus* (panic/fright/surprise), one may feel *song* (justifiable anger) toward the person who caused it. Or following *filengaw* (incapacity/discomfort) one may feel *ma* (shame/embarrassment).

Lutz shows how these schemata can be combined in various ways, and how many of them are important in negotiating roles or forming the bases of joint plans.

Schema 1 is salient in Euro-American folk theory, as well as on Ifaluk. It is the heart of the theory embedded in English emotion terms. We think of emotions as happening to us. We think of them as being largely outside voluntary control, predominantly as experiences of the individual self. This schema states that events cause emotions. It also has come to dominate thinking in European and American psychology, so that much of the research on emotions is about emotion-eliciting events and how they are evaluated.

Schema 2 is that if a certain emotion occurs we may perform a particular action. As Lutz points out, the general form of this schema is common to both Ifaluk and Western cultures; instantiations of it in the two cultures are often quite distinctively different.

In Schema 3, if we experience emotion X, others may experience emotion Y. Here Lutz avers that Ifaluk and American ethnotheory diverge, because in Ifaluk, emotions are primarily interpersonal, whereas in the United States Lutz thinks the more internalizing and subjective folk theory would tend toward seeing emotions as nearly always triggered by external events. So, in the United States, it is not so much that an emotion in one person causes emotions in others but rather that when such effects occur, it is thought that something one person says or does might cause the emotion in the other.

As to Schema 4, that one emotion may lead to another, this too occurs in Euro-American ethnotheory. As Katz (1980) points out, an emotion may be part of a sequence of emotional states in which one mode gives way to another as events unfold or further evaluations occur, perhaps in sequences: Anxiety → anger → sadness. This can appear as emotions following one another in waves, particularly in response to severe events. Such mobility of emotions can be treated in terms of phases of adjustment to certain kinds of events, perhaps most notably to bereavement (cf. Silver & Wortman, 1980), as the event is coped with and cognitively reevaluated. Some kinds of ritual allow such processes to occur in concert with other people.[21] Further reasons for emotions following one another in sequence, though, might be the possibility of switching between basic emotion modes and also the possibilities of changes of semantic interpretation within modes.

It is tempting to suppose that Lutz's schemas may be universal, even though the events that trigger emotions and their relevance to goals may be culturally specific. The triggering of emotions by events, Lutz's Schema 1, has been dealt with. Schema 2 and Schema 3 are more specifically interpersonal. In the next sections, therefore, I shall ask whether these patterns derived from Ifaluk may generalize, and also whether these interpersonal aspects are known about in Western culture.

An analysis of anger

Lutz's Schema 2 is that if we experience emotion X, then we may perform act Y. In both Ifaluk and the West such acts of type Y have social significance. An important work in which this schema is explored is Averill's (1982) book on anger. It draws on historical treatments, on philosophy, on experiments, and on other fields. I will choose just two of his topics. One is at the extreme of human behavior, on the relation of anger to homicide. The other concerns Averill's findings on more ordinary episodes of anger.

Anger and the law of homicide. There are two common kinds of analysis of law. One is of law as more or less explicit commands of a ruler backed by sanctions that may be enforced violently against those who are ruled. The ruler may be a ruling elite, and the law's effects, consciously or unconsciously recognized, may be to benefit some parts of society rather than others. The other conception is of a social contract, a broader consensus of rules to which a whole culture subscribes. It seems likely that the law on homicide is of the consensual kind. Some evidence for this is from a survey by Rossi et al. (1974) assessing the seriousness with which people view various types of killing. There were few differences attributable to different groups in society, of racial background, education, income, and so forth. Subjects ranked 19 types of homicide in an order of seriousness that was close to legal categories. These types included planned killing for a fee, impulsive killing of an acquaintance, killing a pedestrian while driving a car, and so on.

Two major currents have contributed to American law on homicide. One is influenced by Germanic and English law from the middle ages onward, that public procedures should replace traditional individual duties of blood feuds in which people were obliged to avenge deaths of members of their family. The other is the tradition from Greek and Roman law of a moral or mental element, that some killings are more reprehensible than others.

In the mental tradition, American law makes a distinction between murder as the most serious kind of killing carrying the heaviest penalties and manslaughter as less serious and carrying lesser penalties. Murder occurs with malice aforethought. This indicates either that the person had planned the killing in advance, or killed in the course of another crime, as in a robbery. The category also includes the killing of public officials, as police officers in the performance of their duties, though this type of killing has clearly been smuggled into the category meriting the most serious punishments. It was not found by Rossi et al. to be different in seriousness from killing nonofficials. Manslaughter is killing in which there has not been malice aforethought. It includes killing while the perpetrator was angry.

To put it crudely, anger is a vindication of killing. The implication for understanding emotions is that here is a folk theory of anger operationalized for use in courts. According to this theory, anger is not just a feeling. Four requirements have to be met for a verdict to be given of manslaughter based on anger rather than of murder: (1) There must be adequate provocation, and this amounts to establishing in court that the provocation was such as would rouse a reasonable person to anger. (2)

The actual mental state of the accused is taken into account: The killing must have been done in the "heat of passion," not in "cold blood." (3) The idea of cooling time is applied: If a jury judges that the anger had sufficient time to cool, and if, for instance, the accused engaged in deliberate well-planned acts between the provocation and the killing (like making an business call), then the killing would be murder. (4) It has to be shown that the anger was caused by the provocation: There is no mitigation if the intent to kill was formed before the provocation. We find in this codification that, with sufficient provocation to anger, the response to an eliciting event may transgress society's most solemn prohibitions against taking human life. A passion is regarded as legitimate if provocation is adequate. If the provocation is inadequate, no matter how impassioned a person may become, there is no mitigation.

According to this folk theory embedded in law, in one way anger is an involuntary passion. At the same time social rules (e.g., about how long a passion lasts and whether an intention to kill might have been formed before the provocation) are applied strictly to its expression in assessing an act of killing. Moreover, in court, the adequacy of provocation is judged not by whether the person was provoked, but on normative grounds, by whether a reasonable person would have been provoked in those same circumstances.

Averill argues that anger is thus not so much a biological event as a socially constituted temporary role, in which certain rules and responsibilities are redefined.[22] In other words, a person sufficiently and adequately provoked enters an extraordinary social role, which itself has transitional qualities. As English law put it until recently, the kinds of provocation seen as adequate were as follows: Catching one's wife in the act of adultery, being violently assaulted by another, being caught up in a sudden mutual quarrel, and being arrested unlawfully.[23] Under these circumstances, the wrong may be redressed by entering, as it were, though a social membrane with different rules than those that were operating prior to the incident, and taking on the role of an injured party in a way that might result in the death of the person who provoked the anger.

Averill's diary studies of anger. Averill's (1982) studies of anger examine more ordinary incidents. They are a model for research on emotions. In his main study he analyzed structured diaries from 80 randomly chosen married community subjects, aged 21 to 60.[24] He also analyzed 80 diaries from university students, who were single and under 21 years old and who volunteered for the study. The questionnaires were rather detailed, with 88 items, asking subjects also to estimate the number of episodes of anger or annoyance during the previous week. Most of the analyses were on the subjects' descriptions of an incident that made them most angry rather than annoyed during the week, and an incident that made them most annoyed but not angry.

Anger is not an uncommon emotion in Massachusetts. The majority of subjects (66%) reported an angry episode one to two times a week, and 44% an annoying episode at least once a day. These are underestimates, partly due to episodes being forgotten during a weeklong study. In a further study in which people kept daily diaries, Averill found a mean of 7.3 incidents of anger, and 23.5 incidents of annoyance were recorded per week.

Angry episodes were nearly always perceived as having been instigated by another person or a human institution. Of the 6% that were not, the subjects nevertheless spoke in human terms, or with close connection to some human failing. For instance, a plumber who became angry at a trap he had installed that leaked because it had an inconspicuous hairline crack, described his response as follows: "I made the hole in the trap bigger, as if to say, 'That's what you should look like if you are going to leak.'" When describing his motives he said: "Silly, but if I'm doing my job, why can't the trap do its job?" (p. 166).

People provoking anger were most often seen as doing something voluntarily that they had no right to do, or as doing something they could have avoided had they been more careful. The majority of anger-inducing events were described as frustrating or interrupting what subjects were doing. At the same time frustration or interruption was hardly ever the sole cause. Of the 129 subjects who mentioned frustration as being involved, 124 indicated that one or more of the following also applied: violation of important personal expectations, violation of socially accepted ways of behaving, a loss of personal pride, possible or actual property damage, or personal injury. Of those who did not mention frustration the reasons given, in order of frequency, were loss of self-esteem, violation of personal wishes or expectations, and violations of socially accepted ways of behaving.

Episodes of anger were most often provoked by people the subject knew well and liked, such as parents, children, spouses, and friends. Although many people (57%) said that their motives were for getting even for the present incident or for previous wrongs (39%), the most common motive was to assert authority or independence, or to improve the subject's image (63%). Subjects frequently gave as a motive bringing about a change in the instigator, either for their own good (54%) or for the instigator's good (49%) or to strengthen a relationship (46%). Using anger to express dislike occurred (28%), and to break off a relationship (18%), but these motives of dislike and discontinuation were relatively infrequent in comparison with motives for strengthening or readjusting a relationship.

Averill also investigated subjects who had been the targets of anger. This sample was of student volunteers, recruited in parallel with those of the first study. The questionnaire they answered was designed to be as similar as possible to that of the first study. Of the people who had been the targets of anger, 95% agreed that the anger had resulted from something they, the target, had done. Whereas the angry person had perceived the targets as having acted in an unjustified or avoidable way, the main discrepancy was that targets thought they had been justified or that the incident was beyond anyone's control. Evidently, there is room for negotiation – and this may no doubt be related to the finding that among the angry people, more than half subsequently reappraised the incident, with the most common type of reappraisal being a rein-terpretation of guilt or motives of the target.

The target person most usually recognized anger from the other person's tone of voice (89%), facial expression (75%), or body postures or gestures (60%) from the content of what was said (86%), from actions of withdrawal (48%), and aggression (28%), combined with the knowledge of the incidents themselves (63%). Targets were often aware that a particular event would make the person angry, before expressive signs were evident, and 57% of targets said that the anger was somewhat or very much expected. The most common responses of targets were hurt feelings (66%), surprise (63%), and a range of other responses that included apology, defiance, anger, rejection, and denial of responsibility. Over the longer term most targets (76%) said the episode helped them realize their own faults, and 48% said their relationship with the angry person was strengthened.

Approximately two thirds of angry people felt negatively about their anger, and targets typically felt even worse. But despite the subjective dysphoria, 100 of the 160 angry people rated the anger as beneficial, compared with 41 who found it harmful and 19 who found it both or neutral. About 70% of targets rated the angry incident as beneficial.

Averill regards this as the most important result of this research. Anger is unpleasant and distressing for both parties, but both regard it as beneficial. It functions to regulate our relationships. In agreement on this, Jenkins, Smith, and Graham (1989), in a community study of 139 English families, found that 79% of women speaking of marital quarrels that included angry voices raised for at least 10 minutes thought that at least some good came from such quarrels. By contrast, only 41% of their children saw these quarrels as beneficial.

Averill points out that emotions have similar properties to speech acts. They affect those to whom they are directed, and the effects depend on social rules and conventions, as well as on the communication and the circumstances.

Anger, annoyance, and the renegotiation of roles. Averill points out that some emotions accomplish role transitions and some do not. People in his study were able to distinguish anger from annoyance, with anger being more intense, predominantly interpersonal, more likely to involve attributions of blame and the intention for revenge, and being more serious and personally threatening. Averill points out that anger refers to a state of the self where knowledge is forced upon us by our passionate feelings and perhaps by physiological accompaniments. It is hard to ignore. Anger is also an indictment of someone that must not be made without due warrant. It carries an intention. Like the speech acts of promising or threatening, it carries a commitment to action if the behavior or attitude of the target person does not change. By contrast, annoyance does not share these properties to any great extent. A person becoming annoyed does not take a stand on the issue, and there is not the same sense of indictment and commitment to action.

Averill's account indicates that anger is seldom initiated just by unpredictable events. It is primarily an emotion of joint plans, in which the other person has not done his or her part as he or she should. An angry incident may have unpleasant effects, but the consensus is that anger is usually beneficial to relationships.

Although researchers agree that emotions occur frequently in our social relationships, Averill explains what might be meant by emotions being interpersonal. Anger functions to adjust relationships when one participant perceives another as having violated a commitment or as having transgressed a rule that functions to regulate social behavior. Typically, too, anger occurs in relationships that are expected to continue, in role relationships such as husband-wife, friend-friend, or parent-child. These are relationships that are based not just on a single episode of joint planning, but on the expectation that there will be

Table 6. *Role transitions accomplished by or justified by emotions (extension of Table 5)*

Basic emotion	Adult social emotion	Juncture of joint plans or roles	Example of social justification
Happiness	Sexual love, joys of cultural pursuits, delight	Commitment and engagement in joint plans	Falling in love
Sadness	Depression, disappointment	Loss of valued joint plans and goals	Mourning after bereavement
Fear	Conscious anxiety, embarrassment	Lack of confidence in fulfilling roles	Agoraphobic anxiety
Anger	Vengefulness, bitterness	Readjustment of roles or joint expectations	Righteous anger justifying violence
Disgust	Hatred, loathing	Discontinuation of joint plan or disengagement	Anorexic refusals to eat or share meals

further joint plans in an extended series, and that these will be related to one another by characteristics of the participants being known and predictable. In this sense, we see anger as involved in the regulation of roles and in transitions between roles.

Emotions as transitional roles

Averill's idea (1990) is that emotions generally are transitional roles. We can express the idea by extending Table 5, retaining the columns "Basic emotion" and "Adult social emotion" and inserting new columns for junctures in joint plans and for the typical justifications of role transition for the emotions in question. This produces Table 6.

Taking the rows of Table 6 in turn, we see in the first row something that Averill points out: To declare that one loves someone is not just to say one likes that person. It is to commit oneself to that person in a long-term role. It anticipates a future of joint activity, asserts that one will engage in it willingly and wholeheartedly, and carries an expectation of happiness within the role. I will discuss this further in Chapter 8. Such large-scale commitments evidently require an extraordinary justification. In Western society it is called "falling in love." Falling in love has a comparable social structure to the one pointed out by Averill (1985) for anger. Just as an unusual state of passionate anger can be appealed to by people who have killed someone, so people appeal to falling in love as a state that is involuntary and that justifies (evidently) role changes that would otherwise be prohibited and that often seem bizarre. They can involve abandoning children, career, family, as well as a sexual partner to whom commitments had been made.[25]

Moving to the next basic emotion: Sadness occurs with the loss of a role relationship. In its largest and most obvious social form is the grief of bereavement or separation in which the loss involves that part of the self that was engaged in joint plans with another. During mourning, a person is socially justified in absenting herself or himself from other social duties for a while. In Chapter 6, I will discuss such issues further.

In the case of the next basic emotion, fear in its interpersonal sense is often experienced as anxiety. It can result from separation from people to whom one is attached – hence it is an emotion that can warn against embarking on plans without the partner, and often occurs to ensure that the partner does not allow one to be subjected to dangers, real or imaginary. Agoraphobia provides a prototype: Though anxiety is felt by one person it usually constrains another person such as a spouse to be close by on all outings and social interactions. Anxiety is perhaps the most fertile ground of all for symptoms and their transpositions. It can justify many types of social arrangements. Some of these I will discuss in Chapter 7.

Anger is the socially constituted emotion that Averill has discussed most fully. It affords justification for violence in some circumstances and in Chapter 5 I discuss it further.

Disgust has emotions such as hatred, loathing, and contempt as its interpersonal forms. These are emotions of withdrawal from other people, of cessation or dissociation from joint plans. An example of a social justification in which disgust is recognizable in European and American society is anorexia and its milder forms in various refusals to eat, which some adolescents discover as a potent role for controlling their parents.

In so far as emotions provide socially constructed transitional roles, they are of course aspects of the folk theories that I discussed at the beginning of Chapter 2. What we know about love, anger, grief, and the rest provides us with the materials to interpret our experience and to have a hand in creating it. So when I say I am angry, I am not merely consulting an introspective state – though I claim that I do experience such a state when angry. I am also referring to an elaborate theory of anger known to myself and others in my culture, which has implications for me and for the person I am angry at.

Nisbett and Ross (1980) have argued that people are too affected by their implicit theories, and that they use them to make inferences when they would be better attending to the actual causes of behavior. No doubt in many ways this is so, but this slant can give implicit theories a bad name. As Nisbett and Ross acknowledge, these same intuitive theories are bases for many human accomplishments as well as for lapses. As far as emotions go, an accomplishment is to provide a basis of communication consciously with ourselves and less consciously with other people that creates a structure of predictability in interactions.

Direct interpersonal transmission of emotions

Lutz's Schema 3 is that if we experience emotion X, then another person should or might experience emotion Y. In the West we might disattend this kind of schema. What might be relatively unfamiliar is the apparently direct transmission that nonsemantic signals of emotion seem to have among us. This, for instance, is the implication of some of the research on the effect of adult anger on children (as by Cummings, Ianotti & Zahn-Waxler, 1985), reviewed in Chapter 2. According to the communicative theory, nonsemantic emotion signals between people do not need to be thought about or have their significance understood for them to affect us. In adults one way to study this has been to make physiological recordings during social interaction.

Physiological indices of emotion in social interaction. Recently, physiological recording techniques have allowed an increased understanding of how people experiencing emotions in mutual plans communicate these emotional states between each other. Ax (1964) had speculated that empathy, a name for such communication, might be thought of as "an autonomic nervous system state which tends to simulate that of another person" (p. 12). Levenson and Gottman (1983) took this idea further by making recordings of patterns of physiological response in 30 married couples.

Recording sessions took place after the members of each couple had been apart for at least 8 hours. Electrodes were attached to record heart rate, pulse transmission time (a measure of the force of the heartbeat and the distension of the arteries), skin conductance (a measure of the amount of sweat being produced), and general bodily activity. At the same time verbal and nonverbal behavior were recorded on videotape. After 5 minutes of sitting quietly the couple began a conversation. They had been asked to talk about the events of the day as they would if alone together at home. After 15 minutes of this conversation, the recording stopped and both completed some questionnaires, including measures of marital satisfaction. Then there was another recording session of similar length, but this time they discussed a specified problem that they had previously identified as a matter of conflict between them, in an attempt to resolve it or reach a compromise. A few days later, each spouse went again to the laboratory, separately, to view the video recording, to have further physiological recordings made while watching the session, and to make ratings by moving a pointer of how positive or negative were the emotions they remembered experiencing at each point of the recorded conversations.

Levenson and Gottman created a measure of what they call physiological linkage, the extent to which the physiological responses of one spouse predicted those of the other during their discussions. They then related these measures to the measures of marital satisfaction that they had made. There was no relation between physiological linkage and marital satisfaction in the conversations on the events of the day. But in the conversations on conflictual areas, high linkage was strongly related to marital dissatisfaction.[26]

In dissatisfied marriages more negative emotions and fewer positive ones occurred, especially when the topic turned to an area of conflict. Typically, the wife would reciprocate the husband's negative emotions. At the same time, although in conflictual marriages there was little in the way of positive emotions, husbands did not reciprocate any positive emotions that their wives expressed. In satisfied marriages interactions were less constrained.

The results imply that in dissatisfied marriages there was more stereotyping of responses as conflicts escalated. Each person's negative emotions were communicated to the other partner, and seemed directly to cause negative emotions in that partner. This phenomenon may contribute to the sense of being locked into interactions that both partners feel are involuntary and that neither can change.[27] This evidence demonstrates Lutz's Schema 3. To put the hypothesis at its strongest, emotion X in one person can cause another person's emotion Y.

Levenson and Gottman's measures of reciprocation of negative emotions imply that emotions such as anger that causes reciprocal anger and anger that causes fear were being passed between the spouses. Other patterns have also been reported, for example, anxiety communicating anxiety. Minuchin, Rosman, and Baker (1978) reported that anxiety of parents in a conflictual discussion can be passed on to certain kinds of susceptible children. When this has occurred, and the child has psychosomatic effects of this anxiety, the child's physiological anxiety measures continue high while physiological measures of the parents' anxiety decline. This pattern may underlie certain syndromes in which a child may suffer a psychosomatic illness based on anxiety but this is really an indicator of parental dissatisfaction in their marriage. Asthma or certain kinds of psychologically affected diabetes can create life-threatening emergencies, thus distracting everyone from the root cause, which may be an unresolved conflict between parents. It can also function to preserve marriages, as parents can concentrate on their sick child, avoid their conflicts, and defer their resolution indefinitely. But the price of this can be a child whose illness worsens at any time that a parental conflict seems likely to break out.

The ambiguity of emotions

I opened Chapter 1 by saying that we live in two worlds, of nature and culture. In this chapter we find ourselves at the intersection of these worlds. Emotions can be deeply ambiguous. Simultaneously they are happenings that are involuntary with a biological basis and they are justifications for interpersonal actions that must obey social rules.

Emotions are not just *either* physiological mechanisms *or* social meanings. We are caught up in the fine paradox of states that require that they are both, simultaneously. They draw some of their significance precisely from that fact. We know enough, I think, about what goes on between us to realize that when one spouse says to another: "Let's not make love tonight, I've got an awful headache" the real question is not whether that person does or does not have a headache. It is how this is interpreted and incorporated into the interpersonal world. The difference is whether the speech act is "Oh, damn, I've got a headache, I'm sorry" or "Oh, good, I've got a headache. So there." Like headaches, emotions have this quality of ambiguity and I will explore this further in Chapter 7.

Averill illustrates the importance of this ambiguity in his discussion of the law on homicide. In pleading for a verdict of manslaughter a defense counsel must argue that anger occurred as an involuntary natural passion. For the defense to succeed, the killing must have conformed to certain societal rules, including the absence of delay or of a deliberate plan. Comparably, it is hard to imagine people doing in cold blood some of the things they do when in love, a state that is thought of as being largely involuntary, though certain rules must be applied for any justification to be convincing.

And speaking of emotions . . . the pragmatics of emotion terms

I have concentrated in this chapter on the structure of joint planning and on its semantic and nonsemantic bases. But, of course, emotion terms are used in our verbal communications with each other. As well as emotion terms having semantics, we can ask how they are used pragmatically. Again we can look to Tolstoy for some paradigmatic examples.

Anna's statements to Karenin in the carriage on the way home from the races are a renegotiation of her most important commitments. She says "I love him, I am his mistress; I cannot endure you; I am afraid of you, and I hate you" (p. 212). When she says, "I love him," she advises Karenin that her marital commitment is replaced by a commitment to Vronsky. Then, by saying that she is afraid of Karenin, she offers the beginning of a justification for her disengagement from him. By saying that she hates him, she implies that her withdrawal from him will be complete.

This is not simply an announcement of details of Anna's mental state. It has effects of the most profound kind. We understand them by noting that in these cases the verbal utterances offer semantic content for the nonsemantically prompted role changes already in progress. Karenin had for some time been aware of his wife's emotional withdrawal, but when he had spoken of it with her, she had disclaimed it. Her conflicts were such that she both did and did not want the role changes that were taking place. At the races Karenin had interpreted her anxiety about one of the riders correctly. A small gust of contempt blows toward himself in Anna's gesture:

> She glanced for an instant at him, with a look of inquiry, and, slightly frowning turned away again.
> "Oh, I don't care!" she seemed to say to him. (p. 209)

Semantically, what is said in the carriage confirms to Karenin what he has picked up nonsemantically. Words do not just describe feelings. They are needed to build plans, in the way that Power (1979) has shown. Just as "I love you" is a statement of commitment to continuing mutual activity, not just a description of an emotional state, so "I hate you" is a statement of ending commitment, saying joint goals no longer exist, withdrawal is in progress, mutual planning can no longer be assumed.

There are several ways in which emotion terms are used when we speak to each other. This one, which gives semantic content to a role adjustment, is perhaps the most significant for the kind of theory being developed here, but I will end the chapter by giving a brief sketch of the ways in emotion terms are used.

Role adjustment

As I have just indicated, emotion terms function in renegotiating the relationship between the people who are speaking, or adjusting, or explaining the mental state of either person in such a way that it may affect their relationship, temporarily or more permanently. Anna's utterance is an example on the most significant scale. On a minor scale we use expressions like "I'm not cross, I'm just not feeling very well"[28] to clarify aspects of an emotion, reinterpret it, enjoin others to act in various ways with regard to their emotions, and so forth. In this case the speaker was explaining her lack of talkativeness in terms of feeling sick and thus indicating to the hearer that she was not angry with him, that he had not done anything that might require apology, renegotiation, or repair.

Education

A second use of emotion terms is educative. Lutz (1987) recounts an example from Ifaluk: She was chatting with a woman outside her hut when a girl of about four came past, did a little dance, and made a silly face. Lutz was thinking that the girl was rather cute, but her woman companion said: "Don't smile at her – she'll think you are not *song*" (justifiably angry). On Ifaluk, one has to be a bit careful about happiness. As Lutz explains in her Schema 2, it can lead to showing off and misbehaving. Evidently this is what the woman had in mind, in her advice to Lutz, implying that smiling would encourage the little girl. *Song* is felt and expressed toward people who are violating rules. This utterance was educative advice on rules for emotional expression.

Such utterances may be particularly frequent when speaking to children. Here is another example, this time from Europe: "If he's bugging you, sit up at the table." Here a mother was advising her four-year-old son to take the drawing he was doing to a place that was out of reach of his one-year-old brother, who was showing interest in the drawing materials. Here she was both attempting to educate the older child about how to handle a developing interpersonal incident and guarding against its possible escalation.

De Sousa (1980, 1987) has argued that paradigm scenarios of emotion allow us to learn first the occasions for various emotions and then the proper actions in response. De Sousa observes that our folk theory is that emotions motivate responses, but more likely the learning is the other way round. If emotions are primarily based on action readiness, which in turn is based on genetic programs, then what we have to learn are the names for such kinds of readiness and the elaborations and ramifications of the situations in which they arise. Such scenarios are a primary vehicle for education, by parents and in other ways. By means of such scenarios we come to recognize emotions and are able to judge whether or not an emotion is appropriate to a situation. It is in this sense that Hochschild (1979) proposes that in any culture we come to act in relation to feeling rules, for managing our emotions appropriately to situations.[29]

Social comparison

A third use of emotion terms is in social commentary and comparison. As a species we spend a great deal of time discussing and evaluating other people and ourselves. Among the subjects of this evaluation are people's emotions, for example: "He is not a very happy person; He's not interested in other people"; or "She took the huff." Such things tend to be said in evaluation of others, their emotions, and the appropriateness of those emotions.

These attributions have two kinds of purpose. In one kind they allow all concerned to compare themselves with the person being discussed, thus the sentiment "He's not a very happy person" allowed the three hearers of this remark to apply it to themselves. The implication in the context was something like: "We are all interested in other people, and this goes with us being generally happy." In other words, as pointed out by Totman (1979), such conversation, and perhaps particularly gossip, fulfills the important function of generating frequent social comparisons, which allow us constantly to reevaluate and revise cultural

rules of our local language communities, endorsing some of these rules
for ourselves and rejecting others. Thus we can see ourselves and others
as respectworthy or blameworthy.

In another kind of purpose, talk of emotions can be intended to provide hearers with materials for building models of people being discussed, tending to induce beliefs that could influence future joint plans
involving those people. The utterance "She took the huff" was made by
one academic to another about a student whom he had advised on an
academic matter and who had rejected the advice. This utterance gave
advance notice that should any problem arise because of the choice the
student made that she had been warned against it. Her huff (sulky
anger) indicated her unreasonable unwillingness to be guided. Such
utterances use emotions terms as fragments of informal character references.[30]

Narrative

A fourth use is in narrative accounts, for instance: "He was very glad to
have the house." Here the speaker, in casual conversation, was telling a
story of a visitor to London who had made a house exchange, and after
encountering various difficulties on the journey to London found the
house he had borrowed to be very convenient. Uses of emotion terms in
such contexts are more heterogeneous. They may function to explain
behavior, to describe mental outcomes (as in this example), and so on.

Narrative is the means by which we explain ourselves to ourselves
and to each other, particularly when joint plans become problematic.
Because of the inferences that can be made from them about goals and
plans, occurrences of emotions are often fundamental to narrative accounts. The role of emotions in narrative is the subject of the next
chapter.

Conflict and unpredictability

Tragedy also, however, shows something more deeply
disturbing: It shows good people doing bad things,
things otherwise repugnant to their ethical character and
commitments, because of circumstances whose origin
does not lie within them.

Martha Nussbaum
The fragility of goodness, p. 25

In Part I of this book I described how the cognitive system can be
thought of as being made up of quasi-autonomous modules, and how
society is made up of quasi-autonomous individuals. In both cases there
are problems of resolving conflicts of goals and of reevaluating plans
that have not gone as imagined. These problems may appropriately be
thought of as emotional. Part II, broadly speaking, is devoted to the
emotions that arise from conflict. In Chapter 5 the conflicts are those
that arise principally between people. Chapter 6 is concerned principally
with stressful events, sometimes described as conflicts between events
and goals. In Chapter 7, the conflicts are mainly intrapsychic – due to
goals within the individual being contradictory.

In Chapter 1, I described how we can think of the human emotional
system being organized around a small number of basic emotion modes,
perhaps just five. In this second part of the book, each chapter is devoted mainly to a discussion of one of those modes. In Chapter 5 the
principal emotion is anger, and I continue the analysis begun in Chapter
4. Chapter 6 is mainly about sadness, and Chapter 7 mainly about anxiety. (I leave the subject of happiness to Chapter 8.)

One of the threads running through Part II is the involuntariness of
emotions. Each chapter is based on a different type of narrative, fictional
or autobiographical, interpreted as our attempts to come to terms with
our emotions. Certainly narratives about emotions seem to be inescapa-

bly fascinating. Not only are emotions and the vicissitudes of human action the major preoccupation of European and American literature, but it is a social fact that people obsessively attend to stories in a variety of forms. We gossip, read books, watch television. Even the so-called news is presented to us in story form.

Frijda (1988) has described the involuntariness of emotion in terms of 12 laws. Not only do emotions have empirical regularities that may be regarded as laws by social scientists, they act in a law-like way on ourselves. Emotions are "grounded in mechanisms that are not of a voluntary nature and that are only partly under voluntary control. We are subject to our emotions, and we cannot engender emotions at will" (Frijda, 1988, p. 349).

What are Frijda's laws of emotion? They include a law that states emotions arise in response to the meaning of a situation, and one that says they arise in relation to goals. There is also one that says they arise in response to things regarded as real: So the idea of a disaster, perhaps a famine in the Third World, may not concern us. It is only when we are confronted with such a matter in our own lives, or in a way that makes it vivid to us, that our emotions are stirred. Then there is a law that emotions arise in response to changes rather than steady conditions. A law of hedonic asymmetry is that pleasure disappears with continuous satisfaction and emotional pain may endure under persisting adverse conditions, as the adversity continues to violate our goals. This stern and bitter law, as Frijda calls it, exists because emotions signal conditions of the world that have to be responded to. Like the other laws, he asserts, it is implacable.

Among the features of this quasi-involuntary nature are the effects emotions have in our interpersonal relations. At their most involuntary, emotions like anger or anxiety affect relationships where one might have thought there could be negotiation using semantic means. But in negotiations there is nothing so persuasive as the nonnegotiable. To present a proposal as something over which one has no control is a powerful interpersonal maneuver, one that cannot be countered by the other person saying that he or she might like to do this or that on the whole he or she would prefer that.

This is where Chapter 5 starts: The involuntary anger of a Greek hero is employed in an interpersonal maneuver, a sulk, which results in serious reverses for the Greek army in the Trojan War. Perhaps because it is difficult to measure, conflict between and within people has been somewhat resistant to scientific investigation – but it has been at the center of literary explorations of human life and is intimately concerned with emotions. Chapter 5, then, is an exploration of conflictual emotions in the *Iliad*. Such conflicts are also explored in the second part of the chapter, which is on George Eliot's *Middlemarch*, a novel with several themes – one about the interpersonal conflicts derived from projecting expectations onto another person in a love relationship.

Chapter 6 is concerned with stress, with ways in which an emotion can somehow be turned in on oneself and experienced as illness or a psychiatric state. The practical understanding of stress has become one of the major health issues of the modern world. In this chapter I draw on research in which ordinary people narrate significant events in their lives and their reactions to these events. To the extent that people's life plans are important to them, then events that unpredictably affect those plans are experienced as stressful. They give rise to dysphoric emotions and to psychiatric states such as depression, which in turn function in relation with other people.

This status of being inescapable and involuntary is also often achieved by anxiety. This emotion may provide a powerful argument in interpersonal life. And this indeed was what Freud began to suspect when he gave up treating his patients by hypnosis, at which he said he was not very good, and started instead to listen to them as they narrated their stories. Symptoms, as he realized, are not just malfunctions of mechanism, but transformations of anxiety into a rhetorical language, a language of persuasion. In Chapter 7, I offer an analysis of Freud's analysis of Dora. The case history of Dora is one of the seminal texts on intention, emotion, and the ways in which internal conflicts act on emotions. As we may see, the subtlety of these processes goes far beyond anything we can handle by cognitive modeling or in experiments.

In this second part of the book I claim that the emotions depicted by poets and novelists, in the accounts of people being interviewed about life events, and in the narratives of psychoanalysis are recognizable to us. Their recognition depends on making explicit the intuitions of members of European and American culture, in the same kind of way that Chomsky argues that understanding the structure of language requires that we make explicit the intuitions of native speakers. In all three kinds of narrative discussed in this part of the book, what is being made explicit are the goals and customary plans of our relationships. In the end the questions rest upon our assent, on our being able to say, "Yes, we do behave like that, with emotions like that, and with consequences like that."

What poets and novelists have succeeded in doing is to depict emotions: how they occur at certain junctures of intended action, how people are moved involuntarily by strong emotions, how anger escalates into cycles of revenge that are difficult to stop, how love triumphs over difficulties, and so on. When people attest that an account of emotions in literature is true this implies that it is recognizable, that it corresponds to certain schemata that they have. The fact that a poem can have currency for many people, even across cultures or centuries, suggests that certain issues common to people across these cultures are being hinted at.

Although emotions have not been easy to understand, either for individuals or in the collective activity of science, literature has been able to propose: "This is an emotion. This is how it comes about. These are its effects." In the *Iliad*, for instance, discussed in Chapter 5, Homer proposes what effects anger has. In this way, our conceptions of emotions and their interpersonal effects crystallize out of what might otherwise be diffuse and incoherent understandings.

Most of Part II can be read without special technical knowledge. Chapter 6 is more technical than the others, and readers who are less interested in the mechanisms of stress should skip parts as may be appropriate for them.

5. Plans and emotions in fictional narrative

In or about December 1910 human character changed.
Virginia Woolf
Collected essays, Vol. 1, p. 320

Homer and the archaeology of mind

The first three words of Homer's *Iliad* are *Menin aeide, thea* (Of anger sing, goddess). These words invoke the muse to sing about the anger of Achilles against Agamemnon, the leader of the Greek army, and the disastrous effects it had on the Greeks, who had for nine years besieged the city of Troy.

Looking into the *Iliad*, it is as if we are standing on a promontory overlooking an undiscovered country quite different from our own.[1] As we descend into it, we find that the land is peopled by gods and goddesses, by human heroes hardly less godlike, by armies of belligerent men subject to the unpredictabilities of a primitive life, and by occasional women who share the men's beds and tend their homes. Though the male mortals lead lives of action, most curious of all, none of them seems to regard himself as the author of his own thoughts, plans, or emotions.

It was perhaps not the contrast of ourselves with these fierce warriors that Virginia Woolf (1966/1924) had in mind when she said that human character had changed in 1910. Nevertheless, tracing European character through literature to her day indicates that indeed something had changed.[2] She saw this century as being different from the past – now we live in a post-Freudian, post-Proustian, post-Joycean age. Now the outer world is somewhat under control, but the world within has come into clearer focus. Now it is within us that the tumult often seems the fiercest. Now it is within us that implacable deities reign.

225

Nonetheless there are continuities with more ancient European narratives. Let me try and trace them. This chapter is on fictional narrative, accounts we tell ourselves about ourselves. I will consider first the *Iliad*, written some 2,700 years ago,[3] and then an account not much more than 100 years old, George Eliot's *Middlemarch*. In both of these, emotions are the central theme.

Mental terms in the Iliad

Mind, it seems, was not always an aspect of human experience. Though mind, consciousness, and body seem to us to be self-evident givens of existence, they were not for Homer. Mind was, as Snell (1982/1953) said, a discovery. Only once it was made did it seem self-evident. In its discovery it brought itself into being.

In physical archaeology, fragments of buildings and artifacts invite us to reconstruct past ways of life. In the archaeology of the emotions and consciousness, the fragments are those of narrative writing, poetry, and drama. Not just Homer, establishing a tradition of European written literature as he did with a tale of anger, but also other writers have been fascinated by the emotions, perhaps because they are so problematic for us. One might almost imagine that great writers have deliberately set out to explore within the structure of their own cultural theories just why emotions are problematic.

The opening passages of the Iliad. In Homer, terms that are usually translated as mental probably were not mental in his day. Rather, Homer's descriptions are behavioral. The *Iliad* indicates that Homer did not regard the human mind as autonomous. The origins of human action, what I have called here plans, occur in quite other beings, namely, gods. Mortals are not prime movers. At the beginning of the *Iliad*, the idea is stated in plain terms that it is among gods, not mortals, that intentions are formed. After four lines saying that Achilles' wrath had led to the deaths of many Achaeans (Greeks), the poem continues "Thus the plan (*boule*) of Zeus was being brought to fulfillment" (line 5). Then a few lines later: "Which of the gods brought these two [Achilles and Agamemnon] together to fight? The son of Leto and Zeus [Apollo]" (line 8).

What is being stated is something apparently self-evident, just as it might be said, "The President decided to attack," meaning that an autonomous decision of the president in consultation with his advisers led to a particular strategic action. For the archaic Greeks, it was, evidently, equally obvious that we humans are not the source of important plans or decisions. In important matters we are moved by outside agencies. In Homer's epics these agencies are called gods. They are certainly to be taken notice of, though not necessarily revered. A god is not, as modern theists believe, a source of goodness, wisdom, or right thinking. Rather it is a source, projected outward as we would now say,[4] of disturbances in the ordinary flow of life. Of the Greek pantheon, only Athena comes anywhere near being a source of wisdom or love. Nearly all the others are amoral, and often disruptive in their influence, such as the urge of hostile anger that is Ares, or of lust that is Aphrodite.

After the first few lines, Homer sets the scene for the *Iliad:* The Greek army was encamped outside Troy, with ships drawn up on the beach. Agamemnon, the commander in chief, had captured, in plundering another city, the daughter of Chryses. He, a priest of Apollo, had come with a large ransom to reclaim his daughter. Agamemnon speaks harshly to the old man, saying his daughter will be taken home to share his bed. The priest goes off, frightened and powerless. On his way along the beach, he prays that Apollo will avenge his tears.

Apollo hears him and showers arrows of pestilence on the Greek army: Not just inner impulses but what we now call natural events like diseases and storms, also outside human volition, are due to the activity of gods. The Greek army is ravaged by an epidemic. Since the time of Florence Nightingale, modern military commanders have become concerned about hygienic arrangements. On this occasion, though, after the pestilence had raged for nine days, Achilles, who was the Greeks' best warrior, had a different idea suggested to him by the goddess Hera. He was prompted to call a conference. He speaks to the army and asks whether it would not be good to ask a seer why Apollo is angry with them. The seer says it was because Apollo's priest had been dishonored.

Hearing this, Agamemnon becomes furious. He berates the seer, saying that he always speaks evil. He says he prefers the daughter of Chryses to his wife, Clytemnestra. Even so, he will give her back, but only if the others will give him another prize. Achilles tells him that the plunder has been apportioned. Agamemnon replies that, if the Achaeans do not give him someone who he finds equal, he will take Achilles' prize, Briseis, another captured woman. The argument escalates as Achilles calls Agamemnon shameless and reminds him that he, Achilles, only came to this war for Agamemnon's sake. Agamemnon tells Achilles that in that case he should go back home, and moreover, he says, "I will myself come to your hut and take the beautiful Briseis, that prize of yours . . . so that you may fully know how much greater I am than you" (line 184).

Achilles starts to draw his sword to strike at him. At that moment the goddess Athena appears to him. Homer says that she "appeared (*pha-inomeme*) to him alone, and of the rest no man saw her" (line 198). Achilles, in wonderment, sees her. He asks why she has come: "Was it for you to see the *hubris* of Agamemnon? . . . I think . . . he may soon lose his *thumos*" (i.e., lose his life; lines 203–205). Athena replies: "To restrain your anger (*menos*), if you will listen" (line 207).[5] Achilles is persuaded by Athena and says, "A man must observe what you say, goddess . . . whoever obeys the gods, to him do they gladly listen" (line 216).

Homer uses words that tend to be translated anachronistically as mental terms. *Thumos* was an organ of motion, or as Snell puts it, "(e)motion." This was the organ Achilles threatens to deprive Agamemnon of. It was the *thumos* that became agitated in battle, in joy, or in love. Though still echoing in medical terms (e.g., thymus), *thumos* does not now have modern representatives in ordinary English. The word *psuche*, however, lives on in terms like psychology. Since Plato, it has been thought of as mind or soul. In Homer's time it was not mental but meant something like livingness.[6] It could be taken away in battle and could leave through the hole made by a spear or could be coughed out with mouthfuls of blood. In one passage of doubtful authenticity in the *Iliad*, when Achilles sees the ghost of his dead friend Patroclus, in book 23, the *psuche* had an insubstantial existence in Hades. But it did not mean "mind." *Noos* later came to mean intellect, but was for Homer an organ of mental images. But just as Homer tends to speak of organs of the body (e.g., swift or strong limbs) rather than about the body as a whole, he also speaks in the same way about the *noos* and *thumos* as if they were organs, not as if they were aspects of an autonomous mind. Such usages seem to us odd. Now we would tend to speak of a person being swift or athletic, not just the limbs being swift. There is not even a Homeric term for the whole body: *Soma* meant corpse. Just as Homeric people did not speak of limbs as having an impulse to run, they did not attribute plans or impulses to a *noos* or a *thumos* either. A *boule*, a plan, a major decision, or any action that was out of the ordinary was not attributed to a human origin at all. It was attributed to gods.

It is rather shocking to think, following Snell (1982/1953) and a number of others, that the terms that are regularly translated as mental may not have been mental. Certainly, *psuche* was not mental. *Thumos* and *noos*, though quasi-mental, were not the origins of emotions or plans, merely the organs in which some emotions were experienced or images formed.

In an analysis that has much in common with that of Snell, Dodds (1951) has argued that when Homeric people felt themselves moved to do things out of the ordinary, they experienced this as being moved by gods. Dodds describes how, when toward the end of the *Iliad*, Agamemnon apologizes for his part in the quarrel, he says:

> Not I was the cause of this act, but Zeus and Fate and the Erinyes who walk in darkness: they it was who in the assembly put fierce *ate* in my *phrenes*, on that day when I arbitrarily took Achilles' prize from him. So what could I do? The gods will always have their way. (Book 19, line 86, based on Dodds's 1951 translation, p. 3)

Ate is usually translated as blindness, or infatuation. Agamemnon explains: "Since I was blinded by *ate*, and Zeus took away my *phrenes*, I am willing to make my peace, and give compensation beyond counting" (19, line 136, based on Dodds's 1951 translation, p. 3). *Phrenes* is another organ of emotional agitation – as Jaynes (1976) points out, the organ of breathing. Like *thumos*, it is used frequently in the *Iliad* and has a quasi-mental sense. The translation here is usually something like "understanding." Perhaps we would catch the sense by thinking of Agamemnon as saying that his calm breathing was taken away, replaced by breathless anger. Dodds points out that here Agamemnon gives an account of how, because of the passion he was in, he acted wrongly. He offers compensation. But at the same time it was not he who willed it. Here already in the birthplace of European culture is this idea, discussed in Chapter 4 that anger is involuntary, but has consequences such as the obligation to make recompense that one must accept.

The split between agency and intention. Snell describes the *Iliad* and the *Odyssey* as enacted on two stages. One is the main stage, the world of mortals. This is where the action of life takes place, where its joys and sufferings occur. Then, on a sort of balcony above the main stage, are the gods. It is among them that plans are formed and decisions made. Although mortals act, the plans are made by gods.[7]

The gods sit chatting in the great taverna in the sky. In the *Iliad* it is as if they idly watch a divine television set of magical properties on which is being broadcast the Saturday afternoon sports program. One of the features of this device is that the gods themselves can intervene. This may be by setting up the whole plan of the afternoon's game, as Zeus has done. Or may be by destruction of things that take humans much toil to make, but which for the gods may be deleted effortlessly as if from a computer screen, as when Apollo sweeps aside the rampart the Achaeans had built (Book 15, line 355). The magical device allows the gods also to enter, Alice-like, through the screen, to join the mortal world and take part in the game, either by impersonating humans or as themselves, in order to enjoy some of the fighting or other human activities, to advise here or prompt there. On the field of life, young human men act, suffer, and die; women and old men grieve. On Olympos there is emotion, but only of a kind appropriate to a game, as the gods themselves no more suffer and die than we do when we play chess or "Space Invaders." But only on Olympos is action understood in terms of the goals that give it meaning.

As Snell says: "Man does not yet regard himself as the source of his own decisions; that development is reserved for tragedy" (p. 31) in the dramas of Aeschylus and Sophocles written two and a half centuries later. "In Homer every new turn of events is engineered by the gods" (p. 29). In the terms of the communicative theory of emotions, we could say: At every important juncture of a plan a god appears.

Reading the *Iliad* with this in mind, it is indeed as if a new planet swims into our ken.[8] Gods in Homer are not poetic devices or quaint superstitions. They represent a theory of mentality as serviceable then as our modern Western view is to us now that we individuals are captains of our souls, masters of our fate.[9] In the terminology of social psychology, Homer attributed major goals and plans to external agencies, called "gods." In our culture we make internal attributions, seeing ourselves as causing our own actions. But, as Kierkegaard (1944/1844) realized, this has the shocking consequence that now we are responsible for what we do, despite not knowing nearly enough to direct our actions rationally. Our predicament can scarcely do otherwise than precipitate pervasive anxiety.

Dodds (1951), in pursuing arguments similar to Snell's, has pointed out that experiencing emotions as passions has a close relation to madness. In madness, now as then, people sometimes think themselves in touch with divine agencies and feel themselves involuntarily impelled.

Mortals and immortals. In the first 200 lines of the *Iliad*, 11 characters are mentioned. Seven of these are mortals: Achilles, Agamemnon, Briseis,

Calchas the seer, Chryses the priest of Apollo, his daughter who was Agamemnon's prize, and Clytemnestra Agamemnon's wife. Four are immortals: Apollo, Athena, Hera, and Zeus.

Mortals initiate some actions – for instance, Chryses petitions for his daughter and prays to Apollo; Agamemnon acts by repulsing him rudely; Achilles utters a threat and starts to draw his sword. Snell's argument is that all these are more or less predictable, not so much actions as reactions to what was already going on. Neither in these opening passages nor later in the poem is there any suggestion that mortals initiate or bring to fruition long-range plans. Only gods do so: It is Zeus who is described as having a plan (*boule*) that is accomplished. It is Hera who suggests to Achilles that he call a meeting. Athena appears to Achilles in his anger to represent the tribal law that one should not kill the commander in chief. She counters Achilles' more natural impulse to act on his wrath.

To summarize, then: The human actors in the *Iliad*, members of a self-assured, male, feudal aristocracy, are seen here in the midst of a conflict between city-states and between themselves but are impelled by non-human forces. Occasionally, as with Achilles' impulse to draw his sword on Agamemnon, there is a conflict between a human impulse and a cultural imperative. But there are no hidden depths, no awareness for Homeric heroes of anything going on except the evenly illuminated present unfolding before them.[10] Of course the poet has some such awareness, and describes the discussions on Olympos, but the actors themselves are unconscious of these. They are only aware when an outside agency intervenes in the flow of their lives.

The bicameral mind. Jaynes (1976) takes the hypothesis of the unconsciousness of the Homeric heroes a step farther.[11] He argues that when Homer describes how gods appear, as Athena to Achilles, this is to be taken literally. Achilles was having a hallucination brought on by the stress of conflict between his reactive impulse and a tribal injunction. Achilles' main feeling on seeing Athena was wonderment. This pattern of hallucination and the wonderment that it occasions is repeated again and again in the *Iliad*.

Jaynes argues that the Homeric epics chronicle the emergence of European civilization from a state that was just one stage removed from animal unself-consciousness. In this state people were motivated very simply, either by individual motives or by the spoken injunctions of the tribe. He calls this twin basis of self-government bicameral, where bicameral means having two chambers. For an ancient person so governed, one chamber is instinct, individual habits, impulses, and reactions. The other derives from the authoritative imperatives of the tribe, heard at appropriate moments as hallucinations.

Such imperatives would be uttered first by the leaders (kings or queens), then they would be incorporated into socialization processes, passed hierarchically down via heads of families to everyone in the community. They were heard by people in times when societal direction was needed. Because they could be heard even when the ruler who uttered them was not present and continued to be heard even when that ruler was dead, the phenomenon was referred to as the voices of gods. Because new rulers took on the function of uttering the tribal injunctions, which were also heard out of earshot, these rulers were themselves gods.

The people of the ancient city-states of the Indus Valley, of the valley of the Tigris and Euphrates, of Crete, of Egypt, and of the civilizations of Central and South America, most of which flourished between 10,000 and 3,000 years ago, were, according to Jaynes, living in a bicameral state. The appearance of gods was part of a psychological mechanism of a primitive form of social organization replaying social injunctions like a mental tape recording. This type of preliterate organization evolved with people's abilities to live in cities. Indeed, it was essential to that form of life. In such societies, large social groupings had to be organized to undertake the complex tasks of building, agriculture, warfare, and so on.

To put this in terms of the current theory: The form of social organization was the hierarchy, which means sacred rule. It is a simple system, in which plans are implemented, as in the planning trees described in Chapter 1. The only modifications are that long-range goals are always specified from the topmost level, called gods, and the terminal subgoals are usually implemented by different agents, the subject people. One may postulate that such an organization becomes necessary when society goes beyond the limits of face-to-face contact. One can imagine an ancient hierarchy branching downward via the circles of the court of the god-ruler and the heads of families to each individual. Such organizations have left physical vestiges in cities like Knossos, in which a royal palace is surrounded by civic buildings and more peripherally by ordinary dwellings.

Face-to-face contact, or at least acoustic contact, is adequate for animal and, one assumes, for certain kinds of human organization, such as the hunter-gatherer band. With frequent face-to-face contact, including the emotional expressions that accompany it, a group can maintain a cohesiveness of social action. In urban life, buildings create the opportunity for privacy. Additional forms of social organization become necessary. As Jaynes suggests, these were the spoken commands of a ruler, remembered and heard as authoritative injunctions.

Perhaps, says Jaynes, 6,000 or 8,000 years ago, all dwellers in a god-ruled city-state heard voices of dead leaders and their own ancestors, as well as the pronouncements of the current leader and of household leaders, all contributing to a tradition of cultural rule. Certain reminders in the form of images assisted the hallucinated recall of cultural injunctions. Jaynes points out that burying and preserving the dead and placing statues and idols (i.e., gods) in habitations are ubiquitous features of ancient cities.

The *Iliad*, argues Jaynes, marks the end of the bicameral period in Europe, when the voices were fading. Perhaps at that time they were heard less frequently, perhaps only in stress or conflict, as when Achilles started to draw his sword against Agamemnon. Moreover, by this time a class of priests, seers, and oracles had arisen to fill the gap left by the fading voices of authority. The dawning of consciousness is also the dawning of doubt, of the problematic nature of personal responsibility, and of the fact that to us as individual agents the outcomes of our longer range plans are not fully predictable.

Like Snell and Dodds, Jaynes points to the language of the *Iliad* for further clues to ancient mentality during this era when authoritative voices were still heard, but were perhaps growing less distinct or less frequent. He points out that in Homeric epics there were several terms indicating psychosomatic agitation. Most common was *thumos*, general agitation or excitement, and *phrenes*, the apparatus of breathing, which I have already discussed. Then there were *kradie*, meaning the heart, and *etor*, meaning the guts. Each of these terms is associated with emotion and is an easily recognizable type of autonomic activation: trembling, disturbed breathing, pounding of the heart, churning of the guts. In addition, the breathing apparatus, cardiovascular system, and the gastrointestinal tract are each associated with a psychosomatic ailment: asthma, cardiovascular accident, gastric and intestinal disease.

Jaynes argues that although these are often translated as mental terms, neither these terms nor anything else in the *Iliad* indicate that people then were conscious at all. Consciousness, as we know it – that is, self-consciousness – was a later development, involving people experiencing themselves making decisions by reasoning. The gods, who were at first transformations and remembrances of hierarchical tribal rulers, retain some of their externality in the metaphor of their home in Olympos and the upper stage. Three thousand years later they have left their traces in each individual mind.[12]

Emotions when action becomes problematic

The *Iliad* is not just about the anger of Achilles, it is about the repercussions of an angry feud. Paris, one of the sons of King Priam of Troy, had seduced and abducted Helen, wife of King Menelaus of Sparta. As well as being an obvious insult, this act dishonored hospitality, as Paris was being entertained by Menelaus at the time. Menelaus therefore joined with his brother, Agamemnon, king of Mycenae, to raise an army from neighboring city-states. They set off to punish Paris, and the Trojans.

The dramatic setting is a period of 52 days with the war in its tenth year. By now the ships' timbers had begun to rot and the rigging to decay. No doubt the morale of the troops had suffered. In general, the Achaeans had had the better of the fighting, partly due to their best warrior, Achilles. The *Iliad* opens, with the episode of immediate anger within this larger grim and angry war. Its result is that Achilles withdraws from the battle. His mother, Thetis, herself a goddess, visits Achilles as he broods vindictively on his humiliation in the quarrel with Agamemnon and on the removal of his bed partner, Briseis. He asks his mother to intercede on his behalf with Zeus, asking that Agamemnon be chastened by having the Trojans humiliate the Achaeans, forcing them back to their ships on the beach amid much slaughter.

The story is one of battles that are unpredictable, exciting, and finally wracking for the human actors as well as for us readers. At each point when something problematic occurs, a god appears, as we would say an emotion or a decision, to direct the action according to plans made on Olympos. (I give a synopsis of the middle part of the story in note 13.) In the end, as a direct result of the Greeks being humiliated as Achilles has wished, his friend Patroclus is killed by the Trojan hero Hector. The death is engineered by Apollo, prompted by Zeus, who saw the battle going in a way that did not please him. This forces Achilles out of his sulk. He slays Hector and desecrates his body by dragging it in the dust behind his chariot.

The human climax of the story comes in a reworking of the opening scene of Chryses coming with a ransom to reclaim his daughter. Now it is Priam, the aging king of Troy, Hector's father, who comes with a ransom, begging for the return of his son's body. The scene again is staged by Zeus. He sends Thetis to tell Achilles to release Hector's body, and at the same time sends Iris to Priam, instructing him to take a huge ransom to Achilles. Hermes arrives to guide Priam through the Achaean lines in the darkness.

At last, against the backdrop of fearful slaughter comes one of the few moments in the poem that is purely human: a moment of compassion. Priam pleads with Achilles for his son's body, and the two of them begin to weep together for those they have loved, now dead. Achilles asks Priam to sit down, saying: "The gods have spun this thread for wretched mortals, that we should live in pain; while they are without sorrow" (24, line 527). This moment does not last. Priam asks not to be invited to sit while his son's body lies untended. Achilles responds to this by threatening further violence. But the ransom is unloaded from Priam's cart. Achilles himself lifts Hector's body onto the bier, and agrees for the truce to hold until the funeral has taken place. The rites last nine days, as had the rites for Patroclus's death and as had the plague at the beginning of the story. As the *Iliad* ends, we know that Hector's death indicates the imminent destruction of Troy. Achilles' goddess mother has told him that if he takes the path of revenge by killing Hector, then following Hector's death his own will also be certain.

The gods have had an enjoyable time at the battles. Zeus's plan for this group of people is completed, giving the story dramatic unity. The mortals are left mourning their fates.

Has human character changed?

Are Snell, Dodds, and Jaynes right in their analysis of the *Iliad*? If it were possible to strip the text of anachronistic retrojections, would we find that ancient Greek mentality was different from ours? Could preclassical people even be so radically different as to be not conscious at all and not burdened with existential anxiety?

The evidence is thin but suggestive. At its crudest, there are gods in the *Iliad* whose role in the plot we do not find in modern writing. Indeed, we do not find it in Greek literature of the classical era, for example, in tragedy, where the emphasis has changed to personal responsibility in the face of conflicting goals and the impossibility of predicting the results of certain kinds of human action. Moreover, the *Iliad* is neither moral nor psychological in its concerns. Emotions are depicted as occurring at the junctures of plans, but described as agitation, passion, compulsion. The actors experience these agitations and the appearances of gods, and then act. They do not contemplate their own existence.

The emotions of stress and conflict are experienced in relation to actions taken according to god's plans, not to human plans. Homeric Greeks do not decide anything of consequence. They do not suffer remorse or other emotions of the self. They do not agonize over responsibility for their actions. Why should they? They had not chosen these actions. But emotions occur, as I have argued, at just those junctures where the smooth flow of action is interrupted or when goals conflict. So, even if the higher level goals are attributed to outside agencies, emotions to which they relate are experienced by humans.

The *Iliad* is one of the earliest literary proposals that emotions occur at the junctures of plans. The main difference from current literary forms is that each juncture also tended to elicit the appearance of a god. So, when Achilles is anxious about disease ravaging the troops, Hera prompts him to call an assembly. When he is in conflict between his private desire to kill Agamemnon and his feudal duty to the army commander, Athena appears.

Thus conflict and evaluation theories of emotions capture a European folk theory of emotions that has a venerable history. This of course does not mean that this theory is scientifically demonstrated. It does mean that emotions have been seen in this way in European culture for a long time. As the Japanese scholar Ischida (1974), when reflecting on his European experiences after having lived in Germany, remarked, Western civilization is "an odd compound of inexhaustible goodwill and kindness on the one hand and an implacable severity in human relationships on the other" (p. 29). Nowadays the muse may sing as much of wars within as between ourselves, but the themes are all too easily recognizable even with the transformation of character that Virginia Woolf (1966/1924) referred to as occurring in 1910.

Also striking is the fact that rising straight from the pages of the *Iliad* is the kind of theory about anger that Averill (1982) said is embodied in American homicide laws (discussed in Chapter 4). In the *Iliad*, anger is depicted as a passion, outside human control. At the same time it is an action that affects others. It is also a reason for interpersonal violence. These ideas about anger run through European literature starting with the *Iliad*. If we follow Averill's analysis, war is a large-scale, angry response of a whole community. Despite the immeasurable distress it will surely bring, it is thought to have benefits. The causes of the Trojan War, if indeed it was a historical episode, are unknown, but the folk theory expressed by Homer is entirely clear: The war occurred in retributive anger because of the abduction of Helen, a tribal chieftain's wife.

The parallel with Averill's analysis is yet closer. Agamemnon's apology to Achilles and the Achaeans in Book 19 has exactly the same structure as a plea of justified anger that is recognizable in an American law court today. Agamemnon says he did act wrongly, and for that he will give ample compensation, but his anger was not his own doing, he was blinded by an outside agency (Zeus). He pleads appropriate provocation and involuntariness. This is not an excuse, nor is it just Agamemnon's view. As Dodds points out, it is the view of Achilles, too, and of the rest of the Greeks – as well, of course, as the view of the muses, singing to explain how these events came about through the plan of Zeus. Men are affected by passions. Because of them they act involuntarily, but must nevertheless be responsible for the consequences.

The *Iliad* is a mere fragment from an ancient culture. It carries a theory of mentality that is both like and unlike our own. Now as then passions are regarded as involuntary. Both the archaic Greeks and we create our understandings via folk theories of the kind discussed in Chapter 2. So, for Achilles, a plan to call a meeting was an injunction from outside, from a god. For Jane Smith of New York a plan may be a good idea that she herself has had.

We do experience decisions, ideas, words, and so forth coming to mind. The only way we can have these experiences is via the concepts of our implicit theories. According to the communicative theory, emotions arise as communications within the individual or among the immediate community. They themselves have no semantic content. Therefore content needs to be supplied. Typically it is supplied by perceptions or inferences, either from the immediate social context or from cultural or idiosyncratic theories. This is also true of decisions. When we find a decision forming we can even feel the rightness or the risk of it. Whether we attribute it to ourselves as agents or to some external source is a matter that is culturally variable. When it comes to writing or speaking, again one may attribute the words and the way in which they are uttered to oneself. In truth their source is unbeknown to us as agents. Is the theory that writing is the inspiration of muses worse than the theory that it is the autonomous production of an individual mind? More likely, writing and other utterances emerge from a complex history of interaction with a culture and a language community.[14]

George Eliot's *Middlemarch*

Some 2,600 years after Homer, *Middlemarch* was written by George Eliot, who was herself deeply influenced by Greek literature.[15]

For Homer, the strongest emotions took place as psychosomatic agitations each accompanied by the appearance of a god with whom a discussion or a confrontation took place. Each appearance was followed by a new phase of action. For George Eliot, equivalent junctures also elicit emotions. Psychosomatic agitations occur, but so also does a new element. George Eliot's phrase is "inward debate" (p. 383) or "inward dialogue" (p. 444). In her novel, emotions may be expressed or suppressed, desire followed or renounced. In her world, phenomena that we usually think of as having been discovered by Freud some 30 years later, of repression in conflict, projection of expectations onto quite unsuitable people, and displacement of emotions from one object to another, are actively at work. George Eliot depicts all these as consequences of human intentions that involve other people in an incompletely knowable world.

In *Middlemarch*, the fatefulness of human life is due no longer to the will of the gods. Emotions still come unbidden, but now many of the conflicts rage within. Individuality has arrived, but even now it is not in control. Emotions are at work, and for some they can appear as alien forces. For George Eliot, human choice takes on a moral quality. No longer with the certainties of divine direction, people in *Middlemarch* themselves make decisions whose consequences they cannot be sure about.

I shall first summarize a little of the main plot of the story as it touches the principal character, Dorothea, then treat one chapter in more detail, to draw out George Eliot's treatment of emotions and their significance, generally.

The plot of Middlemarch

Middlemarch is the name of an English town based on Coventry. The action begins in September 1829, some 40 years before the time of writing. Its principal characters are two young people, Dorothea and Lydgate.

Dorothea Brooke is an ardent woman of 20. She and her sister, Celia, had come a year previously, after an education in Switzerland, to live with their uncle and guardian. Dorothea wants to enlarge her understanding of the world and to do some good in it. Tertius Lydgate, a 27-year-old doctor, is well bred and full of ideas for research and practice that will relieve human suffering. He arrives in the district after studying in Paris. The lives of these two intertwine, and touch briefly, but although they are the heroine and hero of the novel, they do not become romantically attached.

Lydgate begins his practice quite successfully, sets up his research, and becomes the medical director of a new fever hospital largely financed by the banker Bulstrode, who has an evangelical bent and is not liked in the town. Lydgate falls in love with the town beauty, Rosamund, who sees marriage to him as a social coup, a means to escape the narrowness of her provincial life and to rise above the position of her manufacturer father.

Dorothea, meanwhile, marries an elderly scholar, the Reverend Edward Casaubon, who is researching a compendious work "The key to all mythologies." She admires his erudition, and is excited by the prospect of a world altogether more noble than that of her self-concerned relations and acquaintances. She thinks that he will open to her the door to the serious male world of learning.

On honeymoon in Rome, Casaubon persists in visiting libraries for his research. When making time to show Dorothea the sights, he comments on them with unenthusiastic weariness. She asks him when he will tell her which passages to copy from his rows of notebooks, amassed over many years, to prepare his great work for publication. Having married her because she seemed only capable of admiration, he suddenly sees in this question, the unappreciative public who fail to understand how his work must be infinitely extended. Now in the shape of a wife, she is in a position to observe him closely. Acutely sensitive to the hint of criticism implied by Dorothea hurrying him toward publication, he replies angrily. She is indignant at his response. Both are only partly able to inhibit their anger. Casaubon is unable to bear the possibility that she might form an independent judgment of his work.

Casaubon's young cousin, Will Ladislaw, is financially supported by Casaubon because of a duty to his family. Ladislaw hopes to find something to do with his life, perhaps painting, perhaps writing. He bumps into the Casaubons in Rome, starts to admire Dorothea, and contrives occasions for meeting with her. His admiration is of a sublimated kind, without sexual intent. Nevertheless, their conversations have an openness that contrasts, for Dorothea, with the rigidly controlled quality of her life with Casaubon.

Back in England, there is a second passage of words between Dorothea and Casaubon. He suffers a heart attack. Lydgate attends, and later Dorothea consults him about her husband. Lydgate is perceptive and sympathetic. He counsels that excitement should be avoided. For Dorothea, this means the avoidance of any occasion for further quarrels. Following this intimation of mortality, Casaubon starts at last to prepare his notebooks for publication. He brings pressure on Dorothea to agree to complete the work should he die. Dorothea delays in assenting to this onerous undertaking, and Casaubon dies from another heart attack while waiting for her answer.

After Casaubon's death Dorothea finds that he had made a codicil to his will, forbidding her to marry Ladislaw. This spiteful act contrasts starkly with the generous and wholehearted devotion to Casaubon that Dorothea had maintained throughout her marriage. Her relatives, too, are scandalized by the injustice implied in this. (A synopsis of the middle part of the story, continuing from this point, is given in note 16.)

The long novel resolves in an almost conventional way. Dorothea and Ladislaw do finally marry, after having renounced any interaction with each other partly at least to dispel any indication of scandal for which there was no basis during Casaubon's lifetime. Ladislaw becomes a member of Parliament and Dorothea becomes his helpmeet. Lydgate moves to London and is able to support Rosamund in the luxury she feels she deserves, by means of a fashionable practice. He realizes that unless he conforms to her desires there will be no happiness for either of them. In contrast to the culmination of more romantic novels, neither Dorothea nor Lydgate fulfill the promise or ambitions of their youth.

Dorothea falls short of her aims of becoming widely knowledgeable or of doing the great good work in the world that she had longed for. It was almost impossible for a woman who was 20 in 1829 in Coventry to do so. "Many who knew her thought it a pity that so substantive and rare a creature should have been absorbed into the life of another" (p. 894). Her life was a "mixed result of a young and noble impulse struggling amidst the conditions of an imperfect social state" (p. 896).[17] But, as George Eliot argues, by a personal influence of a kind that is unremarked in history books, Dorothea affected the lives of others in the way that is perhaps more important than anything else in human life.

Lydgate, as George Eliot surmises more harshly, falls short because of a speck of commonness in his character – a kind of arrogance that led him into his conventional marriage and cut him off from those who might have been able to support him. Lydgate was thoughtful in most areas of his life. He might have been warned by a disastrous earlier obsession with an actress in Paris, but he remained unconscious that the roots of his attraction to Rosamund were largely those of a contrived appearance of the kind known as feminine. In marrying her, he acquired, as was the usual male practice, a possession, without being aware that in doing so he was foregoing any possible intellectual or emotional companionship in his marriage.

The structure of story plots

A typical story with a completed plot includes some description or implication of the goals and plans of one or more characters. Such goals constitute the psychological beginning that Aristotle discussed in the *Poetics*. Episodes of the story are then typically based around problems or vicissitudes that occur in these plans, often because of the activities of others. These episodes are Aristotle's middle. Finally, vicissitudes are met in some way, a denouement occurs and the story plan draws toward its end, its *telos*, or outcome. This structure of plan→vicissitude(s) →culmination can be applied to the whole story or at finer levels of detail to each episode.[18]

In *Middlemarch* there are four main plots: of Dorothea, of Lydgate and Rosamund, of Rosamund's brother Fred, and of Bulstrode the banker. Each revolves around plans that are conceived as mutual and that lead to strong emotions as the copies of these plans that are held by each character are discovered to be different from those of others with whom they had mutual arrangements. In these discoveries the structure of the selves of the characters disintegrates to some extent, plans are abandoned or revised, and new selves emerge.

In later European literature the self comes to dominate, perhaps because the individualistic self is such a problematic acquisition, so often essentially contradictory. Casaubon's self, for instance, is proud and ambitious, longing for justification and immortality by showing the world a key to universal understanding. This same self, acting on the basis of a mutual plan, allows Casaubon to marry with almost no understanding whatsoever of Dorothea. He anticipated that she would be sufficiently sensitive to admire his erudition and sufficiently intelligent to be appreciative. When Casaubon's copy of the joint plan failed to match the actual Dorothea, it was his own individualized model of self that suffered damage. Though his self was a social construction, the dissolution of its goals was personally and biologically damaging.

A mixed result of an imperfect world

Middlemarch is arguably one of the best half a dozen English novels. It was enthusiastically received and reviewed by eminent contemporaries. Most famous was Henry James, who wrote: *"Middlemarch* is a treasure house of detail, but it is an indifferent whole" (in Swinden, 1972, p. 61).[19] What James meant is that the subplots of the novel, that is to say, the plans of its various characters, interweave and touch in numerous ways but without constituting an organic whole, as Aristotle had recommended or as Homer achieved in the *Iliad.* So the fatefulness of the lives of this group of people does not have a clear coherence. If we may employ George Eliot's remark about Dorothea's life, the book is a more "mixed result" of people's plans and aspirations interacting with others' often quite different plans in an imperfect and imperfectly knowable world.

George Eliot prepared herself for writing *Middlemarch* by reading history and social science and pondering the processes that affect human destiny.[20] The theme pervades the novel. Lydgate in his research wanted to "pierce the obscurity of those minute processes which prepare human misery and joy" (p. 194). Like Casaubon, he thought there might be some key that would give unity to all. But George Eliot was suspicious of these grand triumphs of mind over unruly actuality. Her book explores how human life is not like that. There are large social forces to be sure, like the coming of industrialization and the railways, progress in medicine, parliamentary reform. These in part form the setting for *Middlemarch.* But individual destinies are also affected by small events, which seem insignificant at the time, as well as by people's more deliberate plans. Humans now are not directed by the far-seeing gods of Homer. They have to fall back on guides to action that are less grandiose and more fallible. Mistakes and miscalculations occur. We all embark on plans without perfect knowledge.

Middlemarch is a story of plans miscarried, or ordinary misunderstanding, of actions taken without the possibility of foresight. Lydgate might have come upon something in his researches that would have allowed him to make progress on the problems of cholera before Snow and Pasteur. Instead, his attention is diverted by sordid financial anxieties in a marriage undertaken for the most conventional of reasons to a woman who cultivated her charm with the view of attracting a man of the better class. Dorothea longed to attain the wide vistas of learning, but found only musty anterooms and cobwebs in Casaubon's mind. Casaubon himself wanted to be appreciated for providing a universal "Key," but overestimated his ability while suspiciously concealing his work from others. *Middlemarch* is a web of interconnections of lives and events.

George Eliot's plot might seem to Henry James to make an indifferent whole.[21] When he wrote his review of *Middlemarch*, however, he was pursuing a private preoccupation. If I may borrow a phrase of Todorov (1977/1971) describing another, similar preoccupation of Henry James: "We rarely have occasion to observe so pure a case of egocentricity presenting itself as universality" (p. 66). James wanted to write a novel that was a perfect whole. In *Portrait of a Lady* he succeeded. It is a suspense story. It is stage-managed by James to conceal from Isabel, its central character, and from us, its readers, the existence and workings of a conspiracy that shapes Isabel's life without her knowledge, and only emerges with the most delicate retardations as the lengthy plot unfolds. James could make his perfect whole by having behind the scenes a single plan that unified the plot. In the same way Homer had won Aristotle's approval of his poem as a creditable whole by the machinery of Zeus's plan directing proceedings.

But what if one wishes, as George Eliot did, to give an account of ordinary conditions of human life and interaction with nothing behind the scenes, of people impelled by the forces of biology and society, and individually directed only by their own imperfect judgments? The account of provincial life that George Eliot gave would necessarily form an indifferent whole in the sense that James achieved.

For George Eliot, human life has no agency behind the scenes. It requires a different set of principles. She proposes that in a world of uncertainty and potential conflict the principles on which our lives depend are an emotional sympathy with others and an openness to our own feelings. "Our good depends on the quality and breadth of our emotion."[22] The construction of an artistic unity by such means needs development of the novel beyond structures that depend on some agency with a top-level goal to which the whole of the plot can be assimilated.

A novel based on sensitivity to emotions

For George Eliot, the world has no knowledgeable agencies directing events. Sensitivity to emotions replaces the Homeric idea of fate as a god's plan behind the scenes. So she sets herself a double task. There is an artistic task of carrying forward the dramatic structure of a novel.

There is also the philosophical task of exploring whether sensitivity to emotions could have properties of interrelating people's lives in an unpredictable and potentially conflictual world.

George Eliot's solutions to these problems involve having Dorothea at one end of an emotional spectrum: passionate, overemotional, even. She is able to experience her emotions rather fully and to transmute setbacks into new plans. At the other end of the spectrum, Casaubon experiences his emotions hardly at all. When he started courting Dorothea he had "determined to abandon himself to the stream of feeling, and perhaps was surprised to find what an exceedingly shallow rill it was . . . he concluded that the poets had much exaggerated the force of masculine passion" (p. 87). Such setbacks were, however, felt by him only as obscure increases in irritability and in psychosomatic illness. In his disappointment in marriage he reverted to his lifelong habit of scrupulous duty.

Plots as plans. In cognitive science, analyses of narrative have generally followed the work of Rumelhart (1975), who proposed the idea of story schemas to explain how sentences are connected to form stories. A story schema is very close to a plan, and can be thought of in terms of a plan tree, as described in Chapter 1.[23]

In narratives, episodes are often connected by emotions signaling a culmination of one phase of a character's plan and making way for a new episode.[24] According to the communicative theory, emotions occur at junctures, often bringing a piece of a plan to an end and initiating a new phase, often also using the schemas that Lutz (1987) has described (see Chapter 4). Stories become interesting precisely because augmented human planning is so problematic. Almost invariably it involves several agents, multiple goals, and uncertain environments. Stories provide paradigm accounts not only of emotions, their eliciting conditions, and consequences, but also of recognizable solutions and nonsolutions to the problems of such a world.

Narratives that involve only one protagonist enacting a simple plan are not good stories.[25] Proper stories, as Rumelhart (1980) has proposed, typically involve a problem and have a problem-solving motif in which the protagonist grapples with the vicissitudes of pursuing a goal in a world that he or she is not fully able to predict. Perhaps we tell ourselves stories to explore the ways these problems can be approached, how unruly elements may be coped with, and how events are made comprehensible by human purposes.

Like Homer, George Eliot portrays phases of action punctuated by emotions. At each juncture she describes emotional expressions – the coloring of a face, the way a person trembles or makes an unconsidered gesture, a tone of voice, the direction of a glance. She also describes when someone suppresses an emotional expression or enters inward debate. Of the 80 chapters in *Middlemarch* none lacks mention of an emotional expression. Minimally it is a smile, often it is a physiological excitation, an emotionally impelled inward dialogue, an action prompted or suppressed by an emotion. In most chapters there are many instances. Often there are detailed descriptions of emotional incidents.

Emotional states often draw each episode of the story to its climax. The emotional state may be a stable mood, implying that an attitude or disposition will continue. Perhaps there is a switch to a different aspect of the plot. Alternatively, an emotion initiates a new phase of action toward the same goals as before or toward goals that have been transformed by new evaluations that have occurred. In their final episodes, stories, including *Middlemarch*, conventionally reach a stable emotional state, that is, either a happy or an unhappy ending. Unstable outcomes imply the initiation of new plans, so that such an ending, like an ending on a dominant seventh chord in music, gives a sense of unresolvedness.

The multiple meanings of narrative. The idea of plots as the plans of a story's characters, with emotions as the points around which the plots turn, neglects an important feature of written narratives: Although emotions of story characters could perhaps be accounted for, what about the emotions of the listener or reader?

Narrative literature has a number of functions in the understanding of emotions. In Chapter 2 I discussed the idea of literature as *mimesis*, simulation, and its function of making explicit cultural intuitions about emotions, a quasi-educative function. There is a yet more important role. To understand this, we can start from the fact that makes it difficult for many to take literature seriously as a means of approaching truth – that disagreement occurs about the interpretation of any narrative. But if narrative is simulation, running on individual minds, nothing else could be expected. There will be no single canonical interpretation. At best, there will be families of interpretation. The text, of course, constrains what is possible, but if each narrative is a simulation creating a world in the mind space of each reader or listener, then each person's interpretation will inevitably be different. Each will arise from a meeting of the text created by the writer with the simulation resources and preoccupations of each individual reader or listener.

Narrative is different from the natural scientific description of technical matters. In reading a scientific paper the aim is precisely to receive an unambiguous meaning. Papers in which several interpretations of findings are possible are rejected by the referees of scientific journals. The goal of natural science is that people in the scientific community converge unanimously on fundamental concepts. By contrast, when reading a narrative an individual reader does not receive but generates explanations. Interpretations can change within a single reading or when rereading. Even in a single reading the issue is not to predict what will happen but to create a range of explanations appropriate to what has happened or what might happen.[26]

Bruner (1986) has argued that multiple meanings are essential to literature. There are meanings at many levels, often simultaneously, for example, the literal, the ethical, the historical, and the mystical – or if we were to adopt Barthes' (1975/1970) five categories: the hermeneutic, the semantic, the symbolic, the proairetic (having to do with action), and that concerning cultural codes. In reading good literature, the text enables us to create our own meanings ranging, as it were, across such categories and their interconnections. We do not receive a constrained meaning. Instead, as Edel (1955) has said, we the readers create what we understand, we accomplish what Barthes calls a "writerly" reading.

Reading in a writerly way enables our conceptions of emotions and their interpersonal effects to crystallize out from diffuse and incoherent feelings, but to remain our own. We compare a literary simulation with our own experience. Literature is a basis, though not the only one, whereby we can begin to acquire a reflective understanding of our emotions.

Literature that is taken seriously within a culture is not enough on its own for us to understand emotions. My argument here is that to understand emotions we need both meaning constraint as provided by science and meaning generation as exemplified in narrative literature, together of course with the other sources of evidence from our own experience and from the many and the wise.

Story structure and discourse structure. Todorov (1977/1971) has argued that two levels of narrative structure must be distinguished. Story structure is the chronological sequence of intentions, actions, and events in the world of the story. It has its own laws, perhaps those described by Rumelhart (1975). Discourse structure is the sequence of events presented in a narrative, and this is subject to all the transformations that writers use including figures of rhetoric, the tenses, aspects, and modes of the narrative. These two levels can themselves be subdivided.

The two levels correspond to even more basic subdivision in language, of topic and predicate: First one refers to something that is given and mutually understood, and then one offers some comment upon it. They also correspond to two different kinds of speech act. Todorov offers the following example from Proust: "He lavished upon me a kindness as superior to Saint-Loup's as the latter's to the affability of a tradesman." The first proposition, up to "kindness," concerns events at the story level. It describes what happened. Subsequently, a different kind of speech act occurs, in which the reader is being addressed with a more general proposition that requires consultation of his or her intuitions about the affability of tradesmen. Of course, as Todorov then explains, these two levels interdigitate in a variety of ways.

Many stories arouse emotions in their readers. Brewer and Lichtenstein (1981) have shown how, while keeping constant the story structure, or as they call it the event structure, they can change the discourse structure. This has large effects on readers' liking for stories and their experience of suspense, surprise, and curiosity. Narratives that simply offer a basic event sequence are not much liked, whereas, for example, when description of a significant outcome is deferred, the narrative is liked better and invokes suspense. Stories are enjoyable insofar as they invoke planlike sequences and set problems, not just for the story characters but for the readers.

Narrative form decouples the event or story sequence from the discourse sequence. In so doing an arena of creativity emerges – not just the writer's creativity but the reader's. Writers invoke the readers' schemata, entrain them in a plot, and allow identification with one or more story characters.[27] In reading we may each create our own narrative, a writerly reading in Barthes' (1975/1970) sense of enabling the reader to become a writer of the text being read, and as Bruner (1986) puts it: "The *great* writer's gift to a reader is to make him a *better* writer" (p. 37; emphasis in the original).

In the discourse structure plans can be made problematic and resolutions presented in ways that may be edifying. But insofar as they also allow recognitions or insights that arouse the reader's emotions and promote reflection on the reader's reactions to the plans in which she or he has become engaged, then the reader is creating the narrative. The emotions are the reader's own and so are the reflections upon them.

Has George Eliot succeeded? George Eliot wrote during the century of the greatest European novelists. But this was also a period of transition between eighteenth-century tales of morality and adventure and the twentieth-century prose of fragmented images and inner lives. The plot of *Middlemarch* is not fragmented, though Henry James claimed it was not unified. People in the book have inner lives, and in this George Eliot accomplishes a great deal in comparison, for instance, with Charles Dickens, whose characters are seen from the outside. In George Eliot's works there emerges a depth of character not approached by previous novelists.

Did George Eliot, however, create in *Middlemarch* the synthesis for which she was striving between her aspirations as an artist and her equally strong philosophical and scientific interest in discerning the role of emotions in human lives that are interdependent but not directed by a unifying agency? I believe she did achieve both these aims. Artistically there is a unity expressed in terms of the spectrum of emotional responsiveness of the major characters in *Middlemarch*, set against a chorus of commentary and gossip of the townspeople and the counterpoint of her own commentary, which I will discuss later. Philosophically and scientifically she was able to illuminate many vicissitudes of emotions.

If we were to neglect for a moment the fragmentation of post-Freudian and post-Joycean narrative that challenges readers to achieve their own unifications, Henry James is surely right in arguing that a novel should achieve unity. Of course he argued that George Eliot had not managed it. But he had his own preoccupations: He was seized by the idea of the reader's attention being captured and suspended by the gradual unfolding of a single plan. He says in his review of *Middlemarch* that he could keenly remember wondering in the early chapters "what turn in the way of form the story would take – that of an organized, molded, balanced composition, gratifying the reader with a sense of design and construction, or a mere chain of episodes, broken into accidental lengths and with no sense of a plan" (James's review of *Middlemarch*, reprinted in Swinden, 1972, p. 60). He, more than anyone writing in English until that time, took hold of the idea of the novel as plan.

James also paid tribute to George Eliot's philosophical intelligence and to her ability to create character – he was one of the few writers to approach her in this ability. But he seems not to have grasped her more revolutionary ideas, either of a different kind of structural unity for a novel or the integrative potential of a theme of responsiveness to our own and other people's emotions.

In a world with no omniscient guiding agency, what guide to actions might there be? George Eliot's answer was that it is our emotions and the way in which we habitually respond to them. So, in portraying a spectrum of such responses against a background of the sometimes unpredictable happenings of ordinary life, she creates an artistic unity. The four subplots of the novel are not coordinated by any single over-arching plan – there can be no such device – but they are coordinated in the minds of readers who come alive to the interrelatedness of the decisions the characters make on their own and each other's emotional lives: Dorothea's responsiveness to her emotions contrasts with Casaubon's repression of emotion, Lydgate's susceptibility to falling in love with a charming woman is in counterpoint with Rosamund's deliberate cultivation of such charm, and so forth. Here we might refer again to Todorov (1977/1971), who sketches what he calls a poetics of prose in terms of such features as the contrasts that George Eliot establishes with her characters. Her fully drawn characters are not mere representatives of moral stances and not "ideal types" in Weber's (1968/1922) sense – they are drawn in a manner that had not been accomplished by novelists before her. They are possible as people in the real world: Each is both understandable as someone with whom we have the utmost intimacy and clearly occupies a position that is recognizable to us in the space of human possibilities.

George Eliot also proposes the philosophical idea that responsiveness to emotions can unify an individual life. Because, in the end, she is interested not just in her characters but in her readers, she is faced with the question of how to structure her novel to allow it to affect them as readers. This implies not just telling a story but modulating the narrative by a complex discourse structure.

Events and discourse in Chapter 29 of Middlemarch

Here I will give an account of Chapter 29 of *Middlemarch* in terms of its event and discourse structure. In Chapter 29, Dorothea and Casaubon quarrel and he has his first heart attack.[28]

Middlemarch has three voices at the discourse level. Most frequent is a voice of external observation, quite closely representing the event structure: "She or he did so and so." Then there is the inward voice of self-reflection or inner experience, not developed fully in the Victorian novel, but developed later by writers like Marcel Proust, James Joyce, and Virginia Woolf. Last is the narrator's voice, which from time to time offers commentary or generalization. George Eliot has been criticized for this narrator's voice, on the grounds that it lends an air of unrealism and godlike omniscience. I shall argue that the narrator's voice has an al-

together different purpose and effect, and that the several voices of this
novel form an essential part of its construction.

Casaubon's heart attack. Chapter 29 starts in the narrator's voice with
Casaubon. Despite Casaubon's age and unprepossessing appearance,
the narrator points out that Casaubon too has a spiritual hunger. He
intended his marriage to fill this hunger and to allow him to leave
behind a copy of himself. But he has not succeeded in that, any more
than he has succeeded in leaving a copy of his "Key to all mythologies."

The narrator's voice continues: Dorothea had seemed more than he
could have wished. Providence had supplied him with someone purely
appreciative and unambitious. But the happiness that he anticipated did
not materialize. His experience had always been of a distrustful shrinking from being known. His energies were lost in self-preoccupation and
narrow scrupulosity. The few articles he had published had not been
warmly received. He felt "that melancholy embitterment which is the
consequence of all excessive claim: Even his religious faith wavered with
his wavering trust in the power of his authorship."

The narrator's voice in this opening section stands in, as it were, for a
more explicit voice of Casaubon's own consciousness. George Eliot lets
us understand that Casaubon's inner voice, if we were to hear it, would
be thin, irritable, and suspicious. Her commentary, perhaps more like
that of a sympathetic psychotherapist, is, I think, the more appropriate
counterpoint to Casaubon's public actions. We may argue that in the
twentieth century authentic inner voices have been developed in the
novel. We may also wonder whether with such an inner voice a Casaubon could be portrayed, or whether with such a voice his own lack of
self-awareness would prohibit readers from developing any more insight into this kind of person than Casaubon had in himself.

The narrator also slips more explicitly into her own role, saying, "For
my part I am very sorry for him. It is an uneasy lot at best to be present
at this great spectacle of life and never to be liberated from a small
hungry shivering self" (p. 314). The narrator continues: When Casaubon
married, the anticipated pleasure did not materialize, but his new state
became another duty to be observed scrupulously. Even drawing Dorothea into use in his research became an effort. Only because of her
insistence did he allow her to take a place in his study and to copy
documents or read aloud to him.

Next comes an incident. This and most the rest of the chapter are described in the voice of external observation. One day Dorothea and Casaubon were in the study, and Casaubon said in a "tone that implied that he was discharging a disagreeable duty" that a letter had come for her, enclosed in one to him. Dorothea glanced at the signature: "'Mr Ladislaw! What can he have to say to me?' she exclaimed, in a tone of pleased surprise" (p. 316). Casaubon, severely pointing to it with his pen, said she may also read the letter that had come for him. "I may as well say beforehand that I must decline the proposal it contains to pay a visit here. I trust I may be excused for desiring an interval of complete freedom from such distractions" (p. 316).

Dorothea was upset by this "ill-tempered anticipation that she should desire visits which might be disagreeable to her husband." She asked, "Why do you attribute to me a wish for anything that would annoy you? . . . Wait at least till I appear to consult my own pleasure apart from yours" (p. 316). In a brief snatch of her inner voice we hear that she had curbed any show of emotion since the argument on her honeymoon, but now Casaubon's gratuitous defense against an unmade complaint "was too sharp a sting to be meditated upon until after it had been resented" (p. 316). Next the voice of outer observation again: He met the flash of her eyes with shock, and said nervously that she was too hasty. She replied that it was he who had been hasty. She thought it ignoble that he did not apologize. He asked that they speak no more of it, "dipped his pen and made as if he would return to his writing, though his hand trembled so much that the words seemed to be written in an unknown character" (p. 317).

Dorothea, without divining the cause of her husband's irritation, rejected the reading of the letters, as one might "hurl away any trash towards which we seem to have been suspected of cupidity," knowing only that they had caused him to offend her. Full of indignation, she sat down to work, but "her hand did not tremble" (p. 317). She felt, and here we return to her consciousness again, that she was forming the letters beautifully, and that she was beginning to understand the Latin that she was copying. In her indignation there was a sense of superiority.

The voice of external observation recounts that after half an hour of silence Dorothea heard the noise of a book falling, and turned quickly to see Casaubon "on the library steps clinging forward as if he were in some bodily distress." She leapt forward, and said with her whole soul melted in to tender alarm, "Can you lean on me dear?" (p. 317). He was still and gasping for breath. When she got him to sit down, he seemed helpless and about to faint. Dorothea rang the bell violently, and he was helped to the couch.

Celia, Dorothea's sister, had been staying in the house. Sir James Chettam, to whom Celia was newly engaged, was at this moment arriving to pay a visit. He was met in the hall with the news that "Mr. Casaubon had had a fit in the library." When he came into the library, Casaubon was recovering. Dorothea was sobbing by his side, but rose and proposed that a doctor be sent for. Lydgate was summoned and came quickly.

When Lydgate had gone, Celia, speaking privately to Sir James, said that it was shocking that Casaubon was ill, but she never did like him, and he was not fond enough of Dorothea. No one else would have had him. Sir James said: "She's a noble creature." He had received a fresh impression of Dorothea's warmheartedness, "stretching her tender arm under her husband's neck, and looking at him with unspeakable sorrow. He did not know how much penitance there was in that sorrow" (p. 319).

Celia went to Dorothea and left Sir James remembering the disgust he had felt at Dorothea's engagement. His own previous courtship of Dorothea had not left bitterness, for he was happy with Celia, but his previous admiration of Dorothea and his chivalrous nature left him with feelings of brotherly friendship toward her.

Emotions and stress

In Chapter 29 of *Middlemarch* we see what is by now a familiar sequence. An event occurs that elicits an emotion: Ladislaw's letters elicit Casaubon's irritation, not so much because of what they are themselves but because of Casaubon's own purposes. But this is not just an individual event, it is interpersonal. He becomes irritable with Dorothea. His emotion evokes an emotion in her – an angry sense of outrage. She knows she has subordinated her wishes to her husband's, suppressing her unhappiness since their first quarrel and curbing her own eager nature. Now he has not only failed to recognize or appreciate this and is ungrateful, but he berates her on a subject of which she is innocent.

For his part, Casaubon finds himself in the aftermath of a honeymoon that has distracted him from his work without having brought him closer to happiness. Now he has become suspicious of Ladislaw. He is

appalled that Dorothea, who had seemed so perfectly to fit his requirements, now exists as an extra burden to be dutifully borne, and responds to his remarks about the letters with unwifely rebelliousness.
Here, then, is the sense of transgression for both participants that is so
typical of anger, and that marks the turning point of the plot in this
episode. In this chapter, the transition takes place from Casaubon's habitual plan of proceeding as usual with his work, though with the added
burden of his wife's accompaniment, to a new phase in which, with the
intimation of his own death and following the promptings of Dorothea,
he will start to prepare at last for publication. The change has the additional bitter twist that he will try to recruit her to the onerous task of
completing this goal should he be unable to finish it.

The quarrel here shares features with the earlier one of the Casaubons'
honeymoon. The plans of two characters, supposedly corresponding,
are revealed by an external event to be quite disparate. The copies that
each has of the joint planning tree do not correspond, and the discrepancy is experienced as an interruption in each individual's sequence of
action. Each individual's goals are thwarted by the failure of the joint
plan. The incongruence is experienced not as a cognitive problem to be
solved but as an insult that threatens the foundations of the self.

The frequency with which this kind of event happens in long-term
relationships, the violence of the emotions involved, and the seriousness with which they are viewed by people who experience them
are significant. The necessarily ad hoc way in which human plans develop from infancy makes it impossible that two people's mental schemata
could ever correspond exactly. At the points when mismatches do occur,
the model of self and other that enables longer term mutual plans to be
established can become sorely strained. As our model of the other is
challenged because expectation is not fulfilled, so our model of self is
threatened, as we can no longer experience that self in the way we had
thought. The cognitive problem of renegotiating a piece of a joint plan
becomes an emotional problem of sustaining a sense of who one is.

These are elements entirely absent from Homer's Achilles. Casaubon's
emotions become problematic to himself. He is in an inner fury. Overtly
he ceases to rail against Dorothea, though a little later we discover that
his resentments and lack of trust continue to work: Casaubon seeks to
exert from Dorothea a promise that she "avoid doing what [he] should
deprecate, and apply [herself] to do what [he] should desire" (p. 518).
He wants her to finish the book he is unable to complete himself, and

has added the spiteful codicil to his will depriving her of an inheritance should she marry Ladislaw, and making plain to all his jealousy of Ladislaw.

The vindictiveness of Achilles is different from that of Casaubon. Achilles remains potent in his anger. The foretelling of his own death is merely the prediction that he will be killed in a further cycle of the same vengeful destructiveness that he had willingly entered. Casaubon has not just others but himself to contend with: He cannot acknowledge himself as vengeful, and the distrustfulness of this self, moreover, makes him unable to be other than suspicious of the affectionate companionship offered by Dorothea. He wreaks vengeance by means of his own death.

How are we to understand emotions in literary narratives?

How do such matters affect us as readers? I want to propose that both Homer and George Eliot have a purpose which in part is educational, but in part is also quite different: to enable readers to approach a particular kind of truth.

Education or propaganda? First the educational part: Homer and George Eliot say, "See, here is the nature of emotions, their causes and effects. We can all learn from this." Their art allows them to do this in a way that is quite different from schoolroom recitation.

The simple educative sense is, I think, clear. It is indeed the propagation of the folk theory of emotions that I have been discussing – that emotions are both involuntary passions elicited by distinctive events and actions that have interpersonal effects. As members of a culture we come, by literature and other means, to adopt those theories that form part of a social apparatus assisting our interaction with others. But the educative function is problematic in the sense that I have discussed in Chapter 2. How do we know what value to place on anything we learn about emotions from Homer or George Eliot? The fact that these works of art arouse emotions in us is itself suspicious. We know too that there are biases in judgments about the self and others, as Nisbett and Ross (1980) have shown. Biases can be exploited, for instance, by rhetorical means of the manipulation of vividness, and such means may distort our rational judgments. Can we distinguish any educative sense from mere cultural propaganda?

If we take the *Iliad*, there had been recent social change, perhaps somewhat as described by Marx and Engels (1970/1932), from social organizations based on the family, via aristocratically ruled city-states such as those of the Myceneans depicted by Homer, toward division of labor, private property, and slave-owning oligarchies such as those of classical Athens. For Athenian readers, the *Iliad* could be seen as endorsing the rights of elites and to legitimize the inequalities of society in order to help maintain itself.

If we see the *Iliad* in such a light, what better than if lords like Achilles and the others are on speaking terms with gods? Some indeed have one parent who is a god. What better than to portray the aristocracy as admirable? As Nietzsche (1977/1878, 1956/1887) pointed out, terms such as good and evil and their development as moral ideas evolved from concepts attaching, respectively, to ruling and slave classes. Such ideas still live on in English where "noble" is a synonym for "good" and "poor" is a synonym for "bad." Seen in such terms one could scarcely have a clearer example of an ideological document than the *Iliad*. Among mortals only male warlords making their predatory way through the world are significant. As Veblen (1948/1899) put it, they occupy the most meritorious status since they do not concern themselves with productive work. Instead, in the development of European society, "Aggression becomes the accredited form of action and booty serves as *prima facie* evidence of successful aggression" (p. 68). Moreover, these men describe decisions not in terms of their own responsibility, but in terms of gods whom only they are in touch with. Ordinary people are not portrayed as speaking with gods. Women are chattels to be fought over, only better than household slaves in that they are mentioned by name. Of course, the *Iliad* is not about the societies of classical times, but perhaps all the better for that. During classical times Homer was widely revered. The setting in an earlier period may have diverted the readers' mind from criticizing messages about the function of honor measured by wealth[29] and the supposedly natural differences between men and women, lords and ordinary people, Greeks and slaves.

One can see *Middlemarch* as middle-class propaganda in a comparable way, though George Eliot herself would have been horrified at the idea. Encouraged by her naturalist partner, George Henry Lewes, she was concerned to create a natural history of human life depicting its whole range without sentimentality, a social science parallel to biological natural histories. So *Middlemarch* was intended as a study of provincial life. In fact, it is a view of scarcely more than half a dozen fully depicted characters.[30] To modern eyes the bias is clear. It is clearly symbolized in

Chapter 34, where the more elevated members of society, including Sir James Chettam, his mother the Dowager Lady Chettam, Dorothea, and Celia, look down from an upper window of the rectory on the procession of townsfolk and tradesmen below, including Rosamund's family, as they enter the church for the funeral of Rosamund's uncle. Below these town worthies in social rank are the tenant farmers and the workers in the new industrial revolution. Below them, in a stratum that has more to do with George Eliot's moral perception than her sociological one, are the loungers and gossipers at the alehouse, the indigent and disreputable.

Unlike some of her contemporaries George Eliot does portray people other than the middle and upper classes, so that in other novels, for instance, she makes craftsmen the main protagonists. My point is that, try as she may, she can, in her educative mode, scarcely hope to avoid spreading the mores of her class and times. And how are we to know that the folk theory of emotions that both Homer and George Eliot expound is not just their own folk theory of emotions? How could we know from *Middlemarch* how far the emotional vicissitudes of Victorian middle-class life were common to the majority and to the burgeoning classes of people working in building, transport, and factories? The answer is that we could not know. Writers write in the pursuit of all sorts of causes, not just for the sake of truth. Unlike science, art has no explicit procedures for converging on truths about the outer world. The individual artist, however great or well intentioned, will be subject to bias, conscious or otherwise. I will show how such biases may be overcome in Chapter 6.

Art and inner truth. Here, however, I propose that as well as this educative sense, subject as it is to bias, there is something else, something that concerns truths in inner worlds. It depends on the ability that an artist has not just to depict emotions but to allow readers to be moved by their own emotions as they read and also to reflect on them. George Eliot struggled to define this: She put her conception in a book review:

> The greatest benefit we owe to the artist, whether painter, poet or novelist, is the extension of our sympathies. Appeals founded on generalizations and statistics require a sympathy ready-made, a moral sentiment already in activity; but a picture of human life such as a great artist can give, surprises even the trivial and the selfish into that attention to what is apart from themselves, which

may be called the raw material of moral sentiment. . . . Art is the nearest thing to life; it is a mode of amplifying experience and extending our contact with our fellow-men beyond the bounds of our personal lot. (George Eliot, 1856; reprinted in Pinney, 1963, p. 270)

George Eliot wanted something beyond the educative. She proposed that the pictures and histories that an artist might give were capable of extending people's sympathies. This meant not just giving them information: A novel should also be moving. It was this, she thought, that would enable readers to transform their conceptions of themselves and others.

She did indeed succeed in this. I would like now to show, using the descriptions of the different voices in the novel, as illustrated by Chapter 29, something of how she accomplished it, in relation to the character of Casaubon.

THE VOICES OF *MIDDLEMARCH:* CHAPTER 29. At the event level, there is one sequence in Chapter 29: the bad-tempered conversation about the letters – the half hour of silence – Casaubon's heart attack – the arrival of others on the scene.

At the discourse level, this chapter has four phases. First are the reflections in the narrative voice on Casaubon's disappointments and habits of mind. Second comes a more nearly observational account, though with brief pieces of Dorothea's inner understandings. It consists of the conversation about the letters that results in the state of repressed anger in Casaubon and the sense of righteous scorn in Dorothea. It ends in Casaubon's heart attack. Third, and also in the observational voice, is the rapid sequence of actions: Dorothea's ringing of the bell, the arrival of Sir James, and then Lydgate. Finally is a brief coda in the observational voice describing Celia and Sir James conversing. This is followed by the narrator's voice, offering an observation on Sir James's feelings toward Dorothea.

MENTAL SCHEMATA. Cognitive analyses of mind have needed the idea of intermediate mental constructions, mental models, representations, or schemata to provide a bridge between the outside world and our actions. Why do we need such an intermediate stage? Because only from such inner representations can our own inferences be generated. Only such inner models could have the links to other structures of knowledge relevant to our purposes and preoccupations. Only models, including models of the self, can fill the gaps and amplify the fragmentary data of our senses of linguistic input to the rounded sense of ourselves living in the world as we know it. Schemata, then, are the means by which we connect ourselves to the world, or to a narrative.

OUTER AND INNER: IDENTIFICATION AND EMPATHY. *Middlemarch* mirrors two levels: The level of the outside world represented by the event sequence of the characters' world and a different level, of the discourse structure, which has a purpose of connecting the scenes of the event world to the minds of readers in different ways. Thus Todorov (1977/1971) points out that there are the two kinds of speech act: one of description and one of appeals to the reader. As Todorov goes on to say, these levels, especially in the hands of a great artist, may interdigitate in a variety of ways.

At its simplest, the first or descriptive part, the plot, is principally that which allows readers to identify with a character – that is to say, to adopt as our own a story character's goals, just as in a game we adopt a goal that the game affords. Although in real life we like to guide our planning routines, in reading, our planning-and-understanding systems are guided by the narrative, and it seems they lend themselves to being steered in this way very well. As to the second part, in which the author appeals, as it were, to the reader, connections are made between the descriptions of events and other aspects of the readers' schemata. In Chapter 29 of *Middlemarch* this occurs somewhat as follows.

First, the narrator discusses with the readers the predicament of Casaubon. His suspiciousness and shrinking from being known make sense of his delays in publishing, of his scholarly way of giving references as he talks, of his endless notes on what is wrong with other scholars' work. By this device the surprising accomplishment of George Eliot is to allow an identification of the reader with Casaubon. Knowing him from within is to understand him, and understanding him means we can to some degree stand in his position.

Next, George Eliot's narrator is able to show how companionship with Dorothea, which had been appealing because of her ready admiration during their courtship, has become alarming after she asked when Casaubon would publish his work for the benefit of others. According to Casaubon's schemata, which we as readers can now share, Dorothea indicated that she had features other than pure appreciativeness. Casaubon's model of Dorothea is contradicted. Now, instead of being bulwark against an unappreciative public, she has become part of that public, but more threateningly because she is in a position to oversee what he is doing. His idea of the joint plan of Dorothea bringing him appreciation and happiness in his old age is lost forever, with all the despair that this brings. He backtracks to his more familiar, more private strategy of behaving with a scrupulous correctness that cannot be criticized. We who might have inklings of the enormity of his life being wrecked in this way may shiver in our pity for him.

EMOTIONS OF IDENTIFICATION. The writer's task includes the invocation of our schemata and creation of the possibility of identifications with the characters. As readers, we run our planning schemata entrained with those of the characters. The communication of emotions will then be of several kinds.

There may be basic identificatory emotions: If a plan such as marriage starts, and if we identify with any of the characters and take on their goals, we feel happy. As Casaubon and Dorothea's marriage begins to fail, the loss is sad. One may postulate that because basic emotions are innate, they may be evoked in others universally. A loss will be understood as a loss and experienced as such if the identification has occurred.

Complex emotions involve the sense of self. Their communication may require the elicitation of emotion-linked individual experience rather than just basic emotions like sadness or anger. Academics, for instance, might more easily identify with Casaubon than people who have not struggled with scholarly work and with the ambivalence of making oneself known through one's research while being apprehensive of a potentially critical and unappreciative public. There is no single term in English for the emotion that Casaubon feels when his sense of being valued for his work is disappointed by Dorothea's question about when he will start preparing for publication. On the other hand, our culture does have a term to describe the threat of sexual loss: Jealousy is one of the emotions that Casaubon feels with the arrival of Ladislaw's letters. Perhaps more of us can resonate with this sense in our own experience.

As Brewer and Lichtenstein (1981) point out, the discourse structure is arranged to allow emotions to be evoked in the reader. A detective story places an outcome near the beginning, and we feel anxiously curious to discover the plan that led up to it. George Eliot relies on a more straightforward curiosity of the what-will-happen-next variety. She allows identification with different characters in turn, and the plot gains momentum with our curiosity about how their lives will unfold and interact. This is the skill of the storyteller, but her greatness involves engaging yet another kind of curiosity, perhaps the kind that is behind many people's interest in psychology. This is of how we might understand those of our reactions that seem not quite comprehensible and those of our actions that occur without apparently being voluntarily willed.

Understanding ourselves

In the scene in the library, George Eliot implies that Casaubon's jealousy of Ladislaw has been displaced from its real origin, his disappointment in his marriage. The emotion is therefore expressed as irritability that can no longer be contained by his rules of behaving with correctness. His irritation floods out. Though not very directly expressed, it starts a serious quarrel. George Eliot, here and throughout the novel, explores consequences of such emotional trajectories, uprushings of feeling that we may experience but that may remain mysterious. Though emotions leap into consciousness, aspects of the goals and plans from which they arise may not be conscious at all.

Models of self have functions that provide the possibility of continuity across episodes of joint planning, the learning of social skills, and engagement in long-term projects. This self is a thread joining our plans, connecting ourselves to our own history and memories of how we started actions in which we find ourselves engaged. George Eliot's characters each have a "self," but these modern selves are not just supported by worldly measurements of honor. Now each is in itself a microcosm, a little inner world of self-with-others who must play their roles in order for life to go on properly. So when people meet it is as if two whole inner worlds must somehow combine or interleave, adding a dimension to the emotions of *Middlemarch* that is absent in the emotions of the *Iliad*.

When Dorothea and Casaubon are disappointed in each other, they are each disappointed in a choice made voluntarily, a choice made in relation to an image of the other's attributes. She chose him for his erudition, so that she could be his student, could give up the triviality of everyday tittle-tattle and engage with the great questions of life. So he becomes installed in her mind as an idealized teacher in relation to herself as willing student. The actual Casaubon must then be constantly compared to this role that he must play opposite to herself. Comparably he chose her as someone purely appreciative, in contrast to those others who had not received his work warmly. She must play the admiring public in relation to himself as great author.

So rather than one person meeting another, as it were directly, each self meets the other in terms of the model of a person they have installed in their minds. As the image of the other is confronted with the plans and actions of an actual other person, image and the actuality may fail to match. The projection of the image of the other is both the erotic fire of being in love and the betrayal as that other turns out to be different than we suppose.

Unlike science, literature does not just speak in the voice of external observation. By reflecting on episodes of emotion in novels such as those of George Eliot, we may extend our sympathies, because this too is our own predicament. Insofar as we have been able to identify with the characters, the love, disappointment, and so on can be our own. Because we run the literary simulation on our own models of self, we can also reflect on such matters in our own lives and interactions.

The purpose of the narrator's voice in *Middlemarch*, then, is not description of a quasi-scientific kind, and not to indicate godlike omniscience. George Eliot does not use her narrator's voice in that way. Instead, she uses it to apply particularities of what has gone on in the event sequence to more general consideration, and to us as readers. If she is right in her sense of the importance of emotions, the effects are no longer cultural propaganda, no longer just a means of educating emotions in the sense of which emotions are appropriate to which events and what their consequences might be. Hers is a means of inviting self-reflection on our model of self, without forcing our interpretations of the events that occur in the story or rigidly programming our emotions as they occur in response to them. This allowing of the reader's own creativity is what distinguishes, I think, great art such as hers from formula written novels whose purpose is largely to program particular emotions in the reader. George Eliot's art allows a kind of experimentation within the self that may promote understanding of our own emotions and their relation to other people.

6. Stress and distress

A crisis consists precisely in the fact that the old is dying
and the new cannot be born; in this interregnum a great
variety of morbid symptoms appears.

Antonio Gramsci
Prison notebooks

Epidemiology and illness

In the wake of disappointments and frustrations in an incompletely
knowable world may come illness, as it did for Casaubon. George Eliot
was able to have Lydgate recognize Casaubon's illness as "fatty degener-
ation of the heart," making a diagnosis that is distinguishable only in
terminology from one that would be made today (coronary heart disease
or atherosclerosis; atheromata are the fatty plaques that form to harden
and obstruct the coronary arteries). Lydgate was also able to describe
how intense emotions could increase the risk of death and could give a
prognosis that again would scarcely differ from today's.

Since the time in which *Middlemarch* was set, some of the most important advances in medicine have come from the epidemiology of physical
disease, and during the last 30 years the epidemiology of psychosomatic
and psychiatric states has come into prominence. This kind of study has
begun to stimulate a fuller understanding of how emotional states may
cause illness.

Epidemiology is the statistical analysis of illnesses as they occur in
everyday life, in different places and in different sections of society. It
began in earnest in the first half of the last century, when fevers such as
typhoid, typhus, and cholera killed large numbers of people and became
of great concern in Europe and elsewhere. In an epidemic that occurred
between November 1831 and May 1832 some 22,000 people died of

cholera in Britain, more than 1 per 1,000 of the population at that time. It was with the possibility of such an epidemic in mind that the fever hospital in Middlemarch was being built. The death rates from cholera stood against a background of yet higher mortality from other causes. At the beginning of the 1840s in Britain the mean life expectancy was 22 years for laborers and 44 for gentry.[1]

Many diseases were thought to be caused by a miasma, a smelly infectiousness of bad air from excreta and the rotting matter that stood around in piles in towns, and would have overwhelmed any modern time-traveler with their disgusting stench. The rapidly growing over-crowded towns of those days had no sewers, and garbage disposal was not as we know it. The miasma theory was based on the salient phenomenon of smell, which was misleading as a clue about how infectious diseases are transmitted.[2]

It was the success of the nineteenth-century epidemiology of infectious diseases that displaced the miasma theory and established a climate for the theory that diseases were caused by microorganisms. John Snow traced an outbreak of cholera on the edge of Soho in London in 1854 to a pump in Broad Street (now Broadwick Street). His evidence implied that cholera was carried by water. He followed this by investigating rates of illness of people drawing water from supplies provided by different water companies. In another outbreak of cholera, people living on one side of a street with water supplied from one company remained well. Those on the other side of the street taking water from another company were dying of cholera. Snow found a cracked earthenware pipe supplying this side that ran near an overflowing cesspool, which was seeping into the water supply.[3]

Snow suspected that cholera was due to a cell that reproduced itself, rather than a poison. Epidemiological work of the kind that he pioneered initiated "the great cleanup" in cities, a revolution quite as extraordinary as any involving shooting and political coups. It included paving streets and building sewers. It prepared medical opinion for the theories of Pasteur and Koch that infectious diseases were caused by bacteria too small to see. At last the reasons for the ravages of such diseases began to be susceptible to human technology.

Now, in a later century, a movement that may perhaps be equally important is beginning. Very large numbers of people, concentrated unevenly in different sections of society, are found to suffer from illnesses related to stress and from psychiatric conditions of depression and anxiety. Just as the idea that infection spread by miasmas gave way to the idea that disease is due to microorganisms carried by water and insects, so now our conceptions of psychiatry are changing.

Textbooks of psychiatry tend to emphasize genetic abnormalities, disordered or fragile personalities, disturbances of the brain's transmitter metabolism, and the possibilities of correcting those disturbances by drugs. If the hypotheses that are now emerging from psychiatric epidemiology are even partly correct, these conceptions will be displaced or accompanied by quite different ideas. In this chapter I shall discuss some of the evidence that stress provokes physical illnesses and causes psychiatric syndromes.

Stress and psychosomatic illness

Crisis means a point of judgment, a turning point. In this chapter I will take a crisis to be a turning point at which a person interprets the progress in some large personal plan as changing for the worse, as when a marriage ends or he or she becomes involuntarily unemployed.

Imposed stress puts a person under strain. Stress can be coped with successfully, either by an action that rescues or reformulates the plan that was threatened or by a mentality or a physiology that allows the imposed strain to be borne. The suggestion of much recent research is that, if a stress is not coped with, the person may suffer psychiatric breakdown or physical illness.[4]

Holmes and Rahe (1967) proposed that psychosocial events, such as bereavements, changes in habits, or major readjustments of ordinary patterns of activity, are stressful. They asked laypeople to rate how stressful each of 43 events was. The events had been chosen from clinical experience as being frequently associated with psychosomatic disorders. Death of a spouse was given as an anchor point scoring 100 points. Then people were asked to rate other kinds of events in relation to it. Thus people made explicit their folk theories of the relative stress of various kinds of happenings. A scale of values of each kind of stressful event was then constructed from the means of the ratings: Being fired from work scored a mean of 47, an outstanding personal achievement 28, taking a vacation 13, and so on.

This scale prompted an acceleration in work on the epidemiology of stress-related illnesses: Scores on this easily administered scale were found to predict rates of illness of various kinds (see, e.g., Rahe & Arthur, 1978; Rahe, 1988). Medical wisdom in many cultures and from ancient times has described associations of illness with failures of people's equilibrium or with actions miscarried. The newer epidemiological work on stress provides an empirical basis in investigating these ideas.

Approaching the issue not by summing effects of several life changes, but by looking at the effects of a specific event, namely, separation from a spouse by bereavement or divorce, commonly agreed to be stressful, we have further indications of effects of stress. Stroebe et al. (1982), for instance, have studied mortality in England and Wales, and compared rates of married people dying from all causes with rates of death among the widowed and divorced. In all age groups over 20, and for both sexes, widowed and divorced people were more likely to die than the married. The effects were generally greater for men than women. As an indication of the size of these effects: In the middle years (40 to 54) there was about a 50% greater chance of widowed or divorced people dying than of married ones. This excess decreased with age to 18% for men and 6% for women between the ages of 70 and 74, when, of course, the total numbers of people dying are high. As to causes, both cancers and heart disease showed differential effects in the widowed and divorced as compared to the married. Such statistics are a starting point. Is it possible to be more specific?

Imbalance and invasion

Despite the advent of scientific medicine, remnants of folk theories remain. In widely separated cultures, folk theoretical concepts in medicine occur, for instance, in conceptions of equilibrium among the different elements of life. In health, these elements are thought to be in balance with each other and with the environment. Illness is a disharmony within the person or between the person and the environment, to be corrected by restoring balance. People in whose lives the elements are not combined harmoniously are susceptible to illness.[5]

The microorganism theory of disease, for which the ground was laid by the epidemiological discoveries of Chadwick, Snow, and others, is the major triumph of modern medicine. Its discovery, unsuspected by folk theories, was that many diseases are caused by infectious bacteria and viruses. Recently, however, the theory of infection by microorganisms is being related again to the older conception of lives maintained in a kind of harmony.[6] The reason is that even the most virulent infections seem not to affect everyone in the same way, so the question arises as to what makes some people susceptible and others not. More illnesses are now thought to be affected by stress than was considered within scientific medicine when infectious diseases were beginning to be understood.

It is now an active research question as to whether stresses that have long been suspected of making people susceptible to disease have a physiological basis in reducing the competence of the immune response system. The ability of the system to respond is itself dependent on the person being in equilibrium.

Some 50 years ago, Selye (1936) proposed that different kinds of stress all have similar physiological effects. He reported that any of a large number of events, including injury, surgical shock, exposure to cold, and even muscular exercise, may provoke a "general adaptation syndrome." In this syndrome the body reacts with a general alarm signaled by a number of somatic symptoms, including rapid secretion of corticosteroids from the adrenals, weight loss, increase in lymphatic tissue, loss of muscle tone, ulceration of the digestive tract, and a fall in body temperature. There follows a phase of resistance, when, if the stress continues, the pituitary increases its production of hormones that stimulate corticosteroids while stopping the secretion of hormones that promote growth. The body shifts its metabolism toward physiologically coping with the continuing emergency. This is accompanied by a loss of the symptoms of the first stage. The third phase is exhaustion: If the stress continues, the resources for physiological coping seem to be depleted and symptoms of the first stage return.

Even the editor of the journal in which Selye published a long article in 1946[7] admitted that Selye's work had at first seemed merely a curiosity, of no medical interest. With the epidemiology of stress-related illnesses, and the realization that stress affects not only hormonal responses but also the body's immune response system, it seems fundamental.

Imposed stress and the immune response system

Stress is now thought to have much wider effects than Selye first discussed. Riley (1981), for instance, has confirmed that, under stress, the adrenal cortical hormones impair the competence of the immune response system. Three kinds of effects occur. First, an impaired immune system can fail to recognize and destroy foreign invaders, including bacteria and viruses, so that the body becomes more susceptible to infectious diseases of all types. Second, changes can occur to the immune system's ability to recognize and hence refrain from attacking the body's own tissue. Some diseases are due to just such failures; in some kinds of arthritis, for instance, the immune system starts to destroy joints. Third, an impaired immune system may fail to destroy some types of growing cancer cells.[8]

Causes of cancer. Cancer is an uncontrolled growth of cells in the body. Usually when cells grow and divide they are controlled by genetic plans that build them into the structure of existing body parts. A malignant cancer is a proliferation of a line of cells that causes damage and leads to symptoms. If it continues, it can result in death. With age, and it seems with stress, cancers are produced at an increased rate and the immune system's ability to detect and destroy them deteriorates.[9]

The efficiency of the immune system seems to be under the control of transmitter substances, hormones including corticosteroids, and peptides. The secretion of these is, in turn, probably controlled by way of the pituitary and hypothalamus. This offers a plausible mechanism for effects of emotional stress.

AVOIDABLE ENVIRONMENTAL CAUSES OF CANCER. Different cancers behave differently, some are now treatable though some usually cause death. Three kinds of cancer – of the lung, lower bowel, and breast – together account for around half of the deaths from cancer at present in the United States. Despite an earlier sense that cancer was caused by genetics, age, or luck, the striking recent finding is that the majority of cancers, including those that are the most frequent killers, are avoidable. As Doll and Peto (1981) point out, this can be inferred from four different kinds of evidence.[10]

First, is the evidence that the prevalence of the commoner cancers differs in different groups of people. Skin cancer is about 200 times as common in Queensland, Australia, as in Bombay, India. Second, incidence rates change when people migrate to a different country. Black Americans have cancer rates similar to those of white Americans and unlike those of black Africans living in regions from which slaves were transported. And the rate of breast cancer in black Americans is more than three times higher than the rate in black Nigerian, and conversely, for cancer of the liver the Nigerian rate is four times higher than the American. Third, there are changes in incidence over time. Between 1950 and 1975 in the United States, the rate of stomach cancer approximately halved, whereas the rate of lung cancer increased by 148%.

Fourth, there is the evidence of scientific experiments on specific causes, for instance, of specific industrial chemicals and radiation now known to cause specific cancers. Workers in some parts of the dye industry have suffered from cancer of the bladder caused by substances with which they worked. Overall, more than 50% and perhaps as many as 80% of cancers are avoidable. They are usually attributed to lifestyle or the environment.

Epidemiologically, in Western nations, by far the most significant causes of death from cancer are from just two sources. Tobacco contributes to about 30% of cancer deaths, mainly lung cancers, but with other types of cancer also being affected. Diet is thought to affect about 35% of cancer deaths, but for reasons that are less well understood. It is likely that dietary factors are not specific carcinogens, although these do occur in some foodstuffs that should be avoided. Major effects are more likely due to grosser attributes of diet, such as amounts of vitamins and perhaps the amount of fat or fiber, which in turn may affect the bacteria that live in the lower bowel. Other causes of cancer death are small in comparison with tobacco and diet. Other factors do have measurable effects. They include alcohol, having many sexual partners, severe or frequent sunburns, and some kinds of occupations.

PROSPECTIVE STUDIES OF STRESS ON MORTALITY. Doll and Peto said in 1981 that direct effects of psychosocial stress on cancer rates or the immune system had not been demonstrated conclusively, and this was echoed by Fox (1982). Typically, research on environmental and on psychosocial risks has not been closely connected. Moreover, the picture is still incomplete. It is confusing partly because so many of the data are correlational and partly because cancer takes years to develop and is therefore not susceptible to quick studies.

Recently, however, prospective studies that may provide causal evidence, and that relate stress to mortality over the appropriate time scale, have started to come in from the work of Grossarth-Maticek and his colleagues. In the first study (Grossarth-Maticek, Bastiaans & Kanazir, 1985), every second household in a small Yugoslavian town was visited. The oldest member, and in some cases another member who was seen as suffering from stress, were given a personality questionnaire. This procedure yielded 1,353 subjects mostly between 59 and 65 years of age. Ten years later, the cause of death of any who had died was assessed. It was found that people who scored highly on a "rational," antiemotional personality trait and who also smoked more than 20 cigarettes a day had died from lung cancer at a high rate (22% of those who had both factors).

Heavy smoking on its own or the antiemotional personality trait on its own did not lead to deaths from cancer.

Subsequently, Grossarth-Maticek has created a somewhat different typology, postulating four general personality types (Grossarth-Maticek, Eysenck & Vetter, 1988). Type 1 can be thought of as dependent on some other person or on some highly valued occupation for emotional well-being, with withdrawal of this source of well-being causing hopelessness and depression. Type 2 are people who have a highly valued goal and feel angry if unable to reach it. Type 3 people tend to shift between reactions of Types 1 and 2. Type 4 has achieved a degree of emotional autonomy. Analyzing their Yugoslavian data using this typology, Grossarth-Maticek et al. found that 46% of Type 1 people had died from cancer and 24% were still alive at 10 years. By contrast, of the Type 4 people, 91% were still alive.

Two further studies have been completed since Grossarth-Maticek has moved to Germany. Grossarth-Maticek, Eysenck, and Vetter (1988) found similar results to those of the Yugoslavian study in a random sample of the population of Heidelberg. In this sample, with a younger mean age, 17% of Type 1 people had died from cancer within 10 years of first contact with the researchers, 2% had died from heart disease, and 72% were still alive. Another study was of a sample of people nominated by those in the random sample as being under stress. Here 38% of the Type 1 people had died from cancer in 10 years, 7% from heart disease, and 38% were still alive. In the Heidelberg samples the autonomous Type 4 people had very low death rates, with only 3% dying.[11] Again in the Heidelberg samples, deaths from lung cancer were mainly among smokers, but of such deaths the large majority were Type 1 people.

As well as this longitudinal research, neuroendocrinological evidence suggests that stress may be a risk. For instance, Schleifer et al. (1983) found that in blood from 15 men who had been recently bereaved the response of lymphocytes to stimulation by foreign substances was significantly reduced for 2 months after the death of the men's spouses. Kennedy, Kiecolt-Glaser, and Glaser (1988) have reviewed evidence of this kind on nondietary effects, including their own work. This evidence indicates impairment of immune response in women who had been separated for a year compared with matched married women.

PSYCHOSOCIAL FACTORS IN THE COURSE OF CANCER AND THE EFFECTS OF PSYCHOTHERAPY. There is work on the effects of psychological and social factors on the course of cancer once it has been diagnosed. Factors affecting regression of cancers may be similar to those affecting their growth. In a healthy person, cancers may start frequently but be inhibited by a competent immune system. Problems arising from such research may be illustrated in relation to breast cancer. Derogatis, Abeloff, and Melisaratos (1979) found that particular kinds of psychological coping were effective in prolonging survival time following the detection of breast cancer. But the question remains unclear, as a more recent and methodologically sophisticated study by Cassileth et al. (1985) on a range of cancers indicated that none of the factors of social support, job and life satisfaction, drug use, perception of health, hopelessness/helplessness, and adjustment to the diagnosis had any effect in prolonging survival time.

Looking at the issue of how cancer proceeds from a different viewpoint based on the occurrence of severe life events, Ramirez et al. (1989) matched 50 women with operable breast cancer who had relapses with 50 who did not have relapses. Matching factors were the type of operation, type of chemotherapy, menopausal state, number of affected lymph nodes, and size and type of cancer. The authors measured the number of severe life events and difficulties that occurred between the date of the original operation and the recurrence, or a equivalent period for the controls, using the Bedford College Life Events and Difficulties Schedule. (Events that are severe are typically bereavements, separations, the breakdown of important relationships, and the like. The method of measuring these is described in a following section of this chapter.) The relative risk of a recurrence of the cancer was significantly increased in women who had suffered severe events or difficulties. Taking each woman with her matched control: There were nine pairs of women in which the one with the recurrence had a severe life event or difficulty when her matched control had not. By comparison, in only one pair did the control woman have a severe life event or difficulty when the woman who had a recurrence did not.

Then there are studies of the outcome of psychological therapy. On the one hand there are some positive effects of therapy. One was found by Grossarth-Maticek and his team (reported by Eysenck, 1988). They chose a subsample of 100 people from their highly stressed Heidelberg sample and randomly assigned 50 to a control group and 50 to a therapy group in which cognitive-behavior therapy was given to help them cope with stresses – essentially to help them turn into autonomous Type 4 people. Preliminary results are that of the therapy group 45 were alive at a 10-year follow-up and of the control group only 19, though the exact causes of death are still under analysis, and details at the time of this writing are not available. In a study in California, Spiegel et al. (1989), also with a 10-year follow-up, found that patients who had metastatic breast cancer and randomly allocated to receive weekly supportive group therapy sessions had their life prolonged by some 18 months compared with control subjects with similar pathology allocated to a condition with the same medical care but without group therapy.

An apparently contrary result of psychosocial therapy was found by Bagnall et al. (1990), who in a nonrandomized trial compared the survival rate of two groups of women with breast cancer. All had conventional treatment, that is, some combination of surgery, radiotherapy, and chemotherapy. There were 334 who had in addition voluntarily attended an alternative medicine center, the Bristol Cancer Help Centre, UK, for a program that included group work and a vegetarian diet. There were 461 companion subjects who had only conventional treatment. The women attending the Bristol Centre were self-selected and on average younger than the comparison sample but group-matched on other physical variables. Several different analyses were made, but surprisingly in all of them the Bristol women fared significantly and substantially worse than the comparison sample. It seems possible that the cause is due either to diet or to the change of diet or lifestyle for those attending the center or to some factor of personality or even to a disappointment at conventional treatment that selectively led women to attend the center. This question will no doubt be debated further.

CONCLUSION. There are two basic kinds of study on which the hypothesis is based that cancer is affected by psychological and social factors. One kind is studies of the effects of psychosocial factors on the onset of cancer. One of the many difficulties with this kind of study is dating the onset of cancer. Cancers may take many years to grow. The important immunologically sensitive step in the process, if there is one, may be a precancerous change that may take many more years to develop into a full-grown cancer. Moreover, small cancers may be present but physically undetected (see e.g., Fox, 1982; Ramirez, 1988). This set of possibilities makes research on factors affecting onset problematic, because not only is it impossible to date when changes that are significant in promoting onset have occurred, but cancerous or precancerous changes could make psychological functioning deteriorate, which in turn might erode relationships with other people. Thus, psychosocial variables found to be associated with cancer could be effects rather than causes.

Even so, the most striking recent epidemiological evidence linking psychological and social factors to onset is that of Grossarth-Maticek et al., which suggests a link because it involved making classifications that predicted outcome 10 years later. This aspect alone makes the work potentially important; but the research is problematic in many respects. One problem in addition to those described in the previous paragraph is that the questionnaire measures used by Grossarth-Maticek, Eysenck, and Vetter (1988) by which their Type 1 people were identified involve such questions as "Do you have a marked tendency to concern yourself lastingly with one emotionally important person or one important aim in life, combined with a strongly marked faithfulness and a desire for belongingness?" (p. 492). Not only are many issues mixed in each item, making it impossible to know which were influential, but none of the items on their Type 1 scale indicates what stresses there actually were or when they occurred.

We also lack demonstrations that the immunological effects of bereavements and separations that have been demonstrated to occur in humans are large enough, or of the kind, to affect human cancer growth in a clinically significant way.

The other kind of studies are those that try to ascertain the time course of cancer as affected by psychosocial factors and the effects of psychosocial therapy. Here evidence is also scanty, but both Grossarth-Maticek's results as reported by Eysenck (1988) and the randomized trial of Spiegel et al. (1989) are sufficiently striking to encourage further work along these lines. The trial by Bagnall et al. (1990) at the Bristol Cancer Help Centre is thought-provoking, but without randomization such trials cannot be taken very seriously.

Overall, the current balance of evidence is that psychological and social factors, perhaps especially those involving severe losses, do affect both onset and course of cancers. These effects may be mediated by the immune response system, and other immune-sensitive illnesses are affected by comparable factors (see also Dorian & Garfinkel, 1987). At the same time neither the factors themselves nor the mechanisms by which they may act are well understood.[12]

Does personality affect risk of coronary heart disease?

If the kind of stress that provokes cancer seems to be a loss of people or objects on which a person might be dependent, a different kind of stress affects coronary heart disease. Friedman and Rosenman (1959) compared the incidence of coronary heart disease in 83 middle-aged American professional men identified by their colleagues as striving intensely to achieve self-selected goals and as having high competitiveness, a strong desire for recognition, and continuous involvement in multiple activities subject to deadlines, hastiness, and extraordinary alertness. Friedman and Rosenman labeled this group Type A, and compared them with 83 men in the same kinds of occupations who were seen by colleagues as having a relative absence of drive, urgency, a desire to compete, or involvement in deadlines. They called this second group Type B.

The main finding was that 23 men (28%) in the Type A group had definite clinical or electrocardiographic evidence of coronary heart disease. Only 3 men in the Type B group had such signs. Type A men had more of several other factors known to be associated with risk of heart disease. They smoked more and they had higher levels of blood cholesterol. These other factors were not sufficient to account for the differences in the incidence of heart disease between the groups.

Subsequently, the Western Collaborative Group Study (Rosenman et al., 1975), which was a prospective study of 1,589 Type A and 1,565 Type B men, essentially confirmed these results: 34 Type A men, who were without symptoms when first seen, died from coronary heart disease within the 8.5-year follow-up period, compared with 16 Type B subjects. On other measures of heart disease, too, Type A men were at roughly twice the risk as Type B men.

In his longitudinal studies, Grossarth-Maticek (Grossarth-Maticek, Bastiaans & Kanazir, 1985; Grossarth-Maticek, Eysenck & Vetter, 1988) defines a Type 2 personality, which is similar to Rosenman and Friedman's Type A, as people for whom some highly valued object (such as a person or job) makes them unhappy and angry if they cannot achieve what they wish, and they are unable to disengage themselves from this object. This type is emotionally opposite to the cancer-prone group, seemingly reacting with anger rather than hopelessness. For them, cancer deaths in the Yugoslavian sample were only 6%, but coronary heart disease was the largest specific cause of death: 29% at the 10-year follow-up. At that time 28% of this type were still alive. In the random population sample from Heidelberg, coronary heart disease again caused high mortality among Type 2 people, with 13.5% of this type having died from it, compared with only 6% from cancer and with 64% still alive. In the stressed Heidelberg sample, 28% had died from coronary heart disease, 2% from cancer, and 48% were still alive.

Just as there are gaps in the evidence on stressful events, so too the idea of susceptibility to coronary heart disease has not gone un-challenged. Type A effects have been weaker when questionnaires have been used rather than Rosenman and Friedman's interview, which in-cludes assessments of nonverbal behavior, and weaker also in non-Cal-ifornian cultures (for reviews, see Steptoe, 1981, and Boman, 1988).[13] Moreover, the predictive role of Type A categorization shows signs of being replaced in the research literature by hostility, which is a part of the original Type A syndrome but which has been found to predict coronary artery disease independently of the Type A classification. So, for instance, Barefoot, Dahlstrom, and Williams (1983) in a 25-year fol-low-up and Shekelle, Gale, and Ostfield (1983) in a 20-year follow-up have found both coronary artery disease and mortality to be predicted by hostility of their subjects measured at the beginning of the research projects.

Two kinds of stress?

In crude terms, the stress of life events such as bereavements occurs because mutual plans are disrupted by external means. By contrast, Friedman and Rosenman's Type A, Grossarth-Maticek's Type 2, or Bare-foot and Shekelle's hostility characteristic can be thought of as an aspect of personality related to constantly creating internal incompatibilities among plans and resources, and hence frustration with things given high priority but not enough resources to accomplish them. These can be thought of as two different kinds of stress. Both can be understood in terms of the problems in planning that have been discussed in this book. Dysphoric signals arise on the one hand because of unpredicted obsta-cles to a plan, and on the other because of difficulty in optimizing plans to achieve many goals with finite resources. What is perhaps surprising is that, for human planners, both kinds of trouble may be accompanied by increased incidence of illness, respectively, of cancer and coronary heart disease.

   There are suggestions that the mechanisms of the two kinds of stress might be different, that the stress of adverse life events is more closely associated with fear or sadness and activation of adrenal-corticoid hor-mones, while the stress of a Type A or hostile person is more closely associated with anger and adrenal medullary hormones. Research on such matters may be suggestive, but at present it is not conclusive (Price, 1982; Frankenhaeuser, 1983; Rahe, 1988).

The psychosocial nature of stress

How could we understand a mechanism that could react to stresses? The most likely kind of explanation is that stresses derive from mismatches between a planner's goals and environmental outcomes or from conflicts among goals. These junctures are signaled by the system and are experienced as dysphoric, as described by conflict theories of emotions. A dysphoric emotion is not, however, necessarily stressful in a way that produces illness. It is only when such an emotion is very intense or long-lasting that we think of it as dangerous. This can occur if a circumstance persists in which goals that are felt to be vital to a person's sense of self cannot be achieved, and if the plans for achieving them cannot be modified. In such circumstance stress of the kind that may provoke illness exists.[14]

Totman (1979, 1985, 1988) has proposed a psychological theory of psychosomatic stress. He argues that most human behavior can be defined as purposeful and meaningful if it has goals that are recognizable by other people in a community. Purely private behavior that has no reference to others and could not draw commentary from others would not be socially meaningful in this sense.

When socially meaningful actions are undertaken we constantly compare them with shared rules, for instance, to be considerate, to work hard, or to be loyal. In terms of the communicative theory of emotions, these rules are among the multiple goals that we try to satisfy in our actions. Not only do we compare our actions with such rules, but much human talk consists of comparing other people's actions with them. This is often called gossip: "She'll regret leaving that job"; "They won't ever be happy in that relationship"; "He should spend more time with the children." Such commentary often includes emotion terms, as discussed at the end of Chapter 4. Not only actions and emotions but also verbal endorsements of action and of emotional responses are compared with implicit cultural rules. Totman argues that without frequent registration of actions and emotions, or verbal endorsements of them, with the rules of the community in which we live, we lose a sense of identity and worth. A lack of frequently registered consistency of purposeful action or verbal endorsements with a community's rules constitutes stress.

Totman goes on to show how, although they are members of a community, different individuals may operate with different rules. We all select from a range of rules that are recognizable within society. We may choose subcommunities of friends who agree with our own set of rules, and we may modify societal rules idiosyncratically.

Some people, moreover, may follow directives rigidly, not adapting to circumstances; others may distort social values defensively, and still others may adopt goals they are not equipped to fulfill. Type A people seem to act in this latter fashion, trying to do more than their resources allow. In yet other people, circumstances such as separations or role changes make it difficult or impossible to carry on well-practiced patterns of social interaction with their accompanying quotas of rule registrations. Yet other people may undergo changes in beliefs and thus adopt new sets of rules. These choices can sever them from social groups that supported a previous structure of well-practiced rule following. Such individuals would then be subject to a decrease in registration with rules and hence are under stress. Put in terms of the communicative theory, we could say that these people were not accomplishing a set of subgoals sanctioned by their immediate community.

In humans, psychosocial stress can, therefore, be defined in terms of failure to stay in register with prevailing social patterns.

Is stress a failure of optimization or a selective pressure?

The body is a system of multiple equilibria. Mammalian life involves simultaneously satisfying multiple goals: to maintain a certain temperature, to maintain the concentration of many different ions, hormones, and other substances, to balance energy production and consumption, and so on. When stress occurs, the body responds as to an emergency, and in doing so, it introduces another goal, to which the body responds. The argument of stress theorists since Selye is that this shifts equilibria toward less adapted states, which carry increased susceptibility both to invading pathogens and immune-related illnesses.

If we accept this, effects of stress on illness are counterintuitive and offer a serious challenge to evolutionary theory, as one would imagine that people who were made ill by stress would have survived less often. Genes causing stress dependence would have been selected against. There seem to be two main possibilities for understanding this.

One is simply that this is a failure of optimization over the range of disparate goals that have to be satisfied by complex physiological systems of mammals. Such an idea seems puzzling, because one can imagine immune response systems that would not be susceptible to psychosocial influences. It seems likely that during the relevant period of human evolution the principal causes of death were different, and occurring on average at an earlier age than now. Also, many of the diseases discussed in this chapter occur to people past child-rearing age, and so are not sensitive to selection pressures.

The other possibility is that the illness-producing effects of stress are adaptive. Totman (1985, 1988) has proposed that the immune system's response to stress may decrease the fitness of individuals who cease to be in register with the social patterns and customs of their community. Stress would therefore tend to maintain social cohesion by making less integrated members of social groups prone to disablement and less likely to survive. The difficulty with this idea is that the group benefits at the expense of individuals who are less good at following social norms. Such mechanisms are hard to understand within the postulates of genetic theory, because selection works on the individual, or on genetically related individuals, rather than the group as such (see, e.g., Dawkins, 1982, 1986). But it may be that during the evolutionary history of the human species, social groups were perhaps made up of genetically related individuals, living, for example, as hunter-gatherers.

In terms of any of these ideas, our understanding has some way to go.

Stress and suffering

Koch's principles showing, for instance, how specific microorganisms can be demonstrated to be the immediate cause of many infectious diseases, are no longer in doubt. Nevertheless, we are amid a revolution of thinking. Questions that have become important are again those epidemiological ones left unanswered by microorganism theories: Why, when plagues swept across the world, did not everybody die? Why did doctors working in sanatoriums not themselves contract tuberculosis? The same goes for noninfectious diseases. Why do some smokers contract lung cancer and others do not? Why do some people die of cardiovascular disease and others eating similar diets stay healthy? Similarly, in psychiatry: Why, when someone has schizophrenia, is there a greater than 50% chance that her or his genetically identical twin will be healthy?

The epidemiological question for the end of the twentieth century is, as Antonovsky (1979) has put it, not so much what causes disease (though this is still important) but how, amid the pathogens showering on us like the arrows of Apollo, does anyone manage to be healthy? Poverty, certain kinds of occupations, diet, multiple factors in the individual's plans and other kinds of relation to the environment, all contribute to the incidence of illness, and not only in relation to pathways for the invasion of pathogens. Yet many people live long lives.

If current research ideas about the pathogenic effects of stress become well established they will require changes in medical treatment. The literature on stress implies that such changes should concern the person's emotions as they emerge in the person's interaction with the world. The main approach of Western medicine to emotions during the last century has been distinctive: Emotions of medical interest have been those of suffering, anxiety, and despair. The medical calling is to reduce suffering, lessen anxiety, and relieve despair. Diminishing pain by anesthetics and analgesics and diminishing dysphoric emotions by tranquilizers and antidepressants are, however, quite different from attending to the meaning of emotions that accompany the stressfulness of many of our plans and the adversity of many people's circumstances. The increased susceptibility to illness that accompanies being poor rather than well off or unemployed rather than employed is not to be relieved by drugs (see Townsend & Davidson, 1982).

Emotional specificity of stress

The nature of research on stress is unsatisfactory from the point of view of any theory of emotions. In research such as Wallbott and Scherer's (1986), for example, people were asked to indicate events that provoked specific emotional episodes of anger, happiness, fear, and so on, together with their responses. Such research has the possibility of revealing whether specific emotions do have similar initiating circumstances and consequences. For stress, we would like to know whether repeated elicitation of certain kinds of emotion can provoke illness.

By contrast, in research on stress any assessment of the role of specific emotions is difficult in at least two ways. First, the role of stress in causing major illnesses via immunological or physiological mechanisms is still controversial. It is possible that mainly minor illnesses are affected and that smaller irritations rather than major events are the best focus of attention.[15] Second, circumstances leading to stresses have, since Selye's work, tended to be treated as equivalent. The only differentiation that has been made systematically is between stresses of life events such as bereavement and stress factors of personality such as Type A or hostility. Dysphoric emotions or even supposed tendencies to such emotions are lumped together in interviews or questionnaire scales to produce total scores. There is as yet only suggestive evidence that adverse life events have their effect via anxiety or sadness, or that Type A behavior is based on anger. Too many emotional factors are at present confounded in this research. It will be important to apply research on normal emotions to these issues of whether particular kinds of emotional life, or higher than usual frequencies of particular emotions, predispose to specific kinds of pathology. It would be worthwhile to ask, for instance, whether social losses or losses of conformity with a social group provoke illness by way of repeated elicitations of the basic emotions of sadness and anxiety, and whether competitive and hostile striving affects heart disease by way of repeated elicitations of anger.

In one area of research the importance of stress as a causative factor is more firmly established. This is in the epidemiology of depression. Although this work too is in its early stages, and still not specific enough for a theory of the circumstances and effects of specific emotions to emerge in more than outline, an important advance in understanding the meanings and specificity of events has been made. In this research people's reactions to specific emotionally significant events are beginning to be understood.

Psychiatric epidemiology

By far the largest amount of psychiatric distress discovered in the community is depression and anxiety. It seems to be caused less by disturbances in people's brains or disorders of their personality than by disruptions in their lives and relationships by stressful events and undermining circumstances.

Psychiatric epidemiology involves standardized psychiatric diagnoses on people in the community and examining the frequencies of diagnosed conditions related to such factors as gender, social class, marital and employment status, number of children in a family, and so on. The important difference from research conducted with samples derived from clinics and hospitals is that community samples are not biased by being made up only of those who have chosen to visit doctors.

In community studies, a psychiatric diagnosis is largely an inventory of people's current emotional state. Psychiatrists describe the condition of people with high scores on such inventories in terms of depression, anxiety states, affective disorder, nonpsychotic psychiatric disorder, and the like. An ordinary understanding of these terms includes the idea of people being caught up in persistent moods of sadness and fear that have made it hard to concentrate on anything else, have made sleep difficult, and have prevented them from living an ordinary life. Psychiatric states are different from ordinary emotions in that they are either intense, long-standing, or difficult to understand or perhaps all of these. Typically, also, they are associated with bodily complaints and ruminations about the self.

An important criterion in community studies is the idea of a case level, approximately equivalent to the severity of symptoms that could take a person to a psychiatric outpatient clinic. Being at case level is experienced as making it impossible to cope with ordinary obligations such as maintaining a job and social relationships. If the condition occurs suddenly, it is referred to as a breakdown. The large majority of people who are diagnosed as cases in this sense are either despairing (depressed) or frightened (anxious) or both.

States involving disorders of thinking (e.g., delusions) or perception (e.g., hallucinations) are much rarer. Such states are generally called psychoses, or, in ordinary terms, madness. The most common nonorganic psychosis is schizophrenia. The usual estimate is that worldwide about 1% of people suffer from schizophrenia during their lifetime.

Such a percentage is known as prevalence: the proportion of a population that has a specific condition at specified level of severity in a given period. Prevalences may be estimated over the subjects' lifetimes, or over one year or one month, or just at the time when the diagnosis was made. In comparison with the 1% lifetime prevalence of schizophrenia, the estimated prevalence of depression and anxiety at the case level is 10.9% in London in one month (see Bebbington et al., 1981, who also quote comparable data from cities in other parts of the world).

Reliable data on psychiatric prevalence are a recent innovation. Diagnostic schemes involve a longish interview in which subjects are asked to describe whether or not they have each of a specified list of symptoms. If they recognize a symptom when asked, the interviewer collects more information about it, asking the respondent to describe it in detail, its frequency, its time course, its severity, the extent to which it prevents them doing ordinary things. Then the severity of a person's condition is assessed on the basis of the number of symptoms and their handicapping effects on the person's life.[16]

As an example here is an item from a research diagnostic interview (the PSE; see note 16) about the symptom of poor concentration: "What has your concentration been like recently?" If the respondent says she or he has not been able to concentrate, the interviewer continues with more detailed probes: "Can you read an article in the paper or watch a TV program right through?" "Do your thoughts drift off so that you can't take things in?" The interviewer continues questioning to establish how troublesome the symptom has been. If it has not seriously interfered with the person's life, it is rated as absent. If it does interfere, questions are asked about whether it has been intense more or less than 50% of the time in the last month, or makes the person unable to read a short article or watch a TV program. If the symptom is present less than 50% of the time, it is rated as moderate; if present more than 50% of the time, it is severe and clinically significant.

A psychiatric symptom is a complaint about one's mental state or some handicapping difficulty: not being able to sleep, feeling panicky, often bursting into tears, feeling fearful that other people intend to harm one. A person with a given number of symptoms at disabling severity can be diagnosed as having a particular kind of disorder, for example, depression or an anxiety state.[17]

The disturbing finding of psychiatric epidemiology is that incapacitating depression and anxiety are common. Unlike schizophrenia, there are very wide variations in prevalence among different sections of the population. As with cancer, the large differences in prevalence indicate that many of these conditions are avoidable. Thus there are differences in prevalence due to social class, unemployment, living in town or city, and so forth (see Oatley & Bolton, 1985).

Perhaps the most striking differences are between the sexes. In the West, approximately twice as many women as men suffer from depression and anxiety, and this is found in most of the countries in which surveys have been made.[18] Lest one think this is due to inherent biological differences, the data may also be broken down by marital status. In a study by Bebbington and others (1981), married men were less symptomatic than the unmarried: The proportion of married men with symptoms at the case level was 2.6%, and for single men it was three times higher, at 8%. For women, the effects of marriage were the reverse: Single women had a prevalence of depression and anxiety of 4.1%, whereas their married counterparts were more than three times more likely to be at the case level, with a prevalence of 18.4%. These sex differences are very marked: In terms of psychiatric distress marriage seems on average a much better prospect for men than for women.

Depression is the most common psychiatric syndrome, and the typical kind of depressive breakdown has a clear onset. It may last for several months with symptoms gradually becoming less intense and occurring less frequently if and when it resolves. Very rarely do nonpsychotic breakdowns occur without symptoms of depression, though there may be symptoms of anxiety too. Anxiety states are the second most common psychiatric condition, and mixtures of anxiety and depression are frequent. When a psychiatric condition has lasted for several years, anxiety symptoms often predominate and can make the sufferer chronically disabled.

How does one interpret these shocking findings, that at any one time perhaps 10% of the adult population in Western cities are unable to cope, and that women are much more likely than men to be suffering in this way, particularly if they are married?

People who find themselves in these states are certainly experiencing emotions. Some of the states that count as symptoms, like autonomic disturbances, or a lack of concentration perhaps due to the salience and distraction of an inner dialogue, are easily seen as manifestations of intense emotions. Emotional states, comparable to the sadness that follows the loss of a loved one, or the kind of fear that soldiers experience in combat, are often accompanied by bodily symptoms such as weight loss, bodily agitation, inability to sleep, and intense tiredness.

Psychiatry is usually thought of as the medical treatment of madness, and madness implies irrationality – that someone is behaving incomprehensibly, in an alien way. One of the achievements of psychiatric epidemiology is that although people detected as cases in community surveys have breakdowns in epidemic proportions, their symptoms are not incomprehensible. They may fail to conform to expectations that people should be happy, but the events and conditions of the lives of ordinary people can make their mental states comprehensible. It may therefore be misleading to call these states emotional disorders. Though people's lives may be in disorder, typically there is no implication of anything wrong with the emotions themselves. People may cry and talk about feeling unbearably sad. They may tremble and feel dread. But usually the reasons for such states are not obscure: They occur when a person suffers an important loss or a threat about something vital, and when it seems impossible that life will get better. Such states visit most of us at some time in our lives. They could visit any of us in some circumstances.

Life events and depression

Most depressive breakdowns are preceded by a serious adversity. It is this that makes breakdowns comprehensible. One of the important pieces of research establishing this relation with adversity was published in 1978, in Brown and Harris's *The Social Origins of Depression*. It brought convincing order into an area where evidence until then had been only suggestive.

Brown and Harris's research

Brown and Harris interviewed 458 women, randomly selected from the voters' list in Camberwell, London. There were 37 women who had onsets of depression or depression and anxiety at the case level.[19] Of these, 33 (89%) were found to have suffered a severe event or a major chronic difficulty in the preceding 38 weeks. In comparison, among the women who did not have symptoms at the case level, only 30% had suffered such an event or difficulty. Though not everyone with a threatening event or difficulty broke down, this large difference strongly implied a causal role of events and difficulties in provoking depressive breakdowns.

The interview that Brown and Harris developed is known as the Life Events and Difficulties Schedule. Examples of events rated as severe included separation or threat of separation from a parent or husband, an unpleasant revelation such as learning that one's husband had been having an affair, a life-threatening illness in someone close, a major material loss such as living in bad housing and learning that one's chances of being re-housed were minimal, and unemployment of the family's breadwinner. Almost all these events implied a sense of disappointment, often clearly expressed by the women themselves. In terms of a theory of plans, an ongoing life plan had been interrupted. In 88% of those who had suffered a severe event, there was an element of loss. Major difficulties were intractable problems that had lasted at least two years, such as living in squalid and overcrowded accommodations with many children, living with a violent husband or father, coping with a chronically sick child, or coping with children constantly in trouble with the police.

Here is an example of a depressive episode, given by Brown and Harris, of a person whose symptoms had reached the case threshold and were preceded by an adverse event, her husband's unemployment.

Mrs. Trent had three small children and was married to a van driver. Her flat had two rooms and a kitchen. A year before the interview, although she had some symptoms of occasional migraine headaches, she felt quite herself. Her third child had been born eight months before the interview, and around the same time her husband lost his job. She didn't worry too much, and he got another job quickly. But after two weeks he was fired from that job too, without any explanation. Seven weeks later her worries had become so severe that she felt tense all the time; she was miserable, had difficulty getting to sleep, and had became irritable with the children. She found it difficult to do the housework, became unable to concentrate, and her appetite declined noticeably. During the next two months these symptoms worsened. She would often cry all day. She got some sleeping pills from her doctor. Her relationship with her husband deteriorated. She lost all interest in sex and thought that her marriage was finished. Three times she packed and walked out but returned because of the children. She was self-deprecatory, felt she couldn't cope, and thought that she might end it all. By three weeks before the interview things had started to get better. She still tended to brood, though her concentration was now good enough for her to watch television, which distracted her. Her sexual relationship with her husband had returned, and indeed was better than before. She had been depressed for five and a half months. She had not consulted her doctor about depression, but about her migraines and it was for these, she said, that the sleeping pills had been prescribed. She thought it would have been wrong to bother her doctor about feeling depressed, since this was clearly related to her financial and marital worries (Brown & Harris, 1978, pp. 28–30).

Among the advances made by Brown and Harris was the construction of a way of interviewing in which people could describe events and difficulties such as these in some detail and from which the severity of these events and difficulties could be estimated. Interviews lasted perhaps an hour and a half, and took place during the same visit on which the subject's psychiatric state was assessed. The interviewer would ask the woman whether each of an exhaustive list of possible events or difficulties had occurred to her during the previous year. For each event and difficulty that the woman described, the interviewer would collect information about its context: Where and when did it happen? Was it expected? What occurred exactly? Who was there? What was said? What followed? What kind of support was available?

Later, at a meeting of the research team, after giving details of the circumstances in which each woman lived, the interviewer described each event and difficulty the woman had experienced. The research team discussed each in turn and rated each event and difficulty by consensus. Events that were focused on the woman herself, that were judged as likely to pose a threat lasting for more than a week, and that were rated on the top two points of a four-point scale of severity were described as severe. The researchers used only biographically relevant information to say how they thought most people would react in these circumstances, not the reaction of the woman herself. They were helped by training in a set of principles for making the ratings, and these principles acted as a sort of statute law. To keep the judgments constant there was also a large dictionary of ratings previously made of events and difficulties, a sort of case law.

Several important innovations were accomplished in this procedure. A largish number of randomly selected people in the ordinary community were given thoughtful and unhurried attention as they talked about their lives and the problems they had experienced in an interview that for the most part they found helpful to themselves. The closest parallel is psychotherapy. The difference from psychotherapy is that Brown and Harris's interviewers had an agenda and the interview had a structure to allow categorization and quantitative analysis of responses.

Most previous attempts to measure stress had used standard scores for particular events, such as Holmes and Rahe's (1967) Social Readjustment Rating Scale, or else personality questionnaires. As described earlier, Holmes and Rahe's scale was popular because of its simplicity of administration and because it predicted illness to some extent. Its results were inconclusive, however, as one might expect from an instrument that is so unfocused. It treats an event as the same for everybody, assumes that everyone has the same understanding of each item, and that effects of quite different events add together.[20]

Verstehen. Brown and Harris operationalized the concept of *Verstehen*, the act of imaginative understanding, of entering into another's lived experience, which Dilthey (1985/1926) and Weber (1968/1922) argued is the necessary operation of any distinctively human science (see also Hughes, 1959). *Verstehen* is the attempt to understand what might have gone on in a personal event, in history, in another culture – or in a novel.

Brown and Harris convene, as it were, a Greek chorus to enter into and comment on each event or difficulty as it affects the life of each protagonist. These protagonists are not members of the nobility, but ordinary people chosen randomly. The procedures allows intuitions about social rules to be articulated and applied in a way that does not oversimplify or distort the significance of events in people's lives, but does allow quantitative analyses to be made.

A further accomplishment is that, just as the procedure allows an essentially subjective *Verstehen* to be applied in the right place, it also allows objectivity its right place. Only events that are probably or certainly independent of the woman's own mental state are included. For instance, Mrs. Trent's husband's loss of his job would be included, because it was clear that her mental state had no influence on it. Her marital difficulties would be excluded because plausibly they were due to her own gathering depression. The threat of the event or difficulty is assessed only on the basis of relatively objective biographical information. It is independent of bias on the part of the interviewer, who might be drawn into the subject's view of the world. The interviewer gives the research team only circumstantial data. They do not know either the woman's attitude toward the event or her psychiatric diagnosis. The ratings are therefore independent of biases that might affect the estimate of severity, either underestimating it because of denial or overestimating it because of depression.

To give an idea of the threshold between severe and nonsevere events, here is an example at the lower end of the range of events rated as severe: "Subject's friend and only confidant left to live in Ireland; she had seen her three times a week." A comparable separation event rated as nonsevere occurred when a woman's husband left to work 70 miles away for three months and did not come back at weekends (Brown & Harris, 1978, p. 310).

An example of a chronic difficulty rated as severe was "The subject is 25 and lives with her husband and three children (aged one, two and three) in one room with one bed. The room is very damp and they share a kitchen. They have extremely poor relations with their landlord who has accused them of stealing food. The landlady's children often make a great noise when her children are trying to sleep" (Brown & Harris, 1978, p. 341).

Rather than people becoming depressed for irrational reasons, this research indicates that they become depressed for understandable reasons. The rating procedure showed that these reasons corresponded closely to the rules and understandings of society, as embodied in the research team's judgment of the kinds of events that are and are not threatening. Although the subjects' own emotional reactions were not used in assessing severity, they corresponded closely to the research team's contextual ratings.[21] One common view is that people become depressed because they distort the meaning of events, an extension of the idea that emotions are irrational (discussed in Chapter 3). In this research it is clear that people's own assessments of severity and unbiased collective intuitions of society are in close register. One might feel hopeless when depressed, but from this research, there is nothing irrational about the reasons for these feelings. Emotions of misery and despair occur at junctures that indicate reverses in people's life plans that are indeed crushing.

Vulnerability. Although nine out of ten women who had breakdowns in Brown and Harris's study had suffered at least one severe event or difficulty, only a fifth of those who experienced such an event or difficulty broke down. Severe events and difficulties provoked depression only in some people, others seemed protected from their impact. Brown and Harris therefore searched in their data for other influences in the lives of those who broke down under stress. They discovered four types that they called vulnerability factors. For the women in this London sample, these factors were (1) the absence of an intimate relationship with someone such as a husband or lover in whom the subject could confide, (2) the subject having lost her mother before age of 11, (3) having three or more children under 14 at home, and (4) being herself without a job outside the home. This last factor operated only in the presence of one of the other three.

Vulnerability factors operated by increasing the risk of breakdown if an event occurred. For instance, of women who had suffered a severe event or difficulty but who had an intimate relationship, only 10% became depressed. Of those who suffered a similar event or difficulty and had a relationship of low intimacy or none, 41% became depressed. Brown and Harris found that vulnerability factors did not increase the risk of breakdowns in the absence of severe events or difficulties.[22]

Severe events and difficulties, in conjunction with vulnerability factors, thus explained much of the incidence of depression among the urban women in Brown and Harris's sample. Approximately 10% of depressive breakdowns seem not related to any clear event or difficulty. But by far the largest proportion of psychiatric distress is occasioned not by anything intrinsically wrong with them, but by serious adversities in people's lives.

The kinds of understanding about the relation of adversity to distress that poets, playwrights, and novelists have given us throughout the ages are confirmed in this research and extended empirically. People suffering severe losses and disappointments feel sad about what is lost, feel angry toward any that might unjustifiably have contributed, and feel anxiety about a bleak future. The syndromes that occur also involve more than emotions. Research diagnostic interviews do not themselves, however, make fine distinctions between emotional states. They are concerned to categorize a medically recognizable syndrome and estimate its severity. Nor does Brown and Harris's Life Events and Difficulties Schedule seek to relate specific emotions to specific kinds of precipitating event. But the work has shown an empirical relation between losses and depression, in which people typically experience dysphoric emotions in an intense form.

In literature, from Gilgamesh to modern novels, intuitions about the relation of events to breakdowns have been explored. Now a quantitative dimension allows a check on whether these insights have not focused just on a kind of relation that happens to catch the literary eye, or perhaps happens only in that small segment of the population who write about themselves. This quantitative dimension adds both new insights and precision to folk theories. Although we know from our own experience some of the value of friends and lovers, Brown and Harris show that an intimate relationship is protective for women against the risk of breakdown in adversity and prompts some new thoughts about how such relationships might help.

Criticisms. Brown and Harris's research has been criticized in several ways. I will discuss three principal criticisms: one from psychiatry, one from a basis in an alternative theory of depression, and one on the basis of the statistics used in this kind of research.

PSYCHIATRIC CRITICISM. People who are discovered in community studies to be depressed are not always psychiatrically ill; they may, according to a medical view, be suffering only from a transient distress that need not be the concern of doctors or psychiatric services. Depressed people in community samples tend to recover, as did Mrs. Trent in the example given earlier. By contrast, people who attend psychiatric hospitals tend to have more symptoms, in a more severe and longer-lasting form.[23] Real depression, according to this idea, is a mental illness with roots in a disordered personality of the sufferer, not in the person's immediate life.

Surprisingly, this criticism by the medical profession is close to a folk theory of such happenings. Mrs. Trent did not want to bother her doctor because it was clear to her that her depression had been caused by her worries about money and her marriage.

This argument may imply a realization of practical limits to the resources of health care systems, but it is not well founded in any other sense. Reasons for the onset of depression have not hitherto been well understood within psychiatry. Only about 10% of the outpatients and a similar proportion of community cases who suffer onsets of depression seem to have had no obvious antecedent in severe events or difficulties. These depressions may be thought of as endogenous, and they remain poorly understood. Certainly, also, it is easier to find people with the most severe symptoms of depression in hospitals, precisely because they have selected themselves from the community, partly because of the intolerability and intractability of their symptoms. The advent of standardized psychiatric diagnoses, however, also means that there is little doubt that people diagnosed in community research are depressed in the traditional psychiatric sense (Brown & Harris, 1986; 1989). Many of the cases do improve within a matter of months,[24] but this does not mean that these people had not broken down.

It is a commonplace of epidemiology that many more cases of almost any condition are discovered in the community than at the clinic. This does not mean that community cases, either of a physical or a psychiatric condition, are not of medical importance. Research diagnostic interviews were introduced because diagnoses by psychiatrists were found to be unreliable for research purposes (Ward et al., 1962). There are no grounds for regarding the depression discovered in the community as fundamentlly different from that discovered in hospitals, or for dismissing disabling cases discovered in the community as of no psychiatric significance. There are grounds for discussing whether depression in general is an illness, to be treated in the way that psychiatric illnesses currently are, that is to say, mainly with drugs, but that is a different matter.

IS ONSET OF DEPRESSION CAUSED BY IRRATIONAL THINKING? It is an ancient view that thinking about things wrongly causes emotional troubles. It is closely related to the idea that emotions themselves are irrational, that they are diseases of the soul, as discussed in Chapter 3. Cognitive-behavior therapists such as Beck (1976) have propounded a modern version, arguing that irrational thought patterns give rise to emotional disorders. The basic argument, as expounded by Beck, is that depressed mood occurs because of irrational thinking. A typical depressogenic thinking pattern can be stated in the form of syllogism, such as the following (adapted from Beck, 1976, p. 100):

Major premise: If my spouse does not love me, I am worthless.
Minor premise: My spouse has spoken to me in a disparaging way.
Conclusion: I am worthless.

If such a minor premise should occur, people automatically reach the conclusion. Feeling sad or depressed may then follow. What has gone wrong, argues Beck, is that the premises are faulty. Here the major premise is absolute, overgeneralized, and exaggerated. Beck and his associates also identify all-or-nothing thinking, preferential attention to instances with negative connotations, inattention to instances with positive connotations, jumping to conclusions, personalization of plausibly impersonal events, and a number of other features as common emotional irrationalities. Cognitive therapy teaches people how to recognize such errors in their thinking and how to avoid them. People who are able to recognize the irrationalities of such thought patterns will avoid reaching such conclusions and will not suffer the inappropriate emotions that result.[25]

Beck's theory is, for practical purposes, indistinguishable from a theory of depression that has become widely accepted among American psychologists, the attributional version of Seligman's helplessness theory (Abramson, Seligman & Teasdale, 1978). According to this theory, depressed mood occurs if one suffers a failure of some kind and if one thinks about it in a particular kind of way. We will become depressed if we make three kinds of causal attribution about the failure: that it is due to internal reasons (i.e., due to oneself rather some external agency); that it is global, of a kind that occurs in all situations, rather than being local to just the current happening; and that the reason for it is stably permanent rather than temporary. There are no empirical criteria that distinguish Beck's theory from the attributional helplessness theory (Coyne & Gotlib, 1983). I will therefore take the Beck-Seligman position to be a single one.

The core argument is that people become depressed who experience a failure to control some important aspect of their world and who then think irrationally about this failure. The argument continues by indicating the strong evidence that cognitive therapy has shown good results in relieving depression, as compared both with antidepressant drugs and with other kinds of psychotherapy (Robinson, Berman & Neimeyer, 1990).

Though thoughts that may be judged irrational are often symptoms of depression, and they may interfere with coping in a crisis, there are empirical reasons to doubt whether irrationality has a distinctive role in causing onset of depression.[26] There are also matters of principle. The Beck-Seligman formulation is that people who think with a certain kind of irrationality are liable to depression, and that rational thinking is a procedure. I have argued in Chapter 3 that analyzing rationality as a procedure is misleading. In addition, Seligman's formulation assumes that the goal of behavior is instrumental control of the environment, including other people. Yet, if the important aspects of the world are personal and social, it is questionable whether either the view that depressogenic thinking is especially irrational or this idea of universal instrumentality is appropriate. Although it is important that we find our own and other people's behavior predictable within limits (Antonovsky, 1979), this is very different from treating other people instrumentally. As I have discussed in Chapter 4, we do not typically make models of others in order to control them. We construct joint plans with others in which we expect them to behave reliably.

The thought patterns identified as irrational in the Beck-Seligman position may not be irrational in all circumstances. The kind of thinking that has been labeled personalized, selective, and absolutist may be adapted to understanding the interpersonal world. People are typically involved in a variety of plans and a variety of roles. Given that these involve inferences about others' intentions, which may not be explicitly expressed, it is not necessarily irrational for us to see a large and personal significance in small indications, for example, lack of an affection in a spouse as indicative of loss of priority that we have in that other person's plans, or the coming to existence of some contrary goals.

In conclusion, we sometimes come to wrong conclusions in the interpersonal domain. And certainly it is easy to find instances of irrational thinking by depressed people. But there is little to indicate that depression at the case level is caused by irrational thinking. The most straightforward understanding of irrationality in relation to depression is to regard certain kinds of irrational thinking as symptoms of depression. As argued by Teasdale (1988) certain perseverating thoughts can prolong depression once onset has occurred.

THE METHODOLOGICAL PROBLEM. Brown and Harris's study (1978) was retrospective: Subjects were seen at a single point in time, and this can be misleading. Replications are important using both the original methods by different research groups and extensions using other methods.

As to replications there have now been at least 10 studies that either use Brown and Harris's methods or methods of comparable rigor in several British and North American communities (Oatley & Bolton, 1985). All of these showed substantially increased risk of depression following severe events or difficulties. Some of the factors that contribute to vulnerability differ in the different samples. All but one study have shown that low social support increases the risk of depression following a severe event or difficulty, and that this increase in risk is more than can be accounted for by the risk associated with low social support on its own.

More recently, longitudinal studies have begun to emerge, following people up over a period of months or years. Bolton and Oatley (1987) studied men who became unemployed. We compared their levels of depression and social support with those of men who remained in stable employment. Men who became unemployed and stayed unemployed over the following 6 to 8 months did indeed become significantly more depressed, and in this group those with few friends and a restricted social network outside work were more likely to become depressed than those with more extensive social networks. Amount of social interaction had no effect on depression among men who stayed employed.

Brown and his colleagues (Brown et al., 1986; Brown, Bifulco, & Harris, 1987) have conducted a prospective study of women with children in London with interviews a year apart. Of 303 women who were not depressed at the first interview, 32 became depressed in the year before the second, and 29 of these 32 were found to have suffered a prior severe event, most within 5 weeks before their breakdown. Almost always the events involved a loss, failure, or disappointment. As in the earlier study, although most people who became depressed had suffered a severe event, only about a fifth of those experiencing a severe event became depressed. Clearly some people were more resilient than others.

In this study it was possible to evaluate features of the woman's life at the first interview and to see how they affected whether an event would provoke breakdown. Women who at the first interview had a conflict of some sort and who later suffered an event related to it were more likely to break down. For example, a woman who had a conflict between her need to work and her desire to be a good mother suffered such a severe event when her school-age daughter became pregnant. It is not difficult to empathize with this woman, thinking that in devoting time to her work she might have neglected her daughter. Women with conflict-related events were more than twice as likely to become depressed as those with events that were similarly severe but unrelated to any preexisting conflict.

Similarly, women who at the first interview were especially committed to a plan or relationship, and who had severe events that damaged such plans, were four times more likely to break down than those who had suffered an event that had not affected a primary commitment. Events that exacerbated a preexisting difficulty also increased risk as compared with events that were unrelated to ongoing difficulties.

Some findings challenged some of the conclusions of the earlier study: Simply having a close relationship was not enough to protect a woman from the impact of an event. The close person must actively have been supportive in a crisis. Some women had such support at the first interview and expected it to continue, but when a crisis occurred, the support did not materialize. They were let down.[27] These women had a much higher rate of breakdown than those for whom expected support materialized. In those who were let down, the husband or other confidant from whom support was expected was deeply involved in the crisis and not available for this reason or would not listen or take the problem seriously. One husband, for instance, whose wife had had an ectopic pregnancy said he "might as well leave."

Indicating a different kind of factor: women who had made self-deprecatory remarks about themselves at the first interview before they were depressed were two and a half times more likely to break down if they suffered a severe event than those who also suffered events but had not made such remarks. Self-deprecating women did not become depressed if crisis support was available.

The authors speculate that, despite this, low self-esteem and low support each may contribute risk while at the same time affecting one another. A generally supportive relationship may help increase a person's estimation of self. At the same time a person with a positive evaluation of self may be in a better position to sustain her relationship with someone so that she does receive support in time of crisis.

A theory of depression

How does one make sense of these phenomena? Mead's and Goffman's theories of role offer the basis of an understanding. Following from their ideas (described in Chapter 4), self can be thought of as an internal model or representation that emerges from our role relationships with others and becomes important in managing future relationships. We maintain a sense of self by continuing interaction in roles. Our most important roles function to fulfill those explicit or implicit roles by which we define our worth.

Life events as role losses

According to Oatley and Bolton (1985), a life event or difficulty that is severe is one that removes from a person the possibility of enacting a role, a mutual plan of long standing that fulfills an important goal. Brown and Harris give a nice illustration of the way in which a sense of self can be involved in the enactment of a mutual plan. Henry VIII's fifth wife committed adultery, or at least let it appear that she had. Contemporary accounts describe the king as being "pierced with pensiveness" and moved to tears before the assembled Council. The French ambassador wrote to his own court that "the King has wonderfully felt the case of the Queen his wife and has certainly shown greater sorrows at her loss, than at the faults, loss or divorce of his preceding wives . . . as yet this King has formed neither plan nor a preference" (Brown & Harris, 1978, pp. 87–88).

Evidently, when previous dissolutions of marriage had been planned by the king they did not give rise to such distress. Only when a plan that he had thought to be mutual and going well was interrupted by his wife did he find himself at a loss, without a plan or a preference for a new partner. He found himself unable to undertake other plans and kingly duties. His preoccupation with himself as husband was carried, inappropriately, into his enactment of his role of king. He became depressed, and in doing so, revealed that he had a high-level goal of seeing himself as a man to whom a wife is faithful.

We experience ourselves primarily within relationships, and build up the experience of self in the process of interacting in mutual plans. Moreover, just as in technical work we build up a set of useful habits, an ordered arrangement of tools and materials, an organized set of models of the world, and a repertoire of skilled subplans, so in long-standing mutual plans we build up repertoires of stored plan segments.

When a larger scale plan of this kind fails, as when the king found that his wife had been unfaithful, the experience of self derived from the plan is no longer available. A whole repertoire of subplans and knowledge becomes useless. If a goal at the top of the hierarchy is damaged, a person may be left without any active plans. If a man lavished love and affection on his wife, then if she should die, there is the serious possibility that he no longer has the means for experiencing himself as an affectionate person. If a woman gains self-respect from her work, then if she loses her job with no possibility of reemployment, she can no longer enact the plans by which she experienced herself as worthy of respect.

One way of thinking about what happens in depression is that, with the loss of a major goal, plans to fulfill that goal revert to earlier plans that had once been successful, perhaps in childhood. These include making gestures of helplessness, appeals for rescue, and the like. The phenomenon is known as regression. In cognitive science, it is recognizable as backtracking to a default plan.

Horowitz (1979) has argued that some losses may reveal attributes of a relationship that is lost. Thus someone who was made strong by the support of another may become depressed with symptoms of feeling weak and being supplicatory. Someone feeling kind and good in a relationship may, following the loss, feel vengeful and hating. The relationship may have defended them against the experience of upsetting motives and the dysphoric emotions that had accompanied them before that relationship.

Vulnerability as lack of alternatives for lost roles

If a severe life event or difficulty is the removal of a plan that satisfied a major self-definition goal, then vulnerability consists in having no alternative plans that could allow the person to fulfill that goal, no subsidiary roles or potential roles that will substitute for what is lost. Theoretically, there are three main possibilities.

One possibility is that a person may suffer a severe life event and have a subsidiary role readily available. Brown and Harris's original idea that an intimate relationship is protective from depression can be interpreted in this way. If a woman has a loss in one area but can still experience herself as worthwhile in an intimate relationship, then the loss may give rise to sadness, anger, or other emotions but not to hopeless despair. In Bolton and Oatley's (1987) study of unemployment, some men were vulnerable in having only a restricted structure of social interaction outside work. These men were more likely than the others to become depressed. Whereas a single intimate relationship is protective for women, for men a structure of less intimate interaction seems to be more protective. In either case, and within the rules, conventions, and expectations of female and male roles in our society, social support means the existence of mutual plans within which people can experience themselves as worthwhile. If the possibility of fulfilling a major goal is lost, these plans provide subsidiary roles that can compensate for those that were lost.

A second possibility is that a person who loses a major role may have no subsidiary roles that will fulfill the same higher level goals, but can readily formulate new plans. Such a person has a sense of self that generalizes across roles, a sense of self-esteem that can bridge toward a new role not yet built. She or he has compiled this sense perhaps from earlier relationships, perhaps from childhood. Such a person faced with a severely threatening event might suffer dysphoric emotions but not depression. One may expect different kinds of phenomena from trying to start new plans. Someone starting a new plan that was similar to the one that was lost might need relatively little reconstruction. The loss would be of a role relationship that was somewhat independent of who occupied it. In *Middlemarch*, Dorothea's neighbors, evidently working on such assumptions, prescribed visits from eligible young men after her husband died. They thought that not being married was the problem. There are some well-known dangers of just moving from one relationship to another, and this idea neglects the fact that individuals literally are irreplaceable. Nevertheless, in terms of depression, such a move can be protective. Events that neutralize previous threatening events do occur, and they can cut short depressive episodes (Bebbington et al., 1984).

The third possibility is that people may have models of themselves compiled perhaps over a life of social interactions that have allowed them to feel loved and valued. Such selves would suffer sadness at losses of individual others who would themselves be unique and irreplaceable. But the core sense of self would not be threatened. People with such a sense of themselves need not, for instance, feel a driving need to start a new role to replace a loss.

Vulnerability to depression, then, has three theoretical levels, according to the alternatives available. A person would be vulnerable if she or he lacked at least one alternative role within which to experience a worthwhile self, the ability and circumstances to generate new plans or to create new role relationships, or the ability to take part in activities felt to be satisfying irrespective of a role that was lost.

Emotional development in childhood

Though most of the recent research on stress has been in adults, per-haps research on children is even more important, as it is generally thought that emotional traumas in childhood have effects that can them-selves be the bases for psychopathology in adult life. Two kinds of research have recently become important.

Children's vulnerability to psychiatric symptoms. First is evidence of stress on children. Though the effects are typically different from those of adulthood, children also suffer symptoms of emotional disturbance such as fears, regression to infantile behavior such as soiling themselves, and antisocial and disruptive activity at home and school.

For children, the events that most frequently provoke such symptoms are not losses of role relationships, but open conflict between parents. Smith and Jenkins (1991) have shown that conflictual marriages raise the rate of psychiatric symptoms significantly among children between 9 and 12 years old, even when other factors that are known to affect the occurrence of such symptoms such as social class and maternal depres-sion are controlled for. It is the communication of angry emotions and open quarrels between their parents that have the harmful effects for children. Divorce, for instance, is not necessarily stressful as such. The stress that occurs results from the parental conflict that accompanies it (Block, Block & Gjerde, 1986). Parental conflict in those who do not divorce has effects on children that are as substantial as comparable levels of conflict in those who do divorce.

As in the research on adult psychiatric symptoms, only a minority of children subjected to stresses develops symptoms. The question arises as why this minority is vulnerable or, conversely, what protects those who do not become symptomatic. For adults, social support seems to be protective. Comparable protection was found for children who had a warm relationship with at least one parent, for those who had a warm relationship with an adult other than a parent, typically a grandparent, and for those who had something for which they received recognition at school (Jenkins & Smith, 1990).

Once again, here is research that indicates the importance of the emo-tional tone of relationships. Parental quarreling can have damaging ef-fects on children, but warm relationships or recognition in another area can protect against adverse effects. It is as if children rely on their parents to be happy in their relationship with each other. Open conflict between parents severely disrupts a child's own emotional life.

Effects of childhood emotional disruption. As well as having parents in conflict, risks to emotional development in childhood also include the child being raised in an institution or having a parent who is mentally ill. Longitudinal studies have been carried out of children at emotional risk who are now in adulthood.

Being raised in an institution leads to difficulties, no doubt because institutions often lack features that are important for emotional development, perhaps especially stable parental attachment figures of the kind described by Bowlby (e.g., 1969). Rutter and his colleagues (Quinton, Rutter & Liddle, 1984; Dowdney et al., 1985) have gone further to ask how this effect is mediated. They have followed into adulthood a sample of children who had this experience and a comparison sample of children from similar backgrounds who were not brought up in institutions. Are any adverse effects that occur due to personalities immutably scarred, or to identifiable circumstances in adulthood?

The institution-raised children did have more difficulties than comparison children, but these were not explained by genetic factors or direct effects of personality development. Rather, they were effects of adverse environments that tended to be created in the life plans of the people concerned. Institution-raised children of both sexes were more affected by environmental circumstances, good or bad, than those of the comparison sample.

The girls in the institution-reared sample were particularly instructive. A higher rate of early pregnancy led, for them, to more difficult problems in adulthood. And less forethought in job planning also led to worse economic circumstances. It was these circumstances that tended to act as life events and difficulties that had adverse effects on them as adults. Those who had formed relationships with unsupportive men were liable to become poor mothers themselves. But those who formed relationships with supportive men became mothers just as good as those from the comparison sample, regardless of their own earlier emotional adjustment: The words of George Eliot at the close of *Middlemarch* come to mind: "The growing good of the world is partly dependent on unhistoric acts; and that things are not so ill with you and me as they might have been, is half owing to the number who lived faithfully a hidden life, and rest in unvisited tombs."

Data of this kind are of fundamental importance in that there has been much discussion of genetics and early environment handicapping people for life. The longitudinal studies of Rutter and his colleagues now bring evidence to bear: Difficulties in people's adult emotional lives are somewhat predictable from family and early environments, but older ideas of "personality" explain little. Effects seem most clearly to be mediated by adverse circumstances, some of which are caused by the person's choices and plans.

Depression as a stimulus to change

Depression in adults, according to my account, is a crisis in a plan that leaves the person without alternative plans for fulfilling a goal that has been lost. Depression feels intolerable. But the function of this intolerability may be to prompt change.

The finding that women suffer about twice as frequently as men from depression and anxiety has implied to some commentators that there is something wrong more often with the personalities of the "weaker" sex. This supposition neglects the fact that men are several times more numerous than women as alcoholics and as persons convicted of crimes.[28] One can imagine that men more often deal with disappointments and conflicts in a more external way. Moreover, although depression can be quite unbearably distressing, it can induce a certain reflectiveness, imply a certain possibility for change. By comparison, it is hard to see that drunkenness or crime has much of this potentiality.

For some people, a crisis is resolved by a change of plan in which a previous goal can continue to be pursued. In depression, however, the most radical kind of crisis is one that questions a high-level goal or a model of self. A person comes to understand something of what went wrong in pursuing that goal, or in the rules and other knowledge that were compiled into the previous models of the self and its interactions with others. In a severe life event, part of the theory that the person was inhabiting is refuted. Depression, in these terms, is the opportunity to construct a new theory. So, although the distress of such depressions may tear us apart, it can also be creative. It acts as a challenge from the real world to the cognitive structure of interpersonal goals, plans, and beliefs. Depression presents an opportunity to learn from mistakes such as assumptions that partners share the same goals when they do not – as when, in *Middlemarch*, it emerged that Dorothea's plan of helping her husband toward publishing his book was different from Casaubon's plan of having her admire the abundance of his industry.

Changes in an implicit theory about oneself, about others with whom one lives, or about one's goals or plans can be retrogressive as well as progressive. Therapists label as defensive changes in which goals or plans become curtailed, in which models of the world and other people are distorted, or in which models of the self are idealized. Depression may have overwhelmingly negative effects, as when people become stuck in depressions that will not change, perhaps partly for the reasons described by Teasdale (1988).

It is hard to believe, however, that depression is purely maladaptive. People can respond to the challenge of depression by making goals and plans more appropriate to circumstances, their models of the world and others more realistic, and their understanding of the properties of models of themselves more explicit. Although the whole of such a process has not been demonstrated, Brown, Adler, and Bifulco (1988) found that people who made "fresh starts" tended to recover more quickly from their depression, and Oatley and Perring (1991) found that after a breakdown, people with at least one plan that had not worked out were likely to remain depressed.[29]

The characteristics of depression

Research diagnostic schemes used in psychiatric epidemiology do not assign much structure to the syndrome of depression. They diagnose a case if the person has severe and persistent dysphoric mood plus some number of other symptoms, irrespective of what these symptoms are. Oatley and Bolton (1985) proposed that depression itself is not an emotion but a syndrome that includes emotions. The theory of life events as losses of role proposes that the structure of this state consists of three components: a cognitive sense of the loss of self, a set of emotions, and a set of plans to replace those lost.

Loss of the sense of self. A sense of self derives from actions being compared with those goals we define ourselves and from other people who behave consistently or inconsistently with models we have of them. When an important role is lost, the loss of a sense of self that occurs can be experienced as not having a self, or of having a self that is unworthy, defective, guilty, or lacking in some respect that seems quite essential. Symptoms can occur of self-denigration, of a self that seems bad or worthless, and cognitive therapists argue that such symptoms are central to depression.

It was this self-reproach that Freud (1957/1917) regarded as pathological and that distinguished melancholia from mourning. It seems that Freud was wrong in trying to use these grounds to distinguish depression from the mourning that follows bereavement. We now know that life events or difficulties are judged to be severe and capable of provoking depression to the extent that they have an impact that is comparable to bereavement. A sense of self derives from important role relationships and it can undergo depressing diminishment when a role is lost and the person is vulnerable in having no alternatives.

Emotions, bodily symptoms, and inward dialogue. Dysphoric emotions are generated by mismatches between outcomes and important goals, and they occur when there are severe events and difficulties. In depression, the two principal features of emotions are bodily symptoms and a salient inner dialogue. Because of the high priority of self-definition goals, mismatches with them can give rise to the autonomic arousal of emotions. Somatic complaints also occur over longer periods in depression. Sleeplessness and weight loss are common. Decreased pleasure in food and sex may be related to the intense emotional disturbances. An inward dialogue can become preoccupying as the problem is obsessively debated, and attempts to understand it or come to terms with it are made. Such preoccupation may underlie the lack of concentration that occurs in depression.

Although depression itself is not an emotion, intense emotions are a salient part of the larger syndrome of depression. A person may experience sadness when contemplating a loss, vengeful anger when thinking about how to repay the wrong, envy at the fortune of others, anxiety in the contemplation of what may happen next, longing for what was lost, and so on. Such emotions can alternate and sweep the person across the emotional scale. Although sadness is the predominant emotion in depression, it is rarely the only one. Anxiety is also common. Finlay-Jones and Brown (1981) have found that it tends to be associated with threats about the future, rather than losses. Severe events and difficulties tend to imply a harsh and even a hopeless future, and so anxiety occurs very frequently. Most intensely, the anxiety is an anticipation of further losses of selfhood.

Strategies of interaction. Modes of interaction with others change in depression. The event or difficulty, and whatever vulnerability factors may be present, indicate to the person that previous plans have failed in some way. People may feel themselves without the possibility of action. They may feel tired, listless, without energy enough to do even small things. Medically, terms such as retardation, inhibition, and anergia are used.

Strategies tend to regress, or backtrack, to earlier modes of interacting, including maneuvers practiced in childhood, such as sulking and attempting to engage others in rescue and comfort. People may feel cut off from others and withdraw from interaction. Alternatively, they may feel a pressing need to discuss the issue, trying to externalize the salient inner dialogue and seeking validation from others. Depression affects other people in the manner discussed by Lutz (1987): An emotion in one person induces an emotion in another. The difficulty in this is that although in some of these inductions the other person does feel sympathy prompting helping and caring responses, in other cases the distress causes anger or a contempt in the other that promotes withdrawal. This seems to have been the result for the husband quoted by Brown et al. (1986), who in the face of his wife's distress at her ectopic pregnancy, said he "might as well leave."

If one is depressed and without positive plans, suicidal thoughts and plans can occur. The implication is that no alternative seem possible. Suicidal plans often have an interpersonal quality: A high proportion of suicides are attempted in circumstances where discovery or rescue is possible.

The metaphor "strategy" for the plans of depression is military, perhaps appropriate because such plans are defensive. The person's self feels as if it has been attacked, and the person seeks to construct means for acting against a world that has become hostile and ungiving when a whole structure of habitual action is no longer available.

The impact of an event

It is now possible to give some answers to the question of why some people suffering a severe event or difficulty become depressed while others do not. Severe events are typically losses of roles by which we define ourselves, or other losses that undermine our self-definition goals. Vulnerability means having no alternative plans, either readily available or that can be constructed. People who are vulnerable are likely to suffer the full syndrome of depression: the loss of sense of self, the dysphoric emotions, and a regression to earlier interpersonal strategies.

People who make active plans, as opposed to depressive or suicidal ones, therefore, may suffer dysphoric emotions but will not suffer from the whole syndrome of depression. For instance, people who embark on plans of vengeance may be sustained by such plans, even though they may have destructive consequences within their own life. Alternatively, someone who has been treated badly in a love affair may decide to have no more sexual relationships of any kind, withdrawing from that area and throwing energy into some other pursuit.

It is often assumed that the process of mourning follows a natural course, with a phase of protest followed by one of resignation or despair. In the phase of protest the person becomes energized, affecting others in emotional ways, in seeking to resolve or cope with the loss and perhaps reunite with whoever was lost. But if these efforts are unsuccessful a phase of resignation and despair may follow (Gilbert, 1984, 1988). Although there are many important studies of the processes of mourning and loss, Silver and Wortman (1980) argue that little systematic, prospective research has been done to establish whether well-defined underlying patterns of response do occur, whether they are similar in response to different types of severe events, and what the factors are in modifying the time course.[30]

For some people, depression does not resolve within a matter of months, and they become chronically depressed. In Brown and Harris's study (1978) 7% of the women had been depressed at the case level for more than a year. Whereas depression can result from loss of a central role, when there are no alternatives, chronic depression results when the sufferer takes up depression and its associated strategies as a role. Strategies of complaining, trying to engage others in rescue and comfort, and the like can themselves become the basis of interactions with others who may themselves reciprocate by acting in complementary roles, perhaps encouraging dependency. Depression has then become itself a basis for action, when nothing else seems possible. Even though it involves symptoms such as the lack of self-worth and dysphoric emotions that continue to bring distressing thoughts to mind, it may appear to the sufferer to be the only possible plan to fulfill goals that remain salient.

The statistics of science and the portraits of art

In Chapter 5 I described how George Eliot had set out in her novels to put forward the social equivalent of natural histories that in Victorian times had become so compelling to biological scientists. Her argument is, however, not straightforward. How do we know that the portrait of human life in such natural histories is accurate? A novelist has the inevitable bias of a single observer without procedures to eliminate this bias or estimate its effects. Invocations of gods, or the adoption of an authorial voice, apparently avoid limitations of human vision and the biases of human cognition. But use of such devices may call into question authors' intentions in not recognizing their own biases.

Complementary contributions of science and art

George Eliot had said: "The greatest benefit we owe to the artist . . . is the extension of our sympathies. Appeals founded on generalizations and statistics require a sympathy ready made" (in Pinney, 1963, p. 270). Research on stress is largely statistical. The statistics of psychiatric epidemiology, for instance, are not influential to someone whose sensibility is not already active. So, on the one hand, statistics may be meaningless to those who are not interested, on the other hand, novels may be moving but biased.[31] Each kind of investigation has a partial effect. In one area, however, of the implications of tragic events, the work of social scientists has converged with that of great novelists. The common element is that of *Verstehen*.

Verstehen applied to making judgments of the impact of life events and difficulties in the lives of people like Mrs. Trent, picked with 457 other women at random from a voters' list, is the same empathy aroused when we read about Casaubon's bitterness or Lydgate's financial and marital difficulties. The emotions that occur in relation to life events and difficulties recorded in the work of Brown and Harris and others share common ground with those that occur when plans of characters in novels undergo adversities. They are judged empathetically, using that same ability to enter into the emotional life of another person. The epidemiological approach makes it possible for events to be categorized and counted in order to diminish the bias and to examine whether and how events can cause breakdowns of physical or mental health.

In psychiatric epidemiology, many of the same issues are at work as in the novel. The argument that such findings tell us nothing new, that we already know upsetting events cause upsets, quite misses the point. Making these observations systematically safeguards against bias that none of us can prevent in our own individual experience. It allows us to test the ordinary intuitions of folk theory, which, though it is capable of distilling experience, is itself liable to biases. Epidemiological psychiatry provides a basis of reliability comparable to that of the epidemiological discoveries of the last century that ushered in our understandings of disease and substantial changes in public health.

George Eliot, in saying that statistics are not enough, identified something important. Nisbett and Ross (1980) argue also that vividness and immediacy of experience are also not enough. For a knowledge of human affairs and of ourselves, we need the evidence about our society collected representatively together with the phenomenological comprehension and vivid self-reflection that is enabled by great works of art, among other things. The two perspectives, each somewhat different, like a stereoscopic view, allow something closer to a three-dimensional understanding of the emotional world. The implications of adverse interpersonal action and unexpected distressing events have for long been the preoccupation of playwrights and novelists. Now, however, the wisdom of artists with the communicative and moving potential of narrative form can be placed in register with empirical data that guard against bias and partiality.[32]

Practical measures

In Victorian Britain the epidemiologists were able to show that public health affected everyone. Aristocracy, politicians, businesspeople, middle and working classes were all subject to infectious diseases. Though the risk was not equal, those in political power could be conducted to the edge of the abyss of public disease. All were able to see how easily they might themselves slip in. The lower-lying parts of London near the river, including Parliament and the royal palaces, were in areas of higher mortality than those at somewhat greater altitude. Though such facts stimulated an interest in dwellings on the higher ground of Hampstead, and made attractive the expensive sanatoriums of Switzerland, they also implied that there was no real possibility of individual escape. Nobody could be safe unless everyone was. No doubt this was a great spur to the astonishing political accomplishment of Victorian sanitary reform, the large-scale building of sewers, the provision of clean water supplies that we now expect to come through pipes to almost every house, the paving of streets, the public collection of garbage.

The findings of the newer epidemiology of psychosomatic illness and psychiatric breakdowns do not have such political appeal. Statistics and other varieties of scientific truth alone do not move anyone whose moral sensibility is not already awakened.

Some technical solutions are possible. Some adversities described in this chapter are avoidable, although technical solutions are not everything in this field where loved ones are irreplaceable, where death remains inevitable, and where life is unpredictable. The middle classes in Europe and America are a demonstration that problems of housing, employment, economic productivity, and distribution are susceptible to technical improvement. So indeed are similar problems globally. It will remain to be seen whether a moral sensibility of the wealthy and more powerful will have effects in improving psychological health worldwide in the next 150 years on a scale comparable to the improvements in physical public health accomplished in industrialized societies during the last 150 years.

7. Freud's cognitive psychology of intention: the case of Dora

Suppose that one dark night I went to a lonely spot and was there attacked by a rough who took away my watch and purse. Since I did not see the robber's face clearly, I laid my complaint at the nearest police station with the words: "Loneliness and darkness have just robbed me of my valuables." The police officer might then say to me: "In what you say you seem to be unjustifiably adopting an extreme mechanistic view. It would be better to represent the facts in this way: 'Under the shield of darkness and favored by loneliness an unknown thief robbed you of your valuables.' In your case the essential task seems to me to be that we should find the thief. Perhaps we shall then be able to recover the booty."

Sigmund Freud
Introductory lectures on psychoanalysis, pp. 45–46

Cognitive psychology as natural science and human science

Work on stress has demonstrated causes of psychopathology in the immediate life of the sufferer, whereas traditionally psychoanalysis is thought of as pointing to such causes far back in childhood. I want here to put a different contrast: If work on stressful life events concentrates mainly on the disappointments of an unknowable world, another area of importance occurs with the problematics of conflicts among goals and the anxiety that such conflicts engender. This is the principal subject of psychoanalysis and of this chapter.

Freud did not propose a theory of emotions as such, but he was influential in founding the psychological theory of goals, of intentions. Because emotions are based on goals and plans, and because, as I have indicated, goal conflict is a source of emotions, Freud's work is fundamental.

307

From its earliest expressions (e.g., Miller, Galanter & Pribram, 1960) cognitive psychology has involved understanding behavior in terms of goals and plans. These in turn can be modeled by computer programs. Since 1960 there has been technical work on computational theories of planning, but less within cognitive psychology that aims to afford insights about ourselves as agents who have goals and make plans.

I have proposed (Oatley, 1987) that psychology is unique among academic disciplines in that it provides a natural scientific basis for useful technological development, while at the same time, within the terms of human and social sciences it aims to be insightful about our human condition. Human science, as an interpretive discipline in the sense outlined by Dilthey (1985/1926), is not so much underrepresented as unintegrated with modern psychology's main edifice based on natural science.

One way in which human science is distinguished from natural science is in the attempt to understand people in terms of intentions that make sense of their actions. What makes human action meaningful is that it is intended. It is this, according to Weber (1968/1922), that sets human science apart from the attempt to understand mechanical causes, as in natural science. It is human intention that requires *Verstehen*, understanding by entering imaginatively into the life of the other (as discussed in Chapter 6).

Cognitive psychology has the potential of combining usefulness and insight. By declaring its interest in goals and plans, it fairly demands integration of natural science and human science: The technical literature on planning needs to be joined to a psychology of human intention and action. Because Freud's work was on intention, his concerns converge with the cognitive psychology of understanding narrative, which I shall discuss. I also claim that his main work on intention is not subject to the kinds of criticism that have been made validly against many of the tenets of psychoanalysis.

A psychology of intention

What might a psychology of intention be about? A full human intention has several elements. It implies a goal or objective, that the goal is conscious, and that it has been explicitly adopted by the agent, who believes that he or she can achieve the goal by means of a possible plan. The idea of intention poses a problem to psychological understanding, however, because although some actions may be fully intended in this sense, others lack some feature of full conscious intention. This lack can make actions puzzling. Often effects are achieved, but it is not clear whether a goal was deliberately adopted or planned for.

I shall use *intention* as a bridge between the term goal, as used in cognitive science, and Freud's *Wunsch* ("wish"). I hope intention, as I shall use it, will span the ambiguity between its basic sense without commitment to the presence of consciousness and its full conscious sense. Freud's therapeutic aim, of course, was to enable basic intentions to become full, conscious intentions.[1]

Freud investigated the implications of intentions that might not be conscious and of multiple intentions. He began to move away from the idea, prevalent in his time as in ours, that psychology was to be understood purely in terms of neural mechanisms (see also Parisi, 1987). This, I think, is the significance of the quotation at the beginning of this chapter. Freud there describes how loss of control over some events of mental life is not to be understood just in terms of mechanism. The thief is a metaphor of deliberate personal agency with a goal and a plan. Freud proposes that if we are to understand our mental life, we should see it as directed by intentions. He stated this early in his therapeutic endeavors: "Once we have discovered the concealed motives . . . nothing that is puzzling or contrary to rule remains in hysterical connections of thought, any more than in normal ones" (Freud & Breuer, 1955/1893–1895, p. 294). This continued to be a guiding idea.

Putting this another way, Freud began to open up a psychology of intention alongside the psychology of mental mechanisms. All his objects of close investigation, such as dreams, slips of the tongue, jokes, psychiatric symptoms, free associations, and states of mind in which one both does and does not know something, are about ambiguous pieces of behavior on the border between the intended and the unintended, in which some but not all the attributes of full conscious intention are present.

Part of Freud's hypothesis about intention was that action does not always have a single causal intent. We are creatures of multiple motives, a point reiterated in cognitive psychology by Neisser (1963), who argued that this places a gulf between us and simulations of mentality by computers. The implication is that cognitive science needs investigations of how multiple goals may be managed (Oatley & Johnson-Laird, 1987).

Perhaps Freud's most far-reaching hypothesis was that conflict of important motives is common and can engender neurosis. To resolve conflicts, we may try to make a motive invisible to other people, and thereby lose sight of it ourselves. It becomes, so to speak, unconscious. The very imagery of this idea, of invisibility and of unconsciousness, indicates the difficulty for an empirical science to conceptualize or investigate this problem. The procedure that Freud initiated, and which has not been negated by subsequent criticism, is that of listening to his patients. If we are interested in mechanisms of mind, then natural scientific methods such as experimentation are appropriate. If we are interested in intention, other methods such as listening become important.

Three main methods allow us to understand intentions. First, we can witness actions, including emotional expressions, and infer intentions (e.g., Heider & Simmel, 1944; Oatley & Yuill, 1985). Second, we can make inferences about how we might intend and feel if we were in the position of the person we wish to understand. This is the sense indicated by Dilthey and Weber, as implied by their term *Verstehen* (discussed in Chapter 6). Third, we can listen to people giving commentaries on their actions in which they will typically include intentions.

Freud employed these methods to varying extents. In particular he stopped inspecting patients to see what was wrong with them and began to listen to them with "evenly suspended attention" (Freud, 1958a/1912, p. 111). It occurred to him that symptoms are not so much seen, but that they speak. To understand them, he must learn their language.

Understanding psychiatric symptoms in terms of intentions required two changes. The first, as Rose (1983) has pointed out, was made by "Charcot whose first contribution to the study of hysteria was to move it out of the category of sexual malingering and into that of a specific and accredited neurological disease" (p. 12). This meant making it visible, an empirical accomplishment.[2] Rose has reproduced a set of pictures that were part of this contribution. They illustrate hysterical features and show results of stimulating patients visually and electrically. Freud then made the next moves. He "questioned . . . the idea that you could know a hysteric by looking at her body," and "rejected the idea that hysteria was an 'independent' clinical entity" (Rose, 1983, p. 12). Rose here develops the idea that to have someone under observation while remaining outside of the circle of gaze is characteristic of a power relationship. Freud's listening to his patients enabled them to tell their stories and take part in dialogues in which symptoms were part of the language being spoken. Despite this, his preference was to sit behind the couch, out of sight.

The case of the missing intentions

In this account* of Freud's psychology of intentions, I will recount the story of Dora (Freud, 1953/1905).[3]

Freud started his case history with the problem of gaps in narrative. He says he began treatment by asking the patient "to give [him] the whole story of [her] life and illness." He continues: "As a matter of fact the patients are incapable of giving such reports about them-selves . . . their communications run dry, leaving gaps unfilled, and riddles unanswered" (p. 16). These gaps in the narrative were funda-mental for Freud, and are, I contend, fundamental also to any psycholo-gy of intentions. What is left out are principally the intentions that would make sense of the stories.

Said Freud: "It still strikes me myself as strange that the case histories I write should read like short stories and that, as one might say, they lack the serious stamp of science" (Freud & Breuer, 1955/1893–1895, p. 160). In Freud's hands the case history became a detective story (cf. Meyer, 1975) in which he set out to solve the puzzles left by the gaps in the patient's narrative. The case history of Dora is the first text in this genre that goes beyond short-story length. It was written by Freud, ostensibly as natural scientist. Between the lines, however, a new world opens up in which the observer-observed relation is accompanied by something quite different.

First, here are the *dramatis personae* of the story:

> *Dora:* The patient, suffering from hysteria. She is aged 18 at the time of the analysis, described at the beginning of the story by Freud as "in the first bloom of youth, a girl of intelligent and engaging looks" (p. 23).
> *Freud:* The analyst, aged 44, armed with a "collection of picklocks" (Freud, 1985, p. 427) for penetrating the unconscious, and hop-ing after several false starts to make a reputation for himself.
> *Dora's father:* A wealthy industrialist living with his wife, son, and daughter (Dora), but having a love affair with Frau K.
> *Dora's mother:* Treated contemptuously by Dora, by Dora's father, and by Freud, who dismisses her as an obsessional housewife of no account.

---

* Except where otherwise indicated, page numbers given in this chapter refer to Freud (1953/1905).

Dora's brother: A year and a half older than Dora, enters the story briefly.

Herr K: Friend of Dora's parents. He connives at Dora's father's affair with his wife, and pays courtly attentions to Dora.

Frau K: Wife of Herr K and lover of Dora's father. She also befriends Dora.

Governesses: In Dora's family and in the K family, who become embroiled in family affairs.

The story of Dora

Dora was referred to Freud by her father, whom Freud had treated in his neurological practice. She was distressed and had been at odds with her parents. She had psychosomatic complaints, including a periodic loss of voice, a nervous cough, and loss of appetite. She had had what seemed like a fit. Now she was irritable and low in spirits. Her parents had found a suicide note in her writing desk, and this had prompted her father to consult Freud.

Dora's father told Freud that Dora's depression and irritability began with an incident two years previously. The family had been staying with the K family, who had a holiday house at the Alpine lakeside resort of L____. On this holiday, Dora had told her mother that Herr K "had had the audacity to make her a proposal while they were on a walk after a trip upon the lake" (p. 25). Dora had then wanted to leave the Ks' house immediately with her father, who was also not staying for long. Frau K had told her father that Dora had been reading sexually explicit books. He told Freud that he thought these had overexcited her. Probably she had imagined the proposal. Immediately we find ourselves in ambiguity. Were Dora's symptoms reactions of a woman to whom an abusive suggestion had been made by a family friend, or of a romantic adolescent imagining sexual liaisons with an older man? Neither explanation seems quite adequate. Freud the detective investigates further.

Dora entreated her father to break off all relations with the Ks, but he was keen to tell Freud how unreasonable this was. He had no very high opinion of Herr K, but he was, he said, bound by ties of honorable friendship to Frau K who had nursed him during an illness some years previously. Freud lets us know that the illness, for which he had treated Dora's father, was probably syphilis.

Here, then, is the setting: A young woman, depressed and with apparently hysterical ailments, is passed by her father to Freud. It turns out that she has been passed around a lot, a bit like a parcel. Dora and Freud become caught up in the story as it emerges in their dialogue. The account we have is, as it were, a second-level account by Freud of this emergence.

The story began to reveal certain possibilities about Dora's intentions and the emotions to which they had given rise. These possibilities at first are indirect, arguably because Dora herself was unable to experience them directly. They were, so to speak, unconscious. They had to be spoken at first in a set of evasions and displacements; to put it more bluntly, in lies. But the lies were beginnings of truths about Dora's important concerns, which, by their discovery, might transform Dora's sense of herself.

In Freud's case histories a pseudonym was given to the protagonist. Dora's real name was Ida Bauer, and something is known about her life (Bernheimer & Kahane, 1985, pp. 33–34). Freud wrote (1906/1901) about how the name Dora had occurred to him, and he analyzed this in the way that he recommended that all such quasi-unintentional occurrences, mistakes, dreams, symptoms, and so on should be analyzed. He let his mind play freely on the name and noticed what occurred to him. What came to mind was an incident concerning a Dora, the name his sister had given to her nursemaid, whose real name was Rosa. Freud had remarked that she was not even allowed to keep her own name. His patient, too, had not been able to keep what was hers. He concluded that this must be the reason why Dora seemed the appropriate pseudonym.

The name Dora was overdetermined. Had Freud pursued this analysis, other associations might have come to mind. With his classical education he might have known that Dora, an abbreviation of Theodora, meant gift of God. With his interest in Jewish scholarship he might also have associated the name with its rhyme, Torah, the holy text to be deciphered by careful contemplation (Bakan, 1958). Dora was a gift to Freud, allowing him to write about how each person is a text to be understood by careful contemplation and detective work. This was the idea indeed with which he was to fulfill his intention of making a reputation for himself.

One of the most insightful ways of reading Dora is to apply ourselves with Lacan (1982/1952) to a close contemplation of Freud's text as a dialogue, or as Lacan calls it, a dialectical exchange. We can then see how this dialogue form is appropriate to an analysis of intentions.

Approaching a truth

Lacan describes Dora's story as a series of dialectical reversals, by which a displaced truth (an evasion) is gradually approached. The account of Dora's father, of how he wanted Freud to relieve Dora of her distress and of her distressingness is followed by what Lacan calls a first development: Dora describes her father's love affair. I follow Lacan's marking of the junctures of the dialogue, but draw attention to different features.

Freud had proposed that hysterics cannot give a coherent account of their story because of gaps due to repression. He said Dora suffered from such gaps. He pointed out that, in contrast to her vagueness about her own life, Dora's memories of her father's affair with Frau K were very distinct. The affair had become obvious to Dora four years earlier, on a holiday taken by the two families in a hotel, which involved changes of rooms by Dora's father and Frau K that would not have been out of place in a theatrical farce.

It was clear to Dora that her father had connived at a relationship between Herr K and herself. This had the effect of keeping both Herr K and herself quiet, while allowing the affair between her father and Frau K to progress. When Dora was still 14, this "odious exchange," as Lacan (p. 65) calls it, had involved Herr K trying to kiss her. She had felt disgust, but suppressed it, or perhaps as Freud surmises, displaced it into symptoms of disinclination for food and ailments of the alimentary canal and respiratory tract. With her disgust displaced, she continued on warm terms with Herr K.

We may wonder whether Dora's father is now handing Dora to Freud, because again the possibility has arisen of her making difficulties for his affair with Frau K.

Dora's denunciation of her father and his affair are followed by what Lacan calls the first dialectical reversal, as Freud, without denying Dora's accusations, asks her whether she might not also be reproaching herself in the same way that she reproached her father. Was she not perhaps also engaged in a cover-up? What was her involvement in all this?

This questioning gives way to a second development, in which it emerges that Dora had wanted the attentions of Herr K. He had sent her "flowers every day for a whole year while he was in the neighbourhood" (p. 35), given her valuable presents, and spent all his spare time in her company. One is reminded of Sartre's (1958/1943) image of bad faith. A woman accepts invitations from a man whom she knows has intentions toward her. When he places his hand on hers she ignores the implication that a decision is called for. Not wishing to break the harmony of the moment, wanting to postpone any decision, she leaves his hand there, but somehow contrives not to notice it. Thus may a conflict of intentions be resolved. At least for a while Dora also does this with Herr K. She is enlivened by their relationship, but somehow, as with the kiss, she displaces its implications.

Not only had Dora connived at her father's affair, but by looking after the Ks' children she had enabled Frau K to spend time with her father. Perhaps her youth kept from her the implications of her involvement. But when, at the age of 16, in the scene by the lake, it occurred to her that Herr K was not just making a proposal but a proposition, she finally was horrified.

These disclosures to Freud allowed her identifications with the adults in the drama to become clearer. Dora had been almost a mother to Herr K's children (with its connotations of being almost Herr K's wife). She had imitated Frau K's way of being ill to avoid certain distasteful duties: Freud indicated how some of Dora's illnesses had motives. Dora had also identified with her father in his relations with Frau K. She said at one point that her father was "a man of means" (p. 47; a translation that catches the connotation would be "a potent man"). The phrase, and Dora's way of expressing it, hinted to Freud that behind it there might be an opposite meaning, that her father was impotent. This Dora confirmed. Asked whether there was not some contradiction with her assertion that her father and Frau K were having an affair, she said, "There was more than one way of obtaining sexual gratification. . . I questioned her further, whether she referred to the use of organs other than the genitals for the purpose of sexual intercourse" (p. 47). There follows talk of oral sex, the first of many discussions between Dora and Freud about sexual practices.

Dora angrily assaults Freud with a crescendo of reproaches against her father while using various means, including the argument of her symptoms, to try to get her father to break with the Ks. What enrages Dora more than anything is her father's idea that Herr K's proposal was just her imagination. Lacan writes that this gives way to a second reversal: Freud observes that this seems like jealousy. Might not such jealousy more appropriately have been expressed by Dora's mother? Dora was behaving as if she were her father's deceived wife. She wanted to be reassured of his love. To do this he must end his affair with Frau K.

The third development begins. Hints occur of Dora's deep attachment to Frau K. They had shared a bedroom on family holidays (Herr K being quartered elsewhere). Frau K had confided in her in terms of closest intimacy. When speaking of Frau K, Dora "used to praise her 'adorable white body' in accents more appropriate to a lover than to a defeated rival" (p. 61). But the question, in Lacan's (1982/1952, p. 67) words, of what "the real value of the object which Frau K [was] for Dora," is never asked. The analysis is unfinished. Dora left after only three months. Lacan's speculation is that in an answer to such a question there would appear an image, hinted at by an early memory of Dora "sucking her left thumb and at the same time tugging with her right hand at the lobe of her brother's ear as he sat quietly beside her" (p. 51). This image was of the object of Dora's desire, a woman. In the memory of autoerotic contentment, the image was of herself, with a male sitting compliantly by.

However, this may be, Dora's quest, seemingly being worked out in a series of transformed repetitions, was to discover how she might find love. This is glimpsed, as in a hall of mirrors, in her attachments to her father, to Herr K, to Frau K, and to Freud himself; in her sexually ambiguous identifications with her father and with Frau K; and in her raptly gazing for two hours in silent admiration at the picture of the Sistine Madonna in a Dresden art gallery.

Dora's intentions

The dialogue returns time and again to Dora's intentions. The interjections of Freud, which mark what Lacan calls the reversals, are psychoanalytic "interpretations." When a gap occurs, the analyst's inference is that something is unconscious. An interpretation is offered to fill the gap.

According to some commentators, interpretations can be anything to fill such gaps, to restore memories. This, however, is misleading. Central to Freud's theory, and to the bridge to cognitive science, is the idea that interpretations are principally about intentions. We are confronted in psychiatric states by actions and mental states occurring apparently involuntarily. Intentions have gone missing. So Freud says to Dora, in effect: "Is there an intention to reproach yourself in the same way that you reproach your father?" and "Are you not jealous, intending as a wife might, that your father ends his affair?" The suggestion is that among Dora's conflicting goals were "I want Herr K's courtship," "I do not want the implications of male sexuality," "I want my father to love me best."

Similar questions are raised by identifications. In an identification, one copies a plan of action, but unlike our identifications with characters as we read stories, this can occur without being motivated by a goal like that of the person from whom it was copied. Here is the same pattern – an action without the intention that makes it a full, voluntary action.

An implication of Freud's interpretations and of Dora's identifications is that Dora was not conscious of her intentions in the story she was recounting. Intentions make actions meaningful and rational. It is the attribution of intentions to actions that allows understanding, *Verstehen*. On the largest scale it is in terms of intentions that the story of our lives may make sense – the alternative being "a tale told by an idiot, full of sound and fury, signifying nothing" (Shakespeare, *Macbeth*, 5, 5).

Intentions as expressed in transferences

Freud proposed that we build up strategies of intention toward others, founded on early relationships. If we have, as Dora had, an untrustworthy father, we practice forms of role relating that are means of coping with such a person. We establish a goal of maintaining a wary distrust in relationships that have similar properties to the earlier one.

In the postscript to Dora's case Freud wrote his first extended hypotheses on transference: A patient transfers to the analyst intentions and phantasies that grew up in relation to people earlier in life. Transferences are "new editions or facsimilies" (p. 116) of the earlier intentions, which replace an earlier figure by the analyst. The patient may act toward the analyst as toward a parent.[4]

Taking up, working through, and resolving transference distinguishes psychoanalytic therapy from other kinds (cf. Strachey, 1934). An analysis is completed by the patient coming to experience how the therapist is not, for instance, another version of a selfishly seductive, ultimately untrustworthy, and disappointing male – not just like father. The patient then might generalize from this and recognize projections that coerce others to conform to such internal models. With the resolution of transference, gaps in the patient's story are filled in. The patient can tell his or her own story, not just be a character in someone else's, for instance, a parent's, story.

It was after the therapy with Dora that Freud's ideas about this issue began to stir. He said it was "easy to learn how to interpret dreams, . . . the patient will . . . always provide the text" (p. 116). But the transference, which is unavoidable, is the latest creation of the disease. It brings the issues directly into the consulting room. Combating it "is by far the hardest part of the whole task" (p. 116). A reason for the difficulty is that although we can often perceive someone's intentions toward a third person, as when we notice a friend becoming sexually attracted to a new acquaintance, it is much harder for us both to take part in a relationship and perceive what we ourselves are intending toward the other, what roles we are entering: the role of the caring parent, the untrustworthy male, the attentive suitor, the confidant.

Dora and Freud found themselves enacting roles that had become habitual, perhaps derived from their earlier lives. For Dora, these roles took hold fatefully. After her disappointments with her father and Herr K, she approached this new older man in hope of his affection, with the charm of a young woman "of intelligent and engaging looks" (p. 23). Freud came to be, for her, a man with whom she might be intimate, who possibly would care about her. A reason why it is difficult to perceive transference implications is that, for the analyst, Freud, Dora just seemed directly "of intelligent and engaging looks." It did not seem: "Here is a woman being attractive to me, and me responding with interest."

Freud did not see all the intentions of the role structures that developed, but he noticed some of them, for instance, that Dora was distrustful. He says she constantly compared him to her father, and "kept anxiously trying to make sure whether [he] was being quite straightforward with her, for her father 'always preferred secrecy and roundabout ways'" (p. 118).

In the end, the prophesy of Dora's distrustfulness was fulfilled. Freud was attentive, but also engrossed in his own concerns. His eagerness to receive the gift of Dora, and to convince others that he had solved the mysteries of mind, indicate his intention of making a name for himself. His concern was to be the clever detective – and for Dora to be a good informant. He was in danger of using Dora as a convenience, as had her father and Herr K. Certainly that is how Dora came to experience him, as another man who let her down.

The idea of transference is that in analysis each finds his or her model of self prompting him or her to engage the other in forms of relating that have less to do with that person than with others from the past. So Dora starts her ambivalent approach to a new older man both hopefully and warily. Freud at first is willing to be a confidant, then he becomes fatherly, then patronizing. Ultimately his ambitions take over.

The context of interpretations

Dora was passed to Freud, and began to describe her father's affair with Frau K. She had a low regard for men. In the transference she might have been asking Freud, as she told him of Herr K's advances and of her father's affair: "Isn't this the kind of thing that men do? Where do you stand in this?" Freud declines the role of family doctor following her father's directions. He lets her know that he will not just pass her back, no longer disrupting family life, no longer threatening damaging disclosures. He takes Dora seriously. He says he "could not in general dispute Dora's characterization of her father" (p. 34). He also notices that Dora has some affection for her father.

Interpretation in psychoanalysis is often described as a technical matter. What is often neglected is that interpretations can only be offered in the context of a relationship between analyst and patient. It was only in the context of respect for Dora that what Freud said would have been acceptable. Without this, it would have been intrusive – at best patronization, at worst bullying. The interpretation in which Dora was asked whether she might not also be reproaching herself, and implying that she had an involvement, was not an intrusion. To have accepted Dora as a parcel passed on by her father, or to have treated her as women are sometimes treated in rape cases, would have had a different effect. To have said: "Very well. I've heard these accusations about your father with Frau K. And I've heard what you've said about Herr K. Don't you think that by accepting presents, and going for long walks with him, you were being provocative?" would have had Dora leave not after three months but before three days.

So the space for a second development opened. Here began the talk of sex. Though aware of some of the aspects of his roles as parent and suitor, Freud had, by taking Dora seriously, entered these in a way that he might not quite have anticipated. In the second development, Freud was taken by surprise. In a footnote to his postscript, Freud said that the longer the interval since the analysis the more probable it seemed to him that the fault in his technique lay in failing "to discover in time . . . that [Dora's] love for Frau K was the strongest unconscious current in her mental life. I ought to have guessed that the main source of her knowledge of sexual matters could have been no one but Frau K" (footnote to p. 120). He was unaware that the transference implication of this was that in becoming Dora's confidant, he became her confidante. He was given the role of a woman with whom intimate subjects could be discussed. Such a confidante was, for Dora, modeled on Frau K, perhaps also on her governesses and perhaps behind them on her mother.

It was within a structure of confiding that the interpretation was made that prompted the second reversal. It would scarcely have been acceptable to Dora in any other context. Freud asked whether Dora's anger at her father's affair and her insistence that he break with the Ks was not jealousy.

It was the third development in which the dialogue became stuck. Freud later wondered why Dora had remained loyal to Frau K, although she too had betrayed Dora by telling her father of the sex books that she had read. One can see why Dora preferred loyalty to Frau K than to other actors in this drama. Later in the case history, Freud interprets Dora's second dream as including the meaning "Men are all so detestable that I would rather not marry" (p. 120). Frau K did not have the detestable qualities of men, and she had avoided being handed around, devalued, replaced.

The third reversal was never reached. Freud identified with Herr K and with the heterosexual conventions of his time. He was not willing to allow himself to take up the role of a woman or to reflect an image like Frau K's for very long. Dora stopped confiding in him, and so from some matters Freud and we his readers are permanently excluded.

Lacan says transference is a stagnation in the analytic discourse, and that interpretation is what allows the discourse to set off again.[5] Based on this idea, we can say that interpretations that are worth making show the involvement of both therapist and patient in the intentions of a role relationship based in the past. So Freud might have said something like: "It seems you are confiding in me in much the same way that you confided in Frau K." When statements of this kind have the quality of something the therapist need not strive to convince the patient of, they can give that person a sense of being recognized in an important way. A new piece of discourse may open, and the dialogue moves from where it had become stuck.

This is not what happened. The transference issue reverted to Freud as the virile male wanting to fill Dora's gaps forcibly, and of her resisting this intrusion – a role structure that was not interpreted. In this role structure Freud could, however, do what he had wanted, interpret Dora's dreams. He could have a go at unpicking the locked doors of Dora's unconscious, and try to penetrate her test. As he said: "The question of whether a woman is 'open' or 'shut' can naturally not be a matter of indifference. It is well known too what sort of 'key' effects the opening in such a case" (footnote to p. 67).

Freud's reversion to this role allowed Dora to experience him poking around in her mind, just the kind of thing she might have expected from a man. Only in his postscript did Freud mention that Dora's transference had turned negative. She had not just been talking about her life "then" and "out there." She had also been saying something to him. Not directly, of course. It isn't easy to speak directly to domineering fathers who prod around while insisting that they rather than you are right. Nonetheless, obliquely, she warned him that all was not well between them.

Multiple intentions and the repercussions of conflict

If intentions are crucial to psychoanalytic narratives, how do we understand conflicts of intention, and how are they handled in cognitive science?

Freud described conflict of intention as inherent in the human condition (see, e.g., Laplanche & Pontalis, 1973). It may be explicit, as between a wish and a forbidding moral imperative, or between two contradictory wishes, as in the ambivalence of affection combined with aggression. It may be implicit, as between a desire and a defense. When conflict is implicit, it may, according to Freud, emerge in neurotic symptoms or in mini-neurotic symptoms (as Grünbaum, 1984, calls them) such as slips of the tongue.

Dreams are central to psychoanalysis because Freud supposed they allow conflicting intentions to be discerned. He wanted to show dream analysis working to practical effect in the case of a sufferer from disabling conflicts. This was what made Dora's case important to him. The center of this case history is the analysis of two dreams. In tracing Freud's psychology of intention we may take up the idea that dreams reveal conflicts.

In Dora's first dream, which she had had on several occasions, she dreamed of a house on fire, of her father standing beside her bed, and of her mother wanting to save her jewel case.

Freud asked Dora to free-associate, to say whatever came to mind when she thought of each image in her dream in turn. He pieced together how it was linked to the scene at L____ by the lake two years earlier, where Herr K had proposed. In giving free associations a new piece of dialogue opened out to confirm that the dream related to the proposal, as Dora described something she had not told Freud before and that filled a gap in her account. It was that after returning after the proposal, she had gone to lie down in her bedroom. She had woken up to find Herr K standing beside her. "Just as you saw your father standing beside your bed in the dream," remarked Freud (p. 66). Dora had been frightened that Herr K might take advantage of her. It had become imperative to get away from the house. That night, she said, she had dreamed this dream for the first time.

The six lines of the dream in Freud's text are followed by 29 pages of virtuoso interpretation. He ranges from the theme of the proposal to the theme of childhood enuresis from which her father used to save her by waking her up at night. Then comes the jewel case, representing the female genitalia, and jewels in the shape of drops to represent both drops of semen and vaginal discharges. Dora had said her mother suffered from discharges, and Freud asked whether she did also. She said she did, and Freud writes that he was surprised she knew that her father had a venereal infection – she assumed that somehow he had passed this unclean affliction on to her.

Freud thought about Dora having been on the verge of sexual exploitation by Herr K, but we as modern readers might think further about her vaginal discharges. It has become clear that sexual abuse of children is frequent. In 19 North American surveys it has been estimated that from 6% to 62% of female children have suffered some form of sexual abuse by the age of 18 (Peters, Wyatt & Finkelhor, 1986). Women who have suffered such abuse have higher levels of anxiety, dissociative states, and other psychiatric disorders than those who have not (Browne & Finkelhor, 1986). Though not all vaginal discharges in children are due to venereal infections, some are, and they suggest at least the possibility of abuse. Freud discussed in a rather muddled way the idea of a hereditary taint of syphilis having been passed on to Dora, but he did not raise the question of her having been infected directly.[6]

Freud steers in another direction, not necessarily incompatible with the foregoing. The analysis moves toward Dora's conflicting intentions: In Dora's dream, her father stands beside her bed, as Herr K had in the house by the lake. She wants her father to save her from danger. The conflict involves wanting her father as a protector, though he is also the one to escape from. It is he who has brought the danger in the first place. Freud is most keen to stress that the danger may also be of her own desires. This is a classical psychoanalytic conflict.

We may be intrigued by Freud's suggestions, but in a detective story there is typically a confession to corroborate the clever detective's reconstruction. Here there is no corroboration. There are even reasons to think that Freud had got it wrong. How is this method sufficient for us to know what the truth might be when the evidence is a story full of gaps, suffused with ambiguities that cannot be resolved?

I have proposed that Freud's major contribution was to found a psychology of intention, but is this contribution not subject to criticisms that are justly made of Freud? In contrast to the interpretations discussed so far, which were corroborated, at least in part, because they led to what Lacan called new developments, some of the interpretations of Dora's first dream are uncorroborated. Freud, indeed, describes Dora as not accepting his interpretation that, although she feared Herr K and her father, she was more afraid of her own desires. We are left with the conclusion that the dream could indicate conflicting wishes as Freud suggests, but it could also indicate Freud's enthusiasm for his own ideas.

I suggest there is other evidence in the Dora case for the existence of conflicting intentions. First we should consider in more detail the criticisms that have been made of Freud's approach.

Criticisms of Freud

The most thorough of Freud's recent critics is Grünbaum (1984, 1986), who has argued that Freud's epistemology is more sophisticated than Popper (1962) and others have credited him with, but that, as we may suspect in Freud's analysis of Dora's first dream, many of his concepts may be contaminated by suggestion.

This problem of suggestive contamination was raised by Freud himself. Psychoanalytic therapy, he said, may be like a relationship of student and teacher, where the compliance of the student can be taken to imply that the teacher is right. In this case psychoanalysis would be no more than "a particularly well-disguised and particularly effective form of suggestive treatment and we should have to attach little weight to all that it tells us about what influences our lives" (Freud, 1963/1916–1917, p. 452).

Freud rebutted this by arguing that psychoanalytic interpretations are validated by whether they tally with something real in the patient. We can know whether this has occurred by conflicts actually being resolved. Grünbaum takes this to be the most important methodological statement in all Freud's work. It provides a criterion that is objective. It does not depend on analysts' accounts of their interpretations or of our understandings of them. Freud thereby committed his epistemology to evidence that psychoanalysis uniquely gives long-term relief of disabling conflicts. This as a valid epistemological warrant.[7]

It is at this point that natural scientific criteria are appropriate. To apply Freud's tally criterion we need to compare, in experimental designs, outcomes for a number of people having psychoanalytic therapy with outcomes for control groups having no therapy or some other therapy. Since Freud's time there have been many such comparisons. They show that psychoanalysis is about as good as other methods, such as behavior therapy (see, e.g., Smith, Glass & Miller, 1980; Lambert, Shapiro & Bergin, 1986).

Thus far, psychoanalysis has therefore not been shown to be unique, but there is a caveat. Perhaps we should not expect effects other than suggestive ones from the usually short therapies studied so far, of which the majority are of 12 hours' duration or less.[8] Psychoanalysts argue that longer periods of therapy are essential for the resolution of transferences and the working through of conflicts. Comparisons of the longer periods of psychotherapy, with random assignment to psychoanalysis or to other therapies or control groups, have not yet been made. It may be, as many analysts maintain, that it takes years rather than months to resolve transferences.

Two criteria for inferring intentions and conflict

Grünbaum concludes that psychoanalysis is alive but not well. In trying to establish foundations of a psychology of intention, however, I propose that we can tackle a more limited problem than whether grand psychoanalytic hypotheses, such as that of the Oedipus complex, should be accepted. This question is whether action can be explained by intentions, and whether humans have multiple intentions that sometimes conflict. Here evidence is less equivocal than we might think from Grünbaum's arguments. I propose that two criteria are available for deciding whether intention and conflict have explanatory functions in narratives – the criteria of consensual understanding and of consistency.

The first criterion is whether, within the conventions of our culture, an intention is generally understood as capable of making sense of actions. We can apply this criterion to Dora's actions of demanding that her father break with the Ks. What is recounted is plausible in the way that is appealed to in a law court. We have no more reason to doubt that Freud is correctly informing us that Dora was clamoring for her father to break with the Ks than to doubt an experimenter who says that certain events occurred. Then, because we understand that jealousy may issue in demands that a rival be excluded, we can infer that when a protagonist insistently demands the breaking off with a third person in this way, jealousy could be involved. This would hold even if the protagonist were unaware of these implications. Dora's behavior is made sense of by jealousy, and hence an intention to maintain an emotional claim on the affections of her father.[9]

The second criterion is stressed by Szasz (1965). This is the principle of consistency: If a person's verbal and nonverbal expressions are at odds, if some elision has occurred, or if the things she or he says contradict one another, such inconsistencies constitute a clue to understanding. They may be explicable in terms of conflicts of multiple motives. Freud, for instance, drew Dora's attention to an omission. How was it that she was so keenly sensitive to her father and Frau K's affair and yet said nothing to anyone at the time about a subject, which evidently concerned her greatly, or mentioned to Freud any discomfort about the events? There is a plausible reason for the omission. Freud supplies something to fill the gap, a suggestion about her own involvement. On this occasion it was admitted by Dora. The suggestion that Dora had an interest in her father's affair was followed by a new development (cf. Freud, 1964/1937), her confiding details of Herr K's courtship of herself. A gap is filled, and the dialogue moves on from where it had become stuck.

These two criteria are close to those used in history or literary criticism. As I discussed in Chapter 2, they admit more ambiguity than the criteria of natural science. Indeed, multiplicity of interpretations is essential to understanding narrative, including psychoanalytic narratives. Otherwise, of course, an analyst would be unable to suggest any plausible alternative interpretation to the one the patient offers. Such narratives nevertheless provide evidence that we would not have from other sources and help us toward an understanding, an understanding of a particular kind. One reason for considering these criteria as important despite their ambiguity is that exact parallels arise in cognitive science, in the problem of computational understanding of narrative.

Cognitive understanding of narratives

When we inspect narratives closely, we find that they all have gaps. A narrative is like a net, with more gaps than substance. Narrative supplies barely sufficient clues for a reader or listener to construct a model of the world described and the trajectory of characters' actions within it. In understanding narrative, we the human readers supply the world from our own knowledge and from our ability to see actions as connected by plans with intentions. When programming computers to understand narratives, programs need similarly to supply such a world of understanding. Then, when there are inferences to be made about what might have prompted a mental state such as an emotion or about gaps, unexpected events, and apparent contradictions in the text, the program makes inferences and builds a model of what is being described.

Wegman (1985) has given an example of this and of the closeness of computational understanding of stories to psychoanalytic understanding. He has used Schank and Abelson's (1978) work to give a computational sketch of processing a Freudian case history. Wegman chose not Dora, but the case history of the British governess Miss Lucy R (Freud & Breuer, 1955/1893–1895).

The case of Miss Lucy R. Schank and Abelson's work includes the idea of scripts, representation of habits or of recurring sequences of events. If a storyteller mentions something that invokes a script, then inferences can be made to fill gaps left by things not mentioned. Wegman uses this to show how inferences can be made from Miss Lucy's story. Lucy was governess to two children of a wealthy widower. She had become depressed, and in telling her story, she described a visit of a lady to her employer. A visit includes arrival, conversation, departure – the sequence can be inferred from a visit script, whether or not specific parts of the sequence are mentioned (cf. Bower & Morrow, 1990).

At the end of the visit Miss Lucy described how the lady visitor kissed Miss Lucy's charges. After the visitor had gone, her employer flew into a rage, threatening to dismiss her if she ever let anybody kiss the children again. The issues for a psychoanalytic interpretation and for ordinary narrative understanding (by computer or human) are similar. What do we make of this unscripted, seemingly inconsistent event in Miss Lucy's account?

Wegman treats it in two stages: First he considers why kissing the children is mentioned. If it is simply a parting ceremony, it would be taken care of by the visit script. That the storyteller mentions it indicates that it may be significant, not standard. A story-understanding program would set a flag to indicate that it may be, as Schank and Abelson say, "weird," and needs to be noticed as such. The program would search its knowledge base for what it knew about kissing. It might find that as well as a greeting or parting, kissing could be a mild health threat, a means of affirming a relationship, a sexual gesture. Next comes Miss Lucy's employer flying into a rage. This, too, cannot be assimilated to a script. The mention of anger would therefore trigger a search for an intention. One inference is that a goal of the angry person has been violated. Another is that the person to whom the anger is directed is the cause of this goal frustration. Again, the program has to search for evidence to fill the gaps.

This is closely similar to Freud's procedures, and related to the two criteria that I have outlined. In Miss Lucy's case, Freud inferred from her depressed state, from incongruities in her story, and by asking her for associations to certain events that she had fallen in love with her employer. Her distress at his anger was because she had longed for more tender exchanges, though she had also been trying to put any such idea out of mind. We can apply the criterion of consensual understanding to Freud's story: Is this the sort of thing that might happen to a young governess working for a widower? Might such an intention, pushed out of mind but crushed by a violent outburst, explain Miss Lucy's depression? Then we can consider the "weird" event of her employer flying into a rage. Here we can apply the criterion of consistency: To resolve the inconsistency we can entertain the idea that Miss Lucy's wealthy employer had become sensitive to possible designs of his lady visitor, and perhaps of Miss Lucy herself. Perhaps he had become suspicious of a woman gaining a foothold in his affections, and perhaps his wealth, via his children.

For any understanding of such a story, including a psychoanalytic or computational one, the issue is to generate a range of interpretations and to select from them those that might fill such gaps as occur. Just as at the center of any detective story is the issue of motive, so at the center of any such gap-filling process is the same question: What intention would make sense of this action? Unless we can answer this we do not understand the story.

Computational work on understanding stories brings together issues that have seemed far apart: mechanism (as in computer programs) and meanings of human actions, the structure of narrative parsed and interpreted, and the content of stories understood by humans, natural science and human science. A connecting link between each pole of these apparent dichotomies is intention.

Natural science and human science. Now comes a possible confusion between natural and human science, or between causal and narrative accounts, which, as Bruner (1986) has argued, work in quite different ways. If, in the natural scientific sense, we ask, for instance, whether Dora had really been jealous and whether this had actually caused her rage and symptoms, we have to say that we do not know. As it happens, this interpretation was at least seriously incomplete. A more convincing possibility, which only emerged in the final session, was that Dora wanted her father to end his affair because she had ended her involvement with Herr K – in which case her emotion should more properly have been interpreted as envy. In the same way we do not know if her vaginal discharges were infections caused by sexual penetration. We cannot exclude alternative hypotheses. More generally, we cannot say from individual psychoanalytic case histories how far conflict is causally associated with symptoms, whether sexual abuse in childhood increases the probability of adult anxiety states, or whether psychoanalysis resolves conflicts. The story form does not validly permit such inferences. For such questions we need empirical inquiries with appropriate controls or comparisons.

Within the terms of human science an interpretation such as Freud made about Dora's jealousy can be acceptable and important in two ways. First, for us readers, it provides a kind of explanation that we might not have thought of ourselves but that would allow us to understand the story, to make sense of Dora's complaints. In other words, the question of intention is not just ambiguous in the sense of whether an action had an intention, it is ambiguous in the sense of what intentions could possibly explain a particular action. Since this is not always obvious, we sometimes need suggestions as to what intentions could fit. As Wilensky (1978) has put it, when understanding a story, it is not that we are trying to predict exactly what will happen next, but that understanding involves summoning a range of explanations to make sense of what does happen. According to this argument such explanations typically concern intentions. Second, there is the effect of an interpretation on the patient. A person to whom an intention is suggested can decide whether it might have contributed to an action. If the interpretation is accepted, it helps the patient build a model of his or her goal structure to which there is conscious access.

In neither case is there any guarantee against suggestive contamination. A reader, by imaginatively entering into the life of the patient, might have felt moved, and might have realized something about people in general and him- or herself in particular. The patient might have had an insight about his or her own intentions. But such insights will be relative to that person. They will be more ambiguous, objectively, than any technical result.

If we as readers are affected by reading the case history this is not because of any context-free or person-independent knowledge being exported beyond the consulting room. As with any story, Dora's case history will have different effects on different people each with his or her particular mental schemata within which the narrative has been interpreted (see the wide range of understandings in Bernheimer & Kahane, 1985). This does not mean that what actually happened to Dora is unimportant. It means that the criteria for judging the truth of what happened from her or her analyst's narrative accounts admit ambiguity. This is acceptable because the inference or interpretation is just one part of the process. The other part is whether the inference admits an increase in personal understanding to any individual, an insight. This is like a weaker application of Freud's tally idea. No symptom may be removed, but something real is touched that can resolve an inner inconsistency, fill an inner gap, of patient or reader.

By contrast, the technical results of natural science can be exported from situations in which they are demonstrated. Their criteria must be completely unambiguous because technical effects must be reproduced entirely independently of personal or other contexts. Quantitative and other formal bases of technical writing are designed precisely to exclude ambiguities.

Personal insight, derived from human science, is thus complementary to technical truth. This is not to say that the methods of human science are forever separated from the quantitative or the empirical. On the contrary, we need to construct links, because as psychologists we are interested in both insight and technical truths. For instance, the method of *Verstehen* has been embedded within empirical studies, and used to test hypotheses about the causes of depression in the important studies of Brown and Harris (discussed in Chapter 6). Starting from the potential insights of case histories, such work can move to generalizations that càn be transmitted to others, as evidence about the etiology of psychiatric symptoms.

In psychoanalytic texts, though, it is primarily by applying the consensual and consistency criteria that readers decide about what went on, and may perhaps derive insights. By such criteria we might regard Freud in Dora's case sometimes as intrusive, sometimes as making an insightful interpretation. By these criteria we may consider whether a new piece of dialogue is reached because a truth, not previously owned, had been established between them, or whether Dora was being a compliant student, or Freud a fanciful storyteller. If what is recounted is consensually comprehensible, and inconsistencies are resolved, what is recounted becomes recognizable as deriving from our human condition. Thereby we may improve our own implicit folk theories of ourselves and others, our own understanding.

Dora's conflicts

If what is recounted in a story or case history becomes implausible, the step of applying it to an understanding of ourselves is not made. We sense, instead, that there is something wrong with the story or the storyteller. Freud says Dora was unable to accept his interpretation of her first dream in terms of a conflict of fear and her own sexual desire. No new piece of dialogue opens up, nor does anything else in the case history corroborate this interpretation. We readers may therefore be reluctant to accept it as insightful.

There is, however, a clearer case of intrapsychic conflict that does have corroboration. It arises at this same point: It is that Dora wanted both to leave her analysis and to stay for a while. As Freud was interpreting Dora's first dream this conflict emerged as transference. He was trying to din into Dora his conclusion that fear and her own sexual desire contributed to her wanting to leave the Ks' house at L____. The beginning of a footnote reads: "I added: 'Moreover, the re-appearance of the dream in the last few days forces me to the conclusion that you consider that the same situation has arisen once again, and that you have decided to give up the treatment – to which, after all, it is only your father who makes you come' " (p. 70).

Because this does not appear in the main text, and because Freud in his postscript explicitly says that he missed these transferential indications (p. 118), we might wonder whether he actually said this to Dora, or whether after writing up the case, he put it in the footnote because that is what he would have liked to have said. Here is a gap larger than those inherent in most stories. Freud had started his account by declaring that some people, hysterics, leave gaps and inconsistencies. Now we find ourselves wondering, not perhaps for the first time in this text, whether he himself might have left important gaps and inconsistencies in his story (Marcus, 1974).

Did Freud mention to Dora any idea that her dream had been triggered by something to do with himself, a piece of negative transference?

We cannot know. At this same point in the story Freud mentions in his text his idea of a positive transference: Dora said the next day that she smelled smoke after waking from the dream. Freud's thought was because her father, Herr K, and he himself were smokers that this put him into the chain, and now she wanted to kiss him! But he does not say that he mentioned this thought to her either, and nothing corroborated the idea about Dora's erotic desire as such. Nevertheless, Freud took it in this way.[10]

Freud's footnote interpretation about Dora wanting to leave, whether it was made or unmade, seems altogether less contentious than the one in the text about Dora's sexual desire. He seemed to have stirred up in Dora a similar response to the one she felt toward Herr K. We cannot know whether she wanted to leave because of fear, because of exasperation, or, as Freud supposed, because of repressed desire. But we are on more reliable ground in thinking that she had decided to leave at this point because two weeks later she corroborated this. This kind of structure, interpretation with corroboration coming later in the dialogue, has recently been proposed as an objective basis for recognizing transference manifestations in transcripts of psychoanalytic sessions (Luborsky, Crits-Christoph & Mellon, 1986).

Dora might have told Freud she was unhappy with how things were going, but she did not. Her dream was a compromise partly resolving her conflict of wanting and not wanting to leave. By means of it she was both telling Freud and not telling him about this.

A strong version of the theory of transference as it has developed since Freud is that there is always an aspect of the patient's narrative that is not just talking about life in the past, or life outside the consulting room, but about what is going on between patient and analyst. After all, the theory goes, the patient speaks to a specific person, not just to anybody or to a tape recorder. Here again is a direct relation of a psychoanalytic issue with cognitive science in the theory that utterances always have more than just semantic content: Utterances are speech acts (Austin, 1962; Searle, 1969; see also Chapter 4) that have a component of intended effect on the hearer. The psychoanalytic version of this idea is that some of the patient's intention is imparted by such speech acts to the analytic relationship from earlier relationships.

When we talk with someone about our relationship with them, we can either do so directly or indirectly. Thus, if Dora had spoken directly, we could imagine her saying something like: "I warn you that if you go on telling me that you are right and I wrong about my being frightened of my own sexual desires, I shall leave." If there is some reason that makes it impossible to be direct, the impulse may not go away. Conflicts may, as they did for Dora, emerge indirectly.

But Freud was only just beginning to suspect this. He preferred the idea that he was an archaeologist of personal prehistory, bringing "to the light of day after their long burial the priceless though mutilated relics of antiquity. I have restored what is missing. . . . I have not omitted to mention in each case where the authentic parts end and my constructions begin" (p. 12). He did not see why Dora should have wanted to resist his conclusions.

Whose intentions?

Freud's case of Dora indicates that human intention is not simple. It is ambiguous. I have argued that intentions are crucial in understanding our actions, and that intentions can conflict. Gaps appear in any narrative, but Freud proposed that those gaps that are associated with distress or with conflict are larger than the usual ones. In the next section, I propose that issues of intentions and their conflicts spread yet further. In Freud's story of Dora, they spread to Freud's intentions, and to ours as readers of such narratives.

Freud's intentions

Dora left after three months, her analysis unfinished, perhaps as Freud suspected later because he had by "premature communication of a solution brought the treatment to an untimely end" (1958b/1912, p. 140). Many people leave consideration of psychoanalysis for a similar reason: Freud's fondness for believing himself to be right. And yet, and yet, . . . for Freud to leave behind such writings as Dora's case is to provide evidence for others to analyze his own text using methods that he himself taught. It is because we are prompted by his work to seek intentions behind actions that we ask: What was Freud's involvement in all this?

Freud called his text a fragment, stating, rather baldly one might think, that it has gaps. He had started his account by saying that the stories of hysterics have gaps. But he too tells a story. We, his readers, discover not just minor gaps, but rather large ones. Might they occur for the same kinds of reasons that he supposed hysterics left gaps, because of conflicts? The unreliability of Freud's narrative affronts us as natural scientists, but it can prompt us as human scientists to apply interpretive methods to it.

Gallup (1982) has indeed applied Freud's method to this text. She describes Dora and Freud's discussions of those sexual practices that would not be mentioned in polite society. Dora, it seems, is willing to discuss these in her analysis. Freud gives away, by small hints, that he is also interested in taking part. Gallup points out that Freud's German text occasionally breaks into French. He describes earnestly how in discussing sexual practices and terms "the best way . . . is to be dry and direct . . . the method furthest removed from the prurience with which the same subjects are handled in 'society.' . . . I call bodily organs and processes by their technical names, and I tell these to the patient if they – the names, I mean – happen to be unknown to her. *J'appelle un chat un chat*" (p. 48).

An English translation might be "I call a spade a spade." But Gallup points out that at the very moment at which Freud denounces prurience he lapses into a figurative expression. "By his terms, this French sentence would seem to be titillating, coy, flirtatious. And to make matters more juicy (less 'dry'), *'chat'* or *'chatte'* can be used as vulgar (vulvar) slang for the female genitalia . . . he takes a French detour and calls a pussy a pussy" (Gallup, 1982, p. 140). Though all who knew him agreed that Freud was an upright man, he was not averse to speaking in intimate terms with an engaging young woman also interested in discussing matters sexual.

Nor is this the only one of Freud's intentions that might be relevant. In the story, there is a torrent of generalizations about sex. We read that the transmission of a "heavy taint . . . syphilis in the male parent is a very relevant factor in the etiology of the neuropathic constitution of children" (footnote 1, p. 20). We hear that bedwetting has "no more likely cause than masturbation, a habit whose importance in the etiology of bedwetting in general is still insufficiently appreciated" (p. 74). We find Freud asserting that "it is well known that gastric pains occur especially often in those who masturbate" (p. 78), and that hysterical symptoms occur when those who have masturbated then give it up.

One would be wanting in historical imagination to regard these assertions as just so much Victorian nonsense. We do not go beyond the evidence of the text, however, to see that Freud intends to announce such generalizations with an air of authority. As Todorov (1975/1971) has pointed out, writers of prose address speech acts to their readers – here we are being told by Freud not just that he has the picklocks for this case in particular, but keys to the etiology of neuroses in general.

Dora had been passed in a circle of male exchange by her father to Herr K and now to Freud. As Marcus (1974) points out, after initially being attracted to this "woman of intelligent and engaging looks" (p. 23), Freud's text implies that he comes to like her less. Perhaps he preferred women to be more pliant. In the end Freud too let her down, perhaps because of another motive, the prospect of at last becoming famous. Constantly in the discourse structure of this text we find Freud first convincing himself of the correctness of his theories, then trying to din his ideas into Dora and then into us his readers.

Can we make sense of the inconsistency between Freud's hope of establishing his discoveries as natural science and his disregard of the usual criteria of such science, by inquiring into his intentions? Freud was, in his own words, a man with a "thirst for grandeur" (Freud, 1953/1900, p. 192), a "conquistador" (Sulloway, 1979, p. 216). Kardiner remembers him saying, some 20 years later, more modestly:

> I have no great interest in therapeutic problems. I'm much too impatient now. I have several handicaps that disqualify me as a great analyst. One of them is that I am too much the father. Second I am much too much occupied with theoretical problems . . . rather than paying attention to the therapeutic problems. (Kardiner, 1977, pp. 68–69)

Dora's second dream

The nature of Freud's involvement is clearest in his account of Dora's second dream: In it, Dora was walking in a strange town, she came home, found a letter from her mother saying that her father was dead, and that she could come if she liked. She visited a station, entered a wood, met a man who said, "Two and a half hours more" (p. 94), and offered to accompany her. Then she reached home to find that her mother had left for the cemetery.

Freud did not finish interpreting this dream because Dora left after only two further sessions. But he inferred that it included a theme of revenge: She wished her father dead.

In her associations Dora recognized the phrase "if you like" (p. 98) as coming from the letter from Frau K that had contained the invitation to

L____. So this dream too led back to the scene by the lake. Another memory opened up about it: Dora remembered that Herr K had said, "I get nothing out of my wife" (p. 98), and that she had slapped his face. She had walked away, intending to return alone around the lake to the Ks' house. She had asked a man how long this would take: "Two and a half hours" (p. 99) was the reply, so she decided to go back on the boat, meeting Herr K again there, where he had apologized to her.

On the third day after this dream, Dora began "with these words: 'Do you know that I am here for the last time today?' – 'How can I know, as you have said nothing to me about it?' – 'Yes, I made up my mind to put up with it till the new year. But I will wait no longer than that to be cured' " (p. 105). Freud asked how long ago she had decided. She said two weeks.

Freud, in a barely believable intuitive leap, remarked that this sounded like the length of notice given to a maidservant or governess, and asked whether anything came to mind about a governess. The great detective had hit upon the right question. Its answer cleared up some of the mystery of Dora's case. She said that there had been a governess of the Ks who gave two weeks notice when they were at L____. She had confided in Dora a day or two before the scene at the lake that Herr K had made advances and had sexual intercourse with her. He had said to her that he got nothing out of his wife.

Said Freud: "These are the very words he used afterwards when he made his proposal to you and you gave him the slap in his face" (p. 106). He inferred that among the causes of Dora's outrage at Herr K was that she was being treated like a governess, a servant. Accompanying this is a footnote to the effect that Dora's father had also said he got nothing from his wife.

Freud explained to Dora that before this she had planned on Herr K divorcing his wife and marrying her. Frau K could then marry her father. Her disappointment was more serious than had previously appeared. No wonder she had been enraged that her father had discounted the idea of Herr K's proposal. Now the reason why she wanted her father to end his affair with Frau K also became clearer. Their affair had become intolerable because it was no longer to be accompanied by her own marriage, which would at last have given her some dignity, some sense of her own intentions being accomplished. Up till then, she had been scarcely more than an object in other people's plans.[11]

Freud suggested that Dora had taken the possibility of a proposal from Herr K seriously for a long time.[12] When it came it was horribly transformed by the governess's confidences. Freud added that Dora "had listened to [him] without any of her usual contradictions. She seemed to be moved" (pp. 108–109).

Freud's postscript

In his postscript, Freud recounts ideas that occurred after Dora left. Included are his discussions of transference. Its implications were only just dawning. "I did not" he said "succeed in mastering the transferences in good time. . . ." He says he should have listened to the "warning that she had better leave my treatment just as she had formerly left Herr K's house." He says he "ought" to have pointed out this piece of transference to her (p. 118).

Again, in Dora's second dream, Freud realized that he ought to have noticed that "two and a half hours" (p. 119) could have been another warning that she was about to leave after another two and a half sessions, simultaneously escaping him and taking revenge. Freud's peevish tone as he explains that he could not clear up all the details of the second dream indicates that she succeeded. Freud was not above getting his revenge too. He wrote the case history up immediately after Dora had left, as if to get it off his chest, and thought that Dora would be "pained if her own case history should accidentally fall into her hands" (pp. 8–9). But he too was conflicted. He sent it to the publishers a few months after writing it, then got them to send it back to him. He did not publish it for another four years.

Freud saw, at the beginning of Dora's analysis, that he was being cast into the role of "her father in her imagination. . . . She was even constantly comparing me with him consciously" (p. 118). He was good at being a benevolent though strict father, but this made it difficult for him to experience negative aspects of the transference, occurring to question either his being right or his paternal rights.

Gallup (1982) describes how despite Freud's immediate grasp of the significance of two weeks as the period of notice given to a governess, he was reluctant to grasp its implications for him. He asked Dora for an association, and neglected a possible insight about himself. Freud was paid for his services, just as governesses are paid. It was Freud who had been given two weeks' notice. It was he who was being thrown out.

Clement and Cixous (cited by Gallup, 1982) use, for this throwing out, the vulgar idiomatic French expression *foutu a la porte* ("chucked out at the door"). "'*Foutre*' which no longer has a literal sense used to [be a term for sexual intercourse].' What Freud could not tolerate was to have been *'foutu a la porte'* " (Gallup, p. 147).

Governesses appear frequently in Freud's works (cf. Miss Lucy R). They were insecure in their employment, liable both to being *foutu*, as was the Ks' governess, and seen as getting up to things. It is not governesses only who are *foutu a la porte*, however, it is women in general. Unconsciousness is not just an individual matter. Whole structures of unconscious attitude and intention pervade cultures. In the Dora case there is a succession of instances in which women are declared nothing. Both Dora's father and Herr K declare that their wives give them nothing, perhaps are nothing. Might not Dora have realized that it was only a matter of time before this fate would befall her too? Is the label of "hysteria" a further attempt to nullify her refusal of the consequences of a kind of male sexuality that turns a woman from a thing into a nothing?

Freud did not want to realize himself in the role of a governess, meaning a nothing. He avoided recognizing that this was what Dora was saying to him, that he too was to be *foutu a la porte*.

The end of Dora

The story of Dora is a tragedy. Neither Dora nor Freud were transformed by their dialogue. Freud recounted how Dora went back to see him 15 months later. He observes that the date was April the first, and also that her visit was prompted by her seeing his name in the newspaper. Freud's editor points out that this was no doubt the news of his appointment to a professorship (footnote to p. 122). An opportunity had arisen to visit the Ks, following the death of one of their children. She told Frau K that she knew of the affair with her father. She got Herr K to admit that the scene by the lake had not been her imagination. This she told her father. She did not resume relations with the K family.

Though Dora's symptoms had improved when she revisited Freud, she was recognized 20 years later by Deutsch (1957) from the story of her early life given by a woman who consulted him. She was pleased to be recognized as the famous Dora, but at that time she was still beset with psychosomatic symptoms and with vaginal discharges that made her feel unclean. Not long after her last visit to Freud she had married. To Deutsch she denounced her husband as "selfish, demanding and ungiving" (1957, p. 161). She was fond of her brother, of the calm childhood memory, by that time a prominent politician. He, though saying that she was a difficult woman "who distrusted people and tried to turn them against each other" (Deutsch, 1957, p. 162), saw her frequently and was kind to her. Some 30 years later still, Dora died of bowel cancer, having emigrated to New York. It shocks us to read, in an echo of what has gone before, that Deutsch's informant of her death utters a phrase of contemptuous dislike, denouncing her as of no account.

Freud went on from publishing Dora's case with the main part of his system in place. He allowed the system to change later so long as he was the one to make the changes. But he himself seems largely to have been unchanged. Among the characteristics that remained unchanged, as Forrester (1984) and others have pointed out, was Freud's unwillingness to see himself as having any aspect of the feminine. In our society, for those with a certain kind of ambition, to be feminine is not such a good role. Ramas (1980) proposed that another implication of Freud finding "Dora" an appropriate pseudonym was that this was the name his sister gave to a servant. Servitude was the metaphor for femininity that came to Freud's mind. To be a woman can mean being passed over, being given a couple of weeks' notice.

Freud's ideas about this matter culminated in his lecture on "Femininity." Although, he says, the hysteric's ideas of male seduction turned out to be largely fantasy, the real cause of all the trouble is the seductive action of the mother. This is grounded in reality. She had actually caressed the child, enclosed it in love, and then in various ways been disappointing. In a breathtakingly chauvinist statement, he says: "Women have made few contributions to the discoveries and inventions in the history of civilization" (Freud, 1964/1933, p. 132), but they may have invented weaving – a kind of cultural equivalent of pubic hair to cover up the shame of having no penis. Freud was not on any account going to be like that. He was going to make sure that he was cock of the roost, and to be quite shameless about it. He continued to be as domineering when his schemes were at stake as he was with Dora. The difference, later on, was that when any substantial disagreement with his views occurred, it was he who gave the dissident notice to quit.[13]

Where does this leave us, I the writer of this, you the reader? What is our involvement? We could do any of the usual things, idealize Freud or dismiss him; identify with Dora and seek to disrupt the orderliness of a patriarchal world, or cockily with Freud make use of that order. I could perhaps write this, and think that in writing I might somehow get the better of Freud. You could read this and see what is wrong with it, and with me. But if we involve ourselves not so much as observers in a commanding position with respect to the observed, if instead we listen to this story, and take part ourselves in it, then a more remarkable thing may happen.

From the dialogue of an outraged woman and an ambitious man in 1900, there may come alive a sense of a movement in which we are all still involved. It is a movement of multiple conflicting intentions for which there is no necessary resolution: of wanting to be loved and respected, but fearing to be made a convenience of, fearing to be *foutu a la porte*. These very conflictual intentions make the story recognizably human, and make their recognition in ourselves able to provoke important insights.

Freud's striking proposal is that in a dialogue that can be retold in story form, about abuses of power, about imperfections and evasions, we can take a few steps toward truths that may be transformative. It was this idea that Freud glimpsed, even if not quite clearly enough to transform himself.

We are not in a position to stand outside all this and say: "Well, Freud was such and such, and Dora was so and so, but I, on the other hand. . . ." Freud, Dora, and we are all involved. The possibility, indicated in this fragment of a story, is that even if truth may not set us entirely free, there may be a possibility of reappropriating missing intentions that we are tempted to project and displace, that tend to be chucked out of the door. By this means we may have some success, though always partial, of coming to know consciously our intentions and integrating them into a model of self.[14]

Telling one's own story: Dorothea and Dora

It may be accidental that George Eliot and Freud, both deeply concerned with the question of transformation of the human personality, should happen on the same name for their protagonists, Dorothea-Dora, gift of God. The differences between the two stories are great. For George Eliot, it was the understanding of other people's stories that was to be part of a new social science, transformative for readers in a way that statistics are not. For Freud, the issue shifts to being able to tell one's own story and understand it. Nonetheless there is a connection.

Novelists tell stories of other people, even when these are partly autobiographical. But now Freud asserts not only that to be psychologically ill is to be unable to tell one's own story, but by telling it in the dialogue of analysis, gaps and incoherences produced by conflicts are filled and resolved.

In the course of a successful treatment this incoherence, incompleteness, and fragmentariness are progressively transmuted as facts, events, and memories are brought to the forefront of the patient's mind . . . nothing less than reality is made, constructed, or reconstructed. A complete story. . . . (Marcus, 1974, p. 71)

We make, as Marcus says, "a fictional construction that is at the same time satisfactory to us in the form of the truth, and as the form of the truth" (p. 72).

And then, as Marcus puts it in a resounding paragraph,

No larger tribute has ever been paid to a culture in which the various narrative and fictional forms had exerted for centuries both moral and philosophical authority and that had produced as one of its chief climaxes the great bourgeois novels of the nineteenth century. Indeed we must see Freud's writings – and method – as themselves part of this culmination, and at the same moment along with the great modernist novels of the twentieth century, as the beginning of the end of that tradition and its authority. Certainly the passages we have just dealt with [about the filling of gaps] contain heroic notions and offer an extension of heroic capabilities . . . at least as a possibility. (p. 72)

The heroic notion is that in the tradition of narrative that started with the epics of Homer, and the audience's *katharsis* of emotions in Greek tragedy, now Freud proposes that it is not just the contemplation of other people's stories that is transformative. It is telling our own stories, not just to be writerly in Barthes' (1975/1970) sense, but ourselves to be authors, to fill the gaps left by our own missing intentions, to construct our own sense of our selves.

I will close this chapter on Freud by examining a little further the contrast with George Eliot, who can be thought of as coming immediately before Freud in this tradition.[15] She proposed that the story form, the novel, was capable of extending people's sympathies, and in *Middlemarch* she set about doing this by recounting stories of Dorothea, Lydgate, and the others. Like the best novelists, George Eliot is able to portray transformation. Most clearly, Dorothea, by her emotional openness is capable of allowing other people's lives to be transformed. *Middlemarch* is about what might be called the emotional influence of Dorothea – her emotional life standing out from those of others and influencing them. This occurs both with specific emotionally significant episodes such as Lydgate being encouraged by Dorothea's trust when he was at his most despairing, and Rosamund being prompted to an uncharacteristic act of generosity when Dorothea rose above her own jealousy. There is also emotional influence in the large, for instance, with Ladislaw coming to love Dorothea and thereby being drawn toward selfless pursuits.

For George Eliot, emotion was at the center: "No life would have been possible for Dorothea which was not filled with emotion." George Eliot remarks that Dorothea's life was neither of grand historical proportions, nor ideally beautiful. In the final words of the novel she says: "But the effect of her being on those around her was incalculably diffusive: for the growing good of the world is partly dependent on unhistoric acts; and that things are not so ill with you and me as they might have been, is half owing to the number who lived faithfully a hidden life, and rest in unvisited tombs."

The history of European literature starting with the *Iliad*, is, like the history of European international relations, all too clearly dominated by cycles of greed, anger, and revenge. In *Middlemarch* George Eliot portrays another influence, also an emotional one though easier to sneer at. She asserts that such an influence has contributed half to our own well-being.

For individual characters in *Middlemarch*, however, there is not much about their own lives that transforms themselves. Forces as stern as those of the *Iliad* drive them toward their destiny. Lydgate's life deteriorates. A speck of commonness in his character becomes amplified by his experiences, and he falls short of what he might have become. Dorothea herself is driven toward two marriages, in both cases with the sense that to achieve her goals she needs a man to enact her purposes. She has no sense that as a woman she could become knowledgeable or do some good in the world by her own efforts.

What is new in Freud, what Marcus calls heroic about Freud's narrative of Dora, what allowed human character to change in 1910, as Virginia Woolf (1966/1924) put it, is not that such forces are absent. They are present with renewed vigor, now with a thoroughly modern name, "the unconscious." What is new is the idea that as well as influencing others emotionally, it is just possible that we might transform ourselves. What Freud suggests is that the cycles of fateful emotional influence, such as those of angry revenge or even the baleful effect of a loveless childhood, can be transmuted, precisely by rendering our own lives into story form. For in this we can both experience our emotions and reflect upon them. We can understand the effects of intention on emotion and action. In this conception of telling a story, emotions have the central function. It is they that can point to the intentions that will fill the gaps.

Displacement of emotions or successive elicitation?

Emotions thus emerge in Freud's story of Dora in a kind of double movement. First, in the fashion that I have described here, they occur because conflicts of goals or evaluations of events have occurred to trigger them. But then, under the press of yet further goals, these emotions are themselves worked upon. They undergo what seem like displacements and distortions. They are changed into terms of a disjointed language of symptoms, particularly when our relationships with others make it difficult to express them.

Thus Freud suggests that Dora's dissatisfactions with her father and with Herr K were transformed into irritability and despair, which were later transferred to Freud. Her disappointment with Freud could also not be spoken of directly, but was itself displaced to occur as transference manifestations in the dreams of danger and revenge.

Basic emotions, then, are first elaborated in ways described by theories of conflict and evaluation, but then they may be transformed, because, in a secondary movement, the expression of these emotions conflicts with yet other concerns. From Freud we understand that an emotion may only be understandable in terms of such doubled series of goal conflicts, which have contributed to it over several stages.

A basic emotion – a joy, a sadness, an anger, a fear, a disgust – may occur with the evaluation of an event in relation to an intention. Although when this happens we may be as clear about its significance as Achilles was about his anger with Agamemnon, another process may occur, the second part of a double movement, making the significance of our emotions unclear to us. When this occurs we may, as Freud pointed out, infer that yet further intentions have intruded. Freud uses the term displacement to describe this effect. The metaphor is of an emotion sliding across the surface of our possible interpretations of events until it fastens upon a constellation that will hold it. When circumstances change, or when a new consideration emerges, an emotion may seem to slide yet again to take up a new place. Though lively, the metaphor of displacement is misleading. An emotion is not an object capable of being displaced. Emotions emerge from evaluations of events and goal conflicts coming into focus: Such evaluations give rise to repeated and interrelated episodes of emotion when we recognize their further implications, as we reflect upon them, or as we talk about them, or as new goals become relevant, or as events unfold.

Thus we may trace the implications of Dora's intentions in the repeated elicitations of her bitterness. In response to Freud's question about her involvement in the cover-up of her father's affair, Dora's original reproachfulness toward her father seems, as Freud would say, to be displaced and comes to rest upon herself. She has had an interest in encouraging her father's love affair with Frau K. Then, a new mental territory of this realization opens up in what Lacan calls the second development about some of her identifications. Her resentments point back toward her sense of betrayal, and beyond that to the fact that her heart had gone out to Herr K. Following the second reversal it seems that an emotion she had been feeling may have been jealousy. It points back to her love for her father. Be he ne'er such a devious person she remains attached to him. The third development points to the attachment of Dora to Frau K. Of all the people she had known, Dora had most desired to be like Frau K. One way to achieve this had been, like Frau K herself, to have an affair. A reappropriation of these implications begins to reconnect her to her actions.

Before a question could be put, to which this was leading, "How is it that you do not feel bitter to Frau K who has also betrayed you, " the analysis veers away. It is left in the more simple structure of Dora feeling vengeful toward men, almost where she started, though now her anger is directed toward Freud. Her plan of gaining some influence within the circle of exchange, of keeping everyone in that circle happy, by Frau K and Herr K divorcing, and her father marrying Frau K and herself marrying Herr K comes to nothing. In the end the men are still in control of things. Her father carries on as usual. And Herr K had simply wanted yet another sexual partner, not a wife.

Are not these displacements really emotions each newly generated as different considerations occur of a more general issue in Dora's life, as new concerns come to be relevant about how she might feel loved? Nothing is being displaced. The series of understandings gives rise to a series of emotions each comprehensible in terms of goals and interpretations of events.

Freud at a turning point in European literature

The European literary tradition starts with Homer's portrayal of gods – later to become the similarly inexorable influences of character, biology, society – providing the goals and some of the plans of human life. In

Western culture our current theory is that we humans create some of our goals as well as devising and enacting the plans. This means that somehow we struggle with goals we only partly know, and are responsible for actions that have effects we can only partly foresee. In the literary tradition we as audiences, choruses, and readers look on as if fascinated by such an extraordinary arrangement. We too become engaged in the action and we experience some of the emotions.

As Marcus (1974) says, the idea that in relating the narrative of one's own life we may become whole is a conception of grandeur and compassion. The idea of facing determinism and our own ignorance, and thereby being able to transcend them, coming after nearly 3,000 years of European literature vindicates our obsession with stories. The aim is to reappropriate those parts of the story that have got away.

The dialogue of therapy, within which such stories emerge, is therefore one of emotions and intentions. Interpretations are not injunctions to the patient to believe something, though Freud often found himself unable to stop lecturing and browbeating his patients. They are remarks about intentions and emotions that, if the patient recognizes them, could conceivably fill gaps. The consciousness that Freud sought to enable in his patients is not a special state of mind. It is an understanding of involvement: "Oh, so that's what I was doing when I. . . ." Consciousness in psychoanalysis is an enlargement of one's understanding: "I hadn't thought of it like that before" (cf. Freud, 1964/1937).

Perhaps fortuitously the etymology of the word consciousness in English suggests mutuality, knowing something with another person: By experiencing our transference feelings we come to know something about what we are up to with another. Certainly, though we can derive insights from our own unaided reflection, much the easiest way is with another person present in person or in a piece of writing, improving the possibilities of rationality in dialogue. In the end, the effect of successful therapy is to allow us to fill some of the gaps in our story and hence to enlarge our knowledge of our goal structures. With an improved model or ourself comes the possibility of being able to act to some extent voluntarily, not just be moved by impersonal forces.

Freud's Dora was not able to keep her own story, just as his sister's maid was not able to keep her own name. Within Freud's own terms this outcome could scarcely have been more tragic. The reason was that in this new kind of dialogue Freud himself was also involved, principally as an ambitious man with a good idea by which he wanted to make his name – and it is a good idea. He manages to fill the gap in his own soul, the gap of his unfulfilled desire for recognition. He fits his intentions together, completes his story. Dora does not. We can scarcely be satisfied by such a result.

Freud was able to hint at the transformative possibilities of becoming whole by fitting one's intentions and actions together in story form. He had not yet achieved the kind of dialogue to which his idea was pointing. Perhaps therapists, or writers, or writerly readers coming afterward may, with the knowledge of these imperfect explorations, achieve it more often. We are not far beyond the inception of this new kind of story form. Perhaps after its fragmentary beginnings it will have a long future, just as more traditional stories of European literature have had a long past.

PART III

Enjoyment and creativity

But my writing is simply a set of experiments in life – an
endeavour to see what our thought and emotion may be
capable of – what stores of motive, actual or hinted as
possible, give promise of a better after which we may
strive.

George Eliot, Letter of 1876

Frijda (1988) asserts that emotions are lawful and often inexorable. Does
this mean, as Homer seems to say, that we are little more than puppets
activated by forces of which we have some but only partial understanding, and where even if we did have an understanding this would not
allow us to choose our actions?

Some philosophers have indeed given us a picture of the human
condition in such terms. Hume (1988/1739), for instance, portrays
human reason as being slave to the passions; but, argues, Frijda, these
laws do not mean we are puppets or slaves. Perhaps Dutch philosophers
are more sanguine than Scottish ones: Frijda recommends the formulation of Spinoza (1955/1675), whose book on ethics contains an important
section on the emotions. Spinoza was the first philosopher to put the
idea about which Part III of this book was written. It is as follows.

Spinoza proposed that everything that is, let us call it nature, is part of
one connected system. Individuals are, as it were, local singularities in
the system, like wrinkles in a piece of cloth. The proper activity of the
human mind within this scheme is to understand this, both generally
and in the detail of our daily lives. When we do this we have what
Spinoza calls active emotions, based on love for what is the case. When
we feel frustrated or resentful about the way the world acts on us,
Spinoza calls these passions, negative emotions, based on hatred, which
rejects what is the case and wants things to be different. Spinoza was

347

thoroughly cognitive in his understanding of both active and passive emotions: Negative emotions, he thought, are really ideas that are false understandings of the nature of things and of our place in the world. To understand, and actively to take part in the world, then is to be happy. To be resentful, frustrated, or hating are ways in which our bodies are affected because our ideas are confused.

Now comes the idea that is striking. Spinoza introduced it for the first time, apparently, into European thinking: Understanding the sources of our will and impulses to action, even though we are not ourselves prime movers, is liberating. Instead of a life of grumbling, discontent, and frustration, we can be at one with ourselves and the world. This, according to Spinoza, is the secret of how to be happy.

This is an important idea. We could only hold it fully, I think, in a profoundly religious state of mind like that of Spinoza himself, that God being perfect cannot be incomplete and therefore that God and the world are one. Or perhaps we must have something like a Buddhist belief. For those of us who are not able to attain such beliefs, who find ourselves occasionally feeling resentful, for instance, there are difficulties – as with all theories of emotions based on essentially Stoic ideas. I will, therefore, not argue for Spinoza's position as such. Nevertheless the last two chapters have much in common with it.

This book has been written around the idea that emotions occur at the junctures of plans, when a goal or a plan needs to be reevaluated, perhaps because everything has not fitted together. This final section treats the question of the integration. Among the principal issues is integration of what Johnson-Laird and I have called basic and semantic parts of emotions.

Chapter 8 is on happiness, in which the processes making for mental fragmentation are in obeyance. To be creatively, wholeheartedly, doing what one is doing is to be happy. One is not doing something while some other part of ourself is worrying about something else. One is not acting under compulsion that one resents. One is not suffering interruption, not being conflicted. To be engaged wholeheartedly, either individually or with someone else, is to experience a particular mental tone. One's mind is filled semantically just with what one is doing, taking care of what happens in the flow of action, meeting what occurs with resources to hand.

Chapter 9 is on the expression of emotion in distinctively human ways, where a central consideration is the integration of basic and semantic parts. I consider the question of how emotions might prompt cognitive change, promote integration of the bits that are unintegrated. Just as new evidence and internal inconsistency prompt changes in scientific theories, the emotions that arise from the unexpected can prompt changes in our private, implicit theories. The question of how emotions can enable cognitive change to occur is explored in two areas. One is the expression of emotional issues in narative art in a way that invites vicarious participation. The other is the expression of emotions to a psychotherapist. In both of these, an element of imagination is involved that is central to the processes of psychological transformation that emotions can prompt.

8. Happiness

Happiness not only needs no justification, . . . it is also
the final test of whether what I am doing is right for me.
Joanna Field
A life of one's own, p. 199

The correspondences of happiness

Freud's story of Dora brings to an end the Victorian era of literature. Although not itself a novel, it can also be thought of as the implicit start of the modern psychological novel, with its subjectivity, its free-associative consciousness, its shifting perspectives of time, and its need, as Edel (1955) and Barthes (1975/1970) have said for the reader to become the author. As Proust put it toward the end of *A la recherche du temps perdu,* reflecting on his work and on the purposes of art – almost as if he had been reading Marcus's (1974) commentary on Freud that I quoted in Chapter 7:

> It would be inaccurate even to say that I thought of those who would read [my book] as "my" readers. For it seemed to me that they would not be "my" readers but readers of their own selves . . . it would be my book, but with its help I would furnish them with the means of reading what lay inside themselves." (Proust, 1981/1912–1922, Part III, p. 1089)

Proust explicitly brought the novel of subjective consciousness to birth, as an invitation to experience the world from inside the mind of another with whom the reader can identify and thereby to understand some of the timeless principles of his or her own mental life.

Toward the end of the overture to Proust's novel, there occurs a fa-

350

mous moment of great happiness. Proust's narrator describes how one day in adulthood his mother gave him some tea and some *petite madeleine* cake.

> And soon, mechanically, dispirited after a dreary day with the prospect of a depressing morrow, I raised to my lips a spoonful of the tea in which I had soaked a morsel of the cake. No sooner had the warm liquid mixed with crumbs touched my palate, than a shudder ran through me, and I stopped, intent upon the extraordinary thing that was happening to me. An exquisite pleasure had invaded my senses, something isolated, detached, with no suggestion of its origin. And at once the vicissitudes of life had become indifferent to me, its disasters innocuous, its brevity illusory – this new sensation having had on me the effect which love has of filling me with a precious essence; or rather this essence was not in me, it *was* me. I had ceased to feel mediocre, contingent, mortal. Whence could it have come to me, this all powerful joy? (Proust, 1912–1922/1981, Part I, p. 45).

In his novel, Proust creates opportunities for reflecting on our own experiences of this and other kinds, and he searches for the meaning of such moments. In part, he identifies them with pieces of autobiographical memory, which cannot be rediscovered deliberately, but which can flood involuntarily into the mind.

There are many descriptions in the psychological literature of memory images closely tied to emotions that had occurred as part of the event that was being remembered.[1] But Proust was not satisfied with the idea that the happiness he felt was simply the recall of the emotion of the moment from the past. The emotion he experienced was an "oceanic" feeling of joy.[2] Neither here, nor in the comparable incidents that Proust's narrator remembers, of being on a train when a railwayman had tapped a wheel, or tripping over an uneven paving stone in Venice, was this oceanic feeling the mood of the moment from which the autobiographical fragment was derived. Nor indeed was it in the prototype of Proust's own experience when in 1909 a servant had given him a cup of tea, and he had recalled with great vividness a garden in which he had played when a child (May, 1977).

In the last volume of *A la recherche du temps perdu* Proust explores the significance of these phenomena. He concludes that such experiences occur only by accident; they cannot be found planfully. The profoundly joyful effect is not due to the event as such. It is due to experiencing the perceptual structure of the event, prompted by a similar sensory experience in the present and reflecting at the very same moment on its meanings, including its context and subsequent significance. Ordinarily we are unable to make this kind of connection. When we contemplate events in advance, our image or model of them is invariably contradicted by reality. When we try to do this in the present, if we think about what is happening or because we are striving after goals, this diminishes our actual experience. But there are moments that can occur when we are not striving. They are remembrances where occasionally there can be complete coincidence of image and experience. These are glimpses of a relation we can have to our world that seems to have a kind of timelessness. At the same time such experiences indicate a fundamental feature of our human psychological constitution, the exploration of which, Proust then goes on to argue, is the purpose of art.[3]

The kind of state to which Proust refers – which is of a quasi-mystical nature outside egoistic striving – may only be attained very rarely. Nevertheless, the theme of correspondence that Proust's narrator discusses, though replayed in quite different keys than that of Proust's novel, recurs time and again in discussions of happiness: correspondence between image and reality, between phenomenon and significance.

Happiness as engagement in action

Aristotle began his *Nichomachean Ethics* by explaining that action has goals: We act "to aim at some good." He states that in some cases the goal in question is a result that the action aims at, but in other cases the activity is not instrumental. The activity itself is the goal. What is the highest of such goals? It is happiness, the goal of a life lived well.

It may seem that when Aristotle discusses *eudaimonia*, the word translated into English as happiness, he is speaking of a concept that is quite different from anything referred to in Euro-American culture by the term happiness. I will argue, however, that there is a relation between *eudaimonia* and the emotion of happiness. Aristotle's discussion in terms of goals and actions is compatible with a cognitive treatment of the subject. He allows us an analysis of happiness that is recognizable in our culture.

Opinions about happiness, of course, differ. Quennell (1988), in an anthology of reflections of writers mainly of the eighteenth and nineteenth centuries, offers a selection of them. He concludes that many of the images of happiness we find in literature do not derive from pursuit of any goal, and certainly not the goal of happiness itself, but from simply being with a loved one,[4] or from a quiet enjoyment of some other kind of activity, or even from perception.

Aristotle offers a method of proceeding which he used in his own analyses, comparing the conceptions of the many and the wise, to try and resolve contradictions and differences. In the case of happiness, in his day as in ours, opinions of the many and the wise varied. He says that popular conceptions then were that happiness is pleasure, or a result of being thought well of in public life, or that it comes with wealth. None of these satisfies Aristotle. Even achieving the goal of goodness does not offer him a definition of happiness, as one can be good while asleep.

Happiness, concludes Aristotle, is an attribute of activity. He goes on to say that it pertains to the whole life, and he develops his famous idea of life lived not at extremes, but with moderation, according to the mean. By this he meant life lived in correspondence with what is right for the individual and his or her own aims, temperament, talents, and circumstances and right for that person's relations with others. In this, of course, it is clear that the happiness of which he speaks is not an emotion, but an attribute of character that, as he says, can be developed by actions of the right kind. We still have this usage in utterances like "He's not a happy person. He's always wanting something he hasn't got."

Nevertheless, Aristotle's identification of happiness with activity, rather than with a goal external to action, is more promising for understanding the emotion of happiness than ideas of happiness as pleasure, or achieving fame, or wealth. We notice that though people often devote themselves to pleasure, fame, and wealth, they are not always happy in achieving them.

Happiness is, of all the emotions, the least easy to understand in terms of conflict theories. Indeed, this may be why, despite a long history, conflict theories of emotion have been dropped, only to be reinvented at intervals. Conflict theories have treated happiness in ways that may be clever, but by leaving something out from ordinary conceptions. They treat happiness in terms of impediments that will in the end be resolved, causing agitations that are interpreted as happy excitement, rather than anxiety. Ingenious and appropriate to their subject matter though some of the theories are – for example, Meyer's (1956) or Gaver and Mandler's (1987) theories of enjoying music or Berscheid's (1982) theory of romantic love – they seem not to apply to all instances of happiness.

Having fun

Aristotle was concerned to understand happiness on the large scale. In more recent times the idea of happiness as connected with action has been discussed by Goffman (1961). Goffman's approach is one that scientists often use to understand something difficult. He simplifies. He analyzed not happiness as such, but its lesser relative, fun.

In his essay "Fun in Games," Goffman inquires about what it is in games that allows us confidently to expect to have fun. The components are these: To play a game we adopt a role the game affords, and act to achieve a goal defined by the game's rules. Goffman goes further and argues that the most instructive games are those with more than one role. Here, the rules define modes of social interaction, for example, competition to win and/or cooperation to achieve some result, and subgoals about how to achieve the overall goal.

Many of the games in which we become happily involved, furthermore, engage us in face-to-face interaction with the other players. We enter the interaction through what Goffman calls a semipermeable membrane that partially encloses the game and sets it off from the rest of the world. Once inside that membrane, a distinctive microworld is ordered according to its own rules. Actions have meaning insofar as they are defined by these rules. It is no good saying, at football, "I just wanted to go on playing when the ball went over the sideline." As the ball crosses the line the game dissolves. It has to be brought into being again by a special kind of startup action.

Rules and roles. Goffman is concerned to use the structure of games to discover the structure of face-to-face encounters more generally. In the rest of this discussion, when I mention games I will refer just to those that involve face-to-face interactions. When we pass through the semipermeable membrane of a game, we become "black," who moves second at chess, or "the top hat," with the chances the dice provide at Monopoly, or "the server" in tennis, or whatever. Real life is different principally in that the rules are not so codified. The roles and semipermeable membranes are there just the same. As I go into my workplace, I take on a role, recognizable to myself and my colleagues. As I sit down for a family meal, I take part in an interaction where the rules of interaction have been highly practiced. Each type of social interaction is surrounded by its own membrane, its own frame. Within each is a microcosm. Unhappy consequences can occur if concerns from another world are imported or if the rules within the membrane are not regarded.[5]

Focused interaction. When I enter what Goffman calls a focused interaction there is an agreed top-level goal within the membrane. In a shop it is buying and selling. Everything in the shop serves its subgoals. I take on the role of customer. Actions having to do with choosing objects for purchase, exchanging money, carrying away the goods, avoiding taking things I have not paid for, all become the focus of interaction and are subject to the rules that obtain within the membrane. Other matters are disattended. If I blow my nose because I have a cold, or worry that I might get a parking ticket, or chat to my friend, none of these is in the official focus of shopping; at most, they are byplays, perhaps embedded within the focused activity. Such actions could, however, be relevant within other membranes: Having a cold may be relevant at work because my colleagues and I may think it best if I went home to bed. Parking tickets are tokens in the role of car user. Chatting is part of the role of friendship.

Superficially this may seem all there is, either to games or the more loosely defined roles and interactions of real life, and we may wonder what this could have to do with happiness. Goffman explores how rules and roles are only part of the issue.

Engagement. The other part is the actor's engagement in the roles afforded. To be a player simply means generating moves that are legal according to the rules of the game. To be a participant is to take on the goals of the game as one's own. Only as a participant will one experience emotions. Only as a participant will one be excited by the possibility of an attack on the queen's side, feel glad to start putting up hotels on one's property, or feel anxious to avoid serving another double fault. Emotions that occur in relation to goals we have adopted are real. One may be engaged in a role, experiencing what happens in it as happening to oneself, and indeed shaping one's selfhood.

Goffman gives an example of this engagement in an excerpt from the autobiography of Sonia Keppel, the daughter of a famous Edwardian beauty:

> Sometimes, King Edward (Kingy) came to tea with Mamma, and was there when I appeared at six o'clock. On such occasions he

and I devised a fascinating game. With a fine disregard for the good condition of his trouser, he would lend me his leg, on which I used to start two bits of bread and butter (butter side down), side by side. Then, bets of a penny each were made (my bet provided by Mamma) and the winning piece of bread and butter depended, of course, on which was the more buttery. The excitement was intense while the contest was on. Sometimes he won, sometimes I did. Although the owner of a Derby winner, Kingy's enthusiasm seemed delightfully unaffected by the quality of his bets. (p. 39)

To have fun in a game is not to be without dysphoric emotions. It is to be identified with the goals provided by one's role, and engaged in actions allowed by the rules, to meet the contingencies of the game with the resources the game provides.

An engine of meaning. The rules of a game, or indeed of any focused interaction in ordinary life allow a world of meaning to be built. As Goffman put it: "A matrix of possible events and a cast of roles through whose enactment the events occur constitute together a field for fateful dramatic action, a plane of being, an engine of meaning, a world in itself" (p. 26).

A distinctive world comes into being within each semipermeable membrane, and has its own history, its own customs that are elaborated as we go along, and it allows for its own generation of meanings. This occurs in games, in conversations, in the life of any community, in the interactions of law, commerce, government. For each participant the extent to which any of these worlds comes alive depends on his or her engagement. This in turn depends on face-to-face interaction within the membrane: "There seems to be no agent more effective than another person in bringing a world for oneself alive or, by a glance, a gesture or a remark, shriveling up the reality in which one is lodged" (p. 41).

Games afford the possibility of engaged participation in activity that generates meaning, in ways that, like life, are partly unpredictable. But games are constructed to avoid some of the stresses that occur in the ordinary world and that lead to illness or despair. One can lead a medieval army in chess, experience our hearts beating as we think we may have outwitted our enemy, but we need suffer neither the fear of our own death nor the guilt of others'. One can be excited to make or lose thousands at Monopoly without being seen as unscrupulous, as reckless, or as a failure and without the possibility that one's children might starve. One can experience the exhilaration of single combat at tennis without oneself or one's opponent being maimed.

Moreover, a game furnishes just the resources needed for its enactment. We can make the required interactions, elaborating plans in the usual ad hoc manner as we go along, confident that the resources we need are at hand, either because they are provided by the game or because they can be provided by acquiring more skill or experience in another episode.

Emotions in the game. We can see further into the enjoyment of games, I think, by following some more of Goffman's analysis. Within the membrane of a game, one can feel frightened, sad, and so on, but this is part of the fun, because, as in the theater, it takes place at one remove. Games remain fun just so long as we are engaged, even when we suffer dysphoric emotions in them. This paradoxical fact is essential to games as it is in the theater: In a game we can exit through the membrane when we have had enough of whatever emotions or action may occur there. A game, in this sense, is not serious.

Games, by means of their rules, embody something basic to human interaction. At the same time they stretch human capacities of mental and motor skills to limits that would be much too problematic in real life. If we had to search through a tree of possibilities of the breadth and depth that occur in chess in many of our decisions, life would become impossibly stressful and anxiety ridden.

Drama and novels similarly point to how we operate just at the edge of our cognitive abilities. In real life, crime, duplicity, and disappointment in love are the stuff of nervous breakdowns. In literature we can experience them and experiment with them in a safer way. Literature offers an emotional version of a laboratory. In both games and novels we are fascinated because we can almost accomplish the cognitive tasks of social interaction that are set for us, but not quite. In games we can try again when we lose. In books and plays we can leave at the end of the story with the furniture of our own lives intact.

We know too that we can guard against emotions in a game by staying unengaged, by just going through the motions, by generating the plans, but not adopting the goals as our own. It is, of course, no accident that in real life the most radical defense described by psychoanalysis is to go through the motions without engagement. This can be successful in avoiding the emotions of being let down in love or of being hurt by others, but the price is a sense of bored futility. Happiness is absent from such a life because it is a life lived without engagement in what one is doing.[6]

Goffman also points out that transactions within any semipermeable membrane depend in part on what we import with us. Because of the official focus, and because of the role we adopt, what we import of ourselves undergoes a redefining transformation. This allows a range of expressiveness within a role. Nuances of meaning can be generated that we do not perhaps create elsewhere, and subtle shifts occur in what we take to be ourselves.

As well as the different selves that can be experienced there is, as it were, a sense of self that remains constant across interactions. What we take from the interaction itself, and what we take from the more constant self, or from other interactions, can generate a wide range of potentially problematic happenings. To import, for instance, concerns of the workplace into a game is to be a killjoy. Goffman points out too that sexual encounters are very dependent on the absence of discordant importations. If some of our multiple goals distract us, we lose the sense of joy in interaction:

> Love making provides us with some extremely useful data, for the engrossing power of such encounters can become a crucial test of the relationship, while local physical happenings are very likely to distract at least one of the partners. And we know that the relation between two persons can become such that, on whatever occasion they meet, they must – like two ex-husbands of the same woman – suppress considerations they are not capable of banishing from the mind, and thus spoil all occasions of interaction with one another. (p. 40)

Ease and tension. Goffman comes close in his essay to describing a version of the conflict theory of emotions. To experience a dysphoric emotion, or tension, as he calls it, is to be less than fully engaged in the encounter one is in, either because of concerns imported from elsewhere or because the encounter itself is unable to sustain engrossment.

Goffman's analysis of roles and encounters, each with its focus and rules, provides us with a picture of life not as individuals, but as dyads or little groups of people interacting, and with each type of interaction having its own goals, rules for plan making and the local knowledge for the necessary model of each microworld. We enter each microworld with a sense of self and a sense of the kind of other to be encountered within that membrane. So cognition is distributed not just between people, it is distributed across a range of semiencapsulated social encounters, each with its own customs, its own local history, its own rules of conduct.

The definition of an encounter can change quite suddenly. We can, as Goffman puts it, "flood out" by bursting into laughter or tears. We see in such possibilities that the definition of each interaction has constantly to be created by the participants, and that when this is not done successfully, tensions may occur and the definition of what is going on may collapse. Redefinitions may recruit the allegiance of other participants, as when everybody laughs at a joke in a formal meeting, or an attempted redefinition may be treated as a temporary distraction, insufficient to change the interpretation of what is going on.

If such matters make for tension and conflict within an encounter, absence of such tension or conflict allows the complete absorption of a person in the interaction. In a game it is indeed precisely this engagement in single-minded activity that we experience as fun. In life this is what we experience as joy, as happiness in Aristotle's sense: Happiness is to be engaged in wholeheartedly in what we are doing.

Happiness in the communicative theory of emotions

From these analyses we can see that happiness can have at least three meanings, Goffman's sense of being engaged in what we are doing by solving problems that arise with resources that are available, the sense of being without dysphoric emotion, and the sense of having achieved something which we wanted. With these senses it is clear how the communicative theory can cope with issues that are problematic for other forms of the conflict theory of emotions. In the communicative theory it is not interruption of a tendency that gives rise to emotion, but any substantial change in the evaluation of progress of any goal or plan. Positive reevaluations of a current plan, for instance, when some unforeseen circumstance is dealt with successfully or some subgoal is achieved, will give rise to a distinctive happy signal. Its effect will be to encourage continuation with that same plan, enabling the person to remain absorbed in what he or she is doing, expecting that unforeseen problems can be solved as they occur, with confidence that all such contingencies can be met from available resources.

Happiness does not occur simply from repeating a habitual pattern. This does not produce any emotion at all. Happy emotions occur in interaction with others or on one's own, when one is engaged wholeheartedly in what one is doing, perhaps solving unforeseen problems as they occur with resources at hand. It occurs when conflicting goals do not distract one. This description is a paraphrase, in cognitive terms, of the concept of engagement in a plan or action, a basic condition of happiness that would be recognizable both to Aristotle and to Goffman.

The communicative theory also postulates the possibility of feeling happy for no particular reason, perhaps when doing nothing at all, perhaps when doing something mundane. One may find oneself "surprised by joy."[7] Here we postulate that a nonsemantic signal on which happiness is based has spread through the system, but the person concerned is not aware of any semantic information about what caused it.[8]

Where and when does happiness occur?

There have been several surveys of happiness, using questionnaire methods. These methods allow one to see, albeit rather roughly, who does and does not feel happy and in what circumstances.

Economic circumstances

The Gallup Organization in 1975 surveyed 8,787 people in countries in North, Central, and South America, Europe, the Middle East, Asia, and Africa (cited and discussed by Freedman, 1978). Countries with the highest proportion of happy citizens, Sweden and Canada, had 95% of people saying they felt generally happy, with other wealthy nations like the United States and West Germany having almost as many. The wording of the questions encouraged overoptimistic estimates of happiness, but despite this the comparisons between countries are striking and important. Countries that are relatively unsuccessful economically (like Britain and Spain) were well below the levels of Sweden and Canada. They had between 60% and 80% of the population rating themselves as happy.

It is shocking, though presumably not a political surprise, that the overwhelming finding of this survey was that in the poorest countries the large majority of people rated themselves as "not too happy," the lowest point offered on the response scale: In India, 80% of people rated themselves in this way, in Colombia the proportion was 76%, and other poor nations had comparable figures.[9]

In countries where the average income is the equivalent of a few hundred dollars a year or less – and this is the income equivalent of

most dwellers on our planet – people are not happy. With such arrangements for so many people, it is impossible to see how they could be
happy, and this simple fact is a constant reproach to us in wealthier
nations. When the primary concern is with basic needs for yourself and
your family and with staying alive, happiness is scarce. The idea that a
simple life without money or possessions is a happy one is generally
romantic nonsense: Poverty means pain, the proximity of death and
illness, starvation, grinding work, lack of any hope of the future being
any better. One has little concern with questions of life's satisfactions.

It is more heartening that within rich countries like the United States,
Freedman (1978) found that, beyond a certain minimum income, money
made relatively little difference to people's happiness, though Argyle
(1987) cites evidence that people of higher socioeconomic status rate
themselves as somewhat happier than those of lower socioeconomic
status.[10]

The effects of relationships

Relationships are a cause for happiness, particularly sexual relationships. Freedman (1978) conducted a large questionnaire survey of
100,000 Americans responding to a request in magazines. One of the
salient findings was that not money, not power, not youth, not health,
but love in marriage was the "thing" that the respondents most closely
associated with happiness. The effect of a sexual relationship is to make
one somewhat more happy.[11] The effect is more marked for men than
women, and stronger for younger people than for older ones. Men
evidently derive more satisfaction from marriage than women, perhaps
because women are, on average, more satisfying to be with than men.
Wives are better at being confidants and give better social support than
husbands (Vanfossen, 1981).[12]

Relationships other than marriage are also associated with happiness.
In particular, friendships have this quality. Children can be a source of
happiness – but they are also associated with higher levels of anxiety
and marital disharmony than are found in marriages without children
(Abbott & Brody, 1985).

Argyle (1987), in his book on questionnaire research on this subject,
regards happiness as personal reflection on satisfactions in various aspects of life. He concludes that relationships increase happiness by
providing the social support that can buffer against stresses that would
tend to produce unhappiness. Also, relationships act positively to en-

hance self-esteem and allow self-disclosure. They are rewarding in matters such as sex and the sharing of activities.[13]

Occasions for happiness

Occasions for happiness may be seen from diary studies. Scherer, Wallbott, and Summerfield (1986), in their report of students describing characteristics of emotions that were recently experienced, say that the most frequent examples occurred in relationships with friends, as, for example: "During a conversation I told my friend that I loved him. Initially he was stunned. Then to my surprise he said he loved me too. The emotion lasted for weeks. I told him how hurt I had been thinking that he might not be interested in me and how foolish we both had been" (p. 52). And "At the beach. A guy was present, we were lying on the beach, sunbathing, taking photographs, and saying nice words to each other" (p. 52). Also, nonsexual meetings can bring happiness: "By sheer chance I met in my old village some acquaintances with whom I have a pleasant, and friendly relationship. My sister was with me. We sat together until 3:00 A.M. and had a pleasant party" (p. 52).

Nonsocial incidents also caused happiness, as passing an exam, getting a job that was desired, and simply enjoying physical pleasures like eating. Oatley and Duncan[14] found very similar types of verbal description in a diary study. We found that episodes of happiness were most often associated with being with other people. More intense descriptions were often associated with sexual relationships, for example, "Very happy and content. (This is corny . . . love is what it felt like. Don't laugh.)" The occasion was "In my flat; with my boyfriend; we came in from the pub, were just talking, cuddling, etc. Just being together."

Frequency of happiness. Among the basic emotion terms that Johnson-Laird and I have postulated, four are of emotions that are usually distressing and only one is not. Of the 590 emotion terms in English that were considered by Johnson-Laird and Oatley (1989), there is a predominance of terms for the usually negative emotions. Frijda (1988), in his law of hedonic asymmetry, implies that happiness is rare and negative emotions more common. As to actual incidents, Oatley and Duncan found that among Scottish students episodes of happiness were common, though negative emotions were twice as frequent.

Effects of happiness

One of the few people working on the effects of happiness on cognitive processing is Isen, who has shown, for example, that people who had just found a dime in a public telephone were more likely to help a stranger who had dropped some papers (Isen & Levin, 1972), and that randomly selected people given a free gift in a shopping mall reported fewer servicing problems with their cars and television sets in an apparently unrelated consumer survey (Isen et al., 1978). These effects of mild happiness would presumably not surprise any public relations person who has given a "free lunch," but the effect is not simple.

More recent work has shown that as well as being more helpful to others, subjects may also be more helpful toward themselves, and this can sometimes conflict with helping others. For example, happy people may be more likely to act in a way that protects their own mood and more likely to avoid taking large risks (Forest et al., 1979; Isen & Patrick, 1983; Isen, 1984).

Effects have also been found on cognitive processing. Remembered material of a pleasant kind is recalled more completely and more readily when subjects are in a happy state induced by success in a computer game, by the Velten mood induction procedure, or by hypnosis than when in neutral or negative toned mood states. (Isen et al., 1978; Velten, 1968; Teasdale & Fogarty, 1979; Bower, 1981). Isen, Daubman, and Nowicki (1987) have found that people are more able to solve a difficult problem when happy. They try out a wider range of solutions. Isen has also found that mild happiness induced either by having subjects process pleasant words, by showing them funny films, or by giving them small gifts of candy induces subjects to make significantly more unusual word associations.

This kind of finding clarifies some of the issues associated with the question of whether emotions are irrational. Many emotions narrow the focus of attention, for instance, fear tends to induce a frightened person to concentrate exclusively in issues of safety. Happiness, according to Isen, can widen the range of possibilities, and hence in certain kinds of tasks improve rationality. This effect is not universal. Thayer (1988) has reported that when people have to make judgments in a situation that involves equity, being happy makes them less fair. Presumably, here it is important to be able to enter empathetically into the plight of unfortunate people, and being happy on one's own account may conflict with this.

The interpersonal structure of happiness

Happiness often occurs in the company of friends and lovers. What, then, can we make of its interpersonal structure? According to Johnson-Laird and myself, being in love is an interpersonal form of happiness, and is indeed a paradigmatic example. When we are in love, our selves expand to include the other. This person becomes just the one person with whom one could possibly share oneself, and the world is transfigured. At the same time, the experience of being in love is a special role that may justify abandoning existing commitments. Simpson, Campbell, and Berscheid (1986), for instance, found that in America a large majority of people thought that they would not marry without being in love, and many felt that a loss of this kind of love would be reason to end a marriage.

Being in love, then, is a temporary role, a kind of happiness connecting one with another person. In our culture it justifies beginning one exclusive relationship and sometimes ending another. Hence, being in love is comparable with the temporary roles provided by other emotions – with grief's withdrawal from social activity, with anger's vengefulness, with social anxiety's concern for safety.

The writing of love

To portray being in love, I have chosen writings from two poets and a novelist spanning the period of European culture over which I have dealt with other emotions.

Sappho. First, three short fragments from Sappho, who wrote perhaps a hundred years after Homer:

> 1. Love the loosener of limbs shakes me again, an inescapable bitter sweet creature.
>
>   Translation, Trypanis (1971), p. 150

> 2. Some say that the most beautiful thing on the black earth
>   is an army of horsemen,
>   others an army of footsoldiers,
>   others a fleet of ships;
>   but I say it is the person you love.
>
>   Translation, Trypanis (1971), p. 151

3. He is a god in my eyes – the man who is allowed
   to sit beside you – he

   who listens intimately to the sweet murmur of
   your voice, the enticing

   laughter that makes my own heart beat fast.
   If I meet you suddenly, I can't

   speak – my tongue is broken; a thin flame runs
   under my skin, seeing nothing,

   hearing only my own ears drumming, I drip
   with sweat; trembling shakes my body

   and I turn paler than dry grass. At such
   times death isn't far from me.

   Translation, Barnard (1958), p. 39

These three fragments, I think, depict vividly some of the experience of being in love. Sappho wrote the first love poetry in the European tradition that has survived.[15] What remains of her work is very fragmentary.

In the first of these fragments, the involuntariness of love is felt in the same terms as Homer depicted the involuntariness of the emotions of war, though now with an individuality that points to a dawning consciousness of self in relation to another person. Love is *Eros*, a creature shaking Sappho's limbs. But, as with so many other emotions, conflicts may not be far away. It is Sappho who first expressed the idea that love is *glucopicron* (sweet-bitter). She knows that as well as delight, it will bring anguish.

The second fragment is about the admiration of love – the one you love is the most beautiful thing on the black earth. Frijda (1988) describes the absoluteness of emotions as one of his laws of emotion. His "law of closure" states that emotions are closed to judgments in relation to other examples of similar events and to the requirements of goals other than their own. When they are at all strong, emotions are complete, beyond external comparison. So the one you love is not just pleasant, with a friendly tone of voice, not just engaging, not just good looking – but the most beautiful of all. Falling in love, each time it happens, is unlike anything that ever has been or ever will be.

The third fragment is astonishing for combining the excitement of sexual attraction with a sparse purity of language. It has a physiological immediacy that is not about mechanisms of the body. It relates to just this person, this loved one, who not only evokes the perturbations of Sappho's being but is their recipient.

John Donne. This poem was most probably written around the end of the sixteenth century.[16]

> Our two soules therefore, which are one,
>   Though I must goe, endure not yet,
> A breach, but an expansion,
>   Like gold to ayery thinnesse beate.
>
> If they be two, they are two so
>   As stiffe twin compasses are two,
> Thy soule the fixt foot, makes no show
> To move, but doth, if the'other doe.
>
> And though it in the center sit,
>   Yet when the other far doth rome,
> It leanes, and hearkens after it,
>   And grows erect, as that comes home.
>
> Such wilt thou be to mee, who must
>   Like th'other foot, obliquely runne;
> Thy firmnes drawes my circle just,
>   And makes me end, where I begunne.
>   John Donne
>   Nonesuch text (1929), p. 37

I first came across this poem read aloud. The person reading it held the book in his left hand, and a compass, an ordinary school compass with a pencil for drawing circles, in his right. As he reached the line: "If they be two, they are two so," he separated the two parts of the compass. Then, as the poem proceeded, he first showed the part with the point staying still while the other moved, then as the pencil part moved, the part with the point inclined toward it. Then it grew erect as the compass was closed. Then it traced a circle starting where it began. The effect was enthralling: Who would think of using such a trifling mechanical contraption as a metaphor for love? But how apt for that sense of two souls whose lives are joined, one self extended to include another.

The poem is called "A valediction: forbidding mourning" and was written in temporary farewell, I suppose when Donne was off on one of his travels, leaving his beloved at home. The joy both have in each other should not turn to sorrow. They remain joined though separated.

Penelope Lively. For the last selection I will not offer a quotation, merely an indication from the central love scene, in Penelope Lively's (1987) novel *Moon Tiger.*[17] Unlike the other literary works I have cited, this is distinctly from the near side of that time line of 1910, separating us from the Victorians, when Virginia Woolf said human character changed. So it is not a book in which the plan of a character provides a central route map of a plot, with the author describing the plan and modulating the discourse structure to nudge the reader into wanting to see what will happen next. It does have some of these properties, but as a modern work, it is both more inward and more fragmentary. The fragments are those of a historian, Claudia Hampton, elderly, dying, in hospital, looking back on her life, with images rising to her mind as she thinks of writing a history of the world.

As one reads one begins to realize that Penelope Lively herself has succeeded in this apparently preposterous idea: She has written a history of the world in a novel of 207 pages, not closely printed. The novel is not a latter day *War and Peace*, but it has the same concern for the intertwining of personal history and the history of peoples. It is made up of fragments of thoughts about the stuff of cultural history, and prehistory, juxtaposed with fragments of Claudia's life. Meaning is not given by a plan, but implied by proximities, inviting us the readers to fill the gaps between the fragments.

The novel's central scene is in Egypt, one of the cradles of civilization, in World War II, one of the wars of current Euro-American civilization. Claudia, at that time a war correspondent, has met a tank officer, Tom. The Moon Tiger of the title is the green coil that slowly burns at night to repel mosquitoes in the insect-laden air of Egypt, dropping lengths of green ash as it burns.

Claudia met Tom by accident. She was in a truck that had broken down in a sandstorm. He and another officer in a jeep came across the truck and they took Claudia back to safety.

An interval . . . then a phone call: Tom has five days' leave. Claudia thinks back to this moment in her life that she spent with him, thinks that history has its facts. So does a life. This, for her was its core.

They arrive at Luxor on the train from Cairo, stayed at the Winter Palace Hotel. They make love more times than she would have thought possible as the sun sliced in stripes through the shutters. Got dressed. Went out to the terrace overlooking the Valley of the Kings. That evening, thought Claudia, was isolated in her head. Or perhaps it was the next or the next. She could not remember the order of the days. They had become fused into one, with the presence of him. She remembers the cane chair that left an imprint on her flesh through the thin cotton dress, and that she felt richer, happier, more alive then than ever before or since. One day they went to visit Karnak, and the tombs, saw statues of the Pharaoh and his wife – who was also his sister. In the tomb Tom's arm is round her shoulders, she feels the heat of him against her breast. She is so erotically possessed that she thinks he might take all her clothes off and lie down with her in the dust.

It seems that for the first time, in the midst of that war, she really saw the country and life of Egypt, saw that it was beautiful. In the small hours she lies awake, with the Moon Tiger glowing in the dark. She lies thinking of nothing. Tom wakes. They talk. She wants to hear his voice. She gets him to tell the story of his life. He does so. It is conventional, idealistic. He leaves out what Claudia calls the interesting bits: who he was with, what he was feeling. He says that until then there had been no interesting bits. He'd thought of it impersonally. Now that was utterly changed. Until then he'd been on his own. They both think that this is not for much longer. She thinks: May this have a happy ending.

How to fall in love

We need some analyses, some commentaries: Falling in love in European literature has often been depicted as being taken over, and it occurs with an almost mechanical sequence, one that is depicted in Lively's account of Claudia falling in love with Tom. Frijda (1988) describes some results of an as yet unpublished questionnaire study of Rombouts that characterizes people's experience of falling in love as follows.

Falling in love first requires some degree of willingness. This may be because of loneliness, sexual need, conscious or unconscious dissatisfaction with one's current state, desire for variety, or the like. Next a particular person excites interest, more or less by accident, again for one of a number of reasons such as novelty, attractiveness, or even mere proximity. This person, the potential love object, then gives some response that suggests interest. It may be sharing a confidence. It may only be a meaningful glance. It may, as with Claudia, result from a rescue from a stranded truck. Then there is a lapse of time, which can be as short as half an hour, during which fantasies can build up. Then it needs scarcely more than a single confirmation, real or imagined, from the other – and one may be in love.

Averill and Boothroyd (1977) inquired whether falling in love in conformity with a romantic ideal of this kind was usual. They offered 85 subjects a brief newspaper account of a young man and young woman, initially strangers, boarding a train in San Francisco on Monday. These two saw each other from seats on either side of the aisle but did not speak until Wednesday. The man later said, "We did most of the talking with our eyes." On Thursday, when they got off the train in Omaha, they had plans to get married. Averill and Boothroyd also reminded their subjects of other accounts of romantic love in literature, such as Romeo and Juliet. About 40% of their subjects said that their most intense experience of love definitely did conform to this romantic ideal, whereas about 40% said it did definitely did not.

There is, of course, a question as to how far this sequence of curious events is itself a cultural construction. Certainly it is described in literature time and again. Not just by Lively in 1987, but by Shakespeare in *Romeo and Juliet* and by Tolstoy in the novel with which I started this book. Anna and Vronsky follow this same sequence. First came a chance meeting at the station of two people who were in some way dissatisfied with their lives, and rather little is said. Then, after an interval of a day or so, Vronsky happened to visit the house where she was staying with her brother and his family. Anna, going from one upper room to another, glanced down from the top of the great staircase and noticed Vronsky in the hall. By chance, at that moment, he glanced up, their eyes met, and Vronsky showed some embarrassment. Some further days passed, during which fantasies could build. Then another meeting at the ball, where they danced and fell in love.

Averill (1985) argues persuasively that falling in love is indeed a cultural construction: Though the newspaper report of the two people falling in love on the train from San Francisco to Omaha was unusual, its close similarity to the romantic ideal made it newsworthy. The sequence of falling in love may even be quite modern – one commentator discussed by Averill dates it from 1274, when Dante fell in love with Beatrice. People, it seems, drawing on the images of love from our culture, invest their own experience with these, and may do so in a way that is both creative and exciting.

Here are some autobiographical accounts from ordinary people:

Humphries (1988) arranged interviews with some 60 elderly people about their experiences of sex in the years between 1900 and 1950. Their experience is largely untouched, I think by academic theories, but not of course untouched by the folk theories of culture. These interviews indicate that though people quite often described themselves as being in love, the sequence described by Rombouts was not salient in their descriptions – though this does not mean that it had been absent. The states of being in love, however, and of having a sexual relationship were vividly remembered. Being in love was very often seen as a passion, with strong involuntary components. A woman factory worker, for instance, talked about her first boyfriend in the 1930s, when she was 19 years old:

> We went steady for some time before anything like sex was mentioned. . . . Then one summer evening we were strolling through some fields, and decided to sit down. We kissed passionately and spoke of our love for each other. . . . It was my first experience of sex although he withdrew just before the climax. . . . I found I quite enjoyed it, and from that time on it happened many times. . . . I can't really say which of us was the keenest. I think we were equal. It was a feeling we couldn't control once we were close to each other. (Humphries, 1988, pp. 26–27)

Then, from another woman: "I became infatuated by that time and then of course, the inevitable happened" (p. 71).

In whatever way falling in love occurs, the state of being in love is, in our society, the very paradigm of happiness: As Claudia says in *Moon Tiger*, it was the one moment in her life when she felt more happy than ever before or after. It may be partly founded on fantasy, but at the same time it connects us more closely than any other adult experience with the reality of another adult person.

As Averill argues, being in love involves not just a sudden onset. The full syndrome also includes physiological arousal, a continuation of the fantasy elements in idealization of the other with a corresponding altruism, and then commitment, as for instance, in marriage. The element of commitment, of course, may become problematic. Like the other plans described in this book, this mutual plan is embarked on with only limited knowledge of the future, and given the brief exposure to the other person specified by the idea of romantic love, also with very little knowledge of that person. As with some other fantasies, projections onto the other may clash with actuality, or even just evaporate, leaving only a sad pool of disappointment or disdain. The sequence that triggers being in love and its fantasy elements can even precipitate the state with most unsuitable people.[18] However celebrated, however mythologized, this it is not a sequence that everyone wants to become involved with.[19]

The state remains, however, as one of the most valued in our culture. As we know, the fantasy may carry the participants through the delights of a sexual encounter with the kind of intensity described by Sappho, extending the self so that one is part of another described by Donne, and the delight of opening into the kind of intimacy with another person described by Lively. Such passions may enable the fantasy to be replaced by finding out who this other person actually is: coming to love that person in the sense of being committed to him or her.

Love and attachment

On what, then, is this powerful fantasy founded? The answer I think was provided by Darwin. I do not know whether anyone before Darwin might have had this idea, or who other than Darwin, with his conception of the persistence of habits from previous generations and from childhood, could have had it before. In his 1872 book on emotions, he wrote the following: "We long to clasp in our arms those whom we tenderly love. We probably owe this desire to inherited habit, in association with the nursing and tending of our children, and with mutual caresses of lovers" (p. 213).

Darwin is saying that the expression of love by caresses is derived from the attachment and nursing of babies by their mothers. He could have afforded, I think, to have been a little clearer here. It would be completely consistent with what he says elsewhere in the book to have said more explicitly that the caresses of adult sexuality derive probably from our experience as infants of clasping our mothers and being caressed by them. But perhaps that thought seemed a bit strong. The idea that adult sexuality is founded on infant sexuality was, of course, not too strong for Freud,[20] but the real clarification comes from the work of Bowlby (e.g., 1969) and Ainsworth (e.g., 1967) on attachment.

The characteristics of attachment. Ainsworth observed that children had a special set of emotional reactions to their mother. She described patterns of attachment behavior in infants in Uganda. With their mothers they behaved quite distinctively and differently from the ways in which they acted with other people. The distinctive behavior patterns were:

1. Differential crying (i.e., with mother as compared with others)
2. Differential smiling
3. Differential vocalization
4. Crying when the mother leaves
5. Following
6. Visual motor orientation
7. Greeting through smiling, crowing, and general excitement
8. Lifting arms in greeting
9. Clapping hands in greeting
10. Scrambling over the mother
11. Burying the face in the mother's lap
12. Approach through locomotion
13. Embracing, hugging, kissing (not seen in Ugandan infants but observed frequently by infants in Western societies)
14. Exploration away from the mother as a secure base
15. Flight to the mother as a haven of safety
16. Clinging

Not all of these are unambiguously emotional, particularly items 5, 6, and 12, but in general Ainsworth describes the structure of a complex of emotional interaction of one person with another – an interaction characterized by what Bowlby called attachment. The emotion mode involved is that of happiness in the presence of the attachment figure, the feeling of safety when that person is present, sadness and anxiety when that person departs.

The proposal Johnson-Laird and I have made (see Table 5) is that a development of the attachment pattern forms the basis for the adult emotion of being in love. The hypothesis is that we need only read down Ainsworth's list of 16 types of attachment behavior, substituting the term lover for mother, and we have a very fair description of someone in love. The fantasy of being in love, then, is the fantasy of the ideal attachment partner, with whom one could be forever safe and happy, just as one could when an infant with an affectionate and attentive parent.

Recently, Hazan and Shaver (1987) have conceptualized romantic love as attachment, and found three major styles of adult love, based on Bowlby's (1969, 1973, 1980) styles of attachment in infancy: secure, avoidant, and anxious/ambivalent. In questionnaire studies it was found that the relative prevalence of these three styles in adulthood is similar to their prevalence in infancy. Also, people's beliefs about love and about the trustworthiness of love partners were related to these styles of attachment. The adult styles were related to what respondents could remember of their relationships with parents. This research therefore indicates that adult love relationships may be due at least in part to the style developed in infancy in relation to parents.

Sexual love is not just the basis for fantasies. It is not just a repetition: It is the basis for adult sexuality, of the joy of each with the other. Sex is not a sensation – according to attachment theory it is a re-creation and extension of loving and being loved that we have experienced as children. Research on resonances with infancy and with our capacity as a mammalian species to become attached to another does not indicate that infant attachment is a straitjacket. It is a foundation that can be built upon.[21]

Role change justified by falling in love. There is a temptation to think of happiness just as an experience or being in love just as a feeling. To do so would neglect the implications that these states have for relationships that are comparable to the role changes of anger discussed in Chapter 4. As well as being an experience, as well as being a passion, being in love is a kind of role, often a transitional one, that enables a person to do things that are out of the ordinary.

The events with which I started this book are like this. Anna Karenina, a respectable wife, separates from her husband. Tolstoy shows how being in love has an interpersonal value that is similar to the one Averill (1982) describes for anger. Love feels very different from anger, but because it is accepted as a passion, as Averill (1985, 1990) explains, it too can function to readjust role relationships that would otherwise be immutable.

Just as anger feels involuntary, so too does falling in love. Anna was open to the attractions of a dashing cavalry officer. This occurred partly, as Tolstoy tells us, because her commitment to Karenin was not wholehearted. She had, consciously or otherwise, that willingness that is needed for falling in love to occur. Then she was enabled to break her commitment to a marriage she had found suffocating. We know too that the price society exacts can be very high. Anna was separated from her child, incurred the obloquy of her former friends, and lost the support of her previous life. Finally, her lack of any acceptable connection with the community of which she had been part contributed to her suicide.

Anna was an aristocrat, shielded against some of the consequences of her actions, particularly financial ones. But the seriousness with which society can view sexuality, particularly women's sexuality, is also glimpsed from the story of Dora (discussed in Chapter 7), who failed to achieve a sustainable role in her relationship with Herr K, as well as in some of the poignant stories of Humphries's book (1988).

For instance, Humphries tells how, in 1930, Ada, from a mining village in the north of England, became pregnant the first time she made love. A marriage was quickly arranged by her parents. Her bridegroom, a young sailor from the neighboring village, did not turn up at the wedding. He had fled to sea. From shame, Ada was turned out of her parents' home to have her baby in a workhouse. In the end, Ada's mother brought up her child as if he were her own son, and Ada was sent to London to work as a servant. Ada, now an elderly woman, wants to tell her son the truth, but thinks it unlikely that she will. "I sent him five pounds for his birthday present and he returns it to me with a note saying 'Spend it on yourself, Sis, you can't afford it,' and it upsets me quite a bit" (p. 16).

Women in particular suffered social destruction in the cause of sexual happiness. Becoming pregnant outside marriage could mean being ostracized if one were upper or middle class, being sent to a workhouse or mental hospital if one were poor. Sex, though enjoyable, was fraught with guilt and with realistic anxiety. Nowadays, perhaps, consequences are different, though often still severe. It needs to be something like an involuntary passion that allows people to brave rupturing their ordinary roles in the community when such punitive consequences are likely.

Nonetheless, and despite the often tragic stories of love, the Euro-American cultural construction of love has its purposes, and its successes. Though unhappiness in marriage is common, continuing commitment in marriage and a relatively happy relationship are commoner. So, for instance, in intensive interviews with husbands and wives of 450 London families with children drawn from 7,000 families as representative of the total population, 81% had marriages rated on the Maudsley Marital Rating Scale (Quinton, Rutter & Rowlands, 1977) as 1, 2, or 3 on the scale's 6 points. Point 1 indicates mutual affection and concern, with no significant tensions or difficulties; 2 means positive and satisfying with some short-lasting tensions; and 3 indicates some concern, though less than for point 2, or longer lasting tensions and difficulties. Lower points on the scale indicate progressively less concern, more open disruption and hostility, quarreling, intractable conflict, indifference, and dislike (Jenkins, 1987).

Consider the problem: How can a man or woman, unable to foresee the future, choose a mate and make a commitment that enables a sustaining relationship for both participants and an affectionate environment for bringing up children?

Emotions prompt commitment to plans or changes of plans. Falling in love is no exception. Becoming married is one of the most momentous mutual plans into which most of us enter. Hence it is appropriate for the emotion that begins it to be elaborated by cultural images and celebrated in song and narrative. The state shows vividly how emotions are not merely biological events. They are not, for instance, like sneezes. There is a biological basis, as I have discussed, but with being in love, as with other emotions, biology is just one element in an elaborate cultural theory. Within such a theory there is every opportunity for creativity and elaboration. Thus can an emotion become not just an interruption, not just a transition, but one of our highest accomplishments.

I argued in Chapter 3 that emotions function when rational solutions are unavailable. Falling in love certainly fits this model. Would it be possible to be more rational about choosing spouses? We could compare the Western folk theory of falling in love with a procedure aimed at increasing rationality, and here I draw on a description given to me by a Pakistani friend when he was about to get married. His parents, over a period of years, thought very carefully about women they knew among a circle of acquaintances and more distant relations such as second cousins. They had his best interests at heart, he said, and they knew him well, perhaps better than he knew himself. He is a person with intellectual interests who was educated and working in the West, and this was something that his parents considered strongly. Among the people they considered were women who had also had a Western education. At the same time parents of prospective brides were undertaking similar considerations. When a likely match was found, then the two sets of parents would discuss the matter, perhaps at considerable length. Then, if a match seemed possible, a brief meeting between the two prospective spouses would be arranged, not for them to get to know each other, but in order that either might apply a veto. This procedure, then, increases the possibility of couples having the same cultural assumptions and for their personalities to be somewhat compatible. Then, after the marriage, my friend explained, spouses would expect to come gradually to love each other.

In the West, it seems, not all but some of us prefer the alternative of falling in love as an initial step, even with a person whose characteristics are largely unknown.

How might one become happy?

To return to happiness more generally: A striking contribution to its understanding was the project of Joanna Field (1934/1952) to study herself in order to find out what made her happy.[22] She had a psychology degree and had worked as an industrial psychologist. She realized that her life was not really as she wanted it to be, and decided "to pick out those moments in daily life which had been particularly happy, and try and record them in words," then: "to go over these records in order to see whether [she] could discover any rules about the conditions in which happiness occurred" (p. 13).

A life of one's own

Joanna Field decided that in her project she needed, like Descartes, to start by doubting everything. She discovered herself to be a different creature than she had imagined. The nature of her project was gradually transformed as she pursued it, though still maintaining its central purpose of discovering what happiness was.

Multiple goals. At the start of Joanna Field's project it had gradually begun to occur to her that her life was not as she wanted it to be. She could remember herself going about "in a half dream state, sometimes discontented but never trying to find out why, vaguely 'making the best of things'" (p. 21). She decided to formulate a plan, to gather facts, as in an experiment: "It was in December 1926, and I expected that after a few weeks or months I would be able to say 'these are the facts of my life, now I'm going to do something about it'" (p. 36). She started by making lists of her goals. They included wanting to achieve something, to be good at her job, to be popular, not to let people down. She soon saw this task was not easy, as "whichever of these aims might be the most important to work for I would not achieve it; for my life was determined, not by any one of them, but by a planless mixture of them all" (p. 26).

Here, then, is a plain statement of the dilemma with which Chapter 1 of this book is concerned. How are we to manage our multiple goals? Joanna Field was uncertain of what guide there might be. She thought that neither books nor her own powers of deduction were likely to be helpful. Not only did she see a gap between what could be learned from books and the actualities of life, but she felt uncertain of her ability to apply knowledge to the problem. This is what prompted her to try to find out about her own life by observation and experiment. "I thought the best way to begin was to keep a diary, noting in it every day when I had been particularly happy. . . if it should turn out that happiness did not matter I should have a chance of finding out what was more important" (p.28).

The result horrified her. She discovered in the diary for one day that her main concern in the morning had been about whether she would be able to get her hair cut before going to work – she managed it and then found that events in the day, some of which included people's reactions to her haircut, seemed equally banal. She felt elated that all had gone well at lunch with F, leaving thinking what an intriguing person she was . . . in the evening she went home and sorted out photos that looked good of herself. She said this observation nearly made her give up the whole enterprise! She accepted the idea that it is important to be unselfish, now here was her observation of herself caught in vanity and self-absorption.

To start with the only happiness she recorded was of things like someone playing the piano, watching the water splashing in the bath, a sudden burst of laughter, or at the zoo finding pleasure in seeing the animals. One day she records: "Exulted in my body and clothes and red skirt, and freedom to do as I choose on Sunday morning" (p. 40).

The project became more rather than less perplexing. She felt disappointed that there were no fixed facts, rather there was a horizon that kept receding. She persevered. She recorded other emotions as well as happiness. Found herself irritated, frustrated, envious. About six months after starting the diary she says many new experiences began to occur, some of them physical, which brought her a new kind of happiness.[23] So: "D's touch soothed me, giving peace throughout my body. . . . I am happy being immersed" (p. 48). They marry and go to the United States. There are few entries until the following year. A year later, still she thinks in her diary about how absurd it is to consider having children because she is so undomestic. All in all the experiment had not brought her as much as she had thought. So next she tried lists of things she liked and things she hated.

After that she decided to study in more detail the moments in which she felt happy, and discovered that expressing these in writing was sometimes like putting "fuel on glowing embers, making flames leap up, and throw light on the surrounding gloom" (p. 69). She also discovered she could make mental gestures of thinking herself into something she was perceiving, as if feeling out into the world. Coming back from America after two years away, she sat on the train, feeling no great emotion in homecoming.

> Then something happened. Perhaps I remembered . . . to feel out into the landscape. I do not remember the precise gesture. But suddenly [the landscape] aroused such a deep resonance in me that I sat, as if meeting a lover, aglow with an almost unbearable delight. (p. 77)[24]

But still her purposes eluded her. She decided at last to turn to books on mental training, which recommended concentration on major aims, but she had still not decided what those were. So she took to keeping a diary record of wants. It brought her no further.

The problem was the very one that I have claimed our emotions help us solve: Her goals were many, and some were contradictory.

> I wanted a great many friends, but had often refused invitations because I hated to feel the beautiful free space of an empty day . . . broken into by social obligations. I had thought I wanted to be a unique individual, but had been filled with shame when anyone disagreed with me. . . . I wanted to be importantly useful in the world, but avoided all opportunities for responsibility. (p. 85)

As I have discussed: One way of organizing such disparate goals is to form a hierarchy. Indeed, this is what Joanna Field tried. Perhaps many of us try it. She had attempted to use her will, making resolutions to impose order by promoting some goals and making others subservient. She found as many of us do that goals can have a life of their own, that they are not so easily organized in this way, that good resolutions often do not count for much. Not only that, but even being methodical did not make it possible to know which goal was the most important to her because this depended so much on mood.

Discovery of inner purpose. At last came a moment when her project changed. Walking by the Thames it came to her what her purpose was: She wanted knowledge of the mind, but not just knowledge. She wrote: "Knowing is no good unless you feel the urgency of the thing. Maybe this is love" (p. 86). Her project ceased being about trying to find out facts so that preconceived purposes could be achieved. It became the gradual discovery of a purpose she did not yet know and an understanding of her own mind.

Now, although she felt she had achieved some insights, and knew something about occasional moments of delight that she experienced, she could not always control these.

> Often when I felt certain I had discovered the little mental act which produced the change I walked on air, exulting that I had found the key to my garden of delight. . . . But most often when I came again the place seemed different, the door overgrown with thorns and my key stuck in the lock. (p. 96)

Two different kinds of attention and thinking. Little by little Joanna Field discovered more about herself. She found she had two kinds of attention. One was narrow and related to ordinary purposes. It noticed just things that related to those purposes. The other was wide and seemingly purposeless. It could enable the sense of going out from the self. She described an example looking at a Cezanne painting: just becoming absorbed in it. It was a type of attention that was not easy to accomplish without busy concerns interfering, but when she did, it brought delight to what she was seeing or doing.

She also discovered two kinds of thinking. One was the kind that we are usually aware of in ourselves, but the other, which she had found at first by just writing down whatever came to her, was of automatic thoughts hovering on the brink of awareness.

Blind thoughts. Joanna Field found that thoughts of the automatic kind were often the subject of her daily preoccupations:

> Oughtn't we ask those people in for tea? That's best, say "Do you ever have time for a cup of tea? Will you come in any day?" We are free all the week, let them choose, will the maid answer the door? will she be too busy? what shall we give them? go into town and buy a cake? will they expect it? can't afford these extras but bread and jam won't do, what does one give people for tea . . . why not something a little unusual, cress sandwiches? but it's too late for cress. (p. 115)

Here is an anxious little train of thought about approaching someone unfamiliar, who has much more money than she has. One cannot help admiring this. Virginia Woolf scarcely did better.[25] But to Joanna Field it was distressing. Not only did such thoughts occupy her frequently, distracting her from what she was doing, but they were completely self-absorbed. She called them blind thoughts because they seemed to proceed in a direction of their own and could contradict each other without any difficulty.

She identified the blind thought patterns with those that Piaget (e.g., 1926) had observed in children. Adults are supposed to have developed beyond these. Now here were these thoughts living on in her adult mind, leaving behind a trail of worries, upsets, bad moods. Because she was barely aware of them before her project, they had remained unknown. Because they were unknown they could not be recognized as the culprits of her moods. The blind thoughts were uninfluenced by external comparisons because many of them remained vague, but once written down they could be seen to be absurd. She caught specimens that she called "butterflies" and decided that the success of her whole enterprise hung on her ability to emerge from the influence of these thought patterns. For every act based on deliberation, she thought there must be dozens that grew out of this self-centered irrational reverie. This chattering mind, she discovered, was a mean mind. It recognized only itself. It set all sorts of impossible standards, and if these were not achieved it reviled her, although it did not tell her it was doing this. When the thoughts could be captured on paper they were seen to be ridiculous.

Escape from blind thoughts. The second part of Joanna Field's book is the story of her escape from these thoughts, which I shall not describe in detail. It included discoveries that the anxieties that drove the automatic thought chatter were based on pervasive fears. Her escape involved discovering the existence within herself of a more secure intuitive basis for living, very different from the method of being swept about by her chattering blind thoughts. She says she could only think of this basis as a kind of wisdom that shaped her life. Following this she discovered that she could take delight not just in things, but in people. Her fear of them, of being taken over, of being criticized, not liked, of losing her "self" began to diminish. Then: "Just as I had, when first beginning to examine my experience, found most of my delights in natural things, I was now finding that I chiefly reckoned each day's catch of happiness in terms of my relationships with others" (p. 193).

It was not, therefore, the quest for her happiness that was self-centered. Rather, she discovered that to be happy was to be able to interact with others with the background volume of self-centered anxieties having been turned down. In the blind thoughts she found that one indulges in a kind of thinking that by its nature denies other people.

Interpersonal influences. Happiness has effects on others. Joanna Field gives an example of her interaction with her baby:

> When trying to persuade my baby to go to sleep I would often wait beside him, absolutely motionless, but my own heart filled with peace. Once I let impatience and annoyance dominate my mind, he would become restless again. This may have been sheer accident of, course, but it happened so many times. (pp. 194–195)

Keeping a diary had allowed her to discover that happiness came when she was most widely aware, and that her anxious blind thoughts were narrowing thoughts. Her happiness was not just a personal matter, but an interpersonal one.

Telling one's own story

Joanna Field succeeded where Dora in Freud's case history had not. She succeeded in telling her own story, filling the gaps in her narrative that had been left because much of what affected her went on just outside her awareness. She sensed that the gaps could be filled and the inconsistencies resolved by paying attention to her emotions, particularly to happiness and to the pervasive fears that militated against other purposes and thereby destroyed the possibility of happiness. She arrived at a model of herself that was her own, that she constructed for herself. This was not the story of herself she had been told or that she had expected. The rules and axioms that she had taken over from parents and education enabled her to survive, but not really to live her own life.

Her method and her solution are hers, not a formula or a solution for everyone. One could say that each person has to discover her or his own set of goals and principles of life and ways of coming to terms with them.

One of the striking things about Joanna Field's book is the clear realization that there is a problem: How could we know which of the many goals and principles or what combination of them would form the basis for a structure that was one's own. Presumably the source of all or most of our goals is outside voluntary control, coming from genetic sources and from childhood. Yet, as adults, we become responsible for our own lives, and conscious resolutions about arranging these goals seem not always to help.

Tragic drama in classical Greece is founded on the realization that as mortals we act without much foreknowledge of the effects of our actions in the outer world, but must take responsibility for them. Joanna Field's book, though written in a very different key, confronts a similar recognition of this problematic core of our life: In our inner world our goals are not necessarily chosen by us, but we come to take responsibility for them.

Joanna Field did not at first understand her emotions, but she had the sense that they would point to something important for her. Her explorations involved giving up some of the calculation of everyday goals and plans, to reach a state that felt goal-less, but nonetheless to be engaged in what she was doing. Now her life had a sense of purpose with which she could identify and in which she felt confidence because it was close to her own understanding of her self. She was able to give up some of the distractions of pervasive fears and start to be happy.

9. Putting emotions into words

It is perfectly true, as philosophers say, that life must be
understood backwards. But they forget the other proposition, that it must be lived forwards.

Søren Kierkegaard
Journals, 1843

Communication and change

Darwin (1872) treated expression as a physiological and behavioral matter. But emotions can be expressed in ways that are more complex than
gestures, in ways that are distinctively human. Darwin said that "the
power of communication . . . by means of language has been of para-
mount importance in the development of man; and the force of language
is much aided by the expressive movements of the face and body" (1872,
p. 354). Because emotions are largely involuntary he doubted whether
the intention of an emotion was ever to communicate. Now that the
concept of communication has broadened, and it is no longer necessary
to see emotions as vestiges, it seems appropriate, as Oatley and Johnson-Laird (1987) propose, to regard them as communicative. Emotions
communicate to ourselves to make ready for appropriate action. They
communicate to others indicating a readiness for certain kinds of action
or interaction.

Putting things into consciousness

One of the effects of an emotion is to make a problem conscious.[1] Perhaps the most salient property of intense emotions is that as well as
producing readiness for action they are preoccupying. They make con-

383

scious any available characteristics of the evaluation that has occurred, directing our attention and holding it.

According to the communicative theory, emotions occur when our plans or goals are reevaluated. The problem is debated in an inward dialogue (deriving from its semantic part) and is experienced with emotional tone (the nonsemantic part). One may find oneself pleasantly preoccupied, as with thoughts of a person to whom one is sexually attracted, or unpleasantly, as in vengefulness or hatred.

If emotions occur when problems arise, we can ask how such problems are solved, or more generally about the nature of cognitive change. If we inhabit our mental schemata, then the question is how our schemata may change when emotions occur. I propose that schemata are prompted to change when they accommodate to something new, or when mistakes occur, just as scientific theories are prompted to change when new or contrary evidence is discovered. When, under the influence of an emotion, a new consideration becomes conscious, perhaps some unrealized effect of our actions, a conflict or a new goal, this implies that our previous schemata are incomplete or even obsolete. We are compelled to attend to such matters.

The compulsiveness of emotions and the ways in which some of them tend to constrain us to a small range of actions seem to indicate that they will interfere with problem solving. But different emotions have different effects on different tasks. It is likely that these effects are related to the urgency and priority of the goals associated with emotions and to the distribution of attention that emotions produce.

Oatley and Johnson-Laird (1987) have argued that emotions may have evolved because thinking takes too long to meet the exigencies of immediate practical problems. The constraining by emotions of readiness within a limited range in certain recognizable situations is an emergency response. But as well as the emergency response there is often a longer lasting conscious preoccupation with the problem that has occurred. In this chapter I consider its possible function in changing cognitive organization.

Disjunction between semantic and nonsemantic parts

The coming of human consciousness has allowed emotions to have effects that have not occurred previously in evolution. These are important now that we think of ourselves as voluntary and autonomous beings. When we act without being fully conscious of our intentions, emotions can function to provide clues that will help us infer what goals were relevant. It is for this reason that emotions are of such central interest in psychotherapy. But why should this be? On the face of it, emotions are simple: Something happens, an emotion is triggered by an evaluation of the event, actions are made ready, expressions occur. The person is also aware of the emotion and can speak about its semantic content.

The argument that I put in this final chapter is that puzzles occur when the basic part of an emotion is not matched by the semantic part.[2] Sometimes fears occur when we do not know what the danger might be. Perhaps an emotion occurs when we wish it did not. Perhaps the semantic part seems inadequate to the problem, or irrelevant, or inappropriate, as Dora's explanations of her feelings toward Herr K seemed inadequate to Freud. I will call such effects disjunction effects. Reflection or discussion of them may reveal something previously unrecognized, may prompt not just immediate actions but insights, changes in the inner world.

Three types of disjunction in emotions

An emotion sometimes occurs where the person concerned does not know what caused it or what to do about it.[3] I will consider three types of disjunction in which our emotions or their implications may seem puzzling, unclear, or inappropriate to us.

Disjunctions when goals are lost

Though emotions of loss are not the easiest to bear, they are not usually difficult to understand. They occur when a plan is interrupted, when a goal is lost and cannot be reinstated. When intense, such emotions engender despair. Though clinical depression is not itself an emotion but a complex that includes emotions, this state including its emotions can seem very puzzling. The way it drives people to suicide is a challenge to any functional view of emotions.

How do disjunctions occur with the emotions of loss? It is not just that these feelings are devastating, though they can be. Disjunctions occur because the nonsemantic part prompts inaction, when ultimately the person concerned must again act even without the goal that has been valued. Sometimes a person is prompted to appeal for rescue to those who are not able to restore what is lost.

George Eliot portrays such an emotion: in Chapter 20 of *Middlemarch.*
Dorothea on her honeymoon is in a handsome apartment in Rome.

> I am sorry to add that she was sobbing bitterly, with such abandon-
> ment to this relief of an oppressed heart as a woman . . . will
> sometimes allow herself when securely alone. . . . Yet Dorothea
> had no distinctly shapen grievance that she could state even to
> herself; and in the midst of her confused thought and passion, the
> mental act that was struggling forth into clearness was a self-accus-
> ing cry that her feeling of desolation was the fault of her own
> spiritual poverty (p. 224).

George Eliot explains: Dorothea had married the man of her choice.
She had not been naive enough to imagine marriage as some new state
of bliss, but had chiefly thought in terms of new duties to a man with a
mind greater than her own. Now the bridal life of this girl with a Puritan
upbringing was made more strange by the passing before her of the
sights of the city of Rome with its "ruins and basilicas, palaces and
collossi, set in the midst of a sordid present, where all that was living
and warm blooded seemed sunk in the deep degeneracy of a supersti-
tion divorced from reverence" (p. 225). George Eliot continues that if
Dorothea had been asked to state the cause, she could only have done so
in some such general words as these.

Here, then, is the phenomenon: Dorothea is desolate, but with no
clear idea why and no conception of what should be done. George
Eliot's sense is different from that of Dorothea. She thinks there is a
reason for the sadness in a realization of disappointment in Dorothea's
marriage. Part of her intention is to convey this to the reader. Perhaps,
George Eliot proposes, it is always like this when the reality replaces
what was imagined. But this does not seem adequate. Casaubon had not
changed – he was just as learned as before. Not only could he still
describe a theory, he could also provide the names of those who held it.
And no man would have been less likely to foster illusions about himself.

George Eliot ends her discussion of the phenomenon by suggesting
that the disappointment must have been because in courtship everything is provisional. The imperfect coherence of the facts that Casaubon
had related in their talks had seemed to Dorothea to be caused by the
broken nature of the time they spent together. She had assumed that the
fragments of learning fitted together: Soon she would accompany Casaubon to an exhilarating high place from which their relation to each

other could be seen. But now what was fresh to her was worn to him. When visiting the sights he commented on them with weariness: "Should you like to go to the Farnesina, Dorothea? It contains celebrated frescoes designed or painted by Raphael, which most persons think it worth while to visit" (p. 229). Dorothea always wanted to know what he cared about. This he seemed unable to say: Instead, he answered in a measured official tone, and nothing seemed to evince eagerness in himself. "There is hardly any contact more depressing to a young ardent creature," says George Eliot, "than that of a mind in which years full of knowledge seem to have issued in a blank absence of interest or sympathy" (p. 229).

At the same time, Casaubon's tenacity in hurrying off with his notebook to libraries did show an eagerness, which is usually taken as a sign of enthusiasm. All the same there was no high ground. Casaubon was lost "among small closets and winding stairs, and in an agitated dimness about the Cabeiri, or in an exposure of other mythologists' ill-considered parallels" (p. 229).

George Eliot conjectures that still all might not have been lost had Dorothea been "encouraged to pour forth her girlish and womanly feeling," but such approaches were met by Casaubon: "Pronouncing her, with unfailing propriety, to be of a most affectionate and truly feminine nature, indicating at the same time by politely reaching a chair for her that he regarded these manifestations as rather crude and startling" (p. 230).

To modern eyes the reasons why the affectionate and spirited Dorothea should feel disappointed in her marriage seem clear enough. Is it only our own sadness that may seem incomprehensible?

In Western society, for many people sadness, and its more brooding relative, depression, usually do pass. As I said in Chapter 6, conditions often change. Adjustments are made. Sadness even has in itself a potentially creative quality, provoking the kind of reflection that fairly drives a person to understanding and working through the causes of a grief. If resources are available, when a period of mourning has disconnected the person from the goal that was lost, building new goals can begin.

Disjunctions arising from conflicts of goals

In many ways, conflicts of goals can be yet harder to come to terms with than emotions of loss. Emotions of anxiety and fear may announce that something is wrong, but what it is may be thoroughly obscure.

Consider the problem faced by Joanna Field. Even when she discovered that her goals were many and contradictory, she still was unaware that her life was strongly affected by pervasive fears. Then, even when she found this, it was difficult to understand the causes of these fears. And even when she discovered a principle that could guide her life, she was able to describe it in only the vaguest terms, as an inner wisdom.

It is usually thought that the sense we have of ourselves is an unproblematic thing. But if Joanna Field's experience is at all common, we may experience something quite different. We have many different goals, triggered into activity by different situations. Some are evoked in contradiction to others, and some give rise to emotions that are not all easy to understand. We as "selves" have had little part in choosing the seemingly ill-assorted array of goals. Nevertheless, it becomes our task to find out about them. We must decide which to commit ourselves to, and how goals might fit together. The implications of our goals may only gradually become clear to us in the course of our life.

There seem to be two ways in which our emotions help in this. First, as Joanna Field discovered, by attending to our emotions we can become aware of some goals, adopted perhaps before explicit conscious reflection. Emotions of happiness may give clues to compatibilities among goals, whereas emotions of anxiety and annoyance may indicate incompatibilities.

Usually there is not complete chaos but underlying themes, perhaps because patterns of upbringing have for most of us had some consistency. Ryle (1982) argues that such themes typically will have organized our goals into rough hierarchy in which the top-level goals have pervasive implications. He calls these self-definition goals. They are built into the model of self, and are rules by which we define ourselves. Dorothea's most important goal that she was able to articulate was something like: "I want to feel passionately engaged in some great good work." Casaubon's, which he would have been unable to voice, was something like, "I must have unqualified admiration for my research which is so complete as to make all others' trivial." Joanna Field discovered hers by means of her project.

Therapeutic wisdom holds that self-definition goals, such as needs to be loved, admired, respected, appreciated, and so on, when applied over too wide a range of relationships, or pursued too insistently within any one relationship, can make for destructive self-absorption and be potent sources of distress. It is also part of this wisdom that such goals and plans are formulated early on, perhaps in relation to a parent. Ryle suggests that goals may be conditionally attached to situations and to outline plans: For instance, "If the other is giving me their full attention I am loved," or "If I work unremittingly I shall be admired," or "If I see sacrifices being made for me, then I know I am loved for myself."

One of the perplexing aspects of human mentality is that such goals need not be conscious. Indeed, they seldom are. Lives may be understood in such terms, but as Freud pointed out, the person is not necessarily able to tell his or her own story in terms of intentions. Ryle puts it that we often know a lot about the structure of lower level goals and their relation to our plans and actions, but we may have only the haziest sense of the upper parts of the goal hierarchy and only a vague conception of its overall structure.

Here, then, are two kinds of phenomenon. First, goals may be various and contradictory, impelling a person now one way, now another, depending on circumstances, and with no clear way of choosing which are most important. Sloman (1990) has said: "One of the tragedies of human life is that insistence [the urgency of an emotional impulse] is not consistently related to importance" (p. 3). Second, if there are themes or coherences among goals they may not be conscious. So emotions deriving from goal conflicts may occur when a circumstance makes a conflict significant, but their semantic content may only be on the edge of awareness or it may be incomprehensible.

Joanna Field found herself with both these problems. First she was confused by the diversity of her conscious goals. Then she discovered one set of goals that all seemed related by a theme, a fear of others, particularly of men and particularly of the criticism that they might make of her. It was this that provided the content of her blind automatic thoughts that determined, as she came to recognize, so many of her choices and feelings.

So it is not so much that we start with a top-level goal as occurs in a technical plan, and that subgoals are elaborated in relation to it as the plan is constructed. Rather, we may acquire goals in a piecemeal way, in different roles, at different times in life, without any necessary interconnections among them. In adulthood we may then find ourselves not consciously knowing about these goals and their interrelations, but confronted by their effects. From these effects, and particularly from the emotions that occur as the goals and plans are monitored, we can begin to build a more or less explicit model of our goal structure. In this model we might describe some higher level regularities that had perhaps been present in our interactions with others but had not been known explicitly to ourselves.

We experience emotions when reevaluations of goals and plans are made, even if the goals are not conscious. An implication of any mismatch is that something needs to be done, first to understand the cognitive structure and then perhaps to change it.

Disjunctions in anger

Both sadness and anxiety communicate primarily to ourselves. But often an emotion prompts us to communicate in some way with others and this too may not be completely understood. Here the paradigmatic emotion is anger.

When two people have a mutual plan, the copy that each holds needs constantly to be compared with that of the other so that when unexpected events occur their implications can be negotiated. This indeed is part of the process of repair postulated by Power's (1979) model of joint planning. Power's robots discuss all plans in terms of proposals, followed by checking and repair. In his microworld, copies of the joint plans are kept in close correspondence. People who are not robots, however, make inferences, and the result of this is that copies can be seriously discrepant.

Most typically anger occurs when one person, according to his or her own copy of the plan, perceives the other to have done something contrary to an agreed goal or to have left undone something that should have been done. For an explication we need only turn again to *Middlemarch*, for the continuation of Chapter 20, that began with Dorothea weeping alone in her apartment.

Dorothea had longed for access to the kind of knowledge that was not available to her as a woman in a provincial town. What was available was marriage. Her copy of the mutual plan of marriage therefore included the idea that having taken her place in companionship at her husband's side, she would be able to gain access to the wide vistas of learning from the high ground that he had already scaled. This ground would open to her view as she helped him with the preparation of his book for publication.

It was mention of publication, soon after Dorothea had been sobbing alone in her room in Rome, that provoked Dorothea and Casaubon's first angry quarrel. He had just announced that their wedding journey was nearing its close. He had made a little speech saying Rome was "one among several cities to which an extreme hyperbole has been applied – 'See Rome and die': but in your case I would propose an emendation and say, 'See Rome as a bride, and live thenceforth a happy wife'" (p. 231).

Dorothea said she hoped he was satisfied with his stay, and said she was looking forward to being able to be useful to him when they got home.

Then came the remark at which a discrepancy became clear: Dorothea asked when he would enlist her aid: "All those rows of volumes – will you not now do what you used to speak of? . . . and begin to write the book that will make your vast knowledge useful to the world? I will write from your dictation, or I will copy and extract what you tell me: I can be of no other use" (p. 232). George Eliot adds, rather archly one might think: "Dorothea in a most unaccountable, darkly feminine manner, ended with a slight sob and eyes full of tears" (p. 232).

George Eliot now uses words very similar to those of Joanna Field: "In Mr Casaubon's ear, Dorothea's voice gave loud emphatic iteration to those muffled suggestions of consciousness which it was possible to explain as mere fancy . . . confused murmurs which we try to call morbid" (p. 232). Casaubon's copy of the joint plan included the proposition that Dorothea would admiringly appreciate his "abundant pen scratches and amplitude of paper" (p. 232) and act as a bulwark against just the kind of scathing critical appraisal that he himself applied to the work of other scholars, and which he feared might be visited on his work if it were published. This bulwark was the more necessary since he had not seen a vista of his subject from any unifying high perspective. Now "this cruel outward accuser was there in the shape of a wife . . . [who] seemed to present herself as a spy watching everything with a malign power of inference" (232–233).

For the first time in their relationship Casaubon became angry. He delivered a speech, that he had often rehearsed mentally to try to silence his imaginary inner critics, to the effect that he knew "the times and seasons adapted to the different stages of a work which is not to be measured by the facile conjectures of ignorant onlookers" (p. 233).

This kind of event in which individual copies of a joint plan prove to be discrepant is recognizable to anyone who has been in a close relationship (cf. also the story of the honeymoon couple described by Laing, Phillipson & Lee, 1966, discussed in Chapter 4). The highly charged emotions that emerge when such discrepancies are revealed occur not just when any kind of plan is interrupted, but when joint plans that were intended to fulfill goals that are vital to our sense of self are nullified. What appears is not just a mistake, but a frightening annihilation of that sense of self that a relationship was meant to sustain.

There may be strong connections between plans and the way in which their goals are taken as defining the self. Because of such connections, junctures can be reached in which any discussion that might question that definition of self cannot occur. The temptation is to suppose that no repair is possible. The other is responsible for the disgraceful breach.

If one is able to open a discussion, the basic emotion mode of anger, with its sense that some transgression has occurred, can be compared with the semantic demand that the other fulfill his or her part of the plan in some specific way. Discrepancies in the two copies of the mutual plan may be compared and modifications made. This indeed is the frequent course of such discussions, as described by Averill's (1982) subjects (discussed in Chapter 4). When this occurs, the emotion has done its work of prompting an interpersonal repair. But, as we all know, further goals may be present to inhibit the expression of anger. It may be thought too dangerous or even too improper to be angry. It is then that disjunctive effects can occur. Dorothea was disappointed, but had been unable to talk about why. In part this was why she had come to be sobbing on her own. Casaubon's maneuver was more destructive. He withdrew into his habitual practice of narrow, pedantic scrupulosity – apparently unaware that he had any part to play other than having made a mistake in allowing anyone into the position of being able to observe his activities at close quarters.

For both Dorothea and Casaubon, disjunctions occurred. She felt disappointment, then a sad despair, not knowing how she had erred beyond her own spiritual poverty. He experienced anger at her question, also not knowing what he had done wrong besides having chosen to take a wife. For neither were emotions coupled closely to any semantic content that could be used to discuss the issue, let alone make a repair.

We might say that what they should have done is to speak to each other, perhaps speak angrily about expectations that had been dashed. But as we know, it is not as easy as that. People, instead, may labor to contain large discrepancies between basic emotion modes and the semantic discourse they utter to themselves and others.

George Eliot proposed that something of the fatefulness of human life is to be understood in terms of such discrepancies and how congruently or openly each person expresses emotions to the self and others. Casaubon is quite unable to express emotions openly or to give reasons for his emotions. Why was this so?

An answer, I think, is given by Joanna Field. Some of our goals remain unconscious, because the moment we are aware of them it becomes clear that they are ridiculous. The admirable quality of Joanna Field's story is that she had the courage to say this. For Casaubon, the equivalent would have been to say: "More than anything I want to become famous for all time by writing a book that will unlock the secrets of all mythologies. But I cannot bear anyone to see what I am doing, because they will see that I have not found the key. Maybe I shall be unable to find it. Perhaps there is no such key." Thoughts of this kind were recognized by Joanna Field as "absurd" as soon as she caught them. Perhaps Casaubon had too much invested in his work for such honesty. Thus are gaps in one's story created. He experienced his love for Dorothea as a very meager emotion, much overrated by poets. He experienced anger, but this experience too was attenuated and the nonverbal expressions of it were at variance with his verbal utterances. Mostly his emotions were incomprehensible to him: a disjunctive effect.

If emotions are communicated to ourselves and others, it seems we can inhibit this communication if we see it conflicting with other goals. But this cure may be worse than the disease. Emotions may need to be expressed for their significance to be recognized. Casaubon might have expressed his fear, but, as George Eliot put it: "His experience was of that pitiable kind which shrinks from pity, and fears most of all that it should be known" (p. 313). By having an additional goal of keeping our more important goals inexplicit, disjunctive effects are created and at the same time become difficult to understand. They cut us off from the potential significance of our emotions and from those other people who might matter to us or who might be able to assist the repairs.

Joining semantic and nonsemantic aspects

Disjunctive effects can occur when an emotion is aroused and some further goal prohibits its expression to ourselves or others. Clear examples are treated extensively by Freud. The effect of suppressing (or repressing) the expression or implications of an emotion may disconnect its nonsemantic parts from its semantic parts. In this way the phenomena that Freud described as displacements and dissociations occur. The person has unruly feelings that do not have comprehensible semantic content.

Semantic and basic parts of emotions in therapy

Dora, whose case is discussed in Chapter 7, bitterly reproached her father. She was preoccupied with demands that he must break off relations with the K family. She tried incessantly to convince Freud that this break was necessary. She felt angry with her father. She was disgusted with the K family and wanted somehow to get rid of them.

She was unaware of why she felt so violently. She experienced the nonsemantic part of her emotions, and some semantic content that she debated in an inward dialogue and expressed to Freud. He suggested further semantic ideas to her. These allowed her an outer view. Just as rationality in science requires a community of scientists who comment on others' work, so in personal life other people, friends, advisers, even therapists, can usefully comment on our ideas and actions from outside the circle of our own schemata.

Transference in the repair of disjunctions. Whereas in the theater or a novel people take part in drama not their own, in psychoanalytic therapy people recount stories that are their own but to someone who is not the person these stories properly concern. Such therapy is about emotions that are apparently displaced.[4]

Transference is the process of projecting emotions and actions inappropriately onto the therapist. It involves importing through the semipermeable membrane of the analytic relationship expectations that are not really appropriate to a relation with an adult person. They are derived from relationships elaborated outside that membrane, typically with parents. The argument is that in psychoanalytic therapy conflicts that were unresolved in earlier relationships, and the emotions associated with them, reemerge in relation to the therapist. They could not originally be spoken of directly. With the therapist there is a possibility of speaking so that the semantic content may become known. Psychoanalytic therapy works by the therapist and patient devoting themselves to understanding how these difficulties have led to symptoms and other inadvertencies. The language of symptoms is translated into semantically based speech that can become conscious. The argument is that in such speaking displacements and repressions will be recognized, conflicts resolved.

As Strachey (1934) has argued, an effective interpretation is one that allows the patient to experience the difference between the actual person of the therapist and the fantasy from the past in terms of which the therapist is being seen. In that moment the person's model of self in relation to this other can undergo change.

Working as a therapist on transference issues is difficult.[5] As Freud said in his postscript to Dora's case, "It is easy to learn how to interpret dreams, to extract from the patient's associations his unconscious thoughts and memories." Combating the transference is "by far the hardest part of the whole task" (1953/1905, p. 116). Perhaps the difficulty is that transferential acts and emotions are so much a part of our every relationship that to pay specific attention to aspects that seem to have been displaced and are not properly part of the current relationship requires skill and judgment. To do so successfully, the therapist must take part in the relationship, not just go through the motions. Simultaneously, she or he must develop understandings of the kind that are usually noticed only from outside relationships. In this way the therapist tries to understand what interpersonal roles she or he is being invited into.

There are many such role relationships, as a patient one might find oneself trying to seduce someone attractive, complain to someone who might do something, appeal to someone wise, confide in someone who will understand, confess to someone who can forgive. All these are, as it were, prompted by emotional needs. They are emotional effects on others of the kind that Lutz (1987) talked about and that were discussed in Chapter 4. The psychoanalytic hypothesis is that not only have the nonverbal aspects of these interpersonal effects become detached from any semantic consciousness, but that in early relationships we may have developed kinds of habitual readiness that can then be replayed in ways that need not have much to do with the person we are with. What is required of the therapist, then, is to take part in the relationship that develops, but not be taken in by these interpersonal emotional effects. The therapist's job is to supply some of the semantic content of what is going on.

Because this can only be done in the context of a relationship that develops, Freud began to recognize that therapy was not a craft, or a *techne*, like most of medicine, in which accurate knowledge allowed a skilled repair of a malfunctioning mechanism.[6] Instead, if neuroses are disorders of intention rather than malfunctions of mechanism, then a different approach is needed – a dialogue about intention. In such dialogues interpretations are suggestions. They are verbal communications about intentions and other semantic aspects of emotions that patients may experience as tallying with something real in them. If they do tally, they make sense of the interpersonal actions.

Direct and indirect speaking. Kierkegaard put it like this:[7]

> The maker of the communication has to present something to the attention of one who knows, that he may judge it, or to one who does not know that he may learn something. But no one bothers about the next consideration, that which makes communication dialectically so difficult, namely, that the recipient is an existing individual, and that this is essential. To stop a man on the street and stand still while talking to him, is not so difficult as to say something to a passerby in passing, without standing still and without delaying the other, without attempting to persuade him to go the same way, but giving him instead an impulse to go precisely his own way. (1846/1941, p. 247)

The possibility of addressing the other in this way seems to derive from love, however much it is transformed or sublimated. As Nagel (1979) has said, writing on the subject of sexual desire: "Desire is therefore not merely the perception of a pre-existing embodiment of the other, but ideally a contribution to his further embodiment which in turn enhances the original subject's sense of himself" (p. 48).

So how might one make communications of the kind that Kierkegaard recommends, that are capable of joining semantic content to some existing but incoherent nonsemantic sense, without trying to coerce, but contributing to that person's own sense of self?

Keats, in a letter of 1818, said, "Poetry should surprise by a fine excess and not by Singularity – it should strike the Reader as wording of his own highest thoughts, and appear almost a Remembrance" (Gittings, 1966, p. 46). Therapeutic interpretations need to have this same quality of being surprising yet familiar. When they do tally with a nonsemantic state in the patient they do strike him or her as being a wording, not perhaps of highest thoughts, but of important thoughts. They bring both a sense of recognition and of being recognized. As Keats said of his axioms of poetry, "You will see how far I am from their center" (Gittings, 1966, p.

46). We need not feel surprised that therapists, who are often lesser poets than Keats, only occasionally find the right words in the flow of therapy.

The therapist in psychoanalytic therapy both is and is not who the patient imagines. Freud was and was not Dora's father with whom she was angry and disappointed. It is this duality that provides the possibility, not quite attained in her case, of bringing together the nonsemantic and semantic parts of interpersonal emotions. If successful a therapist will enable the patient to feel an emotion such as fear or anger intensely – to realize that that emotion still has an influence in relationships quite other than the ones in which it was formed, and to recognize also how its semantic content is linked both to the earlier and the current relationship.

So, to Freud, Dora might have been able to say: "I hate you arranging everything for your own convenience just like my father. And I hate you making me a convenience. I trusted you – but you could only take advantage of me to write more of your wretched books and papers."[8]

Semantic and basic parts of emotions in art

One possibility for understanding emotions in which disjunctions have occurred is, therefore, the kind of situation in which a patient interacts with a therapist who is a surrogate for the person whom the emotions concern. There are difficulties with this kind of therapy, some of which were discussed in Chapter 7. Another and more widely available possibility, open to more people, is narrative art in which a reader or watcher becomes a surrogate, taking the part of a protagonist and experiencing his or her emotions as the story unfolds.[9] In the theater or in a novel, a person enters by identification into a plan that is not her or his own. Because participation is at one remove, as in a game, emotions may be experienced more freely than in real life. Their experience is not prohibited. This enables the possibility of clarification (*katharsis*) where disjunctions exist.

Art as expression of emotions. I wish to propose that art is a form of expression of emotions, and that it enables us to integrate the experience of the basic parts of emotions with semantic contents. I also claim that whereas the kind of truth at which science aims is that theories are improved by coming to correspond more closely with the empirical world,[10] art aims at another kind of truth in which the coherence of our inner theories is more important. An increase in coherence is comparable to that which Freud hinted at when he made his interpretations to Dora or that Joanna Field achieved in her project.

Cognitive science is a relatively new discipline (Gardner, 1985). One of its central procedures is simulation of theories and states of affairs in computer programs. A central procedure of art, too, is simulation that runs on our minds rather than on a computer. The main value of any simulation is in testing the internal consistency of its assumptions, enabling them to be explored and to be improved. Its correspondence with empirical data is important, but secondary, because if the consistency issues are not taken care of the simulation will not run at all.

Aristotle's theory of art as simulation (discussed in Chapter 2) makes it possible to gain some clarification (*katharsis*) of our emotions. Here I will discuss this further, and explore how art allows the phenomenological tone of emotions to occur with clarification of their meanings, so that disjunctions of basic and semantic parts of emotions can be repaired.

I begin my argument with a proposal by Collingwood (1938) that art, properly so called, is the imaginative expression of emotions in a variety of languages. Collingwood was apparently not aware that George Eliot had proposed exactly this idea 70 years previously, in her essay "Form in Art" (1868):

> My concern is here chiefly with poetry which I take in its wider sense as including all literary production of which it is the prerogative & not the reproach that the choice & sequence of images & ideas – that is, of relations & groups of relations – are more or less not only determined by emotion but intended to express it. (Pinney, 1963, p. 434)

In terms of Oatley and Johnson-Laird's theory, we can translate George Eliot's and Collingwood's idea by saying that poetry, or art more generally, is an imaginative expression of the semantic part of an emotion.

Collingwood is rather sweeping in his arguments: Art is, after all, many things, just as science is many things, not capable of being defined exhaustively in a programmatic way. But I think we can regard his proposal about a central prototypical core of art as important, just as philosophers of science have made important proposals about a central core of science that demarcates it from other procedures. Art proper, according to Collingwood, is not representation, not a set of techniques for arousing emotion, not magic, but the expression of an emotion.[11]

Emotions impinge on consciousness and we give off involuntary signs of them in the ways that Darwin described. Adapting Collingwood's argument to the proposal of this book: In many cases we are unable to express emotions semantically to others, in verbal language, for instance. We may find ourselves feeling something but having thoughts that are inarticulate, disjunctive with our feelings. We may experience a disturbance, but be unaware of its meaning. The literary artist is someone who works to express emotions in language with explicit semantic meaning.[12]

This does not mean that a poet would say, "I feel angry." That is to categorize an emotion, not to express it in its individuality. Artistic expression, continues Collingwood, is a creative act; indeed it is *the* fundamental creative act. To create means to make something in a non-technical way, without a predefined goal. Art means making something not from a plan that has already been arranged, practiced, and refined to produce a predictable result.

According to the communicative theory, emotions occur as our goals and plans are being monitored, at junctures when stored actions (i.e., instincts, habits, and techniques) are no longer adequate. Adapting Collingwood's idea of creativity to this theory, we arrive at the following proposal.

EMOTIONS AND CREATIVITY. Emotions occur at junctures where preformed plans and expectations have not worked. If, at such a point, a new piece of action can be made from available resources and skills, we make the necessary modification, carry on with the plan, and tend to experience the juncture joyfully. If, on the other hand, a problem has arisen that cannot be solved with current resources, we experience the juncture as dysphoric. In either case the occasion is one that fairly demands a creative act, which makes sense of what has happened and proposes what is to be done. The artist, then, is someone who can express the semantic aspects of our emotions creatively, in some chosen language, in such a way that sense can be made of emotional experiences.

In dramatic and literary art, we need representations of actions just as scientists need theories, which are themselves representations.[13] In theatrical art we need representations to identify which kinds of actions are at issue, settings in which they are recognizable, and the bases on which outcomes of actions might be consistent with the actions. This does not mean that artistic representations are necessarily parts of a technique of arousing emotions, as Collingwood has claimed. Cognitive science has given us a broader understanding of representation as simulation. My proposal derives from this cognitive approach, that at the theater or when reading an audience or readership runs the simulation offered by the author on their own minds.

Art and truth. Two issues now come into focus concerning theatrical and literary art. The first is how truthful a simulation needs to be to events in the real world. A simulation may be more or less representative of the conditions of human life as it is experienced by different groups of people. This is equivalent to the question of correspondence of theory with evidence in natural science. If a representation of an action or a way of life does not correspond to anything recognizable, or if it strikes false notes, then it will either not be accepted by any public, or it will be criticized perhaps as incompetent, perhaps as tendentious, perhaps as inauthentic. Only if a representation corresponds to people's experience or to the possible will it be able to work as art.

The second issue depends on the first. It concerns self-consistency. It is the question of how, at the junctures of a plot, and the moments of moral decision that confront the characters, do emotions that are aroused in the audience allow clarification, *katharsis*. According to the theory proposed here, they do so because their basic parts can be brought into relation with the semantic parts and judged as to their consistency with each other.

Aristotle said that the important vehicle for transmitting emotions is the plot or story. In other words, if we experience basic emotions in the theater or when reading a novel, this has occurred by a communication that is semantic. In cognitive terms a plot is typically a plan of one or more characters. A plan meets some vicissitude, perhaps a reversal of the fortunes of the protagonist. Communication of emotions to a spectator or reader occurs at such a juncture, because a plot allows a spectator or reader to identify with a character. But then it is our involvement in the plans of the plot that causes our own emotions. Such emotions are not primarily reactions to the nonverbal communications of the actors.

VERSTEHEN IN THE THEATER. The communication that occurs in the theater, or when reading, requires an act of *Verstehen* (understanding reached by imaginatively entering into the life of the character). The plan becomes the spectator's or reader's own in that simulated situation. As this induced plan meets the conclusion, *telos*, toward which the plot steers it, emotions occur to the spectator or reader. A member of the audience at the theater, a listener to poetry, or in our time someone watching a film or reading a novel may bring the semantic effects of action together with the basic emotions that running the simulated plot may have induced. In this way he or she may achieve a *katharsis*, not a purification or a purgation, but a clarification, an increase in self-consistency.

The reason why simulation is closely associated with art is not that it beckons us toward untruth. It functions like the laboratory in science. The laboratory is not the real world. It allows principles of causation to be explored better than in the real world and only later applied outside the laboratory. Psychoanalysis is not the real world. A therapist comes to represent certain kinds of other people in the transference and the patient acts toward her or him in ways that allow the different components of emotions to be reflected upon and integrated. Principles derived from this may then be applied in other relationships. The theater is not the real world. Members of the audience identify with a protagonist, and clarify the significance of emotions and actions. Because of the human and cultural universality of many of the dilemmas of our existence, emotional implications can become our own in the actions of a protagonist, and may generalize beyond the theater.

CATHARSIS. Scheff (1979) proposed a theory that takes up the issue of how drama can be therapeutic. His theory is based on the idea that emotions can in some way be stored, and that as such they can have pathogenic effects. This idea runs counter to all cognitive theories of emotion, in which the postulate would be that circumstances and goals can be remembered and reinterpreted, with emotions not being stored, but occurring when memories are recalled and interpretations are generated. In this case the metaphor of therapy as discharge of stored emotions used by Scheff is inappropriate.

Scheff has proposed that the distance between, as it were, oneself and one's emotions that is created deliberately both in therapy and art is essential to understanding. We may overdistance ourselves from what happens by suppressing emotions and minimizing the importance of our goals, or else underdistance ourselves and be overwhelmed by the distress of traumas that can befall us. Typically these latter kinds of underdistanced traumas can create knots of rigid and unresponsive patterns, formed around an unresolved event – just as Freud argued in his earliest theory of neurosis. But, as Scheff (1979) says:

> When we cry over the fate of Romeo and Juliet, we are reliving our own personal experiences of overwhelming loss, but under new

and less severe conditions. The experience of vicarious loss in a properly designed drama is sufficiently distressful to reawaken the old distress. It is also sufficiently vicarious, however, so that the emotion does not feel overwhelming. (p. 13)

Scheff uses the idea of catharsis as the core concept in this process. It involves re-experiencing an emotion in a form that is not too overwhelming, but sufficiently strong for it to be experienced as an emotion, and at the same time to reevaluate it.[14]

Psychotherapy, ritual, and drama, argues Scheff, are means whereby we may create an aesthetic distance, as he calls it, from events that have been overwhelmingly painful. As I would put it, at that distance there is a good possibility that a basic emotion may both occur and be made sense of semantically. This is an important reason for the cultural creation of forms of ritual, drama, and psychotherapy – they are capable of creating the distance whereby we may both experience our emotions and understand them.[15]

Literary art along with therapy and societal rituals may allow a person to approach inward truths by experiencing an emotional significance having to do with self-knowledge, with past events and relationships, with issues of what might constitute right action for him or herself in society, with consistency of goals. Such nonscientific understandings are not to be devalued in comparison with scientific understandings that relate explicit theories to observable data. Science and these therapeutic arts are complementary. If science has to do with discovering truths about the world, then literary art may have to do with discovering truthfulness within oneself. In understanding emotions scientifically we may discover how we are affected by processes to which we have no conscious access. In understanding disjunctions in our personal emotions we may see that semantic content may be connected with what had been merely inchoate.

EXTENDING OUR SYMPATHIES. How does art allow our personal implicit theories to improve? For George Eliot, art "is a mode of amplifying experience and extending our contact with our fellow-men beyond the bounds of our personal lot" (Pinney, 1963, p. 270). As our implicit theories assimilate new evidence they change, our schemata accommodate. On average this will be for the better, as we are likely to be restricted by self-absorption and a narrowness of vision. So art supplements ordinary life and helps people to construct their own moral sensibility.

In our age people around the world spend much time witnessing narrative accounts of human actions on television. We observe presentations, in story form, lasting a few seconds for a news item or advertisement to a few years for a long-running soap opera. Could George Eliot's proposal, described in the last paragraph, apply as well to the staple fare of television as to the art of a tragedy by Sophocles or Shakespeare? One criterion is that some works can pass between cultures that are widely separated in time and space. But this argument is not strong. Certain aspects of theatrical form act as good projection screens for very different cultural theories: Hamlet in an African village can have a very different interpretation than it does in London.[16] I am not proposing that a story has a single meaning; as discussed in Chapter 5, it has a family of meanings with each interpretation having a relation to the mental schemata of the person making it.

So with George Eliot's suggestion we still have questions. On what can any claim that great artists achieve universality be based, when people differ so much both in their interpretation and assessment of them? How do we distinguish the artist's vision of truth from the advertiser's hyperbole or the hack's column designed to resonate with prejudices of readers in order to sell more newspapers? Is not literary art just more or less pleasant diversion? And how is it that some writings, usually referred to as great literature, achieve amplification of experience, whereas others do not?

COMPARISON WITH OURSELVES. Not everything we see or read is capable of amplifying experience. In the ordinary detective or thriller story a pursuit is joined, fights occur, the wrongdoer is punished. The detective, usually a man with whom the spectators identify, wins respect. One leaves one's seat in the cinema having felt safely anxious and justifiably vengeful, but with cognitive schemata intact. Another diverting piece of male violence has been portrayed and some mild cultural propaganda about the triumph of good has been promoted, probably along with other less obvious cultural assumptions such as that illegality is allowable if you are on the right side. In a love story we may be moved by the tenderness of the tale, but our own capacity for love may be quite unchanged.

In Sophocles' *Oedipus the King*, the play that Aristotle praised as the best example of a well-constructed tragedy, the effect is not so straightforward. The detective turns out, unbeknown to himself, to be the wrongdoer. Insofar as we have been entrained by the plot, insofar as we have identified with Oedipus, we are now invited to take part in the act of recognition. We might find ourselves reflecting upon our own wrong-doings, considering our own multiplicity of motives. This is quite different from the content of ordinary cultural propaganda, partly because the effects it might induce are not programmed by the playwright as a piece of planned technique. It is the comparison between our own and the other's standards that invites a change in our model of self, an accommodation of our schemata, a widening of our experience. No one but ourselves can know in what way this experience will be widened.

On one hand, then, there are techniques or crafts for making culturally recognizable stories carry more or less explicit ideological content and for arousing specific emotions for purposes of amusement or persuasion. On the other hand is narrative that may have similar elements but that challenges our existing schemata, and invites extension of our implicit theories in some way that is not predictable or preintended by the author. Although Sophocles includes cultural propaganda, for the most part he contents himself with inviting the spectator's own reflection, and hence the possibility of enlarging her or his own schemata. As George Eliot says, he surprises even the "trivial and selfish into that attention to what is apart from themselves" (Pinney, 1963, p. 270).

Our more personal theories, those models by which we define ourselves and view others, are like other theories, often quite resistant to change. Many people have remarked how much easier it is to hang on to theories, to disregard or look with contempt at evidence that seems contradictory. Our implicit theories of self are no exception: These were what George Eliot seemed to have in mind when she spoke of how the potentiality of art is to amplify experience and provide raw material for moral sentiment.[17]

If in George Eliot's novels we were merely offered views of characters we had not met personally, and a concurrent discussion with an unusually perceptive companion, this would certainly be instructive. It would not be enough to argue that the novelist's art had some special place in our culture. It would not be enough to raise what any particular novelist had to say above the level of mere opinion. There is, however, something that sets great novels off from lesser ones.

INNER AND OUTER VIEWS. In Chapter 5, I argued that George Eliot's *Middlemarch* was constructed using several different voices, including one of external observation and one of inner reflection. We can thus compare externally viewed actions with inner experiences of these actions. If the artist has been successful, we identify our self with the inner view.

It is principally this comparison with self that allows the reader to be creative in reflection on her or his own life, and as Collingwood has argued, this creativity is central to art. A character who is an aspect of ourself is seen with one more dimension than usual. We do not just see this aspect behaviorally as we usually see others. And we do not just empathize with the character, experiencing it as we usually experience ourselves. Rather a double vision creates an effect comparable to that of *Oedipus the King* in which the searcher turns out to be the person sought, and an effect occurs of allowing us to compare ourselves in our own experience and ourselves as others see us.[18]

George Eliot succeeded as an artist in being able to express emotions in narrative language. The emotions from which *Middlemarch* flowed were of indignation about the restrictions on women in the 1830s, of sorrow for universal accidents of life, and of hope that emotional openness and unselfish acts, though unremarked in history books, will continue to contribute largely to what we value about the human world.

In expressing her emotions, George Eliot created in verbal form the semantic content of occasions, accompaniments, and consequences of her characters' emotions. Also, and unlike those occasions when we are perhaps struggling with our own emotions, she elaborated the two views, outer and inner. They create a tension that draws together basic feelings and semantic content that because of disjunctive effects may be unconnected in us. Thus her readers' emotions may undergo clarification, and cognitive change may occur. This perhaps is what is meant by extending our sympathies.

Clearly, it is necessary for the reader to be engaged. It is the identification of the reader with a character that allows comparisons such as that between inner and outer. Only with such an identification might any discrepancies make a difference, transcending the reader's more usually egocentric perspective not just in the world of the novel but in reality. Or, as Frijda (1988) puts it in one of his laws of emotion, emotions are only elicited by events appraised as real. So, with literature, it is only if the simulation runs with phenomenological vividness in our own minds that it will enable us a readers to be engaged and emotions to occur.

Like many another novelist, George Eliot typically creates each episode of the plot with an emotion as the fulcrum around which the episode turns. Emotions are means by which implications of a character's own plan are communicated to her- or himself and to the other characters in the story. By recognition and empathetic identification the reader experiences comparable emotions and their implications. By evaluating a character's encounters, using the means by which we usually evaluate our own emotions, resonant analogies are set up with encounters of our own. We can then reflect on our experiences of ourselves and others, but now with our experience extended beyond the immediacy of our own life and without the inhibition of expression that some of our own emotions might have.

George Eliot scarcely lets us escape reflecting on our own lives and understandings, because in one of the voices from which she composes *Middlemarch* she continuously offers a generalizing commentary inviting us to reflections beyond each particular incident.

The novel, even in the hands of a keen observer, who like George Eliot endeavored to make her work a vehicle of social science, is well on the arts side of any boundary there might be between arts and science. This difference leaves some scientists skeptical as to the importance of any insights available. Such scientists can point to the widely differing conclusions that are regularly drawn, and compare them with the more unanimously convincing understandings in physics and engineering, where testing against a practical application of knowledge in the world is the criterion of truth. For an engineer or scientist the novel may be entertaining, but it does not find its way out of the "labyrinth of conflicting opinions."[19]

Art, however, points not primarily to correspondences between theory and observation, but within ourselves to a possibility of consistency of what we say, what we feel, and what we do. Just as in Dora's case history I proposed that a warrant for accepting a psychoanalytic understanding was that it could point to an inconsistency and allow it to be resolved, so too does the counterpoint between inner and outer voices in *Middlemarch* or the discrepancy implied by the seeker and the sought in *Oedipus the King*.

The truth toward which such art tends is that we can build conscious knowledge of some of our mental structure, and this allows us to integrate some of the parts rather than allowing them to remain fragmented, isolated, inconsistent. It is better – that is more truthful – that the goal hierarchy and aspects of our knowledge base do not contain gross contradictions, that the nonsemantic and semantic aspects of our emotions correspond, that what we say to others is consonant with what we say to ourselves. Otherwise we may become people on whom neither we ourselves nor others can rely. Art proper, by expressing emotions in a way that elaborates semantic content, enables discrepancies and contradictions to be discovered and resolved.

A poem expressing an emotion

To demonstrate his idea that art is the expression of emotions, Collingwood brought his book to a conclusion with a commentary on a poem that is widely considered the greatest of the modern era: T. S. Eliot's *The Waste Land.* It lacks nothing of the fragmentariness of literary art in a post-Freudian age. It depends on juxtapositions of images, pieces of personal memory, reflections on grand philosophical themes. The gaps are to be filled, of course, by the reader – who will need also have a commentary nearby to explain the more recondite allusions. The emotion this poem expresses is modern despair: The poem speaks to Collingwood of how our civilization has fled from the experience and expression of all emotions save the fear of emotion itself.

I would also like to bring my book to a conclusion with something showing how literary art can express an emotion as Collingwood proposes. In my case, though, what comes to mind is not a poem of despair but a poem to juxtapose, as it were, with Homer's poem of anger and war with which I started Chapter 5. The poem is about love. It is one of the two poems by Sappho on which her reputation rests.[20] Here is a translation:

> Richly-enthroned immortal Aphrodite, daughter of Zeus, weaver of wiles, I pray to you: break not my spirit, Lady, with heartache or anguish;
>
> But hither come, if ever in the past you heard my cry from afar, and marked it, and came, leaving your father's house,
>
> Your golden chariot yoked: sparrows beautiful and swift conveyed you, with rapid wings a-flutter, above the dark earth from heaven through the mid-air;
>
> And soon they were come, and you, Fortunate, with a smile on your immortal face, asked what ails me now, and why am I calling now,
>
> And what in my heart's madness I most desire to have: "Whom now must I persuade to join our friendship's ranks? Who wrongs you, Sappho?
>
> For if she flees, she shall soon pursue; and if she receives not

gifts, yet shall she give; and if she loves not, she shall soon love even against her will."

Come to me now also, and deliver me from cruel anxieties; fulfil all that my heart desires to fulfil, and be yourself my comrade-in-arms.

Translation, Page (1955), p. 4

The poem is in the form of a prayer to Aphrodite, goddess of erotic love, or should we say lust?[21] Sappho asks her to come yet again. As Page points out, the poem repeats three times the word "again," which on its second and third occurrences Page has translated as "now": Perhaps this should be with emphasis "*now*" or "*this* time." So Sappho says to Aphrodite: "When you came to me in the past, you asked 'What is the matter with you *again*, Sappho, and what are you calling me for *again* and whom *again* must I win over to your love?'" (Page (1955), p. 12, emphasis in original).

Sappho is conscious that this repetition may have been tiresome to the goddess – and now she is asking yet again. It is not altogether clear why this is not tiresome to Sappho herself. She sees there is something mechanical in it. Aphrodite comes smiling. Though this goddess is often depicted as smiling, here it seems the smile is ironic. Such repetition without apparently any application of the will is evidently what it is like for mortals. What can one do but smile?

In the fifth stanza Sappho depicts Aphrodite speaking directly to her: "This woman you are pursuing now will soon be pursuing you. Now she is refusing gifts, soon she will be offering gifts to you, and you will be the one who is refusing. Now it's your love that is unrequited. Soon it will be her love for you that is unrequited." Not only are the requests repetitive; even the progress of Sappho's passions can be foreseen.

The emotion Sappho feels is a passion – she has felt it often enough to recognize it. It has enabled her to construct a model of herself. It is clear that this pattern is something to do with herself, not just an external imposition. It is her own proclivity to keep falling in love. And what is worse, although her love starts by being unrequited, usually by the time it has ended it is the other way round. Probably this new person for whom Sappho's need seems now so absolute will be pursuing her when her own ardor has cooled. Best under these circumstances, one might think, to see the passion as likely to be ephemeral, possibly destructive. Despite that, it seems urgent, impossible to ignore. "Please, Aphrodite, join me in this new conquest. Relieve this anguish by making her love me."

Sappho has been widely admired, and widely reviled. The reasons for both attitudes I think are clear.[22] In this poem she may not seem very likable. We might regard her sense that soon it will be she who is pursued as arrogant, her longing for this new conquest as manipulative. But here for the very first time in European literature speaks an inner voice of self. Here is the contrast between inner and outer, here is some of the raw material of what George Eliot called "moral sentiment," which brings some self-knowledge and perhaps an extension of sympathy.

Sappho depicts a voice speaking to her like the voice heard by Achilles when he began to draw his sword, as something external, a goddess. The quotation of the goddess within Sappho's own poem shows that she knows that she knows. For her this is a voice with which to mock herself with the repetition of "again." And now the smile on the face of this goddess is ironical.

In this poem is a seed of possibility that in knowing herself the mortal Sappho may become herself, with an inner life, not just an object acted on by fateful events. The seed of sexual passion might become a way of recognizing that someone else too will be affected by this impulse.

On this occasion, around 600 B.C.E., the sequence about which Sappho wrote may have been played out *again*, just as before, though now with a little more self-knowledge and perhaps some regard for the object of her desire. As well as probably expressing her passion in various ways for this woman, object of her desire, she expresses it in the words of her art. She leaves for us this semantic message, making sense of the emotion of human erotic love, allowing an insight, a possibility of understanding both something about ourselves and our relations with other persons to whom such passions may be directed.

Not just goal-based understanding

In this book, I have suggested that we start with a cognitive treatment of emotions. In the current state of cognitive science this treatment is necessarily based on plans, perhaps such as the plan Sappho had for the woman she desired. Such a basis can help us understand the functions of emotions. But this does not mean that all life is directed by goals that we ourselves set. Had Sappho been merely the vehicle for the goal of yet another sexual conquest, then Aphrodite might appropriately have smiled at this hopelessly robot-like repetitiveness. Fortunately, our technical abilities to plan instrumentally are tempered in our interactions with others by something else. This something else includes the way in which aspects of our plans are confronted by occurrences of emotions upon which we can reflect, which remind us of our finiteness and our egotism.

If poetry is indeed semantic expression of "emotion recollected in tranquillity,"[23] then the possibility occurs from such reflection of something other than an understanding merely of how to achieve a goal that has become problematic.

Robert Burns's image of "best laid schemes" from which the title of my book is taken, is one of goal-directed plans often going wrong. Such plans may sometimes bring us distress rather than the joy they promise. This is indeed the predicament of both mice and men. We do not know enough. Our powers are not extensive enough for our goal-directed plans to go right all the time. We are not gods and our emotions force us to reflect on this fact.

The theories of emotions that have been dominated in Western psychology until recently have assumed emotions to be disturbances of efficient functioning of goal-directed behavior. As such, they have seemed to be distortions of truth, disruptions of rationality. Emotions are indeed disturbing; but in this poem by Sappho, just as in the timeless moments described by Proust, in Joanna Field's recognition that reviewing her consciously set goals did not help her much in understanding herself, in the unfulfilled aspirations of the characters of *Middlemarch*, as well as in many other works of literature, we may see something else of significance.

It is not that emotions distort rationality, but rather, the opposite: In the perturbations of the smooth surface of habit, of plans, of schemes that do not always go as we might have planned, we can sometimes catch a glimpse of something real in us that may point beyond the issue of achieving our next goal.

Epilogue

What is always needed in the appreciation of art, or life,
is the larger perspective.

Alice Walker
In search of our mothers' gardens, p. 5.

Emotions and cognitive change

This book has been concerned broadly with psychology and specifically
with the cognitive psychology of how knowledge is represented and
used in emotional life. The book's questions have implications both for
technology and insight. Emotions are a human solution to problems of
our simultaneous multiple goals, of our limitations and uncertain
knowledge, and of our interactions with others. By contrast, gods and
robots have no contradictions among their goals, and have full powers
and perfect knowledge of their worlds. There is no need for them to
have emotions.

Technically, in computing, distributed problem-solving systems with
quasi-autonomous processes are being designed and organized into
larger systems. If arguments of the kind I have put forward about this
general problem become accepted, then the junctures in action with
which emotions deal, if not emotions themselves, will begin to be seen
as central to cognitive science, not as peripheral. And in the other part of
the psychological domain, in questions of the inner and interpersonal
world, emotions themselves are important. They have been peripheral
to the mainstream of psychology. Now they are becoming more central.

I have concentrated not so much on questions of technology as on
those of insight. Partly this is because I believe a search for insight is
important in most people's interest in psychology and partly because,
despite this, issues of insight are under-represented in the mainstream.

In the prologue I said that among the problems posed by emotions was that of why they should be so preoccupying. The answer that has emerged is that emotions can communicate the need for cognitive change. Learning is still generally regarded as one of the things that mammals do well and human mammals do best. In a system in which cognitive change is more than putting data into prearranged slots, or the adjustment of parameters, very substantial issues are at stake. One cannot enter new goals into a system or integrate much new knowledge without the possibility of repercussions for the whole system. So when a new goal is inserted into a planning sequence it may be necessary to revise what has been done before. On the largest scale a change of goals may make large pieces of existing cognitive structure obsolete, as happens when a person has suffered a severe life event.

Emotions are necessary because the human cognitive system works in a way that is partly ad hoc, with imperfect knowledge both of the environment and of implications of its multiple goals. When certain kinds of unexpected junctures are reached, new goals or new considerations must be entered. The system can expect certain kinds of events in general, though they cannot be anticipated in particular. When these occur the system must rewrite parts of itself as it goes along. Even more difficult than this: The problems raised are like operating a new card index or categorization system. It turns out that our understanding as we start a project is replaced by better ways of thinking about it as we go along, as new considerations or new purposes occur. So it is then not just a matter of adding new cards or changing the structure locally, but possibly of reorganizing large parts of the system, reconciling its parts with each other, even starting again from scratch.

If we are indeed systems that write new pieces of ourselves, this process should be preoccupying – and it is. If we have to integrate diverse parts, then we need a system that occupies our whole attentional consciousness. Emotions do that. If the issue is integration, then a single unified consciousness drawing conclusions from a model of the whole goal structure is needed.

The metaphor of a program that rewrites itself is not complete, but I think it gives the clue as to why emotions remain necessary, why they are not just vestiges of our evolutionary past. If we humans were to reach a stage where we did not have emotions, we would have become static, perfectly adapted to an unchanging world. Some people, and even some cultures, work hard to achieve this, to minimize the unexpected. For most people in European or American society, the goals that do emerge and the events that do occur are not fully foreseeable. New components do not just have local effects. Sometimes as new considerations occur one needs to start again though traces of earlier structures remain.

The theory offered here is designed to allow insight into some features of emotional life: why pieces of structure created in earlier role relationships persist, why they can produce spiky outbursts of emotion as expectations are not fulfilled, why they may be difficult to revise. Pieces of structure may have been useful, but as our lives change other considerations enter, making some habits and interpersonal patterns no longer appropriate.

Thus the shifting pattern of emotional meanings within which we live is intrinsic to us. As new interpretations occur to us, and as new pieces of cognitive structure are built, the significance of what happens to us changes. This also hints at why the emotional life of childhood is so different from that of adults – as we grow older our implicit theories change (cf. Schachtel, 1959) and even improve. Fewer and different things challenge the existing cognitive structure. We become more able to organize the world around us to minimize the need for certain kinds of cognitive change – except, of course, that we can never reduce this to a very low level.

We might derive from sociology or sociobiology the idea that we are corks tossed by the waves of society and genetics. Or we may hold to the opposite folk theory in European and American culture, that each individual is fully master of his or her fate. The fact is, as Kierkegaard supposed, that we live in two worlds simultaneously: a world of social and biological mechanisms that compel us though they are perhaps technically predictable and a world of possibilities limited only by our individual imagination and our preparedness to cooperate with one another. Making a synthesis from these apparent irreconcilables depends on being open to our emotions that bridge the two worlds of necessity and freedom and on building models of ourselves and our goal structures that are accurate. Then, as Spinoza and Freud supposed, we may be liberated from some of the forces that are unbeknown and become one with ourselves, at least some of the time.

To a limited extent, then, as selves in relation to others, we come into a position to steer a little bit. It is not that the world comes under control, but that our own actions and those of others with whom we construct mutual plans become, within limits, predictable and comprehensible, so that we may rely on ourselves and others.

Four bases of understanding emotions

I have argued that literature such as the novel, especially in the hands of such as Tolstoy or George Eliot provides a dimension that is factored out by natural science in its production of person-independent, technically applicable knowledge. Empathetic understanding, the imaginative entry into the life of other people, which Dilthey and Weber called *Verstehen*, is an act from which neither the person understanding nor the one who is to be understood can be factored out. It is an element of phenomenological comprehension in common between social science and narrative literature.

My proposal here is that an understanding of emotions depends on more elements than, say, an understanding in physics. In physics we can identify three elements: events, qualitative descriptions of these events with reliable quantitative measurement, and theories for drawing valid inferences about the events. Though of course theories are held by people, it is generally understood that the truths they express are not dependent on being held by anyone. They transcend human consciousness.[1]

Understanding emotions also depends on events, reliable measurements, and theories. But a human (as opposed to a Martian) understanding needs also a fourth element, that of *Verstehen*, or imaginative reliving, which depends on the production of phenomena in the mind of the person who is striving to understand. As Johnson-Laird and I have argued in our semantic analysis of emotion terms, basic emotions are phenomenological primitives. We understand them from our own experience. If you were emotion-blind, perhaps like a being from another planet, you would no more be able to understand happiness or sadness as emotions than a color-blind person could understand what it was like for something to be red or blue.

The difficulty is that in our quest for understanding emotions, there continues to be a temptation to base understanding on only three of the four necessary elements. Depending on how these are disposed we can find ourselves with quite a rickety structure. So in literature the element of reliable measurement is muted, because the quantitative is missing, because bias occurs, because folk theories are not always sufficient. On the other hand, in laboratory experiments there is often nothing that allows *Verstehen*.

A proper psychological account of emotions needs to be founded on all four of these elements. First there are the events of human emotions, mental and physiological, including our own emotions. Second is description and measurement: The methods include observation, listening, and other more or less reliable measurements of expressions, physiological variables, verbal utterances, and so on assessed across appropriate sampling ranges. Third: Theory is the means by which we can make inferences that go beyond phenomena and measurements. In this book the theory is of multiple goals, of limitations of knowledge and abilities, and of interactions with others. The fourth element is *Verstehen:* It occurs in the phenomenological response to an event in one's own life or to a play or novel, to a description by an anthropologist, to a vignette in a psychological experiment, or when rating a life event in psychiatric epidemiology.

For an understanding of emotions to approach completeness, all four elements must be related to one another, integrated. The assumption of novelists that life turns round episodes of emotion, being expressed or suppressed, is, for instance, not quite enough. It lacks that element of reliable observation across an appropriate sampling range. Scenes of a novel, however striking, however thought-provoking, are not enough.

So the famous opening sentence of *Anna Karenina* "All happy families resemble one another, each unhappy family is unhappy in its own way" catches a certain truth capable of being made sense of. It is meaningful to many of us. But such a truth is not independent of how each of us understands it. It is ambiguous, polysemous. However great Tolstoy was as a novelist, his greatness consisted in part in creating a world in which our imagination could flourish, not so much in describing a constrained world accurately for reliable perceptions.

In the same way Freud telling a story of his patient's conflicts is not enough. We do not always know if the patient was leading Freud on or whether Freud is leading us on. Similarly, Goffman in his idea that joy is engaged participation as in a face-to-face encounter, or a psychologist asking people to recall circumstances that recently made them happy or angry are not in themselves enough. There is no safeguard in these kinds of work against the possibility that people merely recount the cultural rules by which they believe emotions occur and within which they live.

At the same time, an experiment from the psychological laboratory or the survey of a randomly sampled population are also not enough. These are designed to maximize reliability of observation, but their generalization beyond the domain of the data collection is seldom assured. They may be reliable, but are they valid? They may be empirically true but of no importance. They may have impeccable methodology and statistics but be without interest to anyone who is not doing a Ph.D. using the same methods.

My argument is that in the field of understanding emotions the methods that have been valuable are those that articulate several of the four necessary elements and relate these to each other. For a tolerably complete understanding we must bear all four in mind.

George Eliot's work is important for understanding emotions because it allows an imaginative reliving of lives in a different setting from our own. It also relates to the expression of emotions that researchers in the Darwinian tradition had described, as well as to the structure of story plots and plans in theories of cognitive science. Freud's work is important not just because of its development of the idea of *Verstehen*, but also because its explorations of implications of multiple goals that are theoretically important in artificial intelligence. In the epidemiological work of Brown and others, episodes from people's lives are collected and presented in story form – life events. They are judged with *Verstehen* to preserve the element of emotional significance, but they can also be categorized and counted in order to diminish the degree of bias of a single observer. In Ekman's studies of expression, actors pose and relive emotions as they might on the stage, but now their accompanying autonomic reactions can be measured. Each of the approaches articulates more than one aspect, and so assists setting its findings in relation to others.

Plato, I think, had something to answer for if we take emotions to be important in human life. He was distrustful of their influence on reason. Where he did discuss them, as he did the subject of love, it was to show that even the most valued of human emotions were not in themselves very worthy. At best they were means to a greater end – love for a person could be sublimated and turned into love of truth. Such attitudes as these have resonated down the centuries of European culture. And, although he did promote dialogue as a means for approaching truth, and though his mentor Socrates discovered that humans could not know very much, Plato proposed that somewhere, somehow, it was possible to be certain about important truths directly, from a position outside our merely human concerns, unclouded by an earthly viewpoint.[2]

In the domain of emotions there are no fixed points outside our merely human world. If when we build a tripod we find each leg not so sturdy as we thought, perhaps with Aristotle we might consider another way – consistent with the understanding that for us human beings very little is perfectly certain. We could begin to build another kind of structure less dependent on the perfect functioning of every part. We have to live with such structures, in which, because of interconnections of their parts, wholes are more reliable than any of their components.

Events, measurements, theories, emotional experience: these are parts, I think, to be interconnected in creating structures to comprehend human emotions. With them we can begin to understand both outer and inner worlds.

Notes

Prologue

1. Authors usually thought of as founders of the Romantic movement include Goethe and Rousseau on the Continent and Wordsworth in Britain. For instance, Goethe's influential novel of 1774, *The Sorrows of Young Werther*, describes first the passion of Werther for a young woman already promised to another and the joy that his love brings him, then his despair and suicide. Rousseau, in *Confessions* (completed in 1765 and published posthumously in 1781), set out to give a frank description of his emotional life. Many found his candidness shocking. A major landmark in English Romantic literature was Wordsworth's and Coleridge's *Lyrical Ballads*, which appeared in 1798. In the famous preface to the second edition of 1801, enlarged for the third edition of 1802, Wordsworth describes how the poems were written about subjects in which "the passions of men are incorporated with the beautiful and permanent forms of Nature" (Wordsworth, 1984/1802, p. 597). See Drabble (1985) for pointers to principal Romantic authors in English, or one of the many guides to English and Continental literature and philosophy from about 1770 to 1850.
2. Winograd and Flores (1986) describe this Apollonian tradition as rationalist. Their book contains an interesting discussion of this tradition, and their reaction to it.
3. An excellent history of cognitive science is by Gardner (1985), who describes how cognitive scientists have until recently avoided considering emotions in their work. For a more recent view, see for example, the editorial article by Oatley (1987b) introducing the special issue of *Cognition and Emotion* on emotions in cognitive science.
4. Gardner (1985) traces cognitive science back to the epistemological concerns of Plato and forward from the invention of the computer.

Chapter 1

1. The term "man" in the English translation of Kierkegaard's aphorism is probably related etymologically to terms like "mental," with their implications of thinking. Thus an English word meaning "thinking being" seems to have been taken over by the word meaning "adult male human." Though it seems a shame to lose from a book on cognitive psychology a term implying

that human beings are distinguished by thinking, this sexist appropriation will restrain me from using "man" generically.

2. The idea of structure is that used by de Rivera (1977). He follows Piaget's (1971, p. 5) usage of structure meaning a system "characterized by wholeness, the idea of transformation, and the idea of self-regulation."

3. James (1890, Vol. 2) said that "feeling of [bodily] changes as they occur is the emotion" (p. 449), and makes clear that by feeling he means "sensational process" (p. 458). He was canny enough to avoid outright the claim that all emotions are perceptions of internal states, and said his theory applied to "the coarser emotions" in which there were strong organic reverberations, and to the subtler emotions insofar as bodily effects occurred (p. 470). I return to James's theory in Chapter 3.

4. Stephen Draper, on hearing that I was planning to write a book on emotion, told me that such a project was not sensible, and wrote a survey of 10 theories of emotions to show why (Draper, 1985). I have benefited considerably from this and from discussions of it. I take my book to be somewhat successful in that it convinced him that there is evidence for a coherent theory of emotions. I am grateful for his discussion, and in particular for his suggestion that I modify the view I had in the first drafts, that emotions were evaluations of ongoing plans. His suggestion was that both active and nonactive goals must be monitored, and that emotions are indications that some goals may not be integrated with ongoing action. This I think is right and I have adopted it.

5. The schematic idea of emotions as having eliciting conditions, typical accompaniments, and consequences in behavior is becoming widely accepted among workers in the field. See, for example, Ekman (1984), Frijda (1986), and Scherer (1984).

6. In this formulation I follow Helmholtz (1962/1866), who argued that consciousness is the consciousness of certain conclusions of mental inference processes. The processes themselves forever remain unconscious; see also note 17.

7. The notion of a mental model is fundamental to cognitive science. The idea was introduced by Craik (1943). See Oatley (1972) for an introduction to this idea or Johnson-Laird (1983a) for a more advanced account. Mental models are also referred to as schemata (Bartlett, 1932), representations (Oatley, 1978), or implicit theories of aspects of the world. The knowledge embodied in them is not necessarily conscious.

8. Suchman (1987) discusses the implications of plan hierarchies being applicable at any level of detail, and goes on to criticize the idea that action is driven by plans. The augmentations of planning theory that I suggest later are influenced by her analysis.

9. See, for instance, Oatley's (1978) account of Hughlings-Jackson's nineteenth-century proposals about hierarchical organization of the nervous system.

10. An early and well-known planning program from which much subsequent work on planning in artificial intelligence has derived is that of Fikes and Nilsson (1971). Explication of planning is given by Rich (1983), Charniak and McDermott (1985), and Sanford (1985).

11. I have described in this subsection some basic elements of programming style, which can also be applied to planning problems other than programming (cf., e.g., Papert, 1980).

12. Many ideas about technical plans and their properties can be found in Plato, particularly the *Republic*. Although I have made a distinction, the words *techne* and *episteme* are often used interchangeably in Plato's texts. Gardner

(1985) argues that cognitive science is a new development of philosophical themes such as the bases of epistemology that go back to the Greeks. He does not draw this link with Greek treatments of *techne*, though this would strengthen his case.

13. The fact that knowledge does not necessarily generalize was discovered by Socrates in his famous quest to find what the oracle might have meant by saying that no one was wiser than he was. Socrates thought that this could only mean that he was wise enough to know that he did not know everything; he knew he did not have reliable knowledge generally (Plato, *Apology*).

14. Neisser (1963), in a prescient and insightful article on the difference between computational and human intelligence, stressed that human mentality typically involves multiple goals, in comparison with the single top-level goals of computational schemes. Simon (1967) drew on this idea to write one of the first papers in cognitive science on the problem of handling multiple goals, which he took to be coextensive with the problem of emotions occurring in the course of action.

15. Tolstoy's novels are quite remarkably autobiographical, and we can infer this goal of Vronsky's from Tolstoy's own penchant for going out, on the lookout for excitements as it were (Wilson, 1988).

16. *Anna Karenina* is a novel about inner conflict, and of course Freud (e.g., 1963/1916–1917) made such conflict a central explanatory principle of his work; see Chapter 7.

17. The argument from cognitive science, first put by Helmholtz (1962/1866) is that nearly all mental processes and conclusions are unconscious. Consciousness occurs at the tip of a computational iceberg, and Marcel (1983) has elegantly shown how conscious and unconscious mental processes may be separated and have different origins. The function of anything being conscious is not at all clear, though I hope to contribute to its understanding here. See Oatley (1981) for a discussion of unconscious cognitive processes and of their relation to the issue of unconsciousness as described in psychoanalysis. Freud's exposition of the unconscious is well explained in his Introductory Lectures (1963/1916–1917).

18. A sequence of action being triggered in inappropriate circumstances is not uncommon. It has been called vacuum activity by ethologists (Lorenz, 1970).

19. Goffman's (1961) essays are explorations of the problem. I discuss them in Chapter 8.

20. Perring, Oatley, and Smith (1988) found that explicit and implicit conflict may give rise to symptoms of anxiety and depression, particularly among students, including mature students, with women being more affected than men.

21. Distributed agency is the main theme of Chapter 4. Here I just touch on the issues. Plato once again had a sense of an essential problem for the idea of *techne*. The *Republic* is an exploration of how a planned city-state might be envisaged, so that problems of distributed agency are solved. Plato proposes a rigid division of labor between governors who set top-level goals, auxiliaries who have executive and military functions, and workers who each exercise a specific skill. Plato sees the problems as essentially technical, with the idea that rational solutions can be imposed from the top downward. It is this that has drawn such vehement condemnation from Popper (1945).

22. A number of other writers have recently proposed a modular theory of mind. They include Fodor (1983) and Gazzaniga (1988).

23. The term conflict theory seems to have been introduced by Angier (1927) in

his discussion of Dewey's (1894, 1895) work on emotions. The history of the concept is discussed by Mandler (1984).

24. I am most grateful to Stephen Draper, who offered me this image of alarms, and another of emotions as like land mines that we might step on as we journey across no-man's-land, as part of an argument that every goal and plan in a person's repertoire needs monitoring.

   Such a mechanism takes the place of Wilensky's (1983) metaplanning, and has some of the same characteristics. Wilensky does not describe metaplanning as emotional. But he regards it as the principal issue of everyday reasoning about action. One difference is that Wilensky sees metaplanning as a top-level activity with a predictive quality, whereas emotions can arise from a goal at any level being reevaluated in the course of action.

25. Pribram (e.g., 1984) makes a distinction between processes that he calls epicritic, which carry information about time and place, and protocritic, which do not carry such information but merely indicate intensity. This distinction has some features in common with the one between semantic and control signals, though it is based on different considerations. Moreover, Pribram proposes what he calls a multidimensional view of emotions, in which the epicritic-protocritic dimension is one of several, including lability and arousal. Pribram's are general terms intended to characterize both emotions and motivations. Johnson-Laird and I think there is evidence for more discrete emotions than Pribram suggests.

26. The analysis and characteristics of emotions discussed in the following sections has been strongly influenced by Ekman's work, which has itself been driven largely by his research on facial expressions (see Ekman, 1984, for a summary of his theoretical position and empirical findings). Except where I discuss it specifically my treatment is not substantially different from his. I am most grateful to him for discussing issues arising from his work. Further evidence on basic emotions is discussed in Chapter 2.

27. Plutchik (e.g., 1984) has examined the contingencies of mammalian life and proposed basic emotions being triggered by them. He starts with a set of basic adaptive problems derived from ethological considerations suggested by Scott (1958). He then supposes that there are recurring and recognizable circumstances that elicit emotions with distinctive behavioral and functional effects. Campos et al. (1983) have made similar arguments in reviewing the development of emotions in infancy.

   The ontology described in this chapter is based on Johnson-Laird and Oatley (1989), and is also described in Johnson-Laird (1988). Such an ontology depends strongly on Darwin: *Origin of Species* (1859), *Descent of Man* (1871), and *Expression of Emotions* (1872). The more specifically behavioral parts of his work now, of course, form the foundations of ethology (see, e.g., Hinde, 1982). We differ from Plutchik in deriving our analysis primarily from cognitive concerns, in the idea of emotions being specific signals, and in having no commitment to discovering how emotions can be arranged in a pattern in terms of adjacency and opposition. As with our difference from Pribram's view (note 25), we think that there is evidence for much more discrete and specific emotions than are suggested by Plutchik's dimensions.

   Ekman (e.g., 1984) has also suggested that there are specific eliciting conditions for specific emotions, but says that there has been rather little cross-cultural empirical work done on this.

28. See Bowlby (1969, 1973, 1980) for elaboration of the idea of attachment and its implications in infancy and later life. A recent hypothesis relevant to the idea of emotions having specific physiological accompaniments is that of

Panksepp (e.g., 1989), who proposes that endogenous opiates are involved in mediating attachment. The hypothesis is that infants are born in a rather quiet and self-absorbed state, maintained by high levels of circulating opiates. These endogenously produced opiates decline to be replaced by opiates elicited by the interactions of attachment, which are thereby experienced as rewarding. Infantile autism, according to this hypothesis, is associated with a failure of endogenous opiates to decline, hence not allowing those derived from social interaction to replace them.

29. The statements "Ekman said . . ." in this paragraph were from a personal communication (25 March, 1985). On the second point about intensity of specific feelings experienced when making facial expressions, subjects typically scored above the median on nine-point scales, and often within two points of the upper anchor point "the most extreme you have felt in your life." One should note that all the results of Ekman, Levenson, and Friesen's (1983) study are correlational, that is, they show associations among facial expression, autonomic nervous activity, and phenomenology. The study was not designed to define causal relationships between any of these categories.

30. There has been a considerable amount of work on recognition of facial expressions, both of still and moving displays. A basic reference is Ekman (1982). Work has been done cross-culturally (see, e.g., Ekman & Oster, 1982; Ekman, 1989), on infants (see, e.g., Izard, 1971; Harris, 1989), and on non-human primates (see, e.g., Redican, 1982).

31. This paper was followed by Izard and Haynes (1988), who argued that Ekman and Friesen were not the first to find this expression. Ekman and Friesen (1988) replied saying that it was indeed they who showed the expression was unique to contempt and different from that for other emotions, including disgust.

32. The question of negative emotions raises a difficulty that other theorists have pointed out. We have been criticized by Frijda (1987a) and by Ortony and Clore (1989) for arguing for a small set of distinctive basic emotions, rather than just accepting the distinction among emotions as positive and negative. For full replies see Johnson-Laird and Oatley (1988a) and Oatley and Johnson-Laird (1990).

In pondering these criticisms I am unpersuaded by the idea of a primary distinction between emotions as positive or negative if the grounds are of positive or negative valency, as Ortony and colleagues claim, or of pleasure and pain as Frijda (1987a) argues. The reason is that context strongly affects whether people approach or avoid particular emotions, and whether they find them pleasurable or painful. So in ordinary life few people enjoy feeling angry, but in certain sports they may seek the experience of anger. In ordinary life fear and sadness are avoided, but people seek them by reading books and watching films that are thrillers and weepies.

In my view the proper distinction is that made by Gordon (1987) between positive emotions occurring with evaluations of increasing probability of goal attainment and negative emotions occurring when there is decreased probability. With negative emotions, however, there is not a just a single kind of emotion. Rather, as I have argued in this chapter, there are four basic kinds of negative emotion, sadness, anger, fear, and disgust, each signaled by a distinctive kind of decreasing probability of goal attainment.

33. Tomkins (e.g., 1979, 1984) has been influential in proposing that emotions amplify motivations, bringing them into the focus of attention, giving them urgency.

34. I proposed (Oatley, 1972) that the function of sleep was to entrain an animal with the period of the day-night cycle when it was at its best (e.g., being able to see in the light) and showed what principles underlie entrainment (1974). This kind of view of the function of sleep is now generally accepted.

35. Putting it crudely, amphetamines and drugs like heroin and cocaine, in certain doses, invoke happiness. But some drugs taken for recreational reasons sometimes produce bad trips, that is, states of intense fear. For therapeutic uses most attention has been paid to drugs that reduce the intensity of maintained moods. Alcohol and tranquilizers such as the benzodiazepines reduce fear. Antidepressants reduce sadness.

36. Teasdale (1988) has argued that both for etiology and therapeutics the problem in such cases may be thought of as one in which a self-reinforcing cycle is based on a mood, influenced, as Oatley and Johnson-Laird would say, by effects of basic emotion signals that need not relate consciously to events. This mood is based on a maintained mode that biases the system toward accessing certain kinds of semantic message, which then function to maintain the system in the same mode. Therapeutic intervention in this cycle can be either pharmacological or cognitive.

37. Our theoretical difficulty with emotions of withdrawal and rejection is made sharper by Ekman and Friesen's (1986) finding of a unique pancultural facial expression of contempt. This suggests that contempt might be considered basic. According to Oatley and Johnson-Laird (1987) and to Johnson-Laird and Oatley (1989) each basic emotion can occur without any semantic information associated with it – nausea and a nonspecific sense of revulsion have this property for disgust, so for emotions of withdrawal related to food there seems to be no problem. But contempt seems as if it must have an object. We would like to interpret contempt as a basic signal of disgust/hatred at some semantically known person.

   We would argue that although contempt has a distinctive facial expression, this alone does not qualify it as basic. Such an argument would also indicate that embarrassment is basic, as it has a unique, biologically based physiological accompaniment that is also an expression, namely, blushing. Embarrassment, however, is not basic. Its basic signal is fear and its semantic component of being the object of unwelcome attention. See Chapter 2 for a description of the combination of basic emotions with semantic information.

Chapter 2

1. I started the first chapter with a scene in which Anna Karenina experienced a sequence of emotions. I relied on Tolstoy's accounts of them. An empirical argument would be that there are methodologies for studying just these emotions that could yield factual data of a far superior kind (as argued, for instance, by McNaughton, 1989). Physiological monitoring could indicate changes in peripheral circulation and heart rate of actual subjects. One could make video recordings of facial expressions. One could experiment with animals, or make measurements in experimentally induced conditions on humans. One could discuss a neuroscientific theory of what influences the states we call emotions have on behavior.

2. The term intentionality is derived from Brentano's use: a mental phenomenon with "reference to a content, direction towards an object" (Brentano, 1973/1874, p. 88). Intentionality thus means a mental state that will

allow statements that include a predicate in which the term "that" appears or could appear, for example: "He desired that P," "She believed that Q," and so on. Such statements are known in philosophy as propositional attitudes.

An intention in its ordinary sense means a conscious goal with a plan to do something. I will try to maintain the distinction between intentional and intentionality on the one hand as meaning mental aboutness, and intend and intention on the other hand as meaning having conscious goals and plans.

3. This set of propositions may be thought of as similar to Aristotle's idea of a practical syllogism. See *Nichomachean Ethics*, 1146b–1147.

4. Patricia Churchland (1986) vigorously lays out the philosophical basis of a causal neuroscience. She, Paul Churchland, and Stich became known as eliminativists, because they propose accounts that eliminate mentalistic concepts. Stich (e.g., 1988) more recently has left this group, and now takes the view that eliminativism needs to be taken seriously, but that a pluralistic position is more appropriate.

The eliminativist position has been given impetus by the work on neural computation, based on parallel distributed processing, or connectionism (see, e.g., McClelland & Rumelhart, 1986). This view has been energetically opposed by those insisting on the "classical" approach to artificial intelligence, which can appropriately be called symbol processing and in which a level of mental representations intermediate between behavior and neural implementations is regarded as important (see Fodor & Pylyshyn, 1988).

One way of seeing the issue is that the eliminativists insist on accounts in terms of what Aristotle called efficient causes, whereas folk theoretical terms like desire and belief are final causes. See also Averill (1982) for a discussion of the difficulties of functional explanations in this area.

Clark's (1987) argument, in agreement with the one that I develop here, is that both in physics and psychology some folk theories, though not all, indicate a basic competence of mind to mirror nature and social interaction. As such, these theories are not automatically "wrong." They are the places to start in explaining mentality.

5. The decisive blows in the overthrow of Aristotelian physics, which can be thought of as the attempt to make explicit some of our ordinary intuitions in physics, are usually attributed to Galileo. He wrote his famous books, *Two Chief World Systems* and *Two New Sciences* as dialogues between an Aristotelian, Simplicio, and a Copernican, Salviati, with a third person, Sagredo, listening, as it were, impartially.

I get the impression that Aristotle, far from being dismayed by these dialogues, would have approved because although they overthrew many of his conclusions, they drew exactly on the methods he advocated – namely, of taking reputable opinions, trying to resolve differences, and looking for inconsistencies dialectically in order to approach a more general understanding.

Take, for instance, one of the most famous of Galileo's ideas in which he shows that one object weighing 10 times as much as another does not fall faster. The problem with the idea that heavier weights fall faster has nothing much to do with empirical observation, let alone any special instruments – the argument could have been discovered by Aristotle himself. Though the "appearance" of the heavier weight falling faster seems intuitively plausible, it is the idea itself that is self-contradictory.

Here is a loose paraphrase of Galileo's argument: Imagine two iron weights, one of 1 kg and the other 10 kg. According to the intuitive theory, and to Aristotle's conclusion, the 10-kg weight should fall 10 times quicker – and Galileo tells us that we get this idea from feeling that heavier things press down more, and from weighing them in balances. But if the heavier weight fell quicker, then what would happen if we tied the two weights together with a piece of string and let them fall? Presumably the light one should slow down the heavier, and the heavier should speed up the light one, so together they would fall at a rate intermediate between that of the light and heavy weights falling separately. But now what if we tie the weights together very tightly with the string? What if we were to weld them together? We would have created an 11-kg weight, which according to the intuitive theory will fall faster than the 10-kg one. But according to the same theory, the 1-kg slows the 10-kg weight down.

It had to await a human landing on the moon to demonstrate this piece of counterintuition empirically in diluted gravity and zero air resistance – so that a television audience could see objects of different weights being dropped and descending at an equal rate.

6. It can scarcely be argued that psychology has lacked substantial scientific figures during the period of advances in physics. Descartes, for instance, wrote extensively on psychology, as did Helmholtz. A more plausible explanation is that only neurophysiological problems and a limited set of psychological problems, principally in perception, have yielded to methods that have been mainly natural scientific and experimental (cf. also Newell, 1972).

7. This is not a bad motto for the Aristotelian approach. Nevertheless, this quotation is from the mouth of Protagoras, by Plato in *Theaetetus*, 160d: Nussbaum's (1986) translation.

8. Natural scientists insist on separating observations and interpretations. This was a crucial advance, one of the keys to the success of natural science, perhaps the most important maneuver that allows us to stand outside the merely human world of appearances that may deceive. Aristotle's term *phainomena* does not imply any such distinction between observation and interpretation. In this sense *phainomena* need to be treated with caution.

I do not argue against disentangling observation from inference – it is fundamental. Instead, I am arguing that *phainomena* meaning intuitions or ordinary human interpretations also remain fundamentally important. These should not be surrendered either in natural or human science. Without them, understandings are never *our* understandings. Some of the greatest physical scientists, including Galileo and Einstein, were great precisely because they were constantly translating human intuitions into formal or mathematical arguments, and retranslating the results back into intuitions to allow us to perceive the world differently or more fully.

9. Putnam (1975) has shown that none of us know "the truth" about terms we use for natural objects and events. When I say "dog," I am saying "I mean what an expert, perhaps a zoologist, would mean by dog." The term is a placeholder for knowledge that I do not have but that is distributed in the community and that potentially I might have if I were to take up training in zoology.

Two things may happen here. First, the understandings of experts is gradually incorporated into ordinary culture. Perhaps we learn that dogs are animals to be grouped with paramecia and ostriches. Second, there is the realization that perfect knowledge is not possible for the individual. None of us, even experts, can attain it. Rather, science itself is a dialectical matter,

involving creative people and critics, teachers and learners, in a social organization in which, surprisingly, it is possible to talk about things and make
progress despite our ignorance.

   In discussion we can improve understanding, although probably not ever
reaching "the truth." Aristotelian philosophy is not the business of ever
having the correct view, but of comparing various kinds of appearances,
including those of experts, with our own to *approach* progressively better
understandings. This argument is influenced by Popper (e.g., 1962). See also
Chapter 3 for a further discussion on these matters.

10. Aristotle in *On Generation and Corruption,* for instance, gets into what seems
    to modern minds the most extraordinary muddles in explaining how things
    are created and decay. Many things appear, coming from nothing into some-
    thing. They also disappear from something into nothing again. These are
    apparently very salient physical phenomena.

    Aristotle had not much inkling of things and processes that are invisible
    but important. It is not that his reasoning methods as such were misleading,
    but that for problems like this in physics and biology he did not have any
    way of starting with the kinds of appearances that would be crucial for
    unifying explanations. One has to say, of course, that in cosmology trying to
    understand the creation of the universe still gives rise to problems.

    In the field of history, traditionally a discipline of human science, McNeill
    (1977) has argued that people were for many centuries unaware of the
    causes of epidemics. They too did not start with the most important *phai-
    nomena,* and consequently, though they solved many technical problems
    where visible things were at issue, the science and technology of public
    health lagged far behind because important causes were invisible. Not only
    that, continues McNeill, historians also choose salient human phenomena
    from which to start historical explanations, events like battles and treaties. It
    is more likely that many major conquests of cultures were caused mainly by
    disease in which unseen organisms caused ravages to cultures that had not
    acquired immunity.

11. This is an argument made by Humphrey (1983). He supposes that introspec-
    tion is an evolutionarily important means whereby we can consult our self as
    a model of other people, and thereby we are able predict their behavior from
    what we would do in their circumstances. See also Gordon (1987), who
    argues that we are very good at predicting our own behavior, as evidenced
    by our ability to say, "Now I will do x" and then do it. Our competence at
    this is as good or better than that of predicting the success of, say, launching
    a rocket into orbit around the earth. We are also good at simulating certain
    mental states of other people.

12. None of the terms within parentheses in this paragraph refers to emotions,
    according to Johnson-Laird and Oatley (1989).

13. The corpus includes the 196 terms generated by Fehr and Russell's (1984)
    subjects, all the terms of Clore, Ortony, and Foss (1987) that were judged by
    them or their subjects as having an affective component, and the 136 terms
    used by Tiller (1988). From these three corpora we rejected 73 terms as not
    referring properly to emotions – typically they refer to accompaniments of
    emotions, eliciting conditions, bodily states, and so on. Then to the 327
    remaining proper emotion words from these corpora we added 263 that did
    not appear in any of them.

    The idea of componential analyses of emotion terms was explored by
    Aristotle, with much of this discussion being in the *Rhetoric*; see also Forten-

bough (1975). So, for instance, Aristotle describes anger as caused by a belief that one has been insulted, and it is directed at the perpetrator (*Posterior Analytics*, 94a, b). It is diminished by an apology or remedy, and it does not occur at all if one is treated justly (*Rhetoric*, 1380). By contrast, hatred does not have to be caused by an action. It can be felt simply toward a particular kind of person (1382a). Fear is caused by impending harm, and shame by the thought of disgrace (1382–1383).

Spinoza (1955/1675), an early cognitive theorist of emotions, gives in his *Ethics* an impressive componential analysis of emotion terms, taking into account antecedent causes and consequences. Here is an example: "Definition 23: *Envy* is hatred, insofar as it induces a man to be pained by another's good fortune, and to rejoice in another's evil fortune." Spinoza's analysis is based on his theory that there are essentially two kinds of emotions, positive ones based on love that accepts what is the case, and negative ones based on hatred that rejects what is the case.

14. Ortony and Clore (1989) have criticized the specificity of our "don't know why" linguistic test, and we have replied to their criticisms (Oatley & Johnson-Laird, 1990).

15. To hate, according to Johnson-Laird and Oatley (1989), is analyzed as "to feel intense disgust toward someone or something." But if the basic emotions of our theory were to include contempt/disdain, then this would be the basic emotion of hatred – to hate would then be to feel intense contempt/disdain toward someone or something.

16. Wittgenstein (1953) proposed that words have meanings that depend on usage and function within the rules of a public language game. He repealed his earlier (1922) theory that sentences were pictures of the world. He also questioned the possibility that we can ever directly refer to private events. Our view is that terms do not refer directly to private or public events. They refer to our concepts of such events. So, if we have a concept of a particular kind of feeling that typically accompanies a serious loss, then we refer to this as sadness (see also Wierzbicka, 1972).

17. This work includes Ortony, Clore, and Foss (1987), Clore, Ortony, and Foss (1987), Ortony (1987), and Ortony, Clore, and Collins (1988).

18. The prototype concept has become important in psychology through the work of Rosch (e.g., 1973) and in philosophy through the work of Putnam (1975) on stereotypes. It is an important discovery that we understand many things that are natural kinds in terms of prototypes, referring to something in language with terms indicating concepts that we do not understand completely: Such is the inadequacy of our mental models. It is remarkable that we can nevertheless let the other person understand what we are referring to. But this does not mean that everything is a prototype.

Johnson-Laird and I claim that we do know certain things about our own emotions, and that some such matters can be denoted by emotion terms. Our conclusions here are similar to those of Ortony, Clore, and Foss (1987).

19. Fehr and Russell (1984) propose that the concepts of love, fear, anger, and other emotions are captured in scripts that represent their prototypical sequences of events. Frijda's emotion processes are scriptlike in this sense. Fehr and Russell derive the term script from the work of Schank and Abelson (1978), who have used it to designate regularly occurring sequences of events. I discuss the idea of scripts further in Chapter 7.

20. Wierzbicka (1987) has said: "It is not the Aristotelian notion of necessary and sufficient features which causes troubles in semantic analysis; it is the tacit

behaviorist assumption that the necessary and sufficient features should correspond to measurable, objectively ascertainable aspects of external reality" (p. 25). Russell (1991) correctly argues that Johnson-Laird and Oatley's argument about confusing meaning with verification does not apply to Fehr and Russell's (1984) studies because in these, people were judging meanings not anything to do with identification.

21. Johnson-Laird and Oatley have argued that Fehr and Russell's (1984) subjects were not unanimous about whether pride is an emotion, because the noun pride is listed in dictionaries as having several meanings, including (1) a sense of one's own proper dignity or value, and (2) pleasure or satisfaction taken in one's work, achievements, or possessions. Russell (1991) has, however, now offered these two definitions to 117 subjects, asking whether either definition of pride indicates an emotion. In a nice test of what we were claiming he found that subjects were not unanimous in thinking either definition indicated an emotion, and the difference in the numbers of people saying that either definition referred to an emotion was not statistically significant. My sense is that neither definition catches the idea of pride as an emotion, and that Johnson-Laird and myself were wrong in offering this example. A better test in my view would be not to take definitions from a dictionary, but to ask whether "pride" as it appears in the following sentence is an emotion: She experienced pride as she watched her daughter receive her doctoral degree.

Considerations of the meanings associated with words must prompt one to be cautious of psychometric data based wholly on the ratings of single words out of context. Many studies have been based on sorting terms written on cards to see which terms are similar and which different. Among the most influential is that of Russell (1980), who concluded that English emotion terms can be defined in a space of two dimensions, pleasantness and arousal, and that the terms can be arranged in a circle passing through these axes. This is known as the two-dimensional circumflex model of emotion terms.

This model is open to criticisms. Tiller (1988) showed, for instance, in extending Russell's work, that different clusters emerged if people were asked to focus on eliciting situations of emotions or their effects than if they were asked just to sort the terms in an unconstrained way.

Lutz (1982) also used a sorting technique with her subjects on the Pacific atoll of Ifaluk. They did not show an arrangement reminiscent of Russell's, probably, as she points out, because the Ifaluk made their categorizations of emotions mainly on the basis of antecedents, which is consonant with their implicit theory that emotions are not to be thought of as individualized feelings, but as arising in particular interpersonal situations. Instead, the clusters show some similarities to those of Tiller when he asked subjects in Oxford to focus on eliciting situations, but there are also differences as might be expected as the situations that elicit emotions in Oxford and Ifaluk can differ.

According to Johnson-Laird and Oatley (1989) and to Ortony, Clore, and Foss (1987), sorting emotion terms into categories, although it may be helpful as a first step in understanding emotion terms, is not as helpful as it may seem because of the inherent ambiguity of emotion terms when presented alone.

Lutz's and Tiller's results, on Ifaluk and English terms, respectively, both produce clusters that are consonant with our postulate of basic emotions, but they also produce some other clusters that are not easily recognized as grouped by the same basic emotion. For the subjects they shared something else that is salient, for example, a common type of condition capable of eliciting emotions. We do not propose that the basic family to which an emotion belongs is its most salient characteristic to everyone experiencing that emotion. Saliency will depend on the attitude and concerns of the person involved.

22. See, for instance, particularly the book of Frijda (1986), the papers of Ekman, Lazarus, Leventhal, Plutchik, Scherer, and Tomkins in the book edited by Scherer and Ekman (1984), and reviews by Leventhal and Tomarken (1986) and Leventhal and Scherer (1987).

23. Richard Feynman, the physicist, in a television interview (1981) told a story of how when he was a child he spent a lot of time with his father who had an intense interest in the physical world. One day, young Feynman was playing with a toy wagon that had a ball in it. He noticed that when he pulled the wagon the ball rolled toward the back, but when the wagon got stuck on some obstruction the ball rolled forward. Why did that happen? The older Feynman said: "Nobody knows. The general principle is that things that are moving try to keep on moving, and things that are still tend to stand still unless you push on them hard. This tendency is called 'inertia,' but nobody knows why it's true" (p. 635).

As Richard Feynman said, his father knew the difference between knowing the name of something and understanding it, knowing how it works. Inertia is a better concept than impetus in that it has functional significance, but there are still questions about how it works.

24. The fact that a concept acquires currency attests to its usefulness in discourse. It does not insulate it from change. Meanings change considerably: For instance, 500 years ago, according to the Oxford English Dictionary, sad was a contraction of sated, having had one's fill of something. Terms in folk theory will change in the future, and be affected by better understandings, just as the folk theoretical term seeing has been affected by understandings of eyes as imaging devices like cameras. Better understandings of emotions will include clearing up boundaries, which itself will resolve some of the problems of the apparent heterogeneity of emotion terms, as Ortony, Clore, and their colleagues have done and as Johnson-Laird and I have done. Moreover, as the psychology of emotions advances this will have its effect on usage. Some terms that ordinary English speakers might now offer as examples of emotions may not in the future be seen as referring to emotions as our understanding grows. Physics has tidied up our understandings of the phenomena that are affected by the moon. We now think that the moon does affect tides, but not so many people think it affects human personality.

25. In a case that I know of, a woman reported that she made a huge bonfire of all the possessions and all the things she had been given by a co-habitee who had left, although there was no possibility that this would affect his future behavior and although this was not to her material advantage. Gordon (1987) draws on the arguments of Hebb (1946), discussed at the end of the previous section, that behavior can become unpredictable if only behaviorist assumptions are made. Emotion concepts allow greater predictability, and as in the case of the woman with the bonfire they require, I think, that we imagine ourselves in a comparable position. Similar arguments about behavior being prompted by emotions rather than instrumental considerations are also advanced by Frank (1988).

26. Studies in which people either make judgments of stories or vignettes (Roseman, 1984) or in remembered emotional incidents (e.g., Smith & Ellsworth, 1985; Scherer, 1984) involve a greater likelihood of responses generated from emotion folk theories or stereotypes (cf. Bartlett, 1932) if they are asked to judge a story or if they are asked to judge an incident from some time past. By contrast, people asked to make judgments about an emotion while it is happening, as Smith and Ellsworth (1987) have done for students' feelings just before taking an examination and when they received their results, will be less likely to draw on stereotypes than on noticing how they are actually reacting.

27. Schiff and MacDonald (1990) have also found that people performing a difficult task experienced it negatively and show facial expressions more on the left side of the face, and people performing an easy task experienced it positively and made more right-sided facial expressions.

28. Termine and Izard (1988) have found comparable results: Nine-month-old babies mirror their mother's happiness and sadness.

29. One has to say that although Klinnert's (1984) experiment is fascinating in conception, its results fall somewhat short of what might be hoped for. She took a number of measures of whether children approached a novel object when mothers looked happy and approached the mother herself if she looked fearful – but differential movement toward or away from the novel toy did not take place in a systematic way. My sense is that the phenomenon of social referencing as a guide to infant action is real but that the conditions for its laboratory demonstration when mothers pose facial expressions are difficult to accomplish.

30. This method is closely related to one derived from attribution theory (see, e.g., Weiner, 1985).

31. Salzen, Kostek, and Beavan (1986) have shown that photographs displaying different facial expressions can reliably be categorized by both adults and children, not just as to feeling but in terms of what the person was doing. The categories of action included passiveness, attention, aversion, aggression, rejection, protection, and acceptance.

32. Tiller (1988) also had people generate sentences describing antecedents. So for sadness, they created sentences like "The death of my cousin at the age of 40." A different set of subjects was also good at decoding antecedent sentences in terms of what emotions they would tend to elicit.

33. A number of researchers have conducted studies in which they have assessed the appraisals for a range of emotions, and they are reviewed by Scherer (1988). Scherer has said (personal communication) that he was not quite sure where the Oatley and Johnson-Laird theory fitted in with the other evaluation theories he reviewed in his 1988 paper, in the sense of our being inexplicit about the values of a range of attributes in eliciting situations for each emotion. I hope the accompanying text will go some way to explaining this inexplicitness.

34. Interest in feature detection theories in perception has recently been reawakened by the advent of parallel distributed processing models.

35. A fixed action pattern is described by ethologists as a pattern of action hardwired to a particular stimulus pattern that elicits it. This mechanism has been discussed by von Uexkull (1957) in the common tick. At a particular stage in its life cycle a photosensitivity of the skin triggers an upward journey. The tick climbs a bush and hangs on a twig. It lets go when a second trigger occurs, the smell of butyric acid secreted by the sweat glands of all

mammals, which are its hosts. If the tick happens to land on one such, passing underneath the bush, a third trigger becomes operative, the warmth of the mammals' bodies. Propelled by this taxis toward the warmth, the tick burrows through hair or fur to the skin. There it makes a puncture to fill itself with blood. Having done that, it drops off the animal to lay eggs on the earth. This mechanism where each action is triggered by a simple pattern works well in limited worlds. In computation production rules are similar – each action is triggered when a specific pattern is recognized (see, e.g., Charniak & McDermott, 1985).

36. In these experiments Conway and Bekerian (1987) and Conway (1990) also investigated more closely how information about autobiographical incidents during which particular emotions had been experienced is indexed under the appropriate basic emotion. They suggest that emotion concepts are stored in a hierarchy with general semantic knowledge. This corresponds, on my interpretation of their results, to claiming that at the top level is knowledge of cultural folk theory of basic emotions, that happiness is accompanied by feeling active, laughing, and so on. At the next level is what they call basic knowledge. It is also derived from folk theory, that happiness is associated with success, with children playing, with friendships. Then, at the next level are stored both general scripts, of success in meeting a goal, of meeting an old friend, and specific autobiographical events, of passing finals at university, of spending an evening with a particular friend. Nonemotional types of content, by contrast, are less frequently found to be stored in terms of such autobiographical events.

37. We do not, of course, deny that emotions are usually pleasant or unpleasant; we think that a deeper analysis is required. Emotions need to be analyzed in terms of the kind of goal-relevant evaluation that occurs and of the kind of action they make ready.

   Ortony, Clore, and Collins (1988) argue that emotions are "valenced reactions . . . being pleased or displeased, approving or disapproving, and liking or disliking" (p. 191). Oatley and Johnson-Laird (1990) have claimed this is an unsatisfactory basis for understanding emotions because too many things are evaluated in these ways that need have nothing to do with emotions. You can be pleased that it is Friday, you can disapprove of the space program, or you can like potato chips without emotions being elicited. What makes the definition too broad is that statements about the person's goals come too far down Ortony et al.'s decision tree, in their discussion of being pleased or displeased in reaction to events.

   Nor in our view have recent empirical attempts to pursue the idea of positive and negative valences been successful. Thus, Diener and Iran-Nejad (1986) asked subjects to rate moods they had experienced. Ratings indicated that subjects did not simultaneously experience both positive and negative affects, but for each event they made ratings of the same valency, for instance, "happy," "joyful," and "pleased." Diener and Iran-Nejad conclude that this argues against basic emotions, but in favor of pleasant positive and unpleasant negative evaluations being the only irreducible feeling elements. Diener and Iran-Nejad's conclusion is unconvincing to us because all the positive emotions that subjects rated were terms that we would regard as implying a single basic emotion, and this accounts largely for their results. We have also had an exchange of views on this issue with Frijda in *Cognition and Emotion* (Oatley & Johnson-Laird, 1987; Frijda, 1987a; Johnson-Laird & Oatley, 1988; see also Frijda, 1987b).

As I have argued in Chapter 1, there is a meaning of positive and negative emotions that makes sense. It is the one in which an evaluation of an event is positive if a goal is more likely to be attained and negative if less likely.

38. Lakatos himself was skeptical as to whether psychology qualifies as science, and so I must be careful in what I attribute to him. As a development of Popper's (1962) argument that a theory can be refuted by a single decisive observation, the view of Lakatos is that a theory, or as he puts it a "research program," is only ever replaced when a better one comes along. "Better" means being able to explain more of the data that are agreed as being important by the relevant research community. This last proviso, of course, is problematic because new theories prioritize observations that for older ones are insignificant.

Both Lakatos and Popper recognize that science is essentially a social activity with its most important mechanism being Aristotelian public discussion. Some people propose theories. Others propose alternative theories. Yet others, for instance the readers of the scientific literature and the writers of textbooks and reviews, decide among them. See Chapter 3 for further discussion.

39. I find some issues troubling for our theory without being able to see how to resolve them clearly. For instance, is disgust really the basis for hatred, and can it be felt acausally independently of feeling nauseous? Alternatively, is there a basic emotion of interpersonal withdrawal, something like hatred/contempt/disdain? Could surprise and interest be emotions? They seem to have some characteristics of emotions but not others. What about feeling faint at the sight of blood or at an operation? This has very strong autonomic effects, like those of an emotion, but not really the phenomenology of fear. I also find Frijda's (1987a) challenge troubling, that there may really only be pleasantness and unpleasantness, though with gradations and nuances, because it is not easy to see how to resolve a disagreement about phenomenological quality. Sadness, anxiety, and anger are not always unpleasant to me (e.g., when I am at the theater), but although it does not accord with my intuitions, I can see why the idea that these emotions feel primarily "negative" is appealing.

40. If an anthropologist were to report of a culture of humans behaving without emotions and speaking like Mr. Spock, the Vulcan in *Star Trek,* our theory would be wrong – and we would give it up.

41. I propose in Chapter 5 that ancient European writing offers further cross-cultural comparisons.

42. This is not to say that reports from cultures in which people do not express anger are without interest. Nance (1975), for instance, visited the 26 strong group of hunter-gatherers in the Philippines known as the Tasadays. They were discovered by Westerners in 1971. Nance, who spent 73 days with them, wrote: "They are altogether a loving gentle people. They have no weapons, and no apparent aggressive impulses." Descriptions of these people as nonaggressive should not be taken to answer such questions as: Could there really be people who never feel anger? Instead, Nance's description must be read in *contrast* to our assumptions derived from societies in which aggression is quite frequent.

Questions of universals can, of course, be raised, and it is of great interest to do so. For instance, Nance reports a visit of Eibl-Eibesfeldt, who observed "classic" aggressive behavior between toddlers, striking at one another and tugging at opposite ends of a stick. But simply remarking on the frequency or infrequency of an emotion in a society does not in itself indicate any universal.

43. I do not wish to disparage Leff's work in general. His work on how interpersonal emotions expressed by relatives affect relapse rates among people discharged from hospital with a diagnosis of schizophrenia (see, e.g., Leff et al., 1989, for one of the most recent papers in this series) is among the most important in the (Western) psychiatric understanding of schizophrenia. Following Lutz, I do wish to observe that exporting British cultural values is different from assuming one's stance to be objective.

44. Lutz (1985a, 1988a) points out that what counts as a loss, a danger, a difficulty in achieving a goal, and so on is defined within the culture under discussion.

45. The groupings are not very different from ours, but not exactly the five that our theory predicts. But this is probably because, as Lutz points out, her subjects made the categorizations mainly on the basis of distinctive eliciting conditions prevalent in their culture, not, for instance, on the basis of having distinctive phenomenological tones, let alone the attribute that Oatley and Johnson-Laird's theory predicts of being able to occur acausally. This issue is discussed further below.

46. Reviews of cross-cultural work on emotions may be found in Lutz (1988a) and Levy (1984).

47. There was a heavy weighting of European subjects in this study. So far as I can tell from this preliminary report, 18 of the 27 country samples were of native members of Euro-American culture, and none was unaffected by this culture. So cultural differences would tend to be underestimated.

48. There have been, of course, arguments against the rationalist, technological approach to mind, including arguments by people who have contributed notably to the program of cognitive science, for example, Weizenbaum (1979), Searle (1980, 1990), and Winograd (Winograd & Flores, 1986). In addition, Dreyfus (e.g., 1979) with a Heideggerian stance, has maintained a long-standing critical position with respect to artificial intelligence.

49. The project of this book did not start only from narrative literature. My interest in the psychology of emotions started from research in psychiatric epidemiology, interviewing people about the emotional consequences of stressful events in their ordinary lives, and also from psychotherapy. Phil Johnson-Laird's interest was in the semantics of emotion terms in ordinary language. The theory that has informed the book (Oatley & Johnson-Laird, 1987; Johnson-Laird & Oatley, 1989) was conceived jointly by us as cognitive psychologists. The methods of cognitive science involve making intuitions explicit – hence our project to understand cultural intuitions about English emotion terms.

Beginning this book with a novel is in the same spirit, including as it does the idea of making intuitions explicit. I do not wish to dismiss experimental methods in psychology. I merely assert that they are part, not the whole, of the enterprise. In studying emotions, moreover, they come later rather than earlier in the exploration.

50. In recommending an Aristotelian approach to emotions I am not espousing Fortenbough's (1975) argument that he derives from his study of Aristotle's work on emotions. This, in brief, is that by proposing that emotions are caused by evaluations of events, that is, cognitively, Aristotle could maintain that the alogical part of the soul can be communicated with in cognitive terms by the logical part, and hence persuaded by logical (in fact, rhetorical)

considerations. It is true that this is the thrust of Aristotle's main exposition of emotions in the *Rhetoric*, (cf. also note 5 in Chapter 3).

I am more persuaded, however, by Nussbaum's exposition of Aristotle's work on emotions as part of a much broader conception of ethics in a world that cannot be entirely controlled. Her interpretation of Aristotle's work is both more challenging and more relevant to the questions of this book.

51. I am grateful to Simon Garrod, who prompted me to reanalyze a draft of Chapter 5 of this book in terms of simulation rather than description. Sanford and Garrod (1982) have given an extended treatment of the hypothesis that writing is a means of affecting the reader's cognitive schemata.

Ricoeur (1984/1983) has proposed the idea of narrative as simulation running on the reader's mind like this: "What is interpreted in a text is the proposing of a world that I might inhabit and into which I might project my ownmost powers" (p. 81).

52. Aristotle discussed these matters: "Since the plot is a *mimesis* of an action, the latter ought to be both unified and complete, and the component events ought to be so firmly compacted that if any one of them is shifted to another place, or removed, the whole is loosened up and dislocated" (51a1). "The difference between the historian and the poet is not in their utterances being in verse or prose . . . the difference lies in the fact that the historian speaks of what has happened, the poet of the kind of thing that can happen . . . poetry speaks more of universals, history of particulars" (51b1).

Lest one think this old-fashioned, one might first remember that historical facts are partial and need interpretation, and then consider the following by the columnist Murray Kempton: "The novelist can always teach us more than the political scientist, because the realm called fiction is ruled by what is real, and the territory called fact has to make do with the dubieties of the fancied" (1990, p. 35).

53. Fortenbaugh (1975) is entirely typical in this respect. He speaks of "tragedy purging or purifying pity and fear."

54. Emotions elicited might not be the same as those of the characters. This will depend on the perspective that the reader has taken, whether he or she has identified with the protagonist from the inside, as it were, or is an onlooker at the scene (cf. Chapter 5).

55. In Chapter 5, I take this argument further, drawing on the work of George Eliot, who was more explicit than Tolstoy in maintaining a voice outside the action for purposes of the kinds of comparisons that I am describing.

Chapter 3

1. Descartes (1911/1649) proposed that the passions of the soul were "perceptions, feelings or emotions" (Article 27).

2. Mandler (1984, p. 37) remarks that the idea that people who are otherwise free are limited in their autonomy by animal passions is a characteristically nineteenth-century idea. Limitation of individual autonomy by social forces is a twentieth-century idea.

3. For Hume, passions were derived from sensations which then caused ideas of pleasure or pain, which in turn had motivational effects, as well as making associations with related impressions in the self and from memory. Hume, of course, was an empiricist, arguing that all knowledge comes via the senses and that mechanisms of mind are those of associations between

ideas. Modern research on parallel distributed processing (McClelland & Rumelhart, 1986) and on mood-dependent memory (Bower, 1981; Teasdale, 1988) resonates with Hume's ideas. Neu (1977) contrasts Hume's idea of emotions as simple elements derived directly from sensations, with Spinoza's cognitive theory of emotions as based on thoughts and judgments.

4. The Stoic philosophers started with Aristotle's demonstrations that emotions are cognitively based, and discussed how, by changing our judgments about events, emotions can be avoided or minimized. Zeno was the founder of this movement. Chryssippus, perhaps the greatest exponent of stoicism, was responsible for the idea that emotions are false beliefs. As Nussbaum (in press) shows, he was concerned with the conceptualizations of ordinary language, and his analysis of emotions is subtle and convincing. The school continued into Roman times, with Seneca and Marcus Aurelius. Many of its attitudes and doctrines were taken over by Christianity and have survived to modern times.

Averill (1982) discusses Seneca's treatise *On Anger*, which is a typical work, and an early treatise on the psychology of a particular emotion. In modern times, cognitive therapists such as Ellis and Harper (1975) and Beck (1976) take a similar, although philosophically less sophisticated, view, arguing that certain emotions derive from false beliefs – but the focus has shifted from anger to anxiety and depression. Unlike earlier therapies for thought, however, their therapy has been subjected to careful evaluation, with positive results (see, e.g., Robinson, Berman & Neimeyer, 1990).

5. Aristotle's view was that there are two parts of the soul, a rational and a nonrational part (see, e.g., *Politics*). Only the rational part is fit to rule because it can reason about moral issues. The nonrational part is appetitive and emotional.

Fortenbough (1975) has proposed that it was part of Aristotle's program to show in the *Rhetoric* that emotions are based on judgment and hence are not entirely separate from reason: Rhetoric is not appeal to emotions to warp reason, but a way of putting correct arguments in a persuasive way, so that the nonrational part of the soul can listen to reason. Subsequently, in the *Ethics* and *Politics*, Aristotle could then show how the nonrational part of the soul can be influenced for good by the rational part (cf. also note 50 in Chapter 2).

In the *Politics* Aristotle was concerned with the generalized issue of the rational ruler and the nonrational ruled. This relation, he says, is a fact of nature. The same kind of relation, with rulers being rational and the ruled nonrational but capable of being influenced by reason, is very widely found, he says. It occurs between the soul and the body, between the rational and the nonrational parts of the soul, between man and woman, between master and slave, between father and child, and between a king and his subjects.

The *Politics*, then, is a set of intuitions about social relationships, which are recognizable today – all too easily so. In this chapter I hope to show that some of the arguments are false. The reason, I suspect, why this dichotomy of ruler and ruled is laid upon that of rational and nonrational with such apparent facility and without raising, until recently, any very sustained criticism is that the arguments in which it is put assume that the reader or hearer will identify with the ruler and his purposes, and hence with the rational. Now of course, we may wonder what happens if we identify with the emotional part of the soul rather than with calculation, with woman rather than man, with slave rather than master. In the interpersonal cases it is clear that what used to mediate the relation was not rationality but power, which of course is all the more powerful if it is called by another name and is only partly visible.

6. The research program of cognitive science is expected to explain human cognition in terms of its functions and even model it computationally. So if emotions should prove to be functionless we would neither be able to understand them within the terms of cognitive science nor understand aspects of human thinking and action that are affected by emotion.

   A distinction between theories that propose that emotions are primarily functional and those that propose they are nonfunctional could, I think, be useful in assessing emotion theories. The communicative theory is based on the proposal that emotions are functional. Other theorists making such a proposal include Claparede (1928), Izard (1972), de Rivera (1977), Plutchik (1980), Averill (1982), and Tomkins (1984). Some of the theorists who propose that emotions are dysfunctional are discussed in this section.

   My reason for offering this distinction is that many researchers seem reluctant to discuss the question. More typically, emotion theories are classified as cognitive versus biological.

7. James (1884) entitled his famous paper "What is an emotion?" It was expanded into his chapter on "The Emotions" in Volume 2 of the *Principles of Psychology* (1890), which in turn was abridged in the corresponding chapter of the *Briefer Course* (1892), entitled "Emotion." These differences in title may be significant: People who think there is a specific system underlying these phenomena tend to refer to emotions (plural), whereas those who think as James did, that there is no specific system underlying emotions, but that the phenomena are general disturbances, consequences of arousal, side effects, intrusions from lower regions, and the like, tend to refer to emotion (singular).

8. Bermond et al. convincingly give reasons for supposing that their result is more to be trusted than Hohmann's (1962) in which decreases of emotion following spinal injury were reported. Bermond et al. had shorter intervals between interview and injury, more careful equalization of the incidents that triggered the emotion episodes, and they gathered separate information about bodily effects and subjective feelings, whereas Hohmann merely asked about bodily effects. See also Lowe and Carroll (1985), who interviewed 29 people with spinal injuries, asking them to imagine states of eight emotions – affection, anger, enjoyment, excitement, fear, grief, guilt, and hate – and to rate whether the intensity of the feeling had increased, stayed the same, or decreased relative to such feeling before their injury. There were no significant decreases in the intensity of any of the emotions. For affection, there was an increase.

9. Duffy (1941), for instance, describes the disorganizing properties of responses that are ordinarily called emotional within her argument that the term emotion as such is worse than useless for scientific purposes. For a textbook presentation of disrupting or disorganizing influence of emotion, see Atkinson et al. (1990). I take up the issue of stress in Chapter 6.

10. Yerkes and Dodson's 1908 paper was the stimulus for many years of research, with a more modern descendant being Easterbrook (1959). Activation theory was the term used by Lindsley (1951) to integrate behavioral and neurological findings in this area. For some years these issues were very much at the forefront of psychological research on emotions.

11. Leeper's review may seem dated, but many introductory psychology text-

books indicate that the underlying sense of emotion as irrational is still with us. Most textbook writers feel it necessary to have a chapter or at least a section on emotion. In recent years this has tended to include a review of James's and Cannon's theories and a presentation based around Schachter and Singer's (1962) study, which is discussed later in this section. The conclusions of these discussions, as described by Leeper, are that there is something irrational about emotions. More recent, introductory textbooks, although including these elements, have tended also give fuller and more representative presentations of research on the psychology of emotions. Good examples are Bernstein et al. (1988) and Atkinson et al. (1990).

12. See Oatley (1978) for a discussion of Hughlings-Jackson's influence on neuropsychological thinking.

13. From early in his scientific career, Darwin collected copious notes (see, e.g., Gruber, 1974) on the material basis of mind, and after the *Origin of Species*, he planned a book showing how the human species had evolved. It became too large, so that one part became *The Descent of Man* and the other part the *Expression of Emotions*. Both have essentially psychological concerns and they put Darwin with Helmholtz and Freud as one of the three principal founders of modern psychology.

14. See Boakes (1984, p. 204). I thank Bob Boakes for discussion of this issue.

15. The Weismann doctrine is that if a phenotype acquires adaptations to an environment they cannot be transmitted to the genotype. The opposing view is that of Lamarck, who supposed that acquired characteristics could be inherited – Darwin was Lamarckian in his proposals about the inheritance of habits. The Weismann doctrine is embodied in the "central dogma" of molecular genetics, which states that DNA can transmit information to proteins, but proteins cannot compile information into DNA (see, e.g., Dawkins, 1982).

16. In artificial intelligence this effect is implied by the phrase "procedural embodiment of knowledge." It means that knowledge is only usable locally in a procedure serving a particular goal and is not accessible more generally or for other purposes.

17. Bryan and Harter (1897) in a famous paper argued that when habits are built up they require a great deal of conscious attention.

18. I am most grateful to Steve Draper for discussing optimization problems with me. The issue raised here in considering emotional expressions is very general. So, for instance, Reason (1984, 1986a) has argued that optimization for speed and automaticity can lead to lack of discrimination of circumstances that trigger habits in skilled operators. This is responsible for much human error, including many of the serious accidents that occur to aircraft, power stations, and so on.

   Wilensky's (1983) theory of planning also confronts problems of optimization: He sees everyday problems as those of summoning up stored action sequences and the optimization problem as that of orchestrating them to fulfill as many goals as possible. In any system that works in this kind of way some actions that occur will seem inappropriate to some goals.

19. Such attitudes are the tip of a large iceberg. Lutz (1986) nicely catches a range of Euro-American cultural assumptions about emotion, several of them contradicting others. She shows how, as well as occurring in contrast to thought, emotion is the mark of engagement rather than alienation; it occurs as unintended and uncontrollable acts; it implies danger and vulnerability; it corresponds to physicality, to the natural rather than to social

conventions, to subjectivity in contrast to objectivity and as female rather than male.

In my attempt to start the consideration of emotions from the point of view of folk theories, I try to enter the problem not at this level of cultural attitudes, which do indeed contain mistakes and contradictions, but at the level of how meanings of terms in natural language are constructed and of the intentional explanations of emotion and action that occur in discourse such as novels. The contradictoriness and even the objectionable qualities of some of the cultural attitudes described by Lutz in her 1986 paper are among the *phainomena* and opinions that have to compared with each other in order to reach more general principles.

20. Scheff (1979) gives a scholarly and compelling account of Freud and Breuer's (1955/1895) conceptualization of hysteria as an effect of earlier traumatic experience. Scheff argues that Freud and Breuer's lack of therapeutic efficacy may have been because their techniques of allowing patients to relive early traumas were crude. They were unaware, he argues, of the idea of optimum distancing – and their therapy tended to be overdistanced, too verbal. Although they discussed arousal of affect, Scheff surmises that its level was low. For optimal results events must be reexperienced intensely, not just remembered. Moreover, Scheff argues, Freud and Breuer were unaware of the necessity of repeated discharge of emotional tension. With these elements, Scheff argues, therapy based on catharsis can be very effective, and is an essential component of psychotherapy of many kinds.

21. Claparede (1928) makes the point that the objection of saying, "Why not just perceive the heart beating, rather than feeling fear?" is solved by arguing that it is the interpretation of a Gestalt of bodily events that will constitute the emotion.

22. Tomkins's idea is close to Cannon's, taken over from James, that subcortical impulses give tone and color to experience.

23. This is not to argue that adaptation places absolute constraints on organisms; otherwise, animals with separate evolutionary histories but similar niches would always become similar.

24. Both these series of demonstrations are well known, and are discussed at length in works on thinking (e.g., Baron, 1985) and on cognitive science (e.g., Gardner, 1985; Sanford, 1985). I discuss them here briefly and selectively. Nisbett and Ross (1980) have presented another important set of demonstrations of human biases in inference making, extending the methods and insights of Kahneman and Tversky toward social science paradigms, such as attribution and forced compliance. I have discussed these briefly in Chapter 2 and shall return to them at the end of this chapter.

25. For evidence that mental models are used in syllogistic reasoning, see, for example, Johnson-Laird and Bara (1984). Syllogisms as bases for reasoning about beliefs and practical syllogisms as bases for generating rational actions were, of course, the paradigms that Aristotle invented in his explorations of rationality (see, respectively, for instance, in *Prior Analytics* and *Ethics*).

26. The improvement of cognition by social interaction is discussed later in this chapter.

27. See Perrow (1984), Baars (1986), Reason (1986), and Doerner (1987) for recent studies of human error, as well as the research mentioned in the text.

28. De Sousa also asks the question about the function of emotions, wondering why it seems an odd question. As with Frijda's (1986) theory, and my own, he proposes that emotions are attentional, determining salience and priority.

29. We find ourselves again confronted with the classical idea of reliable *episteme* being specific to particular skills in limited domains like mathematics or chess. Other domains have specific criteria that differ from each other. In natural science, Popper (1962) argues that attempting falsification is the basis of rationality and the means to improve theories. For conversation, Grice (1975) argues that his principles of implicature mark the boundaries of rationality. In manufacturing it is rational for a large company to test public acceptability of a new item on a small scale before committing capital to large-scale production, and so on.

30. Although we can invoke automatic action-generating procedures very rapidly when they have been compiled, constructing them is long and error prone. A person trained in first aid, for instance, can keep alive for 30 minutes or more someone whose heart has stopped until an ambulance arrives. But if one sees someone who has collapsed, there is not time to think from first principles even if one has medical knowledge. One needs to enact life-saving plans without thinking, for example, make a couple of basic tests and carry out simple plans like artificially inflating the lungs and manually pumping the heart in the right way.

31. See also Sacerdoti (1977) and Tate (1975).

32. See Dixon (1976). The Strategic Defense Initiative promises to re-create the military blunders of the past in space. Though computer programs can no doubt be written to control individual missiles and other pieces of ordnance, it would be impossible to write a mega-program that would coordinate all of the mechanisms and function properly in an actual conflict. Such a program would inevitably be too large to be bug-free. There would at the most be one opportunity to use this system in earnest, and the types of interactions that could occur would be too many to be predicted or controlled (see, e.g., Patel & Bloembergen, 1987).

33. In some skilled performances potential errors are accompanied by socially established means of detection and correction, as Hutchins (1987) has shown in his study of navigation on the bridge of a ship maneuvering in confined waters. Accompanying this is the means of apprenticeship by which new men are inducted into each skill of the navigation process, so that each comes to know both his own role and, when skilled, also the roles of the other participants with whom he must interact.

34. Psychotherapy could be added to Hutchins's examples of social thinking. Many therapists propose systems of therapy as methods of thinking. Currently, cognitive therapy is based on the idea that neurotic people think in a distorted way and should be taught to think more logically (cf. the Stoics). An alternative view is that therapy depends more on its social structure than on any particular method. Dialogue with another person can help one's thinking. Perhaps dialogue is the primary form of thinking and individual thinking is secondary (cf. Harré, 1983). It is not that people who suffer from so-called emotional disorders necessarily suffer from illogicality of the kind claimed by cognitive therapists (e.g., Beck, 1976). Rather, thinking in a dialogue can expand the range of one's models, apply views from outside one's own mental schemata, and help one to understand some of the implications of one's goal structure.

35. McFarland (1989) has recently argued against basing analyses of behavior on representations of goals. He argues that the issue is more a matter of rule-governed behavior with trade-offs and optimizing over multiple constraints. In contrast to my arguments in Chapter 2, McFarland argues that intentional

language is an inappropriate basis for science in that it is designed to deceive others and oneself. This idea that deception is necessary between individuals is current among students of animal behavior: For humans at least, I believe this to be entirely mistaken, as I explain in Chapter 4. The volume in which McFarland's paper appears is a discussion between biologists and philosophers on the problematics of intentions.

Chapter 4

1. From Burns "To a mouse." A rough translation is "The best constructed plans often don't go straight."
2. I am grateful to George Kiss for pointing out to me that emotional expressions have to be parsed and interpreted. But the parts of the expression do not relate systematically to parts of what is being communicated, so are not like propositions, and do not have semantic content in the usual sense. One does not know what a person is angry about from the structure of the frown. The distinction between semantic and nonsemantic signals is worth maintaining because their intentions are different. The intention of a semantically based speech message is informational: to address some cognitive schema of the hearer, to offer a suggestion about a goal, to supply information. Nonsemantic messages are concerned with the organization of control within the system, and also with invoking a particular mode of interaction among agents for instance to structure a particular role relationship.
3. Compare Weber's (1968/1922) notion of instrumental rationality, discussed in Chapter 3. This and comparable definitions indicate that we make models of other people in order to manipulate them planfully, just as we make models of the physical world. Strategists in various domains from warfare and politics, to business and even sexual relationships, argue that this is possible. Some argue that it is necessary for success in the social world.
4. These are the kinds of emotions postulated by researchers of animal learning, where animals are conceptualized as needing merely to learn the instrumental contingencies of their environment: for example, elation when a reward for running along a runway was larger than the animal was used to (see Zeaman, 1949), and frustration when nonreward occurs when it is expected (see Amsel, 1958).
5. Interfaces for computers are beginning to extend our idea of tools. Although current computers are tools, opportunities are being created to interact with them in ways that are more like our interactions with people, for example, in consulting expert systems.
6. Conversation is seen here as the basic mode of speech. Other kinds of utterance occur of course, as monologues, but except in special circumstances these are unusual or at least derivative from exchanges. In linguistics, however, it has frequently been assumed that a single utterance is the pragmatic unit of analysis.

   It was Austin (1962) who raised a profound and important question: How can an utterance accomplish an intention? We know that physical actions can achieve a goal that is a state of the world: Placing an egg in boiling water for 4 minutes produces a boiled egg. But utterances merely perturb the air. So what is their relation to goals and actions in the physical world?

   Austin proposed how this might occur. Pieces of speech can be uttered with an intention to achieve some state of affairs. Clear examples include "I pronounce you man and wife," in which by convention someone with the correct attributes saying this in the right way at the right time and place succeeds in marrying two people. Such utterances have become known as speech acts (Searle, 1969). Though tentative at first, Austin later argued that all utterances are speech acts. If I say, "It is raining," this is not just a neutral description of a state of affairs. It is a contracted form of "I warn (advise, inform, etc.) you that it is raining." The elided first person, active, indicative verb, warn, advise, and inform implies an intention of the speaker.

The linguistic argument has been that speech acts accomplish things in the mind of the listener because they obey social conventions known to speaker and hearer. So to say, "It is raining" counts as issuing a warning to the listener to take an umbrella, or some such. The speech act is successful if the hearer leaves the house prepared for rain.

Austin coined the idea of illocutionary force to indicate the way in which an utterance is intended to have an effect on its hearer because of its conventional meaning. He added the term perlocutionary force to indicate the effect that the utterance actually has, because of its conventional meaning and because of the accompanying circumstances of its utterance. It remained to Power to show how these effects are not effects like physical effects, achieved with a tool. They are accomplished by both actors cooperating in a joint plan.

In the argument here groups of such acts, typically pairs, are taken as appropriate pragmatic units. Sacks and colleagues call a related pair of utterances an "adjacency pair," based on their analysis of conversation in terms of turn taking (Sacks, Schegloff & Jefferson, 1974). Power and dal Martello (1985) have argued, however, that syntactic considerations like turn taking are not the most appropriate. Rather the organization of dialogue depends on how participants achieve goals. One example is that for several people to talk at once is a waste of effort. It is better to let someone talk, and wait to contradict, make further suggestions, and so on.

A unit of Power's robot conversation is a conversational procedure. Its goal is to accomplish what Draper has called an increment of agreement between the two agents in the service of building and executing their joint plan. It typically consists of two speech acts, such as a request and a reply or a suggestion and assent to it. The procedure ends when it has achieved the increment of agreement that was its goal. In this sense a silence of the right kind can be a reply, typically a negative one.

Recently, Oatley, Draper, and Button (submitted) have applied this analysis to real human conversation, with some success, but showing also that utterances do not always achieve increments of agreement. Often, they add constraints on the interpretation of what has been said before and of what will come later.

7. Routines may call other routines or conversational procedures. Conversational procedures may call other conversational procedures or routines. In the set of utterances 8 to 15, Mary has started a conversational procedure to agree on a plan. This calls the routine to make a plan, which in turn calls the conversational procedure of asking for information.

8. Wittgenstein's earlier theory of meaning held that "the proposition is a picture of reality" (1922, 4.01). In *Philosophical Investigations* (1953), he proposed the alternative idea of language composed of language games, essentially social phenomena. Despite exhortations to make this idea central to social science, by, for instance, Winch (1958), such an application of Wittgen-

stein's idea has remained rather blurred. Power's program shows clearly for the first time, I think, a basis for its application. Power also shows that a language game can be constructed of conversational procedures whose purpose is to build joint planning trees, which in turn serve as the basis of plans to be enacted cooperatively. Referring expressions relate to the world via such planning trees, and hence via actions which may achieve effects.

9. Many mutual relations are established without explicit promises or acknowledgements, however. They arise implicitly by precedent and custom in families, friendships and larger communities, and even in nations.

    The fact that we can feel pride, disappointment, or outrage as we evaluate what has happened even to abstract groupings such as nations suggests that cognitive structures similar to those entered into explicitly with individuals also underlie our participation in these larger groupings. It suggests that plans involving these groupings may also be analyzed in the kind of way that Power has shown. For instance, Rawls (1972) has shown that the principle of justice as fairness in society has an implicit contractual basis.

10. Oatley, Draper, and Button (submitted) have found that laughter signals the recognition by one actor of a discrepancy in joint planning. It functions to promote solidarity. If serious discrepancies occur, or where there is no underlying emotional tone of cooperation, such junctures give rise to anger, which can have quite different effects and consequences, as will be described later in this chapter.

11. Often social emotions are experienced as aspects of a relationship – being in love, for instance, is experienced as relating the self to another and has the effect of including the other within the boundary of the self. It can change one's perception of the other person, and even the physical world. Being angry involves seeing that other person as a transgressor. At the same time the phenomenological, physiological, and other perturbations are felt in the self. In Europe and America, perhaps because of our individualistic philosophy, we seem not to experience emotions as primarily between people.

12. Being engaged to be married in the older conventional sense involves frustration, delay, and restriction, and yet it is usually experienced as happy. Another example of how interruptions and delays can make for positively toned emotions is given by Meyer (1956) in his discussion of emotion in music. Dissonances and the unresolved quality of development sections in musical passages can leave one in delicious suspense, not resolved until the end of the piece.

13. Sociobiologists with their concept of inclusive fitness point to mother and infant each having an interest in the survival of their own genes. Each has an average of 50% of genes in common with the other. In these terms there is potential for cooperation in a joint goal, as well as for conflict of individual goals.

14. Some adult emotions, particularly envy and jealousy, are often attributed to infants by psychoanalytic writers. Although the work of Dunn (e.g., 1987) has shown that behavior characteristic of envy, jealousy, and the like occurs in young children, some psychoanalysts project adultomorphic ideas onto infants without empirical constraint. Envy, for instance, though it is no doubt based on feelings that arise in early childhood as Dunn has shown, and as indeed I am arguing, develops further in adult life and acquires meanings dependent on a consciously recognized representation of self that does not fully emerge until adolescence (see Damon & Hart, 1982), as discussed later in this section.

15. The observations in this paragraph should be taken as shorthand pointers to complex issues that are not well understood, some of them (e.g., the question of the appearance of depression in childhood) are controversial (see Angold, 1988).

16. Though the self in European and American society is highly individualized, there is no sense, I think, from anthropology that people in other societies lack a sense of self. Rather, in some societies the self is more explicitly socially structured. In Bali, for instance, as Geertz (1975) has put it, and as is discussed in Chapter 2, the maintenance of the self depends on social performance from which traces of individuality have been eliminated.

17. Damon and Hart (1982) trace the development of the sense of self through adolescence in the United States. Harris and his colleagues (Harris, 1983) have investigated children's experience of emotion at different ages (see also Harris et al.'s, 1987, discussion of children's emotion understanding in a Nepalese culture). See also the discussion of cross-cultural issues in Chapter 2.

18. This is the conclusion of Johnson-Laird and Oatley (1989), who give an analysis of complex terms, defined as described here, in their analysis of 590 English emotion terms.

19. Freud (1961/1923) developed some of these ideas of the individual mentally importing a monitoring agency from the social world. In this he followed Adam Smith and George Herbert Mead, though he was not clearly influenced by either. Freud's concept of the superego was that of a precipitate of earlier relationships, imbued with the guilt of incestuous oedipal cravings and becoming the basis of conscience. It operates as an agency that sternly monitors and comments upon the self's adult doings in terms of repressive concepts of the father.

20. The idea that emotion is a prototype has been espoused by Shaver et al. (1987), by Fehr and Russell (1984) in the form of scripts, by De Sousa (1980, 1987) in the form of paradigm scenarios, and by Frijda (1986) in the form of the emotion process. The core idea of all these is that there is a sequence of eliciting condition, appraisal, and action, which cohere together in a schematic way, and is recognizable as a particular emotion in a particular culture. Lutz has made an advance in showing that there are several such schemata and how they work in interactions with other people.

21. I am grateful to Catherine Lutz for pointing this out; and inadvertently reminding me of a funeral I attended at which the congregation had been tearless until the daughter of the woman who had died uttered an audible sob, at which point my tears and those of others in the congregation flowed rather freely.

22. One reason why the arguments of Lutz and Averill find resistance is because many are convinced that emotions are fundamentally biological, and even may think that James (1884) was right that emotions are perceptions of bodily states (cf. Tomkins, 1984; Zajonc, Murphy & Inglehart, 1989). Hence emotions cannot, by definition, be socially constructed or interpersonal.

23. Recently in England a normative criterion of judging provocation by what would have made a reasonable person enter a state of passion was introduced formally, replacing these four specific types of provocation.

24. Four of the 80 married community subjects in Averill's study were no longer married at the time of the study. To achieve this number of subjects, 156 people were contacted. Thus a response rate of 54% was achieved in the community study. In the student study 93% responded. (The student sample of persons who had been subjected to someone else's anger, described

later, had a similar response rate.) In all samples there was an equal number of responses from males and females.

25. I have not counted carefully, but my impression is that a very high proportion of contemporary film and television dramas are based on two ideas. One is that justifiable anger at some wrong is transmitted to viewers who are keen to identify with this emotion. The emotion in the hero and the viewers then sanctions actions that are otherwise entirely unacceptable in society, namely, ruthless outpourings of violence. The other is that involuntarily falling in love sanctions behavior that would ordinarily be totally unacceptable, namely, the breaking of all existing commitments, for instance, to a family. In this second case Hollywood is ambivalent in that whereas good always comes of the violence begotten of justified anger it does not always come from the role transitions induced by falling in love – sex often leads to tears.

    Catherine Lutz has pointed out to me (personal communication) that the analysis of emotions implied in Table 6 does not work for some Ifaluk emotions. *Ker*, for instance, is treated as dangerous precisely because it risks breaking off implicit joint plans. I think, however, that this requires extension of the idea that I am proposing, rather than radical change.

26. Levenson and Gottman (1983) report that physiological linkage accounted for 60% of the variance of marital satisfaction, far more than any other factor reported in the literature. For instance, questionnaire measures have only accounted for about 10% of this variance, and observational measures for 25%.

27. A recent review of affect in close relationships, including a discussion of the work of Levenson and Gottman, and concentrating on the effects that affect has on cognition in relationships, is given by Bradbury and Fincham (1987). Ekman (personal communication) has suggested that in interpersonal arguments contempt can guard against escalation at least in oneself, whereas when anger is experienced and expressed both participants tend to become locked into escalating cycles, as described by Levenson and Gottman.

28. Examples of speech acts containing emotion terms in the rest of this chapter come, except where otherwise indicated, from a corpus of utterances that I have collected from conversations I have overheard or in which I have taken part.

29. Hochschild (1983) has gone on to show that many people's employment is dependent on their skill in managing their emotions in ways appropriate to their job – appropriate at least in terms of definitions given by their employers. Such emotion management is especially demanded of women in Euro-American society. In her 1983 book Hochschild describes her study of the emotional training of aircraft cabin personnel, whose job it is to provide a pleasant emotional atmosphere for the passengers.

30. Descriptions of emotional dispositions are expected, and sometimes explicitly requested in formal character references for jobs. It is a recommendation to say, "She is a cheerful person," a damning indictment to say "She is sometimes sulky."

Chapter 5

1. Cf. John Keats: "On first looking into Chapman's Homer." The *Iliad* is, apart from the Bible, probably the most influential work in European literature.

Hammond (1987, p. 7, introduction to the Pelican *Iliad*) describes it as the cornerstone of Western civilization.

2. An impressive tracing of what has changed in European literature since Homer's time has been accomplished by Auerbach (1953/1946).

3. In translations from the *Iliad* I have basically followed A. T. Murray's translation in the Loeb edition of 1924, which is keyed to the Greek text, though I have changed some of the old-fashioned phraseology, altering "thou" to "you" and so forth.

It is thought that the *Iliad* was written around 800 B.C.E. It chronicles an oral tradition that probably drew on experiences of the previous few hundred years, with the poet, if he or she was a single person, incorporating stories from a variety of sources and assembling them into a substantial work of remarkable poetic unity. These stories are thought to be tales of the Mycenaean civilization at its height. At that time social conditions in the eastern Mediterranean and Asia Minor were changing rapidly and frighteningly. There had been unprecedented amounts of travel. There had been natural disasters such as the eruption of Theira. There had been migrations of population, increases in trade, widespread captures of people for use as slaves (of whom Helen may herself have been an example). Diplomatic contact between civilizations as far away as Egypt had begun, as had wars among city-states, such as the war of the Achaeans with Troy in what is now northwest Turkey. As we know from archaeological evidence, one of the strata on the site of Troy was destroyed in a way that is not inconsistent with the story of the *Iliad*. All this occurred around the time that writing began to be used for purposes other than trade, inventories, and laws.

4. Feuerbach (1957/1841) wrote a famous essay on the thesis that God consisted of human characteristics projected outward. He influenced many people, including Nietzsche, Kierkegaard, and George Eliot, who was the translator of his work into English.

5. Jenny Jenkins has pointed out to me that this indicates that even then emotions and external promptings were seen as not entirely involuntary.

6. Cf. Aristotle's discussion of the soul; see my introduction to Part I. Plato expounded the idea that the soul has an intellectual existence apart from the body. That view has remained influential in Western thought.

7. Snell's metaphor of superior gods activating humans on a lower stage is not unique. The Japanese drama form of Bunraku employs a comparable metaphor of people being moved by forces outside themselves (see, e.g., Inoura & Kawatake, 1981). Each character in the play is a slightly less than life-size puppet, activated by three puppeteers dressed in dark cowls, one of whom controls the puppet's torso, head and right arm, one of whom operates its left arm, and the other its legs. Watching a play one sees the actors, that is, the puppets, each being accompanied and controlled by three darkly mysterious figures, rather larger than the puppet.

8. "New planet . . ." John Keats: "On first looking into Chapman's *Homer*."

9. ". . . masters of their fates." Shakespeare: *Julius Caesar*, I, ii, 139. "Captain of my soul." W. E. Henley: *Invictus* (reprinted, 1939).

10. Auerbach (1953/1946) gives this image of the evenly illuminated present, and expresses something of the same intuition as Dodds and Snell about Homeric descriptions, but in different terms. He argues that Homer's descriptions are all external. In other words, this is rather like Harris's (1983) view about young children's theories of emotions, couched in behavioral rather than mental terms. In the *Iliad* all thoughts and feelings are ex-

pressed, and are identical with what is said or done. When Achilles is furious at Agamemnon there is a sharp sense of contempt and imminent violence, but nothing is hidden. All is expressed verbally, in a long speech of denunciation: "You clothed in shamelessness, you of crafty mind, how shall any man of the Achaeans listen to your commands? . . . you dog face . . ." (1, lines 149–171).

11. Jaynes (1976, p. 71) says Snell's work was unknown to him when he conceived his hypothesis.

12. Jaynes's challenging idea of gods as hallucinations, of the dawning of modern consciousness little more than 3,000 years ago, and of the *Iliad* portraying the bicameral voices before they finally faded can be questioned on many grounds. Two places where it may be tested are in writings from Egypt and from the Middle East. From the former, for instance, comes the text: "A debate between a man tired of life and his soul," dating from 1,000 years before Homer, which has apparent subjective elements (see Lichtheim, 1973). From the latter comes cuneiform writing, which includes the "Epic of Gilgamesh" (translated, e.g., by Sanders, 1960), parts of which may have been written 1,500 years earlier than Homer.

This epic, though with a recognizably similar literary atmosphere to the *Iliad*, is in some ways psychologically more sophisticated. It is a story of the difficulties of accepting human mortality, either when a loved friend dies or when one's own death is approaching. In it, Gilgamesh becomes recognizably depressed following his friend Enkido's death. He weeps, he cries, "How can I rest, how can I be at peace?" (p. 97). He wanders in the wilderness. He says, "I would not give up my friend's body for burial, I thought my friend would come back because of my weeping. Since he went, my life is nothing" (p. 98). His cheeks become starved and his face drawn so that people he meets find it hard to believe that he is Gilgamesh the hero-king.

Gods are described in Gilgamesh but differently from the gods in Homer. Their appearances are not interpretable as hallucinations. They appear on rather equal footings with mortals. So, after Gilgamesh and Enkido have slain the evil god Humbaba, the goddess Ishtar wants to make love with Gilgamesh. He rejects her, pointing out how badly she has treated her former lovers. She is furious, and it is her anger that leads to Enkido's death.

Like the *Iliad* there is a sense of the fatefulness of life, but this is expressed not by the continual guidance of gods but by dreams, which precede significant moments in the plot or significant decisions that have to be made. Dreams typically are not immediately understandable to the dreamer. They are therefore recounted to another person who then interprets them. It is as if the workings of one's destiny, of a significant meeting, of the outcome of a battle, of the approach of death are inscrutable so they are marked by a dream that is also inscrutable but that can be interpreted by another person who knows one well.

Jaynes points out that some of the psychologically subjective elements do not occur in at least some of the authentically early fragments of Gilgamesh, and because the cuneiform script in which it is written has not the continuity of Greek, it may be more subject to anachronistic translation. More fragments are being discovered, and if more subjective elements are found unequivocally in versions that are from the early second millennium B.C.E., this would pose difficulties for Jaynes's thesis.

A further difficulty in dating the onset of consciousness is that one can make a good case for its dawning, in the modern individualistic sense, in the

Middle Ages in Europe, and indeed, Morris (1972) makes such a case. More-over, other cultures, particularly Oriental ones, do not necessarily indicate a dichotomy between bicameral and modern mentalities. Rather, they indicate that, as Morris says, and as is discussed in Chapter 2, modern Western mentality is quite eccentrically individualistic. In other cultures people have experienced and do now experience themselves as much more firmly part of the world and of society. The self can be experienced not as an individual apart, but as integrated with the world, connected with agencies and pres-ences, seen and unseen, natural and social. See also note 14 for more specif-ic difficulties with Jaynes's hypothesis of the hallucinated voices of gods.

13. When Achilles retires from the battle, the Achaeans start to lose. Agamem-non's grasp on the leadership also weakens. Achilles had asked Thetis to intercede with Zeus, which she does successfully. Zeus puts his promise to her into effect by sending a false dream to Agamemnon that the gods, having taken sides in the war and having prevented an outright victory so far, are no longer divided. Now Agamemnon will be able to take the Trojans' broad-wayed city. Agamemnon decides to test the morale of the troops by suggesting that they should all leave for home. Only Odysseus, taking temporary command, manages to marshal the insubordinate troops, beating one of the lower ranks with the scepter taken from Agamemnon.

Here we are confronted directly with the *Iliad*'s class propaganda. Lords like Achilles and Agamemnon are described as brave, godlike, and so on, even when behaving appallingly. Theresites, a common soldier who was keen to adopt Agamemnon's suggestion that they should abandon the bat-tle, speaks in favor of return home. He is described as ugly, bandy-legged, and vulgarly abusive. The godlike Odysseus brutally beats him into submis-sion, with the evident approval of people nearby.

Though we expect the battle forthwith, it is delayed. Paris offers a chal-lenge to fight in single combat to determine possession of Helen, and an agreed truce. Menelaus joyfully accepts. They fight; but as Paris is about to be killed, he is covered in a mist by Aphrodite, who whisks him up, and sets him down in his bedroom. Aphrodite continues her work: She speaks to Helen commanding her to go to Paris. Helen argues, but obeys, and then goes to taunt Paris for his defeat by her former husband. He rebukes her and orders her to bed, saying "Never yet has *eros* (desire) so enveloped my *phrenes*, not when at first I snatched you from lovely Sparta" (3, line 442).

Zeus and Hera bicker about what should be the outcome of the war. In the end Athena is dispatched to break the truce by prompting one of the Trojans to shoot an arrow at Menelaus. The battle starts again; and in the course of most of the story it is depicted as swinging first one way then another, with the armies fighting across the plain in front of the city. Finally, with Hector invigorated by the power of Zeus, the Trojans break down the rampart built by the Greeks around their ships on the beach. Hector calls for fire to set light to the ships, when he is seen by Patroclus, the friend of Achilles. Patroclus pleads with Achilles to allow him to dress in his armor, in order to terrify the Trojans. He does this, and the Greeks, now successful again, drive the Trojans back. Patroclus slays Sarpendon of Lycia, a son of Zeus – the most significant death so far in the *Iliad*. Zeus sees this, and sends one of his boys, Apollo, to do the necessary. Patroclus, still raging, kills several more men, but at last Apollo knocks his helmet and armor from him. He is stabbed by a spear, and decides to retreat, but then is seen by Hector, who finishes him off.

Only at this point, toward the end of the *Iliad*, is Achilles again stirred to action, because now among this slaughter the friend he loves has been killed. Achilles is wracked with grief, which again brings a visit from his mother the goddess Thetis. She points out that Zeus had done as he asked. But evidently, even when the gods can to some extent be influenced by mortals, the effects are still unpredictable. In this case Patroclus is slain. Achilles can now think of nothing but to kill Hector.

Thetis replies, weeping: "You are doomed then, my child, to an early death for what you are saying, for immediately after Hector dies, your own death is certain." Achilles then mightily vexed says, "Then let me die directly, since I was not to help my friend when he was slain" (18, line 94).

From this point on, events move toward a fateful climax. Achilles calls another assembly, a parallel with that of the first book. He renounces his quarrel with Agamemnon, who makes the apology that I have described in the text, and his offer of compensation. Then in another cycle of retributive violence Achilles joins the battle, killing many Trojans in fierce fury. No doubt because passions are now running so high on the battlefield, many of the gods leave Olympos and join in the excitement. The Achaean team generally has the better of it. Finally the Trojans are driven back inside their city.

Now again a god, Fate, intervenes by shackling Hector outside the city, and there Achilles came upon him. He pursues Hector three times round the walls of Troy. Zeus wonders whether to save Hector. He gets out his golden scales and Hector's weight sinks downward. The final slaying of Hector takes place, and before he dies he asks for his body to be returned to the Trojans for proper cremation, and he too prophesies Achilles' death. Achilles, instead of responding to Hector's appeal for proper cremation, desecrates his body by dragging it behind his chariot. All this is seen from the city wall by Hector's wife, who laments for herself and their young son, now fatherless.

14. The question of the meaning of gods in Homer is quite unsettled. Among the kinds of theory that have been advanced, are Jaynes's that gods were hallucinations, the theory that they were part of the stylistic apparatus of epics to boost the hyperbolic nostalgia for a golden age when men were real heroes; and the theory that tales such as the *Iliad* serve to legitimate a social order by depicting aristocrats conversing with gods.

The view of gods as hallucinations seems implausible. To postulate so fundamental a change as the dying away of whole hallucinating populations within just a few generations strains credulity. That people lived under the sway of authoritative hierarchies, that such hierarchies had their ways of sounding their precepts in the mind's ear, that mentalities changed at the time that writing began to replace wholly oral traditions – all these are matters of profound importance, but they do not constitute the changes in neurological organization that Jaynes postulates.

As well as the more general reservations about Jaynes's arguments discussed in note 12, counters to Jaynes's specific argument about hallucinated voices include the implication that traces of bicamerality should have been found in the anthropological investigations of the early part of this century, or even now among people not living in hunter-gatherer bands but untouched by transistor radio or hotel. Moreover, priests and oracles seem not to be roles that are transitional between bicamerality and modern consciousness during the twilight of the gods. They seem to appear in all cultures, including those which Jaynes argues were bicameral until most recently, for example, Egypt and the ancient American city-states. Religious practices and priestly function cannot be seen solely as an intermediary yearning after ancestral pronouncements as they fade into indistinctness. Jaynes's arguments about the neurological basis of the voices being in the right hemisphere is even more questionable, but it is not central to the current argument.

The view that gods are stylistic devices trivializes something that is central to the whole of the *Iliad*, although no doubt the process of reconstruction by the storyteller occurred here, as it does elsewhere (cf. Bartlett, 1932).

The view of the gods as ideological legitimation no doubt has substance, and I will discuss it later in this chapter. But it omits questions raised by Snell, Dodds, and Jaynes of why gods need to be invented when so many other kinds of legitimation would do just as well. The explanation that seems preferable within cognitive psychology needs to incorporate something of these last two kinds of explanation, and is close to Snell's view. It is the idea that we inhabit the theories that we hold about ourselves and the world, somewhat as follows.

As Helmholtz (1962/1866) pointed out, the only things we are consciously aware of in mental life are certain conclusions of mental processes. We cannot be aware of the inferential processes by which mental conclusions are reached. When I look at something, say, a building, my conclusions appear to me to relate directly to the outside world, and therefore it is compelling for me to think of the building as being in the outside world. Conclusions that are not about the outside world, and for which there are no consensual referents thus become problematic. What happens, we may ask, when we experience the phenomenology of emotions; experience ourselves coming to decisions; experience solving a problem? The mental conclusions of which we become aware are accompanied by imagery, often of voices debating the issue. Sometimes we find ourselves acting compulsively, intruded upon by thoughts or memories and so on. We have no sense of where any of these conclusions come from. How they occur is unknown. Hence we can begin to explain both the sense that assumptions about such matters are culturally variable, because they are constructed from local folk theories, and the sense in which the nature of such assumptions will seem self-evident to each individual. See also Medcalf's (1981) fascinating essay on the subject of what is experienced as inner and what as outer.

15. *Middlemarch* by George Eliot, the pen name of Mary Anne Evans (later Marian Evans), was first published in parts between December 1871 and December 1872.

16. Dorothea goes into mourning, apparently for her husband but more nearly for the loss which she only now realizes, of the possibility of a more vital kind of relationship that she might have had with Ladislaw. While married, she had not thought of him as more than a friend. Now, as a widow, she comes to love him, but in the proper Victorian manner: Her love is renounced, mainly to rebut the unjust allegation of Casaubon's codicil. Ladislaw realizes this and prepares to leave the town.

Lydgate by now, having married Rosamund, finds he has been living far beyond his means. Financial anxieties cut into his scientific work. Rosamund, who has married partly to live in a grand way, becomes resentfully disappointed in him as he explains that they can no longer live in this manner. Her obstinacy becomes more and more effective in thwarting his plans to save money. They quarrel and she begins to despise him for being less than the amiable, romantic, and all-providing man she had married. Rosamund, to offset her disappointment, starts flirting with Ladislaw, who had become a friend of the Lydgates. She believes in her superiority to all other women and that Ladislaw must therefore be in love with her. Lydgate's financial troubles worsen. In the end, with great reluctance, he asks the disliked philanthropist banker Bulstrode to lend him money. Bulstrode refuses.

Meanwhile, Rosamund's brother, Fred, having failed his exams at Oxford, spends too much time at billiards and loses money in gambling. His expectation of being left a large estate by his uncle is disappointed. It is left to an obscure relative, who then sells it to Bulstrode. An acquaintance of this relative, the disreputable and drunken Raffles comes, via this link, to discover Bulstrode's presence in the neighborhood. He starts blackmailing Bulstrode, whom he knows had become rich from money left to him by his previous wife. Bulstrode had married her following her bereavement from a husband who had made the money dishonestly. The pious Bulstrode's inheritance had involved both disattending this fact and suppressing his knowledge of the whereabouts of a relative of that wife. The relative in question was the mother of Ladislaw. (This unlikely chain of coincidence involving Raffles and Bulstrode's relation to Ladislaw is, in my view, the main flaw in an otherwise engaging plot.)

The blackmailing Raffles keeps returning to Middlemarch, and Bulstrode is terrified that the truth of his past will come out. On his final visit Raffles is suffering from alcoholic poisoning. Bulstrode calls in Lydgate, who warns that further alcohol should not be allowed. He prescribes only very limited quantities of opium to allow him to sleep. Bulstrode nurses Raffles, hoping he will die and not reveal his secret. In the midst of his mental turmoil, Bulstrode changes his mind about lending Lydgate money. He lends Lydgate the thousand pounds that he needs. Bulstrode disobeys Lydgate's medical instructions by allowing his housekeeper to supply Raffles with brandy, and lets her administer a whole phial of opium.

Raffles dies. Lydgate is surprised and wonders whether Bulstrode had disobeyed his medical orders, but says nothing. He is aware that less enlightened medical opinion than his own would have allowed alcohol and prescribed opium freely to treat the delirium that Raffles was in.

Bulstrode was too late in hastening Raffles's death to prevent the story of his own past from emerging. Raffles had bragged about what he knew of Bulstrode while drinking in a nearby town before his last illness had begun. Now the gossip spreads, but with the additional, but unprovable, suspicion that Bulstrode had indeed helped Raffles toward his death. Bulstrode's wife, in great personal generosity, stands by him despite now realizing that he had been a hypocrite throughout their marriage, and that this would mean her own disgrace and isolation. It becomes known that Lydgate had received money from Bulstrode, and the inference is widely drawn that he too was implicated in Raffles's death. For Rosamund, this means a total loss of her position in the town and a culmination of all her disappointment in Lydgate.

Dorothea, believing Lydgate to be honorable, asks him to come and see her. He speaks openly to her about his financial problems, about the loan from Bulstrode, and his unease that because of it he might have been less ready to question Bulstrode about whether he had disobeyed his instructions in the care of Raffles. He knows his practice and his reputation in the town are ruined, but he cannot bring himself to discuss the matter with Rosamund, who, he says, now only wants to leave Middlemarch. He would have to abandon his research and his work at the hospital. Dorothea, with memories of her own unhappy marriage, becomes empathetically aware of the unhappiness of the Lydgates' marriage. The next day she visits their house, intending to encourage Rosamund by telling her that others believe in Lydgate's innocence and urging her to support her husband against the calumny in the town. At the same time she takes a check that will allow Lydgate to repay Bulstrode, and to continue his work.

Dorothea, on entering the Lydgates' house, is horrified to find Ladislaw there with Rosamund and leaves without speaking. She feels betrayed. Only then does she realize how much she had loved Ladislaw and depended on him to be a kind of beacon in her heart. She spends an agonized night not knowing how to act for the right. In the end she decides to go again to Rosamund to plead Lydgate's innocence and urge her to support her husband. She feels jealous of Rosamund, but so scornful of Ladislaw that she is able to lend the energy of this contempt to the project of helping Lydgate. She approaches Rosamund with a sisterly warmth that surprises Rosamund into her only generous action of the book. Rosamund tells Dorothea that Ladislaw had never made any advances to her, and indeed that he had told her that he loved Dorothea.

17. The quotations in this paragraph are from the Finale of the novel, which looks forward, as it were, to the adult lives of the young people who are the story's principal characters.

18. See also Oatley and Yuill (1985), who use this structure to analyze the content of simple stories told by people watching Heider and Simmel's (1944) cartoon film of two triangles and a circle moving around a diagram of a house.

19. George Eliot had other detractors besides Henry James, but they seem to have been in the minority among contemporary reviewers. Critical opinion began to run somewhat against the novel around the turn of the century, but in 1919 Virginia Woolf wrote that it was "a magnificent book, which for all its imperfections is one of the few English novels written for grown-up people." As I understand it, modern opinion is still with Virginia Woolf on this.

20. McSweeney (1984) discusses George Eliot's commitment to the idea of being a social scientist who by giving a clear portrait of human life will enlarge our view of ourselves.

21. Despite his somewhat sniffy review of *Middlemarch,* Henry James was deeply influenced by George Eliot, and indeed modeled *The Portrait of a Lady* on George Eliot's last novel, *Daniel Deronda* (cf. Leavis, 1948).

22. This quotation is from *Middlemarch,* Chapter 47.

23. Schank and Abelson (1978) have proposed similar ideas in terms of scripts. Empirical work has shown that episodes arranged in orders specified by story grammars are easier to remember than those in other orders (see, e.g., Mandler & Johnson, 1977). Some writers have criticized Rumelhart's approach (see, e.g., Black & Wilensky, 1979, and Johnson-Laird, 1983a) on the grounds that stories are to be understood in terms of the connectedness of their content not by syntactic properties. These criticisms focus on only one aspect of Rumelhart's approach. His central concern (see Rumelhart, 1980) was to show that stories were plan-like and analyzable in terms of schemata.

He said he preferred the term story schema to story grammar. The criticism that the idea of story grammars implies a purely syntactic analysis somewhat misses the point. The analysis of stories in terms of goals and plans is now general. See, for instance, Trabasso, van den Broek, and Suh (1989), who have proposed a transition network model to explain the connectedness of stories in terms of goals, plans, and outcomes, and Bower and Morrow (1990), who have shown that parts of a mental model are activated as the focus of action proceeds in the plan of a central character.

24. Dyer (1983, 1987) has argued that emotions occur frequently in stories because they describe goal situations and signal the success or failure of plans. If one wants a straightforward demonstration of the theory of narrative episodes as culminating in emotions, one could scarcely do better than to watch an hour of a popular television soap opera like "Dallas" or "Dynasty." A typical sequence lasts a couple of minutes. It begins with an establishing shot (e.g., the outside of a building). It then moves, perhaps indoors, to a scene of two or more people who either converse in order to thwart one another's plans, or to fall into each other's arms. The sequence then typically ends with a close-up depicting fury or erotic passion. Then on to the next sequence, structured in a similar way.

25. What kinds of plans, then, provide the bases for narratives and stories that are interesting?

Plans in which only a single actor is involved can be called first order. The most basic are the simple plans described in Chapter 1, but accounts of these would scarcely constitute stories. Minimally, an augmented plan that encounters unexpected problems is necessary to engage a reader. As Rumelhart (1980) points out, stories mostly have problem-solving motifs. Mismatches of goals and environment in an active plan give rise to emotions such as frustration and to phases of new planning. Fear can occur with the intrusion into the stream of action of a new goal related to self-preservation. Perhaps the best first-order stories are those of adventure, for example, sailing alone around the world.

Second-order plans are those in which an outcome of the protagonist with whom one identifies is affected by other actors in the same arena but with different goals. I call these second order because a protagonist has to represent her or his own goals and take account of the plans of other actors whose cognitive systems are not transparent. The characters enact plans in the domain of the story in ways that create problems and uncertainties for each other. Military strategy involves second-order plans. The *Iliad* is largely based on them. The Greeks' goals are to sack the city, kill its men, regain Helen, and carry off other women and goods as booty. The Trojans' goal is to drive the Greeks into the sea, burn their ships, and take the booty the Greeks had acquired.

Third-order plans are those that are conceived and carried out with the assumptions of mutuality. I call them third order because the protagonist, say, Jane, knows her own intention, and that of Joan with whom she is cooperating, and believes that Joan knows her intentions. Such plans become problematic when their assumptions turn out to be mistaken. They are inherently social, and they provide the bases of cooperation in society. It is with third-order plans that many of our more intense emotions occur – they form the bases for much literature, both popular and classical. In them, mismatches produce emotions of betrayal, such as the wrath of Achilles as he rages against Agamemnon, or the fury of Casaubon as he rages against himself. Matches include new unions in joint plans, as when Rosamund and Lydgate fall in love.

Stories of spies, of special agents, crime, detection, and even those in which someone turns out not to be who she or he seems indicate a strong human preoccupation with wrongly assumed mutuality and its consequences. There are constant questions of who, if anyone, can be trusted, and in what kinds of plan. In modern thrillers the final emotions may be those of loneliness of a hero, appropriate to people who work by not trusting anyone. More conventionally, in television renderings, at least, the hero returns from ordeals to a sexual episode or to gregarious feelings engendered by a joke.

26. Kim (1988) has argued that there is only one natural scientific explanation of any phenomenon. By contrast, when we are understanding a story, as Wilensky (1978) has pointed out, we do not predict exactly what a character is going to do next. Understanding consists of creating, as the story proceeds, a range of explanations, typically in terms of goals and plans to cover what has happened and what could happen. Successful identification with a character makes the goals and possibilities of action one's own.

27. Poets often concentrate on evoking schemata without plan-like elements. Novelists, too, may dispense with certain components of sequential plots. All these modifications, however, emphasize this distinction made by Todorov (1977/1971) that story structure and discourse structure are conceptually separate.

28. This analysis was conceived independently of Barthes' analysis of a text in *S / Z*, and has quite different intentions. Barthes was explicating the multiplicity of meanings across his five categories of meaning. I am pointing out the distinctively different voices in the discourse structure – comparable to Todorov's (1977/1971) "points of view" (p. 27) – and showing how these different voices relate to the reader.

29. The importance of honor measured by wealth is seen in the ransom offered to Agamemnon by Chryses, in the compensation given to Achilles by Agamemnon to heal the quarrel, and the ransom brought by Priam to redeem his son Hector's body – all of very large size. These ransoms would be familiar cultural codes to classical readers. Achilles' proud and manly self was diminished in honor in the opening quarrel because he knows he is the best warrior but has not received the best of the booty and because in the quarrel with Agamemnon booty he had obtained was taken away. According to this code it would be an appropriate closure for Agamemnon to bring him compensation, and for Priam to acknowledge his power by bringing a large ransom.

I should perhaps not criticize the ancient Greeks for, apparently, swallowing these messages of equating social honor with riches, inasmuch as we may not be much further forward in such matters today. I have been arguing that something has changed in Western personality since the *Iliad*, but perhaps the measurement of personal worth in terms of visible possessions is not it. Adam Smith (1970/1776), observing the first movements of the technological and social machinery that was to produce in a couple of centuries more material wealth than the world had previously seen, noted the emotional aspirations of the very rich in a kind of aside: "With the greater part of rich people, the chief enjoyment of riches consists in the parade of riches, which in their eye is never so complete as when they appear to possess those decisive marks of opulence which nobody can possess but themselves" (p. 277). The most valued things are not those that are useful, but those which are most scarce or most difficult to obtain so that by definition other people would not have them. At the turn of the century the situation was still the same, as Veblen (1899/1948) pointed out how the wealthy showed how they principally enjoyed their riches by removing themselves from the useful generation of wealth and by "conspicuous consumption" and "ostentatious display" of things that were for the most part useless. Today, in magazines and on television we are constantly confronted by the Veblenesque displays of the rich, whether they be oil tycoons, film stars, hotel owners, or junk bond financiers.

In psychological terms Veblen is arguing that incitement to envy and other emotions of social comparison are significant forces in modern society and that these shape important social institutions.

30. Only Dorothea, Casaubon, Lydgate, Fred Vincy, Bulstrode, and, arguably, Rosamund, Ladislaw, and Mary Garth are seen both from outside and in.

Chapter 6

1. See, e.g., Cartwright (1977). The life expectancy figures were compiled by Chadwick in 1842. He was responsible in 1836 for a clause requiring the newly established registration of deaths in Britain to include the cause of death, an important move in epidemiological research.
2. Of course smell is important biologically. We are presumably adapted to detecting foul odors, and our avoidance of them is mediated by the emotion of disgust. Smell was not, however, a good clue to *how* infectious diseases are transmitted.
3. Snow (1936) includes a reprint of his "On the Mode of Communication of Cholera"; see also Pelling (1978) for the history of cholera research in Britain. Death rates in Europe for cholera were lower than for some other diseases, notably tuberculosis, but the manifestations of cholera were so sudden and so shocking that no one could ignore them. Death occurred sometimes within a few hours of being quite healthy. Victims could become so dehydrated that they turned into wizened caricatures of their former selves, discolored because of ruptured capillaries under the skin (McNeill, 1977). Though it affected mostly the poor, the rich and famous were not immune – among the victims were Hegel and Clausewitz.
4. There are immediate difficulties with definitions of stress. One is that an event like divorce may be bad for one person, but good for another. Another is that researchers have different theoretical perspectives, with one seeing stress as something imposed, another seeing it a function of personality, and so on. Nonetheless much important research has been done on the basis of average experiences of stress arising from events and difficulties. A large program of work on psychological coping with stresses has been led by Lazarus (Lazarus, 1966; Lazarus & Folkman, 1984). Physiological coping responses are reviewed by Anisman and Zacharcho (1982).
5. This idea is expounded, for instance, by Eryximachus, the doctor at the drinking party described by Plato. Though the portrayal is ironical, the doctor speaks in a quite recognizable way: "When the elements of which I spoke before, hot and cold and dry and wet, are bound together in love which is orderly, and combined harmoniously in due proportions, man and the other animals thrive and are healthy." *Symposium*, p. 56.

6. Though theories of balance were displaced by theories of infection in West-ern medicine, elements of older theories have lived on. For instance, colds, flu, and pneumonia are thought of as progressively more serious results of imbalances of the person with the environment and in particular of becom-ing too cold or too wet. Precautions need to be taken against cold and wet, which can invade the body if one is not careful and thereby upset its bal-ance. There is a special word for cold air that might be able to affect us: a draft. It may come in via ill-fitting windows, and it is quite different from fresh air, which is important to have in the house and which only comes in when windows are wide open. Cold and wet are prone to enter through specific parts of the body. The neck is particularly vulnerable and needs a special protective garment, the scarf. It is best also to keep ankles from becoming cold, and feet from becoming wet. By contrast, having a cold face or cold hands may be uncomfortable, but coldness or wetness of these parts is not thought to be specifically dangerous. At the same time elements of the infection theory have been incorporated: People are used to the idea of catching a bug. "Bug" is always singular. Being infected with billions of bugs might be too much to contemplate. I am grateful to Mary Sissons for describing to me these and similar features of the folk theories of illness.

7. Editorial letter by Thompson, accompanying Selye (1946): "When Dr. Selye first became interested in this, over ten years ago, it was difficult to see how a series of severe traumata in rats could lead to anything" (p. 231).

8. The mechanisms of AIDS also indicates these three types of immune-related disorder. The HIV undermines the body's immune system and thus makes it susceptible to infections, allows immune-related disorders of the skin and mucous membranes, and allows cancers to develop (Redfield & Burke, 1988; Watson, 1988). This disease is now frightening modern populations as much as plague and cholera did in former times. Because it involves suscep-tibilities to infection and other immune responses, it is possible that the time course of the development of AIDS may depend on stress, though this has not been shown convincingly.

9. Riley's (1981) experiments are among the most interesting in this field. They were on mice, and therefore should not be generalized too freely to humans, but they include direct effects of psychosocial stress on the impairment of immune response and demonstrated effects of this impairment on the growth of implanted cancer cells. Among such effects are that animals made anxious by hearing others being handled and undergoing minor surgical procedures had concentrations of blood corticosteroid hormones that in-creased within minutes, and that female mice stressed by being kept in solitary cages repelled only 60% of implanted lymphosarcomas, whereas when housed with others the regression rate of implanted tumors ranged from 80 to 100%.

10. Doll and Peto (1981) calculate age standardized rates of cancer, that is to say, rates within five-year age bands, separately for men and women, and weighted according to the proportion of the male and female population in each age band. The argument about most cancers being avoidable because their incidence in different groups differs widely is also made by Fox (1982).

11. These studies of Grossarth-Maticek and his collaborators are so striking but so methodologically problematic that they have more than the usual need for replication by independent researchers. Issues to be attended to are that the psychometric instruments used so far are crude, that it is not altogether clear from the reports whether categorization of subjects into types was

made by researchers who were blind to the outcome, or whether the typology finally chosen was just one of many explored at the initial interview. Moreover, one would like to know if, as well as indicating by questionnaire that they were susceptible to stress, for instance, from loss of a valued occupation or of a person to whom they were attached, the subjects had actually suffered such losses.

A claim based on these studies, made by Eysenck (1988), is that the effects of personality on cancer are large compared with those from activities such as smoking, and that smoking has effects mainly in people of specific personality types, who respond to stresses in certain emotional ways that can be changed by therapy.

12. Views of social and epidemiological effects on human illness in addition to those mentioned in the text, include those of Eiser (1982), Cooper (1988), and Brown and Harris (1989); on psychoneuroimmunological mechanisms, see Ader (1981), Baker (1987), and Cox (1988).

13. For a meta-analysis of effects of personality on heart disease and also four other psychosomatic conditions – asthma, ulcers, arthritis, and headache – see Friedman and Booth-Kewley (1987). Of these five types of psychosomatic illness, the effects on coronary heart disease have been found most consistently.

14. See Oatley (1988b) for further exposition of this theory.

15. An alternative to the idea that only major life events are stressful is due to Lazarus's group (e.g., Kanner et al., 1981; Lazarus, 1984). They argue that smaller irritations, called hassles, which are not necessarily serious in themselves, can be cumulatively debilitating and cause minor illnesses. See also Dohrenwend and Shrout (1985) for a critique of Lazarus's work and Lazarus et al.'s (1985) reply.

16. There are several different research diagnostic schemes in use. In the United States these include the Spitzer, Endicott, and Robins (1978) Research Diagnostic Criteria (RDC). In the United Kingdom and in a number of international surveys the Present State Examination (PSE) of Wing, Cooper, and Sartorius (1974) and Wing (1976) has been used. Brown and Harris's (1978) diagnostic scheme is a modification of it. Dean, Surtees, and Sashidharan (1983) present a detailed comparison of the different criteria in a population of women in Edinburgh, Scotland, and find comparable results with the different schemes, though with differences of "case" threshold and some differences in the kinds of symptoms counted as significant. These schemes, although not perfect, end an era of such unreliability in psychiatric diagnosis that epidemiological work of any significance could scarcely be performed.

17. Systems of diagnosis differ slightly in the symptoms they specify as necessary to diagnose a case. The Research Diagnostic Criteria (RDC) for a case of major depressive disorder are based on the following main symptoms: loss of appetite or body weight; difficulties in sleeping – depressed people may sleep less than usual, perhaps waking in the small hours of the morning and being unable to go back to sleep; complaints of tiredness or lack of energy; agitation or slow movements; loss of interest or pleasure in activities that previously were pleasurable; feelings or thoughts of self-reproach or guilt; complaints of indecision, slowed thoughts, or lack of concentration (the latter being described above); and suicide preparations or attempts or recurrent thoughts of suicide. The RDC would recognize a person as being a probable case of major depressive disorder if he or she had a persistent sad

or dejected mood lasting at least a week, plus four of these symptoms at a clinical level, and a definite case with sad or dejected mood and five of these symptoms persisting for two weeks.

The symptoms used in the RDC to identify anxiety states are a persistent anxious mood for at least two weeks. Other anxiety symptoms include a subjective feeling of nervous tension, autonomic symptoms such as palpitations, sweating, blushing, dizziness; difficulty falling asleep; muscular tension or tremors; and subjective foreboding. The RDC also describe a diagnosis of panic attacks that are circumscribed episodes of intense fear accompanied by autonomic symptoms, and often inducing the subject to take drastic action to escape or summon help. Three panic episodes in three weeks are counted as clinically significant.

18. Weissman and Klerman (1977) found a difference in prevalence of depression in most of the countries that have been studied, though these figures were based on people receiving treatment.

19. Diagnoses were based on the Present State Examination of Wing, Cooper, and Sartorius (1974), but with the symptoms needed to indicate depression being slightly different from those of the PSE, and equivalent to a criterion on the PSE ID system about midway between 5 and 6 (see Dean et al., 1983). Though the main focus of their study was on the onset of depression, Brown and Harris (1978) found that 9% of their sample of women had been depressed and/or anxious for more than a year.

20. As Brown and Harris point out, Holmes and Rahe's scale implies that a young man who had gained an open scholarship to Oxford could get a score of 79 points (the sum of end of formal schooling 26, outstanding achievement 28, vacation 13, and Christmas 12). A man whose wife had just left him scores 65. In contrast to such implausible conclusions, Brown and Harris use a procedure in which societal intuitions are focused on the meaning of that event for a person in that specific context. Measures such as those used by Grossarth-Maticek are also deficient in that although they are used to define types in terms of their emotional response to events concerning valued people or goals, there is no confirmation of whether such events have occurred.

21. Brown and Harris report that in community samples the coefficient of agreement between the research team's rating of contextual threat and the subject's own rating of threat was 95%, though this agreement was 84% in people who were psychiatric patients (1978, pp. 113–114).

22. Some women in the sample were particularly vulnerable. They had no intimate relationship and had either lost their own mother before the age of 11 or had three or more children at home. Fourteen of these suffered a severe event or difficulty: Of the six without jobs outside the home, all became depressed; of the eight who had jobs, five became depressed. By contrast, of the nine women in the sample who were equally vulnerable but who did not suffer a severe event or difficulty, none became depressed.

23. See Tennant and Bebbington (1978) and Tennant, Bebbington, and Hurry (1981); see also Oatley and Bolton (1985) and Brown and Harris (1986, 1989) for further discussion.

24. Tennant, Bebbington, and Hurry (1981) found that in 60% of their sample there was an improvement of one unit on the Index of Definition scale of severity on the Present State Examination within 6 weeks. Brown and Harris found, however, that there were as many people who had been symptomat-

ic at the case level for at least a year as had had onsets during the 38 weeks before interview.

25. Beck et al. (1979) is the professional handbook of this kind of therapy for depression, with Burns (1980) a self-help version. Among the interesting features of this kind of therapy is the keeping of diaries of emotions, the situations that elicit them, and the thoughts that come to mind in the inner dialogue.

26. Contrary to much research on cognitive theories of depression, it is best to distinguish clinically significant depression from the mood changes that follow a failure. There is good evidence that people become sad and/or angry when they fail at tasks set by experimenters, or when they fail in tasks like university examinations. There is also evidence that attributions affect mood (see, e.g., Peterson & Seligman, 1984). There is no evidence, however, either that depression of clinical proportions is caused by small-scale failures of plans or is influenced by distorted thinking. The best evidence on the onset of clinical depression is from epidemiological studies of people suffering severe life events such as bereavements, becoming unemployed, and the like. Approximately 90% of depressive breakdowns in the community occur in response to such events. Moreover, because evaluations made by people becoming depressed in response to these events do not differ on average from the evaluations of noninvolved researchers rating the seriousness of the events, we may conclude that people get depressed for good reasons, namely, seriously adverse things happening to them. They do not become depressed because they are thinking about the world in a distinctively irrational way or because of distorted attributions they make about the event. (See also Coyne & Gotlib, 1983; Brewin, 1985, 1988; Teasdale, 1988, for reviews of evidence against the idea that irrational thinking has a specific causal relationship to onset of depression. See also Abramson, Metalsky & Alloy, 1989, for a further reformulation derived from Seligman's theory of depression.)

27. Being let down is not strictly a result of a prospective kind. Though the original support was established at the first interview, being let down as a risk factor was discovered at the second interview.

28. In *The Times* of 16 September 1989, p. 4, some results were reported of an ongoing research study by the British Home Office, on a random sample of 176,000 people born in 1953, 1958, and 1963. Figures from the 1953 cohort, the only ones available at the time of the report, indicated that before their thirty-first birthday, 32.5% of males had been convicted of at least one criminal offense on the "standard list" of crimes brought before magistrates and crown courts. Standard list crimes exclude motoring offenses, drunkenness, and prostitution. The corresponding proportion of women acquiring a criminal record by the age of 31 was 7%. One in eight men had been convicted of theft or handling stolen goods by the age of 21, 1 in 11 had a conviction for burglary, and 1 in 16 for criminal damage.

29. Perring, Oatley, and Smith (1988) have investigated coherence and conflict among people's goals and plans. We found that students with incoherences among their plans and goals were liable to more symptoms than those whose goal structures were more integrated. Incoherences could be resolved if people made more explicit models of their goal structure and could undertake rearrangements to lessen incoherences. In the study by Oatley and Perring (1991), we found a nonsignificant suggestion that among people

recovering from breakdowns those with plans that were more explicit did better.

30. Gilbert (1984, 1988) regards the phases of recovery from a stressful event as having a biological basis, with the activating phase involving increased noradrenaline activity, and the slower-building phase of despair being subserved by systems using acetylcholine transmitters. Such theories make an important bridge to the physiologically based work on stress in the psychosomatic tradition discussed earlier.

31. I am indebted to Paul Ekman for a discussion of the problems of bias, a discussion that occurred when he and I were discussing Goffman's work rather than that of novelists. Ekman's argument that bias is the real problem is for him overwhelming, casting suspicion on the conclusions of any single observer who does not use quantitative methods.

32. There has been an important influence of journalism and in the media more generally in using combinations of narrative and statistical data in ways that awaken sensibility and suggest improvements in the lives of others. The large responses to recent famines in Africa have been an important result of the combination of narrative and statistical depictions by television journalists and others.

Chapter 7

1. The term intention is used in this chapter in the everyday sense to imply wanting to do something, not in the technical philosophical sense of intentionality, which indicates a mental state that is consciously about something. When I refer to that latter sense, as I have in Chapter 2, I have used the terms intentionality or intentional. Of course, intentions as wants are intentional, as are beliefs and those emotions that have semantic content.

2. The main current in psychology is empirical. It involves psychological mechanisms being made visible. Some aspects of emotions and their accompaniments have been made visible in the laboratory on polygraphic recordings, and on video film, for periods long enough to measure them.

   There is, however, a danger that a proper attention to the empirical can overflow into the regrettable attitude of empiricism in which only that which can be made repeatably visible is thought to be real or of any interest. Cognitive science has already declined to adopt that position in the area of linguistics. I here argue that a cognitive theory of emotions requires that it is also declined in studying emotions. We should welcome the visible appearance of emotions in laboratory settings, but we will not be able to understand them without some nonvisualizing approaches as well. Psychoanalysis is an example.

3. We can infer from a letter of Freud to Fliess of 14 October 1900 that he started to see Dora that autumn (Freud, 1985). In a footnote added in 1923, he says he wrote the case up in two weeks immediately after the treatment was broken off on 31 December 1899. He should, of course, have said "December 1900." In his letter to Fliess of 25 January 1901, he says he had finished writing it on the previous day. In that letter, he says he regards it as a continuation of *The Interpretation of Dreams*, and said it was "the subtlest thing [he had] so far written." I think it may well be the subtlest thing he ever wrote.

4. See, for example, Laplanche and Pontalis (1973), who have written on

"transference," as they have on other aspects on the language of psychoanalysis, an authoritative and informative essay, describing Freud's development of the idea and the way the concept is used in psychoanalysis. The
theory of transference can also be applied to relationships other than those
of therapy. In terms of the theory of mutual planning discussed in Chapter
4, transference indicates that joint goals or intentions in any relationship are
always being negotiated.

5. Lacan says an interpretation is therefore a kind of ruse to fill in the emp-
tiness of the deadlock that occurs when the discourse has become stuck.
This is presumably a surrealist joke – the idea of countering the evasions of
the patient with an evasion by the analyst. I hope it is not merely Anglo-
Saxon earnestness on my part to think that this is not the best interpretation
of the nature of interpretation.

6. Is this an example of what Masson (1984) has called an assault on truth?
Masson has argued that Freud suppressed his theory that neurosis was
caused by the trauma of actual sexual abuse in childhood. He accuses Freud
of faintheartedness and intellectual dishonesty. Masson's book has caused a
stir. It contributes to a current debate in which it has become clear that
sexual abuse occurs frequently to children, and can increase the incidence of
pathogenic effects (see, e.g., Peters et al., 1986; Browne & Finkelhor, 1986).
We still, however, know very little of "normal" sexuality in childhood and
families, or its effects.

Although he accompanies his arguments with much brandishing of scholarly apparatus, Masson wants to reduce the issue to a simple dichotomy:
Either neurosis is caused by trauma or by unresolved fantasies. He asserts
that Freud began his psychoanalytic work with the idea that symptoms were
caused by actual sexual traumata, but that in his later work he swerved off
toward the hypothesis that they were caused by sexual fantasies. For Masson, the simple question is this. Did Freud suppress the idea that childhood
seductions are a reality, constructing the subsequent part of his work as an
elaborate subterfuge, which he, Masson, will now entirely discredit?

Alongside meticulous documentation of archival material, Masson makes
leaps entirely based on faith. To give just one example of several, in discussing whether an analyst by concentrating on fantasies may damage the analy-
sand by not confirming that a childhood sexual trauma actually took place,
he says: "A real memory demands some form of validation from the outside
world – denial of these memories by others can lead to a break with reality,
and a psychosis" (p. 133). This, coming at a critical point in the argument,
has no basis whatever in evidence. Does a memory require external validation? Is an analyst in a position to provide it in any case? Do analysts deny
memories? Can denial of memories lead to psychosis? We may not know
answers to any of these questions, and we certainly do not find evidence
about them in Masson's book.

Though Masson's work is stimulating, it sadly misses an opportunity for
any real engagement with the issues of how we are to understand discrepancies between expectation and outcome that are experienced as traumas, or
the discrepancies arising from conflicts between goals in which Freud became more interested in his later work. Masson, with his simple dichotomy
and his juxtaposition of minute historical scholarship with groundless assertion, makes a disappointing contribution to these problems.

Masson argues that Freud began to replace the 1893 hypothesis of actual
sexual traumata soon after announcing it, gradually diminishing its impor-

tance. Indeed, he did. Freud says in a footnote to Dora's case history: "I have gone beyond that [1893] theory, but I have not abandoned it; that is to say I do not today consider that theory incorrect, but incomplete (1953/1905, p. 27). By 1933, he thought that childhood seductions did not take place – "hysterical symptoms are derived from phantasies and not from real occurrences" (1964/1933, p. 120).

It is clear that Freud did, as Masson argues, progressively diminish the significance of actual seduction as he went along. But one might think that Masson protests too much. He does not really convince us that Freud was more intellectually dishonest than any theoretician modifying his theory along lines that seemed to be productive. Plausibly Freud became more interested in those causes of neurosis that were amenable to the kinds of therapy he was developing. It is impossible to say whether Freud was more guilty of faintheartedness about the scandal of childhood seduction, or whether possibilities of new theoretical developments were the more influential. From Freud's own work we could see that both of these could have had an effect, not just one or the other; indeed, it was from Freud's own work that we realize that human motives are seldom unmixed.

My proposal, as indicated in this chapter, is that the method of listening carefully, and with respect, to the narrative accounts that people give of themselves is quite unsuitable for validating or denying incidents in the past. The analyst will hardly ever be in a position to know what actually happened. But the method is suitable for coming to understand intentions and conflicts via the gaps and discrepancies in people's accounts, and hence for providing a basis for interpretations about intentions and conflicts.

Masson is, I think, right that Freud was evasive about his early theory of the traumata of sexual abuse, and, as I indicate in this chapter, this is not the only place he was evasive. This is not, however, a ground for dismissing his work entirely, particularly, as I hope to show, because this case history of Dora is about the bases of such evasions and validates itself partly by Freud himself providing data in his own writing on which his own methods can be used. Freud might have been evasive about his theory of childhood seduction, but he also made a contribution to exploring conflicts of intention.

7. It would be inappropriate here to review the many criticisms of Freud and of psychoanalysis as science. Grünbaum's (1984) book, and the discussion by peer commentators in Grünbaum (1986), provide a good overview of current debate. It is also worth reading Wegman's (1985) account of how cognitive science has made many of the arguments of the typical critique of Freud obsolete.

    Grünbaum's (1984) book must be the most complete and satisfying account yet written of psychoanalytic epistemology. It has, of course its defects, not least an occasional tediousness in the rehearsal of other people's philosophical mistakes and frequent recourse to sarcastic epithets directed toward those with whom Grünbaum disagrees. Its virtues, however, far outweigh these blemishes. Grünbaum succeeds, as nobody before him, in clarifying the epistemological status of psychoanalysis and clearing away the less thorough, and sometimes less thoughtful, contributions of both hermeneutic and empirically minded commentators.

    In brief, Grünbaum's critique is as follows. Psychoanalysis, no less than other putative contributions to natural science and despite Popper's ill-judged strictures, is testable. Indeed, aspects of it have changed in response to evidence. It is, moreover, based on causal hypotheses: notably that repressed childhood wishes can cause adult neuroses. Attempts by hermeneuticists to give an account of psychoanalysis that evade causal structure undermine the psychoanalytic enterprise rather than rescuing it from attacks by empiricists.

Perhaps most fundamentally, Grünbaum argues that evidence from psychoanalytic sessions, which Freud and others saw as providing ample warrant for psychoanalytic claims, is flawed. It is flawed principally because it is open to contamination from suggestion by the analyst. Freud's principal defense against this charge, which he himself took seriously, Grünbaum has dubbed "the tally argument." It was enunciated by Freud in his 1917 lectures: Though a pupil might be suggestible to the arguments of a teacher, interpretations are valid only if they tally with something real in the patient. Suggestion cannot explain the effects of an interpretation if the interpretation does lift a repression or does dissolve a conflict, as to do this, it must tally with something real. Freud claimed this for analysis and denied it to suggestive therapies.

Grünbaum admires the epistemological sophistication and boldness of this criterion, but argues that, among other things, because psychoanalysis has not been demonstrated as the only efficacious treatment of psychoneuroses, the apparent findings of psychoanalysis, for example, of the roots of neuroses in repressed childhood sexuality, must be regarded as open to contamination, consciously or unconsciously by analysts.

My position is that although I regard Freud, Darwin, and Helmholtz as the three founders of psychology, Freud's contribution is not to have discovered the unconscious, childhood sexuality, the Oedipus complex or any other such matter, but was of the kind discussed in this chapter: He began seriously to investigate intentions. Psychoanalytic notions about the etiology of psychopathology provide ideas and intuitions about what factors may affect our lives, but psychoanalytic sessions are not appropriate to testing etiological hypotheses. This needs epidemiological studies and controlled experiments, as indicated in Chapter 6.

8. Smith, Glass, and Miller (1980) found that the average length of therapy in the 475 studies of the outcome of therapy on which they performed their meta-analyses was 15.75 hours, with two thirds of the therapies lasting for 12 hours or less.

9. I am not claiming that Dora actually was jealous. This again would assume more from psychoanalytic method than it can deliver. Indeed, later on in this chapter, I discuss how Dora was probably envious rather than jealous. What I am claiming is that consensually we can accept that jealousy *could* make sense of Dora's behavior at this point. Here, as elsewhere in conversation, the proposal is provisional.

10. Freud does say that though this idea of erotic transference made everything fit together satisfactorily, the characteristics of transference made it insusceptible to definite proof.

11. It is the plausibility of this explanation, I think, that makes Dora's insistence that her father break with the Ks more probably due to envy than jealousy. If she was not now going to accomplish her plan of marrying Herr K, why then should her father and Frau K continue their affair?

12. We might even wonder whether this idea had been hinted at, or discussed, between Dora and Frau K, in their intimate confidences.

13. Cf. his breaches with Adler, Tausk, Jung, Ferenczi, and others (see, e.g., Clark, 1980; Gay, 1988).

14. Despite his ambitions, Freud thought of therapy as having to do with the soul, for example, his remark echoing Hamlet: "It is not so easy to play upon the instrument of the soul."

15. Henry James's *Portrait of a Lady,* itself based on the story of Gwendolen in George Eliot's *Daniel Deronda,* in some respects curiously prefigures Freud's story. This indicates, I think, that George Eliot, Henry James, and Freud had touched a truth about a recurrent condition in European society. In *Portrait of a Lady* Isobel finally realizes that she has been "made a convenience of." With Dora, one is struck all too distinctly with the sense that everyone in the story to whom her heart has gone out has had at least one ulterior motive that was sufficient to betray her. For each person she has been not herself, but an instrument, a convenience. She realizes that she has been used, and this is her complaint to Freud.

Chapter 8

1. As well as the kinds of emotion-laden remembering described by Proust, recall of autobiographical memories accompanied by intense emotions is described widely. It is significant both for theories of emotion and for theories of memory. Perhaps most striking in this regard are the phenomena of cathartic recovery of apparently repressed memories, as described, for instance, by Scheff (1979) and discussed in Chapter 3.

   Autobiographical memories of other kinds also are associated with emotions, as described, for instance, by Linton (1982). She points out, however, that with time the emotional implications of events often change. In hindsight some events have become more important, as meeting a person who later comes to be of great significance, whereas other events, which though emotionally salient at the time, become less emotionally significant. According to the hypothesis offered by Linton, the intensity of an emotion associated with a memory would not only be due to its distinctiveness, but to whether it was integrated with other types of experience – to whether generalization has occurred. In this case, repressed memories of the kind described by Scheff would be associated with emotions that remained intense, partly at least because they have been isolated from other experience and left in an unprocessed state.

   Conway and Bekerian (1987) and Conway (1990) found that when given an emotion word and asked to form an image, people most often formed an image of an autobiographical event that could be dated with some accuracy, and which had the significance of the emotion term they had been prompted with. Promptings with nonemotion terms tended to bring to mind other kinds of image, either of events that could not be dated accurately or images that were not in principle autobiographical.

2. Freud (1961/1930) discussed the "oceanic" feeling, which a friend of his identified with the one true and pervasive religious experience, outside of self and giving meaning to a whole life. Freud said he could not discover this feeling in himself, but he identified it with the oneness of being at the breast with one's mother, which may survive alongside more differentiated feelings of one's separateness from the world and other people. Freud's impulse was to analyze such phenomena by tracing them back to their origins, and hence to make them go away. The impulse behind Proust's conception was

the opposite, that by seeing the commonalities and connections between the past and present, to allow oneself to experience a more general timeless significance of such continuities. I am with Proust on this: Earlier experiences can become invested with successions of meanings that can enrich them, and a whole train of comparable ideas can sometimes form, such that the realization of their very personal significances, perhaps taking one by surprise, can be profoundly important in taking one outside one's ordinary self-absorbed thoughts.

3. In am indebted to May (1977) for an insightful discussion of these issues.

4. In one touching instance, Samuel Johnson, when well into middle age, on being asked by his friend Mrs. Thrale what was the happiest period of his life replied that "it was that year in which he spent one whole evening with Molly Aston. 'That indeed (said he) was not happiness, it was rapture . . .' " (cited by Quennell, 1988, p. 15). Quennell goes on to explain that this happiness derived entirely from conversation, because they were not alone, and Johnson, who was married and a stern moralist, would not expect to win her heart. He would in any case know that because he was far inferior in social class to the baronet's daughter, that even if he had been unmarried anything more than conversation would have been out of the question.

5. Games also differ from real life in that when we play them we know that we can exit through the membrane surrounding them at the end of the game, or indeed if something urgent happens at any moment beforehand – in this sense we may say games are not "real." I discuss this further below.

6. This defensive mechanism is usually described as being schizoid, and is discussed, for instance, by Fairbairn (1952).

7. "Surprised by joy" is the opening phrase of Wordsworth's sonnet *Desideria* (Wordsworth, 1984).

8. Rather in contrast to Wordsworth's phrase, but also attesting to an elicitation of happiness uncaused by any external event, is a description by Wordsworth's contemporary, de Quincy (1822) of his first experience of taking opium: "Here was the secret of happiness . . . happiness might now be bought for a penny and carried in the waistcoat pocket; portable ecstacies might be corked up in a pint bottle."

9. What can one say about such data? It is scarcely a matter for saying, but for doing.

10. In one study, by Diener, Horowitz, and Emmons (1985), it was even found that being very rich had an effect: 49 Americans earning more than $10 million a year claimed to be happy 77% of the time, as compared to randomly chosen control subjects who claimed to be happy 62% of the time. In a money economy, lack of money narrows options for guiding the course of one's life or for coping with adversities.

11. In a meta-analysis of 58 studies, it was found that being married was associated with being happy. The overall correlation between being married and subjective well-being was not high however, at 0.14. (Haring-Hidore et al., 1985).

12. This finding that marriage is better on average for men than women is a very general one; compare, for instance, the results of the differences in the associations of marriage with depression in men and women, discussed in Chapter 6.

13. As to other factors that affect happiness: In wealthy nations, being female rather than male is generally conducive to reporting more satisfaction at all

ages up to 65, at which point men on average become more happy than women (Spreitzer & Snyder, 1974). This change of effect in old age may be because there are more elderly widows than elderly widowers.

In America, Freedman (1978) has found that having a college degree is associated with more happiness than being without one, though otherwise level of education has relatively little effect.

14. In this study, reported in Chapter 2, Oatley and Duncan (1992) asked students to keep structured diaries of episodes of emotions that were either of joy/happiness, sadness/grief, anger/rage, or fear/anxiety. Subjects indicated various characteristics of episodes of these four types of emotion that were sufficiently clear to involve bodily perturbations, noticeable desires to act in an emotional way, or thoughts that were difficult to stop.

15. According to Page (1955), Sappho's reputation rests properly on only two poems, the third selection given here and a longer poem that I quote in Chapter 9. Page also discusses in detail 10 more poems that are in some state of completeness, including the second one given here, which he describes as conventional and of no special interest.

As with many ancient writers, most of what we have are fragments of a few lines here and there, torn from papyrus strips or sometimes derived from quotations by other ancient writers whose work has survived. Relatively little is known about Sappho for certain, except that she and her contemporary Alceus were at the center of a flourishing tradition of lyric poetry on Lesbos. They have become its best known members. Both of them left the island because of political troubles.

Love poetry from the Hebrew tradition that is comparable to Sappho's (e.g., the Song of Songs) is thought to be of a much later date, around the third or fourth century B.C.E.

16. I have omitted the first four stanzas of Donne's poem. The poem's date is uncertain. It may have been written to his wife, Ann More, whom he married secretly in 1601. Their act of getting married seems typical of what can happen with love. The marriage resulted in Donne being imprisoned for a short time. It ruined his promising career in the civil service, and left him in poverty without employment or a dowry. He spent the next 14 years trying to live down the disgrace and trying to find suitable work, depending for his living on friends and patrons.

17. I have chosen this because it is the most recent piece of literary work of high quality I could find in English that takes up the subject of love. It was a worthy winner, I think, of the 1987 Booker Prize for literature.

18. An instance of a strong fantasy element is given in George Eliot's description of Dorothea and Casaubon's relationship. Even in the match that seems more auspicious, of Lydgate and Rosamund, the business of committing oneself to another person is problematic. Though Lydgate and Rosamund experience at first the warm feelings of harmonious interaction, of being in love, George Eliot describes this state with irony, and hints at its unpredicted consequences. Rosamund is caught up in one of those "wonderful mixtures in the world which are all alike called love, and claim the privileges of a sublime rage." Lydgate is "completely mastered by the outrush of tenderness at the sudden belief that this sweet young creature depended on him for her joy . . . left the house an engaged man, whose soul was not his own."

A more recent, though equally memorable depiction of the fantasy element of being in love gradually being replaced by a real relationship is Gabriel Garcia Marquez's *Love in the Time of Cholera* (1989/1985).

19. Erotic love is, of course, not the only kind of love and not necessarily a desirable state. One of the best, and best known, books that makes distinctions about the various kinds of love is by Fromm (1957). He distinguishes erotic love from brotherly and motherly kinds of love, as well as from self-love and love of God.

20. A discussion of Freud's work as being founded on biology and especially influenced both directly by Darwin (including his book on emotions) and indirectly by the general intellectual atmosphere created by Darwin, is given by Sulloway (1979).

21. Hazen and Shaver (1987), for instance, argue that though continuities exist in attachment style, these continuities were stronger between infancy and younger adults than between infancy and older people. Insecurely attached people, for instance, can become more secure. The conception of this research is one of a possibility of change based on new information in adult relationships. Similarly, the work of Rutter and his colleagues (Rutter, 1985; Rutter & Quinton, 1984), discussed in Chapter 6, indicate that women reared in unpropitious circumstances in institutions can make satisfactory adult sexual relationships, which then enable them to become good mothers themselves.

Adult sexual desire can transcend both the infant sense that the other is there for one's own convenience, and the sense that sex is just some kind of appetite. As Nagel (1979) in his essay on "Sexual Perversion" describes, sexuality is about knowing and being known by the other. I will discuss this a little more in Chapter 9.

22. Page numbers in the text are from the 1952 Pelican edition. Joanna Field is the pen name of Marian Milner. Under it she published two more books about self-exploration, by means of writing and painting. She became a well-known psychoanalyst who has also published under her own name.

23. By "physical," Joanna Field presumably meant "sexual." It was not quite polite to write of sex in the 1920s. We can take it, I think, that there were no severe conflicts or impediments, and that her love relationship did not cause the kinds of disruptions that befell Anna Karenina, or Dora in Freud's case history, or Ada from the mining village.

24. This is a very Proustian moment of a profound joy coming unbidden, laden with significance, but without its origins being at all clear. See also note 2.

25. Joanna Field was influenced by modernist literature. She read a good deal. She mentions starting to read James Joyce's *Ulysses* (1922/1986) in the course of her project, and she also quotes from Virginia Woolf. She tried to avoid being influenced by psychoanalysis. She had read Freud as a psychology undergraduate and also had a brief period of psychoanalytic therapy shortly after starting her project, though she said she did not apply psychoanalytic theories to her discoveries.

Despite being very much caught up in the literary and psychological movements of her time, her discoveries are however strikingly fresh and original, very much her own. So was her method of keeping a diary of thoughts and emotions and of listing goals. She said that the one external source of insight that helped her formulations was Piaget's work on children.

Joanna Field's methods have been rediscovered by others, notably Karen

Horney (1942) and Aaron Beck (1976). Beck's therapy is currently among the most highly regarded for its efficacy. Beck made his rediscovery from a patient who related to him that he had a train of automatic self-critical thoughts that ran parallel to the ones he was actually expressing. Beck does not refer to Joanna Field in his 1976 book, but he makes writing down such thoughts in diaries the center of his cognitive therapy.

Chapter 9

1. It is not clear who first had the idea that a function of emotions is to make a problem conscious. Paulhan (1887/1930) certainly remarked that emotions fill the field of consciousness, but the general trend was to see emotions as disorganizing, as manifestations of unadaptedness. Mandler (1984) has attributed to Claparede (1934) the law of awareness, the idea that people become aware of automatic actions when they fail, and he has himself (1985) contributed to developing the idea. But Mead had stated this same idea quite clearly in 1913: "When, however, an essential problem appears, there is some disintegration in this organization [of unselfconscious habit], and different tendencies appear in reflective thought as different voices in conflict" (p. 147). My formulation is influenced by both Mead and Mandler.
2. Oatley and Johnson-Laird (1987) propose that emotions can sometimes occur acausally. I will leave aside from this chapter instances that arise from physiological effects creating nonsemantic signals that are not closely related to goals or events, though they may indeed be puzzling.
3. This kind of effect should perhaps be added to those presented by Nisbett and Ross (1980) in their discussion of causes that have effects on our beliefs or behavior without our being aware of them.
4. If we suffer from disorders of intended action, an analysis of planning and joint planning offered, respectively, in Chapters 1 and 4 suggest three broad kinds of therapy.

   The first would be to offer means of improving people's models of the world and hence their understanding of what would enable plans to work. This might be done by offering knowledge of general principles and specific procedures, or as cognitive therapists do, by giving advice about drawing inferences from models.

   A second method would be to induce people to act in the world in ways that were unaccustomed but nonetheless desirable to them. They would then experience effects of their actions, be in a position to adopt selected effects as goals, practice the necessary action sequences, and be able to assemble them into the kinds of intended plan that they might want. These are the techniques of directive therapies like hypnosis and behavior therapy, in which a wide variety of inducements is used to get the person to act in new ways, and hence experience the effects of these actions.

   The third kind of therapy is represented by psychoanalysis, in which the idea is that it is intentions, or wishes, particularly of the sexual and destructive kind, to which we must reconnect ourselves. To be disconnected from them is not to make emotions such as love and anger go away. Rather, it makes us experience things happening to us that feel alien. We acquire symptoms about which we complain to others, and experience other emotions (like anxiety or despair) that obsess us involuntarily.
5. One difficulty is that if a therapist's model of self is of being attractive,

helpful, wise, understanding, forgiving, and so on, transferences reinforc-
ing these ideas tend to be taken at face value. Freud thought of himself as an
understanding but just father and therefore could not himself recognize
Dora's transferences when they were either of this kind or when they questioned this role. He tended to patronize women, and found it hard to avoid
taking part in an exchange, accepting the gift of Dora to serve his academic
purposes, just as Herr K had accepted her for his sexual purposes.

Although it is the center of psychoanalytic therapy, transference seems to
be recognized and interpreted rather infrequently when actual sessions are
analyzed. For instance, Gill (1982) and Gill and Hoffman (1982) have found
in transcripts that transference interpretations are much less common than
is usually assumed.

In my view, whatever one wishes to criticize Freud for it should not be his
difficulties with transference. He recognized its problems and left sufficient
material for us to see in his writing his not altogether successful struggles
with these issues. So far as I know, being able to act as a transference
therapist is an accomplishment that only a few do well.

6. Dora's story would not have unfolded at all if Freud had seen therapy as a
   technical business, if he had said, for instance, "Now what you are suffering
   from is disgust, and this has led to displacement of affect into the alimentary
   and respiratory tracts, which I will have to try and correct." No. Dora's
   intentions were not to be operated upon like a painful tooth.
7. This quotation from Kierkegaard is the essence of the kind of therapy in
   which the therapist does not foist goals or plans onto the patient. This kind
   of therapy is, instead, a creation of a kind of space in a relationship between
   people by saying something that allows one or both to find their own intentions. It is not a persuading, or an encouragement to identification, or a
   coercion. Kierkegaard called it indirect – nondirective.
8. With Dora, Freud began to recognize transference issues too late to interpret
   them at all fully or to allow Dora to recognize them. She acted toward Freud
   rather as she had with her father and Herr K. She started with a sharp
   suspiciousness, which was then allayed and gave rise to a degree of warm
   companionship. With Freud this second phase included elements of womanly confiding. Dora evidently enjoyed intimate conversations on fascinating subjects with the attentive Freud, but too soon it emerged that, again,
   here was a man for whom other things were more important than the
   relationship with her. She became unwilling. She was unable at this point to
   do anything other than take her usual rather bitter revenge.
9. I have discussed interpretive therapy here in terms of psychoanalysis. But,
   as is well known, there are now hundreds of kinds of psychotherapy, many
   (psychosynthesis, Gestalt therapy, transactional analysis) created as modifications of psychoanalysis, and some formed in reaction or in an attempt to
   rival it, such as Moreno's psychodrama (Greenberg, 1974). An important
   issue with all psychological therapies is, as discussed briefly in Chapter 7,
   whether they are efficacious. In considering this question one cannot do
   better than begin with Smith, Glass, and Miller (1980).

   In psychodrama there is an attempt to synthesize both kinds of methods,
   therapy and art, that I discuss in this chapter as means of reconnecting the
   disjunctions of emotions. In it, too, as with the form of therapy known as
   reevaluation counseling discussed by Scheff (1979), the experience of catharsis is central.
10. One of the central procedures of natural science is the experiment, in which

a theory can be compared with a particular kind of outcome. Other types of outcome are controlled. In an experiment, issues of the internal coherence of the theory are not irrelevant, but they are secondary. In Chapter 6, I proposed that the bias associated with a single novelist's picture of social and emotional problems of life can be compensated for by representatively collected empirical data. Natural science sets out to discover truths that generalize beyond particular observations. The clearest examples of reasonable certainty that we understand something are when we can put the understanding to practical use, construct a technological application. Space scientists can, with some reliability, send a projectile to the moon.

Helmholtz argued with considerable conviction that there is "no possible sense in speaking of any other truth of our ideas except of a practical truth" (1866, p. 19). An image or an idea of an object is not the object itself. Ideas and other representations are symbols that allow us to act with certain effects on the world. When we act we expect a certain change of perceptual input, and it is this comparison between what we expect and the actual, practical, effect that is the basis of truth. "Not only is there in reality no other comparison at all between ideas and things . . . but any other mode of comparison is entirely unthinkable, and has no sense whatever." Only by grasping this idea, continues Helmholtz, can we "escape from the labyrinth of conflicting opinions" (1866, p. 19).

Helmholtz was describing a correspondence theory of truth: Ideas correspond to things. This theory is practical, and it lends itself to the technical, to ordered plans. There are important technical applications that emerge from understanding emotions, for instance, living conditions can be improved in many ways that would enable risks discovered in psychosomatic and psychiatric epidemiology (described in Chapter 6) to be reduced.

In understanding emotions, however this is only half the issue. We do not only have technical purposes. So the idea of reliable understanding needs to be elaborated somewhat.

Hume (1888/1739) argued that there are two criteria for evaluating a body of ideas. First: Do the ideas concern matters of fact, in which case, do they rest on observation and experience? Second: Do they concern relations between ideas, as for example, mathematics and logic? My contention is that in a psychology of emotions we need both of these criteria. The first is provided by natural science and the phenomena of our experience, conforming to correspondence theories of truth. The second is provided at least partly by art, and here we need to talk in terms of consistency theories of truth.

Art clearly does not meet the correspondence criteria of truth of the kind that Helmholtz describes. My proposal is that correspondence issues are adequately dealt with in the way I described in Chapter 6. George Eliot aspired to being a new kind of social scientist. Her vision is more perceptive than that of many, but the necessarily unrepresentative quality of novelists' observations have now been supplemented by the more systematic gathering of epidemiological data. Because the fields of interest overlap in the area of the effects of life events, comparisons can be made.

George Eliot's characterization of emotions is essentially consonant with recent and more representative findings. One might only add that she tended to err on the side of attributing to Dorothea and Lydgate more success in coping with their difficulties than we might expect. Dorothea has little or no social support, yet suffers a number of severe losses without symptoms of depression. This perhaps is what Leavis (1948) means when he writes that

Dorothea is too idealized. Lydgate, moreover, is described as having some suicidal thoughts, but again he does not have a breakdown. One finds it hard to imagine that the small amount of social support he receives from Dorothea is enough to carry him through his despair.

Such considerations are prompted by epidemiological studies, from which we may gain some sense of how far adjustments are needed to the proposals of the novel, to make it correspond with statistical probabilities. Art on its own is not well equipped in this area. It may involve representations and point to external events, but the representations are not put to technical uses. Events and interpretations are not reliably testable.

11. Collingwood proposes that the representational theory of art is flawed. He asserts that it is incorrect to view art as copying life. If art were representation, he says, we would become mere consumers of it. In this we would take part in merely synthetic emotional experiences. Representations, according to him, are not central to art. Indeed they may be antipathetic to art.

A representation, according to Collingwood, is part of a plan, part of a craft or a technique, always a means to an end (cf. my discussion of *techne* in Chapter 1). To undertake a technical activity is always to have a predefined goal, in which the plan for achieving that goal has been codified and rehearsed so as to produce a predictable outcome. The instructions and a diagram for assembling a piece of equipment is a representation, for instance. It allows us to undertake a technical plan to reach a goal that corresponds to that depicted in the representation. Such a technique or craft requires that the understandings of relevant aspects of the world are complete and can be represented adequately. In this way the outcome is indeed predictable.

Some activities that pass for art are not art, proposes Collingwood. They are crafts or techniques, means to an end. The end is that of arousing specific emotions. The emotions might be those of amusement (in a comedy), of thrills (in a thriller), of stirring communal sentiment (in a political speech), or of favorable inclination toward making a purchase (in advertising a product). Such arousal of emotions is not necessarily bad.

When we encounter such techniques in other cultures we sometimes refer to them as magic. Magic is not pseudo science, it is pseudo art. Its goal is to produce a specific emotional effect. When it occurs in our own culture it may just appear as the way to do certain things. Each of us tends to approve of some forms of it, maybe ceremonies that promote a worthwhile purpose, and disapprove of others, which we may call propaganda.

12. Collingwood proposes that art is addressed not primarily to an audience in order to have a particular effect on them, but primarily to oneself to make the emotion intelligible. He says an audience, a reader, a listener, a viewer of art can then take part in this making of sense, in an empathetic way. See also note 13.

13. Important though his central idea is, Collingwood mistakes the role of simulation in art I think, seeing *mimesis* (representation) as Plato did, only as having a purpose in pseudo art, such as diversion, advertising, propaganda, and other forms of social magic. In these activities techniques are employed to have particular emotional effects. Collingwood argues that art is direct unmediated creativity. His dismissal of representation in art is similar to a natural scientist saying: "We do not need theories (representations); all we need is to observe the facts directly."

Collingwood is led to his dismissal of representation in art, I believe, because he defined artistic expression as essentially private. He claimed that an artist creates an expression to make sense of an emotion for himself or herself. We the public can, as it were, look over the artist's shoulder and get a vicarious sense of what is expressed. But this surely is a wrong turning: Art is directed to other people as well as to oneself. If this is accepted, a representation that can be recognized by others is a medium for art, just as are the languages in which art is expressed. These languages are not private. Poetry written in a private language could not be recognized as poetry.

Great art allows the observer or the reader to be creative too – perhaps not so much as the artist, but in a comparable way, hence Barthes' (1975/1970) proposal of reading in a writerly way, as discussed in Chapter 5.

14. According to the account of this book emotions as such cannot be stored. They are not that sort of thing (cf. also Wegman, 1985, who makes a similar point in relation to Freud's ideas of traumata remaining like foreign bodies, continuing to have effects). The effects that tempt one to imagine that emotions can be stored are that traumata are typically met by plans to deal with them, some of which have long-term consequences. Such plans or strategies may include motivated repression, restriction of goals, habits of emotional restraint – indeed, the whole range of defense mechanisms that have been described by psychotherapists. Each defense mechanism seems to have its own emotional price, however. For instance, self-medication of anxiety by alcohol has effects that are well known in destroying relationships. Vietnam veterans reacting to the horror of war, to the death of their comrades, and to the sense of themselves as committing actions that they are ashamed of may reject the society that sent them to a war that made them misfits when they returned. They may take to living outside society. The price is that they can become prey to the effects of solitary life.

At a cathartic session it is not so much that stored emotion is allowed to escape, but that events that were influential in starting up a strategy to cope with certain emotions may be recalled and reevaluated. Scheff is correct in pointing out that the conditions for such recall are special, that they are central to psychotherapeutic practice, and that they include what he describes as creating the right "distance" so that the events are neither so close as to be overwhelming nor so far away that one is uninvolved.

15. In 1979 Scheff did not have the benefit of Nussbaum's (1986) book. If he had, her idea of *katharsis* as clarification may have fitted his account, though he may have thought her idea too verbal for the idea of discharge that he regards as central.

16. Bohannan (1966) recounts how she told the story of Hamlet to a group of elders in a Tiv village in West Africa, believing it to have a universal meaning. The elders also believed that there are universal human meanings, and instructed her on Hamlet. The meaning of the story, they said, was not quite as she had explained. Really it centered on Laertes, who had incurred gambling debts and fines for fighting. He had to raise money quickly. There are only two ways, one was to marry off his sister, but this would be impossible because no one would want to marry a woman with whom Hamlet, heir to the great chief, was in love, because if Hamlet and Ophelia were later to commit adultery together, there would be no recourse. Therefore, Laertes took the second way, to have her killed, and sell her body to the witches.

They said that Bohannan had told the story well. She had not made too many mistakes in her interpretation. Sometime she must tell them more stories from her country. Then they, who were elders, would instruct her in their true meaning so that when she returned to her land her elders would see that she had not just been sitting around in the bush doing nothing, but had been instructed in wisdom by those who know things.

17. Nisbett and Ross (1980) give a useful analysis of the resistance of implicit theories to change: Essentially, people are often more keen to hold on to a theory than to consider evidence that might induce them to change it. Mental schemata change more easily when they are rudimentary, and when we imitate others who can operate impressively in a particular domain or accept instruction from them. Change also occurs more easily when we allow a certain suspension of judgment, a period of theory-free gathering of information. Change can also occur where there is a clear goal and where skills are being learned from the mismatches between aspiration and execution, or when there is a deliberate attempt to make theory explicit to test its implications, and let the real world affect the theory.

I am talking here principally about changing our implicit theories of ourselves because these tend to be self-confirming, and because they tend to interpret everything that happens in their own terms. One can hypothesize that emotions are important in promoting change precisely because they can give a jolt, and they can induce a preoccupation from which it is difficult to escape.

18. The discrepancies between inner and outer are thus similar to those accomplished in nondirective psychotherapy where one also acquires a view from both outside and inside. In these therapies the aim of the therapist is not to exert social influence, by coercion, exhortation, advice, charisma, inducements to idealization, or encouragements to relinquish responsibility to the therapist. Instead, in the relation between client and therapist there occurs a similar kind of tension to that in George Eliot's novels. The patient is enabled both to experience his or her own emotions and to take part in the relationship with anther person who offers something of this outer view "to see oursels as others see us" (Robert Burns, "To a louse"). In the possibility of making the comparison and undertaking the reflection, the possibility occurs of transcending the merely egocentric and the merely compliant.

19. "Labyrinth of conflicting opinions" is Helmholtz's phrase; see note 10.

20. See Page (1955). See also the discussion of Sappho's poetry in Chapter 8.

21. It would be a mistake to think of Aphrodite as love in any sense that implied altruistic aspects that we tend to think of nowadays as attributes of love. Remember her wicked intervention in the *Iliad* when she engineers Paris's escape from the fight with Menelaus that he is losing, then coerces Helen to taunt him with his defeat by her former husband, following which Paris leads Helen off to bed. So instead of being settled by the result of single combat between Paris and Menelaus, as had been agreed, the war is allowed to start up again. See Chapter 5, note 13.

22. The reasons for admiration include the fact that here speaks perhaps the first voice of authentic, personal experience, of a self that is conscious of its own existence in a modern way – though it also has an unmistakable archaic tone. Sappho's voice of individuality seems the first to puzzle over those issues of emotion and free will that continue to puzzle us. Here, too, is a poet whose sparseness of style and clarity of expression are such as to take the breath away and survive translation. In the aggressively male Hellenic world, here, too, is one woman whose work has commanded a respect that survives today, as she said herself: "Dead I will not be forgotten."

The reasons for revilement are that it is a fair inference from her poetry that Sappho had sexual relationships with other women. For some, the fact of her being a woman and a homosexual is cause for celebration (see Wickes, 1977; Benstock, 1986). For others, these same facts are cause for distaste. This disapproval has issued in accusations that she was a prostitute, and it has been met by equally prim attempts to show how Sappho was a priestess and her circle of women a religious group, or that she ran an academic institution in which other women were her graduate students. This same distaste shows, I think, rather clearly in Page's discussion of these issues in which he demonstrates that there are no grounds for speculations that she was either a priestess or a prostitute, but he avers that one has to take seriously the accusation that "she was addicted to the perversion that the modern world names after her native island" (p. 143).

This talk is offensive. Homosexuality is not now illegal in most of Europe and America, and is not regarded as a perversion or psychiatric disorder. Taking up Page's term addicted, a colleague David Hodgson has pointed out to me that the American Psychiatric Association's (1980) manual of disorders DSM III has it about right in deleting homosexuality from the list of sexual disorders that had been in previous editions, while now including being unable to give up smoking as a substance abuse disorder.

23. This phrase is from Wordsworth in his 1802 preface to *Lyrical Ballads*: "I have said that Poetry is the spontaneous overflow of powerful feelings: it takes its origin from emotion recollected in tranquillity. The emotion is contemplated till by a species of reaction the tranquillity disappears, and an emotion, kindred to that which was before the subject of contemplation, is gradually produced and does itself actually exist in the mind" (Wordsworth, 1984, p. 611).

Epilogue

1. In physics a being from another planet might well agree with a human physicist about, say, Ohm's law that resistance is the ratio of voltage to current in an electrical conductor. But many human actions might be quite inexplicable to a Martian. In the social sciences in general we are not just making inferences from observations where the activity of the specific observer has been factored out. A planet or an electrical circuit has, as it were, only an outside. People have an inner life, not just a matter of observation.

It was a contention of European historians and sociologists at the end of the last century and the beginning of this (see, e.g., Hughes, 1959) that the human sciences did not just consist of collecting data and making valid or useful inferences from them. History, sociology, anthropology, and psychology also require that people enter imaginatively into the life they are trying to understand. To understand in this sense is not simply being able mentally to model, say, a mathematical relationship, but to relive for ourselves an event or phenomenon. Otherwise an event is part of the physical, not the human, world. Otherwise history is just happenings, imperfectly recorded, that occurred to people now dead. Sociology is just numbers, cross-tabulations between endless social categories, more or less uncertainly defined. Anthropology is a catalog of social rules of no more use to anyone outside a specific culture than is a Toronto subway token on a London bus. Psychology becomes no more than a set of assertions, more or less specific to context, about the performance characteristics of human automata.

2. This idea of certain knowledge has continued to fascinate European philosophers. So we have Descartes (1968/1637) announcing that, yes, indeed, there is something that cannot be doubted, and the empiricists who tell us that observations made in the right way are not subject to doubt. We are invited to think of knowledge as founded on these pure, hard, undeniable truths, and to think that inferences made validly from them will be similarly certain. What I am proposing for emotions is that we do not have sources of knowledge that are both indisputable and from which everything else of any importance can be validly inferred. Instead, structures made from several different kinds of less certain knowledge related to one another are strong enough to sustain worthwhile understanding.

References

Abbott, D. A., & Brody, G. H. (1985). The relation of child age, gender, and number of children to the marital adjustment of wives. *Journal of Marriage and the Family, 47*, 77–84.

Abramson, L. Y., Metalsky, G. I., & Alloy, L. B. (1989). Hopelessness depression: A theory-based subtype of depression. *Psychological Review, 96*, 358–372.

Abramson, L. Y., Seligman, M. E. P., & Teasdale, J. D. (1978). Learned helplessness in humans: Critique and reformulations. *Journal of Abnormal Psychology, 87*, 49–74.

Ader, R. (Ed.) (1981). *Psychoneuroimmunology.* New York: Academic Press.

Ainsworth, M. D. S. (1967). *Infancy in Uganda: Infant care and the growth of attachment.* Baltimore, MD: Johns Hopkins Press.

American Psychiatric Association (1980). *Diagnostic and statistical manual of mental disorders (DSM III).* Washington, DC.

Amsel, A. (1958). The role of frustrative non-reward in non-continuous reward situations. *Psychological Bulletin, 55*, 102–119.

Angier, R. P. (1927). The conflict theory of emotion. *American Journal of Psychology, 39*, 390–401.

Angold, A. (1988). Depression in childhood and adolescence. 1. Epidemiological aetiological aspects. *British Journal of Psychiatry, 152*, 501–507.

Anisman, H., & Zacharcho, R. M. (1982). Depression: The predisposing influence of stress. *Behavioral and Brain Sciences, 5*, 89–137.

Anthony, H. D. (1960). *Sir Isaac Newton.* London: Abelard-Schuman.

Antonovsky, A. (1979). *Health, stress and coping.* San Francisco: Jossey-Bass.

Argyle, M. (1987). *The Psychology of happiness.* London: Methuen.

Aristotle. *Complete works.* Revised Oxford translation in 2 volumes. Ed. J. Barnes. Princeton, NJ: Princeton University Press, 1984. (Page numbers for quotations follow the usual convention among Aristotle scholars, and are from Bekker's standard edition of the Greek text of 1831.)

  On the soul. Trans. W. S. Hett, Loeb Classical Library. London: Heinemann, 1936.

Armstrong, S., Gleitman, L., & Gleitman, H. (1983). What some concepts might not be. *Cognition, 13*, 263–308.

Atkinson, R. L., Atkinson, R. C., Smith, E. E., & Bem, D. J. (1990). *Introduction to psychology.* San Diego, CA: Harcourt Brace Jovanovich. (Previously under the editorship of E. R. Hilgard.)

Auerbach, E. (1953). *Mimesis: The representation of reality in Western literature.* Princeton, NJ: Princeton University Press. (Original published 1946.)

Austin, J. L. (1962). *How to do things with words.* Oxford: Oxford University Press.

Averill, J. R. (1982). *Anger and aggression: An essay on emotion.* New York: Springer.

—— (1985). The social construction of emotion: With special reference to love. In K. J. Gergen & K. E. Davis (Eds.), *The social construction of the person.* New York: Springer.

—— (1990). Emotions as episodic dispositions, cognitive schemas, and transitory social roles: Steps toward an integrated theory of emotion. *Perspectives in Personality, 3,* Part A, 137–165.

Averill, J. R., & Boothroyd, P. (1977). On falling in love in conformance with the romantic ideal. *Motivation and Emotion, 1,* 235–247.

Ax, A. A. (1964). Goals and methods of psychophysiology. *Psychophysiology, 1,* 8–25.

Baars, B. (Ed.) (1986). *The psychology of error: A window on the mind.* New York: Plenum.

Bagnall, F. S., Easton, D. F., Harris, E., Chilvers, C. E. D., & McElwain, T. J. (1990). Survival of patients with breast cancer attending the Bristol Cancer Help Centre. *Lancet, 336,* 606–610.

Bakan, D. (1958). *Sigmund Freud and the Jewish mystical tradition.* Boston: Beacon.

Baker, G. H. B. (1987). Psychosocial factors and immunity. *Journal of Psychosomatic Research, 31,* 1–10.

Barefoot, J. C., Dahlstrom, W. G., & Williams, R. B. (1983). Hostility, CHD incidence and total mortality: A 25 year follow up study of 255 physicians. *Psychosomatic Medicine, 45,* 59–63.

Barnard, M. (1958). *Sappho: A new translation.* Berkeley: University of California Press.

Baron, J. (1985). *Rationality and intelligence.* Cambridge: Cambridge University Press.

Baron-Cohen, S., Leslie, A. M., & Frith, U. (1985). Does the autistic child have a theory of mind? *Cognition, 21,* 37–46.

Barthes, R. (1975). *S / Z.* Trans. R. Miller. London: Cape (Original work published 1970.)

Bartlett, F. C. (1932). *Remembering: A study in experimental and social psychology.* Cambridge: Cambridge University Press.

Bebbington, P. E., Hurry, J., Tennant, C., Sturt, E., & Wing, J. K. (1981). Epidemiology of mental disorders in Camberwell. *Psychological Medicine, 11,* 561–579.

Bebbington, P. E., Sturt, E., Tennant, C., & Hurry, J. (1984). Misfortune and resilience: A community study of women. *Psychological Medicine, 14,* 347–363.

Beck, A. T. (1976). *Cognitive therapy and the emotional disorders.* New York: Meridian.

Beck, A. T., Rush, A. J., Shaw, B. F., & Emery, G. (1979). *Cognitive therapy of depression.* Chichester: Wiley.

Bell, S. M., & Ainsworth, M. D. S. (1972). Infant crying and maternal responsiveness. *Child Development, 43,* 1171–1190.

Benstock, S. (1986). *Women of the Left Bank, 1900–1940.* Houston: University of Texas Press.

Bermond, B., Fasotti, L., Nieuwenhuyse, B., & Schuerman, J. (1991). Spinal cord lesions, peripheral feedback and intensities of emotional feelings. *Cognition and Emotion, 5,* 201–220.

Bernheimer, C., & Kahane, C. (Eds.) (1985). *In Dora's case: Freud – hysteria – feminism.* New York: Columbia University Press.

Bernstein, D. A., Roy, E. J., Srull, T. K., & Wickens, C. D. (1988). *Psychology.* Boston: Houghton Mifflin.

Berscheid, E. (1982). Attraction and emotion in interpersonal relations. In M. S. Clark and S. T. Fiske (Eds.), *Affect and cognition: The seventeenth annual Carnegie symposium on cognition.* Hillsdale, NJ: Erlbaum.

(1983). Compatibility and emotion. In W. Ickes (Ed.), *Compatible and incompatible relationships* (pp. 143–161). New York: Springer.

Black, J. B., & Wilensky, R. (1979). An evaluation of story grammars. *Cognitive Science, 3*, 213–229.

Blaney, P. H. (1986). Affect and memory: A review. *Psychological Bulletin, 99*, 229–246.

Blass, E. M., Ganchrow, J. R., & Steiner, J. E. (1984). Classical conditioning in newborn humans 2–48 hours of age. *Infant Behavior and Development, 7*, 223–235.

Block, J. H., Block, J., & Gjerde, P. F. (1986). The personality of children prior to divorce: A prospective study. *Child Development, 57*, 827–840.

Boakes, R. (1984). *From Darwin to behaviourism: Psychology and the minds of animals.* Cambridge: Cambridge University Press.

Bohannan, L. (1966). Shakespeare in the bush. *Natural History*, August/September 1–6.

Bolton, W., and Oatley, K. (1987). A longitudinal study of social support and depression in unemployed men. *Psychological Medicine, 17*, 453–460.

Boman, B. (1988). Stress and heart disease. In S. Fisher and J. Reason (Eds.), *Handbook of life stress, cognition and health.* Chichester: Wiley.

Bower, G. H. (1981). Mood and memory. *American Psychologist, 36*, 129–148.

(1987). Commentary on mood and memory. *Behavior Research and Therapy, 25*, 443–455.

Bower, G. H., & Cohen, P. R. (1982). Emotional influences on memory and thinking: Data and theory. In M. S. Clark & S. T. Fiske (Eds.), *Affect and cognition: The seventeenth annual Carnegie symposium on cognition.* Hillsdale, NJ: Erlbaum.

Bower, G. H., & Morrow, D. G. (1990). Mental models and narrative comprehension. *Science, 247*, 44–48.

Bowlby, J. (1969). *Attachment and loss: Vol. 1, Attachment.* London: Hogarth Press.

(1973). *Attachment and loss: Vol. 2, Separation.* London: Hogarth Press.

(1980). *Attachment and loss: Vol. 3, Sadness and depression.* London: Hogarth Press.

Bradbury, T. N., & Fincham, F. D. (1987). Affect and cognition in close relationships. *Cognition and Emotion, 1*, 59–87.

Brennan, S. (1985). The cariacature generator. *Leonardo, 18*, 170–178.

Brentano, F. (1973). *Psychology from an empirical standpoint.* Ed. L. L. McAlister. London: Routledge & Kegan Paul. (First edition of original work published 1874.)

Brewer, W. F., & Lichtenstein, E. H. (1981). Event schemas, story schemas and story grammars. In J. Long & A. Baddeley (Eds.), *Attention and performance 9.* Hillsdale, NJ: Erlbaum.

Brewin, C. R. (1985). Depression and causal attributions: What is their relation? *Psychological Bulletin, 98*, 297–309.

(1988). Explanation and adaptation in adversity. In S. Fisher & J. Reason (Eds.), *Handbook of life stress, cognition and health.* Chichester: Wiley.

Broadbent, D. E., & Broadbent, M. (1988). Anxiety and attentional bias: State and trait. *Cognition and Emotion, 2*, 165–183.

Broadbent, D. E., Cooper, P. F., Fitzgerald, P., & Parkes, K. R. (1982). The

Cognitive Failures Questionnaire (CFQ) and its correlates. *British Journal of Clinical Psychology, 21,* 1–16.

Brown, G. W., Adler, Z., and Bifulco, A. (1988). Life events, difficulties and recovery from chronic depression. *British Journal of Psychiatry, 152,* 487–498.

Brown, G. W., Andrews, B., Harris, T., Adler, Z., & Bridge, L. (1986). Social support, self-esteem and depression. *Psychological Medicine, 16,* 813–831.

Brown, G. W., Bifulco, A., and Harris, T. (1987). Life events, vulnerability and onset of depression: Some refinements. *British Journal of Psychiatry, 150,* 30–42.

Brown, G. W., & Harris, T. O. (1978). *The social origins of depression.* London: Tavistock.

(1986). Establishing causal links: The Bedford College studies of depression. In H. Katshnig (Ed.), *Life events and psychiatric disorders.* Cambridge: Cambridge University Press.

(Eds.) (1989). *Life events and illness.* London: Unwin Hyman.

Browne, A., & Finkelhor, D. (1986). Initial and long-term effects: A review of the research. In D. Finkelhor et al., *A sourcebook on child sexual abuse.* Beverly Hills, CA: Sage.

Bruner, J. (1986). *Actual minds, possible worlds.* Cambridge, MA: Harvard University Press.

Bryan, W. L., & Harter, N. (1897). Studies in the physiology and psychology of telegraphic language. *Psychological Review, 6,* 345–375.

Burns, D. D. (1980). *Feeling good: The new mood therapy.* New York: Signet.

Burns, R. (1904). *The poetical works of Robert Burns.* Ed. J. L. Robertson. Oxford: Oxford University Press.

Campos, J. J., Barrett, K. C., Lamb, M., Goldsmith, H. H., & Stenberg, C. (1983). Socioemotional development. In P. H. Mussen (General Ed.), *Handbook of child psychology, Vol. 2.* (Eds. M. N. Haith & J. J. Campos), *Infancy and developmental psychology.* New York: Wiley.

Campos, J. J., Hiatt, S., Ramsay, D., Henderson, C., & Svejda, M. (1978). The emergence of fear of heights. In M. Lewis & L. Rosenblum (Eds.), *The development of affect.* New York: Plenum.

Cannon, W. B. (1927). The James-Lange theory of emotion: A critical examination and an alternative theory. *American Journal of Psychology, 39,* 106–124.

Cartwright, F. F. (1977). *A social history of medicine.* New York: Longman.

Carver, C. S., & Scheier, M. F. (1990). Origins and functions of positive and negative affect: A control process view. *Psychological Review, 97,* 19–35.

Cassileth, B. R., Lusk, E. J., Miller, D. S., Brown, L. L., & Miller, C. (1985). Psychosocial correlates of survival in advanced malignant disease? *New England Journal of Medicine, 312,* 1551–1555.

Charniak, E., & McDermott, D. (1985). *Introduction to artificial intelligence.* Reading, MA: Addison-Wesley.

Chomsky, N. (1957). *Syntactic structures.* The Hague: Mouton.

(1965). *Aspects of the theory of syntax.* Cambridge, MA: MIT Press.

Churchland, Patricia S. (1986). *Neurophilosophy.* Cambridge, MA: MIT Press.

Churchland, Paul M. (1984). *Matter and consciousness.* Cambridge, MA: MIT Press.

Claparede, E. (1928). Feelings and emotions. In M. L. Reymert (Ed.), *Feelings and emotions.* Worcester, MA: Clark University Press.

(1934). *La genese de l'hypothese.* Geneva: Kundig.

Clark, A. (1987). From folk psychology to naive psychology. *Cognitive Science, 11,* 139–154.

Clark, R. W. (1980). *Freud: The man and the cause.* London: Cape.

Clore, G. L., Ortony, A., & Foss, M. A. (1987). The psychological foundations of the affective lexicon. *Journal of Personality and Social Psychology, 53,* 751–766.

Clowes, M. B., & Oatley, K. (1979). Scripts and themes: A course in cognitive psychology. Unpublished mimeo. Brighton: University of Sussex, 1979.

Collingwood, R. G. (1938). *The principles of art.* London: Oxford University Press.

Conway, M. A. (1990). Conceptual representation of emotions: The role of autobiographical memories. In K. J. Gilhooly, M. T. G. Keene, R. H. Logie, & G. Erdos (Eds.), *Lines of thinking: Reflections on the psychology of thought. Vol. 2. Skills, emotion, creative processes, individual differences and teaching thinking.* Chichester: Wiley.

Conway, M. A., & Bekerian, D. A. (1987). Situational knowledge and emotions. *Cognition and Emotion, 1,* 145–191.

Cooley, C. (1902). *Human nature and the social order.* New York: Scribner.

Cooper, C. L. (1988). Personality, life stress and cancerous disease. In S. Fisher & J. Reason (Eds.), *Handbook of life stress, cognition and health.* Chichester: Wiley.

Cox, J. R., & Griggs, R. A. (1982). The effects of experience on performance in Wason's selection task. *Memory and Cognition, 10,* 496–502.

Cox, T. (1988). Psychological factors in stress and health. In S. Fisher & J. Reason (Eds.), *Handbook of life stress, cognition and health.* Chichester: Wiley.

Coyne, J. C., & Gotlib, I. H. (1983). The role of cognition in depression: A critical appraisal. *Psychological Bulletin, 94,* 472–505.

Craik, K. J. W. (1943). *The nature of explanation.* Cambridge: Cambridge University Press.

Cummings, E. M., Ianotti, R. J., & Zahn-Waxler, C. (1985). Influence of conflict between adults on the emotions and aggression of young children. *Developmental Psychology, 21,* 495–507.

Damon, W., & Hart, D. (1982). The development of self-understanding from infancy through adolescence. *Child Development, 53,* 841–864.

Darwin, C. (1859). *On the origin of species by means of natural selection.* London: Murray.

(1871). *The descent of man and selection in relation to sex.* London: Murray.

(1872). *The expression of the emotions in man and the animals.* Reprinted Chicago: University of Chicago Press, 1965.

Davis, P. J. (1988). Physiological and subjective effects of catharsis: A case report. *Cognition and Emotion, 2,* 19–28.

Dawkins, R. (1982). *The extended phenotype: The gene as the unit of selection.* San Francisco: Freeman.

(1986). *The blind watchmaker.* London: Longmans.

Dean, C., Surtees, P. G., & Sashidharan, S. P. (1983). Comparison of research diagnostic systems in an Edinburgh community sample. *British Journal of Psychiatry, 142,* 247–256.

De Quincy, T. (1822). *Confessions of an English opium eater.* Reprinted London: Grant Richards, 1902.

De Rivera, J. (1977). *A structural theory of the emotions.* New York: International Universities Press.

Derogatis, L. R., Abeloff, M. D., & Melisaratos, N. (1979). Psychological coping mechanisms and survival time in metastatic breast cancer. *Journal of the American Medical Association, 242,* 1504–1508.

Descartes, R. (1911). *Passions de l'ame.* In E. L. Haldane & G. R. Ross (Ed. and

Trans.), *The philosophical works of Descartes*. Cambridge: Cambridge University Press. (Original published 1649.)

(1968). *Discourse on method*. Trans. F. E. Sutcliffe. Harmondsworth: Penguin. (Original published 1637.)

De Sousa, R. (1980). The rationality of emotions. In A. O. Rorty (Ed.), *Explaining emotions*. Berkeley: University of California Press.

(1987). *The rationality of emotions*. Cambridge, MA: MIT Press.

Deutsch, F. (1957). A footnote to Freud's "Fragment of an analysis of a case of hysteria." *Psychoanalytic Quarterly, 26,* 159–167.

Dewey, J. (1894). The theory of emotions. I. Emotional attitudes. *Psychological Review, 1,* 553–569.

(1895). The theory of emotions. II. The significance of emotions. *Psychological Review, 2,* 13–32.

(1933). *How we think: A restatement of the relation of reflective thinking to the educative process*. Boston: Heath.

Diener, E., Horowitz, J., & Emmons, R. A. (1985). Happiness of the very wealthy. *Social Indicators Research, 16,* 263–274.

Diener, E., & Iran-Nejad, A. (1986). The relationship in experience between various types of affect. *Journal of Personality and Social Psychology, 53,* 751–756.

Dilthey, W. (1985). Excerpts from *Draft for a critique of historical reason*. In K. Mueller-Vollmer (Ed.), *The hermeneutics reader* (pp. 149–164). Oxford: Blackwell. (Original published 1926.)

Dixon, N. (1976). *The psychology of military incompetence*. London: Cape.

Dodds, E. R. (1951). *The Greeks and the irrational*. Berkeley: University of California Press.

Doerner, D. (1987). On the difficulties people have in dealing with complexity. In J. Rasmussen, K. Duncan, & J. Leplat (Eds.), *New technology and human error*. Chichester: Wiley.

Dohrenwend, B. P., & Shrout, P. E. (1985). "Hassles" in the conceptualization and measurement of life stress variables. *American Psychologist, 40,* 780–785.

Doll, R., & Peto, R. (1981). *The causes of cancer*. Oxford: Oxford University Press.

Donne, J. (1929). *Complete poetry and selected prose*. Ed. J. Hayward, London: Nonesuch Press. (Poems originally published 1633.)

(1967). *John Donne: Selected prose*. Oxford: Oxford University Press. (Sermon preached at St. Paul's on Easter Day 1628.)

Dorian, B., & Garfinkel, P. E. (1987). Stress, immunity and illness – A review. *Psychological Medicine, 17,* 393–407.

Dowdney, L., Skuse, D., Rutter, M., Quinton, D., & Mrazek, D. (1985). The nature and qualities of parenting provided by women raised in institutions. *Journal of Child Psychology and Psychiatry, 26,* 599–625.

Drabble, M. (1985). *The Oxford companion to English literature*. Oxford: Oxford University Press.

Draper, S. W. (1985). A micro-survey of ten theories of emotion. Unpublished technical memorandum. University of Sussex.

Draper, S. W., & Oatley, K. (In preparation). *The structure of intelligent doing.*

Dreyfus, H. (1979). *What computers can't do: The limits of artificial intelligence*. New York: Harper & Row.

Duffy, E. (1941). An explanation of "emotional" phenomena without the use of the concept "emotion." *Journal of General Psychology, 25,* 283–293.

Dunn, J. (1987). Understanding feelings: The early stages. In J. Bruner & H.

Haste (Eds.), *Making sense: The child's construction of the world.* London: Methuen.

(1988). *The beginnings of social understanding.* Oxford: Blackwell.

Dunn, J., & Kendrick, C. (1982). *Siblings: Love, envy and understanding.* Cambridge, MA: Harvard University Press.

Dunn, J., Kendrick, C., & MacNamee, R. (1981). The reaction of first born children to the birth of a sibling: Mothers' reports. *Journal of Child Psychology and Psychiatry, 22,* 1–18.

Dutton, D. G., & Aron, A. P. (1974). Some evidence for heightened sexual attraction under conditions of high anxiety. *Journal of Personality and Social Psychology, 30,* 510–517.

Dyer, M. G. (1983). The role of affect in narratives. *Cognitive Science, 7,* 211–242.

(1987). Emotions and their computations: Three computer models. *Cognition and Emotion, 1,* 323–347.

Easterbrook, J. A. (1959). The effects of emotion on cue utilization and the organization of behavior. *Psychological Review, 66,* 183–201.

Edel, L. (1955). *The modern psychological novel.* New York: Grosset & Dunlap.

Eibl-Eibesfeldt, I. (1972). Similarities and differences between cultures in expressive movements. In R. A. Hinde. (Ed.), *Non-verbal communication* (pp. 297–312). Cambridge: Cambridge University Press.

Eiser, J. R. (Ed.) (1982). *Social psychology and behavioural medicine.* Chichester: Wiley.

Ekman, P. (1973). Cross-cultural studies of facial expression. In P. Ekman (Ed.), *Darwin and facial expression: A century of research in review.* New York: Academic Press.

(Ed.) (1982). *Emotion in the human face.* 2nd ed. Cambridge: Cambridge University Press.

(1984). Expression and the nature of emotion. In K. Scherer & P. Ekman (Eds.), *Approaches to emotion.* Hillsdale, NJ: Erlbaum.

(1989). The argument and evidence about universals in facial expressions of emotion. In H. Wagner & A. Manstead (Eds.), *Handbook of social psychophysiology.* Chichester: Wiley.

Ekman, P., & Friesen, W. V. (1971). Constants across culture in the face and emotion. *Journal of Personality and Social Psychology, 17,* 124–129.

(1976). Pictures of facial affect. Palo Alto, CA: Consulting Psychologists Press.

(1986). A new pan-cultural facial expression of emotion. *Motivation and Emotion, 10*(2), 159–168.

(1988). Who knows what about contempt: A reply to Izard and Haynes. *Motivation and Emotion, 12*(1), 17–21.

Ekman, P., Friesen, W. V., & Ellsworth, P. (1982a). Conceptual ambiguities. In P. Ekman (Ed.), *Emotion in the human face.* 2nd ed. Cambridge: Cambridge University Press.

(1982b). What emotion categories or dimensions can observers judge from facial behavior? In P. Ekman (Ed.), *Emotion in the human face,* 2nd ed. Cambridge: Cambridge University Press.

Ekman, P., Friesen, W. V., & Simons, R. V. (1985). Is the startle reaction an emotion? *Journal of Personality and Social Psychology, 49,* 1416–1426.

Ekman, P., Levenson, R. W., & Friesen, W. V. (1983). Autonomic nervous activity distinguishes among emotions. *Science, 221,* 1208–1210.

Ekman, P., & Oster, H. (1982). Review of research. In P. Ekman (Ed.), *Emotion in the human face,* 2nd ed. Cambridge: Cambridge University Press.

Eliot, G. (1856). The natural history of German life. *Westminster Review.* Reprinted in T. Pinney (Ed.), *Essays of George Eliot.* New York: Columbia University Press, 1963.

 (1871–72). *Middlemarch: A study of provincial life.* Edinburgh: Blackwood. (Page numbers from Penguin English Library Edition. Harmondsworth: Penguin, 1965.)

 (1876). *Daniel Deronda.* Edinburgh: Blackwood.

 (1985). *Selections from George Eliot's letters.* Ed. G. S. Haight. New Haven, CT: Yale University Press.

Eliot, T. S. (1922). *The waste land.* London: Faber & Faber.

Ellis, A., & Harper, R. A. (1975). *A new guide to rational living.* Englewood Cliffs, NJ: Prentice-Hall.

Ellsworth, P. C., & Smith, C. A. (1988a). From appraisal to emotion: Differences among unpleasant feelings. *Motivation and Emotion, 12,* 271–302.

 (1988b). Shades of joy: Patterns of appraisal differentiating pleasant emotions. *Cognition and Emotion, 2,* 301–331.

Emde, R. N. (1983). The prerepresentational self and its affective core. *Psychoanalytic Study of the Child, 38,* 165–192.

Etcoff, N. (1990). Categorical perception of facial expressions. Paper presented to the fifth annual meeting of the International Society for Research on Emotions, Rutgers University, NJ, 25–28 July.

Eysenck, H. J. (1988). Personality, stress and cancer: Prediction and prophylaxis. *British Journal of Medical Psychology, 61,* 57–75.

Fairbairn, W. R. D. (1952). *Psychoanalytic studies of the personality.* London: Routledge & Kegan Paul.

Fehr, B., & Russell, J. A. (1984). Concept of emotion viewed from a prototype perspective. *Journal of Experimental Psychology: General, 113,* 464–486.

Feuerbach, L. (1957). *The essence of Christianity.* Trans. G. Eliot. New York: Harper & Row. (Original published 1841.)

Feynman, R. (1981). The pleasure of finding things out. *The Listener,* November 26, 635–636.

Field, J. (1934). *A life of one's own.* London: Chatto & Windus. (Revised ed. Harmondsworth: Pelican, 1952.)

Field, T., & Fogel, A. (1982). *Emotion and early interaction.* Hillsdale, NJ: Erlbaum.

Field, T., Woodson, R., Greenberg, R., & Cohen, D. (1982). Discrimination and imitation of facial expressions by neonates. *Science, 218,* 179–181.

Fikes, R. E., & Nilsson, N. J. (1971). STRIPS: A new approach to the application of theorem proving to problem solving. *Artificial Intelligence, 2,* 189–208.

Finlay-Jones, R., & Brown, G. W. (1981). Types of stressful life event and the onset of anxiety and depressive disorders. *Psychological Medicine, 11,* 803–815.

Fodor, J. A. (1983). *The modularity of mind.* Cambridge, MA: MIT Bradford Books.

Fodor, J. A., & Pylyshyn, Z. (1988). Connectionism and cognitive architecture: A critical analysis. *Cognition, 28,* 3–71.

Forest, D., Clark, M. S., Mills, J., & Isen, A. M. (1979). Helping as a function of feeling state and nature of the helping behavior. *Motivation and Emotion, 3,* 161–169.

Forrester, J. (1984). Freud, Dora and the untold pleasures of psychoanalysis. In L. Appignanesi (Ed.), *Desire* (pp. 4–9). London: Institute of Contemporary Arts.

Fortenbough, W. W. (1975) *Aristotle on emotion.* London: Duckworth.

Fox, B. H. (1982). Endogenous psychosocial factors in cross-national cancer incidence. In J. R. Eiser (Ed.), *Social psychology and behavioral medicine.* Chichester: Wiley.

Frank, R. H. (1988). *Passion within reason: The strategic role of the emotions.* New York: Norton.

Frankenhaeuser, M. (1983). The sympathetic-adrenal and pituitary adrenal response to challenge: Comparison between the sexes. In T. M. Dembroski, T. Schmidt, & G. Blumchen (Eds.), *Biobehavioral bases of coronary heart disease.* Basel: Karger.

Freedman, J. L. (1978). *Happy people: What happiness is, who has it and why.* New York: Harcourt Brace Jovanovich.

Freud, S. (1953). *The interpretation of dreams (Part 1).* In J. Strachey (Ed. and Trans.), *The standard edition of the complete psychological works of Sigmund Freud* (Vol. 4). London: Hogarth Press. (Original published 1900.)

(1953). Fragment of an analysis of a case of hysteria ("Dora"). In J. Strachey (Ed. and Trans.), *The standard edition of the complete psychological works of Sigmund Freud* (Vol. 7, pp. 1–122). London: Hogarth Press. (Original published 1905.)

(1957). *Mourning and melancholia.* J. Riviere (Trans.), *The standard edition of the complete psychological works of Sigmund Freud* (Vol. 14, pp. 237–258). London: Hogarth Press. (Original published 1917.)

(1958a). Recommendations for physicians on the psychoanalytic method of treatment. In J. Strachey (Ed. and Trans.), *The standard edition of the complete psychological works of Sigmund Freud* (Vol. 12, 107–120). London: Hogarth Press. (Original published 1912.)

(1958b). On beginning treatment. In J. Strachey (Ed. and Trans.), *The standard edition of the complete psychological works of Sigmund Freud* (Vol. 12, pp. 121–144). London: Hogarth Press. (Original published 1912.)

(1960). *The psychopathology of everyday life.* In J. Strachey (Ed.). A. Tyson (Trans.), *The standard edition of the complete psychological works of Sigmund Freud* (Vol. 6). London: Hogarth Press. (Original published 1901.)

(1961). *The ego and the id.* J. Riviere (Trans.), *The standard edition of the complete psychological works of Sigmund Freud* (Vol. 19). London: Hogarth Press. (Original published 1923.)

(1961). *Civilization and its discontents. The standard edition of the complete psychological works of Sigmund Freud* (Vol. 21, pp. 57–145). London: Hogarth Press. (Original published 1930.)

(1963). *Introductory lectures on psychoanalysis (Parts 1 and 2).* In J. Strachey (Ed. and Trans.), *The standard edition of the complete psychological works of Sigmund Freud* (Vol. 15). London: Hogarth Press. (Original published 1915–1916.)

(1963). *Introductory lectures on psychoanalysis (Part 3).* In J. Strachey (Ed. and Trans.), *The standard edition of the complete psychological works of Sigmund Freud* (Vol. 16). London: Hogarth Press. (Original published 1916–1917.)

(1964). *New introductory lectures on psychoanalysis.* In J. Strachey (Ed. and Trans.), *The standard edition of the complete psychological works of Sigmund Freud* (Vol. 22). London: Hogarth Press. (Original published 1933.)

(1964). On constructions. In J. Strachey (Ed. and Trans.), *The standard edition of the complete psychological works of Sigmund Freud* (Vol. 20, pp. 254–269). London: Hogarth Press. (Original published 1937.)

(1985). *The complete letters of Sigmund Freud to Wilhelm Fliess, 1887–1904.* Ed. and Trans. J. M. Masson. Cambridge, MA: Harvard University Press.

Freud, S., & Breuer, J. (1955). *Studies on hysteria*. In J. Strachey & A. Strachey (Ed. and Trans.), *The standard edition of the complete psychological works of Sigmund Freud* (Vol. 2). London: Hogarth Press. (Original published 1895.)

Frick, R. W. (1985). Communicating emotion: The role of prosodic features. *Psychological Bulletin, 97*, 412–429.

Friedman, H. S., & Booth-Kewley, S. (1987). The "disease-prone personality": A meta-analytic view of the construct. *American Psychologist, 42*(6), 539–555.

Friedman, M., & Rosenman, R. H. (1959). Association of specific overt behavior pattern with blood cardiovascular findings. *Journal of the American Medical Association, 169*, 1286–1295.

Frijda, N. H. (1986). *The emotions*. Cambridge: Cambridge University Press.

(1987a). Comment on Oatley and Johnson-Laird's "Towards a cognitive theory of emotions." *Cognition and Emotion, 1*, 51–59.

(1987b). Emotion, cognitive structure and action tendency. *Cognition and Emotion, 1*, 115–143.

(1988). The laws of emotion. *American Psychologist, 43*, 349–358.

Frijda, N. H., Kuipers, P., & ter Schure, E. (1989). Relations among emotion, appraisal, and emotional action readiness. *Journal of Personality and Social Psychology, 57*, 212–228.

Frijda, N. H., Mesquita, B., Sonnemans, J., & van Goozen, S. (1991). The duration of affective phenomena or emotions, sentiments and passions. In K. T. Strongman (Ed.), *International Review of Studies on Emotion, Vol. 1*. Chichester: Wiley.

Frijda, N. H., & Swagerman, J. (1987). Can computers feel? Theory and design of an emotional system. *Cognition and Emotion, 1*, 235–257.

Fromm, E. (1957). *The art of loving*. London: Allen & Unwin.

Galileo Galilei. (1914). *Dialogues concerning two new sciences*. Trans. H. Crew & G. de Santillana. Evanston, IL: Northwestern University Press. (Original published 1638.)

(1953). *Dialogue concerning two chief world systems – Ptolomaic and Copernican*. Trans. S. Drake. Berkeley: University of California Press. (Original published 1632.)

Gallup, J. (1982). *Feminism and psychoanalysis: The daughter's seduction*. London: Macmillan.

Gardner, D., Harris, P. L., Ohmoto, M., & Hamazaki, T. (1988). Japanese children's understanding of the distinction between real and apparent emotion. *International Journal of Behavioural Development, 11*, 203–218.

Gardner, H. (1985). *The mind's new science: A history of the cognitive revolution*. New York: Basic Books.

Gaver, W. W., & Mandler, G. (1987). Play it again Sam: On liking music. *Cognition and Emotion, 1*(3), 259–282.

Gay, P. (1988). *Freud: A life for our time*. London: Dent.

Gazzaniga, M. S. (1988). Brain modularity: Towards a philosophy of conscious experience. In A. J. Marcel & E. Bisiach (Eds.), *Consciousness in contemporary science*. Oxford: Oxford University Press.

Geertz, C. (1975). On the nature of anthropological understanding. *American Scientist, 63*, 47–53.

Gilbert, P. (1984). *Depression: From psychology to brain state*. Hillsdale, NJ: Erlbaum.

(1988). Psychobiological interaction in depression. In S. Fisher & J. Reason (Eds.), *Handbook of life stress, cognition and health*. Chichester: Wiley.

Gill, M. M. (1982). *Analysis of transference. Vol. 1.* New York: International Universities Press.

Gill, M. M., & Hoffman, I. Z. (1982). *Analysis of transference. Vol. 2.* New York: International Universities Press.

Gittings, R. (Ed.) (1966). *Selected poems and letters of Keats.* London: Heineman.

Goethe, J. W. (1989). *The sorrows of young Werther.* Trans. M. Hulse. Harmondsworth: Penguin Books. (Original published 1774.)

Goffman, E. (1961). Fun in games. In *Encounters: Two studies in the sociology of interaction.* Indianapolis, IN: Bobbs-Merrill.

Gordon, R. M. (1987). *The structure of emotions: Investigations in cognitive philosophy.* Cambridge: Cambridge University Press.

Graham, P. J., Rutter, M., & George, S. (1973). Temperamental characteristics as predictors of behavior disorders. *American Journal of Orthopsychiatry, 43,* 328–339.

Gramsci, A. (1971). *Selections from the prison notebooks.* Ed. & Trans. Q. Hoare & G. N. Smith. London: Lawrence & Wishart.

Gray, J. A. (1982). *The neuropsychology of anxiety: An enquiry into the functions of the septo-hippocampal system.* Oxford: Oxford University Press.

Greenberg, I. A. (1974). *Psychodrama: Theory and therapy.* New York: Behavioral Publications.

Grice, H. P. (1975). Logic and conversation. In P. Cole & J. L. Morgan (Eds.), *Syntax and semantics. 3. Speech/Acts.* New York: Academic Press.

Grossarth-Maticek, R., Bastiaans, J., & Kanazir, D. T. (1985). Psychosocial factors as strong predictors of mortality from cancer, ischaemic heart disease and stroke: The Yugoslav prospective study. *Journal of Psychosomatic Research, 29,* 167–176.

Grossarth-Maticek, R., Eysenck, H. J., & Vetter, H. (1988). Personality type, smoking habit and their interaction as predictors of cancer and coronary heart disease. *Personality and Individual Differences, 9,* 479–495.

Gruber, H. E. (1974). *Darwin on man: A psychological study of scientific creativity, together with Darwin's early and unpublished notebooks.* London: Wildwood House.

Grünbaum, A. (1984). *The foundations of psychoanalysis: A philosophical critique.* Berkeley: University of California Press.

(1986). Precis of *The foundations of psychoanalysis: A philosophical critique. Behavioral and Brain Sciences, 9,* 217–284.

Haight, G. S. (1985). *Selections from George Eliot's letters.* New Haven, CT: Yale University Press.

Hallowell, A. I. (1955). *Culture and experience.* Philadelphia: University of Pennsylvania Press.

Hammond, M. (1987). Introduction. In M. Hammond (Ed. and Trans.), *The Iliad: A new prose translation.* Harmondsworth: Penguin.

Haring-Hidore, M., Stock, W. A., Okun, M. A., & Witter, R. A. (1985). Marital status and subjective well-being: A research synthesis. *Journal of Marriage and the Family, 47,* 947–953.

Harré, R. (1983). *Personal being.* Oxford: Blackwell.

(Ed.) (1986). *The social construction of emotions.* Oxford: Blackwell.

Harris, P. L. (1983). Children's understanding of the link between situation and emotion. *Journal of Experimental Child Psychology, 36,* 490–509.

(1989). *Children and emotion: The development of psychological understanding.* Oxford: Blackwell.

Harris, P. L., Donnelly, K., Guz, G. R., & Pitt-Watson, R. (1986). Children's understanding of the distinction between real and apparent emotion. *Child Development, 57,* 895–909.

Harris, P. L., Guz, G. R., Lipian, M. S., & Man-Shu, Z. (1985). Insight into the time course of emotion among Western and Chinese children. *Child Development, 56,* 972–988.

Harris, P. L., Olthof, T., & Terwogt, M. M. (1981). Children's knowledge of emotion. *Journal of Child Psychology and Psychiatry, 22,* 247–261.

Harris, P. L., Olthof, T., Terwogt, M. M., & Hardman, C. E. (1987). Children's knowledge of the situations that provoke emotion. *International Journal of Behavioural Development, 10*(3), 319–343.

Harter, S., & Whitesell, N. (1989). Developmental changes in children's emotion concepts. In C. Saarni & P. L. Harris (Eds.), *Children's understanding of emotions.* New York: Cambridge University Press.

Haviland, J., & Lelwicka, M. (1987). The induced affect response: 10-week-old infants' responses to three emotional expressions. *Developmental Psychology, 23,* 97–104.

Hazan, C., & Shaver, P. (1987). Romantic love conceptualized as an attachment process. *Journal of Personality and Social Psychology, 52,* 511–524.

Hebb, D. O. (1946). Emotion in man and animal: An analysis of the intuitive process of recognition. *Psychological Review, 53,* 88–106.

Heider, F., & Simmel, H. (1944). An experimental study in apparent behavior. *American Journal of Psychology, 57,* 243–259.

Helmholtz, H. (1962). *Treatise on physiological optics, Vol. 3.* Ed. J. P. C. Southall. New York: Dover. (Original published 1866.)

Henley, W. E. (1939). *Invictus.* In A. Quiller-Couch (Ed.), *Oxford Book of English Verse, New Edition.* Oxford: Oxford University Press.

Hiatt, L. R. (1978). Classification of the emotions. In L. R. Hiatt (Ed.), *Australian aboriginal concepts.* Canberra: Australian Institute of Aboriginal Studies.

Hinde, R. A. (1982). *Ethology: Its nature and relations with other sciences.* London: Fontana.

Hochschild, A. R. (1979). Emotion work, feeling rules, and social structure. *American Journal of Sociology, 85,* 551–575.

(1983). *The managed heart: The commercialization of human feeling.* Berkeley: University of California Press.

Hoffman, M. (1978). Towards a theory of empathetic arousal and development. In M. Lewis & L. Rosenblum (Eds.), *The development of affect.* New York: Plenum.

(1986). Affect, cognition and motivation. In E. T. Higgins & R. M. Sorrentino (Eds.), *Handbook of social behaviour* (pp. 244–280). New York: Guilford.

Hohmann, G. W. (1962). Some effects of spinal cord lesions on experienced emotional feelings. *Psychophysiology, 3,* 143–156.

Holmes, T. H., & Rahe, R. H. (1967). The social readjustment rating scale. *Journal of Psychosomatic Research, 11,* 213–218.

Homer. *Iliad.* Two volumes, with an English translation by A. T. Murray. Loeb Classical Library, Nos. 170 and 171. London: Heineman, 1924.

Horney, K. (1942). *Self-Analysis.* London: Routledge & Kegan Paul.

Horowitz, M. J. (1979). Depressive disorders in response to loss. In I. G. Sarason & C. D. Spielberger (Eds.), *Stress and anxiety. Vol. 6.* New York: Wiley.

Howell, S. (1981). Rules not words. In P. Heelas & A. Lock (Eds.), *Indigenous psychologies: The anthropology of the self.* London: Academic Press.

Hudson, W. D. (1980). The rational system of beliefs. In D. Martin, J. Orme

Mills, & W. S. F. Pickering (Eds.), *Sociology and theology: Alliance and conflict.* Hassocks: Harvester Press.

Hughes, H. S. (1959). *Consciousness and society: The reorientation of European social thought, 1890–1930.* London: MacGibbon & Kee.

Hume, D. (1888). *Treatise of human nature.* Oxford: Oxford University Press. (Original published 1739.)

Humphrey, N. (1983). *Consciousness regained: Nature's psychologists.* Oxford: Oxford University Press.

Humphries, S. (1988). *A secret world of sex: Forbidden fruit – the British experience, 1900–1950.* London: Sidgewick & Jackson.

Hutchins, E. (1985). The social organization of distributed cognition. Unpublished manuscript.

(1987). Learning to navigate. Manuscript prepared for the Workshop on Context, Cognition, and Activity, Stenungsund, Sweden.

Inhelder, B., & Piaget, J. (1958). *The growth of logical thinking from childhood to adolescence.* London: Routledge & Kegan Paul.

Inoura, Y., & Kawatake, T. (1981). *The traditional theater of Japan.* New York: Weatherall.

Ischida, E. (1974). The culture of love and hate. In T. S. Lebra & W. P. Lebra (Eds.), *Japanese culture and behavior: Selected readings.* Honolulu: University of Hawaii Press.

Isen, A. M. (1984). Toward understanding the role of affect in cognition. T. Wyer & T. Srull (Eds.), *Handbook of social cognition.* Hillsdale, NJ: Erlbaum.

Isen, A. M., Daubman, K. A., & Nowicki, G. P. (1987). Positive affect facilitates creative problem solving. *Journal of Personality and Social Psychology, 52,* 1122–1131.

Isen, A. M., & Levin, P. F. (1972). The effect of feeling good on helping: Cookies and kindness. *Journal of Personality and Social Psychology, 21,* 384–388.

Isen, A. M., & Patrick, R. (1983). The effect of positive feelings on risk taking: When the chips are down. *Organizational Behavior & Human Performance, 31,* 194–202.

Isen, A. M., Shalker, T., Clark, M., & Karp, L. (1978). Affect, accessibility of material in memory and behavior: A cognitive loop? *Journal of Personality and Social Psychology, 36,* 1–12.

Izard, C. E. (1971). *The face of emotion.* New York: Appleton Century Crofts.

(1972). *Patterns of emotions: A new analysis of anxiety and depression.* New York: Academic Press.

Izard, C. E., & Haynes, O. M. (1988). On the form and universality of the contempt expression: A challenge to Ekman and Frieson's claim of discovery. *Motivation and Emotion, 12,* 1–16.

Izard, C. E., Huebner, R., McGinness, G., & Dougherty, L. (1980). The young infant's ability to produce discrete emotion expressions. *Developmental Psychology, 16,* 132–140.

Izard, C. E., Malatesta, C. Z., & Camras, L. A. (1991). Conceptualising early infant affect: Emotions as fact, fiction or artifact? In K. Strongman (Ed.), *International Review of Research on Emotion.* Chichester: Wiley.

James, H. (1873). Review of George Eliot's *Middlemarch.* Reprinted in P. Swinden (Ed.), *George Eliot, Middlemarch: A casebook.* London: Macmillan, 1972.

(1881). *The portrait of a lady.* Reprinted. Harmondsworth: Penguin, 1963.

James, W. (1884). What is an emotion? *Mind, 9,* 188–205.

(1890). *The principles of psychology.* New York: Holt.

(1892). *Psychology: Briefer course.* New York: Holt.

Jaynes, J. (1976). *The origin of consciousness in the breakdown of the bicameral mind.* London: Allen Lane.

Jenkins, H., & Ward, W. (1965). Judgements of contingency between responses and outcomes. *Psychological Monographs, 79*, Whole No. 594.

Jenkins, J. M. (1987). Protective factors and coping strategies of children living in disharmonious homes. Ph.D. thesis, Institute of Child Health, University of London.

Jenkins, J. M., & Smith, M. A. (1990). Factors protecting children living in disharmonious homes: Maternal reports. *Journal of the American Academy of Child and Adolescent Psychiatry, 29*, 60–69.

Jenkins, J. M., Smith, M. A., & Graham (1989). Coping with parental quarrels. *Journal of the American Academy of Child and Adolescent Psychiatry, 28*, 182–189.

Johnson, W. F., Emde, R. N., Pannabecker, B. J., Stenberg, C. R., & Davis, M. H. (1982). Maternal perception of infant emotion from birth through 18 months. *Infant Behavior and Development, 5*, 313–322.

Johnson-Laird, P. N. (1983a). *Mental models: Towards a cognitive science of language, inference and consciousness.* Cambridge: Cambridge University Press.

(1983b). A computational analysis of consciousness. *Cognition and Brain Theory, 6*, 499–508.

(1988). *The computer and the mind: An introduction to cognitive science.* London: Fontana.

Johnson-Laird, P. N., & Bara, B. (1984). Syllogistic inference. *Cognition, 16*, 1–61.

Johnson-Laird, P. N., Legrenzi, P., & Sonino-Legrenzi, M. (1972). Reasoning and a sense of reality. *British Journal of Psychology, 63*, 395–400.

Johnson-Laird, P. N., & Oatley, K. (1988a). Are there only two primitive emotions? A reply to Frijda. *Cognition and Emotion, 2*, 89–93.

(1988b). Il significato delle emozioni: Una teoria e un' analisi semantica. In V. D'Urso e R. Trentin (a cura di), *Psicologia delle emozioni.* Bologna: Il Mulino.

(1989). The meaning of emotions: Analysis of a semantic field. *Cognition and Emotion, 3*, 81–123.

Joyce, J. (1922). *Ulysses.* Reprinted. London: Bodley Head, 1986.

Kahneman, D., Slovic, P., & Tversky, A. (1982). *Judgement under uncertainty: Heuristics and biasses.* Cambridge: Cambridge University Press.

Kanner, A. D., Coyne, J. C., Schaefer, C., & Lazarus, R. S. (1981). Comparison of two modes of stress measurement: Daily hassles and uplifts versus major life events. *Journal of Behavioural Medicine, 4*, 1–39.

Kardiner, A. (1977). *My analysis with Freud: Reminiscences.* New York: Norton.

Katz, J. M. (1980). Discrepancy, arousal and labelling: Towards a psychosocial theory of emotion. *Sociological Inquiry, 50*, 147–156.

Keats, J. (1816). On first looking into Chapman's Homer. In R. Gittings (Ed.), *Selected poems and letters of Keats.* London: Heineman, 1966.

(1818). Letter to John Taylor, 27 February, 1818. In R. Gittings (Ed.), *Selected poems and letters of Keats.* London: Heineman, 1966.

Kempton, M. (1990). Keeping up with the news. *New York Review of Books, 36*, Nos. 21 and 22, January 18.

Kenealy, P. (1988). Validation of a music mood induction procedure: Some preliminary findings. *Cognition and Emotion, 2*, 41–48.

Kennedy, S., Kiecolt-Glaser, J. K., & Glaser, R. (1988). Immunological consequences of acute and chronic stressors: Mediating role of interpersonal relationships. *British Journal of Medical Psychology, 61*(1), 77–85.

Kierkegaard, Søren. (1938). *The journals of Søren Kierkegaard.* Ed. and Trans. A. Dru. London: Oxford University Press.

(1941). *Concluding unscientific postscript*. Trans. D. F. Swenson & W. Lowrie. Princeton, NJ: Princeton University Press. (Original published 1846.)

(1941). *The sickness unto death*. Trans. W. Lowrie. Princeton, NJ: Princeton University Press. (Original published 1849.)

(1944). *The concept of dread*. Ed. and Trans. W. Lowrie. Princeton, NJ: Princeton University Press. (Original published 1844.)

Kim, J. (1988). Paper presented for research group on "Mind and Brain," organized by Peter Bieri and Ekhart Scherer, Zentrum fur interdisziplinare Forschung, University of Bielefeld.

Klinnert, M. (1984). The regulation of infant behavior by maternal facial expression. *Infant Behavior and Development*, 7, 447–465.

Lacan, J. (1982). Intervention on transference. Trans. J. Rose. In J. Mitchell & J. Rose (Eds.), *Feminine sexuality: Jacques Lacan and the Ecole Freudienne* (pp. 61–73). London: Macmillan (Original published 1952.)

Laing, R. D., Phillipson, H., & Lee, A. R. (1966). *Interpersonal perception: A theory and a method of research*. London: Tavistock.

Lakatos, I. (1978). *The methodology of scientific research programmes: Philosophical papers, Vol. 1*. Ed. J. Worrall & G. Currie. Cambridge: Cambridge University Press.

Lambert, M. J., Shapiro, D. A., & Bergin, A. E. (1986). The effectiveness of psychotherapy. In S. L. Garfield & A. E. Bergin (Eds.), *Handbook of psychotherapy and behavior change: An empirical analysis* (3rd ed.). New York: Wiley.

Laplanche, J., & Pontalis, J-B. (1973). *The language of psychoanalysis*. Trans. D. Nicholson-Smith. London: Hogarth Press.

Lazarus, R. S. (1966). *Psychological stress and the coping process*. New York: McGraw-Hill.

(1984). Puzzles in the study of daily hassles. *Journal of Behavioural Medicine*, 7, 375–389.

Lazarus, R. S., DeLongis, A., Folkman, S., & Gruen, R. (1985). Stress and adaptational outcomes: The problem of confounded measures. *American Psychologist*, 40, 770–779.

Lazarus, R. S., & Folkman, S. (1984). *Stress, appraisal and coping*. New York: Springer.

Leavis, F. D. (1948). *The great tradition*. London: Chatto & Windus.

Leeper, R. W. (1948). A motivational theory of emotion to replace "emotion as a disorganised response." *Psychological Review*, 55, 5–21.

Leff, J. (1981). *Psychiatry around the globe: A transcultural view*. New York: Dekker.

Leff, J., Berkovitz, R., Shavit, N., Strachan, A., Glass, I., & Vaughn, C. (1989). A trial of family therapy versus a relative group for schizophrenia. *British Journal of Psychiatry*, 154, 58–66.

Leslie, A. M., & Frith, U. (1990). Prospects for a neuropsychology of autism: Hobson's choice. *Psychological Review*, 97, 122–131.

Levenson, R. W., & Gottman, J. M. (1983). Marital interaction: Physiological linkage and affective exchange. *Journal of Personality and Social Psychology*, 45, 587–597.

Leventhal, H., & Scherer, K. (1987). The relationship of emotion to cognition: A functional approach to a semantic controversy. *Cognition and Emotion*, 1, 3–28.

Leventhal, H., & Tomarken, A. J. (1986). Emotion: Today's problems. In M. R. Rosenzweig and L. W. Porter (Eds.), *Annual Review of Psychology*. Palo Alto, CA: Annual Reviews.

Levy, R. I. (1984). Emotion, knowing, and culture. In R. A. Shweder & R. A. LeVine (Eds.), *Culture theory: Essays on mind, self and emotion*. Cambridge: Cambridge University Press.

Lichtheim, M. (1973). *Ancient Egyptian literature. Vol. 1. The old and middle kingdoms*. Berkeley: University of California Press.

Lindsley, D. B. (1951). Emotion. In S. S. Stevens (Ed.), *Handbook of experimental psychology*. New York: Wiley.

Linton, M. (1982). Transformations of memory in everyday life. In U. Neisser (Ed.), *Memory observed*. San Francisco: Freeman.

Linton, R. (1936). *The study of man*. New York: Appleton-Century.

Lively, P. (1987). *Moon Tiger*. London: Andre Deutsch.

Lorenz, K. (1967). *On aggression*. Trans. M. Latzke. London: Methuen. (Original published 1963.)

(1970). *Studies in animal and human behavior*. Trans. R. Martin. Cambridge, MA: Harvard University Press.

Lowe, J., & Carroll, D. (1985). The effects of spinal injury on the intensity of emotional experience. *British Journal of Clinical Psychology, 14*, 135–136.

Luborsky, L., Crits-Christoph, P., & Mellon, J. (1986). Advent of objective measures of the transference concept. *Journal of Clinical and Consulting Psychology, 54*, 39–47.

Lucas, D. (1984). Everyday memory lapses. Ph.D. thesis, University of Manchester.

Lutz, C. (1982). The domain of emotion words on Ifaluk. *American Ethnologist, 9*, 113–128.

(1985a). Depression and the translation of emotion words. In A. Kleinman & B. Good (Eds.), *Culture and depression: Studies in the anthropology and cross-cultural psychology of affect and disorder*. Berkeley: University of California Press.

(1985b). Ethnopsychology compared to what? Explaining behavior and consciousness among the Ifaluk. In G. White & J. T. Kirkpatrick (Eds.), *Person, self, and experience: Exploring Pacific ethnopsychologies*. Berkeley: University of California Press.

(1986). Emotion, thought and estrangement: Emotion as a cultural category. *Cultural Anthropology, 1*, 287–309.

(1987). Goals, events and understanding in Ifaluk emotion theory. In D. Holland & N. Quinn (Eds.), *Cultural models in language and thought*. Cambridge: Cambridge University Press.

(1988a). Ethnographic perspectives on the emotion lexicon. In V. Hamilton, G. H. Bower & N. H. Frijda (Eds.), *Cognitive perspectives on emotion and motivation*. Dordrecht: Kluwer.

(1988b). *Unnatural emotions: Everyday sentiments on a Micronesian atoll and their challenge to Western theory*. Chicago: Chicago University Press.

McClelland, J. L., & Rumelhart, D. E. (Eds.) (1986). *Parallel distributed processing: Explorations in the microstructure of cognition. Vols. 1 and 2*. Cambridge, MA: MIT Press.

McFarland, D. J. (1985). *Animal behaviour*. London: Longman.

(1989). Goals, no-goals and own goals. In A. Montefiore & D. Noble (Eds.), *Goals, no-goals and own goals*. London: Unwin Hyman.

MacLeod, C., Mathews, A., & Tata, P. (1986). Attentional bias in emotional disorders. *Journal of Abnormal Psychology, 95*, 15–20.

McNaughton, N. (1989). *Biology and emotion*. Cambridge: Cambridge University Press.

McNeill, W. H. (1977). *Plagues and peoples*. Oxford: Blackwell.

McSweeney, K. (1984). *Middlemarch*. London: Allen & Unwin.

Main, M., & George, C. (1985). Responses of abused and disadvantaged toddlers to distress in agemates: A study in the day-care setting. *Developmental Psychology, 21,* 407–412.

Malatesta, C. Z., & Culver, L. C. (1984). Change and continuity in the affective themes of adult women. In C. Z. Malatesta & C. Izard (Eds.), *Emotion in adult development*. Beverly Hills, CA: Sage.

Mandler, G. (1964). The interruption of behavior. *Nebraska Symposium on Motivation. Vol. 12.* Lincoln: University of Nebraska Press.

(1975). *Mind and emotion*. New York: Wiley.

(1984). *Mind and body: Psychology of emotions and stress*. New York: Norton.

(1985). *Cognitive psychology: An essay in cognitive science*. Hillsdale, NJ: Erlbaum.

Mandler, J. M., & Johnson, L. S. (1977). Remembrance of things parsed: Story structure and recall. *Cognitive Psychology, 9,* 111–191.

Manktelow, K. I., & Evans, J. St. B. J. (1979). Facilitation of reasoning by realism: Effect or non-effect? *British Journal of Psychology, 70,* 477–488.

Manstead, A. S. R., & Wagner, H. L. (1981). Arousal, cognition and emotion: An appraisal of two-factor theory. *Current Psychological Reviews, 1,* 35–54.

Marcel, A. J. (1983). Conscious and unconscious perception: An approach to the relations between phenomenal experience and perceptual processes. *Cognitive Psychology, 15,* 238–300.

Marcus, S. (1974). Freud and Dora: Story, history, case history. *Partisan Review.* Winter.

Marquez, G. G. (1989). *Love in the time of cholera*. Harmondsworth: Penguin. (Original published 1985.)

Marr, D. (1982). *Vision*. San Francisco: Freeman.

Marshall, S. L. A. (1978). *Men against fire*. Gloucester, MA: Peter Smith.

Marx, K., & Engels, F. (1970). *The German ideology*. London: Lawrence & Wishart. (Original published 1932, although the authors had tried to find a publisher in the 1840s, without success, leaving it "to the gnawing of the mice.")

Masson, J. M. (1984). *Freud: The assault on truth*. London: Faber.

May, K. M. (1977). *Out of the maelstrom: Psychology and the novel in the twentieth century*. London: Elek.

Mead, G. H. (1912). The mechanism of social consciousness. Reprinted in A. J. Reck (Ed.), *Selected writings of George Herbert Mead*. Indianapolis: Bobbs-Merrill, 1964.

(1913). The social self. Reprinted in A. J. Reck (Ed.), *Selected writings of George Herbert Mead*. Indianapolis, IN: Bobbs-Merrill, 1964.

Medcalf, S. (1981). Inner and outer. In S. Medcalf (Ed.), *The later middle ages.* London: Methuen.

Meyer, L. B. (1956). *Emotion and meaning in music*. Chicago: University of Chicago Press.

Meyer, N. (1975). *The seven percent solution*. London: Hodder & Stoughton.

Miller, G. A., Galanter, E., & Pribram, K. H. (1960). *Plans and the structure of behavior*. New York: Holt, Rinehart & Winston.

Miller, G. A., & Johnson-Laird, P. N. (1976). *Language and perception*. Cambridge: Cambridge University Press.

Minsky, M. (1986). *The society of mind*. New York: Simon & Schuster.

Minuchin, S., Rosman, B. L., & Baker, L. (1978). *Psychosomatic families: Anorexia nervosa in context*. Cambridge, MA: Harvard University Press.

Morris, C. (1972). *The discovery of the individual 1050–1200*. London: S.P.C.K.

Mowrer, O. H. (1960). *Learning theory and behavior.* New York: Wiley.
Nagel, T. (1979). *Mortal questions.* Cambridge: Cambridge University Press.
Nance, J. (1975). *The gentle Tasaday.* New York: Harcourt Brace Jovanovich.
Neisser, U. (1963). The imitation of man by machine. *Science, 139,* 193–197.
Neu, J. (1977). *Emotion, thought and therapy.* London: Routledge & Kegan Paul.
Newell, A. (1972). You can't play 20 questions with nature and win. In W. G. Chase (Ed.), *Visual information processing.* New York: Academic Press.
Nietzsche, F. (1956). *The birth of tragedy* and *The genealogy of morals.* Garden City, NY: Doubleday Anchor. (Original published, respectively, 1872 and 1887.)
——— (1977). *A Nietzsche reader.* Trans. R. J. Hollingdale. Harmondsworth: Penguin. (Original work *Human, all too human* published 1878.)
Nisbett, R. E., & Ross, L. (1980). *Human inference: Strategies and shortcomings of social judgment.* Englewood Cliffs, NJ: Prentice-Hall.
Nisbett, R. E., & Wilson, T. D. (1977). Telling more than we can know: Verbal reports on mental processes. *Psychological Review, 84,* 231–259.
Norman, D. A. (1981). Categorization of action slips. *Psychological Review, 88,* 1–15.
Nussbaum, M. C. (1986). *The fragility of goodness: Luck and ethics in Greek tragedy and philosophy.* Cambridge: Cambridge University Press.
——— (Forthcoming). The stoics on the extirpation of the passions.
Oatley, K. (1972). *Brain mechanisms and mind.* London: Thames & Hudson.
——— (1974). Circadian rhythms and representations of the environment in motivational systems. In D. J. McFarland (Ed.), *Motivational control systems analysis.* London: Academic Press.
——— (1978). *Perceptions and representations: The theoretical bases of brain research.* London: Methuen.
——— (1981). Representing ourselves: Mental schemata, computational metaphors, and the nature of consciousness. In G. Underwood & R. Stevens (Eds.), *Aspects of consciousness. Vol. 2.* London: Academic Press.
——— (1987a). Experiments and experience: Usefulness and insight in psychology. In H. Beloff & A. M. Colman (Eds.), *Psychology Survey, 6.* Leicester: British Psychological Society.
——— (Ed.) (1987b). *Cognitive science and the understanding of emotions.* Special issue of *Cognition and Emotion.* Hillsdale, NJ: Erlbaum.
——— (1988a). Plans and the communicative function of emotions: A cognitive theory. In V. Hamilton, G. H. Bower, & N. H. Frijda (Eds.), *Cognitive perspectives on emotion and motivation. NATO ASI Series D, No. 44.* Dordrecht: Kluwer.
——— (1988b). Life events, social cognition and depression. In S. Fisher & J. Reason (Eds.), *Handbook of life stress, cognition and health* (pp. 543–557). Chichester: Wiley.
——— (1989). The importance of being emotional. *New Scientist,* 18 August, 33–36.
Oatley, K., & Bolton, W. (1985). A social-cognitive theory of depression in reaction to life events. *Psychological Review, 92,* 372–388.
Oatley, K., Draper, S. W., & Button, C. G. Goals in conversation: Increments of agreement and the satisfaction of constraints. (Submitted.)
Oatley, K., & Duncan, E. (1992). Structured diaries for emotions in daily life. In K. T. Strongman (Ed.), *International Review of Studies on Emotion, Vol. 2.* Chichester: Wiley.
Oatley, K., & Jenkins, J. M. (1992). Human emotions: Function and dysfunction. *Annual Review of Psychology, 43.* (In press.)

Oatley, K., & Johnson-Laird, P. N. (1987). Towards a cognitive theory of emotions. *Cognition and Emotion, 1*, 29–50.

(1990). Semantic primitives for emotions. *Cognition and Emotion, 4*, 129–143.

Oatley, K., & Perring, C. (1991). A longitudinal study of psychological and social factors affecting recovery from psychiatric breakdowns. *British Journal of Psychiatry, 158*, 28–32.

Oatley, K., Sullivan, G. D., & Hogg, D. (1988). Drawing visual conclusions from analogy: A theory of preprocessing, cues and schemata in the perception of three dimensional objects. *Journal of Intelligent Systems, 1*, 97–133.

Oatley, K., & Yuill, N. (1985). Perception of personal and inter-personal action in a cartoon film. *British Journal of Social Psychology, 24*, 115–124.

Ortony, A. (1987). Is guilt an emotion? *Cognition and Emotion, 1*, 283–298.

Ortony, A., & Clore, G. L. (1989). Emotions, moods, and conscious awareness: Comment on Johnson-Laird and Oatley's "The language of emotions: An analysis of a semantic field." *Cognition and Emotion, 3*, 125–137.

Ortony, A., Clore, G. L., & Collins, A. (1988). *The cognitive structure of emotions.* New York: Cambridge University Press.

Ortony, A., Clore, G. L., & Foss, M. A. (1987). The referential structure of the affective lexicon. *Cognitive Science, 11*, 361–384.

Ortony, A., & Turner, T. J. (1990). What's basic about basic emotions? *Psychological Review, 74*, 315–431.

Page, D. (1955). *Sappho and Alcaeus: An introduction to the study of ancient Lesbian poetry.* Oxford: Oxford University Press.

Panksepp, J. (1982). Towards a general psychobiological theory of emotions. *Behavioral and Brain Sciences, 5*, 407–467.

(1989). The psychobiology of emotions: The animal side of human feelings. *Experimental Brain Research, 18*, 31–55.

Papert, S. (1980). *Mindstorms: Children, computers and powerful ideas.* Hassocks: Harvester.

Parisi, T. (1987). Why Freud failed: Some implications for neurophysiology and sociobiology. *American Psychologist, 42*, 235–245.

Patel, C. K. N., & Bloembergen, N. (1987). Strategic defense and directed energy weapons. *Scientific American, 257*(3), 31–37.

Paulhan, F. (1887). *The laws of feeling.* English translation 1930. London: Kegan-Paul, French, Trubner & Co.

Pelling, M. (1978). *Cholera, fever and English medicine 1825–65.* Oxford: Oxford University Press.

Perring, C., Oatley, K., & Smith, J. (1988). Psychiatric symptoms and conflict among personal plans. *British Journal of Medical Psychology, 61*, 167–177.

Perrow, C. (1984). *Normal accidents: Living with high risk technologies.* New York: Basic Books.

Peters, S. D., Wyatt, G. E., & Finkelhor, D. (1986). Prevalence. In D. Finkelhor et al., *A sourcebook on child sexual abuse.* Beverly Hills, CA: Sage.

Peterson, C., & Seligman, M. E. P. (1984). Causal explanations as a risk factor for depression. *Psychological Review, 91*, 347–374.

Pfeifer, R. (1988). Artificial intelligence models of emotion. In V. Hamilton, G. H. Bower, & N. H. Frijda (Eds.), *Cognitive perspective on emotion and motivation. NATO ASI Series D, No. 44.* Dordrecht: Kluwer.

Piaget, J. (1926). *Language and thought of the child.* London: Kegan Paul.

(1971). *Structuralism.* London: Routledge & Kegan Paul. (Original published 1968.)

Pinney, T. (Ed.) (1963). *Essays of George Eliot.* New York: Columbia University Press.

Plato. *Apology.* In *The last days of Socrates.* Trans. H. Tredennick. Harmondsworth: Penguin, 1954.

The republic. Trans. D. Lee. Harmondsworth: Penguin, 1955.

The symposium. Trans. W. Hamilton. Harmondsworth: Penguin, 1951.

Theaetetus. In *Dialogues of Plato.* Trans. B. Jowett. Oxford: Oxford University Press, 1871.

Plutchik, R. (1962). *The emotions: Facts, theories and a new model.* New York: Random House.

(1980). A general psychoevolutionary theory of emotion. In R. Plutchik & H. Kellerman (Eds.), *Emotion: Theory, research and experience. Vol. 1. Theories of emotion* (pp. 3–33). New York: Academic Press.

(1984). Emotions: A general psychoevolutionary theory. In K. R. Scherer & P. Ekman (Eds.), *Approaches to emotion* (pp. 197–219). Hillsdale, NJ: Erlbaum.

Popper, K. R. (1945). *The open society and its enemies. Vol. 1. Plato.* London: Routledge.

(1962). *Conjectures and refutations.* New York: Basic Books.

Pound, A., Cox, A. D., Puckering, C., & Mills, M. (1985). The impact of maternal depression on young children. In J. E. Stevenson (Ed.), *Recent research in developmental psychopathology.* Oxford: Pergamon.

Power, R. (1979). The organization of purposeful dialogues. *Linguistics, 17,* 107–152.

Power, R., & dal Martello, M. F. (1985). Some criticisms of Sacks, Schegloff, and Jefferson on turn taking. Unpublished manuscript.

Pribram, K. (1984). Emotion: A neurobehavioral analysis. In K. Scherer & P. Ekman (Eds.), *Approaches to emotion.* Hillsdale, NJ: Erlbaum.

Price, V. A. (1982). *Type A behavior pattern: A model for research and practice.* New York: Academic Press.

Proust, M. (1981). *Remembrance of things past.* Trans. C. K. Scott Moncrieff, T. Kilmartin, & A. Mayor. London: Chatto & Windus. (Original *A la recherche du temps perdu* published in eight parts between 1913 and 1927.)

Putnam, H. (1975). The meaning of meaning. In K. Gunderson (Ed.), *Language, mind and knowledge.* Minnesota Studies in the Philosophy of Science. Vol. 7. Minneapolis: University of Minnesota Press.

Quennell, P. (1988). *The pursuit of happiness.* Oxford: Oxford University Press.

Quinton, D., Rutter, M., & Liddle, C. (1984). Institutional rearing, parental difficulties and marital support. *Psychological Medicine, 14,* 107–124.

Quinton, D., Rutter, M., & Rowlands, O. (1977). An evaluation of an interview assessment of marriage. *Psychological Medicine, 6,* 577–586.

Rahe, R. H. (1988). Recent life changes and coronary heart disease: 10 years' research. In S. Fisher and J. Reason (Eds.), *Handbook of life stress, cognition and health.* Chichester: Wiley.

Rahe, R. H., & Arthur, R. J. (1978). Life change and illness studies. *Journal of Human Stress, 41,* 3–15.

Ramas, M. (1980). Freud's Dora, Dora's hysteria. *Feminist Studies, 6,* 472–510.

Ramirez, A. J. (1988). Life events and cancer: Conceptual and methodological issues. In M. Watson, S. Greer, & C. Thomas (Eds.), *Psychosocial oncology.* Oxford: Pergamon.

Ramirez, A. J., Craig, T. K. J., Watson, J. P., Fentiman, I. S., North, W. R. S., & Rubens, R. D. (1989). Stress and relapse of breast cancer. *British Medical Journal, 298,* 291–293.

Rawls, J. (1972). *A theory of justice.* Oxford: Oxford University Press.

Reason, J. T. (1984). Absent mindedness. In J. Nicholson & H. Beloff (Eds.), *Psychology Survey, No. 5.* Leicester: British Psychological Society.

(1986). Cognitive underspecification: Its varieties and consequences. In B. Baars (Ed.), *The psychology of error: A window on the mind.* New York: Plenum.

(1987). The Chernobyl errors. *Bulletin of the British Psychological Society, 40,* 201–206.

(1988). Stress and cognitive failure. In S. Fisher and J. Reason (Eds.), *Handbook of life stress, cognition and health.* Chichester: Wiley.

Reason, J. T., & Mycielska, K. (1982). *Absent minded: The psychology of mental lapses and everyday errors.* Englewood Cliffs, NJ: Prentice-Hall.

Redfield, R. R., & Burke, D. S. (1988). HIV infection: The clinical picture. *Scientific American, 259*(4), 70–78.

Redican, W. K. (1982). In P. Ekman (Ed.), *Emotion in the human face,* 2nd ed. Cambridge: Cambridge University Press.

Reisenzein, R. (1983). The Schachter theory of emotion: Two decades later. *Psychological Bulletin, 94,* 239–264.

Rich, E. (1983). *Artificial intelligence.* London: McGraw-Hill.

Ricoeur, P. (1984). *Time and narrative. Vol. 1.* Trans. K. McLaughlin & D. Pellauer. Chicago: University of Chicago Press. (Original published 1983.)

Riley, V. (1981). Psychoneuroendocrine influences on immunocompetence and neoplasia. *Science, 212,* 1100–1109.

Roberts, R. C. (1988). What is an emotion: A sketch. *Philosophical Review, 97,* 183–209.

Robinson, L. A., Berman, J. S., & Neimeyer, R. A. (1990). Psychotherapy for the treatment of depression: A comprehensive review of controlled outcome studies. *Psychological Bulletin, 108,* 30–49.

Rosch, E. (1973). Natural categories. *Cognitive Psychology, 4,* 328–350.

Rose, J. (1983). Femininity and its discontents. *Feminist Review,* no. 14, 1–21.

Roseman, I. (1984). Cognitive determinants of emotion: A structural theory. *Review of Personality and Social Psychology, 5,* 11–36.

Rosenman, R. H., Brand, R. J., Jenkins, C. D., Friedman, M., Straus, R., & Wurm, M. (1975). Coronary heart disease in the Western collaborative group study. *Journal of the American Medical Association, 233,* 872–877.

Rosenstein, D., & Oster, H. (1988). Differential facial responses to four basic tastes in newborns. *Child Development, 59,* 1555–1568.

Rossi, P. H., Waite, E., Bose, C. E., & Berk, R. E. (1974). Seriousness of crimes: Normative structure and individual differences. *American Sociological Review, 39,* 224–237.

Rousseau, J-J. (1953). *The confessions.* Trans. J. M. Cohen. Harmondsworth: Penguin. (Original published 1781.)

Rozin, P., & Fallon, A. E. (1987). A perspective on disgust. *Psychological Review, 94,* 23–41.

Rumelhart, D. E. (1975). Notes on a schema for stories. In D. G. Bobrow & A. M. Collins (Eds.), *Representation and understanding: Studies in cognitive science.* New York: Academic Press.

(1980). On evaluating story grammars. *Cognitive Science, 4,* 313–316.

Russell, J. A. (1980). A circumplex model of affect. *Journal of Personality and Social Psychology, 39,* 1161–1178.

(1991). In defense of a prototype approach to emotion concepts. *Journal of Personality and Social Psychology, 60,* 37–47.

Rutter, M. (1985). Resilience in the face of adversity: Protective factors and resistance to psychiatric disorder. *British Journal of Psychiatry.* 147, 598–611.

Rutter, M., & Quinton, D. (1984). Long term follow up of women institutionalised in childhood: Factors promoting good functioning in adult life. *British Journal of Developmental Psychology, 18,* 225–234.

Ryle, A. (1982). *Psychotherapy: A cognitive integration of theory and practice.* London: Academic Press.

Sacerdoti, E. D. (1977). *A structure for plans and behavior.* Amsterdam: Elsevier.

Sacks, H., Schegloff, E. A., & Jefferson, G. (1974). A simplest systematics for the organization of turn taking in conversation. *Language, 50,* 696–735.

Salzen, E. A., Kostek, E. A., & Beavan, D. J. (1986). The perception of action versus feeling in facial expression. In H. D. Ellis (Ed.), *Aspects of face processing.* Dordrecht: Nijhoff.

Sanders, N. K. (Trans.) (1960). *The epic of Gilgamesh.* Harmondsworth: Penguin.

Sanford, A. J. (1985). *Cognition and cognitive psychology.* London: Weidenfeld & Nicolson.

Sanford, A. J., & Garrod, S. C. (1982). *Understanding written language.* Chichester: Wiley.

Sappho. *Sappho and Alcaeus: An introduction to the study of Ancient Lesbian poetry.* Trans. D. Page. Oxford: Oxford University Press, 1955.

Sartre, J.-P. (1958). *Being and nothingness: An essay on phenomenological ontology.* Trans. H. E. Barnes. London: Methuen. (Original published 1943.)

Schachtel, E. G. (1959). *Metamorphosis: On the development of affect, perception, attention and memory.* New York: Basic Books.

Schachter, S., & Singer, J. (1962). Cognitive, social and physiological determinants of emotional state. *Psychological Review, 69,* 379–399.

Schank, R. C., & Abelson, R. P. (1978). *Scripts, goals, plans and understanding.* Hillsdale, NJ: Erlbaum.

Scheff, T. J. (1979). *Catharsis in healing ritual and drama.* Berkeley: University of California Press.

Scherer, K. R. (1984). Emotion as a multi-component process: A model and some cross-cultural data. In P. Shaver (Ed.), *Review of personality and social psychology. 5. Emotions, relationships, and health.* Beverly Hills, CA: Sage.

(1985). Vocal affect signalling: A comparative approach. In J. S. Rosenblatt, C. Beer, M. C. Busnel, & P. J. B. Slater (Eds.), *Advances in the study of behavior. Vol. 15.* New York: Academic Press.

(1988). Criteria for emotion antecedent appraisal: A review. In V. Hamilton, G. H. Bower, & N. H. Frijda (Eds.), *Cognitive perspectives on emotion and motivation.* Kluwer: Dordrecht.

(1990). Computer program demonstrated at the fifth annual meeting of the International Society for Research on Emotions, Rutgers University, NJ, 25–28 July.

Scherer, K. R., & Ekman, P. (Eds.) (1984). *Approaches to emotion.* Hillsdale, NJ: Erlbaum.

Scherer, K. R., Wallbott, H. G., & Summerfield, A. B. (Eds.) (1986). *Experiencing emotion: A cross-cultural study.* Cambridge: Cambridge University Press.

Schiff, B. B., & Lamon, M. (1989). Inducing emotion by unilateral contraction of facial muscles: A new look at hemispheric specialization and the experience of emotion. *Neuropsychologia, 27,* 923–925.

Schiff, B. B., & MacDonald, B. (1990). Facial asymmetries in the spontaneous response to positive and negative emotional arousal. *Neuropsychologia, 28,* 777–785.

Schleifer, S. J., Kelier, S. E., Camerino, M., Thornton, J. C., & Stein, M. (1983). Suppression of lymphocyte stimulation following bereavement. *Journal of the American Medical Association, 250,* 374–377.

Scott, J. P. (1958). *Animal behavior.* Chicago: University of Chicago Press.

Searle, J. R. (1969). *Speech acts: An essay in the philosophy of language.* Cambridge: Cambridge University Press.

(1980). Minds, brains and programs. *Brain and Behavioral Sciences, 3,* 417–457.

(1990). Could a machine think? *Scientific American,* January.

Seitz, D. E. (1913). *Whistler stories.* New York: Harper and Brothers.

Selfridge, O. (1959). Pandemonium: A paradigm for learning. In *Mechanisation of thought processes.* London: HM Stationery Office.

Seligman, M. E. P. (1975). Helplessness: On depression, development and death. San Francisco: Freeman.

Selman, R. (1980). *The growth of interpersonal understanding.* New York: Academic Press.

Seyfarth, R. M., Cheney, D. L., & Marler, P. (1980). Verbet monkey alarm calls: Semantic communication in a free-ranging primate. *Animal Behaviour, 28,* 1070–1094.

Seyle, H. (1936). A syndrome produced by diverse nocuous agents. *Nature, 138,* 32.

(1946). The general adaptation syndrome and the diseases of adaptation. *Journal of Clinical Endocrinology, 6,* 117–231.

Shakespeare, W. (1981). *Julius Caesar.* Ed. S. F. Johnson. In *Complete Pelican Shakespeare: The tragedies.* Harmondsworth: Penguin. (Original published 1623.)

(1981). *Macbeth.* Ed. A. Harbage. In *Complete Pelican Shakespeare: The tragedies.* Harmondsworth: Penguin. (Original published 1623.)

(1981). *Romeo and Juliet.* Ed. J. E. Hankins. In *Complete Pelican Shakespeare: The tragedies.* Harmondsworth: Penguin. (Original published 1599.)

Shaver, P., Schwartz, J., Kirson, D., & O'Connor, C. (1987). Emotion knowledge: Further exploration of a prototype approach. *Journal of Personality and Social Psychology, 52,* 1061–1086.

Shekelle, R. B., Gale, M., & Ostfield, A. (1983). Hostility, risk of coronary heart disease and mortality. *Psychosomatic Medicine, 45,* 109–114.

Silver, R. L., & Wortman, C. B. (1980). Coping with undesirable life events. In J. E. Garber & M. E. P. Seligman (Eds.), *Human helplessness: Theory and applications.* London: Academic Press.

Simon, H. A. (1967). Motivational and emotional controls of cognition. *Psychological Review, 74,* 29–39.

Simpson, J. A., Campbell, B., & Berscheid, E. (1986). The association between romantic love and marriage: Kephart 1967 twice revisited. *Personality and Social Psychology Bulletin, 12,* 363–372.

Sloman, A. (1987). Motives, mechanisms and emotions. *Cognition and Emotion, 1,* 217–233.

(1990). Prolegomena of a theory of communication and affect. NATO Advanced Research Workshop on Computational Theories of Communication and Their Applications, Trentino, 5–9 November.

Smetana, J. G. (1981). Preschool children's conception of moral and social rules. *Child Development, 52,* 1333–1336.

Smith, A. (1970). *The wealth of nations,* abridged edition. Ed. A. Skinner. Harmondsworth: Pelican. (Original published 1776.)

(1976). *The theory of moral sentiments.* Oxford: Oxford University Press. (Original published 1759.)

Smith, C. A., & Ellsworth, P. C. (1985). Patterns of cognitive appraisal in emotion. *Journal of Personality and Social Psychology, 48,* 813–838.
    (1987). Patterns of appraisal and emotion in relation to taking an exam. *Journal of Personality and Social Psychology, 52,* 475–488.
Smith, M. A., & Jenkins, J. M. (1991). The effects of marital disharmony on prepubertal children. *Journal of Abnormal Child Psychology.* (In press.)
Smith, M. L., Glass, G. V., & Miller, T. I. (1980). *The benefits of psychotherapy.* Baltimore, MD: Johns Hopkins University Press.
Smith, R. (1967). Heart rate of pilots flying aircraft on scheduled airline routes. *Aerospace Medicine, 38,* 1117–1119.
Snell, B. (1982). *The discovery of the mind in Greek philosophy and literature.* New York: Dover. (Original published 1953.)
Snow, J. (1936). *Snow on cholera: Being a reprint of two papers by John Snow MD.* New York: Hafner.
Sophocles. *Oedipus the king.* In Trans. E. F. Watling. *Sophocles: The Theban plays.* Harmondsworth: Penguin, 1947.
Spiegel, D., Bloom, J. R., Kraemer, H. C., & Gotthall, E. (1989). Effect of psychosocial treatment on survival of patients with metastatic breast cancer. *Lancet,* October 14, 888–891.
Spinoza, B. (1955). *The ethics.* Trans. R. H. M. Elwes. New York: Dover. (Original published 1675.)
Spitzer, R. L., Endicott, J., & Robins, E. (1978). Research diagnostic criteria: Rationale and reliability. *Archives of General Psychiatry, 35,* 773–782.
Spreitzer, E., & Snyder, E. E. (1974). Correlates of life satisfaction among the aged. *Journal of Gerontology, 29,* 119–127.
Stein, N. L., & Levine, L. J. (1989). The causal organisation of emotional knowledge: A developmental study. *Cognition and Emotion, 3,* 343–378.
    (1990). Making sense out of emotion: The representation and use of goal-structured knowledge. In N. L. Stein, B. L. Leventhal & T. Trabasso (Eds.), *Psychological and biological approaches to emotion.* Hillsdale, NJ: Erlbaum.
Stenberg, C., Campos, J. J., & Emde, R. (1983). The facial expression of anger in seven-month-old infants. *Child Development, 54,* 178–184.
Steptoe, A. (1981). *Psychological factors in cardiovascular disorders.* London: Academic Press.
Stewart, K. (1969). Dream theory in Malaya. In C. Tart (Ed.), *Altered states of consciousness.* New York: Wiley.
Stich, S. (1983). *From folk psychology to cognitive science.* Cambridge, MA: MIT Press.
    (1988). Paper presented for research group on "Mind and Brain," organized by Peter Bieri and Ekhart Scherer, Zentrum fur interdisziplinare Forschung, University of Bielefeld.
Strachey, J. (1934). The nature of the therapeutic action of psychoanalysis. *International Journal of Psychoanalysis, 15,* 127–159.
Stroebe, W., Stroebe, M. S., Gergen, K. J., & Gergen, M. (1982). The effects of bereavement on mortality: A social psychological analysis. In J. R. Eiser (Ed.), *Social psychology and behavioral medicine.* Chichester: Wiley.
Strongman, K. T. (1978). *The psychology of emotion,* 2nd ed. Chichester: Wiley.
Suchman, L. A. (1987). *Plans and situated actions: The problem of human-machine communication.* Cambridge: Cambridge University Press.
Sulloway, F. J. (1979). *Freud, biologist of the mind: Beyond the psychoanalytic legend.* New York: Basic Books.

Sussman, G. J. (1975). *A computer model of skill acquisition.* New York: American Elsevier.

Swinden, P. (Ed.) (1972). *George Eliot – Middlemarch: A casebook.* London: Macmillan.

Szasz, T. S. (1965). *The ethics of psychoanalysis: The theory and method of autonomous psychotherapy.* New York: Basic Books.

Tate, A. (1975). Interacting goals and their use. *Proceedings of the Fourth International Joint Conference on Artificial Intelligence.* Tbilisi, Georgia, USSR.

Teasdale, J. D. (1988). Cognitive vulnerability to persistent depression. *Cognition and Emotion, 2*(3), 247–274.

Teasdale, J. D., & Fogarty, S. J. (1979). Differential effects of induced mood on retrieval of pleasant and unpleasant events from episodic memory. *Journal of Abnormal Psychology, 88,* 248–257.

Tennant, C., & Bebbington, P. E. (1978). The social causation of depression: A critique of the work of Brown and his colleagues. *Psychological Medicine, 8,* 565–575.

Tennant, C., Bebbington, P. E., & Hurry, J. (1981). The role of life events in depressive illness: Is there a substantial causal relation? *Psychological Medicine, 11,* 379–389.

Termine, N. T., & Izard, C. E. (1988). Infants' responses to their mothers' expressions of joy and sadness. *Developmental Psychology, 24,* 223–229.

Thayer, J. F. (1988). Relations between cognitive style and affect: Implications for cognitive-behavior therapy. Paper presented to World Congress of Behavior Therapy 88, Edinburgh, 5–10 September.

Thompson, K. W. (1946). Editorial on accompanying paper by Selye. *Journal of Clinical Endocrinology, 6,* 231.

Tiller, D. K. (1988). Structure in the affective lexicon. D.Phil. thesis, University of Oxford.

Tinbergen, N. (1951). *The study of instinct.* Oxford: Oxford University Press.

Todorov, T. (1977). *The poetics of prose.* Trans. R. Howard. Oxford: Blackwell. (Original published 1971.)

Tolstoy, L. (1980). *Anna Karenina.* Trans. L. Maude & A. Maude. Oxford: Oxford University Press. The world's classics. (Original published 1877.)

(1982). *War and peace.* Trans. R. Edmunds. Harmondsworth: Penguin. (Original published 1865–1869.)

Tomkins, S. S. (1979). Script theory: Differential magnification of affect. *Nebraska Symposium on Motivation, 26,* 201–240.

(1984). Affect theory. In K. R. Scherer & P. Ekman (Eds.), *Approaches to Emotion.* Hillsdale, NJ: Erlbaum.

Totman, R. (1979). *Social causes of illness.* London: Souvenir Press.

(1985). *Social and biological roles of language.* London: Academic Press.

(1988). Stress, language and illness. In S. Fisher & J. Reason (Eds.), *Handbook of life stress, cognition and health.* Chichester: Wiley.

Townsend, P., & Davidson, N. (Eds.) (1982). *Inequalities in health: The Black report.* Harmondsworth: Penguin.

Trabasso, T., van den Broek, P., & Suh, S. Y. (1989). Logical necessity and transitivity of causal relations in stories. *Discourse Processes, 12,* 1–25.

Trevarthen, C. (1979). Communication and cooperation in early infancy: A description of primary intersunjectivity. In M. Bullowa (Ed.), *Before speech: The beginning of interpersonal communication.* Cambridge: Cambridge University Press.

(1984). Emotions in infancy: Regulators of contact and relationship with persons. In K. R. Scherer & P. Ekman (Eds.), *Approaches to emotion*. Hillsdale, NJ: Erlbaum.

Trypanis, C. A. (1971). *The Penguin book of Greek verse*. Harmondsworth: Penguin.

Tyhurst, J. S. (1951). Individual reactions to community disorder. *American Journal of Psychiatry, 107,* 764–769.

Vanfossen, B. E. (1981). Sex differences in the mental health effects of spouse support and equity. *Journal of Health and Social Behavior, 22,* 130–143.

Veblen, T. (1899). *The theory of the leisure class: An economic study of institutions.* Reprinted. London: Allen & Unwin, 1948.

Velten, E. (1968). A laboratory task for induction of mood states. *Behavior Research and Therapy, 6,* 473–482.

von Uexkull, J. (1957). A stroll through the world of animals and men. In C. H. Schiller (Ed.), *Instinctive behavior: The development of the modern concept.* London: Methuen.

Walker, A. (1984). *In search of our mothers' gardens.* San Diego, CA: Harcourt Brace Jovanvich.

Wall, P. D., & Melzack, R. (1984). *Textbook of pain.* Edinburgh: Churchill-Livingstone.

Wallbott, H. G., & Scherer, K. R. (1986). How universal and specific is emotional experience? Evidence from 27 countries on five continents. *Social Science Information, 25,* 763–795.

Ward, C. H., Beck, A. T., Mendelson, M., Mock, J. E., & Erbough, J. K. (1962). The psychiatric nomenclature. *Archives of General Psychiatry, 7,* 198–205.

Wason, P. (1960). On the failure to eliminate hypotheses in a conceptual task. *Quarterly Journal of Experimental Psychology, 12,* 129–140.

(1968). Reasoning about a rule. *Quarterly Journal of Experimental Psychology, 20,* 273–281.

(1983). Reason and rationality in the selection task. In J. St. B. Evans (Ed.), *Thinking and reasoning: Psychological approaches.* London: Routledge & Kegan Paul.

Watson, J. D. (Chairman) (1988). Report of the presidential commission on the human immunodeficiency virus epidemic. Washington, DC: U.S. Government Printing Office.

Weber, M. (1963). *The sociology of religion.* English trans. Boston: Beacon Press. (Original published 1922.)

(1968). *Economy and society: An outline of interpretive sociology.* G. Roth & C. Wittich (Eds.), New York: Bedminster Press. (Original published 1922.)

Wegman, C. (1985). *Psychoanalysis and cognitive psychology: A formulation of Freud's earliest theory.* London: Academic Press.

Weiner, B. (1985). An attributional theory of achievement motivation and emotion. *Psychological Review, 92,* 548–573.

Weissman, M. M., & Klerman, G. L. (1977). Sex differences and the epidemiology of depression. *Archives of General Psychiatry, 34,* 98–112.

Weizenbaum, J. (1979). *Computer power and human reason: From judgment to calculation.* San Francisco: Freeman.

White, G. M. (1980). Conceptual universals in interpersonal language. *American Anthropologist, 82,* 334–360.

Wickes, G. (1977). *The Amazon of letters: The life and loves of Natalie Barney.* London: Allen.

Wierzbicka, A. (1972). *Semantic primitives.* Frankfurt: Athenäum Verlag.

(1987). "Prototypes save": On the uses and abuses of the concept "prototype" in current linguistics, philosophy and psychology. Unpublished manuscript, Australian National University, Department of Linguistics, Canberra, Australia.

Wilensky, R. (1978). *Understanding goal based stories.* Research report 140. New Haven, CT: Yale University Department of Computer Science.

(1983). *Planning and understanding: A computational approach to human reasoning.* Reading, MA: Addison-Wesley.

Wilson, A. N. (1988). *Tolstoy.* London: Hamish Hamilton.

Wilson, T. D., Laser, P. S., & Stone, J. L. (1982). Judging the predictors of one's mood. Accuracy and the use of shared theories. *Journal of Experimental Social Psychology, 18*, 537–556.

Wimmer, H., & Perner, J. (1983). Beliefs about beliefs: Representations and constraining function of wrong beliefs in young children's understanding of deception. *Cognition, 13*, 103–128.

Winch, P. (1958). *The idea of a social science and its relation to philosophy.* London: Routledge & Kegan Paul.

Wing, J. K. (1976). A technique for studying psychiatric morbidity in inpatient and outpatient series, and in general population surveys. *Psychological Medicine, 6*, 577–588.

Wing, J. K., Cooper, J. E., & Sartorius, N. (1974). *The description and classification of psychiatric symptoms: An instruction manual for the PSE and CATEGO system.* Cambridge: Cambridge University Press, 1974.

Winnicott, D. W. (1971). *Playing and reality.* Harmondsworth: Penguin.

Winograd, T., & Flores, C. F. (1986). *Understanding computers and cognition: A new foundation for design.* Norwood, NJ: Ablex.

Wittgenstein, L. (1922). *Tractatus logico-philosophicus.* London: Routledge & Kegan Paul.

(1953). *Philosophical investigations.* Oxford: Blackwell.

Wolf, M. E., & Mosnaim, A. (Eds.) (1990). *Posttraumatic stress disorder: Etiology, phenomenology and treatment.* Washington, DC: American Psychiatric Press.

Woodworth, R. S. (1945). *Psychology: A study of mental life,* 16th ed. London: Methuen.

Woolf, V. (1919). Remarks on *Middlemarch. Times Literary Supplement,* 20 November, excerpt reprinted in Swinden, P. (Ed.) (1972), *George Eliot – Middlemarch: A casebook.* London: Macmillan.

(1966). Mr Bennett and Mrs Brown. In *Collected essays.* Vol 1. London: Hogarth Press. (Originally read as a paper 1924.)

Wordsworth, W. (1984). *The Oxford authors: William Wordsworth.* Ed. S. Gill. Oxford: Oxford University Press.

Yerkes, R. M., & Dodson, J. D. (1908). The relation of strength of stimulus to rapidity of habit formation. *Journal of Comparative and Neurological Psychology, 18*, 458–482.

Zahn-Waxler, C., & Radke-Yarrow, M. (1982). The development of altruism: Alternative research strategies. In N. Eisenberg-Berg (Ed.), *The development of prosocial behavior.* New York: Academic Press.

Zajonc, R. B. (1985). Emotion and facial efference: A theory reclaimed. *Science, 228*, 15–21.

Zajonc, R. B., Murphy, S. T., & Inglehart, M. (1989). Feeling and facial efference: Implications of the vascular theory of emotion. *Psychological Review, 96*, 395–416.

Zanna, M. P., Kiesler, C. A., and Pilkonis, P. A. (1970). Positive and negative affect established by classical conditioning. *Journal of Personality and Social Psychology, 14,* 321–328.

Zeaman, D. (1949). Response latency as a function of the amount of reinforcement. *Journal of Experimental Psychology, 39,* 466–483.

Author index

Subject index

abused children, emotional responses in, 97–98, 322, 328
accidents, caused by human error, 157–160
accretion and development, of behavior, 143–144
action, situated, 35
action readiness, emotion-triggered, 19–20, 23, 30
adrenaline, in studies on emotional arousal, 136–137
affective lexicon, 82–83
aggression, studies on, 113, 433n42
AIDS, 456n8
alarms, emotional monitoring systems as, 50, 51, 422n24
anger
  action-readiness, 20
  analysis of, 189–190, 206–212
  as basic emotion, 6, 19, 103, 105
  communication of, 96
  cross-cultural studies on, 112, 433n42
  development of, 192
  diary studies of, 208–211
  disjunctions in, 390–393
  effect on skin temperature, 21
  film and television portrayal of, 445n25
  homicide law and, 207–208, 236
  involuntariness of, 207–208, 229
  occurrence and transitions caused by, 55
  in pathological states, 65
  renegotiation of roles with, 211–212

role transition accomplished by, 213
targets of, 210
animals, emotion studies on, 104, 441n4, see also chimpanzees, emotion studies on; monkeys, alarm calls in
Anna Karenina (Tolstoy)
  depiction of emotions in, 7, 14–16, 21, 22, 24, 37–43, 49, 67, 70, 71, 76, 78, 125, 126, 128, 130–131, 176–177, 196–198, 217–218, 369, 373–374, 415, 424n1
  plot and plans in, 25–27, 28, 32, 67, 176–177, 190, 421n16
annoyance, 211–212
anorexia nervosa, 65, 66, 212, 213
anxiety, 92, 212, 213
  as basic emotion, 6, 19
  in children, 216
  explicit and implicit conflict, 223, 421n20
  free-floating, 64
  psychiatric epidemiology of, 279–282
anxiety states, 65
  from child sexual abuse, 97–98, 322, 328
  as psychiatric disorder, 282
  symptoms of, 457n17
  in women, 299
Aphrodite, 408, 409, 448n13, 473n21
Aristotelian methods, 72, 73, 425n5, 426n9, 427n10
  applied to understanding of emo-